Growth Theory
Volume I

The International Library of Critical Writings in Economics

Series Editor: Mark Blaug
Professor Emeritus, University of London
Consultant Professor, University of Buckingham
Visiting Professor, University of Exeter

1. Multinational Corporations
   Mark Casson

2. The Economics of Innovation
   Christopher Freeman

3. Entrepreneurship
   Mark Casson

4. International Investment
   Peter J. Buckley

5. Game Theory in Economics
   Ariel Rubinstein

6. The History of Economic Thought
   Mark Blaug

7. Monetary Theory
   Thomas Mayer

8. Joint Production of Commodities
   Neri Salvadori and Ian Steedman

9. Industrial Organization
   Oliver E. Williamson

10. Growth Theory (Volumes I, II and III)
    R. Becker and E. Burmeister

11. Microeconomics: Theoretical and Applied (Volumes I, II and III)
    Robert E. Kuenne

Growth Theory
Volume I

Descriptive Growth Theories

Edited by

R. Becker

Professor of Economics
Indiana University, Bloomington

and

E. Burmeister

Commonwealth Professor of Economics
University of Virginia
Research Professor of Economics
Duke University

EDWARD ELGAR

Published by
Edward Elgar Publishing Limited
Gower House
Croft Road
Aldershot
Hants GU11 3HR
England

Edward Elgar Publishing Company
Old Post Road
Brookfield
Vermont 05036
USA

British Library Cataloguing in Publication Data
Growth theory. – (The International library of critical
writings in economics, v. 10).
1. Economic growth
I. Becker, Robert A. *1950–* II. Burmeister, Edwin III.
Series
339.5

Library of Congress Cataloging-in-Publication Data

Growth theory / edited by R. Becker and E. Burmeister.
p. cm. – (The International library of critical writings in
economics ; 10)
1. Economic development. 2. Technological innovations – Economic
aspects. I. Becker, R. (Robert) II. Burmeister, Edwin.
III. Series.
HD75.G77 1991
338.9'001–dc20

ISBN 1 85278 189 0 (3 volume set)

Printed in Great Britain by Galliard (Printers) Ltd, Great Yarmouth

Contents

Acknowledgements

The editors and publishers wish to thank the following who have kindly given permission for the use of copyright material.

American Economic Association for articles: E. Burmeister (1974), 'Synthesizing the Neo-Austrian and Alternative Approaches to Capital Theory: A Survey', *Journal of Economic Literature*, **12**, 413–56; E.S. Phelps (1965), 'Second Essay on the Golden Rule of Accumulation', *American Economic Review*, **55** (4), pp 793–814.

Econometric Society for articles: E. Burmeister, C. Caton, A.R. Dobell and S. Ross (1973), 'The ''Saddlepoint Property'' and the Structure of Dynamic Heterogeneous Capital Good Models', *Econometrica*, **41** (1), 79–95; F.R. Chang (1988), 'The Inverse Optimum Problem: A Dynamic Programming Approach', *Econometrica*, **56** (1), 147–72.

Elsevier Science Publishers B.V. for articles and excerpt: R.E. Lucas (1988), 'On the Mechanics of Economic Development', *Journal of Monetary Economics*, **22**, 3–42; P.A. Samuelson (1965), 'A Theory of Induced Innovation Along Kennedy-Weisäcker Lines', *Review of Economics and Statistics*, **47** (4), 343–56; E. Burmeister (1976), 'Real Wicksell Effects and Regular Economies', from *Essays in Modern Capital Theory*, M. Brown and P. Zarembka (eds), 145–64.

International Economic Review for article: E. Burmeister (1968), 'The Role of the Jacobian Determinant in the Two-Sector Model', *International Economic Review*, **9** (2), 195–203.

John Wiley & Sons, Inc. for articles: R.M. Solow (1956), 'A Contribution to the Theory of Economic Growth', *Quarterly Journal of Economics*, **70** (1), 65–94; F.H. Hahn (1966), 'Equilibrium Dynamics with Heterogeneous Capital Goods', *Quarterly Journal of Economics*, **80** (4), pp 633–46; M. Bruno, E. Burmeister and E. Sheshinski (1966), 'The Nature and Implications of the Reswitching of Techniques', *Quarterly Journal of Economics*, **80** (4), 526–53.

Macmillan Publishing Company (New York) for excerpt: E. Burmeister and A.R. Dobell (1970), 'Money and Economic Growth', from *Mathematical Theories of Economic Growth*, Chapter 6, 156–201.

Review of Economic Studies Ltd for articles: H. Uzawa (1961), 'On a Two-Sector Model of Economic Growth', *Review of Economic Studies*, **29** (78), 40–47: K.J. Arrow (1962), 'The Economic Implications of Learning by Doing', *Review of Economic Studies*, **29** (80), 155–73; C. Bliss (1968), 'On Putty-Clay', *Review of Economic Studies*, **35** (103), 105–32;

P.A. Diamond (1965), 'Disembodied Technical Change in a Two-Sector Model', *Review of Economic Studies*, **90** (2), 161–8.

University of Chicago Press for article: P.M. Romer (1986), 'Increasing Returns and Long-Run Growth', *Journal of Political Economy*, **94** (5), 1002–37.

Every effort has been made to trace all the copyright holders but if any have been inadvertently overlooked the publishers will be pleased to make the necessary arrangement at the first opportunity.

The publishers wish to thank the Library of the London School of Economics and Political Science and the Librarian and Staff at The Alfred Marshall Library, Cambridge University for their assistance in obtaining these articles. In addition they would also like to thank Robert M. Boyling and his staff at the Photographic Unit, University of London Library for their assistance with these and other volumes in the series.

Introduction

This three-volume work provides a comprehensive selection of the most important articles on growth theory. The readings in Volume I address theories that attempt to explain the stylized facts of growth. Volume II focuses on normative models of the growth process. Volume III integrates the positive analysis found in the first volume with the welfare approach found in the second volume. Taken together, the volumes depict the development of growth models from the early aggregative theory without explicitly optimizing agents to the current practice of formulating growth models with an explicit microeconomic foundation for consumption and investment decisions. Both the questions and methods of the new equilibrium approach to growth theory are adapted from optimal growth theory. In this sense the descriptive and normative theories are intertwined and elements of both points of view may be found in each of the three volumes.

In 1956 Robert M. Solow published 'A Contribution to the Theory of Economic Growth'. This thirty-page paper provides the intellectual and historical roots for much of the work reprinted in these three volumes. There is, of course, much of importance that we could not include; Solow's 1956 paper impacted on virtually every field of economics, especially development, financial economics, international trade, monetary economics, public finance, and resource economics. In 1987 Solow was awarded the Nobel Prize in economics.

Solow's seminal contribution was the concept of economic equilibrium over time as summarized by his differential equation describing the evolution of an economy's capital stock:

$$\dot{K}(t) = sF[K(t), L(t)] ,$$

where K is the stock of a single type of capital good, L is labour input, s is the savings rate, t denotes time, and F[.] is the aggregate production function, assumed to have the usual neoclassical properties. This differential equation – along with other assumptions – completely determines the evolution of an economy over time. In particular, questions such as the convergence (or divergence) of a growth path to a dynamic equilibrium or steady-state can be addressed. Part I contains such models with a single type of capital good.

Solow made the simplifying assumption that aggregate saving is a constant fraction, s, of aggregate income. But what values of s are desirable in some economic sense? The papers of Phelps and Chang investigate this question. Phelps explores the existence of an ideal savings rate across stationary states. The result is the famous Golden-Rule of growth theory. Chang studies the question of whether a particular savings function could be the endogenously determined savings rate for some optimizing, infinitely-lived central planner. His specification of the model allows for technological uncertainty; his optimizing solution is also consistent with the planner holding rational expectations about the future.

More recently, papers by Lucas and Romer have extended Solow's analysis to allow for external economies of scale on an aggregate level. That is, even if individual agents believe that they face constant returns to scale, their collective decisions can lead to increasing returns for the economy as a whole. The resulting dynamic paths do not necessarily converge to a steady-state, and they need not be Pareto optimal. These models help to explain why growth rates differ across countries, and they are potentially of great importance for questions of economic development. The Lucas and Romer contributions are representative of the 'new growth theory' which tries to forge a link between growth, development, demography, and the accumulation of physical as well as human capital. Their articles also focus on equilibrium paths with explicitly optimizing agents. This theme will be the focal point of the studies found in Volume III.

The selections in Part II extend the basic Solow framework in another direction by allowing two or more economic sectors. Three different types of models arise:

(i) Two-sector models with one capital good and a distinctly different consumption good, each produced in different sectors of the economy with different neoclassical production functions.
(ii) Models in which money is added to the original Solow model.
(iii) Models with one (or more) consumption good and more than one distinctly different type of capital good, all of which are produced in different sectors of the economy.

Even with models of type (i), the simple conclusions from Solow's model become more complex: there may be more than one steady-state equilibrium, unstable growth paths are possible, and full-employment cyclical behaviour can occur. When wealth may be held in more than one asset, as in either models with one capital good and money or in models with many different types of capital goods, the dynamic behaviour changes drastically. For example, in models with one consumption good and n different types of capital goods, n differential equations are needed to describe dynamic behaviour:

$$\dot{k}_i = f_i(k_1,\ldots,k_n, p_1,\ldots,p_n) , \qquad i = 1,\ldots,n,$$

and

$$\dot{p}_i = h_i(k_1,\ldots,k_n, p_1,\ldots,p_n) , \qquad i = 1,\ldots,n.$$

Here k_i denotes the per capita stock of the i-th type capital good and p_i denotes the price of the i-th type capital good in terms of the consumption good. A unique dynamic rest point or steady-state for this system of 2n differential equations is generally a saddlepoint, and Hahn pointed out that such systems are not stable unless the vector of initial prices is exactly right – the 'Hahn instability problem'. However, in these models a *unique* stable path from arbitrary initial conditions does not always exist; Burmeister, Caton, Dobell, and Ross showed that there can be many stable paths, a first example of nonuniqueness in dynamic rational expectations (perfect foresight) models. The dynamic stability problems associated with this class of models can be dealt with by including a good deal of maximizing behaviour on the part of a representative agent, as in Volume II, or on the part of many agents whose collective actions give rise to equilibrium models, as in Volume III.

The existence of many types of capital goods not only causes problems for dynamics, but it also leads to the so-called 'capital theory or Cambridge controversies'. This debate centred on the comparison of alternative steady-state equilibria, and it turns out that these comparisons can violate some of the basic neoclassical intuition stemming from Solow's original growth model. Part III deals with these issues, and one lesson to be learned is that it is treacherous to hold the belief that *all* the important economic implications from a simple model are valid in a more complex world.

Questions of technological change are addressed in Part IV. If per capita consumption is to increase over time, as is observed empirically, then Solow's model must be modified to allow for improving production possibilities over time. Such technological improvements can be modelled by postulating that given levels of capital and labour inputs become more efficient in production with the passage of time, and the success of Solow's neoclassical growth theory is due, in part, to the labour-augmenting technical change variant of the model. Briefly, the following observations on long-run growth patterns hold (at least for advanced industrial economies) and are explained by the Solow model with labour-augmenting technological change:

(i) The investment-output ratio is constant.
(ii) The capital-output ratio is constant.
(iii) The capital-labour ratio and output-labour ratios are rising at a constant rate.
(iv) The rate of interest is constant.
(v) The real wage is rising at a constant rate.
(vi) The relative shares of capital and labour are constant.

Alternative models of technological change entail the notion that more efficient machines that embody the most modern technology are the source of increasing productivity. In this case technological improvement occurs only with new investment in new machines, so that an increase in investment will increase economic growth, as in the paper by Bliss. Finally, technological change may arise because workers learn from experience and therefore can produce the n-th unit of output with fewer hours than the (n-1)-st unit. This idea was put forth in Arrow's pathbreaking 'learning-by-doing' paper.

The papers reprinted in Volume I merely provide a foundation for studying the modern theory of economic growth, and our selections reflect our judgements as to what constitutes a sound foundation. We believe that the subjects treated here are essential for a proper economic understanding of the more complex economic questions dealt with in Volumes II and III.

Part I
One-Sector Models

[1]

A CONTRIBUTION TO THE THEORY OF ECONOMIC GROWTH

By Robert M. Solow

I. Introduction

All theory depends on assumptions which are not quite true. That is what makes it theory. The art of successful theorizing is to make the inevitable simplifying assumptions in such a way that the final results are not very sensitive.[1] A "crucial" assumption is one on which the conclusions do depend sensitively, and it is important that crucial assumptions be reasonably realistic. When the results of a theory seem to flow specifically from a special crucial assumption, then if the assumption is dubious, the results are suspect.

I wish to argue that something like this is true of the Harrod-Domar model of economic growth. The characteristic and powerful conclusion of the Harrod-Domar line of thought is that even for the long run the economic system is at best balanced on a knife-edge of equilibrium growth. Were the magnitudes of the key parameters — the savings ratio, the capital-output ratio, the rate of increase of the labor force — to slip ever so slightly from dead center, the consequence would be either growing unemployment or prolonged inflation. In Harrod's terms the critical question of balance boils down to a comparison between the natural rate of growth which depends, in the absence of technological change, on the increase of the labor force, and the warranted rate of growth which depends on the saving and investing habits of households and firms.

But this fundamental opposition of warranted and natural rates turns out in the end to flow from the crucial assumption that production takes place under conditions of *fixed proportions.* There is no possibility of substituting labor for capital in production. If this assumption is abandoned, the knife-edge notion of unstable balance seems to go with it. Indeed it is hardly surprising that such a gross

1. Thus transport costs were merely a negligible complication to Ricardian trade theory, but a vital characteristic of reality to von Thünen.

rigidity in one part of the system should entail lack of flexibility in another.

A remarkable characteristic of the Harrod-Domar model is that it consistently studies long-run problems with the usual short-run tools. One usually thinks of the long run as the domain of the neoclassical analysis, the land of the margin. Instead Harrod and Domar talk of the long run in terms of the multiplier, the accelerator, "the" capital coefficient. The bulk of this paper is devoted to a model of long-run growth which accepts all the Harrod-Domar assumptions except that of fixed proportions. Instead I suppose that the single composite commodity is produced by labor and capital under the standard neoclassical conditions. The adaptation of the system to an exogenously given rate of increase of the labor force is worked out in some detail, to see if the Harrod instability appears. The price-wage-interest reactions play an important role in this neoclassical adjustment process, so they are analyzed too. Then some of the other rigid assumptions are relaxed slightly to see what qualitative changes result: neutral technological change is allowed, and an interest-elastic savings schedule. Finally the consequences of certain more "Keynesian" relations and rigidities are briefly considered.

II. A Model of Long-Run Growth

There is only one commodity, output as a whole, whose rate of production is designated $Y(t)$. Thus we can speak unambiguously of the community's real income. Part of each instant's output is consumed and the rest is saved and invested. The fraction of output saved is a constant s, so that the rate of saving is $sY(t)$. The community's stock of capital $K(t)$ takes the form of an accumulation of the composite commodity. Net investment is then just the rate of increase of this capital stock dK/dt or $\dot{K}$, so we have the basic identity at every instant of time:

$$\dot{K} = sY. \tag{1}$$

Output is produced with the help of two factors of production, capital and labor, whose rate of input is $L(t)$. Technological possibilities are represented by a production function

$$Y = F(K,L). \tag{2}$$

Output is to be understood as net output after making good the depreciation of capital. About production all we will say at the moment is that it shows constant returns to scale. Hence the production function is homogeneous of first degree. This amounts to assuming that there is no scarce nonaugmentable resource like land. Constant returns to scale seems the natural assumption to make in a theory of growth. The scarce-land case would lead to decreasing returns to scale in capital and labor and the model would become more Ricardian.[2]

Inserting (2) in (1) we get

$$\dot{K} = sF(K,L). \tag{3}$$

This is one equation in two unknowns. One way to close the system would be to add a demand-for-labor equation: marginal physical productivity of labor equals real wage rate; and a supply-of-labor equation. The latter could take the general form of making labor supply a function of the real wage, or more classically of putting the real wage equal to a conventional subsistence level. In any case there would be three equations in the three unknowns K, L, real wage.

Instead we proceed more in the spirit of the Harrod model. As a result of exogenous population growth the labor force increases at a constant relative rate n. In the absence of technological change n is Harrod's natural rate of growth. Thus:

$$L(t) = L_0e^{nt}. \tag{4}$$

In (3) L stands for total employment; in (4) L stands for the available supply of labor. By identifying the two we are assuming that full employment is perpetually maintained. When we insert (4) in (3) to get

$$\dot{K} = sF(K,L_0e^{nt}) \tag{5}$$

we have the basic equation which determines the time path of capital accumulation that must be followed if all available labor is to be employed.

Alternatively (4) can be looked at as a supply curve of labor. It says that the exponentially growing labor force is offered for employment completely inelastically. The labor supply curve is a vertical

2. See, for example, Haavelmo: *A Study in the Theory of Economic Evolution* (Amsterdam, 1954), pp. 9–11. Not all "underdeveloped" countries are areas of land shortage. Ethiopia is a counterexample. One can imagine the theory as applying as long as arable land can be hacked out of the wilderness at essentially constant cost.

line which shifts to the right in time as the labor force grows according to (4). Then the real wage rate adjusts so that all available labor is employed, and the marginal productivity equation determines the wage rate which will actually rule.[3]

In summary, (5) is a differential equation in the single variable $K(t)$. Its solution gives the only time profile of the community's capital stock which will fully employ the available labor. Once we know the time path of capital stock and that of the labor force, we can compute from the production function the corresponding time path of real output. The marginal productivity equation determines the time path of the real wage rate. There is also involved an assumption of full employment of the available stock of capital. At any point of time the pre-existing stock of capital (the result of previous accumulation) is inelastically supplied. Hence there is a similar marginal productivity equation for capital which determines the real rental per unit of time for the services of capital stock. The process can be viewed in this way: at any moment of time the available labor supply is given by (4) and the available stock of capital is also a datum. Since the real return to factors will adjust to bring about full employment of labor and capital we can use the production function (2) to find the current rate of output. Then the propensity to save tells us how much of net output will be saved and invested. Hence we know the net accumulation of capital during the current period. Added to the already accumulated stock this gives the capital available for the next period, and the whole process can be repeated.

III. Possible Growth Patterns

To see if there is always a capital accumulation path consistent with any rate of growth of the labor force, we must study the differential equation (5) for the qualitative nature of its solutions. Naturally without specifying the exact shape of the production function we can't hope to find the exact solution. But certain broad properties are surprisingly easy to isolate, even graphically.

To do so we introduce a new variable $r = \frac{K}{L}$, the ratio of capital to labor. Hence we have $K = rL = rL_0e^{nt}$. Differentiating with respect to time we get

$$\dot{K} = L_0e^{nt}\dot{r} + nrL_0e^{nt}.$$

3. The complete set of three equations consists of (3), (4) and $\frac{\partial F(K,L)}{\partial L} = w$.

Substitute this in (5):

$$(\dot{r} + nr)L_0e^{nt} = sF(K, L_0e^{nt}).$$

But because of constant returns to scale we can divide both variables in F by $L = L_0e^{nt}$ provided we multiply F by the same factor. Thus

$$(\dot{r} + nr)L_0e^{nt} = sL_0e^{nt}F\left(\frac{K}{L_0e^{nt}}, 1\right)$$

and dividing out the common factor we arrive finally at

$$\dot{r} = sF(r,1) - nr. \tag{6}$$

Here we have a differential equation involving the capital-labor ratio alone.

This fundamental equation can be reached somewhat less formally. Since $r = \frac{K}{L}$, the relative rate of change of r is the difference between the relative rates of change of K and L. That is:

$$\frac{\dot{r}}{r} = \frac{\dot{K}}{K} - \frac{\dot{L}}{L}.$$

Now first of all $\frac{\dot{L}}{L} = n$. Secondly $\dot{K} = sF(K,L)$. Making these substitutions:

$$\dot{r} = r\,\frac{sF(K,L)}{K} - nr.$$

Now divide L out of F as before, note that $\frac{L}{K} = \frac{1}{r}$, and we get (6) again.

The function $F(r,1)$ appearing in (6) is easy to interpret. It is the total product curve as varying amounts r of capital are employed with one unit of labor. Alternatively it gives output per worker as a function of capital per worker. Thus (6) states that the rate of change of the capital-labor ratio is the difference of two terms, one representing the increment of capital and one the increment of labor.

When $\dot{r} = 0$, the capital-labor ratio is a constant, and the capital stock must be expanding at the same rate as the labor force, namely n.

(The warranted rate of growth, warranted by the appropriate real rate of return to capital, equals the natural rate.) In Figure I, the ray through the origin with slope n represents the function nr. The other curve is the function $sF(r,1)$. It is here drawn to pass through the origin and convex upward: no output unless both inputs are positive, and diminishing marginal productivity of capital, as would be the case, for example, with the Cobb-Douglas function. At the point of intersection $nr = sF(r,1)$ and $\dot{r} = 0$. If the capital-labor ratio r^* should ever be established, it will be maintained, and capital and labor will grow thenceforward in proportion. By constant returns to

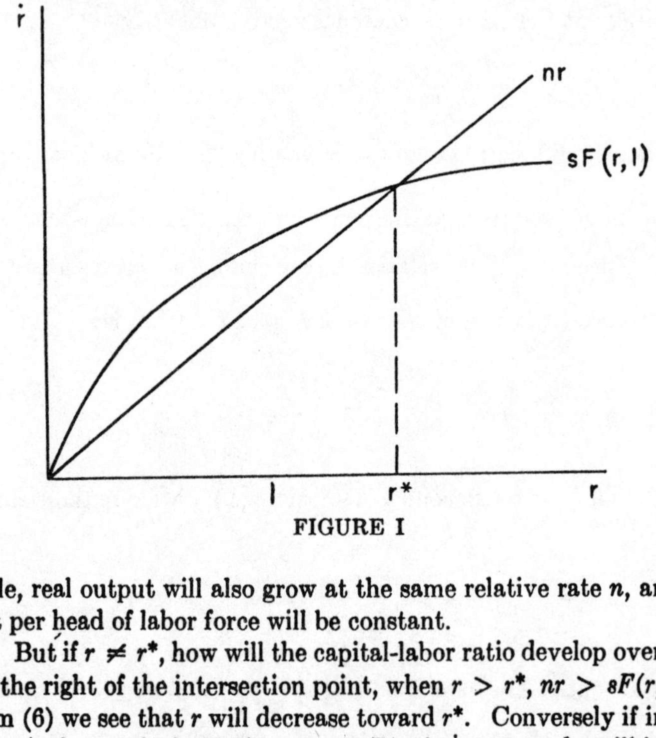

FIGURE I

scale, real output will also grow at the same relative rate n, and output per head of labor force will be constant.

But if $r \neq r^*$, how will the capital-labor ratio develop over time? To the right of the intersection point, when $r > r^*$, $nr > sF(r,1)$ and from (6) we see that r will decrease toward r^*. Conversely if initially $r < r^*$, the graph shows that $nr < sF(r,1)$, $\dot{r} > 0$, and r will increase toward r^*. Thus the equilibrium value r^* is *stable*. Whatever the initial value of the capital-labor ratio, the system will develop *toward* a state of balanced growth at the natural rate. The time path of capital and output will not be exactly exponential except asymptotically.[4] If the initial capital stock is below the equilibrium ratio,

4. There is an exception to this. If $K = 0$, $r = 0$ and the system can't get started; with no capital there is no output and hence no accumulation. But this

capital and output will grow at a faster pace than the labor force until the equilibrium ratio is approached. If the initial ratio is above the equilibrium value, capital and output will grow more slowly than the labor force. The growth of output is always intermediate between those of labor and capital.

Of course the strong stability shown in Figure I is not inevitable. The steady adjustment of capital and output to a state of balanced growth comes about because of the way I have drawn the productivity curve $F(r,1)$. Many other configurations are a priori possible. For example in Figure II there are three intersection points. Inspec-

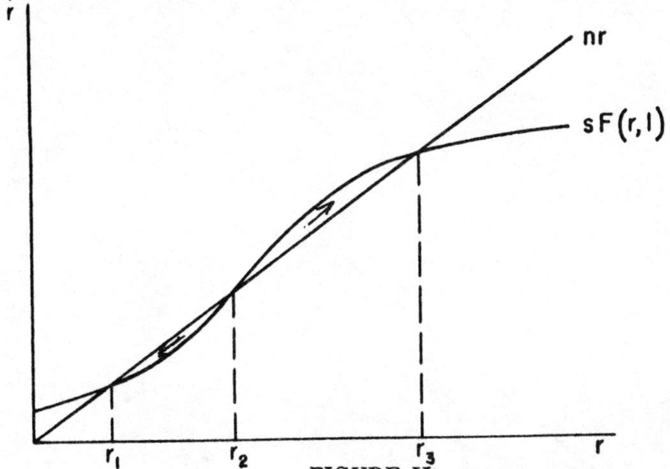

FIGURE II

tion will show that r_1 and r_3 are stable, r_2 is not. Depending on the initially observed capital-labor ratio, the system will develop either to balanced growth at capital-labor ratio r_1 or r_3. In either case labor supply, capital stock and real output will asymptotically expand at rate n, but around r_1 there is less capital than around r_3, hence the level of output per head will be lower in the former case than in the latter. The relevant balanced growth equilibrium is at r_1 for an initial ratio anywhere between 0 and r_2, it is at r_3 for any initial ratio greater than r_2. The ratio r_2 is itself an equilibrium growth ratio, but an unstable one; any accidental disturbance will be magnified over time. Figure II has been drawn so that production is possible without capital; hence the origin is not an equilibrium "growth" configuration.

Even Figure II does not exhaust the possibilities. It is possible

equilibrium is unstable: the slightest windfall capital accumulation will start the system off toward r^*.

that no balanced growth equilibrium might exist.[5] *Any* nondecreasing function $F(r,1)$ can be converted into a constant returns to scale production function simply by multiplying it by L; the reader can construct a wide variety of such curves and examine the resulting solutions to (6). In Figure III are shown two possibilities, together

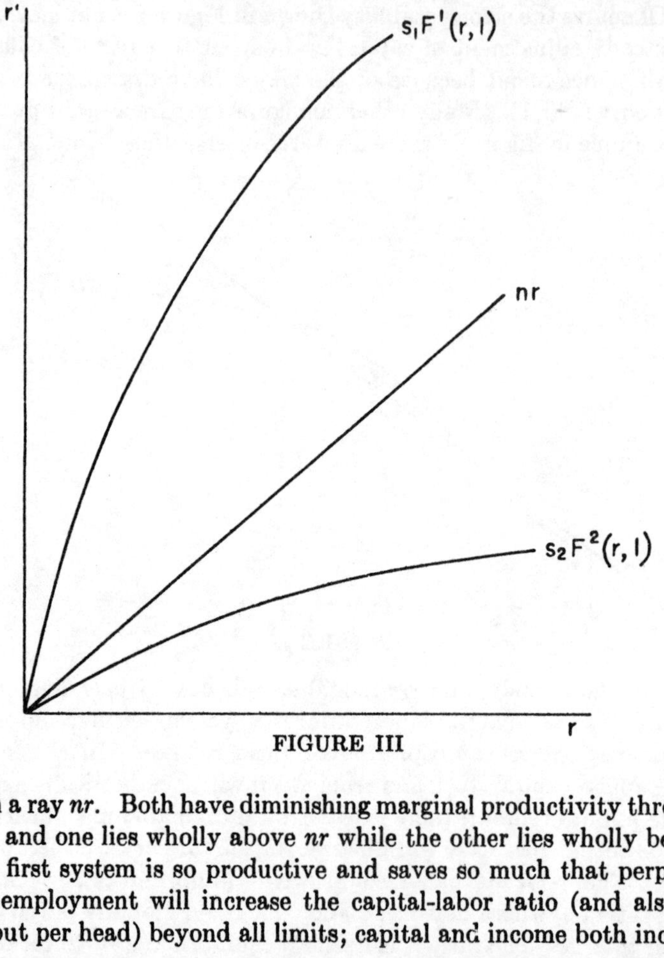

FIGURE III

with a ray nr. Both have diminishing marginal productivity throughout, and one lies wholly above nr while the other lies wholly below.[6] The first system is so productive and saves so much that perpetual full employment will increase the capital-labor ratio (and also the output per head) beyond all limits; capital and income both increase

5. This seems to contradict a theorem in R. M. Solow and P. A. Samuelson: "Balanced Growth under Constant Returns to Scale," *Econometrica*, XXI (1953), 412–24, but the contradiction is only apparent. It was there assumed that every commodity had positive marginal productivity in the production of each commodity. Here capital cannot be used to produce labor.

6. The equation of the first might be $s_1F^1(r,1) = nr + \sqrt{r}$, that of the second $s_2F^2(r,1) = \dfrac{nr}{r+1}$

more rapidly than the labor supply. The second system is so unproductive that the full employment path leads only to forever diminishing income per capita. Since net investment is always positive and labor supply is increasing, aggregate income can only rise.

The basic conclusion of this analysis is that, when production takes place under the usual neoclassical conditions of variable proportions and constant returns to scale, no simple opposition between natural and warranted rates of growth is possible. There may not be — in fact in the case of the Cobb-Douglas function there never can be — any knife-edge. The system can adjust to any given rate of growth of the labor force, and eventually approach a state of steady proportional expansion.

IV. Examples

In this section I propose very briefly to work out three examples, three simple choices of the shape of the production function for which it is possible to solve the basic differential equation (6) explicitly.

Example 1: Fixed Proportions. This is the Harrod-Domar case. It takes a units of capital to produce a unit of output; and b units of labor. Thus a is an acceleration coefficient. Of course, a unit of output can be produced with *more* capital and/or labor than this (the isoquants are right-angled corners); the first bottleneck to be reached limits the rate of output. This can be expressed in the form (2) by saying

$$Y = F(K,L) = \min\left(\frac{K}{a}, \frac{L}{b}\right)$$

where "min (. . .)" means the smaller of the numbers in parentheses. The basic differential equation (6) becomes

$$\dot{r} = s \min\left(\frac{r}{a}, \frac{1}{b}\right) - nr.$$

Evidently for very small r we must have $\frac{r}{a} < \frac{1}{b}$, so that in this range $\dot{r} = \frac{sr}{a} - nr = \left(\frac{s}{a} - n\right)r$. But when $\frac{r}{a} \geqq \frac{1}{b}$, i.e., $r \geqq \frac{a}{b}$, the equation becomes $\dot{r} = \frac{s}{b} - nr$. It is easier to see how this works graphically. In Figure IV the function $s \min\left(\frac{r}{a}, \frac{1}{b}\right)$ is represented by a broken line: the ray from the origin with slope $\frac{s}{a}$ until r reaches the value $\frac{a}{b}$, and then a horizontal line at height $\frac{s}{b}$. In the Harrod model $\frac{s}{a}$ is the warranted rate of growth.

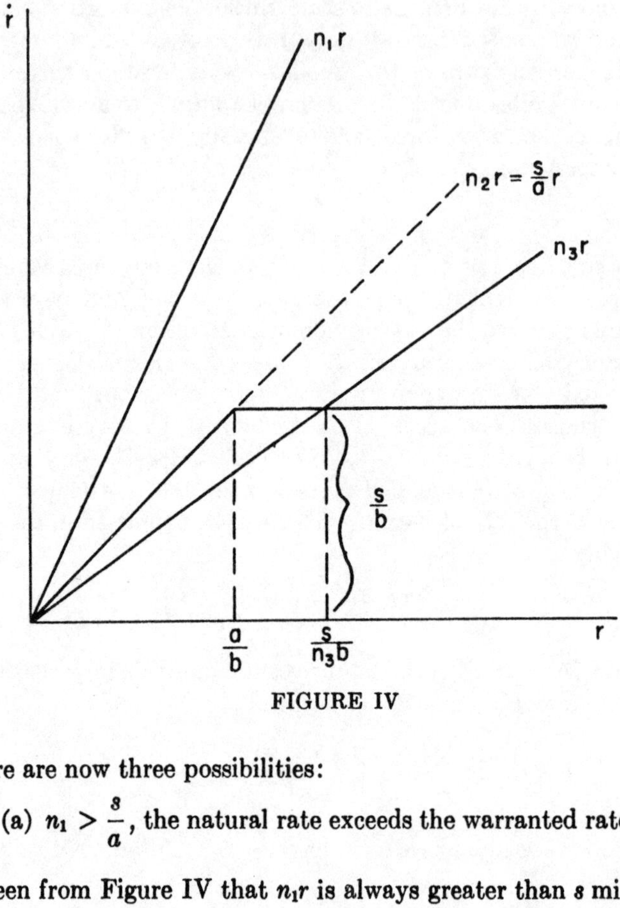

FIGURE IV

There are now three possibilities:

(a) $n_1 > \frac{s}{a}$, the natural rate exceeds the warranted rate. It can be seen from Figure IV that $n_1 r$ is always greater than $s \min\left(\frac{r}{a}, \frac{1}{b}\right)$, so that r always decreases. Suppose the initial value of the capital-labor ratio is $r_0 > \frac{a}{b}$, then $\dot{r} = \frac{s}{b} - n_1 r$, whose solution is $r = \left(r_0 - \frac{s}{n_1 b}\right)e^{-n_1 t} + \frac{s}{n_1 b}$. Thus r decreases toward $\frac{s}{n_1 b}$ which is in turn less than $\frac{a}{b}$. At an easily calculable point of time t_1, r reaches $\frac{a}{b}$. From then on $\dot{r} = \left(\frac{s}{a} - n_1\right) r$, whose solution is $r = \frac{a}{b} e^{\left(\frac{s}{a} - n_1\right)(t - t_1)}$. Since $\frac{s}{a} < n_1$, r will decrease toward zero. At time t_1, when $r = \frac{a}{b}$ the labor supply and capital stock are in balance. From then on as the capital-labor ratio decreases labor becomes redundant, and the extent of the redundancy grows. The amount of unemployment can be calculated from the fact that $K = rL_0e^{nt}$ remembering that, when capital is the bottleneck factor, output is $\frac{K}{a}$ and *employment* is $b\frac{K}{a}$.

(b) $n_2 = \frac{s}{a}$, the warranted and natural rates are equal. If initially $r > \frac{a}{b}$ so that labor is the bottleneck, then r decreases to $\frac{a}{b}$ and stays there. If initially $r < \frac{a}{b}$, then r remains constant over time, in a sort of neutral equilibrium. Capital stock and labor supply grow at a common rate n_2; whatever *percentage* redundancy of labor there was initially is preserved.

(c) $n_3 < \frac{s}{a}$, the warranted rate exceeds the natural rate. Formally the solution is exactly as in case (a) with n_3 replacing n_1. There is a stable equilibrium capital output ratio at $r = \frac{s}{n_3 b}$. But here capital is redundant as can be seen from the fact that the marginal productivity of capital has fallen to zero. The proportion of the capital stock actually employed in equilibrium growth is $\frac{an_3}{s}$. But since the capital stock is growing (at a rate asymptotically equal to n_3) the absolute amount of excess capacity is growing, too. This appearance of redundancy independent of any price-wage movements is a consequence of fixed proportions, and lends the Harrod-Domar model its characteristic of rigid balance.

At the very least one can imagine a production function such that if r exceeds a critical value r_{max}, the marginal product of capital falls to zero, and if r falls short of another critical value r_{min}, the marginal product of labor falls to zero. For intermediate capital-labor ratios the isoquants are as usual. Figure IV would begin with a linear portion for $0 \leqq r \leqq r_{min}$, then have a phase like Figure I for $r_{min} \leqq r \leqq r_{max}$, then end with a horizontal stretch for $r > r_{max}$. There would be a whole *zone* of labor-supply growth rates which would lead to an equilibrium like that of Figure I. For values of n below this zone the end result would be redundancy of capital, for values of n above this zone, redundancy of labor. To the extent that in the long run factor proportions are widely variable the intermediate zone of growth rates will be wide.

Example 2: The Cobb-Douglas Function. The properties of the function $Y = K^a L^{1-a}$ are too well known to need comment here. Figure I describes the situation regardless of the choice of the parameters a and n. The marginal productivity of capital rises indefinitely as the capital-labor ratio decreases, so that the curve $sF(r,1)$ must rise above the ray nr. But since $a < 1$, the curve must eventually cross the ray from above and subsequently remain below. Thus the asymptotic behavior of the system is always balanced growth at the natural rate.

The differential equation (6) is in this case $\dot{r} = sr^a - nr$. It is actually easier to go back to the untransformed equation (5), which now reads

$$\dot{K} = sK^a(L_0 e^{nt})^{1-a}\,. \tag{7}$$

This can be integrated directly and the solution is:

$$K(t) = \left[K_0^b - \frac{s}{n} L_0^b + \frac{s}{n} L_0^b e^{nbt} \right]^{\frac{1}{b}}$$

where $b = 1 - a$, and K_0 is the initial capital stock. It is easily seen that as t becomes large, $K(t)$ grows essentially like $\left(\frac{s}{n}\right)^{1/b} L_0 e^{nt}$, namely at the same rate of growth as the labor force. The equilibrium value of the capital-labor ratio is $r^* = \left(\frac{s}{n}\right)^{1/b}$. This can be verified by putting $\dot{r} = 0$ in (6). Reasonably enough this equilibrium ratio is larger the higher the savings ratio and the lower the rate of increase of the labor supply.

It is easy enough to work out the time path of real output from the production function itself. Obviously asymptotically Y must behave like K and L, that is, grow at relative rate n. Real income per head of labor force, Y/L, tends to the value $(s/n)^{a/b}$. Indeed with the Cobb-Douglas function it is always true that $Y/L = (K/L)^a = r^a$. It follows at once that the equilibrium value of K/Y is s/n. But K/Y is the "capital coefficient" in Harrod's terms, say C. Then in the long-run equilibrium growth we will have $C = s/n$ or $n = s/C$: the natural rate equals "the" warranted rate, not as an odd piece of luck but as a consequence of demand-supply adjustments.

Example 3. A whole family of constant-returns-to-scale production functions is given by $Y = (aK^p + L^p)^{1/p}$. It differs from the Cobb-Douglas family in that production is possible with only one factor. But it shares the property that if $p < 1$, the marginal productivity of capital becomes infinitely great as the capital-labor ratio declines toward zero. If $p > 1$, the isoquants have the "wrong" convexity; when $p = 1$, the isoquants are straight lines, perfect substitutability; I will restrict myself to the case of $0 < p < 1$ which gives the usual diminishing marginal returns. Otherwise it is hardly sensible to insist on full employment of both factors.

In particular consider $p = 1/2$ so that the production function becomes

$$Y = (a\sqrt{K} + \sqrt{L})^2 = a^2K + L + 2a\sqrt{KL}\,.$$

The basic differential equation is

$$\dot{r} = s(a\sqrt{r} + 1)^2 - nr. \tag{8}$$

This can be written:

$$\dot{r} = s\left[(a^2 - n/s)r + 2a\sqrt{r} + 1\right] = s(A\sqrt{r} + 1)(B\sqrt{r} + 1)$$

where $A = a - \sqrt{n/s}$ and $B = a + \sqrt{n/s}$. The solution has to be given implicitly:

$$\left(\frac{A\sqrt{r} + 1}{A\sqrt{r_0} + 1}\right)^{1/A} \left(\frac{B\sqrt{r} + 1}{B\sqrt{r_0} + 1}\right)^{-1/B} = e^{\sqrt{ns}\,t} \tag{9}$$

Once again it is easier to refer to a diagram. There are two possibilities, illustrated in Figure V. The curve $sF(r,1)$ begins at a height s when $r = 0$. If $sa^2 > n$, there is no balanced growth equilibrium: the capital-labor ratio increases indefinitely and so does real output per head. The system is highly productive and saves-invests enough at full employment to expand very rapidly. If $sa^2 < n$, there is a stable balanced growth equilibrium, which is reached according to the solution (9). The equilibrium capital-labor ratio can be found by putting $\dot{r} = 0$ in (8); it is $r^* = (1/\sqrt{n/s} - a)^2$. It can be further calculated that the income per head prevailing in the limiting state of growth is $1/(1 - a\sqrt{s/n})^2$. That is, real income per head of labor force will rise to this value if it starts below, or vice versa.

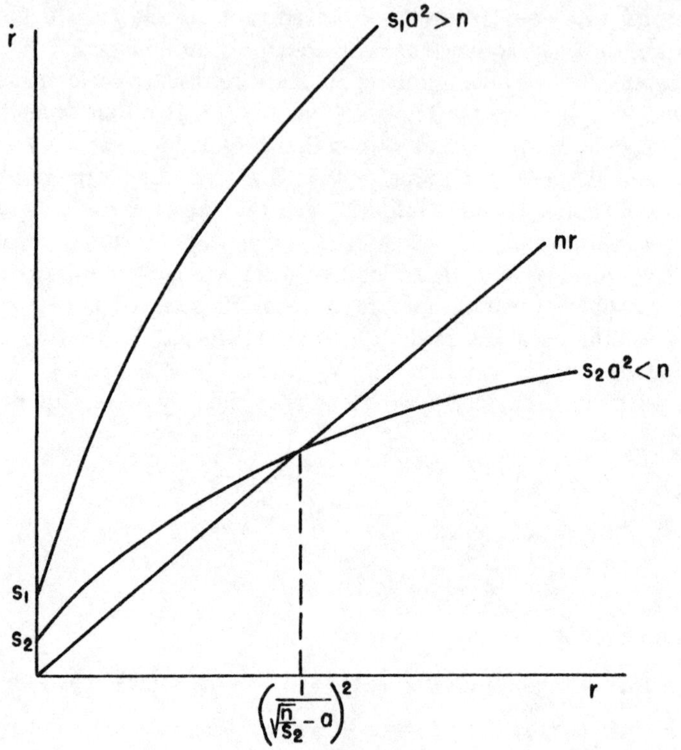

FIGURE V

V. Behavior of Interest and Wage Rates

The growth paths discussed in the previous sections can be looked at in two ways. From one point of view they have no causal significance but simply indicate the course that capital accumulation and real output would have to take if neither unemployment nor excess capacity are to appear. From another point of view, however, we can ask what kind of market behavior will cause the model economy to follow the path of equilibrium growth. In this direction it has already been assumed that both the growing labor force and the existing capital stock are thrown on the market inelastically, with the real wage and the real rental of capital adjusting instantaneously so as to clear the market. If saving and investment decisions are made independently, however, some additional marginal-efficiency-of-capital conditions have to be satisfied. The purpose of this section is to set out the price-wage-interest behavior appropriate to the growth paths sketched earlier.

There are four prices involved in the system: (1) the selling price of a unit of real output (and since real output serves also as capital this is the transfer price of a unit of capital stock) $p(t)$; (2) the money wage rate $w(t)$; (3) the money rental per unit of time of a unit of capital stock $q(t)$; (4) the rate of interest $i(t)$. One of these we can eliminate immediately. In the real system we are working with there is nothing to determine the absolute price level. Hence we can take $p(t)$, the price of real output, as given. Sometimes it will be convenient to imagine p as constant.

In a competitive economy the real wage and real rental are determined by the traditional marginal-productivity equations:

$$(10) \qquad \frac{\partial F}{\partial L} = \frac{w}{p}$$

and

$$(11) \qquad \frac{\partial F}{\partial K} = \frac{q}{p}.$$

Note in passing that with constant returns to scale the marginal productivities depend only on the capital-labor ratio r, and not on any scale quantities.[7]

7. In the polar case of pure competition, even if the individual firms have U-shaped average cost curves we can imagine changes in aggregate output taking place solely by the entry and exit of identical optimal-size firms. Then aggregate output is produced at constant cost; and in fact, because of the large number of relatively small firms each producing at approximately constant cost for small variations, we can without substantial error define an aggregate production function which will show constant returns to scale. There will be minor deviations since this aggregate production function is not strictly valid for variations in output smaller than the size of an optimal firm. But this lumpiness can for long-run analysis be treated as negligible.

One naturally thinks of adapting the model to the more general assumption of universal monopolistic competition. But the above device fails. If the industry consists of identical firms in identical large-group tangency equilibria then, subject to the restriction that output changes occur only via changes in the number of firms, one can perhaps define a constant-cost aggregate production function. But now this construct is largely irrelevant, for even if we are willing to overlook

The real rental on capital q/p is an own-rate of interest — it is the return on capital in units of capital stock. An owner of capital can by renting and reinvesting increase his holdings like compound interest at the *variable* instantaneous rate q/p, i.e., like $e^{\int_0^t q/p dt}$. Under conditions of perfect arbitrage there is a well-known close relationship between the money rate of interest and the commodity own-rate, namely

$$(12) \qquad i(t) = \frac{q(t)}{p(t)} + \frac{\dot{p}(t)}{p(t)}.$$

If the price level is in fact constant, the own-rate and the interest rate will coincide. If the price level is falling, the own-rate must exceed the interest rate to induce people to hold commodities. That the exact relation is as in (12) can be seen in several ways. For example, the owner of \$1 at time t has two options: he can lend the money for a short space of time, say until $t + h$ and earn approximately $i(t)h$ in interest, or he can buy $1/p$ units of output, earn rentals of $(q/p)h$ and then sell. In the first case he will own $1 + i(t)h$ at the end of the period; in the second case he will have $(q(t)/p(t))h + p(t + h)/p(t)$. In equilibrium these two amounts must be equal

$$1 + i(t)h = \frac{q(t)}{p(t)}h + \frac{p(t+h)}{p(t)}$$

or

$$i(t)h = \frac{q(t)}{p(t)}h + \frac{p(t+h) - p(t)}{p(t)}.$$

Dividing both sides by h and letting h tend to zero we get (12). Thus this condition equalizes the attractiveness of holding wealth in the form of capital stock or loanable funds.

Another way of deriving (12) and gaining some insight into its role in our model is to note that $p(t)$, the transfer price of a unit of capital, must equal the present value of its future stream of net

its discontinuity and treat it as differentiable, the partial derivatives of such a function will not be the marginal productivities to which the individual firms respond. Each firm is on the falling branch of its unit cost curve, whereas in the competitive case each firm was actually producing at locally constant costs. The difficult problem remains of introducing monopolistic competition into aggregative models. For example, the value-of-marginal-product equations in the text would have to go over into marginal-revenue-product relations, which in turn would require the explicit presence of demand curves. Much further experimentation is needed here, with greater realism the reward.

rentals. Thus with perfect foresight into future rentals and interest rates:

$$p(t) = \int_t^\infty q(u)e^{-\int_t^u i(s)ds}\,du\,.$$

Differentiating with respect to time yields (12). Thus within the narrow confines of our model (in particular, absence of risk, a fixed average propensity to save, and no monetary complications) the money rate of interest and the return to holders of capital will stand in just the relation required to induce the community to hold the

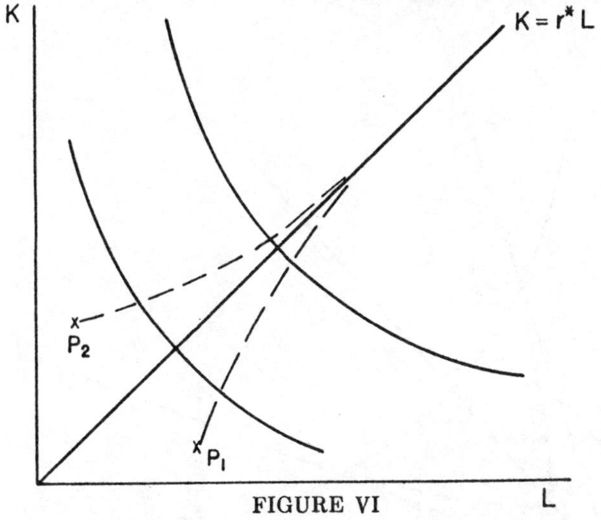

FIGURE VI

capital stock in existence. The absence of risk and uncertainty shows itself particularly in the absence of asset preferences.

Given the absolute price level $p(t)$, equations (10)–(12) determine the other three price variables, whose behavior can thus be calculated once the particular growth path is known.

Before indicating how the calculations would go in the examples of section IV, it is possible to get a general view diagrammatically, particularly when there is a stable balanced growth equilibrium. In Figure VI is drawn the ordinary isoquant map of the production function $F(K,L)$, and some possible kinds of growth paths. A given capital-labor ratio r^* is represented in Figure VI by a ray from the origin, with slope r^*. Suppose there is a stable asymptotic ratio r^*; then all growth paths issuing from arbitrary initial conditions approach the ray in the limit. Two such paths are shown, issuing from initial points P_1 and P_2. Since back in Figure I the approach of r to r^* was monotonic, the paths must look as shown in Figure VI. We see that if the initial capital-labor ratio is higher than the equilibrium value, the ratio falls and vice versa.

Figure VII corresponds to Figure II. There are three "equilibrium" rays, but the inner one is unstable. The inner ray is the dividing line among initial conditions which lead to one of the stable rays and those which lead to the other. All paths, of course, lead upward and to the right, without bending back; K and L always

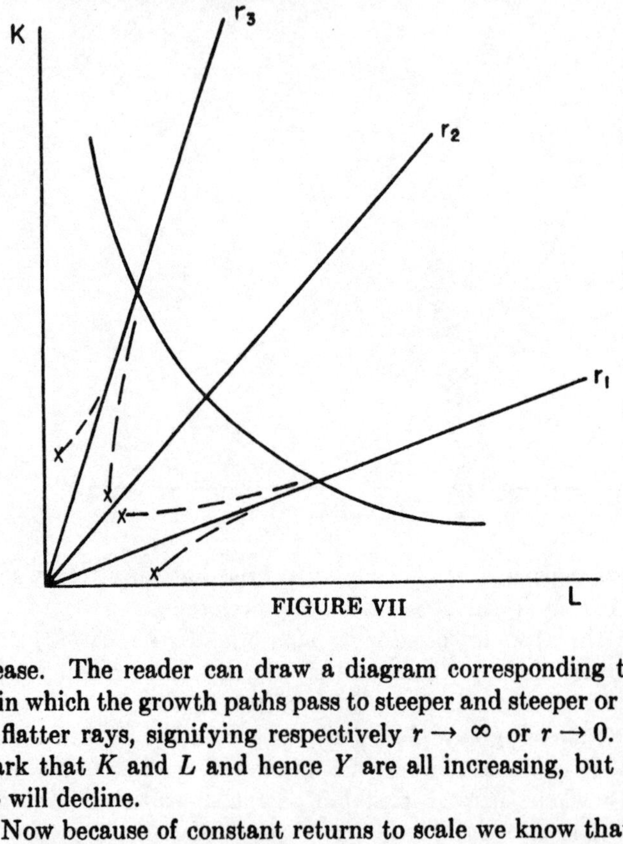

FIGURE VII

increase. The reader can draw a diagram corresponding to Figure III, in which the growth paths pass to steeper and steeper or to flatter and flatter rays, signifying respectively $r \rightarrow \infty$ or $r \rightarrow 0$. Again I remark that K and L and hence Y are all increasing, but if $r \rightarrow 0$, Y/L will decline.

Now because of constant returns to scale we know that along a ray from the origin, the slope of the isoquants is constant. This expresses the fact that marginal products depend only on the factor ratio. But in competition the slope of the isoquant reflects the ratio of the factor prices. Thus to a stable r^* as in Figure VI corresponds an equilibrium ratio w/q. Moreover, if the isoquants have the normal convexity, it is apparent that as r rises to r^*, the ratio w/q rises to its limiting value, and vice versa if r is falling.

In the unstable case, where r tends to infinity or zero it may be that w/q tends to infinity or zero. If, on the other hand, the isoquants reach the axes with slopes intermediate between the vertical and horizontal, the factor price ratio w/q will tend to a finite limit.

It might also be useful to point out that the slope of the curve $F(r,1)$ is the marginal productivity of capital at the corresponding value of r. Thus the course of the real rental q/p can be traced out in Figures I, II, and III. Remember that in those diagrams $F(r,1)$ has been reduced by the factor s, hence so has the slope of the curve. $F(r,1)$ itself represents Y/L, output per unit of labor, as a function of the capital-labor ratio.

In general if a stable growth path exists, the fall in the real wage or real rental needed to get to it may not be catastrophic at all. If there is an initial shortage of labor (compared with the equilibrium ratio) the real wage will have to fall. The higher the rate of increase of the labor force and the lower the propensity to save, the lower the equilibrium ratio and hence the more the real wage will have to fall. But the fall is not indefinite. I owe to John Chipman the remark that this result directly contradicts Harrod's position[8] that a perpetually falling rate of interest would be needed to maintain equilibrium.

Catastrophic changes in factor prices do occur in the Harrod-Domar case, but again as a consequence of the special assumption of fixed proportions. I have elsewhere discussed price behavior in the Harrod model[9] but I there described price level and interest rate and omitted consideration of factor prices. Actually there is little to say. The isoquants in the Harrod case are right-angled corners and this tells the whole story. Referring back to Figure IV, if the observed capital-labor ratio is bigger than a/b, then capital is absolutely redundant, its marginal product is zero, and the whole value of output is imputed to labor. Thus $q = 0$, and $bw = p$, so $w = p/b$. If the observed r is less than a/b labor is absolutely redundant and $w = 0$, so $q = p/a$. If labor and capital should just be in balance, $r = a/b$, then obviously it is not possible to impute any specific fraction of output to labor or capital separately. All we can be sure of is that the total value of a unit of output p will be imputed back to the

8. In his comments on an article by Pilvin, this *Journal*, Nov. 1953, p. 545.

9. R. M. Solow, "A Note on Price Level and Interest Rate in a Growth Model," *Review of Economic Studies*, No. 54 (1953–54), pp. 74–78.

composite dose of a units of capital and b units of labor (both factors are scarce). Hence w and q can have any values subject only to the condition $aq + bw = p, aq/p + bw/p = 1$. Thus in Figure IV anywhere but at $r = a/b$ either capital or labor must be redundant, and at a/b factor prices are indeterminate. And it is only in special circumstances that $r = a/b$.

Next consider the Cobb-Douglas case: $Y = K^aL^{1-a}$ and $q/p = a(K/L)^{a-1} = ar^{a-1}$. Hence $w/q = \frac{1-a}{a} r$. The exact time paths of the real factor prices can be calculated without difficulty from the solution to (7), but are of no special interest. We saw earlier, however, that the limiting capital-labor ratio is $(s/n)^{1/1-a}$. Hence the equilibrium real wage rate is $(1 - a)(s/n)^{a/1-a}$, and the equilibrium real rental is an/s. These conclusions are qualitatively just what we should expect. As always with the Cobb-Douglas function the share of labor in real output is constant.

Our third example provides one bit of variety. From $Y = (a\sqrt{K} + \sqrt{L})^2$ we can compute that $\partial Y/\partial L = a\sqrt{\frac{K}{L}} + 1 = a\sqrt{r} + 1$. In the case where a balanced growth equilibrium exists (see end of section IV) $r^* = \left(\frac{1}{\sqrt{n/s} - a}\right)^2$; therefore the limiting real wage is $w/p = \frac{1}{\sqrt{n/s} - a} + 1 = \frac{1}{1 - a\sqrt{s/n}}$. It was calculated earlier that in equilibrium growth $Y/L = \left(\frac{1}{1 - a\sqrt{s/n}}\right)^2$. But the relative share of labor is $(w/p)(L/Y) = 1 - a\sqrt{s/n}$. This is unlike the Cobb-Douglas case, where the relative shares are independent of s and n, depending only on the production function. Here we see that *in equilibrium growth* the relative share of labor is the greater the greater the rate of increase of the labor force and the smaller the propensity to save. In fact as one would expect, the faster the labor force increases the lower is the real wage in the equilibrium state of balanced growth; but the lower real wage still leaves the larger labor force a greater share of real income.

VI. Extensions

Neutral Technological Change. Perfectly arbitrary changes over time in the production function can be contemplated in principle, but are hardly likely to lead to systematic conclusions. An especially easy kind of technological change is that which simply multiplies the production function by an increasing scale factor. Thus we alter (2) to read

$$Y = A(t)F(K,L). \tag{13}$$

The isoquant map remains unchanged but the output number attached to each isoquant is multiplied by $A(t)$. The way in which the (now ever-changing) equilibrium capital-labor ratio is affected can be seen on a diagram like Figure I by "blowing up" the function $sF(r,1)$.

The Cobb-Douglas case works out very simply. Take $A(t) = e^{gt}$ and then the basic differential equation becomes

$$\dot{K} = se^{gt}K^a(L_0e^{nt})^{1-a} = sK^aL_0{}^{1-a}e^{(n(1-a)+g)t},$$

whose solution is

$$K(t) = \left[K_0{}^b - \frac{bs}{nb+g}L_0{}^b + \frac{bs}{nb+g}L_0{}^b e^{(nb+g)t}\right]^{1/b}$$

where again $b = 1 - a$. In the long run the capital stock increases at the relative rate $n + g/b$ (compared with n in the case of no technological change). The eventual rate of increase of real output is $n + ag/b$. This is not only faster than n but (if $a > 1/2$) may even be faster than $n + g$. The reason, of course, is that higher real output means more saving and investment, which compounds the rate of growth still more. Indeed now the capital-labor ratio never reaches an equilibrium value but grows forever. The ever-increasing investment capacity is, of course, not matched by any speeding up of the growth of the labor force. Hence K/L gets bigger, eventually growing at the rate g/b. If the initial capital-labor ratio is very high, it might fall initially, but eventually it turns around and its asymptotic behavior is as described.

Since the capital-labor ratio eventually rises without limit, it follows that the real wage must eventually rise and keep rising. On the other hand, the special property of the Cobb-Douglas function is that the relative share of labor is constant at $1 - a$. The other essential structural facts follow from what has already been said: for example, since Y eventually grows at rate $n + ag/b$ and K at rate $n + g/b$, the capital coefficient K/Y grows at rate $n + g/b - n - ag/b = g$.

The Supply of Labor. In general one would want to make the supply of labor a function of the real wage rate and time (since the labor force is growing). We have made the special assumption that $L = L_0e^{nt}$, i.e., that the labor-supply curve is completely inelastic with respect to the real wage and shifts to the right with the size of the labor force. We could generalize this somewhat by assuming that whatever the size of the labor force the proportion offered depends on the real wage. Specifically

$$L = L_0e^{nt}\left(\frac{w}{p}\right)^h. \tag{14}$$

Another way of describing this assumption is to note that it is a scale blow-up of a constant elasticity curve. In a detailed analysis this particular labor supply pattern would have to be modified at very high real wages, since given the size of the labor force there is an upper limit to the amount of labor that can be supplied, and (14) does not reflect this.

Our old differential equation (6) for the capital-labor ratio now becomes somewhat more complicated. Namely if we make the price level constant, for simplicity:

$$\dot{r} = sF(r,1) - nr - h\frac{\dot{w}}{w}. \tag{6a}$$

To (6a) we must append the marginal productivity condition (10) $\frac{\partial F}{\partial L} = \frac{w}{p}$. Since the marginal product of labor depends only on r, we can eliminate w.

But generality leads to complications, and instead I turn again to the tractable Cobb-Douglas function. For that case (10) becomes

$$\frac{w}{p} = (1 - a)r^a$$

and hence

$$\frac{\dot{w}}{w} = a\frac{\dot{r}}{r}.$$

After a little manipulation (6a) can be written

$$\dot{r} = (sF(r,1) - nr)\left(1 + \frac{ah}{r}\right)^{-1},$$

which gives some insight into how an elastic labor supply changes things. In the first place, an equilibrium state of balanced growth still exists, when the right-hand side becomes zero, and it is still stable, approached from any initial conditions. Moreover, the equilibrium capital-labor ratio is *unchanged;* since $\dot{r}$ becomes zero exactly where it did before. This will not always happen, of course; it is a consequence of the special supply-of-labor schedule (14). Since r behaves in much the same way so will all those quantities which depend only on r, such as the real wage.

The reader who cares to work out the details can show that over the long run capital stock and real output will grow at the same rate n as the labor force.

If we assume quite generally that $L = G(t,w/p)$ then (6) will take the form

(6b) $$\dot{r} = sF(r,1) - \frac{r}{G}\left(\frac{\partial G}{\partial t} + \dot{w}\,\frac{\partial G}{\partial\left(\frac{w}{p}\right)}\right).$$

If $\dot{r} = 0$, then $\dot{w} = 0$, and the equilibrium capital-labor ratio is determined by

$$sF(r,1) = \frac{r}{G}\,\frac{\partial G}{\partial t}.$$

Unless $1/G\ \partial G/\partial t$ should happen always to equal n, as in the case with (14), the equilibrium capital-labor ratio *will* be affected by the introduction of an elastic labor supply.

Variable Saving Ratio. Up to now, whatever else has been happening in the model there has always been growth of both labor force and capital stock. The growth of the labor force was exogenously given, while growth in the capital stock was inevitable because the savings ratio was taken as an absolute constant. As long as real income was positive, positive net capital formation must result. This rules out the possibility of a Ricardo-Mill stationary state, and suggests the experiment of letting the rate of saving depend on the yield of capital. If savings can fall to zero when income is positive, it becomes possible for net investment to cease and for the capital stock, at least, to become stationary. There will still be growth of the labor force, however; it would take us too far afield to go wholly classical with a theory of population growth and a fixed supply of land.

The simplest way to let the interest rate or yield on capital influence the volume of savings is to make the fraction of income saved depend on the real return to owners of capital. Thus total savings is $s(q/p)Y$. Under constant returns to scale and competition, the real rental will depend only on the capital-labor ratio, hence we can easily convert the savings ratio into a function of r.

Everyone is familiar with the inconclusive discussions, both abstract and econometrical, as to whether the rate of interest really has any independent effect on the volume of saving, and if so, in what direction. For the purposes of this experiment, however, the natural assumption to make is that the savings ratio depends positively on the yield of capital (and hence inversely on the capital-labor ratio).

For convenience let me skip the step of passing from q/p to r via marginal productivity, and simply write savings as $s(r)Y$. Then the only modification in the theory is that the fundamental equation (6) becomes

$$\dot{r} = s(r)F(r,1) - nr\,. \tag{6c}$$

The graphical treatment is much the same as before, except that we must allow for the variable factor $s(r)$. It may be that for sufficiently large r, $s(r)$ becomes zero. (This will be the case only if, first, there is a real rental so low that saving stops, and second, if the production function is such that a very high capital-labor ratio will drive the real return down to that critical value. The latter condition is not satisfied by all production functions.) If so, $s(r)F(r,1)$ will be zero for all sufficiently large r. If $F(0,1) = 0$, i.e., if no production is possible without capital, then $s(r)F(r,1)$ must come down to zero again at the origin, no matter how high the savings ratio is. But this is not inevitable either. Figure VIII gives a possible picture. As usual r^*, the equilibrium capital-labor ratio, is found by putting $\dot{r} = 0$ in (6c). In Figure VIII the equilibrium is stable and eventually capital and output will grow at the same rate as the labor force.

In general if $s(r)$ does vanish for large r, this eliminates the possibility of a runaway indefinite increase in the capital-labor ratio as in Figure III. The savings ratio *need* not go to zero to do this, but if it should, we are guaranteed that the last intersection with nr is a stable one.

If we compare any particular $s(r)$ with a constant saving ratio, the two curves will cross at the value of r for which $s(r)$ equals the old constant ratio. To the right the new curve will lie below (since I am assuming that $s(r)$ is a decreasing function) and to the left it will lie above the old curve. It is easily seen by example that the equilibrium r^* may be either larger or smaller than it was before. A wide variety of shapes and patterns is possible, but the net effect tends to be stabilizing: when the capital-labor ratio is high, saving is cut down; when it is low, saving is stimulated. There is still no possibility of a stationary state: should r get so high as to choke off

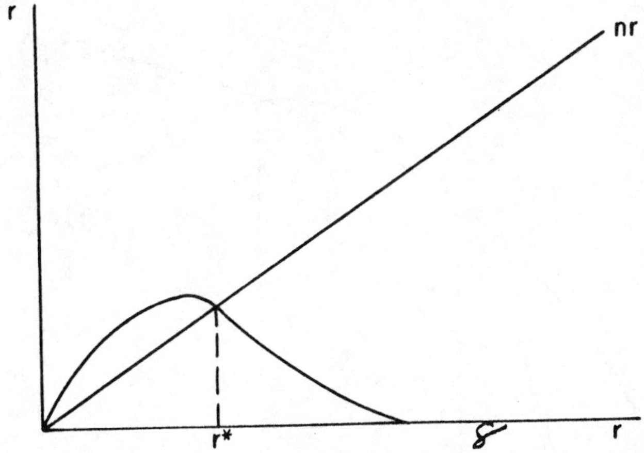

FIGURE VIII

saving and net capital formation, the continual growth of the labor force must eventually reduce it.

Taxation. My colleague, E. C. Brown, points out to me that all the above analysis can be extended to accommodate the effects of a personal income tax. In the simplest case, suppose the state levies a proportional income tax at the rate t. If the revenues are directed wholly into capital formation, the savings-investment identity (1) becomes

$$\dot{K} = s(1 - t)Y + tY = (s(1 - t) + t)Y.$$

That is, the effective savings ratio is *increased* from s to $s + t(1 - s)$. If the proceeds of the tax are directly consumed, the savings ratio is *decreased* from s to $s(1 - t)$. If a fraction v of the tax proceeds is invested and the rest consumed, the savings ratio changes to

$s + (v - s)t$ which is larger or smaller than s according as the state invests a larger or smaller fraction of its income than the private economy. The effects can be traced on diagrams such as Figure I: the curve $sF(r,1)$ is uniformly blown up or contracted and the equilibrium capital-labor ratio is correspondingly shifted. Non-proportional taxes can be incorporated with more difficulty, but would produce more interesting twists in the diagrams. Naturally the presence of an income tax will affect the price-wage relationships in the obvious way.

Variable Population Growth. Instead of treating the relative rate of population increase as a constant, we can more classically make it

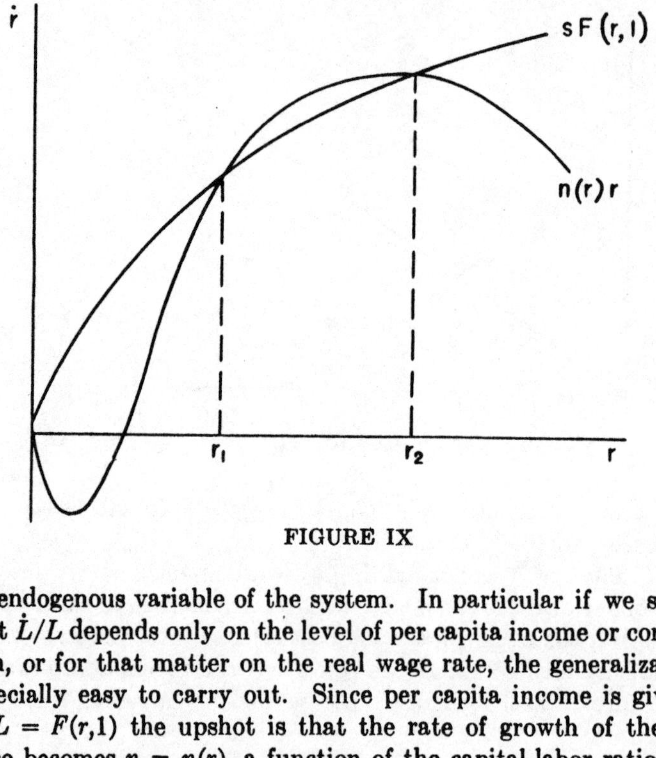

FIGURE IX

an endogenous variable of the system. In particular if we suppose that $\dot{L}/L$ depends only on the level of per capita income or consumption, or for that matter on the real wage rate, the generalization is especially easy to carry out. Since per capita income is given by $Y/L = F(r,1)$ the upshot is that the rate of growth of the labor force becomes $n = n(r)$, a function of the capital-labor ratio alone. The basic differential equation becomes

$$\dot{r} = sF(r,1) - n(r)r.$$

Graphically the only difference is that the ray nr is twisted into a curve, whose shape depends on the exact nature of the dependence between population growth and real income, and between real income and the capital-labor ratio.

Suppose, for example, that for very low levels of income per head or the real wage population tends to decrease; for higher levels of income it begins to increase; and that for still higher levels of income the rate of population growth levels off and starts to decline. The result may be something like Figure IX. The equilibrium capital-labor ratio r_1 is stable, but r_2 is unstable. The accompanying levels of per capita income can be read off from the shape of $F(r,1)$. If the initial capital-labor ratio is less than r_2, the system will of itself tend to return to r_1. If the initial ratio could somehow be boosted above the critical level r_2, a self-sustaining process of increasing per capita income would be set off (and population would still be growing). The interesting thing about this case is that it shows how, in the total absence of indivisibilities or of increasing returns, a situation may still arise in which small-scale capital accumulation only leads back to stagnation but a major burst of investment can lift the system into a self-generating expansion of income and capital per head. The reader can work out still other possibilities.

VII. Qualifications

Everything above is the neoclassical side of the coin. Most especially it is full employment economics — in the dual aspect of equilibrium condition and frictionless, competitive, causal system. All the difficulties and rigidities which go into modern Keynesian income analysis have been shunted aside. It is not my contention that these problems don't exist, nor that they are of no significance in the long run. My purpose was to examine what might be called the tightrope view of economic growth and to see where more flexible assumptions about production would lead a simple model. Underemployment and excess capacity or their opposites can still be attributed to any of the old causes of deficient or excess aggregate demand, but less readily to any deviation from a narrow "balance."

In this concluding section I want merely to mention some of the more elementary obstacles to full employment and indicate how they impinge on the neoclassical model.[1]

Rigid Wages. This assumption about the supply of labor is just the reverse of the one made earlier. The real wage is held at some

1. A much more complete and elegant analysis of these important problems is to be found in a paper by James Tobin in the *Journal of Political Economy*, LXII (1955), 103–15.

arbitrary level $\left(\frac{\bar{w}}{p}\right)$. The level of employment must be such as to keep the marginal product of labor at this level. Since the marginal productivities depend only on the capital-labor ratio, it follows that fixing the real wage fixes r at, say, $\bar{r}$. Thus $K/L = \bar{r}$. Now there is no point in using r as our variable so we go back to (3) which in view of the last sentence becomes

$$\bar{r}\dot{L} = sF(\bar{r}L,L)\,,$$

or

$$\frac{\dot{L}}{L} = \frac{s}{\bar{r}}\,F(\bar{r},1).$$

This says that *employment* will increase exponentially at the rate $(s/r)F(\bar{r},1)$. If this rate falls short of n, the rate of growth of the labor force, unemployment will develop and increase. If $s/\bar{r}F(\bar{r},1) > n$, labor shortage will be the outcome and presumably the real wage will eventually become flexible upward. What this boils down to is that if $(\bar{w}/p)$ corresponds to a capital-labor ratio that would normally tend to decrease ($\dot{r} < 0$), unemployment develops, and vice versa. In the diagrams, $s/\bar{r}F(\bar{r},1)$ is just the slope of the ray from the origin to the $sF(r,1)$ curve at $\bar{r}$. If this slope is flatter than n, unemployment develops; if steeper, labor shortage develops.

Liquidity Preference. This is much too complicated a subject to be treated carefully here. Moreover the paper by Tobin just mentioned contains a new and penetrating analysis of the dynamics connected with asset preferences. I simply note here, however crudely, the point of contact with the neoclassical model.

Again taking the general price level as constant (which is now an unnatural thing to do), the transactions demand for money will depend on real output Y and the choice between holding cash and holding capital stock will depend on the real rental q/p. With a given quantity of money this provides a relation between Y and q/p or, essentially, between K and L, e.g.,

$$\text{(15)} \qquad \bar{M} = Q\left(Y, \frac{q}{p}\right) = Q(F(K,L),\, F_K(K,L)\,)$$

where now K represents capital *in use.* On the earlier assumption of full employment of labor via flexible wages, we can put $L = L_0e^{nt}$, and solve (15) for $K(t)$, or employed capital equipment. From $K(t)$ and L we can compute $Y(t)$ and hence total saving $sY(t)$. But this represents net investment (wealth not held as cash must be held as capital). The given initial stock of capital and the flow of investment determine the available capital stock which can be compared with $K(t)$ to measure the excess supply or demand for the services of capital.

In the famous "trap" case where the demand for idle balances becomes infinitely elastic at some positive rate of interest, we have a rigid factor price which can be treated much as rigid wages were treated above. The result will be underutilization of capital if the interest rate becomes rigid somewhere above the level corresponding to the equilibrium capital-labor ratio.

But it is exactly here that the futility of trying to describe this situation in terms of a "real" neoclassical model becomes glaringly evident. Because now one can no longer bypass the direct leverage of monetary factors on real consumption and investment. When the issue is the allocation of asset-holdings between cash and capital stock, the price of the composite commodity becomes an important variable and there is no dodging the need for a monetary dynamics.

Policy Implications. This is hardly the place to discuss the bearing of the previous highly abstract analysis on the practical problems of economic stabilization. I have been deliberately as neoclassical as you can get. Some part of this rubs off on the policy side. It may take deliberate action to maintain full employment. But the multiplicity of routes to full employment, via tax, expenditure, and monetary policies, leaves the nation *some* leeway to choose whether it wants high employment with relatively heavy capital formation, low consumption, rapid growth; or the reverse, or some mixture. I do not mean to suggest that this kind of policy (for example: cheap money and a budget surplus) can be carried on without serious strains. But one of the advantages of this more flexible model of growth is that it provides a theoretical counterpart to these practical possibilities.[2]

Uncertainty, etc. No credible theory of investment can be built on the assumption of perfect foresight and arbitrage over time. There are only too many reasons why net investment should be at

2. See the paper by Paul A. Samuelson in *Income Stabilization for a Developing Democracy*, ed. Millikan (New Haven, 1953), p. 577. Similar thoughts have been expressed by William Vickrey in his essay in *Post-Keynesian Economics*, ed. Kurihara (New Brunswick, 1954).

times insensitive to current changes in the real return to capital, at other times oversensitive. All these cobwebs and some others have been brushed aside throughout this essay. In the context, this is perhaps justifiable.

Robert M. Solow.

Massachusetts Institute of Technology

[2]

SECOND ESSAY ON THE GOLDEN RULE OF ACCUMULATION

By Edmund S. Phelps*

Four years ago, I presented a theorem on maximal consumption in a golden age [7]. The same theorem was discovered and published by Allais [1], Desrousseaux [3], Mrs. Robinson [10], Swan [15], and von Weizsäcker [17].[1] The theorem established may be expressed as follows:

> If there exists a golden-age growth path[2] on which the social net rate of return to investment equals the rate of growth (hence, in one class of models, the fraction of output saved equals the capital elasticity of output)—or, in market terms, a golden-age path on which the competitive interest rate equals the growth rate and hence gross investment equals the gross competitive earnings of capital—then this golden age produces a path of consumption which is uniformly higher than the consumption path associated with any other golden age.

The consumption-maximizing golden age will be referred to in this paper, as in [7], as the Golden Rule or GR path.

The papers cited raise two sorts of questions. The first concerns the conditions for the existence of the GR path. Some of the papers (including my own) erroneously suggest that the GR path can exist only in "neoclassical" models, i.e., models in which capital and labor are continuously substitutable. Some of the papers leave the false impression that the GR path exists only if there is no technical progress, while my own paper errs with respect to the type of technical progress which permits a GR path. The first part of this paper examines in two kinds of models the conditions for the existence of the GR path. We show, as a few writers have indicated, that the GR path may exist in the un-

* The author is associate professor of economics at Yale University. He owes a great debt to Tjalling C. Koopmans who contributed the basis for the theorems established in the second part of this paper. David Cass, Peter A. Diamond, Paul A. Samuelson, and Robert M. Solow made useful comments on an earlier draft. The author alone is responsible for any errors in the final product.

[1] Mention should also be made of an unpublished paper by Beckmann [2] in which the theorem is proved for the Cobb-Douglas case and the dissertation of Srinivasan [14] in which the existence of a state of maximum per capita consumption with a growing labor force is shown. All these authors made the finding independently, circa 1960.

[2] By a golden-age path we mean a growth path in which literally every variable changes (if at all) at a constant relative rate. It follows immediately that if investment is positive then output, investment, and consumption must all grow at the same (constant) rate. Various other properties can be derived.

neoclassical Harrod-Domar model as well as in the neoclassical model. And we show that a positive-investment GR path can exist only if technical progress can be described as purely "labor-augmenting."

Question also arises as to the normative significance of the theorem. We called the saving rule prevailing on the consumption-maximizing golden-age path the Golden Rule of Accumulation because, on that path, each "generation" saves (on behalf of future generations as it were) that fraction of income which it would have past generations save, subject to the constraint that all generations past and present are to save the same fraction of income. But no proof of the "optimality" of the GR path was given nor was any suggestion of its optimality seriously intended. Society need not confine itself to golden-age paths (should they exist) nor aim to achieve golden-age growth asymptotically. And even if some golden-age path should be utility-maximizing (at least for some initial conditions) the rate of time preference may make that path different from the GR path. It was evidently reflections such as these which led Pearce [6] and Samuelson [11] to doubt whether the GR path has any important normative significance at all.

In the second part of this paper it will be shown, however, that, whether or not it is "optimal," the GR path has the following important normative property: Any growth path on which, at some point in time and forever after, the capital-output ratio always exceeds its GR level by at least some constant amount—equivalently, any path which eventually keeps the social net rate of return to investment (or competitive rate of interest) permanently below its GR value by at least some finite amount—is *dynamically inefficient* in the sense that there always exists another path which, starting from the same initial capital stock, produces more consumption at least some of the time and never less consumption. This is the proposition conjectured by the author in reply to Pearce [8]. Its proof here is based on a proof provided by Tjalling C. Koopmans. The significance of the theorem is this: no path which is dynamically inefficient can be optimal; hence no path which transgresses the GR path in the manner described can be optimal. (Warning: It is only paths which so transgress the GR path for *infinitely long time* that can be shown to be dynamically inefficient.)

Since the conditions for a GR path are stringent, this theorem is only of theoretical interest. But we are able to prove analogous theorems even when no golden-age path, and hence no GR path, need exist. Thus we show that the possibility of "excessive capital deepening," despite a continuously positive rate of interest, is quite general.

A fuller summary of the paper and some concluding remarks close the paper.

I. *Existence of the Golden-Rule Path*

Section A will study the neoclassical and the Harrod-Domar models on the postulate that technical progress can be described as solely labor-augmenting. Section B will show that a GR path can exist only if technical progress can be described as labor-augmenting.

A. *Labor-Augmenting Technical Progress*

In both the neoclassical and Harrod-Domar cases, output, $Q(t)$, is a continuous function of capital, $K(t)$, labor, $L(t)$, and time:

$$Q(t) = F[K(t), e^{\lambda t}L(t)], \qquad \lambda \geq 0. \tag{1}$$

It is assumed here that technical progress can be described as solely labor-augmenting—time enters only in the second (labor) argument of the function—and that labor augmentation occurs at the constant exponential rate λ. The function is supposed to be homogeneous of degree one (constant returns to scale).

We suppose that the labor force grows exponentially at rate γ:

$$L(t) = L_0e^{\gamma t}, \qquad \gamma \geq 0. \tag{2}$$

Capital is taken to be subject to exponential decay at rate δ, so that if $I(t)$ denotes the rate of gross investment:

$$I(t) = \dot{K}(t) + \delta K(t), \qquad \delta \geq 0. \tag{3}$$

Finally, consumption, $C(t)$, is the difference between output and gross investment:

$$C(t) = Q(t) - I(t), \qquad C(t) \geq 0. \tag{4}$$

The neoclassical case. We suppose now that the production function has the following "neoclassical" properties: it is twice differentiable (smooth marginal products), it is strictly concave (diminishing marginal products), and it has everywhere positive first derivatives (marginal products). That is,

$$\frac{\partial F}{\partial K} > 0, \qquad \frac{\partial F}{\partial L} > 0; \qquad \frac{\partial^2 F}{\partial K^2} < 0, \qquad \frac{\partial^2 F}{\partial L^2} < 0. \tag{1a}$$

By virtue of constant returns to scale and (2):

$$Q(t) = L_0e^{(\gamma+\lambda)t}F\left[\frac{K(t)}{L_0e^{(\gamma+\lambda)t}}, 1\right]. \tag{5}$$

Hence, if we let $k(t)$ denote capital per unit "effective labor,"

(6) $$k(t) = \frac{K(t)}{L_0 e^{(\gamma+\lambda)t}},$$

and if we define

(7) $$f(k(t)) = F[k(t), 1],$$

we can express the production function for all t as

(8) $$Q(t) = L_0 e^{(\gamma+\lambda)t} f(k(t)), \qquad f'(k(t)) > 0, \qquad f''(k(t)) < 0.$$

We show now that if $k(t)$ is equal to any positive constant $k>0$, then the economy will grow in the manner of a golden age, provided of course that the constraint $I(t) \leq Q(t)$ is satisfied.

Clearly, output will grow exponentially at rate $g=\gamma+\lambda$,

(9) $$Q(t) = L_0 e^{(\gamma+\lambda)t} f(k) = Q(0)e^{gt},$$

as will the capital stock:

(10) $$K(t) = L_0 e^{(\gamma+\lambda)t} k = K(0)e^{gt}.$$

Hence, from (3) and the relation $\dot{K}(t)=gK(t)$, investment will also grow at the rate g:

(11) $$I(t) = (g+\delta)K(0)e^{gt} = (g+\delta)L_0 k e^{gt}.$$

Since investment and output will grow at the same rate, g, so will consumption, $C(t)$, (where $C(t)=Q(t)-I(t)$)

(12) $$C(t) = [Q(0) - (g+\delta)K(0)]e^{gt} = [f(k) - (g+\delta)k]L_0 e^{gt}.$$

The gross investment-output ratio, s, will be constant:

(13) $$s = \frac{I(t)}{Q(t)} = \frac{(g+\delta)K(0)}{Q(0)} = \frac{(g+\delta)k}{f(k)}.$$

So will the marginal productivity of capital,

$$\frac{\partial F(K(t), e^{\lambda t}L(t))}{\partial K}:$$

(14) $$\frac{\partial F}{\partial K} = \frac{\partial F\left(\frac{K(t)}{L_0 e^{(\gamma+\lambda)t}}, 1\right)}{\partial\left(\frac{K(t)}{L_0 e^{(\gamma+\lambda)t}}\right)} = f'(k).$$

And so will the share of gross output going to capital, a, if capital receives its marginal product:

$$a = \frac{\partial F}{\partial K} \frac{K(t)}{Q(t)} = \frac{f'(k)k}{f(k)} \cdot \tag{15}$$

Conversely, it can be shown that every golden-age path in which investment is positive implies a constant value of $k(t) > 0$ and a growth rate equal to $\gamma+\lambda$.[3] Therefore, a golden age with positive investment occurs if and only if $k(t) = k$, a constant.

Hence, in every golden age with positive investment, the growth rate of output, investment, and consumption is $\gamma+\lambda$. These golden-age consumption paths are therefore logarithmically parallel. Associated with each golden age is a certain value of s, of $\partial F/\partial K$, of $K(0)$ and of k. Let us assume for the moment (we drop this assumption later) that the golden age yielding the maximal consumption path, if such exists, is one in which k, and hence $K(0)$, is greater than zero. We assume, in other words, that if a maximum exists, it is an *interior* one rather than a corner maximum at $k=0$. Then, for every t, the derivative of $C(t)$ with respect to $K(0)$ in (12) must be zero on the GR path:

$$\frac{\partial C(t)}{\partial K(0)} = \frac{\partial F}{\partial K} - (g + \delta) = 0. \tag{16}$$

Equivalently, one can differentiate (12) with respect to k to obtain:

$$f'(k) - (g + \delta) = 0. \tag{16a}$$

That is, on this assumption, the marginal product of capital will equal $g+\delta$ on the GR path (if it exists).[4] Transposing terms in (16), we have:

$$\frac{\partial F}{\partial K} - \delta = g. \tag{17}$$

The left-hand side of (17) is the social net rate of return to investment.[5] Hence this result states that if an *interior* golden-age consumption maxi-

[3] In a golden age, if investment is positive, then investment, consumption, and output must all grow at the same constant relative rate, denoted g. Hence $Q(t) = Q(0)e^{gt}$ and $I(t) = I(0)e^{gt}$. And capital must grow at some constant relative rate, denoted h. Hence $\dot{K}(t) = hK(t)$. Therefore, by (3), $I(t) = (h+\delta)K(t)$ which implies $h=g$. But if $K(t) = K(0)e^{gt}$ then, from (1) and the postulate that $\partial F/\partial L > 0$, if follows that $g=\gamma+\lambda$, hence that $k(t)$ is constant.

[4] A common-sense explanation of (16) has been provided by Solow [13]. Imagine that capital is initially free but that we are to invest so as to maintain a golden age once the initial capital stock has been chosen. Consider a small increase of initial capital, $\Delta K(0)$. The rules of the game require that we then increase the rate of investment by $\Delta I(0) = (g+\delta)\Delta K(0)$ to make capital grow at rate g. The increase of initial capital will increase output by $\Delta Q(0) = (\partial F/\partial K)\Delta K(0)$. Hence consumption will increase by $\Delta C(0) = \Delta Q(0) - \Delta I(0) = [(\partial F/\partial K) - (g+\delta)]\Delta K(0)$. As long as $(\partial F/\partial K) > g+\delta$ it pays to accept more capital. The consumption-maximizing golden age is reached when $K(0)$ has increased to the point where $(\partial F/\partial K) - (g+\delta) = 0$.

mum exists, it is where the social net rate of return to investment equals the golden-age growth rate. This is the first (and most general) way to characterize the GR path in purely technological terms.

The other technological characterization is obtained by multiplying both sides of (17) by $K(t)/Q(t)$ and rearranging terms:

$$\frac{\partial F}{\partial K}\frac{K(t)}{Q(t)} = (g+\delta)\frac{K(t)}{Q(t)} = \frac{I(t)}{Q(t)}. \tag{18}$$

Hence

$$s = \frac{\partial F}{\partial K}\frac{K(t)}{Q(t)}. \tag{19}$$

This states that on the interior GR path the saving ratio is equal to the elasticity of output with respect to capital. (This was the characterization of the GR path employed by Swan and the present author; of course, such a capital elasticity exists only in one-commodity models in which output is a function of "capital.")

Conditions (17) and (19) can be translated into "market" terms if the economy is purely competitive and free of externalities in production. On these assumptions, $\partial F/\partial K$ is the gross rental rate of capital and $(\partial F/\partial K)-\delta$ is the (equilibrium) rate of interest. Then (17) implies that on the interior GR path the interest rate is equal to the golden-age growth rate. (19) implies that the saving ratio equals capital's gross relative share, or that net investment equals net profits.

Now we shall investigate the conditions for the existence of the GR path. For this purpose we adapt, in Figure 1, a diagram first presented by Pearce [6] and later employed by Koopmans [5]. It is a diagram of the relation between $K(0)$ and $C(0)$ in a golden age as given by (1) and (12):

$$C(0) = F[K(0), L_0] - (g+\delta)K(0). \tag{20}$$

(Some readers may wish to diagram $c=f(k)-(g+\delta)k$ where c is consumption per unit effective labor force and observe that c is maximal where k is such that $f'(k)=g+\delta$.)

Figure 1 depicts a golden-age consumption maximum at $K(0)=\hat{K}(0)$ where $(\partial F/\partial K)=g+\delta$. It is easy to see from the diagram, however, that there are two cases in which no such interior GR maximum exists.

[5] By the (instantaneous) social net rate of return to investment at time t we mean

$$\lim_{h\to 0}\left\{\left[\frac{\partial C(t+h)}{\partial C(t)}-1\right]\Big/h\right\}.$$

For a discussion of the rate of return to investment see Solow [12].

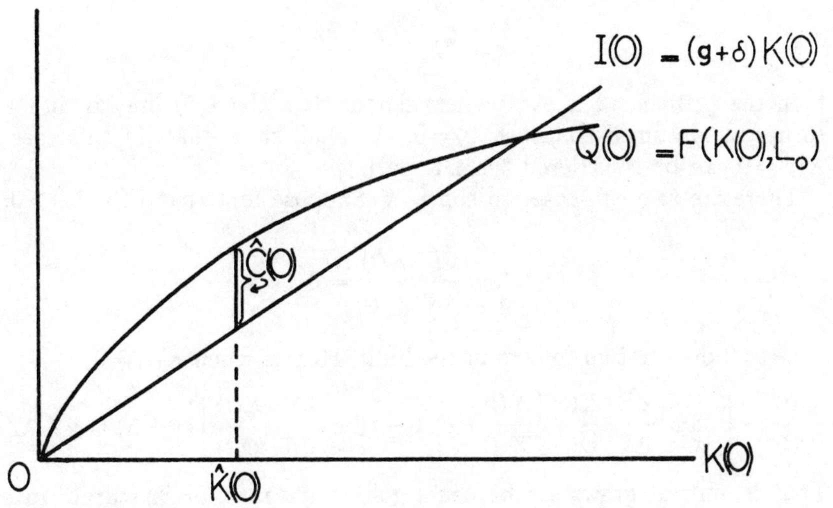

FIGURE 1

In one case, neither an interior nor a corner maximum exists. This is the case in which

$$\lim_{K\to\infty} \frac{\partial F}{\partial K} > g + \delta;$$

then the $Q(0)$ curve is everywhere steeper than the $I(0)$ line so that the distance between them always increases with $K(0)$. It is easy to see that this case implies

$$\lim_{K\to\infty} \frac{Q(0)}{K(0)} \geq g + \delta.$$

While our assumptions on the production function do not exclude this possibility, it can be shown however that, if $g+\delta>0$, this case can arise only if positive output can be produced without labor. Proof: $(Q/K)=F(1, L/K)$. Hence

$$\lim_{K\to\infty} \frac{Q}{K} = F(1, 0).$$

But $F(1, 0)=0$ if $F(K, 0)=0$. Hence

$$\lim_{K\to\infty} \frac{Q}{K} \geq g + \delta > 0$$

only if labor is not required for positive production.

The other case in which no interior maximum exists occurs when

$$\lim_{K\to 0} \frac{\partial F}{\partial K} \leq g + \delta;$$

then the $Q(0)$ curve is everywhere flatter than the $I(0)$ line so that a corner maximum exists at $K(0)=0$. We shall show that, in this case, $K(t)=0$ can be considered the GR path.

There are two sub-cases to consider. Suppose first that $F(0, L_0)>0$. Then

$$\lim_{K\to 0} \frac{\partial F}{\partial K}\cdot\frac{K(t)}{Q(t)} = 0$$

since $Q(t)$ does not go to zero in the limit. Hence, when $K(t)=0$;

$$\frac{\dot{Q}(t)}{Q(t)} = \left[\lim_{K\to 0} \frac{\partial F}{\partial K}\cdot\frac{K(t)}{Q(t)}\right]\frac{\dot{K}(t)}{K(t)} + \left[1 - \lim_{K\to 0} \frac{\partial F}{\partial K}\,\frac{K(t)}{Q(t)}\right](\gamma+\lambda) = \gamma+\lambda.$$

That is, output grows at the usual golden-age rate, or "natural" rate $\gamma+\lambda$. So does consumption. This golden-age path, $C(t)=F(0, L_0)e^{gt}$, is maximal and hence it is the GR path since

$$\lim_{K\to 0} \frac{\partial F}{\partial K} \leq g + \delta;$$

investment would have to increase more than output to maintain a golden age with positive $k(t)$.[6]

The other sub-case is $F(0, L_0)=0$. In this case the $Q(0)$ curve lies uniformly below the $I(0)$ line (since they both start from the origin and $I(0)$ rises more steeply from the start). This implies that no golden age with $K(0)>0$ is possible for it would require $I(t)>Q(t)$. But $K(t)=0$ clearly implies a "golden age" for then $C(t)=Q(t)=I(t)=F(0, L_0e^{(\lambda+\gamma)t})=0$. Since this is the only golden age that exists, it is the maximal golden age and hence the GR path.

Summarizing, if labor is required for positive output and $g+\delta>0$ then a GR path always exists in the model under consideration. If there exists a golden-age capital path $K(t)=K(0)e^{gt}$ such that $(\partial F/\partial K)=g+\delta$ then this is the GR path; if there does not exist such a path then $K(t)=0$ is the GR path. In short, $K(t)=K(0)e^{gt}$ produces the GR path if $(\partial F/\partial K)=g+\delta$ for some $K(0)>0$ or if $(\partial F/\partial K)\leq g+\delta$ when $K(0)=0$.

The Harrod-Domar case. To illustrate the fact that no neoclassical assumptions are required for the existence of the GR path, we now drop the assumptions of twice differentiability, strict concavity and everywhere positive marginal products and specialize (1) to the Harrod-

[6] Note that on this GR path, where $K(t)=0$, the saving ratio and capital's relative share are equal, since they are both equal to zero. But the interest rate may be less than the growth rate.

Domar case:

$$Q(t) = \min\left[\alpha K(t),\ \beta e^{\lambda t} L(t)\right]. \tag{1b}$$

We retain equations (2), (3), and (4).

By virtue of (2) and the constant returns to scale implied by (lb):

$$Q(t) = L_0 e^{(\gamma+\lambda)t} \min\left[\alpha \frac{K(t)}{L_0 e^{(\gamma+\lambda)t}},\ \beta\right] \tag{21}$$

or

$$Q(t) = L_0 e^{(\gamma+\lambda)t} \min\left[\alpha k(t),\ \beta\right]. \tag{21a}$$

It is easy to show again that if $k(t)$ is equal to any constant $k > 0$ then, provided the restraint $I(t) \leq Q(t)$ is satisfied, golden-age growth results. Clearly output, capital and investment will grow at the constant rate $g = \gamma + \lambda$; hence, so will consumption. As before, $s = (g+\delta)K(0)/Q(0)$; if $\alpha K(0) \leq \beta L_0$ (meaning that capital is not in surplus) then $(K(0)/Q(0)) = 1/\alpha$ and if $\alpha K(0) > \beta L_0$ then $(K(0)/Q(0)) = (K(0)/\beta L_0)$. $\partial F/\partial K$ will be constant, either equal to α (if labor is in surplus) or zero (if capital is in surplus).

Conversely, $k(t)$ is constant in every golden age with positive investment. If investment (hence output and consumption) is growing at some constant rate, g, and capital is growing exponentially then capital must also be growing at rate g. Now if g were less than $\gamma + \lambda$, then labor would become redundant (if it was not initially) and the unemployment ratio would grow nonexponentially, which contradicts the notion of a golden age; if g were greater than $\gamma + \lambda$, then labor would eventually become scarce (if it were not initially) and growth of output at the rate g would then be impossible Hence, in a golden age with positive investment, capital grows at the rate $\gamma + \lambda$ and $k(t)$ is therefore constant. Therefore, golden-age growth with positive investment occurs if and only if $k(t)$ is constant.

To investigate the GR path we use Figure 2 which differs from Figure 1 only in that, in (20), we have substituted the Harrod-Domar function $\min\left[\alpha K(0),\ \beta L_0\right]$ for $F[K(0),\ L_0]$:

$$C(0) = \min\left[\alpha K(0),\ \beta L_0\right] - (g + \delta)K(0). \tag{20'}$$

The diagram depicts an interior golden-age consumption maximum at $K(0) = \beta L_0/\alpha$. At this point the capital stock is just large enough to employ the entire labor force. A larger capital stock would put capital in surplus; a smaller stock would cause a surplus of labor. In the Harrod-Domar model, therefore, the interior GR path, if it exists, is the golden-age path in which there is full employment of both labor and capital.

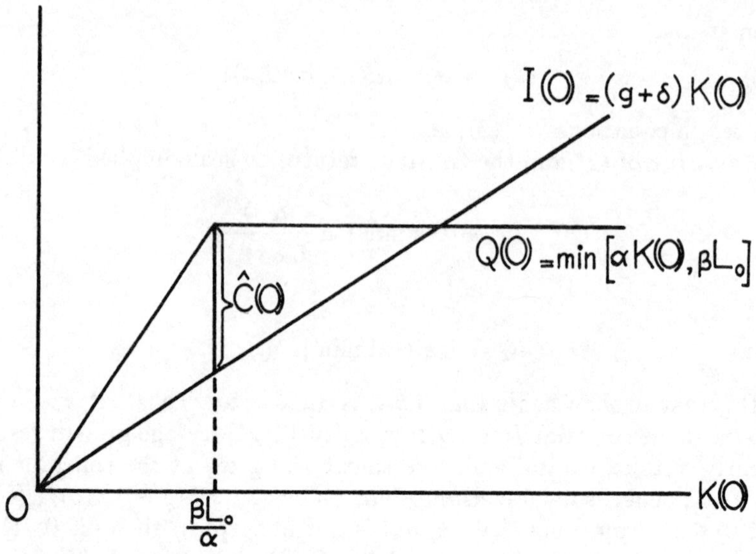

FIGURE 2

What of the usual characterizations of the GR path in terms of the interest rate and capital's relative share? On the interior GR path the saving ratio is $(g+\delta)/\alpha$ and the growth rate $\gamma+\delta$. But relative shares and the rate of interest are indeterminate: we can say only that capital's share is between zero and one and that the interest rate is between zero and $\alpha-\delta$. But it is true that this interior GR path is the only golden-age path with positive investment in which it is possible that the saving ratio equal capital's share and the interest rate equal the growth rate; for in all other positive-investment golden ages capital's relative share and the interest rate are determinate and do not satisfy these equalities. Thus it remains valid that if there exists a golden age in which the interest rate equals the growth rate and the saving ratio equals capital's relative share, then this golden-age path is the GR path. Hence the Golden Rule theorem applies to the Harrod-Domar model as well as to the neoclassical model. (See Robinson [10] and Samuelson [11] for similar comments on more complicated fixed-coefficient models.)

As in the neoclassical case, however, an interior GR path may not exist. Figure 2 shows that if $\alpha<g+\delta$ then no golden age with positive investment exists, hence no interior GR path. In this case the "golden age" $K(t)=Q(t)=I(t)=C(t)=0$ is the only possible golden age; hence it can be regarded as the GR path.

Note that, in the Harrod-Domar case, either an interior or a corner GR path must exist since positive labor input is required for positive output.

B. *The Necessity that Technical Progress Be Labor-Augmenting*

The necessity that any technical progress be describable as labor-augmenting for the existence of a positive-investment (interior) GR path follows from analyses of technical progress by Diamond [4], Robinson [9] and Uzawa [16]. I shall merely indicate one line of proof.

The existence of an interior GR path depends upon the existence of a continuum of logarithmically parallel growth paths on which output, consumption, and investment all grow at some common exponential rate, say g. Since investment grows at rate g and has always been doing so, capital also grows at rate g on each of the paths.

Suppose that the production function is neoclassical (see (1a)) and is homogeneous of degree one:

$$Q(t) = F[K(t), L(t); t]. \tag{22}$$

Differentiating this totally with respect to time and dividing the resulting equation by $Q(t)$ yields

$$\frac{\dot{Q}(t)}{Q(t)} = a(t)\frac{\dot{K}(t)}{K(t)} + [1 - a(t)]\frac{\dot{L}(t)}{L(t)} + \frac{F_t}{Q(t)} \tag{23}$$

where $a(t)$, capital's relative share at t, denotes $(\partial F/\partial K)/(K(t)/Q(t))$, so that, by Euler's theorem, $1-a(t)=(\partial F/\partial L)/(L(t)/Q(t))=$ labor's share. $F_t/Q(t)=(\partial F/\partial t)/Q(t)$ is the relative rate of technical progress at time t.

If the aforementioned parallel paths exist, we may substitute g for $Q(t)/Q(t)$ and $\dot{K}(t)/K(t)$ and obtain

$$\frac{F_t/Q(t)}{1 - a(t)} = g - \frac{\dot{L}(t)}{L(t)} = \Phi(t). \tag{24}$$

Hence, the rate of technical progress expressed as a ratio to labor's relative share is a function solely of time (independent of the capital-labor ratio) if these parallel paths exist.

Diamond [4] has shown the equivalence of the property expressed in (24) and the Harrod-neutrality, for all K, L, and t, of the technical progress represented by $F[K(t), L(t); t]$. (By definition, progress is Harrod-neutral if and only if relative shares or the capital-output ratio are constant over time for a constant rate of interest or marginal product of capital.)

Now the Robinson-Uzawa theorem [9] [16] proves that if technical progress is everywhere Harrod-neutral then technical progress can be described as purely labor-augmenting:[7]

[7] There are cases in which Harrod-neutral progress can be described as capital-augmenting. The Cobb-Douglas function is such a case (and the only case under constant returns to scale) for the function $K^{\alpha}[A(t)L]^{1-\alpha}$ can be written $[B(t)K]^{\alpha}L^{1-\alpha}$.

$$Q(t) = F[K(t), L(t); t] = G[K(t), A(t)L(t)]. \tag{25}$$

All this proves that, if an interior GR path exists, any technical progress present must be describable as labor-augmenting.

Note that if $Q(t)$ and $K(t)$ both grow exponentially at rate g then, by constant returns to scale, $A(t)L(t)$ or "effective labor" must also grow exponentially at rate g. (It is not essential that $A(t)$ and $L(t)$ each grow exponentially.)

Labor augmentation is, of course, a very restrictive type of technical progress. But the notion of the Golden Rule path has considerable heuristic value even if progress cannot be described as labor-augmenting or even as "factor-augmenting" in general. It will be shown in the next part of this paper that there still exists in these cases a critical path—which we call the Quasi-Golden-Rule path—having, in one respect, the same normative significance as the GR path.

II. *Inefficient Growth Paths*

The preceding analysis can be made to show immediately that some golden-age paths are inefficient. Consider any golden age in which the capital-effective labor ratio forever exceeds its GR value. It will be dominated by a policy of immediately gobbling up the "excess" capital and forever after maintaining the capital-effective labor ratio at its GR value, i.e., following the GR path; such a policy will clearly make consumption higher at every point in time. It follows that any investment policy which at some point permanently fixes the capital-effective labor ratio at a level exceeding the GR level is inefficient and therefore cannot be optimal (since a policy to be optimal must be optimal at every stage).

In the author's reply to Pearce an obvious generalization of this result to non-golden-age paths was conjectured: "Any policy which causes the capital-output ratio [equivalently, the capital-effective labor ratio, since the one ratio is a monotonically increasing function of the other] permanently to exceed—always by some minimum finite amount—its GR level is inefficient and hence cannot be optimal" [8, p. 1099]. A proof of this conjecture was later communicated to the author by Tjalling Koopmans. In what follows we present what is essentially Koopmans' proof and then employ the technique to prove an analogous theorem for the case in which technical progress must be described as (at least partially) capital-augmenting, for the case of nonexponential labor growth and factor augmentation, and finally for the case in which technical progress cannot necessarily be described as factor-augmenting.

We confine our analysis to the neoclassical production function, although the theorems proved clearly carry over to the Harrod-Domar production function.

A. *Pure Labor Augmentation at a Constant Rate*

Suppose first that technical progress can be described as solely labor-augmenting and that the rate of labor augmentation is a constant, λ. Then, as was shown above, when $k(t)$ is fixed, the consumption path is given by the equation

$$C(t) = [f(k) - (\gamma + \lambda + \delta)k]L_0e^{(\gamma+\lambda)t} \tag{12}$$

where $f'(k)>0, f''(k)<0$.

We show now that if $k(t)$ is not fixed, then the consumption path is given by the equation

$$C(t) = [f(k(t)) - (\gamma + \lambda + \delta)k(t) - \dot{k}(t)]L_0e^{(\gamma+\lambda)t} \tag{26}$$

Proof: From (3), (4), and (9) we have

$$C(t) + \dot{K}(t) + \delta K(t) = L_0e^{(\gamma+\lambda)t}f(k(t)) \tag{27}$$

or

$$\frac{C(t)}{L_0e^{(\gamma+\lambda)t}} = f(k(t)) - \delta k(t) - \frac{\dot{K}(t)}{L_0e^{(\gamma+\lambda)t}}\cdot \tag{28}$$

Now, differentiating $k(t)$ with respect to time, we have

$$\dot{k}(t) = \frac{\dot{K}(t)}{L_0e^{(\gamma+\lambda)t}} - (\gamma + \lambda)\frac{K(t)}{L_0e^{(\gamma+\lambda)t}} \tag{29}$$

or

$$\frac{\dot{K}(t)}{L_0e^{(\gamma+\lambda)t}} = \dot{k}(t) + (\gamma + \lambda)k(t). \tag{30}$$

Substituting (30) into (28) yields (26).

Assume now that there exists a GR path, hence a GR value of $k(t)$, say $\hat{k}$. For simplicity only, we assume that the GR maximum is an interior one so that $\hat{k}$ is determined by the equation, derived from (12) (see also (16a)):

$$f'(\hat{k}) = \gamma + \lambda + \delta. \tag{31}$$

As a consequence of (31), the expression $f(k)-(\gamma+\lambda+\delta)k$ is monotonically increasing in k up to $k=\hat{k}$ and monotonically decreasing in k for all $k>\hat{k}$.

Consider now any capital-path which "violates" the Golden Rule in that, at some point in time (perhaps initially) and thereafter, it keeps the capital-effective labor ratio in excess of its GR value by at least some positive, constant amount. That is, consider any path $k(t)$ such that, for all $t \geq t_0 \geq 0$,

$$k(t) \geq \hat{k} + \epsilon, \qquad \epsilon > 0 \text{ and independent of } t. \tag{32}$$

Then the following theorem can be proved:

> Any path satisfying (32) is "dynamically inefficient" or (equivalently) "dominated," for there always exists another path which, starting from the same initial capital stock, provides more consumption at least some of the time and never less consumption.

Proof: Define another path, $k^*(t)$, such that

$$k^*(t) = \begin{cases} k(t), & 0 \leq t < t_0; \\ k(t) - \epsilon, & t \geq t_0. \end{cases} \tag{33}$$

In the first interval, $0 \leq t \leq t_0$, the two paths are identical so that $C^*(t) = C(t)$ in this interval (which will not exist if $t_0 = 0$). At $t = t_0$, the starred path gives a discontinuous consumption bonus, for an amount of capital equal to $\epsilon L_0 e^{g t_0}$ is instantly consumed so as to make $k^*(t) = k(t) - \epsilon$ at $t = t_0$. In the remaining interval, $t > t_0$, the difference between the consumption rate offered by the starred path and the path specified in (32) is implied by (26) to be

$$\begin{aligned} C^*(t) - C(t) = \{ & [f(k^*(t)) - (\gamma + \lambda + \delta)k^*(t) - \dot{k}^*(t)] \\ & - [f(k(t)) - (\gamma + \lambda + \delta)k(t) - \dot{k}(t)]\} L_0 e^{(\gamma+\lambda)t}. \end{aligned} \tag{34}$$

But observe that, for all $t > t_0$, $\dot{k}^*(t) = \dot{k}(t)$ since the two paths differ after t_0 by only a constant, ϵ. Hence (33) and (34) imply

$$\begin{aligned} C^*(t) - C(t) = \{ & [f(k^*(t)) - (\gamma + \lambda + \delta)k^*(t)] \\ & - [f(k(t)) - (\gamma + \lambda + \delta)k(t)]\} L_0 e^{(\gamma+\lambda)t}. \end{aligned} \tag{35}$$

The righthand side of (35) is strictly positive for all $t > t_0$ since $k^*(t) \geq \hat{k}$, $k(t) > k^*(t)$ and $f(k) - (\gamma + \lambda + \delta)k$ is strictly decreasing in k for all $k > \hat{k}$. Hence, in the interval $t > t_0$ the starred path gives more consumption at every point in time. Therefore, the starred path dominates the other path for it is never worse and is better for all $t \geq t_0$.

To elaborate a little on the last step of the proof, note that $k^*(t) \geq \hat{k}$ because $k^*(t)$ is only ϵ smaller than $k(t)$ and the latter is at least ϵ larger than $\hat{k}$ for all t. Figure 3 illustrates why $f(k^*(t)) - (\gamma + \lambda + \delta)k^*(t) > f(k(t)) - (\gamma + \lambda + \delta)k(t)$ for any $t > t_0$.

The theorem can be expressed in another way. Since the social net rate of return to investment (and the competitive rate of interest), $f'(k(t)) - \delta$, is a monotonically decreasing function of $k(t)$ and independent of time, an equivalent proposition is that any growth path which keeps the rate of return to investment forever and finitely below its GR value (the golden-age growth rate on the assumption expressed by (31)

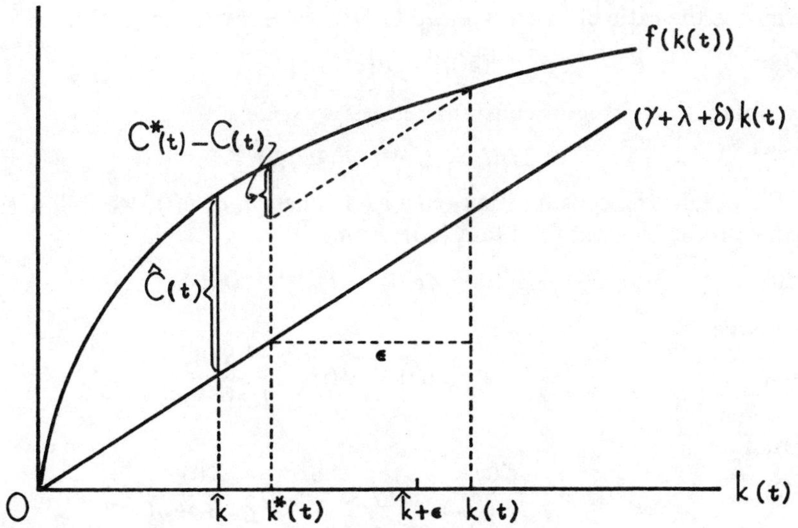

FIGURE 3

is dynamically inefficient. Or the proposition can be expressed in terms of the capital-output ratio, as we first conjectured it.

Another remark is that the neoclassical assumptions $f'(k)>0$ and $f''(k)<0$ for all k are far stronger than necessary for the theorem. If $f''(k)=0$ for all $k>\hat{k}$, for example (where $\hat{k}$ is now defined as the smallest k for which $f'(k)=(\gamma+\lambda+\delta)$), then, while the two paths will yield the same consumption path after t_0, the starred path still offers the consumption bonus at t_0, and hence dominates the other path. Secondly, the theorem is trivial in the Harrod-Domar case, where $f'(k)=0$ for $k>\hat{k}$, for it simply means that any path which keeps capital permanently in surplus is inefficient, and this hardly needs proving.

B. *Factor-Augmenting Progress*

We turn now to the case in which technical progress can be described as factor-augmenting and may be partially or wholly capital-augmenting. Suppose that the rate of capital augmentation is a constant, $\mu \geq 0$. And suppose once again that we have a neoclassical production function. Then

$$Q(t) = F[e^{\mu t}K(t), e^{\lambda t}L(t)], \qquad \mu \geq 0, \lambda \geq 0. \tag{36}$$

In the spirit of the first part of this paper, we define

$$k(t) = \frac{K(t)}{L_0 e^{(\gamma+\lambda-\mu)t}}, \tag{37}$$

which is the ratio of "effective capital" to "effective labor," and

$$f(k(t)) = F[k(t), 1] \tag{38}$$

to obtain, by virtue of constant returns to scale,

$$Q(t) = L_0 e^{(\gamma+\lambda)t} f(k(t)). \tag{39}$$

To obtain the consumption path as a function of $k(t)$, we follow the same procedure used to obtain (26). From

$$C(t) + \dot{K}(t) + \delta K(t) = L_0 e^{(\gamma+\lambda)t} f(k(t)) \tag{40}$$

we have

$$\frac{C(t)}{L_0 e^{(\gamma+\lambda-\mu)t}} = e^{\mu t} f(k(t)) - \delta k(t) - \frac{\dot{K}(t)}{L_0 e^{(\gamma+\lambda-\mu)t}} \cdot \tag{41}$$

From

$$\dot{k}(t) = \frac{\dot{K}(t)}{L_0 e^{(\gamma+\lambda-\mu)t}} - (\gamma + \lambda - \mu) \frac{K(t)}{L_0 e^{(\gamma+\lambda-\mu)t}} \tag{42}$$

we have

$$\frac{\dot{K}}{L_0 e^{(\gamma+\lambda-\mu)t}} = \dot{k}(t) + (\gamma + \lambda - \mu) k(t). \tag{43}$$

Hence, from (41) and (43),

$$C(t) = \{e^{\mu t} f(k(t)) - (\gamma + \lambda + \delta - \mu) k(t) - \dot{k}(t)\} L_0 e^{(\gamma+\lambda-\mu)t}. \tag{44}$$

(If $\mu = 0$, we obtain (26) again.)

Now we define $\hat{k}(t)$ as the value of $k(t)$ which, for fixed $\dot{k}(t)$ and a particular t, maximizes $C(t)$. For simplicity only we assume an interior maximum is attained so that $\hat{k}(t)$ is defined by[8]

$$e^{\mu t} f'(\hat{k}(t)) = \gamma + \lambda + \delta - \mu. \tag{45}$$

Of course, $e^{\mu t} f'(k(t))$ is just the marginal productivity of capital at time t.[9] Hence the path $\hat{k}(t)$ defined by (45) is a constant interest-rate path in which the (competitive) interest rate is $e^{\mu t} f'(k(t)) - \delta = \gamma + \lambda - \mu$.

We know that $\hat{k}(t)$ is not the GR path; no family of golden-age paths exist when $\mu > 0$, and hence no GR path exists. Nevertheless we shall dub this path the Quasi-Golden-Rule path. For we shall demonstrate

[8] If $f'(k) > 0$ for all k, as we assume, then $\gamma + \lambda - \mu > 0$ is required for the existence of such a value of $k(t)$.

Note that $\hat{k}(r)$ must be increasing over time if $\mu > 0$; and if $\lambda + \delta - \mu > 0$, then so must $\hat{K}(t)$, by (37).

[9] $$\frac{\partial F(e^{\mu t} K(t), e^{\lambda t} L(t))}{\partial K(t)} = e^{\mu t} \frac{\partial F\left(\frac{e^{\mu t} K(t)}{e^{(\gamma+\lambda)t} L_0}, 1\right)}{\partial \left(\frac{e^{\mu t} K(t)}{e^{(\gamma+\lambda)t} L_0}\right)} = e^{\mu t} f'(k(t)).$$

that it is like the GR path in the following respect: Any path which, at some point in time and forever after, keeps the ratio of effective capital to effective labor in excess of the Quasi-GR value of that ratio, $\hat{k}(t)$, is dynamically inefficient.[10]

Such a path is one which causes $k(t)$ to satisfy, for all $t \geq t_0 \geq 0$,

$$k(t) \geq \hat{k}(t) + \epsilon, \qquad \epsilon > 0 \quad \text{and} \quad \text{constant}. \tag{46}$$

We show now that the following path dominates any such path:

$$k^*(t) = \begin{cases} k(t), & 0 < t < t_0; \\ k(t) - \epsilon, & t \geq t_0. \end{cases} \tag{47}$$

Comparing the associated consumption paths, we observe first that the two paths yield identical consumption paths until t_0. At this point the starred path yields a consumption bonus, unlike the other path. Subsequently, $\dot{k}^*(t) = \dot{k}(t)$, since, for $t > t_0$, $k^*(t)$ and $k(t)$ differ only by the constant, ϵ. Hence for all $t > t_0$,

$$\begin{aligned} C^*(t) - C(t) = \{ & [e^{\mu t} f(k^*(t)) - (\gamma + \lambda + \delta - \mu) k^*(t)] \\ & - [e^{\mu t} f(k(t)) - (\gamma + \lambda + \delta - \mu) k(t)] \} L_0 e^{(\gamma+\lambda-\mu)t}. \end{aligned} \tag{48}$$

The right-hand side of (48) must be positive for every t, since $k(t) > k^*(t) \geq \hat{k}(t)$, and $e^{\mu t} f(k(t)) - (\gamma+\lambda+\delta-\mu)k(t)$ is, for every t, monotonically decreasing in $k(t)$ in the range $k(t) > \hat{k}(t)$ (since $\hat{k}(t)$ is maximal and $f''(k(t)) < 0$). Hence, the starred path dominates the path which transgresses the Quasi-Golden-Rule path. Therefore, any path which violates the Quasi-Golden-Rule path in the manner described in (46) is dynamically inefficient.[11]

[10] While the Quasi-GR path does not dominate other constant interest-rate paths, it does dominate all $k(t)$ paths parallel to it so it is in fact a Generalized Golden Rule path.

[11] We have just shown that (46), that is, $k(t) \geq \hat{k}(t) + \epsilon$, is a sufficient condition that a $k(t)$ path be dominated by another path on which $k(t)$ is smaller by a constant amount. We show here that $k(t) > \hat{k}(t)$ is necessary that a path $k(t)$ be dominated *in this way*; but that $k(t) > \hat{k}(t)$ is not sufficient for such dominance.

First we show that every $k(t)$ path so dominated is a path along which $e^{\mu t} f'(k(t)) < \gamma + \lambda + \delta - \mu$, and hence $k(t) > \hat{k}(t)$, for all $t \geq t_0$.

Proof: Choose any path $k(t) \geq 0$ and suppose that it is dominated by another path $k^*(t) = k(t) - \epsilon$, $\epsilon > 0$ for $t \geq t_0$. Then, for every $t \geq t_0$ we have

$$\begin{aligned} C^*(t) - C(t) = \{ & [e^{\mu t} f(k(t) - \epsilon) - (\gamma + \lambda + \delta - \mu)(k(t) - \epsilon)] \\ & - [e^{\mu t} f(k(t)) - (\gamma + \lambda + \delta - \mu) k(t)] \} L_0 e^{(\gamma+\lambda-\mu)t} \geq 0. \end{aligned}$$

Then it is immediately clear that, for every $t \geq t_0$, $k(t)$ must exceed $\hat{k}(t)$; that is, $k(t)$ must lie on the right side of the hill whose peak occurs at $k(t) = \hat{k}(t)$, i.e., where $e^{\mu t} f(k(t)) - (\gamma+\lambda+\delta-\mu)k(t)$ is at a maximum.

This proves that $k(t) > \hat{k}(t)$ is a necessary condition that a path be dominated in the manner described. We show next that $k(t) > \hat{k}(t)$ is not a sufficient condition. Consider a path $k(t) > \hat{k}(t)$ with

$$\lim_{t \to \infty} [k(t) - \hat{k}(t)] = 0.$$

We can relax without difficulty the assumptions that the labor force and the technology increase at constant rates. Further, we may allow the depreciation rate at time t, $\delta(t)$, (the same for capital goods of every age) to vary with time. Write

$$Q(t) = F[B(t)K(t),\ A(t)L(t)] \tag{49}$$

where $A(t)$, $B(t)$ and $L(t)$ are continuously differentiable functions of time. Then, defining $k(t)=B(t)K(t)/A(t)L(t)$, one can easily derive

$$C(t) = \left\{B(t)f(k(t)) - \left[\frac{\dot{L}(t)}{L(t)} + \frac{\dot{A}(t)}{A(t)} + \delta(t) - \frac{\dot{B}(t)}{B(t)}\right]k(t) - \dot{k}(t)\right\} \cdot \frac{A(t)L(t)}{B(t)} \tag{50}$$

where $f(k(t))=F[k(t), 1]$.

Next we define the Generalized Quasi-GR path, $\hat{k}(t)$, by

$$B(t)f'(\hat{k}(t)) = \frac{\dot{L}(t)}{L(t)} + \frac{\dot{A}(t)}{A(t)} + \delta(t) - \frac{\dot{B}(t)}{B(t)} \cdot \tag{51}$$

This may be a variable interest-rate path.

It can then be shown, in precisely the same manner as before, that any path which makes $k(t) \geq \hat{k}(t)+\epsilon$, $\epsilon>0$, is dynamically inefficient.[12]

Then, for any $\epsilon>0$ and sufficiently large t,

$$C^*(t) - C(t) = \{[e^{\mu t}f(k(t) - \epsilon) - (\gamma + \lambda + \delta - \mu)(k(t) - \epsilon)] - [e^{\mu t}f(k(t)) - (\gamma + \lambda + \delta - \mu)k(t)]\} L_0 e^{(\gamma+\lambda-\mu)t} < 0$$

since, for any $\epsilon>0$,

$$\lim_{t\to\infty} [k(t) - \epsilon - \hat{k}(t)] < 0$$

and

$$[e^{\mu t}f(k(t)) - (\gamma + \lambda + \delta - \mu)k(t)] < [e^{\mu t}f(\hat{k}(t)) - (\gamma + \lambda + \delta - \mu)\hat{k}(t)] \quad \text{whenever } k(t) < \hat{k}(t).$$

Hence, $k(t) > \hat{k}(t)$ is not a sufficient condition that the path $k(t)$ be dominated.

It does not follow that (46) is necessary for a path to be dominated by a path described in (47), although that can probably be shown, at least on certain additional assumptions. In any case, it should be emphasized, however, that (46) is not a necessary condition for a $k(t)$ path to be dominated in *any* way. In other words, it is not argued that (46) is a necessary condition for dynamical inefficiency; it has only been suggested in the present paragraph that (46) is a necessary condition for a path to be dominated by a path which relates to it in the particular way specified in (47).

[12] In the purely labor-augmenting case, our theorems imply that all paths which keep the interest rate always finitely below the GR or Quasi-GR value are dynamically inefficient, provided that $(\dot{L}(t)/L(t)+(\dot{A}(t)/A(t))+\delta(t)$ has an upper bound. For if, for all t, $r(t) \leq \hat{r}(t) - \eta$, $\eta>0$, where $r(t)=f'(k(t))-\delta(t)$ and $\hat{r}(t)=f'(\hat{k}(t))-\delta(t)=(\dot{L}(t)/L(t))+(\dot{A}(t)/A(t))$, then $f'(\hat{k}(t))-f'(k(t)) \geq \eta$; but if $f''(k)<0$ and $f'(\hat{k}(t))$ is bounded from above (because $(\dot{L}(t)/L(t))+(\dot{A}(t)/A(t))+\delta(t)$ is bounded), then it follows that $k(t) \geq \hat{k}(t)+\epsilon$ for some constant $\epsilon>0$.

But if there is capital-augmenting progress and $B(t)\to\infty$ as $t\to\infty$, then our theorems do

Note that if technical progress is Hicks-neutral, so that

$$Q(t) = A(t)\, F[K(t), L(t)]$$

then, since (by constant returns to scale)

$$A(t)\, F[K(t), L(t)] = F[A(t) | K(t), A(t)\, L(t)],$$

we have $B(t) = A(t)$ and $(\dot{B}(t)/B(t)) = (\dot{A}(t)/A(t))$ in (51). In this case, the interest rate path corresponding to the Generalized Quasi-GR path is the same as for the case of no technical progress; the interest rate at t equals $\dot{L}(t)/L(t)$.

This observation suggests that if rates of factor augmentation are not defined then the Generalized Quasi-GR interest rate path is just the path of $\dot{L}(t)/L(t)$. We now demonstrate this.

C. *Nonfactor-Augmenting Progress*

Here we write the neoclassical production function in the form

(52) $$Q(t) = F[K(t), L(t); t].$$ (52)

Then, by constant returns to scale,

(53) $$Q(t) = L(t) f(k(t); t)$$

where

(54) $$k(t) = \frac{K(t)}{L(t)}$$

and

(55) $$f(k(t); t) = F\left[\frac{K(t)}{L(t)}, 1; t\right].$$

From (53), (3) and (4) we have

(56) $$\frac{C(t)}{L(t)} = f(k(t); t) - \delta k(t) - \frac{\dot{K}(t)}{L(t)}.$$

From (54) we have

(57) $$\dot{k}(t) = \frac{\dot{K}(t)}{L(t)} - \frac{\dot{L}(t)}{L(t)} k(t).$$

---

not imply that all paths which keep the interest rate finitely below the Quasi-GR value are dynamically inefficient. To see this, consider a path such that $r(t) \leq \hat{r}(t) - \eta$, $\eta > 0$, where now $r(t) = B(t) f'(k(t)) - \delta(t)$ and $\hat{r}(t) = B(t) f'(\hat{k}(t)) - \delta(t) = (\dot{L}(t)/L(t)) + (\dot{A}(t)/A(t)) - (\dot{B}(t)/B(t))$. Then $f'(\hat{k}(t)) - f'(k(t)) \geq \eta / B(t)$. If $B(t) \to \infty$ as $t \to \infty$ then, while $k(t) > \hat{k}(t)$ for all t, $k(t) \to \hat{k}(t)$ as $t \to \infty$ is possible. Hence "$k(t) \geq \hat{k}(t) + \epsilon$, $\epsilon > 0$" is not necessarily true of such a path, so the inefficiency of all such low-interest-rate paths is not implied. For $k(t) > \hat{k}(t)$ is not a sufficient condition that a path $k(t)$ be dominated, as the preceding footnote showed.

Equations (56) and (57) yield

$$C(t) = \left\{f(k(t); t) - \left[\frac{\dot{L}(t)}{L(t)} + \delta\right] k(t) - \dot{k}(t)\right\} L(t). \tag{58}$$

It is clear now that the Generalized Quasi-GR path, $\hat{k}(t)$, is defined by

$$f_k(\hat{k}(t); t) = \frac{\dot{L}(t)}{L(t)} + \delta. \tag{59}$$

It can be shown, by the same method that we have been using, that any path which, at t_0 and forever after, keeps $k(t) \geq \hat{k}(t) + \epsilon$ is dominated by a path $k^*(t) = k(t)$, $t < t_0$, $k^*(t) = k(t) - \epsilon$, $t \geq t_0$, so that such a path is dynamically inefficient.

Note that the interest rate, $f_k - \delta$, associated with the Generalized Quasi-GR path is the path of $\dot{L}(t)/L(t)$ which is independent of t. Hence if technical progress cannot be described in purely input-augmenting terms then the critical interest rate path is just the path of $\dot{L}(t)/L(t)$.

III. *Concluding Remarks*

It was demonstrated that a Golden-Rule path, that is, a consumption maximizing golden-age path, always exists in the neoclassical and Harrod-Domar models if the labor force increases at a constant rate, the depreciation rate is constant, technical progress, if any, is purely labor-augmenting, labor augmentation occurs at a constant rate, and positive labor is required for positive output. It was also demonstrated that a positive-investment GR path exists only if any technical progress present can be described as purely labor-augmenting.

It was then shown that any path which permanently deepens capital in excess of the GR path is dynamically inefficient—it is dominated with respect to consumption by another path. Further, if labor augmentation or labor-force growth is nonexponential or if technical progress cannot be described as purely labor-augmenting, then, while no GR path will exist, there may exist a Generalized Quasi-GR path having the same property, namely, that any path which permanently deepens capital in excess of that path is dynamically inefficient. (Note that such paths do not exhaust the class of dynamically inefficient paths. For example, even if no Quasi-GR path exists, the growth path produced by a permanently unitary saving ratio is clearly dynamically inefficient.)

Concerning the significance of these findings, I believe that it is of considerable theoretical interest to know that certain growth paths, even growth paths with continuously positive interest rate and less-than-unitary saving ratio, are dynamically inefficient. The practical importance of these findings is arguable. Beware of the weakness of what has been proved here. The growth paths shown to be dynamically inefficient are paths on which capital is excessive *forever*, that is, for infinite time. Whatever a nation does over a finite time cannot be shown to be dynamically inefficient in the sense of this paper; for what the nation does subsequently may save the entire growth path from being dominated.[13] At best, the economist armed with this paper can say to a country—be it a Soviet-type economy or a capitalist economy—that its public policies and private propensities are such that, if not *eventually* changed, dynamical inefficiency will result. But he cannot say that these policies must be changed within the year or in the next billion years. Such wisdom is not without practical value, I think. But it is to be hoped that some day economists will have stronger recommendations to make in the area of growth policy.

References

1. M. Allais, "The Influence of the Capital-Output Ratio on Real National Income," *Econometrica*, Oct. 1962, *30*, 700–728.
2. M. J. Beckmann, "Economic Growth and Wicksell's Cumulative Process," Cowles Foundation Discussion Paper 120, June 1961.
3. J. Desrousseaux, "Expansion Stable et taux d'intérêt optimal," *Annales de Mines*, Nov. 1961, 31–46.
4. P. A. Diamond, "Disembodied Technical Progress in a One-Sector Model," *Internat. Econ. Rev.*, May 1965, *6*.
5. T. C. Koopmans, "On the Concept of Optimal Economic Growth," Cowles Foundation Discussion Paper 163, Dec. 1963.
6. I. F. Pearce, "The End of the Golden Age in Solovia," *Amer. Econ. Rev.*, Dec. 1962, *52*, 1088–97.
7. E. S. Phelps, "The Golden Rule of Accumulation," *Amer. Econ. Rev.*, Sept. 1961, *51*, 638–43.
8. ———, "The End of the Golden Age in Solovia: Comment," *Amer. Econ. Rev.*, Dec. 1962, *52*, 1097–99.
9. J. Robinson, "The Classification of Inventions," *Rev. Econ. Stud.*, Feb. 1938, *5*, 139–142.
10. ———, "A Neoclassical Theorem," *Rev. Econ. Stud.*, June 1962, *29*, 219–26.
11. P. A. Samuelson, "Comment," *Rev. Econ. Stud.*, June 1962, *29*, 251–54.
12. R. M. Solow, *Capital Theory and the Rate of Return*. Amsterdam 1963.
13. ———, "Comment," *Rev. Econ. Stud.*, June 1962, *29*, 255–57.

[13] This observation leads to another qualification. In a world of uncertainty, as Pearce has observed [6], an economy may rationally deepen capital "excessively" in order to possess a "war chest" of capital for consumption in the event of an earthquake, a war, and other probabilistic phenomena. If these events never occur, so that the war chest is never consumed and capital is always "excessive," then, while the war chest strategy will be regretted from hindsight, it cannot be said to be irrational. But I doubt that such uncertainties are of sufficient quantitative importance to justify an appreciable war chest.

14. T. N. SRINIVASAN, "Investment Criteria and the Choice of Techniques of Production," *Yale Econ. Essays*, Spring 1962, *2*, 59–115.
15. T. W. SWAN, "Of Golden Ages and Production Functions," in K. Berrill, ed., *Economic Development with Special Reference to East Asia*, New York, 1964, pp. 3–16.
16. H. UZAWA, "Neutral Inventions and the Stability of Growth Equilibrium," *Rev. Econ. Stud.*, Feb. 1961, *28*, 117–24.
17. C. C. VON WEIZSÄCKER, *Wachstum, Zins und Optimale Investifionsquote*. Basel 1962.

[3]

Econometrica, Vol. 56, No. 1 (January, 1988), 147–172

THE INVERSE OPTIMAL PROBLEM: A DYNAMIC PROGRAMMING APPROACH

BY FWU-RANQ CHANG[1]

The paper solves the stochastic inverse optimal problem. Dynamic programming is used to transform the original problem into a differential equation. Such an equation is well-defined (with probability one) if the production function is sufficiently concave at infinity. When the production function has a finite slope at the origin, we show that a solution to the aforementioned problem exists for a twice continuously differentiable, strictly increasing consumption function provided the savings function, starting from the origin, is steep initially and flat eventually. Three well-known consumption functions, linear (in the capital-labor ratio), Keynesian, and Cantabrigian, are also studied within the stochastic framework. A well-known result in discrete time models—that a logarithmic utility function and a Cobb-Douglas production function imply a Keynesian consumption function—does not carry through to the continuous time case.

KEYWORDS: Optimal growth, stochastic differential equations, Ito's lemma, Bellman equation, comparison theorems, structural compatibility, dynamic integrability problems.

1. INTRODUCTION

A TYPICAL OPTIMAL GROWTH MODEL can be formulated as follows: Given preferences (represented by a utility function and a discount rate) and opportunities (represented by a descriptive growth equation), find an optimal policy function (represented by a consumption function) that maximizes the discounted aggregate utility. The inverse optimal problem is the "inverse" of the above optimal problem: Given a descriptive growth equation and a behavioral (observable) consumption function, find a utility function and a discount rate so that the given consumption function is indeed a solution to the associated optimal growth model. Obviously, the inverse optimal problem is a dynamic integrability problem in the growth context.

A solution to the inverse optimal problem provides a theoretical foundation for the use of certain savings functions in both empirical and policy-oriented macroeconomic models. It rationalizes the choice of the optimizing models, especially the class of *cardinal* utility functions, representing these savings functions (Kurz (1969, p. 189)). It also blurs the distinction between a positive theory and a normative theory (Wan (1971, p. 267)). In fact, it enables us to "transform the descriptive into the normative case" (Hahn (1985, p. 273)). Furthermore, if the given consumption function were to be *structural*, a fundamental question in macroeconomics, then a solution of the inverse optimal problem provides a description of the underlying preference structure.

[1] I would like to thank Robert Becker, John Boyd, William Brock, Nicolas Spulber and two anonymous referees for their comments and suggestions. I would also like to thank Indiana University for financial support through an Outstanding Young Faculty Award. This paper was presented at the 1986 Winter Meeting of the Econometric Society at New Orleans, LA. Naturally, all remaining errors are my own.

Previous studies on the inverse optimal problem and dynamic integrability problems were done most notably by Kurz (1968, 1969), Hahn (1968, 1985), Brock (1975), and Dechert (1977). However, their contributions were mainly in models without uncertainty. The purpose of this paper is to solve the one-sector stochastic inverse optimal problem. More fundamentally, it suggests a general methodology for dynamic integrability problems. It is noted that, using Ito's lemma,[2] uncertainty is summarized as an additional term in the Bellman equation[3] of a continuous time model. In particular, the Bellman equation is formulated without the conditional expectation operator. This observation enables us to treat both the deterministic and the stochastic cases on an equal footing. By contrast, in a discrete time model with uncertainty, the Euler equation is a martingale equation. In general, there is no unified approach applicable to both cases.

Our strategy has two components. First, we reduce the inverse optimal problem to a differential equation, the fundamental equation, which governs the functional form of utility. It should be emphasized that the derivation of the fundamental equation, be that deterministic or stochastic, follows the same principle. We show that, with probability one, the fundamental equation is well-defined when the production function is sufficiently concave at infinity. This condition is the stochastic version of a condition in the deterministic model that the slope of the production function is eventually smaller than the population growth rate.

Second, we show that the fundamental equation has a solution. There are two approaches to solving a differential equation. One is the finding of a set of sufficient conditions for the existence of solutions; the other is the actual construction of a solution. In the stochastic case, however, the fundamental equation is of the *second* order. Complications arise, especially when that differential equation has singular points.[4] To rule out these singularities, we need conditions closely resembling those for the existence of a steady state distribution. Furthermore, a solution (a utility function) to a second order equation is, in general, not globally concave. More structural restrictions are, thus, called for. By contrast, no such restrictions are necessary and its solution is technically easier in the deterministic case, because the equation is of the *first* order and the singular point can be made regular.

We begin with studying the class of production functions with a finite slope at the origin, which includes CES production functions with the elasticity of substitution less than unity. It was shown, by Chang and Malliaris (1987), that the solution of the Solow equation derived from this production technology exists and is unique. Furthermore, it is the class of production functions for which both

[2] See Appendix A for a self-contained exposition on Ito's lemma and related stochastic calculus concepts.

[3] See Appendix B for a self-contained derivation of the Bellman equation from the Principle of Optimality.

[4] A singular point of a second order differential equation is a point at which the coefficient of the second order term vanishes. See, for example, Birkhoff and Rota (1978).

the marginal propensities to consume and to save, at the origin, can be made finite. This consideration is especially important when the consumption function in question is Keynesian or linear in the capital-labor ratio. Then, we find a set of sufficient conditions for the existence of solutions to the inverse optimal problem under uncertainty for a given twice continuously differentiable, monotonically increasing consumption function. These conditions together imply that the savings function, starting from the origin, is steep initially but flat eventually. They are employed to ensure the global concavity of the utility function. Incidentally, the utility function thus obtained is *three* times continuously differentiable, as a result of applying Ito's lemma.

Next, consider a production function that has an infinite slope at the origin. We use the alternative approach of direct construction of a solution in this case. To do so, we solve each differential equation individually, taking population dynamics as given. Three well-known consumption functions are studied: linear (in the capital-labor ratio), Keynesian (linear in output), and Cantabrigian (one consumes all wage income). Given a Cobb-Douglas production function, we derive the closed form solutions to the stochastic inverse optimal problem in all three cases. All solution utility functions exhibit constant relative risk aversion, if the relative risk aversion at the initial point is properly chosen and is tied to the elasticity of production or the saving rate.

The fundamental equation of the inverse optimal problem also enables us to check the structural compatibility of preferences, technologies, and policy functions. For example, a Cobb-Douglas production function and a logarithmic utility function imply a Keynesian consumption function in discrete time Ramsey models. See, for example, Mirman and Zilcha (1975). In continuous time models, however, we show that logarithmic utility functions are structurally incompatible with either logarithmic or Cobb-Douglas production functions, if the consumption function in question is Keynesian.

Is the solution to the inverse optimal problem unique? In consumer theory, demand functions are invariant under monotonically increasing transformations. In deterministic intertemporal optimization models with additively separable utility functions, the equivalent of this proposition is that optimal policy functions are invariant under *affine* transformations. In that case, the set of utility functions that imply a given consumption function can be obtained by specifying two initial conditions: the value of the utility, and that of the marginal utility. In stochastic models, a third parameter (the second derivative of the utility function) emerges as a result of applying Ito's lemma. While this parameter is not completely free because of the conditions imposed to ensure the global concavity of the utility function, it nevertheless adds a new dimension to the set of solutions.

The one-sector deterministic inverse optimal problem is also solved and interpreted in the same vein. This problem was first studied by Kurz (1969) who uses the Hamiltonian to derive the fundamental equation, by simultaneous solution of the state and the co-state equations. It is a formidable task to eliminate variables when we have a pair of stochastic differential equations in hand.[5] However, the deterministic case is a much simpler problem because the fundamental equation is of the first order and the steady state, if it exists, is unique and a single point, not a distribution as in the stochastic case. Stronger results are thus obtained; the sufficient conditions for the solvability of the problem are also *necessary*.

The paper is organized as follows. In Section 2, we set up the problem and derive the fundamental differential equation. In Section 3, we state and prove the main existence theorem. In Section 4, three special consumption functions are analyzed in the context of the inverse optimal problem under uncertainty. In Section 5, we return to the deterministic case to bring out the full power of our solution technique and to illustrate the complications that result when uncertainty enters the model. In Section 6, we close with some concluding remarks and discuss briefly the inverse optimal problem of multi-sector models.

2. THE STOCHASTIC INVERSE OPTIMAL PROBLEM

2.1. *Problem Stated*

We assume a one-sector neoclassical growth model, in the tradition of Solow (1956), with the production function $F(K, L)$ exhibiting a constant returns to scale technology, where $K(t)$ denotes the capital stock and $L(t)$ denotes the labor at time t. The capital accumulation equation is

$$(1) \qquad \dot{K} = F(K(t), L(t)) - C(t),$$

where $C(t)$ is the consumption at time t and $\dot{K}(t)$ is the time derivative of $K(t)$. Let $k = K/L$ be the capital-labor ratio. Assuming an instantaneous multiplier, i.e., $\dot{K}(t) = I(t) =$ investment $=$ savings, the Solow growth equation is given by

$$(2) \qquad \dot{k}(t) = f(k) - c - nk,$$

where $c(t) = C(t)/L(t)$, n is the exogeneously given population growth rate, and $f(k) = F(K/L, 1)$ is the per capita output. The production function $f(k)$ is assumed to be twice continuously differentiable, strictly increasing and concave in k.

Under uncertainty, the law of motion governing the growth path depends on the source of uncertainty. Assume that the variations in population size follow a stochastic differential equation

$$(3) \qquad dL = nL\,dt + \sigma L\,dz,$$

where z is the standard Wiener process, the continuous time version of a random walk. Equation (3) says that the instantaneous growth rate of population has a mean n and a variance σ^2. In other words, population is expected to grow exponentially with independently identically distributed shocks around the trend

[5] Bismut (1973, pp. 401–403) provides a stochastic version of the Hamiltonian system. Its relation to dynamic programming is still via defining the costate variable as the partial derivative of the value function with respect to the state variable.

line. Using Ito's lemma, the stochastic Solow equation is

$$(4a) \qquad dk = \left[f(k) - (n - \sigma^2)k - c\right] dt - \sigma k\, dz.$$

See, for example, Merton (1975) or Appendix A. When $\sigma = 0$, equation (4a) is the usual Solow equation: $dk/dt = f(k) - nk - c$. In that case, the "maintenance requirement," nk, is the minimum investment required to keep the capital-labor ratio from declining, since population grows at the exponential rate n. If, on the other hand, the source of uncertainty is a Harrod-neutral technological progress following the law of motion

$$dA = aA\, dt + bA\, dz, \qquad \text{where } a, b \text{ are constants,}$$

then the stochastic Solow equation can similarly be derived as

$$(4b) \qquad dk = \left[f(k) - (a + n - b^2)k - c\right] dt - bk\, dz,$$

where $L^*(t) = A(t)L(t)$ = efficiency units of labor and $k = K/L^*$ = capital per efficiency unit of labor. The inverse optimal problem, then, can be stated as follows: Find a utility function $U(c)$ and a constant discount rate $\rho \geqslant 0$ such that the given $c = h(k)$ is the *optimal* policy function to the following optimization problem:

$$(5) \qquad \max_c E_0 \int_0^\infty e^{-\rho t} U(c)\, dt$$

subject to (4a) or (4b), and $k(0) = k_0$ is a given distribution.

Except for changing parameters and interpretations (e.g., the deterministic maintenance requirement is $(a + n)k$), there is no structural difference between equations (4a) and (4b). For the purpose of exposition, we shall only refer to (4a) in what follows.

To complete the description of the inverse optimal problem under uncertainty, we have to specify the class of consumption functions and impose a restriction on technology. Consumption functions, $c = h(k) \geqslant 0$, for $k \geqslant 0$, are assumed to be *twice* continuously differentiable, strictly increasing in k, i.e., $h'(k) > 0$, for all $k > 0$. In addition, a no-borrowing condition is imposed, i.e., $c < f(k)$, for all $k > 0$, and $h(0) = f(0) = 0$. Further restrictions on the limiting behavior of consumption at $k = 0$ and $k = \infty$ will be imposed later when necessary. Existence of the second derivative $h''(k)$ is needed for technical reasons—a typical feature when one uses stochastic calculus.

Recall that, in a deterministic growth model, the slope of the concave production function is assumed to be less than the population growth rate as the capital-labor ratio goes to infinity so that consumption will converge to the steady state. See, for example, Wan (1971). Under uncertainty, we need a condition relating the production function and the population dynamics so as to ensure the capital-labor ratio will not, with a positive probability, go to infinity in finite time. Denote $f'(\infty) = \lim_{k \to \infty} f'(k) \geqslant 0$. We need the following assumption:

Assumption (A1): $f'(\infty) < n - \sigma^2/2$.

Since $f'(\infty) \geqslant 0$, Assumption (A1) implies that

(6) $\quad n > \sigma^2/2,$

a condition employed by Merton (1975) and Chang and Malliaris (1987) for the existence of a steady state distribution. When $\sigma = 0$, Assumption (A1) is the deterministic condition discussed above. Furthermore, given a production function, the population growth rate must be greater than $f'(\infty) + \sigma^2/2$. Given the technology, we need a larger expected population growth rate to balance an increment in shocks.

2.2. *The Fundamental Equation*

Assume we are given a consumption function $c = h(k)$. If it were indeed implied by some utility maximizing problem, it must satisfy the corresponding necessary conditions. The objective of this subsection is to analyze the nature of these conditions. In fact, we shall transform the necessary conditions into a differential equation defined entirely in terms $U(c)$, its derivatives, and the discount rate ρ.

Let the current value of the indirect utility function be

(7) $$J(k, \tau) = \max_c E_\tau \int_\tau^\infty e^{-\rho(t-\tau)} U(c)\, dt,$$

subject to (4a) and $k(\tau) = k$.

Clearly, $J(k, \tau)$ is independent of τ and is subsequently written as $J(k)$. A necessary condition is the Bellman equation

(8) $$0 = \max_c \{ [f(k) - (n - \sigma^2)k - c] J'(k) + \sigma^2 k^2 J''(k)/2 - \rho J(k) + U(c) \}.$$

Usually, it is no trivial task to verify that equation (8) has a solution.[6] However, we are "endowed" with a consumption function and, therefore, the existence of an optimal control is automatic. Furthermore, the given consumption function must satisfy equation (8) without the maximization notation, namely,

(8′) $$0 = [f(k) - (n - \sigma^2)k - c] J'(k) + \sigma^2 k^2 J''(k)/2 - \rho J(k) + U(c).$$

Then the question is: For a given consumption function $c = h(k)$, can we find two functions $J(k)$ and $U(c)$ and a discount rate ρ satisfying (8′), for $k > 0$?

The problem would be more manageable if we could express either J or U in terms of another. The presence of $U(c)$ in (8′) tells us that equation (8′) is not yet defined entirely in terms of $J(k)$ and its derivatives. We can, however, remove such an obstacle by differentiating (8′) with respect to k one more time, using the

[6] See the discussion on the *verification theorem* in Appendix B.

fact that the two utility functions are linked by the first order necessary condition of (8), i.e.,

(9) $$J'(k) = U'(c), \quad \text{for} \quad k > 0.$$

In so doing, we have to assume the utility function is three-times continuously differentiable. Then, the fundamental differential equation for our analysis is

(10) $$(\sigma^2/2)k^2J'''(k) + M(k)J''(k) + \gamma(k)J'(k) = 0,$$

or, expressed in terms of $U(c)$ and its derivatives

(10′) $$0 = \alpha(k)U'''(c) + \beta(k)U''(c) + \gamma(k)U'(c),$$

where

(11a) $$M(k) = f(k) - (n - 2\sigma^2)k - h(k),$$

(11b) $$\alpha(k) = \sigma^2k^2[h'(k)]^2/2,$$

(11c) $$\beta(k) = [f(k) - (n - 2\sigma^2)k - h(k)]h'(k) + \sigma^2k^2h''(k)/2,$$

(11d) $$\gamma(k) = f'(k) - (n + \rho - \sigma^2).$$

Equation (10′) is obtained by substituting into (10) equation (9) and its variants

(9′) $$J''(k) = U''(c)h'(k), \quad \text{for} \quad k > 0, \quad \text{and}$$

(9″) $$J'''(k) = U'''(c)[h'(k)]^2 + U''(c)h''(k), \quad \text{for} \quad k > 0.$$

Notice that equation (10′) is written in *both* variables c and k, instead of using $k = h^{-1}(c)$. We maintain this mixture of variables for two reasons. First, it distinguishes the utility function to be found from those already given (the production technology, the population dynamics, and the behavioral function). This separation is particularly useful when we try to solve the inverse optimal problem by a direct construction of a solution, as we shall see in Section 4. Second, it simplifies the reference of our results to previous studies, in particular to Kurz (1969), as we shall see in Section 5.

In summary, if $c = h(k)$ were derived from some utility function $U(c)$ and discount rate ρ, then together they must satisfy equations (10)–(11d). This reduces the problem to solving a second order linear (in $J'(k)$) differential equation (10).

To complete the description of equation (10), we have to determine the domain of the indirect utility function $J(k)$. Our objective is to show that the capital-labor ratio $k \in (0, \infty)$. But, there are complications. First, $k = 0$ is a singular point of the differential equation (10). Should the law of motion (4a) degenerate to zero in finite time with a positive probability, we have a singular equation to solve. Second, if there is a positive probability of the capital-labor ratio $k(t)$ exploding (i.e., $k(t) = \infty$) in finite time, equation (10) is not defined after the explosion time. To obtain a well-defined equation (10) on $(0, \infty)$, *with probability one*, we have to show that $k = 0$ and $k = \infty$ are *inaccessible* boundaries of (4a) in the sense that $\text{Prob}\{k > N\} \to 0$ and $\text{Prob}\{k < 1/N\} \to 0$, as $N \to \infty$. In fact, we shall demonstrate that the growth path $k(t)$ implied by equation (4a) is positive, with probability one, if the initial capital stock is positive, and that $k=\infty$ is an inaccessible boundary if Assumption (A1) is satisfied.

First, we look at $k=0$. As shown in Appendix A, the stochastic process satisfying the following geometric Brownian motion

$$(12) \qquad dk(t) = -(n-\sigma^2)k(t)\,dt - \sigma k(t)\,dz,$$

is given by

$$(13) \qquad k(t) = k(0)\exp\left\{\int_0^t -(n-\sigma^2/2)\,ds - \int_0^t \sigma\,dz(s)\right\} > 0,$$

provided $k(0)>0$. Equations (4a) and (12) differ only in their drifts. Since no borrowing is allowed, i.e., $c<f(k)$, the addition of $[f(k)-c]\,dt$ to (12) can only shift the value of $k(t)$ upward. That is, $k(t)>0$ for all t with probability one, and $k=0$ is inaccessible.

To show that $k=\infty$ is an inaccessible boundary, we transform (4a), via $x=\log k$, into

$$(14) \qquad dx = q(x)\,dt - \sigma\,dz,$$

where $q(x)=e^{-x}[f(e^x)-h(e^x)]-(n-\sigma^2/2)$. Using Assumption (A1), we see that $q(x)$ becomes negative as $x\to\infty$. (It is obvious if $f(k)$ is bounded from above. Otherwise, use l'Hospital's rule.) By continuity, there exists an $\bar{x}$ such that, for all $x\in[\bar{x},\infty]$, we have $q(x)<\delta$, for some $\delta<0$. The rest of the proof repeats Merton's argument (1975, p. 391, Appendix B) that $k=\infty$ is an inaccessible boundary of equation (4a). Thus, we have the following proposition.

Proposition 1: *Under Assumption* (*A*1), *with probability one, equation* (10) *is well-defined on* $(0,\infty)$ *for all* t.

2.3. *The Undiscounted Case*

The issue of finite expected utility arises when there is no discounting. As in the deterministic case, the model is addressed in the spirit of overtaking principle. We shall take c^* as the optimal policy function associated with the steady state distribution k^*. For a detailed analysis on this stochastic Ramsey problem, the reader is referred to Merton (1975, Section 5).

Let the indirect utility function of the maximized expected utility be

$$J(k,\tau) = \sup_c E_\tau \int_\tau^\infty [U(c)-U(c^*)]\,dt$$

subject to (4a) and $k(\tau)=k$.

Again, J is independent of time and is written as $J(k)$, which satisfies the Bellman equation

$$(15) \qquad 0 = \max_c \left\{[f(k)-(n-\sigma^2)k-c]J' + \sigma^2k^2J''/2 + U(c) - E_0U(c^*)\right\}.$$

The term $E_0U(c^*)$ enters the equation because (15) is obtained by passing the conditional expectation through the Taylor series expansion of the indirect utility function. Since c^* is independent of the initial distribution k, $E_0U(c^*) = b$ (the bliss level) is a constant. Repeating the procedure of (8)–(10), we have, once again, equation (10) with coefficients (11a) and

$$\text{(11d}'\text{)} \qquad \gamma(k) = f'(k) - (n - \sigma^2).$$

3. AN EXISTENCE THEOREM

A second order linear differential equation with two initial conditions is an *initial value problem*. Such a problem has a unique solution, if the coefficients are continuous in the domain. See, for example, Birkhoff and Rota (1978, Chapters 2 and 6). Equation (10′) is such an equation in $U'(c)$. Two initial conditions are $U'(c_0)$ and $U''(c_0)$ for some c_0. It would appear that, once $U'(c_0)$ and $U''(c_0)$ are given, the unique solution to (10′) is the desired marginal utility function. It certainly captures the notion that the utility function $U(c)$ is not unique, and that adding a constant to $U(c)$ is another solution. However, such a solution does not, in general, satisfy $U'(c) > 0$ and $U''(c) < 0$ for *all* $c > 0$. We might, then, end up with a utility function that fails to satisfy the second order necessary condition of (8), i.e., $U''(c) \leqslant 0$. Thus, more structural restrictions are in order. For this purpose, we need the following assumptions:

ASSUMPTION (A2): $f'(0) - h'(0) > n - \sigma^2/2$.

ASSUMPTION (A3): $f'(\infty) - h'(\infty) < n - 2\sigma^2$.

First, from (6), Assumption (A2) implies $f'(0) - h'(0) > 0$, i.e., the savings function $f(k) - h(k)$ has a positive slope at the origin. In fact, it states that, at a low level of the capital-labor ratio, the slope of the savings function, $f(k) - h(k)$, is greater than that of the "maintenance requirement" $(n - \sigma^2/2)k$, i.e., the savings function lies above the maintenance requirement initially. This bounded slope condition is employed by Chang and Malliaris (1987) to prove the existence of a steady state distribution for the class of production functions with $f'(0) < \infty$. Assumption (A3), on the other hand, states that the savings function eventually crosses from above *another* "maintenance line" $(n - 2\sigma^2)k$. Since we do not assume a constant savings ratio, both assumptions have to be stated in terms of the slopes of the savings function. When $\sigma = 0$ and the saving rate is a constant, these conditions become the well-known Solow conditions. In that case, Assumption (A3) is redundant, since it is implied by Assumption (A1). Notice that there are two maintenance requirements: $(n - 2\sigma^2)k$ and $(n - \sigma^2/2)k$. This is typical in stochastic models.

Although the condition $f'(0) = \infty$ obviously satisfies Assumption (A2) when $h'(0) < \infty$, the nature of the problem is quite different. It raises the issue of the functional value of $h'(0)$. If the consumption function is Keynesian or linear in k, then the marginal propensity to save at $k=0$ is infinity. It may take a utility function with $U'(0)=\infty$ to prevent the consumption path from degenerating to zero in finite time. In fact, all examples provided in the next section exhibit this property. Most importantly, our proof relies heavily on the finiteness of $h'(0)$. Thus, in this section, we concentrate on the case that $f'(0)<\infty$ and $h'(0)<\infty$.

Before we formally state and prove the theorem, we shall go over the intuition heuristically. As pointed out earlier, not all initial conditions ensure a utility function that is concave on the entire domain. When that happens, the utility function will no longer exhibit risk aversion. It suggests that assigning initial conditions with a "sufficiently large" degree of absolute risk aversion may prevent the utility function from reaching the forbidden region. Our theorem confirms and formalizes this intuition.

Recall that when a differential equation cannot be solved in terms of elementary functions, a common technique is to compare the unknown solutions of the given equation with the known solutions of another. Results of this type are referred to as *comparison theorems*; they may sometimes also be discussed under the heading of *differential inequalities*. For convenience, we list the results pertinent to our analysis.

THEOREM A:[7] *Let F satisfy a Lipschitz condition on any closed sub-interval of* $x \geqslant a$. *If f satisfies the differential inequality* $f'(x) \leqslant F(x, f(x))$, *for all* $x \geqslant a$, *and if g is a solution of* $y' = F(x, y)$ *satisfying the initial condition* $g(a) \geqslant f(a)$, *then* $g(x) \geqslant f(x)$, *for* $x \geqslant a$.

The intuition is this: A head start and a consistently higher speed always keep one ahead. More precisely, for any two functions, the one with a larger (or equal) initial condition *and* a larger slope everywhere to the right must have a larger functional value than another everywhere to the right.

An immediate corollary of the above theorem is the following:

THEOREM B: *Let F satisfy a Lipschitz condition on any closed interval* $[b, a]$, *where* $0<b<a$. *If the function f satisfies the differential inequality* $f' \leqslant F(x, f(x))$ *on* $(0, a]$, *and if g is a solution of* $y' = F(x, y)$ *satisfying the initial condition* $g(a)<f(a)$, *then* $g(x) \leqslant f(x)$ *on* $(0, a]$.

PROOF: Assume otherwise; let z be such that $g(z)>f(z)$. Then, on the interval $[z, a]$, $g'(x) \geqslant f'(x)$ implies that $g(x) \geqslant f(x)$, by Theorem A, which contradicts the initial condition. *Q.E.D.*

[7] Theorem A is a modified version of Theorem 7 of Birkhoff and Rota (1978, Ch. 1). In their original statement, the Lipschitz condition is satisfied on $x \geqslant a$, and the initial condition is an equality $f(a)=g(a)$. The proof can be constructed as follows. Assume the contrary. There exist $x_1 \in (a, \infty)$ such that $f(x_1) > g(x_1)$. By continuity, let $[x_0, x_1]$ be the largest interval on which $f(x) \geqslant g(x)$. Clearly $x_0 \geqslant a$. Then apply the Lipschitz condition *on that interval* to obtain a contradiction in exactly the same way as their proof. The only difference between the proofs is the choice of x_0.

The intuition is this: The one who is consistently faster yet cannot catch up with another must have started behind. That is, given any two functions, the one with a larger initial condition but a smaller slope everywhere to the left must be larger everywhere to the left. If we interpret the slope to the left as a rate of reduction, then Theorem B states that the function with a higher value and a smaller rate of reduction everywhere to the left must have a higher value everywhere to the left.

Another useful mathematical notion is the *Poincaré phase-plane* which provides the geometric intuition for our analysis. See, for example, Birkhoff and Rota (1978). Expressed in the (U', U'')-plane, if the solution utility function is strictly increasing and concave, then the entire solution must lie in the fourth quadrant of the Poincaré phase-plane. In particular, the solution path should never cross the axes. A sufficient condition for such a result is that the ratio of U' and U'' never changes sign, given that the initial point $(U'(c_0), U''(c_0))$ is already in the fourth quadrant.

THEOREM: *Let the production technology $f(k)$ and the consumption function $h(k)$ be twice continuously differentiable, monotonically increasing. Under Assumptions $(A1)$, $(A2)$ and $(A3)$, the inverse optimal problem under uncertainty has a solution.*

PROOF: It suffices to show $J'(k) > 0$ and $J''(k) < 0$ on $(0, \infty)$. Denote the absolute risk aversion of the indirect utility function by

$$(16) \qquad v(k) = -J''(k)/J'(k), \quad k > 0.$$

It is a known mathematical fact that $J'(k)$ is a solution to (10) with $J'(k) > 0$ for all $k > 0$ if and only if $v(k)$ is a solution to the *Riccati* equation

$$(17) \qquad v'(k) = [v(k)]^2 - (2/\sigma^2)[M(k)/k][v(k)/k] + (2/\sigma^2)\gamma(k)/k^2.$$

See, for example, Birkhoff and Rota (1978, p. 44). It remains to show that the function $v(k) > 0$ on $(0, \infty)$, because it implies that the vector $(J'(k), J''(k))$ never leaves the fourth quadrant of the (J', J'')-plane.

First, we examine the solution of (17) in the neighborhood of $k = 0$, the interval $(0, a]$, for some small $a > 0$. Consider the function $g(k) = Ak^{-1}$, with $A > 0$. Clearly, $g(k) > 0$ on $(0, a]$. Our objective is to show that $g(k)$ satisfies the differential inequality

$$(18) \qquad g'(k) \geqslant [g(k)]^2 - (2/\sigma^2)(M(k)/k)[g(k)/k] + (2/\sigma^2)\gamma(k)/k^2.$$

Since the right-hand side of (18) is a polynomial in g and has continuously differentiable coefficients, the Lipschitz condition is satisfied. If the initial condition of $v(a)$ is so chosen that $v(a) > g(a)$, then, by Theorem B, $v(k) \geqslant g(k) > 0$ on $(0, a]$, and the case of small k is satisfied.

To this end, we choose the discount rate

$$(19) \qquad h'(0) < \rho \leqslant h'(0) + \sigma^2/2.$$

Then $\gamma(0) = f'(0) - (n + \rho - \sigma^2) \geqslant f'(0) - (n - \sigma^2/2) - h'(0) > 0$, by Assumption (A2). Since $f(0) = h(0)$, using l'Hospital's rule, as $k \to 0$, $M(k)/k \to M'(0) = f'(0) - (n - 2\sigma^2) - h'(0) > 0$, the last inequality is due to Assumption (A2). By the continuity of $M(k)/k$, for any small $\varepsilon > 0$, there is some $a > 0$ such that $M(k)/k \geqslant M'(0) - \varepsilon > 0$ on $(0, a]$. Since $\gamma(k)$ is decreasing in $(0, a]$, the comparison equation we are looking for is

$$g'(k) = [g(k)]^2 - (2/\sigma^2)(M'(0) - \varepsilon)[g(k)/k] + (2/\sigma^2)\gamma(0)/k^2.$$

Clearly, $g(k) = Ak^{-1}$, $A > 0$, is a solution of the above equation, if A is a *positive* root of the following quadratic equation

(20) $$X^2 - [(2/\sigma^2)(M'(0) - \varepsilon) - 1]X + (2/\sigma^2)\gamma(0) = 0.$$

A sufficient condition is that the coefficient of the linear term of (20) is negative and the discriminant is positive, i.e.,

(21a) $$(2/\sigma^2)(M'(0) - \varepsilon) - 1 > 0, \quad \text{and}$$

(21b) $$[(2/\sigma^2)(M'(0) - \varepsilon) - 1]^2 - 4[(2/\sigma^2)\gamma(0)] > 0.$$

But, then, by the first inequality of (19),

$$M'(0) = \gamma(0) + \sigma^2 + \rho - h'(0) > \gamma(0) + \sigma^2.$$

It follows that

$$(2/\sigma^2)M'(0) - 1 > (2/\sigma^2)\gamma(0) + 1 > 1,$$

and, hence, (21a) is satisfied as long as $\varepsilon < \sigma^2/2$. Furthermore,

$$\begin{aligned} &[(2/\sigma^2)M'(0) - 1]^2 - 4(2/\sigma^2)\gamma(0) \\ &\quad > [(2/\sigma^2)\gamma(0) + 1]^2 - 4(2/\sigma^2)\gamma(0) \\ &\quad = [(2/\sigma^2)\gamma(0) - 1]^2 \geqslant 0. \end{aligned}$$

Thus, (21b) is valid for small $\varepsilon > 0$. This establishes the fact that $v(k) > 0$ for small $k > 0$.

Now, we concentrate on $[a, \infty)$. Define a function $R(k)$ on $[a, \infty)$ by

$$R(k) = \exp\left\{-\int_a^k (2/\sigma^2)M(x)/x^2\,dx\right\}.$$

Clearly, $R(k) > 0$ and $R'(k) = R(k)[-(2/\sigma^2)M(k)/k^2]$. Then, a change of variable $u(k) = v(k)/R(k)$ implies that $u(k)$ satisfies

$$u'(k) = R(k)[u(k)]^2 + (2/\sigma^2)\gamma(k)/[R(k)k^2],$$

if $v(k)$ satisfies (17). It suffices to show that there is a function $w(k)$ everywhere *positive* on $[a, \infty)$ satisfying the equation

(22) $$w'(k) = (2/\sigma^2)\gamma(k)/[R(k)k^2].$$

For, then, by Theorem A, $u(k) \geqslant w(k) > 0$ on $[a, \infty)$ provided we choose an initial condition $v_1 = v(a) = u(a) \geqslant w(a)$, since $R(a) = 1$.

However, equation (22) is a first-order differential equation; general solutions are of the form

$$w(k) = w(a) + \int_a^k (2/\sigma^2)\gamma(x)/[x^2R(x)]\,dx.$$

If $\gamma(k) \geqslant 0$ on $[a, \infty)$, then any initial condition $w(a) > 0$ ensures $w(k) > 0$ on $[a, \infty)$, and we are done. It leaves us with the case that $\gamma(k) < 0$ on some interval (b, ∞), $b > a$. Since $\gamma(k)$ is decreasing in k, the point b is the one satisfying $\gamma(b) = 0$. Then the question is reduced to: Is the integral

$$I = \int_b^\infty \gamma(x)/[x^2R(x)]\,dx > -\infty?$$

If the answer is yes, then we simply choose $w(a) > -I$ and the problem is solved.

Our strategy is the following: Since $\gamma(k)$ is decreasing in k and since $\gamma(\infty) = f'(\infty) - (n + \rho - \sigma^2)$ is negative and is finite, $0 > \gamma(k) > \gamma(\infty)$, on the interval (b, ∞). Then the integral I is bounded from below by

$$I > \gamma(\infty)\int_b^\infty x^{-2}[R(x)]^{-1}\,dx.$$

If we can show that $R(k)$ is bounded below by $R(k) \geqslant A_1 k^N$, for some positive constants A_1 and N, then we can bound the integral I by

$$I > A_1^{-1}\gamma(\infty)\int_b^\infty x^{-2-N}\,dx > -\infty,$$

and we are done. [Note that there are inequality reversals in the derivation.]

To this end, we have to compute $R(k)$. Rewrite $R(k) = \exp\{-(2/\sigma^2)H(k)\}$, where the function

$$H(k) = \int_a^k M(x)/x^2\,dx = [-M(x)/x]\Big|_a^k + \int_a^k M'(x)/x\,dx,$$

using integration by parts. By Assumption (A3),

$$M'(k) \to f'(\infty) - h'(\infty) - (n - 2\sigma^2) < 0, \quad \text{as} \quad k \to \infty.$$

It follows that both $M'(k)$ and $M(k)/k$ are uniformly bounded on $[a, \infty)$ and for sufficiently large k, $M'(k) < 0$. Let $N > 0$ be such that $M'(k) \leqslant -(\sigma^2/2)N < 0$ on some interval $[z, \infty)$. Clearly,

$$H(k) = M(a)/a - M(k)/k + \int_a^z M'(x)/x\,dx + \int_z^k M'(x)/x\,dx.$$

The first three terms on the right-hand side of the above equation are bounded, say, by the same constant $B > 0$, which depends on the choice of z. Then

$$H(k) \leqslant 3B + (\sigma^2/2)(-N)(\log k - \log z),$$

and

$$R(k) = \exp\{(-H(k))(2/\sigma^2)\} \geqslant A_1 k^N,$$

for some constant A_1, as claimed. This shows the integral I is bounded away from $-\infty$.

Since the choice of $v(a)$ uniquely determines the value of $v(k_0)$, where $k_0 = h^{-1}(c_0)$, the minimal value of $v(k_0)$, v_2, is chosen accordingly. The theorem is proved when we choose the initial condition $v_0 = \max\{v_1, v_2\}$. *Q.E.D.*

An immediate corollary of the theorem is the following:

COROLLARY: *Under the assumptions of the theorem, the relative risk aversion of the indirect utility function, which is a solution to the inverse optimal problem, is necessarily bounded below in the neighborhood of the origin. Similarly, the absolute risk aversion of the utility function, which is a solution to the inverse optimal problem, approaches* ∞ *as* c *approaches zero.*

PROOF: From the construction of v and g, we have

$$-kJ''(k)/J'(k) = kv(k) \geqslant kg(k) = A > 0,$$

and

$$-U''(c)/U'(c) = v(k)/h'(k) \geqslant g(k)/h'(k) \to \infty, \quad \text{as} \quad k \to 0.$$

Q.E.D.

The mathematical reason for the boundedness condition of the discount rate, i.e., equation (19), is to ensure that $\gamma(0) > 0$ and that (20) has a positive root. However, this choice has a very useful economic interpretation as well. Since the return is bounded for all levels of investment, i.e., $f'(0) < \infty$, we need a discount rate small enough to encourage investment for future consumption and, hence, the upper bound of ρ. In fact,

$$\gamma(0) = f'(0) - (n - \sigma^2) - \rho > 0,$$

means a positive rate of *net* return to zero investment (net of the maintenance rate $n - \sigma^2$ and the discount rate ρ, of course). Since f is concave, it does not pay to have a positive investment if $\gamma(0) \leqslant 0$. Our upper bound of ρ thus provides an incentive to save. On the other hand, if the discount rate is too small, deferred consumption is possible and we may have corner solutions. Thus, a lower bound on ρ is needed to encourage current consumption. But the condition that ensures equation (20) has a positive root is $M'(0) > \gamma(0) + \sigma^2$, which is precisely a rewriting of $\rho > h'(0)$, the first inequality of (19). Notice that the marginal propensity to consume at the origin, $h'(0)$, measures the units of consumption required for the economy to come out of $k = 0$. It is, therefore, the cost of transferring resources to current consumption at $k = 0$. Since the discount rate ρ measures the value loss of deferred consumption, the first inequality of (19) says nothing but that it is cheaper to consume something now. Hence, the possibility of corner solutions is ruled out. In conclusion, we choose the discount rate neither too large nor too small to avoid corner solutions and to keep the capital accumulation process going.

The Corollary imposes a very weak condition on the relationship between $U'(0)$ and $U''(0)$. Many popular utility functions are, thus, included. The most prominent is the class of constant relative risk aversion functions. To see this, we observe the equality

$$-U''(c)/U'(c) = [-cU''(c)/U'(c)](1/c),$$

and apply the Corollary. It also includes the case that the marginal utility at the origin is finite, i.e., $U'(0) < \infty$, provided $U''(0) = -\infty$. Typically, we use $U'(0) = \infty$ as a sufficient condition for interior solutions. When $U'(0) < \infty$, it may raise some concerns about the possibility of corner solutions. However, as discussed in the preceding paragraph, our choice of the discount rate (which ensures $U''(0) = -\infty$) eliminates this possibility.

A natural question at this point is the uniqueness of the solution. We have shown that the solution to the inverse optimal problem requires carefully chosen initial conditions $U'(c_0)$ and $U''(c_0)$. Together with $U(c_0)$, there is a three-parameter family of utility functions associated with a given consumption function. This plethora of solutions may seem puzzling. In consumer theory, however, demand functions are invariant under any monotonically increasing transformation of the utility function. In a deterministic intertemporal optimization model with a separably additive utility function, the equivalent of this proposition—the *ordinality* of the preference structure—is that the optimal policy function is invariant under any *affine* transformation of the utility function. That is, there are two free parameters. They are designated by the initial values $U(c_0)$ and $U'(c_0)$. In stochastic models, a third parameter (the second derivative of the utility, $U''(c_0)$) emerges as a result of applying Ito's Lemma. As shown in the proof, the choice of $U''(c_0)$ is not completely free, because it is constrained to ensure global concavity of $U(c)$. It adds, nevertheless, a new dimension to the solution set, because we only specify a *minimal* value of $-U''(c_0)$.

4. SPECIAL CONSUMPTION FUNCTIONS

We now turn to the case $f'(0) = \infty$. It includes Inada-type production functions and, in particular, Cobb-Douglas production functions. Our strategy is to tie the initial conditions to the production technology or the savings function. Three well-known consumption functions are studied, when the production function is of Cobb-Douglas form.

EXAMPLE 1: Let the consumption function be *linear* in k, i.e., $c = bk$, for some $b > 0$. Clearly, $h'' = 0$ in this case, and equation (10′) is simplified as

$$(\sigma^2/2)c^2U'''(c) + [f(k)/k - (n + b - 2\sigma^2)]cU''(c) + [f'(k) - (n + \rho - \sigma^2)]U'(c) = 0. \tag{23}$$

The strategy to solve equation (23) is to break it into two parts: the part related to the production technology is

$$-\frac{cU''(c)}{U'(c)}=\frac{kf'(k)}{f(k)}, \tag{24}$$

and the part independent of technology is

$$(\sigma^2/2)c^2U'''(c)-(n+b-2\sigma^2)cU''(c)-(n+\rho-\sigma^2)U'(c)=0. \tag{25}$$

Equation (25) is an *Euler's homogeneous differential equation* whose solutions are of the form c^{ε}, where ε is a constant satisfying an *indicial equation*. See, for example, Birkhoff and Rota (1978, p. 61). This particular solution fits perfectly with equation (24) if the production function is of constant elasticity, where the elasticity of production is defined as $kf'(k)/f(k)$.

Let the elasticity of production be $\varepsilon<1$, i.e., $F(K, L)$ is of Cobb-Douglas form. Then the solution to (24) is given by

$$U(c)=Bc^{1-\varepsilon}+\text{constant}, \quad \text{where} \quad B>0, \tag{26}$$

provided the initial conditions are so constrained with the production technology that $c_0U''(c_0)/U'(c_0)=\varepsilon$. This condition eliminates $U''(c_0)$ as a free parameter. Notice, equation (26) also solves (25) if we choose

$$\rho=(\sigma^2/2)(1-\varepsilon)(2-\varepsilon)+[b\varepsilon-(1-\varepsilon)n]. \tag{27}$$

The coefficient $\rho \geqslant 0$ if and only if

$$b \geqslant [(1-\varepsilon)/\varepsilon][n-(2-\varepsilon)(\sigma^2/2)]. \tag{28}$$

The constant $(1-\varepsilon)/\varepsilon$ is the ratio of wage share to rental share, LF_L/KF_K, since $F_L=f(k)-kf'(k)$ and $F_K=f'(k)$. This ratio of wage share to rental share is the wage-rental ratio $\omega=F_L/F_K$ divided by the capital-labor ratio k. Thus, equation (28) says that, when $\sigma=0$, $c=bk \geqslant \omega n$, i.e., per capita consumption has a lower bound that is given by the product of wage-rental ratio ω and the population growth rate n. In conclusion, we have shown the following:

PROPOSITION 2: *Suppose the production technology is Cobb-Douglas, i.e.,* $f(k)=Ak^{\varepsilon}$, *and the initial conditions on the utility function exhibit constant relative risk aversion,* $c_0U''(c_0)/U'(c_0)=\varepsilon$. *Then, the solutions to the inverse optimal problem for the class of linear (in the capital-labor ratio) consumption functions, where the constant proportion b satisfies* (28), *are the discount rate* (27) *and constant relative risk aversion utility functions* (26).

EXAMPLE 2: Consider the Keynesian consumption function with a constant savings rate s, i.e., $c=h(k)=(1-s)f(k)$. Then equation (10′) becomes

$$\left(\frac{\sigma^2}{2}\right)\left(\frac{kf'}{f}\right)^2 c^2U'''(c) + \left\{\left[\frac{sf}{k}-(n-2\sigma^2)\right]\left(\frac{kf'}{f}\right)+\left(\frac{\sigma^2}{2}\right)\left(\frac{k^2f''}{f}\right)\right\}cU''(c) + [f'(k)-(n+\rho-\sigma^2)]U'(c)=0. \tag{29}$$

As in Example 1, we assume the production function is of the Cobb-Douglas form, i.e., $kf'(k)/f(k) = \varepsilon < 1$ is a constant. Then $k^2 f''(k)/f(k) = -\varepsilon(1-\varepsilon)$, and equation (29) becomes

$$(30)\qquad (\sigma^2\varepsilon^2/2)c^2U'''(c) + \{[sf(k)/k - (n - 2\sigma^2)] - (\sigma^2/2)(1-\varepsilon)\}\varepsilon c U''(c) + [f'(k) - (n + \rho - \sigma^2)]U'(c) = 0,$$

which is similar to (23). Assume the initial conditions $U'(c_0)$ and $U''(c_0)$ are so constrained to the savings rate that $c_0U''(c_0)/U'(c_0) = -1/s$. Again, this condition eliminates $U''(c_0)$ as a free parameter. Then, by solving the counterpart of (24), namely,

$$(31)\qquad -\frac{cU''(c)}{U'(c)} = \frac{kf'(k)}{s\varepsilon f(k)} = \frac{1}{s},$$

we find the desired utility functions are of the form

$$(32)\qquad U(c) = Bc^{1-1/s} + \text{constant}, \quad \text{where} \quad B < 0.$$

Again, (32) solves the counterpart of (25), the Euler's homogeneous equation,

$$(33)\qquad (\sigma^2\varepsilon^2/2)c^2U'''(c) - [(n - 2\sigma^2) + (\sigma^2/2)(1-\varepsilon)]\varepsilon c U''(c) - (n + \rho - \sigma^2)U'(c) = 0,$$

if we choose

$$(34)\qquad \rho = (n/s)(\varepsilon - s) + (\varepsilon - s)(\varepsilon - 2s)\sigma^2/(2s^2).$$

Again, the coefficient $\rho > 0$ if $2s \leqslant \varepsilon$. In the event of $\sigma = 0$, only $s < \varepsilon$ is needed. Thus, we have the following proposition:

PROPOSITION 3: *Assume the savings rate s is bounded from below by 2ε, where ε is the elasticity of production. Then the inverse optimal problem of a Keynesian consumption function is solvable and the utility function is of constant relative risk aversion $1/s$, if the initial conditions satisfy $c_0U''(c_0)/U'(c_0) = 1/s$. In this case, the relative risk aversion is an increasing function of the marginal propensity to consume, $1-s$.*

Let us conclude this example by pointing out a result in discrete time models not valid in continuous time. According to Mirman and Zilcha (1975), in a discrete time Ramsey problem, a logarithmic utility function together with a Cobb-Douglas production technology implies that the consumption function is Keynesian. Actually, *no* logarithmic utility function can be a solution to the inverse optimal problem if the consumption function in question is Keynesian. To see it, let $U(c) = B\log c + \text{constant}$. Then equation (30) becomes

$$(30')\qquad (1-s)\varepsilon k^{\varepsilon-1} + \text{constant terms} = 0.$$

Since (30′) must be valid for all k, the conditions $\varepsilon > 0$ and $s < 1$ are incompatible with any logarithmic utility function. Similarly, logarithmic utility functions and logarithmic production functions do *not* generate Keynesian consumption functions, because (29) is reduced to

$$(29') \qquad n + \rho - \sigma^2 = \frac{1}{k}(1 - s) + \text{function of } \log k.$$

Thus, the use of Keynesian consumption functions in macroeconomic models should be more a special case than a general result.

EXAMPLE 3: Let $c = h(k) = f - kf'$ be the Cambridge consumption function, i.e., one consumes all wage income. Assuming a Cobb-Douglas production technology as before, the consumption function is simplified to $c = (1 - \varepsilon)f(k)$, which is just another Keynesian consumption function with savings rate ε. Then the derivations in Example 2 suggest that $\rho = 0$, from (34), and

$$(35) \qquad U(c) = Bc^{1-1/\varepsilon} + \text{constant}, \quad \text{where} \quad B < 0.$$

5. DETERMINISTIC CASE REVISITED

The deterministic inverse optimal problem is: Find a utility function $U(c)$, and a constant discount rate $\rho \geqslant 0$, such that $c = h(k)$ is the *optimal* solution to the problem

$$(36) \qquad \max_c \int_0^\infty e^{-\rho t} U(c)\, dt$$

$$\text{subject to } \dot{k} = f(k) - nk - c \text{ and } k(0) = k_0 \text{ is given,}$$

where $U(c)$ is a strictly concave, twice continuously differentiable function. The conditions imposed on $c = h(k)$ are:

$$(37) \qquad h(k) \text{ is continuously differentiable and } h'(k) > 0.$$

By setting $\sigma = 0$, the fundamental differential equation (10′) is reduced to a first order differential equation

$$(38) \qquad [f(k) - nk - c]h'(k)U''(c) + [f'(k) - (n + \rho)]U'(c) = 0.$$

In this case, we have only *two* free parameters, $U(c_0)$ and $U'(c_0)$. Indeed, it restates that the optimal policy functions are invariant under *affine* transformations.

CASE (i): Suppose there is no steady state, i.e., $\dot{k} > 0$. Given any consumption function satisfying (37), (38) can be written as

$$(39) \qquad U''(c) + g(k)U'(c) = 0,$$

where

$$(40) \qquad g(k) = \frac{f'(k) - (n + \rho)}{[f(k) - nk - c]h'(k)}.$$

Clearly,

(41) $$U'(c) = U'(c_0)\exp\left\{\int_{c_0}^{c} g(h^{-1}(x))\,dx\right\}$$

is a solution. By specifying $U(c_0)$ and $U'(c_0)$, we obtain a two-parameter family of solutions. The exponential form of (41) tells us that $U'(c) > 0$ for all c if $U'(c_0) > 0$. To ensure $U''(c) < 0$ for all c, we need $g(k) > 0$ for all k. The following condition will be sufficient:

(42) $$f'(k) > n \quad \text{for all } k.$$

In this case, we choose $\rho \geqslant 0$ such that $f'(k) > n + \rho$, for all k. In this case, the desired utility function is of the form (41).

Conversely, if there exist $\rho \geqslant 0$ and a concave utility function $U(c)$ so that a consumption function $c = h(k)$ satisfying (37) is the optimal policy function, then equation (39) must also be satisfied as implied by the Bellman equation. Since $U' > 0$, $U'' < 0$, $h' > 0$ and $\dot{k} > 0$, it must be the case that $f'(k) > (n + \rho) \geqslant n$, i.e., (42) is satisfied. Thus we have the following proposition:

PROPOSITION 4: *Assume there is no steady state to the equation $\dot{k} = f(k) - nk - c$. Then the inverse optimal problem for any consumption function satisfying (37) is solvable if and only if (42) is satisfied.*

CASE (ii): Suppose there is a steady state k^*, i.e., $\dot{k} = 0$ at k^*. It can be regarded as a special case of our main theorem in Section 3. The co-state variable p is defined as $p = J'(k)$, which satisfies the following equation:

(43) $$\dot{p} = -p[f'(k) - (n + \rho)].$$

Since the state variable is in equilibrium, the co-state variable must also be in equilibrium, i.e., $f'(k^*) = n + \rho$. For a given ρ, there is only one k^*, by the concavity of f. Thus, the coefficients of (38) have a *singular* point of order one at k^*. Our objective is to show that such a singular point can be made *regular*. To this end, we first factor out $(k - k^*)$ from (38) to obtain

(44) $$G(k)h'(k)U''(c) + H(k)U'(c) = 0,$$

where

(45a) $$G(k) = \frac{f(k) - nk - h(k)}{k - k^*}, \quad k \neq k^*, \quad \text{and}$$

(45b) $$H(k) = \frac{f'(k) - (n + \rho)}{k - k^*}, \quad k \neq k^*.$$

Next, we define $G(k^*)$ and $H(k^*)$. By l'Hospital's rule, $H(k^*) = f''(k^*) < 0$ and $G(k^*) = f'(k^*) - n - h'(k^*)$. To ensure the concavity of $U(c)$ *in the neighborhood* of k^*, we need $G(k^*) < 0$. This suggests that the condition we are looking for is

(46) $$f'(k^*) - n - h'(k^*) < 0.$$

Equation (46) says that, at the steady state k^*, the savings function crosses the population maintenance requirement line $m = nk$ from above. This is, in fact, a simplified version of the joint Assumptions (A1) and (A2). (Note that Assumption (A3) is implied by (A1) in this case.)

To maintain the global concavity of $U(c)$, we shall show that $G(k) < 0$ and $H(k) < 0$, for all $k > 0$. For this purpose, we need

$$(47) \qquad f'(k^*) \geqslant n.$$

From (47), we define $\rho \geqslant 0$ such that $f'(k^*) = n + \rho$. By the concavity of f, $H(k) < 0$ for all k. Since there is only one steady state, which satisfies $\dot{k} = f(k) - nk - h(k) = 0$, the condition $G(k) < 0$ in the neighborhood of k^* implies that $\dot{k} > 0$ for all $k < k^*$ and $\dot{k} < 0$ for all $k > k^*$. It follows immediately that $G(k) < 0$, for all k.

Now we are ready to study the inverse optimal problem in this case. Given $c = h(k)$ satisfying (37), the corresponding Bellman equation implies equation (44), which is defined on all k. Under (46) and (47), we can choose a discount rate $\rho \geqslant 0$ satisfying $f'(k^*) = n + \rho$ as before, and a concave utility function (41) with a modification that, at the steady state k^*, $g(k^*) = H(k^*)/[G(k^*)h'(k^*)]$. Conversely, given $\rho \geqslant 0$ and $U(c)$ are solutions to the inverse optimal problem for any consumption function satisfying (37), equation (44) follows from the theory of optimal growth. Since k^* is *the* steady state, $f'(k^*) = n + \rho \geqslant n$, i.e., (47), because ρ is nonnegative. As seen before, the concavity of f implies $H(k) < 0$ for all k. Then $G(k)$ must also be negative for all k, by the concavity of $U(c)$. In particular, $0 > G(k^*) = f'(k^*) - n - h'(k^*)$, i.e., (46) is satisfied. In summary, we have the following proposition:

PROPOSITION 5: *Assume there is a steady state to $\dot{k} = f(k) - nk - c$. Then the inverse optimal problem for any consumption function satisfying* (37) *is solvable if and only if conditions* (46) *and* (47) *are satisfied.*

The results in this section are also obtained by Kurz (1969), who uses the Hamiltonian system to derive the fundamental differential equation (38). In the process of doing so, he simultaneously solves the state and the co-state equations, $\dot{k} = f(k) - nk - h(k)$ and $\dot{p} = -p[f'(k) - (n + \rho)]$. By contrast, equation (38) falls out immediately from the Bellman equation. Furthermore, under uncertainty, it is a formidable task to solve a pair of stochastic differential equations—especially when trying to use the approach of eliminating variables.

In a related study on dynamic integrability problems, Brock (1975) finds a set of necessary and sufficient conditions on the coefficients of a second order differential equation

$$(48) \qquad a(k, \dot{k}, t)\ddot{k} + b(k, \dot{k}, t)\dot{k} + c(k, \dot{k}, t) = 0$$

so that (48) is *the* Euler equation for some calculus of variations problem. For the deterministic inverse optimal problem, the corresponding equation is

$$(49)\qquad -U''(c)\ddot{k} + U''(c)[f'(k) - n]\dot{k} + U'(c)[f'(k) - (n+\rho)] = 0.$$

(Recall that the co-state variable is defined by $p = J'(k) = U'(c)$. Using the co-state equation, we have $U''(c)\dot{c} = \dot{p} = -U'(c)[f'(k) - (n+\rho)]$. On the other hand, differentiating the state equation with respect to t, we have an equation relating $\dot{c}$ to $\ddot{k}$, i.e., $\ddot{k} = [f'(k) - n]\dot{k} - \dot{c}$. Eliminating $\dot{c}$, we derive (49).) As a general principle, Brock suggests a method of recovering the objective function $U(c, t)$. Specifically, in addition to functions a, b, c, we have to construct three auxiliary functions from which another three functions $P(k, \dot{k}, t)$, $Q(k, \dot{k}, t)$, and $R(k, \dot{k}, t)$ can be defined such that the objective function $U(c, t)$ becomes the *line* integral of P, Q, and R. The method is general, systematic, and useful to solve many problems. However, it faces similar difficulties as when applying the Hamiltonian to stochastic models.

6. CONCLUDING REMARKS

The technique of stochastic dynamic programming has, of course, its limitations. For example, it may not be a satisfactory method for proving the existence of an optimal policy function because of the usual compactness assumption on the value set of admissible controls, as noted by Cox and Huang (1986). Nevertheless, it has the advantage of solving the stochastic inverse optimal problems: specifically, it enables us to derive with ease the fundamental differential equation governing the functional form of utility. The method is also useful for the study of other dynamic integrability problems. For example, within the framework of the permanent income hypothesis, we may examine the theoretic foundation of any given consumption function, in particular, those already empirically tested, say, by Bhalla (1980). Possible extensions of this paper also include the inverse optimal problem of a one-sector model with money and those of multi-sector models.

In the case of multi-sector models, Hahn (1985, p. 6 and Ch. 14) argues that the inverse optimal problem is generally not solvable, especially within his framework of one consumption good and several capital goods. Our solution technique provides some insights on the difficulties of the problem. Notice that the technique of expressing the indirect utility function in terms of the direct utility, or vice versa, is no longer applicable if the number of consumption goods is different from that of capital goods. But, if the two numbers are the same, then (9) can be written in gradient vector forms and (9′) involves Hessian matrices and the Jacobian of policy functions. Then the existence of solutions of the vector-valued fundamental equation can similarly be studied, even though closed form solutions may not be easy to come by. In that case, the practical use of the equation is, perhaps, in the verification of the structural compatibility of preferences, technologies, and policy functions.

Finally, as shown in Section 5, sufficient conditions for the solvability of the deterministic one-sector inverse optimal problem are also necessary. In that case, the postulated consumption function can also be generated by a perfect foresight competitive equilibrium, by the equivalence principle. See, for example, Lucas (1978), Becker (1981), Cox, Ingersoll, and Ross (1985). It would be interesting to know whether this result can be extended to the stochastic case or not. Is there a rational expectations equivalence principle for infinite horizon one-sector as well as multi-sector models? (As a matter of fact, the difficulty is the necessity of the *transversality condition*.) This is still an open question.

Department of Economics, Indiana University, Bloomington, IN 47405, U.S.A.

Manuscript received January, 1986; final revision received November, 1986.

APPENDIX A

ITO'S LEMMA AND RELATED CONCEPTS[8]

The simplest way to describe a Wiener process $\{z_t: t \geq 0\}$ is that it is the continuous time version of a *random walk*. In a heuristic discussion, Cox and Miller (1965, Ch. 5) demonstrate that if the time interval Δt of a random walk approaches zero, then the limiting process is Gaussian with both mean and variance linearly proportional to the elapsed time $t - t_0$, where t_0 is the initial time. This sets the stage for the following formal definition:

DEFINITION: A stochastic process $\{z_t: t \geq 0\}$ on a probability space $(\Omega, \mathcal{F}, \mathcal{P})$ is a (standard) *Wiener process* (or a Brownian motion) if the following conditions are satisfied: (i) The increments are independent, i.e., if $0 \leq t_0 \leq t_1 \leq \cdots \leq t_k$, then the differences $\Delta z_j = z(t_j) - z(t_{j-1})$, $j = 1, 2, \ldots, k$, are independent random variables. Furthermore, Δz_j is normally distributed with mean 0 and variance $t_j - t_{j-1}$. (ii) For each $\omega \in \Omega$, the *sample path* (or the *realization*) $z_t(\omega)$ is continuous in t. In addition, $z_0(\omega) = 0$, with probability one, by convention.

Condition (i) is commonly employed in many empirical studies, which assume that shocks are i.i.d. and are normally distributed. However, the standard deviation of Δz_j is proportional to $\sqrt{t_j - t_{j-1}}$. This particular property accounts for the major difference between Ito's differentiation rule and the classic calculus. Another unusual property is this: With probability one, $z_t(\omega)$ is *nowhere differentiable* in t, even though $z_t(\omega)$ is continuous in t, as defined in (ii). Thus, the time derivative of $z_t(\omega)$, $dz_t(\omega)/dt$, does *not* exist except possibly on a set of probability zero.

A stochastic differential equation, denoted by

$$dX_t = f(X_t, t)\,dt + \sigma(X_t, t)\,dz_t, \tag{A.1}$$

is defined in terms of a stochastic *integral* equation

$$X_t = X_{t_0} + \int_{t_0}^{t} f(X_s, s)\,ds + \int_{t_0}^{t} \sigma(X_s, s)\,dz_s, \tag{A.2}$$

because, as pointed out earlier, dz_t/dt does not exist, with probability 1. The function $f(X_t, t)$ is called the *drift*, while $\sigma^2(X_t, t)$ is called the (instantaneous) *variance*. When the drift and the variance are independent of t, the corresponding equation is called *autonomous* and is written as

$$dX_t = f(X_t)\,dt + \sigma(X_t)\,dz. \tag{A.3}$$

The first integral of (A.2) is defined as the usual Riemann integral. The second integral, however, is defined as follows: Given a partition of $[t_0, t]$, $t_0 < t_1 < t_2 < \cdots < t_k = t$, the Riemann sum of the

[8] The reader is referred to Malliaris and Brock (1982) for other applications, and to McKean (1969) and Arnold (1974) for a rigorous presentation. The reader is also referred to Elliot (1982) and Chung and Williams (1983) for general stochastic integrations.

second integral of (A.2) is

(A.4) $$\sum_{j=1}^{k} \sigma(X_{\tau_j}, \tau_j)(z(t_j) - z(t_{j-1})),$$

where τ_j is an intermediate point, i.e., $\tau_j = (1-a)t_{j-1} + at_j$, $0 \leqslant a \leqslant 1$. An *Ito integral* is obtained by setting $a = 0$, i.e., the intermediate points are the *left endpoints* of the subintervals of a partition. Such an integral is a Lebesgue integral.

Formally, given a probability space $(\Omega, \mathscr{F}, \mathscr{P})$ and a Wiener process $\{z_t\}$, let $\{\mathscr{F}_t\}$ be an increasing family of σ-fields such that $\mathscr{F}_t$ contains the σ-field generated by $\{z_s : s \leqslant t\}$ and is independent of the σ-field generated by $\{z_s - z_t : t \leqslant s < \infty\}$. Such a family $\{\mathscr{F}_t\}$ is called *non-anticipating* with respect to z_t. Intuitively, its independence condition tells us that nothing in the future is anticipated (nonanticipating). The integrand $\sigma(X_s, s)$ belongs to the class of functions that are, for all $s \in [t_0, t]$, (i) nonanticipating with respect to $\{\mathscr{F}_s\}$, i.e., σ is $\mathscr{F}_s$-measurable and (ii) square integrable, i.e.,

(A.5) $$\int_{t_0}^{t} |\sigma(X_s, s)|^2 \, ds < \infty, \quad \text{with probability 1.}$$

Let X_t be a diffusion process satisfying an autonomous stochastic differential equation (A.3). Suppose $Y_t = H(X_t)$, where $H(\cdot)$ is a "smooth" function. A natural inquiry is this: Does Y_t satisfy some stochastic differential equation? Ito's Lemma provides such a differentiation rule.

ITO'S LEMMA: *If $H(\cdot)$ is twice continuously differentiable, then $Y_t = H(X_t)$ satisfies the following stochastic differential equation*:

(A.6) $$\begin{aligned} dY_t &= H'(X_t)\, dX_t + (1/2) H''(X_t)(dX_t)^2 \\ &= \left[H'(X_t) f(X_t) + (1/2) H''(X_t) \sigma^2(X_t)\right] dt + H'(X_t) \sigma(X_t)\, dz_t. \end{aligned}$$

Note: This important lemma can best be understood by using the convention $dz = \sqrt{dt}$. This is because the proof of the lemma is based on a Taylor series expansion and those terms having an order higher than dt, e.g., $[dX_t]^3$ is of order $(dt)^{3/2}$, become negligible as $dt \to 0$. Thus, "operational" rules for Ito's Lemma are: $(dz)^2 = dt$ and $(dz)(dt) = 0$. Notice, Ito's differentiation rule differs from the classic differentiation rule in that there is an "extra" term in the first equality of (A.6), $(1/2) H''(X_t)(dX_t)^2$.

Higher dimensional versions of Ito's Lemma can similarly be derived. Let X_t, Y_t follow the stochastic differential equations

(A.7) $$dX_t = f(X_t)\, dt + \sigma(X_t)\, dz,$$

(A.8) $$dY_t = g(X_t)\, dt + v(X_t)\, dz,$$

respectively. Notice that we assume shocks to X and Y follow the *same* Wiener process simply for convenience. More general results can be obtained though. Assume $W_t = H(X_t, Y_t)$, where H is twice continuously differentiable in both coordinates. Then write down the quadratic expansion

$$\begin{aligned} dW_t &= H_X\, dX_t + H_Y\, dY_t + (1/2) H_{XX}(dX_t)^2 + H_{XY}(dX)(dY) + (1/2) H_{YY}(dY_t)^2 \\ &= H_X(f\,dt + \sigma\, dz) + H_Y(g\,dt + v\,dz) + \left[(1/2)\sigma^2 H_{XX} + \sigma v H_{XY} + (1/2) v^2 H_{YY}\right] dt. \end{aligned}$$

Thus, the two-dimensional Ito's Lemma is

(A.9) $$dW_t = \left[f H_X + g H_Y + (1/2)\sigma^2 H_{XX} + \sigma v H_{XY} + (1/2) v^2 H_{YY}\right] dt + (\sigma H_X + v H_Y)\, dz.$$

EXAMPLE 1: *Derivation of the stochastic Solow equation* (4*a*). First, rewrite the capital accumulation equation (1) as $dK = [F(K, L) - C]\, dt$. Since L satisfies $dL = nL\, dt + \sigma L\, dz$, the usual Taylor series expansion of k, treating $k = K/L$ as a function of K and L, is

(A.10) $$d(K/L) = dK/L - (K/L^2)\, dL + (K/L^3)(dL)^2.$$

Two second order terms $(dK)^2$ and $(dK)(dL)$ are ignored, because $(dK)^2$ is of order $(dt)^2$ and

$(dK)(dL)$ is of order $(dt)^{3/2}$. Since $dK/L = [f(k) - c]\,dt$, we have

$$\begin{aligned} dk &= [f(k) - c]\,dt - k(dL/L) + k(dL/L)^2 \\ &= \big[f(k) - c - (n - \sigma^2)k\big]\,dt - \sigma k\,dz, \end{aligned} \tag{A.11}$$

which is our (4a).

EXAMPLE 2: *Derivation of equation* (13). Let $y = \log k$. By Ito's Lemma,

$$\begin{aligned} dy &= dk/k - [(1/(2k^2))](dk)^2 = dk/k - (1/2)(dk/k)^2 \\ &= \big[-(n - \sigma^2)\,dt - \sigma\,dz\big] - (1/2)\sigma^2\,dt = -(n - \sigma^2/2)\,dt - \sigma\,dz. \end{aligned} \tag{A.12}$$

Thus, the solution of (A.12) is

$$y(t) = y(0) + \int_0^t -(n - \sigma^2/2)\,ds - \int_0^t \sigma\,dz_s. \tag{A.13}$$

Since $k(t) = \exp\{y(t)\}$ and $k(0) = \exp\{y(0)\}$, equation (13) is obtained by taking the exponential on both sides of (A.13).

APPENDIX B

THE BELLMAN EQUATION AND THE VERIFICATION THEOREM[9]

Consider the Solow growth equation

$$dk = \big[f(k) - (n - \sigma^2)k - c\big]\,dt - \sigma k\,dz. \tag{4a}$$

It states that the capital-labor ratio k (the state process) evolves according to a stochastic differential equation, once the consumption pattern c (the control law) is chosen. For different control laws, the state processes follow different laws of motion. A stochastic differential equation that admits controls in the drift or the variance is called a *controlled stochastic differential equation* and the corresponding state process is called a *controlled diffusion process*. Incidentally, such a control law is a feedback control.

Recall that a fundamental concept in control theory is the Principle of Optimality, which usually appears in the form of a *recurrence equation*. For an intertemporal optimization problem (5), which maximizes an objective function subject to a controlled stochastic differential equation (4a), the Principle of Optimality states that

$$J(k) = \max_{\substack{c_t \\ 0 \leq t \leq \Delta t}} E_k\left\{\int_0^{\Delta t} e^{-\rho t}U(c_t)\,dt + \max_{\substack{c_t \\ \Delta t \leq t < \infty}} E_{k+\Delta k}\int_{\Delta t}^{\infty} e^{-\rho t}U(c_t)\,dt\right\}, \tag{B.1}$$

where E_k indicates that the initial state is k. In what follows, we shall derive the Bellman equation, using an elementary mathematical argument. Our exposition is based on Kushner (1971).

Using the intermediate value theorem, the first integral of (B.1) can be simplified as

$$\int_0^{\Delta t} e^{-\rho t}U(c_t)\,dt = e^{-\rho\theta\Delta t}U(c_{\theta\Delta t})\,\Delta t, \tag{B.2}$$

where $\theta = \theta(\omega)$, $\omega \in \Omega$, and $0 \leq \theta \leq 1$. Using change of variables, $s = t - \Delta t$, the second integral of (B.1) becomes

$$\begin{aligned} \max_{\substack{c_t \\ \Delta t \leq t < \infty}} E_{k+\Delta k}\int_{\Delta t}^{\infty} e^{-\rho t}U(c_t)\,dt &= \max_{\substack{c_{s+\Delta t} \\ 0 \leq s < \infty}} E_{k+\Delta k}\int_0^{\infty} e^{-\rho(s+\Delta t)}U(c_{s+\Delta t})\,ds \\ &= e^{-\rho\Delta t} \max_{\substack{c_s \\ 0 \leq s < \infty}} E_{k+\Delta k}\int_0^{\infty} e^{-\rho s}U(c_s)\,ds \\ &= e^{-\rho\Delta t}J(k + \Delta k). \end{aligned} \tag{B.3}$$

[9] For a more general and rigorous presentation, the reader is referred to Kushner (1971) and Fleming and Rishel (1975).

The second equality of (P.3) is obtained by relabelling $c_{s+\Delta t}$ as c_s. Now we can rewrite (B.1) as

(B.4) $$0 = \max_c E_k\{e^{-\rho\theta\Delta t}U(c_{\theta\Delta t})\,\Delta t + e^{-\rho\Delta t}J(k+\Delta k) - J(k)\}.$$

For sufficiently small Δt, $e^{-\rho\Delta t} = 1 - \rho\Delta t$. Thus,

(B.6) $$e^{-\rho\Delta t}J(k+\Delta k) - J(k) = J(k+\Delta k) - J(k) - \rho\Delta t J(k+\Delta k).$$

Notice that, by Ito's lemma,

$$J(k+\Delta k) - J(k) = \Delta J(k) = J'(k)\,\Delta k + (1/2)J''(k)(\Delta k)^2.$$

Taking the conditional expectation, we have

(B.7) $$E_k[J(k+\Delta k) - J(k)] = \{J'(k)[f(k) - (n-\sigma^2) - c] + (1/2)\sigma^2 k^2 J''(k)\}\,\Delta t.$$

Substitute (B.7) into (B.4). Dividing (B.4) by Δt and setting $\Delta t \to 0$, we have

(8) $$0 = \max_c\{[f(k) - (n-\sigma^2)k - c]J'(k) + \sigma^2 k^2 J''(k)/2 - \rho J(k) + U(c)\},$$

since $k + \Delta k \to k$, $\theta\Delta t \to 0$ and $c_{\theta\Delta t} \to c$.

Two factors are responsible for equation (8). One is the very nature of continuous time, which enables us to take the limit as $\Delta t \to 0$. The other is equation (B.7) (and, implicitly, Ito's Lemma), which enables us to get rid of the conditional expectation operator, E_k, since $E_k(\Delta k)^2 = \sigma^2 k^2\,\Delta t$. By contrast, a discrete time model under uncertainty, the Euler equation for optimality always involves some conditional expectations.

According to Fleming and Rishel (1975, Ch. 6), a sufficient condition for a maximum in the theory of stochastic control is called a *verification theorem*. Such a condition requires the existence of an optimal control and the existence of a well behaved indirect utility function for the Bellman equation. This sufficient condition becomes necessary under the *compactness* assumption (the value set of admissible controls is compact) and assumptions that, loosely speaking, require that both taste parameters and the coefficients of the controlled stochastic differential equation are smooth functions. All but the compactness assumption are automatically satisfied in many economic models. However, the typical assumption of a frictionless capital market, which implies the linearity of the admissible set, makes the compactness condition less satisfactory. For a detailed analysis on this subject, the reader is referred to Cox and Huang (1986).

REFERENCES

ARNOLD, L. (1974): *Stochastic Differential Equations: Theory and Applications*. New York: John Wiley and Sons.

BECKER, R. (1981): "The Duality of a Dynamic Model of Equilibrium and an Optimal Growth Model: The Heterogeneous Capital Goods Case," *Quarterly Journal of Economics*, 96, 271–300.

BHALLA, S. (1980): "The Measurement of Permanent Income and Its Application to Savings Behavior," *Journal of Political Economy*, 88, 722–744.

BIRKHOFF, G., AND G. ROTA (1978): *Ordinary Differential Equations*, 3rd Edition. New York: John Wiley and Sons.

BISMUT, J-M. (1973): "Conjugate Convex Functions in Optimal Stochastic Control," *Journal of Mathematical Analysis and Applications*, 44, 384–404.

BROCK, W. A. (1975): "Some Results on Dynamic Integrability," Report 7551, Center for Mathematical Studies in Business and Economics, University of Chicago.

CHANG, F-R, AND A. G. MALLIARIS (1987): "Asymptotic Growth under Uncertainty: Existence and Uniqueness," *Review of Economic Studies*, 54, 169–174.

CHUNG, K. L., AND R. WILLIAMS (1983): *Introduction to Stochastic Integration*. Boston: Birkhauser.

COX, D. R., AND H. D. MILLER (1965): *The Theory of Stochastic Processes*. New York: John Wiley and Sons.

COX, J., AND C. HUANG (1986): "A Variational Problem Arising in Financial Economics with an Application to a Portfolio Turnpike Theorem," Working Paper, Sloan School of Management, Massachusetts Institute of Technology.

COX, J., J. INGERSOLL, AND S. ROSS (1985): "An Intertemporal General Equilibrium Model of Asset Prices," *Econometrica*, 53, 363–384.
DECHERT, W. D. (1977): "Optimal Control Problems from Second-Order Difference Equations," *Journal of Economic Theory*, 19, 50–63.
ELLIOT, R. J. (1982): *Stochastic Calculus and Applications*. New York: Springer-Verlag.
FLEMING, W. H., AND R. W. RISHEL (1975): *Deterministic and Stochastic Optimal Control*. New York: Springer-Verlag.
HAHN, F. (1968): "On Warranted Growth Paths," *Review of Economic Studies*, 35, 175–184. It also appears as Chapter 14 in Hahn (1985).
——— (1985): *Money, Growth and Stability*. Cambridge, Mass.: The MIT Press.
KURZ, M. (1968): "The General Instability of a Class of Competitive Growth Processes," *Review of Economic Studies*, 35, 155–174.
——— (1969): "On the Inverse Optimal Problem," in *Mathematical Systems Theory and Economics I*, ed. by H. W. Kuhn and G. P. Szegö. Berlin: Springer-Verlag.
KUSHNER, H. J. (1971): *Introduction to Stochastic Control*. New York: Holt, Rinehart and Winston.
LUCAS, R. E. (1978): "Asset Prices in an Exchange Economy," *Econometrica*, 46, 1429–1445.
MALLIARIS, A. G., AND W. BROCK (1982): *Stochastic Methods in Economics and Finance*. Amsterdam: North-Holland.
MCKEAN, H. P., JR. (1969): *Stochastic Integrals*. New York: Academic Press.
MERTON, R. (1975): "An Asymptotic Theory of Growth Under Uncertainty," *Review of Economic Studies*, 42, 375–393.
MIRMAN, L., AND I. ZILCHA (1975): "On Optimal Growth Under Uncertainty," *Journal of Economic Theory*, 11, 329–339.
SOLOW, R. (1956): "A Contribution to the Theory of Economic Growth," *Quarterly Journal of Economics*, 70, 65–94.
WAN, H. Y., JR. (1971): *Economic Growth*. New York: Harcourt Brace Jovanovich, Inc.

[4]

Journal of Monetary Economics 22 (1988) 3–42. North-Holland

ON THE MECHANICS OF ECONOMIC DEVELOPMENT*

Robert E. LUCAS, Jr.

University of Chicago, Chicago, IL 60637, USA

Received August 1987, final version received February 1988

This paper considers the prospects for constructing a neoclassical theory of growth and international trade that is consistent with some of the main features of economic development. Three models are considered and compared to evidence: a model emphasizing physical capital accumulation and technological change, a model emphasizing human capital accumulation through schooling, and a model emphasizing specialized human capital accumulation through learning-by-doing.

1. Introduction

By the problem of economic development I mean simply the problem of accounting for the observed pattern, across countries and across time, in levels and rates of growth of per capita income. This may seem too narrow a definition, and perhaps it is, but thinking about income patterns will necessarily involve us in thinking about many other aspects of societies too, so I would suggest that we withhold judgment on the scope of this definition until we have a clearer idea of where it leads us.

The main features of levels and rates of growth of national incomes are well enough known to all of us, but I want to begin with a few numbers, so as to set a quantitative tone and to keep us from getting mired in the wrong kind of details. Unless I say otherwise, all figures are from the World Bank's *World Development Report* of 1983.

The diversity across countries in measured per capita income levels is literally too great to be believed. Compared to the 1980 average for what the World Bank calls the 'industrial market economies' (Ireland up through Switzerland) of U.S. $10,000, India's per capita income is $240, Haiti's is $270,

*This paper was originally written for the Marshall Lectures, given at Cambridge University in 1985. I am very grateful to the Cambridge faculty for this honor, and also for the invitation's long lead time, which gave me the opportunity to think through a new topic with the stimulus of so distinguished an audience in prospect. Since then, versions of this lecture have been given as the David Horowitz Lectures in Israel, the W.A. Mackintosh Lecture at Queens University, the Carl Snyder Memorial Lecture at the University of California at Santa Barbara, the Chung-Hua Lecture in Taipei, the Nancy Schwartz Lecture at Northwestern University, and the Lionel McKenzie Lecture at the University of Rochester. I have also based several seminars on various parts of this material.

and so on for the rest of the very poorest countries. This is a difference of a factor of 40 in living standards! These latter figures are too low to sustain life in, say, England or the United States, so they cannot be taken at face value and I will avoid hanging too much on their exact magnitudes. But I do not think anyone will argue that there is not enormous diversity in living standards.[1]

Rates of growth of real per capita GNP are also diverse, even over sustained periods. For 1960–80 we observe, for example: India, 1.4% per year; Egypt, 3.4%; South Korea, 7.0%; Japan, 7.1%; the United States, 2.3%; the industrial economies averaged 3.6%. To obtain from growth rates the number of years it takes for incomes to double, divide these numbers into 69 (the log of 2 times 100). Then Indian incomes will double every 50 years; Korean every 10. An Indian will, on average, be twice as well off as his grandfather; a Korean 32 times. These differences are at least as striking as differences in income levels, and in some respects more trustworthy, since within-country income comparisons are easier to draw than across-country comparisons.

I have not calculated a correlation across countries between income levels and rates of growth, but it would not be far from zero. (The poorest countries tend to have the lowest growth; the wealthiest next; the 'middle-income' countries highest.) The generalizations that strike the eye have to do with variability within these broad groups: the rich countries show little diversity (Japan excepted – else it would not have been classed as a rich country in 1980 at all). Within the poor countries (low and middle income) there is enormous variability.[2]

Within the advanced countries, growth rates tend to be very stable over long periods of time, provided one averages over periods long enough to eliminate business-cycle effects (or corrects for short-term fluctuations in some other way). For poorer countries, however, there are many examples of sudden, large changes in growth rates, both up and down. Some of these changes are no doubt due to political or military disruption: Angola's total GDP growth fell from 4.8 in the 60s to −9.2 in the 70s; Iran's fell from 11.3 to 2.5, comparing the same two periods. I do not think we need to look to economic theory for an account of either of *these* declines. There are also some striking examples

[1] The income estimates reported in Summers and Heston (1984) are more satisfactory than those in the World Development Reports. In 1975 U.S. dollars, these authors estimate 1980 U.S. real GDP per capita at $8000, and for the industrialized economies as a group, $5900. The comparable figures for India and Haiti are $460 and $500, respectively. Income differences of a factor of 16 are certainly smaller, and I think more accurate, than a factor of 40, but I think they are still fairly described as exhibiting 'enormous diversity'.

[2] Baumol (1986) summarizes evidence, mainly from Maddison (1982) indicating apparent convergence during this century to a common path of the income levels of the wealthiest countries. But De Long (1987) shows that this effect is entirely due to 'selection bias': If one examines the countries with the highest income levels at the *beginning* of the century (as opposed to currently, as in Maddison's 'sample') the data show apparent *divergence*!

of sharp increases in growth rates. The four East Asian 'miracles' of South Korea, Taiwan, Hong Kong and Singapore are the most familiar: for the 1960–80 period, per capita income in these economies grew at rates of 7.0, 6.5, 6.8 and 7.5, respectively, compared to much lower rates in the 1950's and earlier.[3,4] Between the 60s and the 70s, Indonesia's GDP growth increased from 3.9 to 7.5; Syria's from 4.6 to 10.0.

I do not see how one can look at figures like these without seeing them as representing *possibilities*. Is there some action a government of India could take that would lead the Indian economy to grow like Indonesia's or Egypt's? If so, *what*, exactly? If not, what is it about the 'nature of India' that makes it so? The consequences for human welfare involved in questions like these are simply staggering: Once one starts to think about them, it is hard to think about anything else.

This is what we need a theory of economic development *for*: to provide some kind of framework for organizing facts like these, for judging which represent opportunities and which necessities. But the term 'theory' is used in so many different ways, even within economics, that if I do not clarify what I mean by it early on, the gap between what I think I am saying and what you think you are hearing will grow too wide for us to have a serious discussion. I prefer to use the term 'theory' in a very narrow sense, to refer to an explicit dynamic system, something that can be put on a computer and *run*. This is what I mean by the 'mechanics' of economic development – the construction of a mechanical, artificial world, populated by the interacting robots that economics typically studies, that is capable of exhibiting behavior the gross features of which resemble those of the actual world that I have just described. My lectures will be occupied with one such construction, and it will take some work: It is easy to set out models of economic growth based on reasonable-looking axioms that predict the cessation of growth in a few decades, or that predict the rapid convergence of the living standards of different economies to a common level, or that otherwise produce logically possible outcomes that bear no resemblance to the outcomes produced by actual economic systems. On the other hand, there is no doubt that there must be mechanics other than the ones I will describe that would fit the facts about as well as mine. This is why I have titled the lectures '*On* the Mechanics ...' rather than simply '*The* Mechanics of Economic Development'. At some point, then, the study of development will need to involve working out the implications of competing theories for data other than those they were constructed to fit, and testing these implications against observation. But this is getting far ahead of the

[3]The World Bank no longer transmits data for Taiwan. The figure 6.5 in the text is from Harberger (1984, table 1, p. 9).

[4]According to Heston and Summers (1984), Taiwan's per-capita GDP growth rate in the 1950s was 3.6. South Korea's was 1.7 from 1953 to 1960.

story I have to tell, which will involve leaving many important questions open even at the purely theoretical level and will touch upon questions of empirical testing hardly at all.

My plan is as follows. I will begin with an application of a now-standard neoclassical model to the study of twentieth century U.S. growth, closely following the work of Robert Solow, Edward Denison and many others. I will then ask, somewhat unfairly, whether this model *as it stands* is an adequate model of economic development, concluding that it is not. Next, I will consider two adaptations of this standard model to include the effects of human capital accumulation. The first retains the one-sector character of the original model and focuses on the interaction of physical and human capital accumulation. The second examines a two-good system that admits specialized human capital of different kinds and offers interesting possibilities for the interaction of trade and development. Finally, I will turn to a discussion of what has been arrived at and of what is yet to be done.

In general, I will be focusing on various aspects of what economists, using the term very broadly, call the 'technology'. I will be abstracting altogether from the economics of demography, taking population growth as a given throughout. This is a serious omission, for which I can only offer the excuse that a serious discussion of demographic issues would be at least as difficult as the issues I will be discussing and I have neither the time nor the knowledge to do both. I hope the interactions between these topics are not such that they cannot usefully be considered separately, at least in a preliminary way.[5]

I will also be abstracting from all monetary matters, treating all exchange as though it involved goods-for-goods. In general, I believe that the importance of financial matters is very badly over-stressed in popular and even much professional discussion and so am not inclined to be apologetic for going to the other extreme. Yet insofar as the development of financial institutions is a limiting factor in development more generally conceived I will be falsifying the picture, and I have no clear idea as to how badly. But one cannot theorize about everything at once. I had better get on with what I do have to say.

2. Neoclassical growth theory: Review

The example, or model, of a successful theory that I will try to build on is the theory of economic growth that Robert Solow and Edward Denison developed and applied to twentieth century U.S. experience. This theory will serve as a basis for further discussion in three ways: as an example of the *form* that I believe useful aggregative theories must take, as an opportunity to

[5] Becker and Barro (1985) is the first attempt known to me to analyze fertility and capital accumulation decisions *simultaneously* within a general equilibrium framework. Tamura (1986) contains further results along this line.

explain exactly what theories of this form can tell us that other kinds of theories cannot, and as a possible theory of economic development. In this third capacity, the theory will be seen to fail badly, but also suggestively. Following up on these suggestions will occupy the remainder of the lectures.

Both Solow and Denison were attempting to account for the main features of U.S. economic growth, not to provide a theory of economic development, and their work was directed at a very different set of observations from the cross-country comparisons I cited in my introduction. The most useful summary is provided in Denison's 1961 monograph, *The Sources of Economic Growth in the United States*. Unless otherwise mentioned, this is the source for the figures I will cite next.

During the 1909–57 period covered in Denison's study, U.S. real output grew at an annual rate of 2.9%, employed manhours at 1.3%, and capital stock at 2.4%. The remarkable feature of these figures, as compared to those cited earlier, is their *stability* over time. Even if one takes as a starting point the trough of the Great Depression (1933) output growth to 1957 averages only 5%. If business-cycle effects are removed in any reasonable way (say, by using peak-to-peak growth rates) U.S. output growth is within half a percentage point of 3% annually for any sizeable subperiod for which we have data.

Solow (1956) was able to account for this stability, and also for some of the relative magnitudes of these growth rates, with a very simple but also easily refineable model.[6] There are many variations of this model in print. I will set out a particularly simple one that is chosen also to serve some later purposes. I will do so without much comment on its assumed structure: There is no point in arguing over a model's assumptions until one is clear on what questions it will be used to answer.

We consider a closed economy with competitive markets, with identical, rational agents and a constant returns technology. At date t there are $N(t)$ persons or, equivalently, manhours devoted to production. The exogenously given rate of growth of $N(t)$ is λ. Real, per-capita consumption is a stream $c(t)$, $t \geq 0$, of units of a single good. Preferences over (per-capita) consumption streams are given by

$$\int_0^\infty \mathrm{e}^{-\rho t} \frac{1}{1-\sigma}\left[c(t)^{1-\sigma}-1\right] N(t)\,\mathrm{d}t, \tag{1}$$

[6] Solow's 1956 paper stimulated a vast literature in the 1960s, exploring many variations on the original one-sector structure. See Burmeister and Dobell (1970) for an excellent introduction and survey. By putting a relatively simple version to empirical use, as I shall shortly do, I do not intend a negative comment on this body of research. On the contrary, it is exactly this kind of theoretical experimentation with alternative assumptions that is needed to give one the confidence that working with a particular, simple parameterization may, for the specific purpose at hand, be adequate.

where the discount rate ρ and the coefficient of (relative) risk aversion σ are both positive.[7]

Production per capita of the one good is divided into consumption $c(t)$ and capital accumulation. If we let $K(t)$ denote the total stock of capital, and $\dot{K}(t)$ its rate of change, then total output is $N(t)c(t)+\dot{K}(t)$. [Here $\dot{K}(t)$ is net investment and total output $N(t)c(t)+\dot{K}(t)$ is identified with net national product.] Production is assumed to depend on the levels of capital and labor inputs and on the level $A(t)$ of the 'technology', according to

$$N(t)c(t)+\dot{K}(t)=A(t)K(t)^{\beta}N(t)^{1-\beta}, \tag{2}$$

where $0<\beta<1$ and where the exogenously given rate of technical change, $\dot{A}/A$, is $\mu>0$.

The resource allocation problem faced by this simple economy is simply to choose a time path $c(t)$ for per-capita consumption. Given a path $c(t)$ and an initial capital stock $K(0)$, the technology (2) then implies a time path $K(t)$ for capital. The paths $A(t)$ and $N(t)$ are given exogenously. One way to think about this allocation problem is to think of choosing $c(t)$ at each date, given the values of $K(t)$, $A(t)$ and $N(t)$ that have been attained by that date. Evidently, it will not be optimal to choose $c(t)$ to maximize current-period utility, $N(t)[1/(1-\sigma)][c(t)-1]^{1-\sigma}$, for the choice that achieves this is to set net investment $\dot{K}(t)$ equal to zero (or, if feasible, negative): One needs to set some *value* or *price* on increments to capital. A central construct in the study of *optimal* allocations, allocations that maximize utility (1) subject to the technology (2), is the *current-value Hamiltonian* H defined by

$$H(K,\theta,c,t)=\frac{N}{1-\sigma}[c^{1-\sigma}-1]+\theta[AK^{\beta}N^{1-\beta}-Nc],$$

which is just the sum of current-period utility and [from (2)] the rate of increase of capital, the latter valued at the 'price' $\theta(t)$. An optimal allocation must maximize the expression H at each date t, provided the price $\theta(t)$ is correctly chosen.

The first-order condition for maximizing H with respect to c is

$$c^{-\sigma}=\theta, \tag{3}$$

which is to say that goods must be so allocated at each date as to be equally valuable, on the margin, used either as consumption or as investment. It is

[7] The inverse σ^{-1} of the coefficient of risk aversion is sometimes called the intertemporal elasticity of substitution. Since all the models considered in this paper are deterministic, this latter terminology may be more suitable.

known that the price $\theta(t)$ must satisfy

$$\dot{\theta}(t) = \rho\theta(t) - \frac{\partial}{\partial K} H(K(t), \theta(t), c(t), t)$$

$$= \left[\rho - \beta A(t) N(t)^{1-\beta} K(t)^{\beta-1}\right] \theta(t), \tag{4}$$

at each date t if the solution $c(t)$ to (3) is to yield an optimal *path* $(c(t))_{t=0}^{\infty}$.

Now if (3) is used to express $c(t)$ as a function $\theta(t)$, and this function $\theta^{-1/\sigma}$ is substituted in place of $c(t)$ in (2) and (4), these two equations are a pair of first-order differential equations in $K(t)$ and its 'price' $\theta(t)$. Solving this system, there will be a one-parameter family of paths $(K(t), \theta(t))$, satisfying the given initial condition on $K(0)$. The *unique* member of this family that satisfies the transversality condition:

$$\lim_{t \to \infty} e^{-\rho t} \theta(t) K(t) = 0 \tag{5}$$

is the optimal path. I am hoping that this application of Pontryagin's Maximum Principle, essentially taken from David Cass (1961), is familiar to most of you. I will be applying these same ideas repeatedly in what follows.

For this particular model, with convex preferences and technology and with no external effects of any kind, it is also known and not at all surprising that the *optimal* program characterized by (2), (3), (4) and (5) is also the unique *competitive equilibrium* program, provided either that all trading is consummated in advance, Arrow–Debreu style, *or* (and this is the interpretation I favor) that consumers and firms have rational expectations about future prices. In this deterministic context, rational expectations just means perfect foresight. For my purposes, it is this equilibrium interpretation that is most interesting: I intend to use the model as a positive theory of U.S. economic growth.

In order to do this, we will need to work out the predictions of the model in more detail, which involves solving the differential equation system so we can see what the equilibrium time paths look like and compare them to observations like Denison's. Rather than carry this analysis through to completion, I will work out the properties of a *particular* solution to the system and then just indicate briefly how the rest of the answer can be found in Cass's paper.

Let us construct from (2), (3) and (4) the system's *balanced growth path*: the particular solution $(K(t), \theta(t), c(t))$ such that the rates of growth of each of these variables is constant. (I have never been sure exactly what it is that is 'balanced' along such a path, but we need a term for solutions with this constant growth rate property and this is as good as any.) Let κ denote the rate of growth of per-capita consumption, $\dot{c}(t)/c(t)$, on a balanced growth path. Then from (3), we have $\dot{\theta}(t)/\theta(t) = -\sigma\kappa$. Then from (4), we must have

$$\beta A(t) N(t)^{1-\beta} K(t)^{\beta-1} = \rho + \sigma\kappa. \tag{6}$$

That is, along the balanced path, the marginal product of capital must equal the constant value $\rho + \sigma\kappa$. With this Cobb–Douglas technology, the marginal product of capital is proportional to the average product, so that dividing (2) through by $K(t)$ and applying (6) we obtain

$$\frac{N(t)c(t)}{K(t)} + \frac{\dot{K}(t)}{K(t)} = A(t) K(t)^{\beta-1} N(t)^{1-\beta} = \frac{\rho + \sigma\kappa}{\beta}. \tag{7}$$

By definition of a balanced path, $\dot{K}(t)/K(t)$ is constant so (7) implies that $N(t)c(t)/K(t)$ is constant or, differentiating, that

$$\frac{\dot{K}(t)}{K(t)} = \frac{\dot{N}(t)}{N(t)} + \frac{\dot{c}(t)}{c(t)} = \kappa + \lambda. \tag{8}$$

Thus per-capita consumption and per-capita capital grow at the common rate κ. To *solve* for this common rate, differentiate either (6) or (7) to obtain

$$\kappa = \frac{\mu}{1-\beta}. \tag{9}$$

Then (7) may be solved to obtain the constant, balanced consumption–capital ratio $N(t)c(t)/K(t)$ or, which is equivalent and slightly easier to interpret, the constant, balanced net savings rate s defined by

$$s = \frac{\dot{K}(t)}{N(t)c(t) + \dot{K}(t)} = \frac{\beta(\kappa + \lambda)}{\rho + \sigma\kappa}. \tag{10}$$

Hence along a balanced path, the rate of growth of per-capita magnitudes is simply proportional to the given rate of technical change, μ, where the constant of proportionality is the inverse of labor's share, $1 - \beta$. The rate of time preference ρ and the degree of risk aversion σ have no bearing on this long-run growth rate. Low time preference ρ and low risk aversion σ induce a high savings rate s, and high savings is, in turn, associated with relatively high output *levels* on a balanced path. A thrifty society will, in the long run, be wealthier than an impatient one, but it will not grow faster.

In order that the balanced path characterized by (9) and (10) satisfy the transversality condition (5), it is necessary that $\rho + \sigma\kappa > \kappa + \lambda$. [From (10), one sees that this is the same as requiring the savings rate to be less than capital's share.] Under this condition, an economy that begins on the balanced path will find it optimal to stay there. What of economies that begin *off* the balanced path – surely the normal case? Cass showed – and this is exactly why the balanced path is interesting to us – that for *any* initial capital $K(0) > 0$, the optimal capital–consumption path $(K(t), c(t))$ will converge to the balanced path asymptotically. That is, the balanced path will be a good approximation to any actual path 'most' of the time.

Now given the taste and technology parameters (ρ, σ, λ, β and μ) (9) and (10) can be solved for the asymptotic growth rate κ of capital, consumption and real output, and the savings rate s that they imply. Moreover, it would be straightforward to calculate numerically the approach to the balanced path from any initial capital level $K(0)$. This is the exercise that an idealized planner would go through.

Our interest in the model is positive, not normative, so we want to go in the opposite direction and try to infer the underlying preferences and technology from what we can observe. I will outline this, taking the balanced path as the model's prediction for the behavior of the U.S. economy during the entire (1909–57) period covered by Denison's study.[8] From this point of view, Denison's estimates provide a value of 0.013 for λ, and two values, 0.029 and 0.024 for $\kappa + \lambda$, depending on whether we use output or capital growth rates (which the model predicts to be equal). In the tradition of statistical inference, let us average to get $\kappa + \lambda = 0.027$. The theory predicts that $1 - \beta$ should equal labor's share in national income, about 0.75 in the U.S., averaging over the entire 1909–57 period. The savings rate (net investment over NNP) is fairly constant at 0.10. Then (9) implies an estimate of 0.0105 for μ. Eq. (10) implies that the preference parameters ρ and σ satisfy

$$\rho + (0.014)\sigma = 0.0675.$$

(The parameters ρ and σ are not separately identified along a smooth consumption path, so this is as far as we can go with the sample averages I have provided.)

These are the parameter values that give the theoretical model its best fit to the U.S. data. How good a fit *is* it? Either output growth is underpredicted or capital growth overpredicted, as remarked earlier (and in the theory of growth, a half a percentage point is a *large* discrepancy). There are interesting secular changes in manhours per household that the model assumes away, and labor's share is secularly rising (in all growing economies), not constant as assumed. There is, in short, much room for improvement, even in accounting for the secular changes the model was designed to fit, and indeed, a fuller review of

[8] With the parameter values described in this paragraph, the half-life of the approximate linear system associated with this model is about eleven years.

the literature would reveal interesting progress on these and many other fronts.[9] A model as explicit as this one, by the very nakedness of its simplifying assumptions, invites criticism and suggests refinements to itself. This is exactly why we prefer explicitness, or why I think we ought to.

Even granted its limitations, the simple neoclassical model has made basic contributions to our thinking about economic growth. Qualitatively, it emphasizes a distinction between 'growth effects' – changes in parameters that alter growth rates along balanced paths – and 'level effects' – changes that raise or lower balanced growth paths without affecting their slope – that is fundamental in thinking about policy changes. Solow's 1956 conclusion that changes in savings rates are level effects (which transposes in the present context to the conclusion that changes in the discount rate, ρ, are level effects) was startling at the time, and remains widely and very unfortunately neglected today. The influential idea that changes in the tax structure that make savings more attractive can have large, sustained effects on an economy's growth rate sounds so reasonable, and it may even be true, but it is a clear implication of the theory we have that it is not.

Even sophisticated discussions of economic growth can often be confusing as to what are thought to be level effects and what growth effects. Thus Krueger (1983) and Harberger (1984), in their recent, very useful surveys of the growth experiences of poor countries, both identify inefficient barriers to trade as a limitation on growth, and their removal as a key explanation of several rapid growth episodes. The facts Krueger and Harberger summarize are not in dispute, but under the neoclassical model just reviewed one would not expect the removal of inefficient trade barriers to induce sustained increases in growth rates. Removal of trade barriers is, on this theory, a level effect, analogous to the one-time shifting upward in production possibilities, and not a growth effect. Of course, level effects can be drawn out through time through adjustment costs of various kinds, but not so as to produce increases in growth rates that are both large and sustained. Thus the removal of an inefficiency that reduced output by five percent (an enormous effect) spread out over ten years in simply a one-half of one percent annual growth rate stimulus. Inefficiencies are important and their removal certainly desirable, but the familiar ones are level effects, not growth effects. (This is exactly why it is not paradoxical that centrally planned economies, with allocative inefficiencies of legendary proportions, grow about as fast as market economies.) The empirical connections between trade policies and economic growth that

[9]In particular, there is much evidence that capital stock growth, as measured by Denison, understates true capital growth due to the failure to correct price deflators for quality improvements. See, for example, Griliches and Jorgenson (1967) or Gordon (1971). These errors may well account for all of the 0.005 discrepancy noted in the text (or more!).

Boxall (1986) develops a modification of the Solow–Cass model in which labor supply is variable, and which has the potential (at least) to account for long-run changes in manhours.

Krueger and Harberger document are of evident importance, but they seem to me to pose a real paradox to the neoclassical theory we have, not a confirmation of it.

The main contributions of the neoclassical framework, far more important than its contributions to the clarity of purely qualitative discussions, stem from its ability to *quantify* the effects of various influences on growth. Denison's monograph lists dozens of policy changes, some fanciful and many others seriously proposed at the time he wrote, associating with each of them rough upper bounds on their likely effects on U.S. growth.[10] In the main, the theory adds little to what common sense would tell us about the *direction* of each effect – it is easy enough to guess which changes stimulate production, hence savings, and hence (at least for a time) economic growth. Yet most such changes, quantified, have *trivial* effects: The growth rate of an entire economy is not an easy thing to move around.

Economic growth, being a summary measure of all of the activities of an entire society, necessarily depends, in some way, on everything that goes on in a society. Societies differ in many easily observed ways, and it is easy to identify various economic and cultural peculiarities and imagine that they are keys to growth performance. For this, as Jacobs (1984) rightly observes, we do not need economic theory: 'Perceptive tourists will do as well.' The role of theory is not to catalogue the obvious, but to help us to sort out effects that are crucial, quantitatively, from those that can be set aside. Solow and Denison's work shows how this can be done in studying the growth of the U.S. economy, and of other advanced economies as well. I take success at this level to be a worthy objective for the theory of economic development.

3. Neoclassical growth theory: Assessment

It seems to be universally agreed that the model I have just reviewed is not a theory of economic development. Indeed, I suppose this is why we think of 'growth' and 'development' as distinct fields, with growth theory defined as those aspects of economic growth we have some understanding of, and development defined as those we don't. I do not disagree with this judgment, but a more specific idea of exactly where the model falls short will be useful in thinking about alternatives.

If we were to attempt to use the Solow–Denison framework to account for the diversity in income levels and rates of growth we observe in the world today, we would begin, theoretically, by imagining a world consisting of many

[10] Denison (1961, ch. 24). My favorite example is number 4 in this 'menu of choices available to increase the growth rate': '0.03 points [i.e., 0.03 of one percentage point] maximum potential ... Eliminate all crime and rehabilitate all criminals.' This example and many others in this chapter are pointed rebukes to those in the 1960s who tried to advance their favorite (and often worthy) causes by claiming ties to economic growth.

economies of the sort we have just described, assuming something about the way they interact, working out the dynamics of this new model, and comparing them to observations. This is actually much easier than it sounds (there isn't much to the theory of international trade when everyone produces the same, single good!), so let us think it through.

The key assumptions involve factor mobility: Are people and capital free to move? It is easiest to start with the assumption of *no* mobility, since then we can treat each country as an isolated system, just like the one we have just worked out. In this case, the model predicts that countries with the same preferences and technology will converge to identical levels of income and asymptotic rates of growth. Since this prediction does not accord at all well with what we observe, if we want to fit the theory to observed cross-country variations, we will need to postulate appropriate variations in the parameters (ρ, σ, λ, β and μ) and/or assume that countries differ according to their initial technology levels, $A(0)$. Or we can obtain additional theoretical flexibility by treating countries as differently situated relative to their steady-state paths. Let me review these possibilities briefly.

Population growth, λ, and income shares going to labor, $1-\beta$, do of course differ across countries, but neither varies in such a way as to provide an account of income differentials. Countries with rapid population growth are not systematically poorer than countries with slow-growing populations, as the theory predicts, either cross-sectionally today or historically. There are, certainly, interesting empirical connections between economic variables (narrowly defined) and birth and death rates, but I am fully persuaded by the work of Becker (1981) and others that these connections are best understood as arising from the way decisions to maintain life and to initiate it *respond* to economic conditions. Similarly, poor countries have lower labor shares than wealthy countries, indicating to me that elasticities of substitution in production are below unity (contrary to the Cobb–Douglas assumption I am using in these examples), but the prediction (9) that poorer countries should therefore grow more rapidly is not confirmed by experience.

The parameters ρ and σ are, as observed earlier, not separately identified, but if their joint values differed over countries in such a way as to account for income differences, poor countries would have systematically much higher (risk-corrected) interest rates than rich countries. Even if this were true, I would be inclined to seek other explanations. Looking ahead, we would like also to be able to account for sudden large changes in growth rates of individual countries. Do we want a theory that focuses attention on spontaneous shifts in people's discount rates or degree of risk aversion? Such theories are hard to refute, but I will leave it to others to work this side of the street.

Consideration of off-steady-state behavior would open up some new possibilities, possibly bringing the theory into better conformity with observation, but I do not view this route as at all promising. Off steady states, (9) need not hold and capital and output growth rates need not be either equal or constant, but it still follows from the technology (2) that output growth (g_{yt}, say) and capital growth (g_{kt}, say), both per capita, obey

$$g_{yt} = \beta g_{kt} + \mu.$$

But g_{yt} and g_{kt} can both be measured, and it is well established that for no value of β that is close to observed capital shares is it the case that $g_{yt} - \beta g_{kt}$ is even approximately uniform across countries. Here 'Denison's Law' works against us: the insensitivity of growth rates to variations in the model's underlying parameters, as reviewed earlier, makes it hard to use the theory to account for large variations across countries or across time. To conclude that even large changes in 'thriftiness' would not induce large changes in U.S. growth rates is really the same as concluding that differences in Japanese and U.S. thriftiness cannot account for much of the difference in these two economies' growth rates. By assigning so great a role to 'technology' as a source of growth, the theory is obliged to assign correspondingly minor roles to everything else, and so has very little ability to account for the wide diversity in growth rates that we observe.

Consider, then, variations across countries in 'technology' – its level and rate of change. This seems to me to be the one factor isolated by the neoclassical model that has the potential to account for wide differences in income levels and growth rates. This point of departure certainly does accord with everyday usage. We say that Japan is technologically more advanced than China, or that Korea is undergoing unusually rapid technical change, and such statements seem to mean something (and I think they do). But they cannot mean that the 'stock of useful knowledge' [in Kuznets's (1959) terminology] is higher in Japan than in China, or that it is growing more rapidly in Korea than elsewhere. 'Human knowledge' is just human, not Japanese or Chinese or Korean. I think when we talk in this way about differences in 'technology' across countries we are not talking about 'knowledge' in general, but about the knowledge of particular people, or perhaps particular subcultures of people. If so, then while it is not exactly wrong to describe these differences by an exogenous, exponential term like $A(t)$ neither is it useful to do so. We want a formalism that leads us to think about individual decisions to acquire knowledge, and about the consequences of these decisions for productivity. The body of theory that does this is called the theory of 'human capital', and I am going to draw extensively on this theory in the remainder of these lectures. For the moment, however, I simply want to impose the terminological convention that 'technology' – its level and rate of change – will be used to refer to something common to all countries, something 'pure' or 'disembodied', something whose determinants are outside the bounds of our current inquiry.

In the absence of differences in pure technology then, and under the assumption of no factor mobility, the neoclassical model predicts a strong tendency to income equality and equality in growth rates, tendencies we can observe within countries and, perhaps, within the wealthiest countries taken as a group, but which simply cannot be seen in the world at large. When factor mobility is permitted, this prediction is very powerfully reinforced. Factors of production, capital or labor or both, will flow to the highest returns, which is to say where each is relatively scarce. Capital–labor ratios will move rapidly to equality, and with them factor prices. Indeed, these predictions survive differences in preference parameters and population growth rates. In the model as stated, it makes no difference whether labor moves to join capital or the other way around. (Indeed, we know that with a many-good technology, factor price equalization can be achieved without mobility in *either* factor of production.)

The eighteenth and nineteenth century histories of the Americas, Australia and South and East Africa provide illustrations of the strength of these forces for equality, and of the ability of even simple neo-classical models to account for important economic events. If we replace the labor–capital technology of the Solow model with a land–labor technology of the same form, and treat labor as the mobile factor and land as the immobile, we obtain a model that predicts exactly the immigration flows that occurred and for exactly the reason – factor price differentials – that motivated these historical flows. Though this simple deterministic model abstracts from considerations of risk and many other elements that surely played a role in actual migration decisions, this abstraction is evidently not a fatal one.

In the present century, of course, immigration has been largely shut off, so it is not surprising that this land–labor model, with labor mobile, no longer gives an adequate account of actual movements in factors and factor prices. What *is* surprising, it seems to me, is that capital movements do not perform the same functions. Within the United States, for example, we have seen southern labor move north to produce automobiles. We have also seen textile mills move from New England south (to 'move' a factory, one lets it run down and builds its replacement somewhere else: it takes some time, but then, so does moving families) to achieve this same end of combining capital with relatively low wage labor. Economically, it makes no difference which factor is mobile, so long as one is.

Why, then, should the closing down of international labor mobility have slowed down, or even have much affected, the tendencies toward factor price equalization predicted by neoclassical theory, tendencies that have proved to be so powerful historically? If it is profitable to move a textile mill from New England to South Carolina, why is it not more profitable still to move it to Mexico? The fact that we do see *some* capital movement toward low-income countries is not an adequate answer to this question, for the theory predicts that *all* new investment should be so located until such time as return and real wage differentials are erased. Indeed, why did these capital movements not take place during the colonial age, under political and military arrangements that eliminated (or long postponed) the 'political risk' that is so frequently cited as a factor working against capital mobility? I do not have a satisfactory answer to this question, but it seems to me a major – perhaps *the* major – discrepancy between the predictions of neoclassical theory and the patterns of trade we observe. Dealing with this issue is surely a minimal requirement for a theory of economic development.

4. Human capital and growth

To this point, I have reviewed an example of the neoclassical model of growth, compared it to certain facts of U.S. economic history, and indicated why I want to use this theory as a kind of model, or image, of what I think is possible and useful for a theory of economic development. I have also described what seem to me two central reasons why this theory is not, as it stands, a useful theory of economic development: its apparent inability to account for observed diversity across countries and its strong and evidently counterfactual prediction that international trade should induce rapid movement toward equality in capital–labor ratios and factor prices. These observations set the stage for what I would like to do in the rest of the lectures.

Rather than take on both problems at once, I will begin by considering an alternative, or at least a complementary, engine of growth to the 'technological change' that serves this purpose in the Solow model, retaining for the moment the other features of that model (in particular, its closed character). I will do this by adding what Schultz (1963) and Becker (1964) call 'human capital' to the model, doing so in a way that is very close technically to similarly motivated models of Arrow (1962), Uzawa (1965) and Romer (1986).

By an individual's 'human capital' I will mean, for the purposes of this section, simply his general skill level, so that a worker with human capital $h(t)$ is the productive equivalent of two workers with $\frac{1}{2}h(t)$ each, or a half-time worker with $2h(t)$. The theory of human capital focuses on the fact that the way an individual allocates his time over various activities in the current period affects his productivity, or his $h(t)$ level, in future periods. Introducing human capital into the model, then, involves spelling out both the way human capital levels affect current production and the way the current time allocation affects the accumulation of human capital. Depending on one's objectives, there are many ways to formulate both these aspects of the 'technology'. Let us begin with the following, simple assumptions.

Suppose there are N workers in total, with skill levels h ranging from 0 to infinity. Let there be $N(h)$ workers with skill level h, so that $N = \int_0^\infty N(h)\,dh$. Suppose a worker with skill h devotes the fraction $u(h)$ of his non-leisure time to current production, and the remaining $1 - u(h)$ to human capital accumulation. Then the effective workforce in production – the analogue to $N(t)$ in (2) – is the sum $N^e = \int_0^\infty u(h)N(h)h\,dh$ of the skill-weighted manhours devoted to current production. Thus if output as a function of total capital K

and effective labor N^e is $F(K, N^e)$, the hourly wage of a worker at skill h is $F_N(K, N^e)h$ and his total earnings are $F_N(K, N^e)hu(h)$.

In addition to the effects of an individual's human capital on his own productivity – what I will call the *internal effect* of human capital – I want to consider an *external effect*. Specifically, let the *average* level of skill or human capital, defined by

$$h_a = \frac{\int_0^\infty hN(h)\,\mathrm{d}h}{\int_0^\infty N(h)\,\mathrm{d}h},$$

also contribute to the productivity of all factors of production (in a way that I will spell out shortly). I call this h_a effect external, because though all benefit from it, no individual human capital accumulation decision can have an appreciable effect on h_a, so no one will take it into account in deciding how to allocate his time.

Now it will simplify the analysis considerably to follow the preceding analysis and treat all workers in the economy as being identical. In this case, if all workers have skill level h and all choose the time allocation u, the effective workforce is just $N^e = uhN$, and the average skill level h_a is just h. Even so, I will continue to use the notation h_a for the latter, to emphasize the distinction between internal and external effects. Then the description (2) of the technology of goods production is replaced by

$$N(t)c(t) + \dot{K}(t) = AK(t)^\beta [u(t)h(t)N(t)]^{1-\beta} h_a(t)^\gamma, \tag{11}$$

where the term $h_a(t)^\gamma$ is intended to capture the external effects of human capital, and where the technology level A is now assumed to be constant.

To complete the model, the effort $1 - u(t)$ devoted to the accumulation of human capital must be linked to the rate of change in its level, $h(t)$. Everything hinges on exactly how this is done. Let us begin by postulating a technology relating the growth of human capital, $\dot{h}(t)$, to the level already attained and the effort devoted to acquiring more, say:

$$\dot{h}(t) = h(t)^\zeta G(1 - u(t)), \tag{12}$$

where G is increasing, with $G(0) = 0$. Now if we take $\zeta < 1$ in this formulation, so that there is diminishing returns to the accumulation of human capital, it is easy to see that human capital cannot serve as an alternative engine of growth to the technology term $A(t)$. To see this, note that, since $u(t) \geq 0$, (12) implies that

$$\frac{\dot{h}(t)}{h(t)} \leq h(t)^{\zeta-1} G(1),$$

so that $\dot{h}(t)/h(t)$ must eventually tend to zero as $h(t)$ grows no matter how much effort is devoted to accumulating it. This formulation would simply complicate the original Solow model without offering any genuinely new possibilities.

Uzawa (1965) worked out a model very similar to this one [he assumed $\gamma = 0$ and $U(c) = c$] under the assumption that the right-hand side of (12) is *linear* in $u(t)$ ($\zeta = 1$). The striking feature of his solution, and the feature that recommends his formulation to us, is that it exhibits sustained per-capita income growth from endogenous human capital accumulation alone: no external 'engine of growth' is required.

Uzawa's linearity assumption might appear to be a dead-end (for our present purposes) because we seem to see diminishing returns in observed, individual patterns of human capital accumulation: people accumulate it rapidly early in life, then less rapidly, then not at all – as though each additional percentage increment were harder to gain than the preceding one. But an alternative explanation for *this* observation is simply that an individual's lifetime is finite, so that the return to increments falls with time. Rosen (1976) showed that a technology like (12), with $\zeta = 1$, is consistent with the evidence we have on individual earnings. I will adapt the Uzawa–Rosen formulation here, assuming for simplicity that the function G is linear:

$$\dot{h}(t) = h(t)\delta[1 - u(t)]. \tag{13}$$

According to (13), if no effort is devoted to human capital accumulation, $[u(t) = 1]$, then none accumulates. If all effort is devoted to this purpose $[u(t) = 0]$, $h(t)$ grows at its maximal rate δ. In between these extremes, there are *no* diminishing returns to the stock $h(t)$: A given *percentage* increase in $h(t)$ requires the same effort, no matter what level of $h(t)$ has already been attained.

It is a digression I will not pursue, but it would take some work to go from a human capital technology of the form (13), applied to each finite-lived individual (as in Rosen's theory), to this same technology applied to an entire infinitely-lived typical household or family. For example, if each individual acquired human capital as in Rosen's model but if *none* of this capital were passed on to younger generations, the 'household's' stock would (with a fixed demography) stay constant. To obtain (13) for a family, one needs to assume both that each individual's capital follows this equation *and* that the initial level each new member begins with is proportional to (not equal to!) the level already attained by older members of the family. This is simply one instance of a general fact that I will emphasize again and again: that human capital accumulation is a *social* activity, involving *groups* of people in a way that has no counterpart in the accumulation of physical capital.

Aside from these changes in the technology, expressed in (11) and (13) to incorporate human capital and its accumulation, the model to be discussed is identical to the Solow model. The system is closed, population grows at the fixed rate λ, and the typical household has the preferences (1). Let us proceed to the analysis of this new model.[11]

In the presence of the external effect $h_a(t)^\gamma$, it will not be the case that optimal growth paths and competitive equilibrium paths coincide. Hence we cannot construct the equilibrium by studying the same hypothetical planning problem used to study Solow's model. But by following Romer's analysis of a very similar model, we can obtain the optimal and equilibrium paths separately, and compare them. This is what I will now do.

By an *optimal* path, I will mean a choice of $K(t)$, $h(t)$, $H_a(t)$, $c(t)$ and $u(t)$ that maximizes utility (1) subject to (11) and (13), *and* subject to the constraint $h(t) = h_a(t)$ for all t. This is a problem similar in general structure to the one we reviewed in section 2, and I will turn to it in a moment.

By an *equilibrium* path, I mean something more complicated. First, take a path $h_a(t)$, $t \geq 0$, to be given, like the exogenous technology path $A(t)$ in the Solow model. Given $h_a(t)$, consider the problem the private sector, consisting of atomistic households and firms, would solve if each agent *expected* the average level of human capital to follow the path $h_a(t)$. That is, consider the problem of choosing $h(t)$, $k(t)$, $c(t)$ and $u(t)$ so as to maximize (1) subject to (11) and (13), taking $h_a(t)$ as exogenously determined. When the solution path $h(t)$ for this problem coincides with the given path $h_a(t)$ – so that actual and expected behavior are the same – we say that the system is in equilibrium.[12]

The current-value Hamiltonian for the optimal problem, with 'prices' $\theta_1(t)$ and $\theta_2(t)$ used to value increments to physical and human capital respectively, is

$$H(K, h, \theta_1, \theta_2, c, u, t)$$

$$= \frac{N}{1-\sigma}(c^{1-\sigma} - 1) + \theta_1\left[AK^\beta(uNh)^{1-\beta}h^\gamma - Nc\right]$$

$$+ \theta_2[\delta h(1-u)].$$

In this model, there are two decision variables – consumption, $c(t)$, and the time devoted to production, $u(t)$ – and these are (in an optimal program)

[11] The model discussed in this section (in contrast to the model of section 2) has not been fully analyzed in the literature. The text gives a self-contained derivation of the main features of balanced paths. The treatment of behavior off balanced paths is largely conjecture, based on parallels with Uzawa (1965) and Romer (1986).

[12] This formulation of equilibrium behavior in the presence of external effects is taken from Arrow (1962) and Romer (1986). Romer actually carries out the study of the fixed-point problem in a space of $h(t)$, $t \geq 0$, paths. Here I follow Arrow and confine explicit analysis to balanced paths only.

selected so as to maximize H. The first-order conditions for this problem are thus:

$$c^{-\sigma} = \theta_1, \tag{14}$$

and

$$\theta_1(1-\beta)AK^{\beta}(uNh)^{-\beta}Nh^{1+\gamma} = \theta_2\delta h. \tag{15}$$

On the margin, goods must be equally valuable in their two uses – consumption and capital accumulation [eq. (14)] – and time must be equally valuable in its two uses – production and human capital accumulation [eq. (15)].

The rates of change of the prices θ_1 and θ_2 of the two kinds of capital are given by

$$\dot{\theta}_1 = \rho\theta_1 - \theta_1\beta AK^{\beta-1}(uNh)^{1-\beta}h^{\gamma}, \tag{16}$$

$$\dot{\theta}_2 = \rho\theta_2 - \theta_1(1-\beta+\gamma)AK^{\beta}(uN)^{1-\beta}h^{-\beta+\gamma} - \theta_2\delta(1-u). \tag{17}$$

Then eqs. (11) and (13) and (14)–(17), together with two transversality conditions that I will not state here, implicitly describe the optimal evolution of $K(t)$ and $h(t)$ from any initial mix of these two kinds of capital.

In the *equilibrium*, the private sector 'solves' a control problem of essentially this same form, but with the term $h_a(t)^{\gamma}$ in (11) taken as given. Market clearing then requires that $h_a(t) = h(t)$ for all t, so that (11), (13), (14), (15) and (16) are necessary conditions for equilibrium as well as for optimal paths. But eq. (17) no longer holds: It is precisely in the valuation of human capital that optimal and equilibrium allocations differ. For the private sector, in equilibrium, (17) is replaced by

$$\dot{\theta}_2 = \rho\theta_2 - \theta_1(1-\beta)AK^{\beta}(uN)^{1-\beta}h^{-\beta}h_a^{\gamma} - \theta_2\delta(1-u).$$

Since market clearing implies $(h(t) = h_a(t)$ for all t, this can be written as

$$\dot{\theta}_2 = \rho\theta_2 - \theta_1(a-\beta)AK^{\beta}(uN)^{1-\beta}h^{-\beta+\gamma} - \theta_2\delta(1-u). \tag{18}$$

Note that, if $\gamma = 0$, (17) and (18) are the same. It is the presence of the external effect $\gamma > 0$ that creates a divergence between the 'social' valuation formula (17) and the private valuation (18).

As with the simpler Solow model, the easiest way to characterize both optimal and equilibrium paths is to begin by seeking balanced growth solutions of both systems: solutions on which consumption and both kinds of capital are growing at constant percentage rates, the prices of the two kinds of capital are declining at constant rates, and the time allocation variable $u(t)$ is constant. Let us start by considering features that optimal and equilibrium paths have in common [by setting aside (17) and (18)].

Let κ denote $\dot{c}(t)/c(t)$, as before, so that (14) and (16) again imply the marginal productivity of capital condition:

$$\beta AK(t)^{\beta-1}(u(t)h(t)N(t))^{1-\beta}h(t)^{\gamma}=\rho+\sigma\kappa, \tag{19}$$

which is the analogue to condition (6). As in the earlier model, it is easy to verify that $K(t)$ must grow at the rate $\kappa+\lambda$ and that the savings rate s is constant, on a balanced path, at the value given by (10). For the derivation of these facts concerning physical capital accumulation, it is immaterial whether $h(t)$ is a matter of choice or an exogenous force as was technological change in the earlier model.

Now if we let $\nu=\dot{h}(t)/h(t)$ on a balanced path, it is clear from (13) that

$$\nu=\delta(1-u), \tag{20}$$

and from differentiating (19) that κ, the common growth rate of consumption and per-capita capital is

$$\kappa=\left(\frac{1-\beta+\gamma}{1-\beta}\right)\nu. \tag{21}$$

Thus with $h(t)$ growing at the fixed rate ν, $(1-\beta+\gamma)\nu$ plays the role of the exogenous rate of technological change μ in the earlier model.

Turning to the determinants of the rate of growth ν of human capital, one sees from differentiating both first-order conditions (14) and (15) and substituting for $\dot{\theta}_1/\theta_1$ that

$$\frac{\dot{\theta}_2}{\theta_2}=(\beta-\sigma)\kappa-(\beta-\gamma)\nu+\lambda. \tag{22}$$

At this point, the analyses of the efficient and equilibrium paths diverge. Focusing first on the efficient path, use (17) and (15) to obtain

$$\frac{\dot{\theta}_2}{\theta_2}=\rho-\delta-\frac{\gamma}{1-\beta}\delta u. \tag{23}$$

Now substitute for u from (20), eliminate $\dot{\theta}_2/\theta_2$ between (22) and (23), and solve for ν in terms of κ. Then eliminating κ between this equation and (21) gives the solution for the *efficient* rate of human capital growth, which I will call ν^*:

$$\nu^* = \sigma^{-1}\left[\delta - \frac{1-\beta}{1-\beta+\gamma}(\rho-\lambda)\right]. \tag{24}$$

Along an equilibrium balanced path (18) holds in place of (17) so that in place of (23) we have

$$\frac{\dot{\theta}_2}{\theta_2} = \rho - \delta. \tag{25}$$

Then by the same procedure used to derive the efficient growth rate ν^* from (23), we can obtain from (25) the equilibrium growth rate ν:

$$\nu = [\sigma(1-\beta+\gamma)-\gamma]^{-1}[(1-\beta)(\delta-(\rho-\lambda))]. \tag{26}$$

[For the formulas (24) and (26) to apply, the rates ν and ν^* must not exceed the maximum feasible rate δ. This restriction can be seen to require

$$\sigma \geq 1 - \frac{1-\beta}{1-\beta+\gamma}\,\frac{\rho-\lambda}{\delta}, \tag{27}$$

so the model cannot apply at levels of risk aversion that are too low (that is, if the intertemporal substitutability of consumption is too high).[13] When (27) holds with equality, $\nu = \nu^* = \delta$; when the inequality is strict, $\nu^* > \nu$, as one would expect.]

Eqs. (24) and (26) give, respectively, the efficient and the competitive equilibrium growth rates of human capital along a balanced path. In either case, this growth increases with the effectiveness δ of investment in human capital and declines with increases in the discount rate ρ. (Here at last is a connection between 'thriftiness' and growth!) In either case, (21) gives the corresponding rate of growth of physical capital, per capita. Notice that the theory predicts sustained growth whether or not the external effect γ is positive. If $\gamma = 0$, $\kappa = \nu$, while if $\gamma > 0$, $\kappa > \nu$, so that the external effect induces more rapid physical than human capital growth.

For the case $\sigma = 1$, the difference between efficient and equilibrium human capital growth rates is, subtracting (26) from (24),

$$\nu^* - \nu = \frac{\gamma}{1-\beta+\gamma}(\rho-\lambda).$$

[13] If utility is too nearly linear (σ is too near zero) and if δ is high enough, consumers will keep postponing consumption forever. [This does not occur in Uzawa's model, even though he assumes $\sigma = 0$, because he introduces diminishing returns to $1 - u(t)$ in his version of (13).]

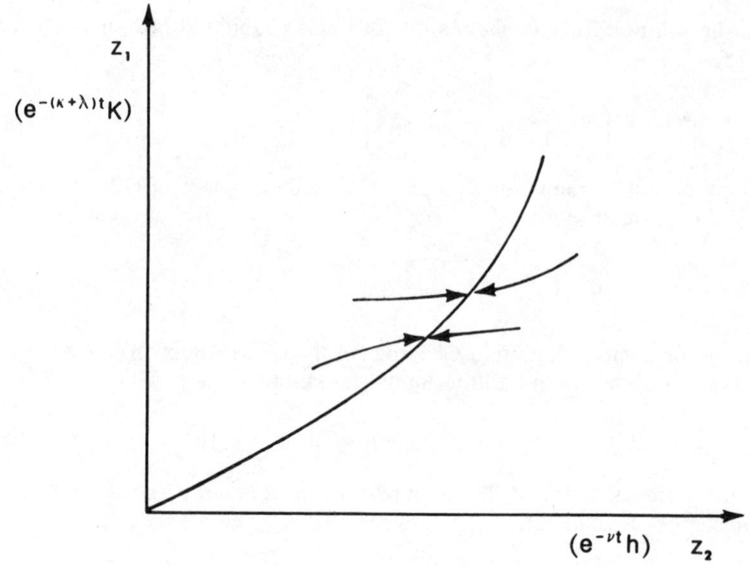

Fig. 1

Thus the inefficiency is small when either the external effect is small ($\gamma \simeq 0$) or the discount rate is low ($\rho - \lambda \simeq 0$).

Eqs. (21), (24) and (26) describe the asymptotic rates of change of both kinds of capital, under both efficient and equilibrium regimes. What can be said about the *levels* of these variables? As in the original model, this information is implicit in the marginal productivity condition for capital, eq. (19). In the original model, this condition – or rather its analogue, eq. (6) – determined a unique long-run value of the normalized variable $z(t) = e^{-(\kappa+\lambda)t}K(t)$. In the present, two-capital model, this condition defines a curve linking the *two* normalized variables $z_1(t) = e^{-(\kappa+\lambda)t}K(t)$ and $z_2(t) = e^{-\nu t}h(t)$. Inserting these variables into (19) in place of $K(t)$ and $h(t)$ and applying the formula (21) for κ, we obtain

$$\left(\beta A N_0^{1-\beta} u^{1-\beta}\right) z_1^{\beta-1} z_2^{1-\beta+\gamma} = \rho + \sigma\kappa. \tag{28}$$

It is a fact that *all* pairs (z_1, z_2) satisfying (28) correspond to balanced paths. Let us ask first what this locus of (normalized) capital combinations looks like, and second what this means for the dynamics of the system.

Fig. 1 shows the curve defined by (28). With no external effect ($\gamma = 0$) it is a straight line through the origin; otherwise ($\gamma > 0$) it is convex. The position of the curve depends on u and κ, which from (20) and (21) can be expressed as functions of ν. Using this fact one can see that increases in ν shift the curve to the right. Thus an efficient economy, on a balanced path, will have a higher level of human capital (z_2) for any given level of physical capital (z_1), since $\nu^* > \nu$.

The dynamics of this system are not as well understood as those of the one-good model, but I would conjecture that for any initial configuration $(K(0), h(0))$ of the two kinds of capital, the solution paths (of either the efficient or the equilibrium system) $(z_1(t), z_2(t))$ will converge to *some* point on the curve in fig. 1, but that this asymptotic position will depend on the initial position. The arrows in fig. 1 illustrate some possible trajectories. Under these dynamics, then, an economy beginning with low levels of human and physical capital will remain *permanently* below an initially better endowed economy.

The curve in fig. 1 is *defined* as the locus of long-run capital pairs (K, h) such that the marginal product of capital has the common value $\rho + \sigma\kappa$ given by the right side of (19). Along this curve, then, returns to capital are constant and also constant over time even though capital stocks of both kinds are growing. In the absence of the external effect γ, it will also be true that the real wage rate for labor of a given skill level (the marginal product of labor) is constant along the curve in fig. 1. This may be verified simply by calculating the marginal product of labor from (11) and making the appropriate substitutions.

In the general case, where $\gamma \geq 0$, the real wage increases as one moves up the curve in fig. 1. Along this curve, we have the elasticity formula

$$\frac{K}{w}\frac{\partial w}{\partial K} = \frac{(1+\beta)\gamma}{1-\beta+\gamma},$$

so that wealthier countries have higher wages than poorer ones for labor of any given skill. (Of course, workers in wealthy countries are typically also more skilled than workers in poor countries.) In all countries, wages at each skill level grow at the rate

$$\omega = \frac{\gamma}{1-\beta}\nu.$$

Then taking skill growth into account as well, wages grow at

$$\omega + \nu = \frac{1-\beta+\gamma}{1-\beta}\nu = \kappa,$$

or at a rate equal to the growth rate in the per-capita stock of physical capital.

The version of the model I propose to fit to, or estimate from, U.S. time series is the equilibrium solution (21), (26) and (10). As in the discussion of Solow's version λ, κ, β and s are estimated, from Denison (1961), at 0.013, 0.014, 0.25 and 0.1, respectively. Denison also provides an estimate of 0.009 for the annual growth rate of human capital over his period, an estimate based mainly on the changing composition of the workforce by levels of education and on observations on the relative earnings of differently schooled workers. I will use this 0.009 figure as an estimate of ν, which amounts to assuming that human capital is accumulated to the point where its private return equals its social (and private) cost. (Since schooling is heavily subsidized in the U.S., this assumption may seem way off, but surely most of the subsidy is directed at early schooling that would be acquired by virtually everyone anyway, and so does not affect the margins relevant for my calculations.) Then the idea is to use (10), (21) and (26) to estimate ρ, σ, γ and δ.

As was the case in the Solow model, ρ and σ cannot separately be identified along steady-state paths, but eq. (10) (which can be derived for this model in exactly the same way as I derived it for the model of section 2) implies $\rho + \sigma\kappa = 0.0675$. Eq. (21) implies $\gamma = 0.417$. Combining eqs. (21) and (26) yields a relationship involving γ, ν, β, δ, λ and $\rho + \sigma\kappa$, but not ρ or σ separately. This relationship yields an estimate for δ of 0.05. The implied fraction of time devoted to goods production is then, from (20), $u = 0.82$.

Given these parameter estimates, the *efficient* rate of human capital growth can be calculated, as a function of σ, from (24). It is: $\nu^* = 0.009 + 0.0146/\sigma$. Table 1 gives some values of this function and the associated values of u^* and $\kappa^* = (1.556)\nu^*$. Under log utility ($\sigma = 1$), then, the U.S. economy 'ought' to devote nearly three times as much effort to human capital accumulations as it does, and 'ought' to enjoy growth in per-capita consumption about two full percentage points higher than it has had in the past.

One could as easily fit this model to U.S. data under the assumption that *all* returns to human capital are internal, or that $\gamma = 0$. In this case ν, ν^* and κ have the common value, from (21), (24) and (26), $\sigma^{-1}[\delta - (\rho - \lambda)]$, and the *ratio* of physical to human capital will converge to a value that is independent of initial conditions (the curve in fig. 1 will be a straight line). Identifying this common growth rate with Denison's 0.014 estimate for κ implies a u value of 0.72, or that 28% of effective workers' time is spent in human capital

Table 1

σ	ν^*	u^*	κ^*
1	0.024	0.52	0.037
2	0.016	0.68	0.025
3	0.014	0.72	0.022

accumulation. Accepting Denison's estimate of a 0.009 growth rate of human capital due to schooling, this would leave 0.005 to be attributed to other forms, say on-the-job training that is distinct from productive activities.

What can be concluded from these exercises? Normatively, it seems to me, very little: The model I have just described has *exactly* the same ability to fit U.S. data as does the Solow model, in which equilibrium and efficient growth rates coincide. Moreover, it is clear that the two models can be merged [by re-introducing exogenous technical change into (11)] to yield a whole class of intermediate models that also fit data in this same rough sense. I am simply generating new possibilities, in the hope of obtaining a theoretical account of cross-country *differences* in income levels and growth rates. Since the model just examined is consistent with the *permanent* maintenance of per-capita income differentials of any size (though not with differences in growth rates) some progress toward this objective has been made. But before returning to empirical issues in more detail, I would like to generate another, quite different, example of a system in which human capital plays a central role.

5. Learning-by-doing and comparative advantage

The model I have just worked through treats the decision to accumulate human capital as equivalent to a decision to withdraw effort from production – to go to school, say. As many economists have observed, on-the-job-training or learning-by-doing appear to be at least as important as schooling in the formation of human capital. It would not be difficult to incorporate such effects into the previous model, but it is easier to think about one thing at a time so I will just set out an example of a system (again, for the moment, closed) in which *all* human capital accumulation is learning-by-doing. Doing this will involve thinking about economies with many consumption goods, which will open up interesting new possibilities for interactions between international trade and economic growth.[14]

Let there be two consumption goods, c_1 and c_2, and no physical capital. For simplicity, let population be constant. The ith good is produced with the Ricardian technology:

$$c_i(t) = h_i(t)u_i(t)N(t), \qquad i = 1,2, \tag{29}$$

where $h_i(t)$ is human capital specialized to the production of good i and $u_i(t)$ is the fraction of the workforce devoted to producing good i (so $u_i \geq 0$ and $u_1 + u_2 = 1$). Of course, it would not be at all difficult to incorporate physical capital into this model, with (29) replaced by something like (11) for each good i. Later on, I will conjecture the behavior of such a hybrid model, but it will be simpler for now to abstract from capital.

[14] The formulation of learning used in this section is taken from Krugman (1985).

In order to let $h_i(t)$ be interpreted as a result of learning-by-doing, assume that the growth of $h_i(t)$ increases with the effort $u_i(t)$ devoted to producing good i (as opposed to increasing with the effort *withdrawn* from production). A simple way to do this is

$$\dot{h}_i(t) = h_i(t)\delta_i u_i(t). \tag{30}$$

To be specific, assume that $\delta_1 > \delta_2$, so that good 1 is taken to be the 'high-technology' good. For the sake of discussion, assume at one extreme that the effects of $h_i(t)$ in (29) and (30) are entirely external: production and skill accumulation for each good depend on the average skill level in that industry only.

As was the case with (13), the equation for human capital accumulation in the model discussed earlier, (30) seems to violate the diminishing returns we observe in studies of productivity growth for particular products. Learning-by-doing in any particular activity occurs rapidly at first, then more slowly, then not at all. Yet as in the preceding discussion, if we simply incorporate diminishing returns into (30), human capital will lose its status as an engine of growth (and hence its interest for the present discussion). What I want (30) to 'stand for', then, is an environment in which new goods are continually being introduced, with diminishing returns to learning on each of them separately, and with human capital specialized to old goods being 'inherited' in some way by new goods. In other words, one would like to consider the inheritance of human capital within 'families' of goods as well as within families of people.[15]

Under these assumptions of no physical capital accumulation and purely external human capital accumulation, the individual consumer has no inter-temporal tradeoffs to decide on, so all we need to know about his preferences is his current-period utility function. I will assume a constant elasticity of substitution form:

$$U(c_1, c_2) = \left[\alpha_1 c_1^{-\rho} + \alpha_2 c_2^{-\rho}\right]^{-1/\rho}, \tag{31}$$

where $\alpha_i \geq 0$, $\alpha_1 + \alpha_2 = 1$, $\rho > -1$, and $\sigma = 1/(1+\rho)$ is the elasticity of substitution between c_1 and c_2. (Please note that the parameters ρ and σ represent completely different aspects of preferences in this section from those they represented in sections 2–4.) With technology and preferences given by (29)–(31), I will first work out the equilibrium under autarchy and then turn to international trade considerations.

Take the first good as numeraire, and let $(1, q)$ be the equilibrium prices in a closed economy. Then q must equal the marginal rate of substitution in

[15] Stokey (1987) formulates a model of learning on an infinite family of produced and potentially producible goods that captures exactly these features.

consumption, or

$$q = \frac{U_2(c_1,c_2)}{U_1(c_1,c_2)} = \frac{\alpha_2}{\alpha_1}\left(\frac{c_2}{c_1}\right)^{-(1+\rho)}.$$

Solving for the consumption ratio,

$$\frac{c_2}{c_1} = \left(\frac{\alpha_2}{\alpha_1}\right)^{\sigma} q^{-\sigma}. \tag{32}$$

Hence both goods will be produced, so that (29) plus profit maximization implies that relative prices are dictated by the human capital endowments: $q = h_1/h_2$. Then (29) and (32) together give the equilibrium workforce allocation as a function of these endowments,

$$\frac{c_2}{c_1} = \frac{u_2 h_2}{u_1 h_1} = \left(\frac{\alpha_2}{\alpha_1}\right)^{\sigma}\left(\frac{h_2}{h_1}\right)^{\sigma},$$

or

$$\frac{1-u_1}{u_1} = \left(\frac{\alpha_2}{\alpha_1}\right)^{\sigma}\left(\frac{h_2}{h_1}\right)^{\sigma-1}. \tag{33}$$

The dynamics of this closed economy are then determined by inserting this information into eq. (30). Solving first for the autarchy price path, $q(t) = h_1(t)/h_2(t)$, we have

$$\frac{1}{q}\frac{dq}{dt} = \frac{1}{h_1}\frac{dh_1}{dt} - \frac{1}{h_2}\frac{dh_2}{dt} = \delta_1 u_1 - \delta_2(1-u_1),$$

or

$$\frac{1}{q}\frac{dq}{dt} = (\delta_1+\delta_2)\left[1 + \left(\frac{\alpha_2}{\alpha_1}\right)^{\sigma} q^{1-\sigma}\right]^{-1} - \delta_2. \tag{34}$$

Solving this first-order equation for $q(t) = h_1(t)/h_2(t)$, given the initial endowments $h_1(0)$ and $h_2(0)$, determines the workforce allocation at each date [from (33)] and hence, from (30), the paths of $h_1(t)$ and $h_2(t)$ separately.

It will come as no surprise to trade theorists that the analysis of (34) breaks down into three cases, depending on the elasticity of substitution σ between the two goods. I will argue below, on the basis of trade considerations, that the interesting case for us is when $\sigma > 1$, so that c_1 and c_2 are assumed to be good

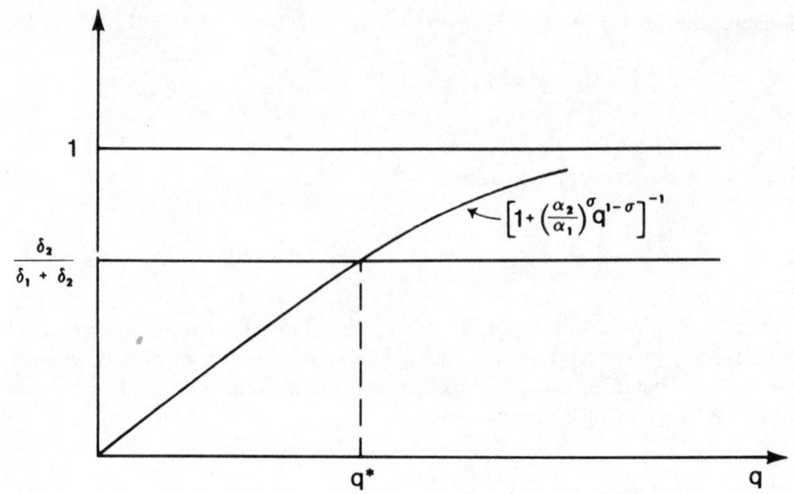

Fig. 2

substitutes. But in order to make this case, we need all three possibilities in front of us. Refer to fig. 2.

The figure is drawn for the case $\sigma > 1$, in which case the function $[1 + (\alpha_2/\alpha_1)^{\sigma} q^{1-\sigma}]^{-1}$ has the depicted upward slope. To the left of q^*, $dq/dt < 0$, so $q(t)$ tends to 0. To the right, $dq/dt > 0$, so $q(t)$ grows without bound. Thus the system in autarchy converges to specialization in one of the two goods [unless $q(0) = q^*$]. The choice of *which* good to specialize in is dictated by initial conditions. If we are initially good at producing c_1 [if $q(0) > q^*$], we produce a lot of it, get relatively better and better at producing more of it, eventually, since c_1 and c_2 are good substitutes, producing vanishingly small amounts of c_2.

If the goods are poor substitutes, $\sigma < 1$, the curve in fig. 2 slopes down and q^* becomes a *stable* stationary point. At this point, the workforce is so allocated as to equate $\delta_1 u_1$ and $\delta_2 u_2$.

In the borderline case of $\sigma = 1$, the curve is flat. The workforce is initially allocated as dictated by the demand weights, $ui = \alpha_i$, $i = 1,2$, and this allocation is maintained forever. The autarchy price grows (or shrinks) at the constant rate $(1/q)(dq/dt) = \alpha_1\delta_1 - \alpha_2\delta_2$ forever.

As we learn how to produce computers more and more cheaply, then, we can substitute in their favor and consume more calculations and fewer potatoes, or we can use this benefit to release resources from computer production so as to consume more potatoes as well. The choice we take, not surprisingly, depends on whether these two goods are good substitutes or poor ones.

As was the case with the human capital model of the preceding section, it is obvious that the equilibrium paths we have just calculated will *not* be efficient. Since learning effects are assumed to be external, agents do not take them into account. If they did, they would allocate labor toward the 'high δ_i' good, relative to an equilibrium allocation, so as to take advantage of its higher growth potential.

Thus, except for the absence of physical capital, this closed economy model captures very much the same economics as does the preceding one. In both cases, the accumulation of human capital involves a sacrifice of current utility. In the first model, this sacrifice takes the form of a decrease in current consumption. In the second, it takes the form of a less desirable *mix* of current consumption goods than could be obtained with slower human capital growth. In both models the equilibrium growth rate falls short of the efficient rate and yields lower welfare. A subsidy to schooling would improve matters in the first. In the second, in language that is current in the United States, an 'industrial policy' focused on 'picking winners' (that is, subsidizing the production of high $\alpha_i\delta_i$ goods) would be called for. In the model, 'picking winners' is easy. If only it were so in reality!

The introduction of international trade into this second model leads to possibilities that I think are of real interest, though I have only begun to think them through analytically. The simplest kind of world to think about is one with perfectly free trade in the two final goods and with a continuum of small countries, since in that case prices in all countries will equal world prices $(1, p)$, say, and each country will take p as given. Fig. 3 gives a snapshot of this world at a single point in time. The contour lines in this figure are intended to depict a joint distribution of countries by their initial human capital endowments. A country is a point (h_1, h_2), and the distribution indicates the concentration of countries at various endowment levels.

At a given world price p, countries above the indicated line are producers of good 2, since for them $h_1/h_2 < p$ and they maximize the value of their production by specializing in this good. Countries below the line specialize in producing good 1, for the same reason. Then for each p one can calculate world supply of good 1 by summing (or integrating) the h_1 values below this price line, and the world supply of good 2 by summing the h_2 values above the line. Clearly, the supply of good 2 is an increasing function of p and of good 1 a decreasing function, so that the ratio c_2/c_1 of total quantities supplied increases as p increases.

Now world relative demand, with identical homothetic preferences, is just the same decreasing function of p that described each country's demand in the autarchic case: $c_2/c_1 = (\alpha_2/\alpha_1)^{\sigma} p^{-\sigma}$. Hence this static model determines the equilibrium world relative price p uniquely. Let us turn to the dynamics.

Those countries above the price line in fig. 3 are producing only good 2, so their h_1 endowments remain fixed while their h_2 endowments grow at the rate δ_2. Each country below the price line will produce only good 1, so that its h_2 is

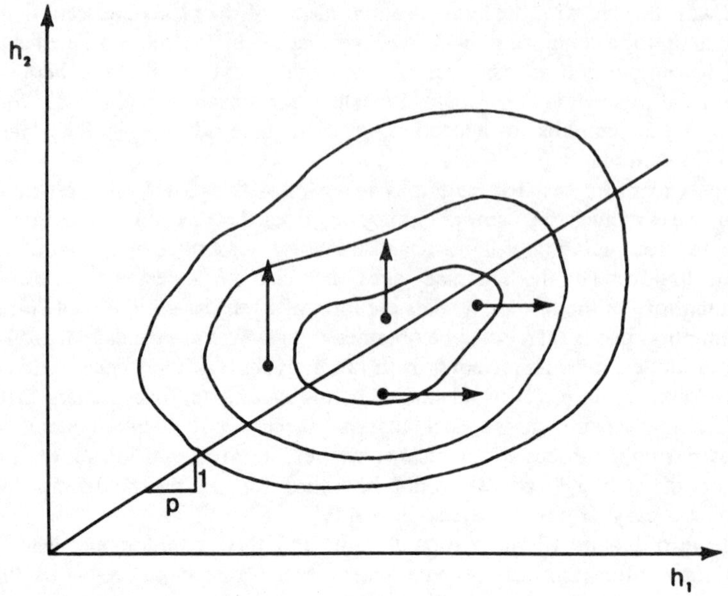

Fig. 3

constant while h_1 grows at the rate δ_1. Thus each country's (h_1, h_2) coordinates are changing as indicated by the arrows in fig. 3, altering the distribution of endowments that determines goods supplies over time. These movements obviously intensify the comparative advantages that led each country to specialize in the first place. On the other hand, as the endowment distribution changes, so does the equilibrium price p. Is it possible that these price movements will induce any country to switch its specialization from one good to the other?

A little reflection suggest that if anyone switches, it will have to be a producer of the high-δ good: good 1. The terms of trade are moving against good 1 (in the absence of switching) since its supply is growing faster. The issue again turns on the degree of substitutability between the two goods. If σ is low, the terms of trade may deteriorate so fast that a marginal good 1 producer may switch to producing good 2: he is getting relatively better at producing good 1, but not fast enough. The inequality that rules this possibility out is

$$\sigma \geq 1 - \frac{\delta_2}{\delta_1}. \tag{35}$$

I have already said that I think $\sigma > 1$ is the interesting case, so I want to accept (35) for the rest of the discussion.

Under (35) – that is, with no producer switching – we can read the dynamics of prices right off the relative demand schedule:

$$\frac{1}{p}\frac{\mathrm{d}p}{\mathrm{d}t} = \frac{\delta_1 - \delta_2}{\sigma}. \tag{36}$$

With relative price movements determined, the growth rates of real output in all countries is also determined. Measured in units of good 1, output of the good 1 producers grows at the rate δ_1. Output of the good 2 producers, also measured in units of good 1, grows at the rate $\delta_2 + (1/p)(\mathrm{d}p/\mathrm{d}t) = \delta_2 + (\delta_1 - \delta_2)/\sigma$. In general, then countries in equilibrium will undergo constant but not equal growth rates of real output.

Which countries will grow fastest? The condition that producers of the high-δ good, good 1, will have faster real growth is just

$$\delta_1 > \delta_2 + \frac{\delta_1 - \delta_2}{\sigma},$$

which is equivalent to the condition: $\sigma > 1$. That is, producing (having a comparative advantage in) high-learning goods will lead to higher-than-average real growth *only* if the two goods are good substitutes. Since it is exactly this possibility that the model is designed to capture, the case $\sigma > 1$ seems to me the only one of potential interest. If the terms-of-trade effects of technological change dominated the direct effects on productivity (which would be the case if $\sigma < 1$), those countries with rapid technological change would enjoy the slowest real income growth. There may be instances of such 'immiserizing growth', but if so they are surely the exceptions, not the rule. (These are the 'trade considerations' I mentioned earlier.)

This simple model shares with the model of section 4 the prediction of constant, endogenously determined real growth rates. In addition, it offers the possibility of different growth rates across countries, though differences that are not systematically related to income levels. In the equilibrium of the model, production patterns are dictated by comparative advantage: Each country produces goods for which its human capital endowment suits it. Given a learning technology like (30), countries accumulate skills by doing what they are already good at doing, intensifying whatever comparative advantage they begin with. This aspect of the theory will tend to lock in place an initial pattern of production, with rates of output growth variable across countries but stable within each country. There is no doubt that we observe forces for stability of this type, but there seem to be offsetting forces in reality that this model does not capture.

One of these has to do with the composition of demand. With homothetic utility the composition of world demand will remain fixed as income grows. In fact, we know that income elasticities for important classes of goods differ significantly from unity (contrary to the assumption of homotheticity). (We know, for example, that demand shifts systematically away from food consumption as income grows.) This force will 'create' comparative advantages in the production of other goods as time passes, altering world production patterns and growth rates as it does.

Another, I would guess more important, force has to do with the continual introduction of new goods and the fall-off of learning rates on old goods. By modeling learning as occuring at fixed rates on a fixed set of goods, I have here abstracted from important sources of change in world trade patterns. Modifying the model to incorporate possibilities of these two types is an entirely practical idea, given current theoretical technology, but the general equilibrium possibilities for such a modified system have not as yet been worked out.[16]

The present model provides a simple context for discussing two popular 'strategies' for economic development: 'import substitution' and 'export promotion'. Consider first a country with $q = h_1/h_2$ currently to the right of q^* in fig. 2, but with (h_1, h_2) lying above the equilibrium world price price line in fig. 3. Under free trade, this country will specialize in the production of good 2 forever. Under autarchy (which is just the extreme version of an import substitution policy) this country will specialize in producing good 1. Eventually its expertise in this protected industry will grow to the point where it will have a comparative advantage in good 1 under free trade, and the maintenance of autarchy will no longer serve any purpose, but this need not be so from the beginning.

I hasten to add that this is only one theoretical possibility among many. Another possibility is an initial q value below q^* in fig. 2. In this case, autarchy will not provide nurture for the infant industry, but will rather permanently cut off the country from consuming the high-learning good. Within the context of this model, then, there is no substance-free way to deduce useful guides for trade and development policies. One needs to know something about the actual technological possibilities for producing different goods in different places in order to arrive at definite conclusions.

I take an 'export promotion' strategy to mean something slightly different: the manipulation through taxes and subsidies of the terms of trade p faced by a country's producers. With this kind of flexibility, one need not simply choose between world price p and autarchy price q, but can rather set any production incentives and hence choose any growth rate between the two extremes in the free trade equilibrium. Obviously, even with this flexibility it does not follow

[16] Again, see Stokey (1987).

that 'growth-increasing' and 'welfare-improving' policies will necessarily coincide, but they certainly might.

My objective in this section has been to offer one example of a theoretical model in which rates of growth differ across countries, and not to offer policy advice. The case for infant industry protection based on external effects that this model formalizes is the classic one, and it does not become either more or less valid, empirically, by being embedded in a slightly new framework. But is it possible, I wonder, to account for the large cross-country differences in growth rates that we observe in a theoretical model that does *not* involve external effects of the sort I have postulated here? I have not seen it done.

6. Cities and growth

My concern to this point has been almost exclusively with the aggregate mechanics of economic development, and I am afraid the discussion in these lectures will not get much beyond these mechanics. But I believe a successful theory of development (or of anything else) has to involve more than aggregative modeling, and I would like both to explain what I mean by this and to indicate where one might look to extend the analysis to a deeper and more productive level.

The engine of growth in the models of sections 4 and 5 is *human capital.* Within the context of these two models, human capital is simply an unobservable magnitude or force, with certain assumed properties, that I have postulated in order to account for some observed features of aggregative behavior. If these features of behavior were *all* of the observable consequences of the idea of human capital, then I think it would make little difference if we simply re-named this force, say, the Protestant ethic or the Spirit of History or just 'factor X'. After all, we can no more directly measure the amount of human capital a society has, or the rate at which it is growing, than we can measure the degree to which a society is imbued with the Protestant ethic.

But this is *not* all we know about human capital. This same force, admittedly unobservable, has also been used to account for a vast number of phenomena involving the way people allocate their time, the way individuals' earnings evolve over their lifetimes, aspects of the formation, maintenance and dissolution of relationships within families, firms and other organizations, and so on. The idea of human capital may have seemed ethereal when it was first introduced – at least, it did to me – but after two decades of research applications of human capital theory we have learned to 'see' it in a wide variety of phenomena, just as meteorology has taught us to 'see' the advent of a warm front in a bank of clouds or 'feel' it in the mugginess of the air.

Indeed, for me the development of the theory of human capital has very much altered the way I think about physical capital. We can, after all, no more directly measure a society's holdings of physical capital than we can its human capital. The fiction of 'counting machines' is helpful in certain abstract contexts but not at all operational or useful in actual economies – even primitive ones. If this was the issue in the famous 'two Cambridges' controversy, then it has long since been resolved in favor of this side of the Atlantic.[17] Physical capital, too, is best viewed as a force, not directly observable, that we postulate in order to account in a unified way for certain things we *can* observe: that goods are produced that yield no immediate benefit to consumers, that the production of these goods enhances labor productivity in future periods, and so on.

The fact that the postulates of both human and physical capital have many observable implications outside the contexts of aggregate models is important in specific, quantitative ways, in addition to simply giving aggregative theorists a sense of having 'microeconomic foundations'. For example, in my application of a human capital model to U.S. aggregative figures, I matched the U.S. observations to the predictions of a competitive model (as opposed to an efficient one) in spite of the fact that education, in the U.S., involves vast government intervention and is obviously not a competitive industry in any descriptive sense. Why not instead identify the observed paths with the model's efficient trajectories? The aggregative data have *no* ability to discriminate between these two hypotheses, so this choice would have yielded as good a 'fit' as the one I made. At this point, I appealed to the observation that most education subsidies are infra-marginal from the individual's point of view. This observation could stand considerable refinement before it could really settle this particular issue, but the point is that aggregate models based on constructs that have implications for data *other* than aggregates – models with 'microeconomic foundations' if you like – permit us to bring evidence to bear on questions of aggregative importance that cannot be resolved with aggregate theory and observations alone. Without the ability to do this, we can do little more than extrapolate past trends into the future, and then be caught by surprise every time one of these trends changes.

The particular aggregate models I have set out utilize the idea of human capital quite centrally, but assign a central role as well to what I have been calling the *external effects* of human capital. This latter force is, it seems to me, on a quite different footing from the idea of human capital generally: The twenty years of research I have referred to earlier is almost exclusively concerned with the *internal* effects of human capital, or with investments in human capital the returns to which accrue to the individual (or his immediate family). If it is this research that permits us to 'see' human capital, then the external effects of this capital must be viewed as remaining largely invisible, or visible at the aggregative level only. For example, in section 4 I arrived at an estimate of $\gamma = 0.4$ for the elasticity of U.S. output with respect to the external effects of human capital on production. Does this seem a plausible number?

[17] That is, the English side.

Or, putting the question in a better way: Is $\gamma = 0.4$ consistent with other evidence? But *what* other evidence? I do not know the answer to this question, but it is so central that I want to spend some time thinking about where the answer may be found. In doing so, I will be following very closely the lead of Jane Jacobs, whose remarkable book *The Economy of Cities* (1969) seems to me mainly and convincingly concerned (though she does not use this terminology) with the external effects of human capital.

I have been concerned with modeling the economic growth of *nations*, considered either singly or as linked through trade. In part, this was a response to the form of the observations I cited at the beginning: Most of our data come in the form of national time series, so 'fitting the facts' is taken to mean fitting national summary facts. For considering effects of changes in policies the nation is again the natural unit, for the most important fiscal and commercial policies are national and affect national economies in a uniform way. But from the viewpoint of a *technology* – like (11) – through which the average skill level of a group of people is assumed to affect the productivity of each individual within the group, a *national* economy is a completely arbitrary unit to consider. Surely if Puerto Rico were to become the fifty-first state this would not, by itself, alter the productivity of the people now located in Puerto Rico, even though it would sharply increase the average level of human capital of those politically defined as their fellow citizens. The external effects that the term h_a^γ in (11) is intended to capture have to do with the influences people have on the productivity of others, so the *scope* of such effects must have to do with the ways various groups of people interact, which may be affected by political boundaries but are certainly an entirely different matter conceptually.

Once this question of the scope of external effects is raised, it is clear that it cannot have a single correct answer. Many such effects can be internalized within small groups of people – firms or families. By dealing with an infinitely-lived family as a typical agent, I have assumed that such effects are dealt with at the non-market level and so create no gap between private and social returns. At the other extreme, basic discoveries that immediately become common property – the development of a new mathematical result say – are human capital in the sense that they arise from resources allocated to such discoveries that could instead have been used to produce current consumption, but to most countries as well as to most individual agents they appear 'exogenous' and would be better modelled as $A(t)$ in section 2 than as $h_a(t)$ in section 4.

If it were easy to classify most external productivity effects as either global in scope or as so localized as to be internalizable at the level of the family or the firm, then I think a model that incorporated internal human capital effects only plus other effects treated as exogenous technical change would be adequate. Such a model would fit time series from advanced countries about as well as any I have advanced, being an intermediate model to those I discussed in sections 2 and 4, which were in turn not distinguishable on such data alone.

Such a model would, I think, have difficulty reconciling observed pressures for immigration with the absence of equivalent capital flows, but perhaps this anomaly could be accounted for in some other way.

But we *know* from ordinary experience that there are group interactions that are central to individual productivity and that involve groups larger than the immediate family and smaller than the human race as a whole. Most of what we know we learn from other people. We pay tuition to a few of these teachers, either directly or indirectly by accepting lower pay so we can hand around them, but most of it we get for free, and often in ways that are mutual – without a distinction between student and teacher. Certainly in our own profession, the benefits of colleagues from whom we hope to learn are tangible enough to lead us to spend a considerable fraction of our time fighting over who they shall be, and another fraction travelling to talk with those we wish we could have as colleagues but cannot. We know this kind of external effect is common to all the arts and sciences – the 'creative professions'. All of intellectual history is the history of such effects.

But, as Jacobs has rightly emphasized and illustrated with hundreds of concrete examples, much of economic life is 'creative' in much the same way as is 'art' and 'science'. New York City's garment district, financial district, diamond district, advertising district and many more are as much intellectual centers as is Columbia or New York University. The specific ideas exchanged in these centers differ, of course, from those exchanged in academic circles, but the process is much the same. To an outsider, it even *looks* the same: A collection of people doing pretty much the same thing, each emphasizing his own originality and uniqueness.

Considerations such as these may convince one of the existence of external human capital, and even that it is an important element in the growth of knowledge. But they do not easily lend themselves to quantification. Here again I find Jacobs's work highly suggestive. Her emphasis on the role of cities in economic growth stems from the observation that a city, economically, is like the nucleus of an atom: If we postulate only the usual list of economic forces, cities should fly apart. The theory of production contains nothing to hold a city together. A city is simply a collection of factors of production – capital, people and land – and land is always far cheaper outside cities than inside. Why don't capital and people move outside, combining themselves with cheaper land and thereby increasing profits? Of course, people like to live near shopping and shops need to be located near their customers, but circular considerations of this kind explain only shopping centers, not cities. Cities are centered on wholesale trade and primary producers, and a theory that accounts for their existence has to explain why these producers are apparently choosing high rather than low cost modes of operation.

It seems to me that the 'force' we need to postulate account for the central role of cities in economic life is of exactly the same character as the 'external human capital' I have postulated as a force to account for certain features of aggregative development. If so, then land rents should provide an indirect measure of this force, in much the same way that schooling-induced earnings differentials provide a measure of the productive effects of internal human capital. It would require a much more detailed theory of the external effects of human capital than anything I have provided to make use of the information in urban land rents (just as one needs a more detailed theory of human capital than that in section 4 to utilize the information in earnings data), but the general logic is the same in the two cases. What can people be paying Manhattan or downtown Chicago rents *for*, if not for being near other people?

7. Conclusions

My aim, as I said at the beginning of these lectures, has been to try to find what I called 'mechanics' suitable for the study of economic development: that is, a system of differential equations the solution to which imitates some of the main features of the economic behavior we observe in the world economy. This enterprise has been taken about as far as I am able to take it, at present, so I will stop and try to sum up what the main features of these mechanics are and the sense in which they conform to what we observe.

The model that I think is central was developed in section 4. It is a system with a given rate of population growth but which is acted on by no other outside or exogenous forces. There are two kinds of capital, or state variables, in the system: physical capital that is accumulated and utilized in production under a familiar neoclassical technology, and human capital that enhances the productivity or both labor and physical capital, and that is accumulated according to a 'law' having the crucial property that a constant level of effort produces a constant growth rate of the stock, independent of the level already attained.

The dynamics of this system, viewed as a single, closed economy, are as follows. Asymptotically, the marginal product of physical capital tends to a constant, given essentially by the rate of time preference. This fact, which with one kind of capital defines the long-run stock of that capital, in the two-capital model of section 4 defines a curve in the 'physical capital–human capital plane'. The system will converge to this curve from any initial configuration of capital stocks, but the particular point to which it converges will depend on initial conditions. Economies that are initially poor will remain poor, relatively, though their long-run rate of income growth will be the same as that of initially (and permanently) wealthier economies. A world consisting of such economies, then, each operating autarchically, would exhibit uniform rates of growth across countries and would maintain a perfectly stable distribution of income and wealth over time.

If trade in capital goods is introduced into this model world economy, with labor assumed immobile, there will be no tendency to trade, which is to say no systematic tendency for borrowing and lending relationships to emerge between rich and poor countries. Put another way, the long-run relationship between the two kinds of capital that holds in each country implies the same marginal productivity of physical capital, no matter what the level of capital that has been accumulated. The picture I have given for a world of closed economies thus carries over without change to a world with free trade in capital goods.

If labor mobility is introduced, everything hinges on whether the effects of human capital are internal – affecting the productivity of its 'owner' only – or whether they have external benefits that spill over from one person to another. In the latter case, and only in the latter case, the wage rate of labor at any given skill level will increase with the wealth of the country in which he is employed. Then if labor can move, it will move, flowing in general from poor countries to wealthy ones.

The model I have described fits the evidence of the last century for the U.S. economy as well as the now standard neoclassical model of Solow and Denison, which is to say, remarkably well. This is of course no accident, for the mechanics I have been developing have been modeled as closely as possible on theirs. It also fits, about as well, what seem to me the main features of the world economy: very wide diversity in income levels across countries, sustained growth in per-capita incomes at all income levels (though not, of course, in each country at each income level), and the absence of any marked tendency for growth rates to differ systematically at different levels of income. The model is also consistent with the enormous pressures for immigration that we observe in the world, even with its extreme assumptions that assign no importance to differences in endowments of natural resources and that permit perfectly free trade in capital and consumption goods. As long as people at each skill level are more productive in high human capital environments, such pressures are predicted to exist and nothing but the movement of people can relieve them.

Though the model of section 4 seems capable of accounting for *average* rates of growth, it contains no forces to account for diversity over countries or over time within a country (except for arbitrary shifts in tastes or technology). Section 5 develops a two-commodity elaboration of this model that offers more possibilities. In this set-up, human capital accumulation is taken to be specific to the production of particular goods, and is acquired on-the-job or through learning-by-doing. If different goods are taken to have different potentials for human capital growth, then the same considerations of comparative advantage that determine which goods get produced where will also dictate each country's rate of human capital growth. The model thus admits the possibility of wide and sustained differences in growth rates across countries, differences that one would not expect to be systematically linked to each country's initial capital *levels*.

With a fixed set of goods, which was the only case I considered, this account of cross-country differences does not leave room for within-country changes in growth rates. The comparative advantages that dictate a country's initial production mix will simply be intensified over time by human capital accumulation. But I conjecture that a more satisfactory treatment of product-specific learning would involve modeling the continuous introduction of new goods, with learning potentials on any particular good declining with the amount produced. There is no doubt that we observe this kind of effect occuring in reality on particular product lines. If it could be captured in a tractable aggregative model, this would introduce a factor continuously shaking up an existing pattern of comparative advantages, and offer some interesting possibilities for shifts over time in a country's growth rate, within the same general equilibrium framework used in section 5.

If such an analysis of trade-related shifts in growth rates should turn out to possible, this would be interesting, because the dramatic recent development success stories, the 'growth miracles' of Korea, Taiwan, Hong Kong and Singapore (not to mention the ongoing miracle of Japan) have all been associated with increases in exports, and more suggestively still, with exports of goods not formerly produced in these countries. There is surely no strain in thinking that a model stressing the effects of learning-by-doing is likely to shed light on these events.

A successful theory of economic development clearly needs, in the first place, mechanics that are consistent with sustained growth and with sustained diversity in income levels. This was the objective of section 4. But there is no one pattern of growth to which all economies conform, so a useful theory needs also to capture some forces for change in these patterns, and a mechanics that permits these forces to operate. This is a harder task, certainly not carried out in the analysis I have worked through, but I think the analysis of section 5 is a promising beginning.

Acknowledgements

The fact that a fairly well known economist is willing to speak so broadly on a topic of such enormous importance, about which he obviously knows very little, has proved a great stimulus to discussion whenever these lectures have been given. I have received many more interesting reactions than I will ever be able to follow up on, or even to acknowledge. But I would like to thank Nancy Stokey for her criticism of preliminary drafts, Arnold Harberger, Jane Jacobs, Akiva Offenbacher, Theodore Schultz and Robert Solow for their comments, Richard Manning for his very able assistance, and Edward Prescott and Sherwin Rosen for stimulating discussions of all aspects of economic development over many years before and after these lectures were first given.

Finally, I would like to thank Robert King and Charles Plosser for encouraging the publication of this awkwardly-sized (too long for an article, too short for a book) paper. In response to their suggestions, I have retained the lecture style in this version, making for the most part only minimal changes. (Section 5 is the only exception: I found a much better framework than the one used in the original, and so have replaced much of the original text.) Their hope, and mine, is that without being definitive on any aspect of the problem we may be productively provocative on many.

References

Arrow, Kenneth J., 1962, The economic implications of learning by doing, Review of Economic Studies 29, 155–173.

Baumol, William J., 1986, Productivity growth, convergence, and welfare: What the long-run data show, American Economic Review 76, 1072–1085.

Becker, Gary S., 1964, Human capital (Columbia University Press for the National Bureau of Economic Research, New York).

Becker, Gary S., 1981, A treatise on the family (Harvard University Press, Cambridge, MA).

Becker, Gary S. and Robert J. Barro, 1985, A reformulation of the economic theory of fertility, Unpublished working paper (University of Chicago, Chicago, IL).

Boxall, Peter J., 1986, Labor and population in a growth model, Unpublished doctoral dissertation (University of Chicago, Chicago, IL).

Burmeister, Edwin and A. Rodney Dobell, 1970, Mathematical theories of economic growth (Macmillan, New York).

DeLong, Bradford, 1987, Have productivity levels converged?, Unpublished working paper (MIT, Cambridge, MA).

Denison, Edward F., 1961, The sources of economic growth in the United States (Committee for Economic Development, New York).

Gordon, Robert J., 1971, Measurement bias in price indexes for capital goods, Review of Income and Wealth, Income and wealth series 17.

Griliches, Zvi and Dale W. Jorgenson, 1967, The explanation of productivity change, Review of Economic Studies 34, 249–282.

Harberger, Arnold C., ed., 1984, World economic growth (ICS Press, San Francisco, CA).

Jacobs, Jane, 1969, The economy of cities (Random House, New York).

Jacobs, Jane, 1984, Cities and the wealth of nations (Random House, New York).

Krueger, Anne O., 1983, The developing countries' role in the world economy, Lecture given at the University of Chicago, Chicago, IL.

Krugman, Paul, 1985, The narrow moving band, the Dutch disease and the competitive consequences of Mrs. Thatcher: Notes on trade in the presence of dynamic scale economies, Unpublished working paper (MIT, Cambridge, MA).

Kuznets, Simon, 1959, Six lectures on economic growth (The Free Press, Glencoe).

Maddison, Angus, 1982, Phases of capitalist development (Oxford University Press, New York).

Romer, Paul M., 1986, Increasing returns and long-run growth, Journal of Political Economy 94, 1002–1037.

Rosen, Sherwin, 1976, A theory of life earnings, Journal of Political Economy 84, 545–567.

Schultz, Theodore W., 1963, The economic value of education (Columbia University Press, New York).

Stokey, Nancy L., 1987, Learning-by-doing and the introduction of new goods, Unpublished working paper (Northwestern University, Evanston, IL).

Summers, Robert and Alan Heston, 1984, Improved international comparisons of real product and its composition: 1950–1980, Review of Income and Wealth, Income and wealth series 30.

Tamura, Robert, 1986, On the existence of multiple steady states in one sector growth models with intergenerational altruism, Unpublished working paper (University of Chicago, Chicago, IL).

Uzawa, Hirofumi, 1965, Optimum technical change in an aggregative model of economic growth, International Economic Review 6, 18–31.

[5]

Increasing Returns and Long-Run Growth

Paul M. Romer

University of Rochester

This paper presents a fully specified model of long-run growth in which knowledge is assumed to be an input in production that has increasing marginal productivity. It is essentially a competitive equilibrium model with endogenous technological change. In contrast to models based on diminishing returns, growth rates can be increasing over time, the effects of small disturbances can be amplified by the actions of private agents, and large countries may always grow faster than small countries. Long-run evidence is offered in support of the empirical relevance of these possibilities.

I. Introduction

Because of its simplicity, the aggregate growth model analyzed by Ramsey (1928), Cass (1965), and Koopmans (1965) continues to form the basis for much of the intuition economists have about long-run growth. The rate of return on investment and the rate of growth of per capita output are expected to be decreasing functions of the level of the per capita capital stock. Over time, wage rates and capital-labor ratios across different countries are expected to converge. Consequently, initial conditions or current disturbances have no long-run effect on the level of output and consumption. For example, an exog-

This paper is based on work from my dissertation (Romer 1983). An earlier version of this paper circulated under the title "Externalities and Increasing Returns in Dynamic Competitive Analysis." At various stages I have benefited from comments by James J. Heckman, Charles M. Kahn, Robert G. King, Robert E. Lucas, Jr., Sergio Rebelo, Sherwin Rosen, José A. Scheinkman (the chairman of my thesis committee), and the referees. The usual disclaimer applies. I gratefully acknowledge the support of NSF grant no. SES-8320007 during the completion of this work.

[*Journal of Political Economy*, 1986, vol. 94, no. 5]

enous reduction in the stock of capital in a given country will cause prices for capital assets to increase and will therefore induce an offsetting increase in investment. In the absence of technological change, per capita output should converge to a steady-state value with no per capita growth. All these presumptions follow directly from the assumption of diminishing returns to per capita capital in the production of per capita output.

The model proposed here offers an alternative view of long-run prospects for growth. In a fully specified competitive equilibrium, per capita output can grow without bound, possibly at a rate that is monotonically increasing over time. The rate of investment and the rate of return on capital may increase rather than decrease with increases in the capital stock. The level of per capita output in different countries need not converge; growth may be persistently slower in less developed countries and may even fail to take place at all. These results do not depend on any kind of exogenously specified technical change or differences between countries. Preferences and the technology are stationary and identical. Even the size of the population can be held constant. What is crucial for all of these results is a departure from the usual assumption of diminishing returns.

While exogenous technological change is ruled out, the model here can be viewed as an equilibrium model of endogenous technological change in which long-run growth is driven primarily by the accumulation of knowledge by forward-looking, profit-maximizing agents. This focus on knowledge as the basic form of capital suggests natural changes in the formulation of the standard aggregate growth model. In contrast to physical capital that can be produced one for one from forgone output, new knowledge is assumed to be the product of a research technology that exhibits diminishing returns. That is, given the stock of knowledge at a point in time, doubling the inputs into research will not double the amount of new knowledge produced. In addition, investment in knowledge suggests a natural externality. The creation of new knowledge by one firm is assumed to have a positive external effect on the production possibilities of other firms because knowledge cannot be perfectly patented or kept secret. Most important, production of consumption goods as a function of the stock of knowledge and other inputs exhibits increasing returns; more precisely, knowledge may have an increasing marginal product. In contrast to models in which capital exhibits diminishing marginal productivity, knowledge will grow without bound. Even if all other inputs are held constant, it will not be optimal to stop at some steady state where knowledge is constant and no new research is undertaken.

These three elements—externalities, increasing returns in the production of output, and decreasing returns in the production of new knowledge—combine to produce a well-specified competitive equilibrium model of growth. Despite the presence of increasing returns, a competitive equilibrium with externalities will exist. This equilibrium is not Pareto optimal, but it is the outcome of a well-behaved positive model and is capable of explaining historical growth in the absence of government intervention. The presence of the externalities is essential for the existence of an equilibrium. Diminishing returns in the production of knowledge are required to ensure that consumption and utility do not grow too fast. But the key feature in the reversal of the standard results about growth is the assumption of increasing rather than decreasing marginal productivity of the intangible capital good knowledge.

The paper is organized as follows. Section II traces briefly the history of the idea that increasing returns are important to the explanation of long-run growth and describes some of the conceptual difficulties that impeded progress toward a formal model that relied on increasing returns. Section III presents empirical evidence in support of the model proposed here. Section IV presents a stripped-down, two-period version of the model that illustrates the tools that are used to analyze an equilibrium with externalities and increasing returns. Section V presents the analysis of the infinite-horizon, continuous-time version of the model, characterizing the social optimum and the competitive equilibrium, both with and without optimal taxes.

The primary motivation for the choice of continuous time and the restriction to a single state variable is the ease with which qualitative results can be derived using the geometry of the phase plane. In particular, once functional forms for production and preferences have been specified, useful qualitative information about the dynamics of the social optimum or the suboptimal competitive equilibrium can be extracted using simple algebra. Section VI presents several examples that illustrate the extent to which conventional presumptions about growth rates, asset prices, and cross-country comparisons may be reversed in this kind of economy.

II. Historical Origins and Relation to Earlier Work

The idea that increasing returns are central to the explanation of long-run growth is at least as old as Adam Smith's story of the pin factory. With the introduction by Alfred Marshall of the distinction between internal and external economies, it appeared that this explanation could be given a consistent, competitive equilibrium interpretation. The most prominent such attempt was made by Allyn Young in his 1928 presidential address to the Economics and Statistics section of the British Association for the Advancement of Science

(Young 1969). Subsequent economists (e.g., Hicks 1960; Kaldor 1981) have credited Young with a fundamental insight about growth, but because of the verbal nature of his argument and the difficulty of formulating explicit dynamic models, no formal model embodying that insight was developed.

Because of the technical difficulties presented by dynamic models, Marshall's concept of increasing returns that are external to a firm but internal to an industry was most widely used in static models, especially in the field of international trade. In the 1920s the logical consistency and relevance of these models began to be seriously challenged, in particular by Frank Knight, who had been a student of Young's at Cornell.[1] Subsequent work demonstrated that it is possible to construct consistent, general equilibrium models with perfect competition, increasing returns, and externalities (see, e.g., Chipman 1970). Yet Knight was at least partially correct in objecting that the concept of increasing returns that are external to the firm was vacuous, an "empty economic box" (Knight 1925). Following Smith, Marshall, and Young, most authors justified the existence of increasing returns on the basis of increasing specialization and the division of labor. It is now clear that these changes in the organization of production cannot be rigorously treated as technological externalities. Formally, increased specialization opens new markets and introduces new goods. All producers in the industry may benefit from the introduction of these goods, but they are goods, not technological externalities.[2]

Despite the objections raised by Knight, static models of increasing returns with externalities have been widely used in international trade. Typically, firm output is simply assumed to be increasing, or unit cost decreasing, in aggregate industry output. See Helpman (1984) for a recent survey. Renewed interest in dynamic models of growth driven by increasing returns was sparked in the 1960s following the publication of Arrow's (1962) paper on learning by doing. In his model, the productivity of a given firm is assumed to be an increasing function of cumulative aggregate investment for the industry. Avoiding the issues of specialization and the division of labor, Arrow argued that increasing returns arise because new knowledge is discovered as investment and production take place. The increasing returns were external to individual firms because such knowledge became publicly known.

To formalize his model, Arrow had to face two problems that arise

[1] For an account of the development of Young's ideas and of his correspondence with Knight, see Blitch (1983).

[2] For a treatment of increasing returns based on specialization, see Ethier (1982). Although the model there is essentially static, it demonstrates how specialization can be introduced in a differentiated products framework under imperfect competition.

in any optimizing model of growth in the presence of increasing returns. The first, familiar from static models, concerns the existence of a competitive equilibrium; as is now clear, if the increasing returns are external to the firm, an equilibrium can exist. The second problem, unique to dynamic optimizing models, concerns the existence of a social optimum and the finiteness of objective functions. In a standard optimizing growth model that maximizes a discounted sum or integral over an infinite horizon, the presence of increasing returns raises the possibility that feasible consumption paths may grow so fast that the objective function is not finite. An optimum can fail to exist even in the sense of an overtaking criterion. In the model of Arrow and its elaborations by Levhari (1966*a*, 1966*b*) and Sheshinski (1967), this difficulty is avoided by assuming that output as a function of capital and labor exhibits increasing returns to scale but that the marginal product of capital is diminishing given a fixed supply of labor. As a result, the rate of growth of output is limited by the rate of growth of the labor force. Interpreted as an aggregate model of growth (rather than as a model of a specific industry), this model leads to the empirically questionable implication that the rate of growth of per capita output is a monotonically increasing function of the rate of growth of the population. Like conventional models with diminishing returns, it predicts that the rate of growth in per capita consumption must go to zero in an economy with zero population growth.

The model proposed here departs from both the Ramsey-Cass-Koopmans model and the Arrow model by assuming that knowledge is a capital good with an increasing marginal product. Production of the consumption good is assumed to be globally convex, not concave, as a function of stock of knowledge when all other inputs are held constant. A finite-valued social optimum is guaranteed to exist because of diminishing returns in the research technology, which imply the existence of a maximum, technologically feasible rate of growth for knowledge. This is turn implies the existence of a maximum feasible rate of growth for per capita output. Over time, the rate of growth of output may be monotonically increasing, but it cannot exceed this upper bound.

Uzawa (1965) describes an optimizing growth model in which both intangible human capital and physical capital can be produced. In some respects, the human capital resembles knowledge as described in this paper, but Uzawa's model does not possess any form of increasing returns to scale. Instead, it considers a borderline case of constant returns to scale with linear production of human capital. In this case, unbounded growth is possible. Asymptotically, output and both types of capital grow at the same constant rate. Other optimizing models took the rate of technological change as exogenously given (e.g., Shell

1967*b*). Various descriptive models of growth with elements similar to those used here were also proposed during the 1960s (e.g., Phelps 1966; von Wiezsäcker 1966; Shell 1967*a*). Knowledge is accumulated by devoting resources to research. Production of consumption goods exhibits constant returns as a function of tangible inputs (e.g., physical capital and labor) and therefore exhibits increasing returns as a function of tangible and intangible inputs. Privately produced knowledge is in some cases assumed to be partially revealed to other agents in the economy. Because the descriptive models do not use explicit objective functions, questions of existence are generally avoided, and a full welfare analysis is not possible. Moreover, these models tend to be relatively restrictive, usually constructed so that the analysis could be carried out in terms of steady states and constant growth rate paths.

Continuous-time optimization problems with some form of increasing returns are studied in papers by Weitzman (1970), Dixit, Mirrlees, and Stern (1975), and Skiba (1978). Similar issues are considered for discrete-time models in Majumdar and Mitra (1982, 1983) and Dechert and Nishimura (1983). These papers differ from the model here primarily because they are not concerned with the existence of a competitive equilibrium. Moreover, in all these papers, the technical approach used to prove the existence of an optimum is different from that used here. They rely on either bounded instantaneous utility $U(c)$ or bounds on the degree of increasing returns in the problem; for example, the production function $f(k)$ is assumed to be such that $f(k)/k$ is bounded from above. The results here do not rely on either of these kinds of restrictions; in fact, one of the most interesting examples analyzed in Section VI violates both of these restrictions. Instead, the approach used here relies on the assumptions made concerning the research technology; the diminishing returns in research will limit the rate of growth of the state variable. A general proof that restrictions on the rate of growth of the state variable are sufficient to prove the existence of an optimum for a continuous-time maximization problem with nonconvexities is given in Romer (1986).

Because an equilibrium for the model proposed here is a competitive equilibrium with externalities, the analysis is formally similar to that used in dynamic models with more conventional kinds of externalities (e.g., Brock 1977; Hochman and Hochman 1980). It also has a close formal similarity to perfect-foresight Sidrauski models of money demand and inflation (Brock 1975) and to symmetric Nash equilibria for dynamic games (e.g., Hansen, Epple, and Roberds 1985). In each case, an equilibrium is calculated not by solving a social planning problem but rather by considering the maximization problem of an individual agent who takes as given the path of some endogenously determined aggregate variable. In the conventional analysis of externalities, the focus is generally on the social optimum and the set of taxes necessary to support it as a competitive equilibrium. While this question is addressed for this growth model, the discussion places more stress on the characterization of the competitive equilibrium without intervention since it is the most reasonable positive model of observed historical growth. One of the main contributions of this paper is to demonstrate how the analysis of this kind of suboptimal equilibrium can proceed using familiar tools like a phase plane even though the equations describing the equilibrium cannot be derived from any stationary maximization problem.

III. Motivation and Evidence

Because theories of long-run growth assume away any variation in output attributable to business cycles, it is difficult to judge the empirical success of these theories. Even if one could resolve the theoretical ambiguity about how to filter the cycles out of the data and to extract the component that growth theory seeks to explain, the longest available time series do not have enough observations to allow precise estimates of low-frequency components or long-run trends. When data aggregated into decades rather than years are used, the pattern of growth in the United States is quite variable and is apparently still influenced by cyclical movements in output (see fig. 1). Cross-country comparisons of growth rates are complicated by the difficulty of controlling for political and social variables that appear to strongly influence the growth process. With these qualifications in mind, it is useful to ask whether there is anything in the data that should cause economists to choose a model with diminishing returns, falling rates of growth, and convergence across countries rather than an alternative without these features.

Consider first the long-run trend in the growth rate of productivity or per capita gross domestic product (GDP). One revealing way to consider the long-run evidence is to distinguish at any point in time between the country that is the "leader," that is, that has the highest level of productivity, and all other countries. Growth for a country that is not a leader will reflect at least in part the process of imitation and transmission of existing knowledge, whereas the growth rate of the leader gives some indication of growth at the frontier of knowledge. Using GDP per man-hour as his measure of productivity, Maddison (1982) identifies three countries that have been leaders since 1700, the Netherlands, the United Kingdom, and the United States. Table 1 reports his estimates of the rate of growth of productivity in each country during the interval when it was the leader. When the

TABLE 1

PRODUCTIVITY GROWTH RATES FOR LEADING COUNTRIES

Lead Country	Interval	Annual Average Compound Growth Rate of GDP per Man-Hour (%)
Netherlands	1700–1785	−.07
United Kingdom	1785–1820	.5
United Kingdom	1820–90	1.4
United States	1890–1979	2.3

SOURCE.—Maddison (1982).

productivity growth rate is measured over intervals several decades long and compared over almost 3 centuries, the evidence clearly suggests that it has been increasing, not decreasing. The rate of growth of productivity increases monotonically from essentially zero growth in eighteenth-century Netherlands to 2.3 percent per year since 1890 in the United States.

Similar evidence is apparent from data for individual countries over shorter horizons. Table 2 reports growth rates in per capita GDP for the United States over five subperiods from 1800 to 1978. (The raw data used here are from Maddison [1979].) These rates also suggest a positive rather than a negative trend, but measuring growth rates over 40-year intervals hides a substantial amount of year-to-year or even decade-to-decade variation in the rate of growth. Figure 1 presents the average growth rate over the interval 1800–1839 (for which no intervening data are available) and for the subsequent 14 decades. Identifying a long-run trend in rates measured over decades is more problematical in this case, but it is straightforward to apply a simple nonparametric test for trend.

Table 3 reports the results of this kind of test for trend in the per capita rate of growth in GDP for several countries using raw data

TABLE 2

PER CAPITA GROWTH IN THE UNITED STATES

Interval	Average Annual Compound Growth Rate of Real per Capita GDP (%)
1800–1840	.58
1840–80	1.44
1880–1920	1.78
1920–60	1.68
1960–78	2.47

SOURCE.—Raw data are from Maddison (1979).

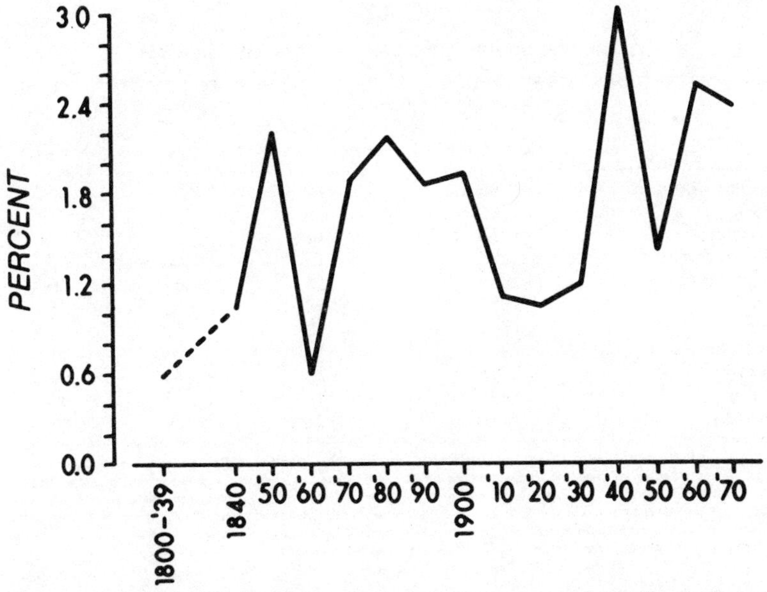

FIG. 1.—Average annual compound growth rate of per capita GDP in the United States for the interval 1800–1839 and for 14 subsequent decades. Data are taken from Maddison (1979).

from Maddison (1979). The sample includes all countries for which continuous observations on per capita GDP are available starting no later than 1870. As for the data for the United States graphed in figure 1, the growth rates used in the test for trend are measured over decades where possible. The statistic π gives the sample estimate of the probability that, for any two randomly chosen decades, the later decade has a higher growth rate.

Despite the variability evident from figure 1, the test for trend for the United States permits the rejection of the null hypothesis of a nonpositive trend at conventional significance levels. This is true even though growth over the 4 decades from 1800 to 1839 is treated as a single observation. However, rejection of the null hypothesis depends critically on the use of a sufficiently long data series. If we drop the observation on growth between 1800 and 1839, the estimate of π drops from .68 to .63 and the p-value increases from .03 to .11.[3] If we further restrict attention to the 11 decades from 1870 to 1978, π drops to .56 and the p-value increases to .29, so it is not surprising that studies that focus on the period since 1870 tend to emphasize the

[3] The p-value gives the probability of observing a value of π at least as large as the reported value under the null hypothesis that the true probability is .5.

TABLE 3

A TEST FOR TREND IN PER CAPITA GDP GROWTH RATES

	Date of First Observation	Number of Observations	π	p-Value
United Kingdom	1700	20	.63	.06
France	1700	18	.69	.01
Denmark	1818	16	.70	.02
United States	1800	15	.68	.03
Germany	1850	13	.67	.06
Sweden	1861	12	.58	.25
Italy	1861	12	.76	.01
Australia	1861	12	.64	.11
Norway	1865	12	.81	.002
Japan	1870	11	.67	.07
Canada	1870	11	.64	.12

NOTE.—π is the sample estimate for each country of the probability that, for any two growth rates, the later one is larger. The p-value is the probability of observing a value of π at least as large as the observed value under the null hypothesis that the true probability is .5. Except in the early years when data are sparse, per capita rates of growth of GDP were measured over successive decades. (Only two observations on growth rates are available for France prior to 1820; for the United Kingdom, only two prior to 1800; for the United States, only one from 1800 to 1840.) For the calculation of the p-value, see Kendall (1962). Data are from Maddison (1979).

constancy of growth rates in the United States. Rejection does not appear to depend on the use of the rate of growth in per capita GDP rather than the rate of growth of productivity. Reliable measures of the work force prior to 1840 are not available, but using data from Kuznets (1971) for the period 1840–1960 and from the 1984 Economic Report of the President for 1960–80, one can construct a similar test for trend in the rate of growth of productivity over successive decades. The results of this test, π equal to .64 with a p-value of .10, correspond closely to those noted above for growth in per capita GDP over the similar interval, 1840–1978.

Over the entire sample of 11 countries, the estimated value for π ranges from .58 to .81, with a p-value that ranges from .25 to .002. Five out of 11 of the p-values are less than .05, permitting rejection at the 5 percent level in a one-sided test of the null hypothesis that there is a nonpositive trend in the growth rate; eight out of 11 permit rejection at the 10 percent level.

For less developed countries, no comparable long-run statistics on per capita income are available. Reynolds (1983) gives an overview of the pattern of development in such countries. Given the paucity of precise data for less developed countries, he focuses on the "turning point" at which a country first begins to exhibit a persistent upward trend in per capita income. The timing of this transition and the pace of subsequent growth are strongly influenced by the variations in the world economy. A general pattern of historically unprecedented growth for the world economy is evident starting in the last part of the 1800s and continuing to the present. This general pattern is interrupted by a significant slowdown during the years between the two world wars and by a remarkable surge from roughly 1950 to 1973. Worldwide growth since 1973 has been slow only by comparison with that surge and appears to have returned to the high rates that prevailed in the period from the late 1800s to 1914.

Although all less developed countries are affected by the worldwide economy, the effects are not uniform. For our purposes, the key observation is that those countries with more extensive prior development appear to benefit more from periods of rapid worldwide growth and suffer less during any slowdown. That is, growth rates appear to be increasing not only as a function of calendar time but also as a function of the level of development. The observation that more developed countries appear to grow relatively faster extends to a comparison of industrialized versus less developed countries as well. In the period from 1950 to 1980, when official estimates for GDP are generally available, Reynolds reports that the median rate of growth of per capita income for his sample of 41 less developed countries was 2.3 percent, "clearly below the median for the OECD countries for the same period" (p. 975).

If it is true that growth rates are not negatively correlated with the level of per capita output or capital, then there should be no tendency for the dispersion in the (logarithm of the)[4] level of per capita income to decrease over time. There should be no tendency toward convergence. This contradicts a widespread impression that convergence in this sense has been evident, especially since the Second World War. Streissler (1979) offers evidence about the source of this impression and its robustness. For each year from 1950 to 1974, he measures the variance across countries of the logarithm of the level of per capita income. In a sample of ex post industrialized countries, those countries with a level of per capita income of at least $2,700 in 1974, clear evidence of a decrease in the dispersion over time is apparent. In a sample of ex ante industrialized countries, countries with a per capita income of at least $350 in 1950, no evidence of a decrease in the variance is apparent. The first sample differs from the second because it includes Japan and excludes Argentina, Chile, Ireland, Puerto Rico, and Venezuela. As one would expect, truncating the sample at the end biases the trend toward decreasing dispersion (and

[4] Examining the dispersion in the logarithm of the level of per capita income, not dispersion in the level itself, is the correct way to test for convergence in the growth rates. If the rate of growth were constant across countries that start from different levels, the dispersion in the logarithm of the levels will stay constant, but dispersion in the levels will increase.

at the beginning toward increasing dispersion). When a sample of all possible countries is used, there is no evidence of a decrease in variance, but the interpretation of this result is complicated by the changing number of countries in the sample in each year due to data limitations.

Baumol (1985) reports similar results. When countries are grouped into industrialized, intermediate, centrally planned, and less developed economies, he argues that there is a tendency toward convergence in the level of productivity within groups, even though there is no tendency toward overall convergence. The tendency toward convergence is clear only in his group of industrialized economies, which corresponds closely to the sample of ex post industrialized countries considered by Streissler. In any case, he finds no obvious pattern in his entire sample of countries; if anything, there is a weak tendency toward divergence.[5]

The other kind of evidence that bears directly on the assumption of increasing returns in production comes from growth accounting exercises and the estimation of aggregate production functions. Economists believe that virtually all technical change is endogenous, the outcome of deliberate actions taken by economic agents. If so and if production exhibits constant returns to scale, one would expect to be able to account for the rate of growth of output in terms of the rates of growth of all inputs. The difficulty in implementing a direct test of this assertion lies in correctly measuring all the inputs to production, especially for intangible capital inputs such as knowledge. In a comprehensive attempt to account for the rates of growth in output in terms of rates of growth of all inputs, including human and nonhuman, tangible and intangible stocks of capital, Kendrick (1976) concluded that rates of growth of inputs are not sufficient to explain the rate of growth of output in the 40-year interval 1929–69. For various sectors and levels of aggregation, the rate of growth of output is 1.06–1.30 times the appropriate aggregate measure of the rate of growth for inputs. This kind of estimate is subject to substantial, unquantified uncertainty and cannot be taken as decisive support for the presence of increasing returns. But given the repeated failure of this kind of growth accounting exercise, there is no basis in the data for excluding the possibility that aggregate production functions are best described as exhibiting increasing returns.

[5] Baumol (1985) argues that the convergence he observes among the industrialized countries results from a transmission process for knowledge that takes place among the industrialized countries but does not extend to centrally planned or less developed countries. He would not agree that the apparent convergence is an artifact of an ex post choice of the industrialized countries. Since he does not treat this issue directly, it is difficult to resolve it from his data. He does admit that his groupings are "somewhat arbitrary."

IV. A Simple Two-Period Model

Even in the presence of increasing returns and externalities, calculating a social optimum is conceptually straightforward since it is equivalent to solving a maximization problem. Standard mathematical results can be used to show that a maximum exists and to characterize the solution by means of a set of necessary conditions. Despite the presence of global increasing returns, the model here does have a social optimum. The next section illustrates how it can be supported as a competitive equilibrium using a natural set of taxes and subsidies. This optimum is of theoretical and normative interest, but it cannot be a serious candidate for describing the observed long-run behavior of per capita output. To the extent that appropriate taxes and subsidies have been used at all, they are a quite recent phenomenon.

The model here also has an equilibrium in the absence of any governmental intervention. Much of the emphasis in what follows focuses on how to characterize the qualitative features of this suboptimal dynamic equilibrium. Although it is suboptimal, the competitive equilibrium does satisfy a constrained optimality criterion that can be used to simplify the analysis much as the study of the social optimization problem simplifies the analysis in standard growth models.

The use of a constrained or restricted optimization problem is not a new approach to the analysis of a suboptimal dynamic equilibrium. For example, it has been widely used in the perfect-foresight models of inflation. Nonetheless, it is useful to describe this method in some detail because previous applications do not highlight the generality of the approach and because the dynamic setting tends to obscure its basic simplicity. Hence, I start by calculating a competitive equilibrium for a greatly simplified version of the growth model.

Specifically, consider a discrete-time model of growth with two periods. Let each of S identical consumers have a twice continuously differentiable, strictly concave utility function $U(c_1, c_2)$, defined over consumption of a single output good in periods 1 and 2. Let each consumer be given an initial endowment of the output good in period 1. Suppose that production of consumption goods in period 2 is a function of the state of knowledge, denoted by k, and a set of additional factors such as physical capital, labor, and so forth, denoted by a vector $\mathbf{x}$.[6] To restrict attention to a choice problem that is essentially

[6] For most of the subsequent discussion, k will be treated as a stock of disembodied knowledge, i.e., knowledge in books. This is merely an expositional convenience and is not essential. For example, if one wants to assume that all knowledge is embodied in some kind of tangible capital such as conventional physical capital or human capital, k can be reinterpreted throughout as a composite good made up of both knowledge and the tangible capital good.

one-dimensional, assume that only the stock of knowledge can be augmented; the factors represented by $\mathbf{x}$ are available in fixed supply. To capture the basic idea that there is a trade-off between consumption today and knowledge that can be used to produce more consumption tomorrow, assume that there is a research technology that produces knowledge from forgone consumption in period 1. Because the economy here has only two periods, we need not be concerned with the problem that arises in an infinite-horizon model when consumption grows too fast and discounted utility goes to infinity. Thus we do not need diminishing returns in research to limit the rate of growth of knowledge, and we can choose a simple linear technology with units such that one unit of forgone consumption produces one unit of knowledge. A more realistic diminishing returns research technology is described in the infinite-horizon model presented in the next section.

Since newly produced private knowledge can be only partially kept secret and cannot be patented, we can represent the technology of firm i in terms of a twice continuously differentiable production function F that depends on the firm-specific inputs k_i and $\mathbf{x}_i$ and on the aggregate level of knowledge in the economy. If N is the number of firms, define this aggregate level of knowledge as $K = \Sigma_{i=1}^{N} k_i$.

The first major assumption on the production function $F(k_i, K, \mathbf{x}_i)$ is that, for any fixed value of K, F is concave as a function of k_i and $\mathbf{x}_i$. Without this assumption, a competitive equilibrium will not exist in general. Once concavity is granted, there is little loss of generality in assuming that F is homogeneous of degree one as a function of k_i and $\mathbf{x}_i$ when K is held constant; any concave function can be extended to be homogeneous of degree one by adding an additional factor to the vector $\mathbf{x}$ if necessary (Rockafellar 1970, p. 67). McKenzie (1959) refers to this additional factor as an entrepreneurial factor. It can be interpreted as an accounting device that transforms any profits into factor payments.

By the homogeneity of F in k_i and $\mathbf{x}_i$ and by the assumption that F is increasing in the aggregate stock of knowledge, K, it follows that F exhibits increasing returns to scale. For any $\psi > 1$,

$$F(\psi k_i, \psi K, \psi \mathbf{x}_i) > F(\psi k_i, K, \psi \mathbf{x}_i) = \psi F(k_i, K, \mathbf{x}_i).$$

The second major assumption strengthens this considerably. It requires that F exhibit global increasing marginal productivity of knowledge from a social point of view. That is, for any fixed $\mathbf{x}$, assume that $F(k, Nk, \mathbf{x})$, production per firm available to a dictator who can set economywide values for k, is convex in k, not concave. This strengthening of the assumption of increasing returns is what distinguishes the production function used here from the one used in the models of Arrow, Levhari, and Sheshinski.

The equilibrium for the two-period model is a standard competitive equilibrium with externalities. Each firm maximizes profits taking K, the aggregate level of knowledge, as given. Consumers supply part of their endowment of output goods and all the other factors $\mathbf{x}$ to firms in period 1. With the proceeds, they purchase output goods in period 2. Consumers and firms maximize taking prices as given. As usual, the assumption that agents treat prices and the aggregate level K as given could be rationalized in a model with a continuum of agents. Here, it is treated as the usual approximation for a large but finite number of agents. Because of the externality, all firms could benefit from a collusive agreement to invest more in research. Although this agreement would be Pareto-improving in this model, it cannot be supported for the same reasons that collusive agreements fail in models without externalities. Each firm would have an incentive to shirk, not investing its share of output in research. Even if all existing firms could be compelled to comply, for example, by an economywide merger, new entrants would still be able to free-ride and undermine the equilibrium.

Because of the assumed homogeneity of F with respect to factors that receive compensation, profits for firms will be zero and the scale and number of firms will be indeterminate. Consequently, we can simplify the notation by restricting attention to an equilibrium in which the number of firms, N, equals the number of consumers, S. Then per firm and per capita values coincide. Assuming that all firms operate at the same level of output, we can omit firm-specific subscripts.

Let $\bar{\mathbf{x}}$ denote the per capita (and per firm) endowment of the factors that cannot be augmented; let $\bar{e}$ denote the per capita endowment of the output good in period 1. To calculate an equilibrium, define a family of restricted maximization problems indexed by K:

$$
\begin{aligned}
P(K):\quad & \max_{k\in[0,\,\bar{e}]} && U(c_1, c_2)\\
& \text{subject to} && c_1 \le \bar{e} - k,\\
& && c_2 \le F(k, K, \mathbf{x}),\\
& && \mathbf{x} \le \bar{\mathbf{x}}.
\end{aligned}
$$

Since U is strictly concave and $F(k, K, \mathbf{x})$ is concave in k and $\mathbf{x}$ for each value of K, $P(K)$ will have a unique solution k for each value of K. (The solution for $\mathbf{x}$ is trivially $\bar{\mathbf{x}}$.) In general, the implied values for c_1, c_2, and k have no economic meaning. If K differs from Sk, then $F(k, K, \bar{\mathbf{x}})$ is not a feasible level of per capita consumption in period 2. Equilibrium requires that the aggregate level of knowledge that is achieved in the economy be consistent with the level that is assumed when firms make production decisions. If we define a function $\Gamma: \mathbf{R} \to \mathbf{R}$ that sends K into S times the value of k that achieves the maximum for the problem $P(K)$, this suggests fixed points of Γ as candidates for equilibria.

To see that any fixed point K^* of Γ can indeed be supported as a competitive equilibrium, observe that $P(K^*)$ is a concave maximization problem with solution $k^* = K^*/S$, $c_1^* = \bar{e} - k^*$, and $c_2^* = F(k^*, Sk^*, \bar{\mathbf{x}})$. Since it is concave, standard necessary conditions for concave problems apply. Let $\mathcal{L}$ denote a Lagrangian for $P(K^*)$ with multipliers p_1, p_2, and w:

$$\mathcal{L} = U(c_1, c_2) + p_1(\bar{e} - k - c_1) + p_2[F(k, K, \mathbf{x}) - c_2] + w(\bar{\mathbf{x}} - \mathbf{x}).$$

When an interior solution is assumed, familiar arguments show that $p_j = D_jU(c_1^*, c_2^*)$ for $j = 1, 2$, that $p_1 = p_2D_1F(k^*, Sk^*, \bar{\mathbf{x}})$, and that $w = p_2D_3F(k^*, Sk^*, \bar{\mathbf{x}})$.[7] As always, the shadow prices w and p_j can be interpreted as equilibrium prices. To see this, consider first the maximization problem of the firm: $\max_k p_2F(k, Sk^*, \mathbf{x}) - p_1k - w \cdot \mathbf{x}$. Since the firm takes both prices and the aggregate level Sk^* as given, a trivial application of the sufficient conditions for a concave maximization problem demonstrates that k^* and $\bar{\mathbf{x}}$ are optimal choices for the firm. By the homogeneity of F with respect to its first and third arguments, profits will be zero at these values. Consider next the problem of the consumer. Income to the consumer will be the value of the endowment, $I = p_1\bar{e} + w \cdot \bar{\mathbf{x}} = p_2F(k^*, Sk^*, \bar{\mathbf{x}}) + p_1(\bar{e} - k^*)$. (The second equality follows from the homogeneity of F in k and $\mathbf{x}$.) When the necessary conditions $p_j = D_jU(c_1^*, c_2^*)$ from the problem $P(K^*)$ are used, it follows immediately that c_1^* and c_2^* are solutions to the problem max $U(c_1, c_2)$ subject to the budget constraint $p_1c_1 + p_2c_2 \leq I$. Note that the marginal rate of substitution for consumers will equal the private marginal rate of transformation perceived by firms, $D_1U(c_1^*, c_2^*)/D_2U(c_1^*, c_2^*) = D_1F(k^*, Sk^*, \bar{\mathbf{x}})$. Because of the externality, this differs from the true marginal rate of transformation for the economy, $D_1F(k^*, Sk^*, \bar{\mathbf{x}}) + SD_2F(k^*, Sk^*, \bar{\mathbf{x}})$.

Arguments along these lines can be used quite generally to show that a fixed point of a mapping like Γ defined by a family of concave problems $P(K)$ can be supported as a competitive equilibrium with externalities. The necessary conditions from a version of the Kuhn-Tucker theorem generate shadow prices associated with any solution to $P(K)$. The sufficient conditions for the problems of the consumer and the firm can then be used to show that the quantities from the

[7] Here, D denotes a derivative, D_i the partial derivative with respect to the ith argument.

solution will be chosen in an equilibrium in which these prices are taken as given. Conversely, an argument similar to the usual proof of the Pareto optimality of competitive equilibrium can be used to show that any competitive equilibrium with externalities for this kind of economy will satisfy the restricted optimality condition implicit in the problem $P(K)$ (Romer 1983). That is, if K^* is an equilibrium value of aggregate knowledge, then K^*/S will solve the problem $P(K^*)$. Thus equilibria are equivalent to fixed points of the function Γ.

This allows an important simplification because it is straightforward to characterize fixed points of Γ in terms of the underlying functions U and F. Substituting the constraints from $P(K)$ into the objective and using the fact that $\mathbf{x}$ will be chosen to be $\hat{\mathbf{x}}$, define a new function $V(k, K) = U(\bar{e} - k, F(k, K, \hat{\mathbf{x}}))$. Because of the increasing marginal productivity of knowledge, V is not a concave function; but for any fixed K, it is concave in k. Then the optimal choice of k in any problem $P(K)$ is determined by the equation $D_1V(k, K) = 0$. Fixed points of Γ are then given by substituting Sk for K and solving $D_1V(k, Sk) = 0$. Given functional forms for U and F, this equation can immediately be written in explicit form. The analysis can therefore exploit a three-way equivalence between competitive equilibria with externalities, fixed points of Γ, and solutions to an explicit equation $D_1V(k, Sk) = 0$.

The key observation in this analysis is that equilibrium quantities can be characterized as the solution to a concave maximization problem. Then prices can be generated from shadow prices or multipliers for this problem. The complete statement of the problem must be sought simultaneously with its solution because the statement involves the equilibrium quantities. But since $P(K)$ is a family of concave problems, solving simultaneously for the statement of the problem and for its solution amounts to making a simple substitution in a first-order condition.

V. Infinite-Horizon Growth

A. *Description of the Model*

The analysis of the infinite-horizon growth model in continuous time proceeds exactly as in the two-period example above. Individual firms are assumed to have technologies that depend on a path $K(t)$, $t \geq 0$, for aggregate knowledge. For an arbitrary path K, we can consider an artificial planning problem $P_\infty(K)$ that maximizes the utility of a representative consumer subject to the technology implied by the path K. Assume that preferences over the single consumption good take the usual additively separable, discounted form, $\int_0^\infty U(c(t))e^{-\delta t}dt$, with $\delta >$

0. The function U is defined over the positive real numbers and can have $U(0)$ equal to a finite number or to $-\infty$, for example, when $U(c) = \ln(c)$. Following the notation from the last section, let $F(k(t), K(t), \mathbf{x}(t))$ denote the instantaneous rate of output for a firm as a function of firm-specific knowledge at time t, economywide aggregate knowledge at time t, and the level of all other inputs at t. As before, we will assume that all agents take prices as given and that firms take the aggregate path for knowledge as given.

Additional knowledge can be produced by forgoing current consumption, but the trade-off is no longer assumed to be one-for-one. By investing an amount I of forgone consumption in research, a firm with a current stock of private knowledge k induces a rate of growth $\dot{k} = G(I, k)$. The function G is assumed to be concave and homogeneous of degree one; the accumulation equation can therefore be rewritten in terms of proportional rates of growth, $\dot{k}/k = g(I/k)$, with $g(y) = G(y, 1)$. A crucial additional assumption is that g is bounded from above by a constant α. This imposes a strong form of diminishing returns in research. Given the private stock of knowledge, the marginal product of additional investment in research, Dg, falls so rapidly that g is bounded. An inessential but natural assumption is that g is bounded from below by the value $g(0) = 0$. Knowledge does not depreciate, so zero research implies zero change in k; moreover, existing knowledge cannot be converted back into consumption goods. As a normalization to fix the units of knowledge, we can specify that $Dg(0) = 1$; one unit of knowledge is the amount that would be produced by investing one unit of consumption goods at an arbitrarily slow rate.

Assume as before that factors other than knowledge are in fixed supply. This implies that physical capital, labor, and the size of the population are held constant. If labor were the only other factor in the model, exponential population growth could be allowed at the cost of additional notation; but as was emphasized in the discussion of previous models, a key distinguishing feature of this model is that population growth is not necessary for unbounded growth in per capita income. For simplicity it is left out. Allowing for accumulation of physical capital would be of more interest, but the presence of two state variables would preclude the simple geometric characterization of the dynamics that is possible in the case of one state variable. If knowledge and physical capital are assumed to be used in fixed proportions in production, the variable $k(t)$ can be interpreted as a composite capital good. (This is essentially the approach used by Arrow [1962] in the learning-by-doing model.) Given increasing marginal productivity of knowledge, increasing marginal productivity of a composite k would still be possible if the increasing marginal productivity of knowledge were sufficient to outweigh the decreasing marginal productivity associated with the physical capital.

Within the restrictions imposed by tractability and simplicity, the assumptions on the technology attempt to capture important features of actual technologies. As noted in Section II, estimated aggregate production functions do appear to exhibit some form of increasing returns to scale. Assuming that the increasing returns arise because of increasing marginal productivity of knowledge accords with the plausible conjecture that, even with fixed population and fixed physical capital, knowledge will never reach a level where its marginal product is so low that it is no longer worth the trouble it takes to do research. If the marginal product of knowledge were truly diminishing, this would imply that Newton, Darwin, and their contemporaries mined the richest veins of ideas and that scientists now must sift through the tailings and extract ideas from low-grade ore. That knowledge has an important public good characteristic is generally recognized.[8] That the production of new knowledge exhibits some form of diminishing marginal productivity at any point in time should not be controversial. For example, even though it may be possible to develop the knowledge needed to produce usable energy from nuclear fusion by devoting less than 1 percent of annual gross national product (GNP) to the research effort over a period of 20 years, it is likely that this knowledge could not be produced by next year regardless of the size of the current research effort.

B. *Existence and Characterization of a Social Optimum*

Before using necessary conditions to characterize the solutions to either the social optimization problem, denoted as PS_∞, or any of the artificial optimization problems $P_\infty(K)$, I must verify that these problems have solutions. First I state the problems precisely. Let k_0 denote the initial stock of knowledge per firm for the economy. As in the last section, I will always work with the same number of firms and consumers. Because the choice of $\mathbf{x} = \bar{\mathbf{x}}$ is trivial, I suppress this argument, writing $f(k, K) = F(k, K, \bar{\mathbf{x}})$. Also, let $\mathcal{F}(k) = f(k, Sk) = F(k, Sk, \bar{\mathbf{x}})$ denote the globally convex (per capita) production function that would be faced by a social planner. In all problems that follow, the constraint $\dot{k}(t) \geq 0$ for all $t \geq 0$ and the initial condition $k(0) = k_0$ will be understood:

[8] See, e.g., Bernstein and Nadiri (1983) for estimates from the chemical industry suggesting that spillover effects can be quite large.

$$PS_\infty: \quad \max \int_0^\infty U(c(t))e^{-\delta t}dt$$

$$\text{subject to } \frac{\dot{k}(t)}{k(t)} = g\left(\frac{\mathcal{F}(k(t)) - c(t)}{k(t)}\right);$$

$$P_\infty(K): \quad \max \int_0^\infty U(c(t))e^{-\delta t}dt$$

$$\text{subject to } \frac{\dot{k}(t)}{k(t)} = g\left(\frac{f(k(t), K(t)) - c(t)}{k(t)}\right).$$

Note that the only difference between these two problems lies in the specification of the production function. In the first case, it is convex and invariant over time. In the second, it is concave but depends on time through its dependence on the path $K(t)$. I can now state the theorem that guarantees the existence of solutions to each of these problems.

THEOREM 1. Assume that each of U, f, and g is a continuous real-valued function defined on a subset of the real line. Assume that U and g are concave. Suppose that $\mathcal{F}(k) = f(k, Sk)$ satisfies a bound $\mathcal{F}(k) \leq \mu + k^\rho$ and that $g(z)$ satisfies the bounds $0 \leq g(\mathbf{x}) \leq \alpha$ for real numbers μ, ρ, and α. Then if $\alpha\rho$ is less than the discount factor δ, PS_∞ has a finite-valued solution, and $P_\infty(K)$ has a finite-valued solution for any path $K(t)$ such that $K(t) \leq K(0)e^{\alpha t}$.

The proof, given in an appendix available on request, amounts to a check that the conditions of theorem 1 in Romer (1986) are satisfied. Note that if α is less than δ the inequality $\alpha\rho < \delta$ allows for $\rho > 1$. Thus the socially feasible production function $\mathcal{F}$ can be globally convex in k, with a marginal social product and an average social product of knowledge that increase without bound.

The analysis of the social planning problem PS_∞ in terms of a current-valued Hamiltonian and a phase plane follows along familiar lines (see, e.g., Arrow 1967; Cass and Shell 1976*a*, 1976*b*). Define $H(k, \lambda) = \max_c U(c) + \lambda\{kg([\mathcal{F}(k) - c]/k)\}$. For simplicity, assume that the functions U, f, and g are twice continuously differentiable. The first-order necessary conditions for a path $k(t)$ to be a maximum for PS_∞ are that there exists a path $\lambda(t)$ such that the system of first-order differential equations $\dot{k} = D_2H(k, \lambda)$ and $\dot{\lambda} = \delta\lambda - D_1H(k, \lambda)$ are satisfied and that the paths satisfy two boundary conditions: the initial condition on k and the transversality condition at infinity, $\lim_{t\to\infty} \lambda(t)k(t)e^{-\delta t} = 0$.[9]

[9] Proving the necessity of the transversality condition for a maximization problem that is not concave takes relatively sophisticated mathematical methods. Ekeland and

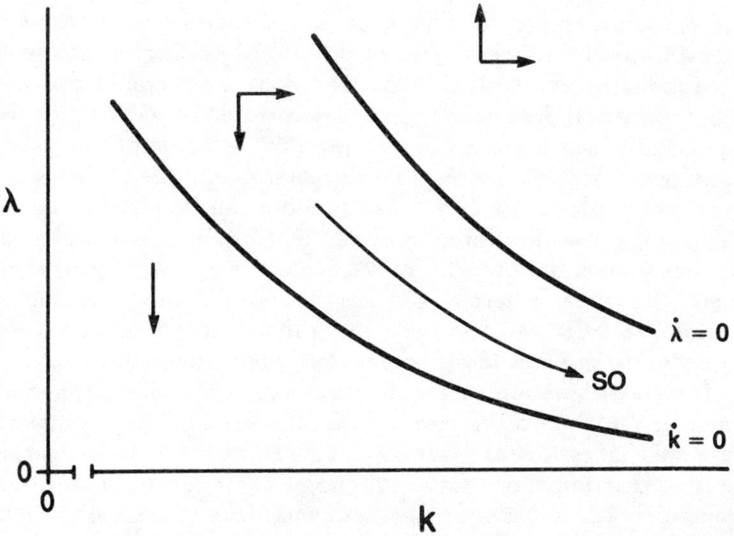

FIG. 2.—Geometry of the phase plane for a typical social optimum. Arrows indicate directions of trajectories in different sections of the plane. The rate of change of the stock of knowledge, $\dot{k}$, is zero everywhere on or below the locus denoted by $\dot{k} = 0$; *SO* denotes the socially optimal trajectory that stays everywhere between the lines $\dot{\lambda} = 0$ and $\dot{k} = 0$.

Under the assumption that $\lim_{c \to 0} DU(c) = \infty$, maximizing over c in the definition of $H(k, \lambda)$ implies that $DU(c) = \lambda Dg([\mathcal{F}(k) - c]/k)$ whenever the constraint $\dot{k} \geq 0$ is not binding; otherwise, $c = \mathcal{F}(k)$. This gives c as a function of k and λ. Substituting this expression in the equations for $\dot{k}$ and $\dot{\lambda}$ gives a system of first-order equations that depends only on k and λ.

Because of the restriction that $\dot{k}$ be nonnegative, the plane can be divided into two regions defined by $\dot{k} = 0$ and $\dot{k} \geq 0$ (see fig. 2). In a convenient abuse of the terminology, I will refer to the locus of points dividing these two regions as the $\dot{k} = 0$ locus. Along this locus, both the conditions $c = \mathcal{F}(k)$ and $DU(c) = \lambda Dg([\mathcal{F}(k) - c]/k)$ must hold. Thus the $\dot{k} = 0$ locus is defined by the equation $DU(\mathcal{F}(k)) = \lambda$. By the concavity of U, it must be a nonincreasing curve in the k-λ plane.

As usual, the equation $\dot{\lambda} = 0$ defines a simple locus in the plane. When the derivative $D_1H(k, \lambda)$ is evaluated along the $\dot{k} = 0$ locus, the equation for $\dot{\lambda}$ there can be written $\dot{\lambda}/\lambda = \delta - D\mathcal{F}(k)$. If $D\mathcal{F}$ increases without bound, there exists a value of $\hat{k}$ such that $D\mathcal{F}(k) > \delta$ for all k

Scheinkman (1983) prove the necessity of the transversality condition for nonconcave discrete-time problems. In continuous time, a proof that requires a local Lipschitz condition is given by Aubin and Clarke (1979).

larger than $\hat{k}$, and for all such k, the $\dot{\lambda} = 0$ locus lies above the $\dot{k} = 0$ locus. It may be either upward or downward sloping. If $\mathcal{F}$ were concave and satisfied the usual Inada conditions, $\dot{\lambda} = 0$ would cross $\dot{k} = 0$ from above and the resulting steady state would be stable in the usual saddle-point sense. Here, $\dot{\lambda} = 0$ may cross $\dot{k} = 0$ either from above or from below. If $D\mathcal{F}(k)$ is everywhere greater than δ, the $\dot{\lambda} = 0$ locus lies everywhere above the $\dot{k} = 0$ locus, and $\hat{k}$ can be taken to be zero. (This is the case illustrated in fig. 2.) Starting from any initial value greater than $\hat{k}$, the optimal trajectory $(\lambda(t), k(t))$, $t \geq 0$, must remain above the region where $\dot{k} = 0$. Any trajectory that crosses into this region can be shown to violate the transversality condition. Consequently, $k(t)$ grows without bound along the optimal trajectory.

This social optimum cannot be supported as a competitive equilibrium in the absence of government intervention. Any competitive firm that takes $K(t)$ as given and is faced with the social marginal products as competitive prices will choose not to remain at the optimal quantities even if it expects all other firms to do so. Each firm will face a private marginal product of knowledge (measured in terms of current output goods) equal to $D_1 f$; but the true shadow price of capital will be $D_1 f + SD_2 f > D_1 f$. Given this difference, each firm would choose to acquire less than the socially optimal amount of knowledge.

C. *Existence and Characterization of the Competitive Equilibrium*

Under a general set of conditions, this economy can be shown to have a suboptimal equilibrium in the absence of any intervention. It is completely analogous to the equilibrium for the two-period model. As in that model, it is straightforward to show that there is a three-way equivalence between competitive equilibria, fixed points of the mapping that sends a path $K(t)$ into S times the solution to $P_\infty(K)$, and solutions to an equation of the form $D_1 V(k, Sk) = 0$.[10] In the infinite-horizon case, this equation consists of a system of differential equations, which can be represented in terms of a phase plane, and a set of boundary conditions.

To derive these equations, consider the necessary conditions for the concave problem $P_\infty(K)$. Define a Hamiltonian, denoted as $\tilde{H}$ to distinguish it from the Hamiltonian H for the social planning problem PS_∞:

[10] An explicit proof of this result is given in Romer (1983). The method of proof is exactly as outlined in the two-period model. A generalized Kuhn-Tucker theorem is used to derive the necessary conditions that yield shadow prices for the maximization problems $P_\infty(K)$. Suppose K^* is a fixed point. If the consumer and the firm are faced with the shadow prices associated with $P_\infty(K^*)$, the sufficient conditions for their maximization problems are shown to be satisfied at the quantities that solve $P_\infty(K^*)$.

$$\tilde{H}(k, \lambda, K) = \max_{c} U(c) + \lambda\left[kg\left(\frac{f(k, K) - c}{k}\right)\right].$$

Then the necessary conditions for $k(t)$ to be a solution to $P_\infty(K)$ are that there exists a path $\lambda(t)$ such that $\dot{k}(t) = D_2\tilde{H}(k(t), \lambda(t), K(t))$ and $\dot{\lambda}(t) = \delta\lambda(t) - D_1\tilde{H}(k(t), \lambda(t), K(t))$ and such that the paths $k(t)$ and $\lambda(t)$ satisfy the boundary conditions $k(0) = k_0$ and $\lim_{t\to\infty} \lambda(t)k(t)e^{-\delta t} = 0$. Substituting $Sk(t)$ for $K(t)$ yields an autonomous system of differential equations, $\dot{k}(t) = D_2\tilde{H}(k(t), \lambda(t), Sk(t))$, $\dot{\lambda}(t) = \delta\lambda(t) - D_1\tilde{H}(k(t), \lambda(t), Sk(t))$, that can be characterized using the phase plane. The two boundary conditions must still hold. Any paths for $k(t)$ and $\lambda(t)$ that satisfy these equations and the boundary conditions will correspond to a competitive equilibrium, and all competitive equilibria can be characterized this way.

Before considering phase diagrams, I must show that a competitive equilibrium exists for some class of models. Standard results concerning the existence of solutions of differential equations can be used to prove that the equations for $\dot{\lambda}$ and $\dot{k}$ determine a unique trajectory through any point (k, λ) in the phase plane. The difficulty arises in showing that for any given value of k_0 there exists some value of λ_0 such that the transversality condition at infinity is satisfied along the trajectory through (k_0, λ_0). As opposed to the case in which these equations are generated by a concave maximization problem known to have a solution, there is no assurance that such a λ_0 exists.

The basic idea in the proof that such a λ_0 exists, and hence that a competitive equilibrium exists, is illustrated in example 1 from the next section. To state the general result, I need additional conditions that characterize the asymptotic behavior of the functions f and g. This is accomplished by means of an asymptotic exponent as defined by Brock and Gale (1969). Given a function $h(y)$, define the asymptotic exponent e of h as $e = \lim_{y\to\infty} \log_y|h(y)|$. Roughly speaking, $h(y)$ behaves asymptotically like the power function y^e. Also, recall that α is the maximal rate of growth for k implied by the research technology.

THEOREM 2. In addition to the assumptions of theorem 1, assume that U, f, and g are twice continuously differentiable. Assume also that $\mathcal{F}(k) = f(k, Sk)$ has an asymptotic exponent ρ such that $\rho > 1$ and $\alpha\rho < \delta$. Finally, assume that $Dg(\mathbf{x})$ has an asymptotic exponent strictly less than -1. Let $\bar{k}$ be such that $D_1 f(k, Sk) > \delta$ for all $k > \bar{k}$. Then if $k_0 > \bar{k}$, there exists a competitive equilibrium with externalities in which $c(t)$ and $k(t)$ grow without bound.

The proof is given in Romer (1983, theorem 3). The assumption on the asymptotic growth of $\mathcal{F}$ is self-explanatory. The assumption on the asymptotic exponent of Dg is sufficient to ensure the boundedness of g. The condition on $D_1 f$ will be satisfied in most cases in which $\mathcal{F}(k)$

$= f(k, Sk)$ is convex. Examples of functions satisfying these assumptions are given in the next section.

Once the conditions for the existence of a competitive equilibrium have been established, the analysis reduces once again to the study of the phase plane summarizing the information in the differential equations. In many respects, this analysis is similar to that for the social optimum for this economy. The phase plane can once again be divided into regions where $\dot{k} = 0$ and $\dot{k} > 0$. Since by definition $\mathcal{F}(k) = f(k, Sk)$, the equations for c as a function of k and λ will be identical to those in the social optimum: $DU(c) = \lambda Dg([f(k, Sk) - c]/k)$ if $\dot{k} > 0$, $c = f(k, Sk)$ if $\dot{k} = 0$. As a result, the boundary locus for the region $\dot{k} = 0$ will also be identical with that from the social optimum. The only difference arises in the equation for $\dot{\lambda}$. Although the equality $H(k, \lambda) = \tilde{H}(k, \lambda, Sk)$ does hold, the derivatives $D_1H(k, \lambda)$ and $D_1\tilde{H}(k, \lambda, Sk)$ differ. In the first case, a term involving the expression $D\mathcal{F}(k) = D_1f(k, Sk) + SD_2f(k, Sk)$ will appear. In the second case, only the first part of this expression, $D_1f(k, Sk)$, appears. Therefore, $D_1H(k, \lambda)$ is always larger than $D_1\tilde{H}(k, \lambda, Sk)$. Consequently, the $\dot{\lambda} = 0$ locus for the competitive equilibrium must lie below that for the social optimum.

As was true of the social optimum, the $\dot{\lambda} = 0$ locus can be either upward or downward sloping. If $D_1f(k, Sk) > \delta$ for all k greater than some value $\tilde{k}$, the $\dot{\lambda} = 0$ locus will lie above $\dot{k} = 0$ for values of k to the right of $\tilde{k}$. Then the qualitative analysis is the same as that presented for the social optimum. Starting from an initial value $k_0 > \tilde{k}$, the only candidate paths for equilibria are ones that stay above the $\dot{k} = 0$ region; as before, paths that cross into this region will violate the transversality condition. A trajectory lying everywhere in the region where $\dot{k} > 0$ can fail to have $k(t)$ grow without bound only if the trajectory asymptotically approaches a critical point where $\dot{\lambda}$ and $\dot{k}$ are both zero, but no such point exists to the right of $\tilde{k}$. Hence, all the trajectories that are possible candidates for an equilibrium have paths for $k(t)$ that grow without bound. The existence result in theorem 2 shows that at least one such path satisfies the transversality condition at infinity.

D. *Welfare Analysis of the Competitive Equilibrium*

The welfare analysis of the competitive equilibrium is quite simple. The intuition from simple static models with externalities or from the two-period model presented in Section III carries over intact to the dynamic model here. In the calculation of the marginal productivity of knowledge, each firm recognizes the private return to knowledge, $D_1f(k, Sk)$, but neglects the effect due to the change in the aggregate level, $SD_2f(k, Sk)$; an increase in k induces a positive external effect

$D_2 f(k, Sk)$ on each of the S firms in the economy. Consequently, the amount of consumption at any point in time is too high in the competitive equilibrium and the amount of research is too low. Any intervention that shifts the allocation of current goods away from consumption and toward research will be welfare-improving. As in any model with externalities, the government can achieve Pareto improvements not available to private agents because its powers of coercion can be used to overcome problems of shirking.

If the government has access to lump-sum taxation, any number of subsidy schemes will support the social optimum. Along the paths $k^*(t)$ and $\lambda^*(t)$ from the social optimum, taxes and subsidies must be chosen so that the first partial derivative of the Hamiltonian for the competitive equilibrium with taxes equals the first partial derivative of the Hamiltonian for the social planning problem; that is, the taxes and subsidies must be chosen so that the after-tax private marginal product of knowledge is equal to the social marginal product. This can be accomplished by subsidizing holdings of k, subsidizing accumulation $\dot{k}$, or subsidizing output and taxing factors of production other than k. The simplest scheme is for the government to pay a time-varying subsidy of $\sigma_1(t)$ units of consumption goods for each unit of knowledge held by the firm. If this subsidy is chosen to be equal to the term neglected by private agents, $\sigma_1(t) = SD_2 f(k^*(t), Sk^*(t))$, private and social marginal products will be equal. A subsidy $\sigma_2(t)$ paid to a firm for each unit of goods invested in research would be easier to implement but is harder to characterize. In general, solving for $\sigma_2(t)$ requires the solution of a system of differential equations that depends on the path for $k^*(t)$. In the special case in which production takes the form $f(k, K) = k^{\nu}K^{\gamma}$, the optimal subsidy can be shown to be constant, $\sigma_2 = \gamma/(\nu + \gamma)$. (This calculation is also included in the app. available on request.)

While it is clear that the social marginal product of knowledge is greater than the private marginal product in the no-intervention competitive equilibrium, this does not necessarily imply that interest rates in the socially optimal competitive equilibrium with taxes will be higher than in the suboptimal equilibrium. In each case, the real interest rate on loans made in units of output goods can be written as $r(t) = -(\dot{p}/p)$, where $p(t) = e^{-\delta t}DU(c(t))$ is the present value price for consumption goods at date t. When utility takes the constant elasticity form $U(c) = [c^{(1-\theta)} - 1]/(1 - \theta)$, this reduces to $r(t) = \delta + \theta(\dot{c}/c)$. In the linear utility case in which $\theta = 0$, r will equal δ regardless of the path for consumption and in particular will be the same in the two equilibria. This can occur even though the marginal productivity of knowledge differs because the price of knowledge in terms of consumption goods (equal to the marginal rate of transformation between knowledge and consumption goods) can vary. Holders of knowledge earn capital gains and losses as well as a direct return equal to the private marginal productivity of knowledge. In the case of linear utility, these capital gains and losses adjust so that interest rates stay the same.

This logical point notwithstanding, it is likely that interest rates will be higher in the social optimum. On average, $\dot{c}/c$ will be higher in the social optimum; higher initial rates of investment with lower initial consumption must ultimately lead to higher levels of consumption. If there is any curvature in the utility function U, so that θ is positive, interest rates in the optimum will be greater than in the no-intervention equilibrium. In contrast to the usual presumption, cost-benefit calculations in a suboptimal equilibrium should use a social rate of discount that is higher than the market rate of interest.

VI. Examples

To illustrate the range of behavior possible in this kind of model, this section examines specific functional forms for the utility function U, the production function f, and the function g describing the research technology. Because the goal is to reach qualitative conclusions with a minimum of algebra, the choice of functional form will be guided primarily by analytical convenience. For the production function, assume that f takes the form noted above, $f(k, K) = k^{\nu}K^{\gamma}$. This is convenient because it implies that the ratio of the private and social marginal products,

$$\frac{D_1 f(k, Sk)}{D_1 f(k, Sk) + SD_2 f(k, Sk)} = \frac{\nu}{\nu + \gamma},$$

is constant. Nonincreasing private marginal productivity implies that $0 < \nu \leq 1$; increasing social marginal productivity implies that $1 < \gamma + \nu$. With these parameter values, this functional form is reasonable only for large values of k. For small values of k, the private and social marginal productivity of knowledge is implausibly small; at $k = 0$, they are both zero. This causes no problem provided we take a moderately large initial k_0 as given. An analysis starting from k_0 close to zero would have to use a more complicated (and more reasonable) functional form for f.

Recall that the rate of increase of the stock of knowledge is written in the homogeneous form $\dot{k} = G(I, k) = kg(I/k)$, where I is output minus consumption. The requirements on the concave function g are the normalization $Dg(0) = 1$ and the bound $g(I/k) < \alpha$ for all I/k. An analytically simple form satisfying these requirements is $g(z) = \alpha z/(\alpha + z)$. Recalling that δ is the discount rate, note that the bound required for the existence of a social optimum as given in theorem 1 requires the additional restriction that $\alpha(\nu + \gamma) < \delta$. Given the stated parameter restrictions, it is easy to verify that f and g satisfy all the requirements of theorems 1 and 2.

A. *Example 1*

With this specification of the technology for the economy, we can readily examine the qualitative behavior of the model for logarithmic utility $U(c) = \ln(c)$. The Hamiltonian can then be written as

$$\tilde{H}(k, \lambda, K, c) = \ln(c) + \lambda k g\left(\frac{f(k, K) - c}{k}\right).$$

Along (the boundary of the region in which) $\dot{k} = 0$, $Dg(0) = 1$ implies that $c = \lambda^{-1}$, so $\dot{k} = 0$ is determined by the equation

$$\lambda = [f(k, Sk)]^{-1} = S^{-\gamma}k^{-(\nu+\gamma)}.$$

The exact form for the locus $\dot{\lambda} = 0$ is algebraically complicated, but it is straightforward to show that, for large k, $\dot{\lambda} = 0$ lies above the $\dot{k} = 0$ locus since $D_1 f(k, Sk)$ will be greater than δ. Also, if we define the curve L_1 in the phase plane by the equation $\lambda = [1/(\delta - \alpha)]k^{-1}$, the $\dot{\lambda} = 0$ locus must cross L_1 from above as indicated in figure 3. (Details are given in the app. available on request.) Thus $\dot{k} = 0$ behaves as k to the power $-(\nu + \gamma) < -1$, and $\dot{\lambda} = 0$ is eventually trapped between $\dot{k} = 0$ and a line described by k to the power -1. In figure 3, representative trajectories t_1 and t_2 together with the competitive equilibrium trajectory CE are used to indicate the direction of trajectories in the various parts of the plane instead of the usual arrows.

Because the line L_1 is of the form $\lambda = [1/(\delta - \alpha)]k^{-1}$, any trajectory that eventually remains below L_1 will satisfy the transversality condition $\lim_{t\to\infty} e^{-\delta t}k(t)\lambda(t) = 0$. Given the geometry of the phase plane, it is clear that there must exist a trajectory that always remains between the loci $\dot{\lambda} = 0$ and $\dot{k} = 0$. Given the initial value k_0, index by the value of λ all the trajectories that start at a point (k_0, λ) between the two loci. The set of λ's corresponding to trajectories that cross $\dot{\lambda} = 0$ can have no smallest value, the set of λ's that correspond to trajectories that cross $\dot{k} = 0$ can have no largest value, and the two sets must be disjoint. Thus there exists a value λ_0 such that the trajectory through (k_0, λ_0) crosses neither locus and must therefore correspond to an equilibrium.[11]

[11] This is the essence of the proof of theorem 2.

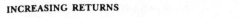

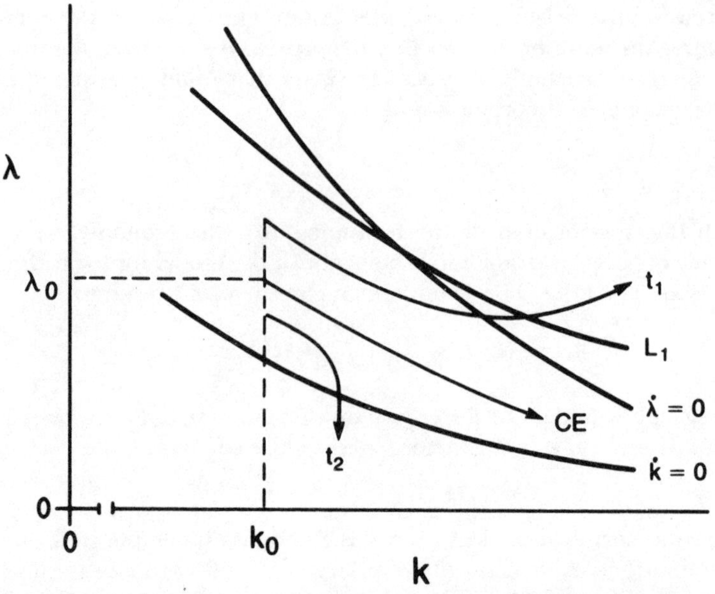

FIG. 3.—Geometry of the competitive equilibrium for example 1. The line L_1 is defined by the equation $\lambda = 1/(\delta - \alpha)k$; t_1 and t_2 denote representative trajectories in the phase plane; *CE* denotes the competitive equilibrium trajectory, which stays everywhere between the $\dot{\lambda} = 0$ and $\dot{k} = 0$ loci; λ_0 denotes the initial shadow price of knowledge corresponding to the initial stock of knowledge k_0.

In fact, the path resembles a conventional equilibrium in which the trajectory remains between the $\dot{\lambda} = 0$ and $\dot{k} = 0$ loci as it converges to a saddle point, although here it is as if the saddle point has been moved infinitely far to the right. Since the optimal trajectory cannot stop, capital grows without bound. Since the trajectory is downward sloping and since consumption is increasing in k and decreasing in λ, it is easy to see that consumption also grows without bound. Because of the difficulty of the algebra, it is not easy to describe the asymptotic rates of growth.

B. *Example 2*

Suppose now that utility is linear, $U(c) = c$. In the algebra and in the phase plane for this case, we can ignore the restriction $c \geq 0$ since it will not be binding in the region of interest. Maximizing out c from the Hamiltonian $\tilde{H}(k, \lambda, K, c) = c + \lambda k g((f - c)/k)$ implies that $c = f - \alpha k(\lambda^{.5} - 1)$. Then $f - c$ is positive (hence $\dot{k}$ is positive) if and only if $\lambda > 1$.

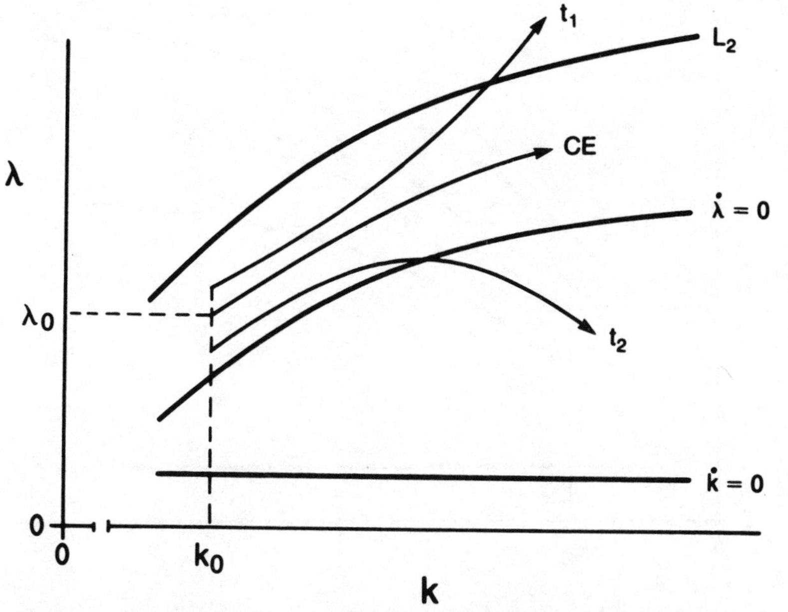

FIG. 4.—Geometry of the competitive equilibrium for example 2. The line L_2 is defined by an equation of the form $\lambda = Ak^{\nu+\gamma-1}$; t_1 and t_2 denote representative trajectories in the phase plane; *CE* denotes the competitive equilibrium trajectory that stays everywhere between L_2 and $\dot{\lambda} = 0$; λ_0 denotes the initial shadow price of knowledge.

In this example, it is possible to put tighter bounds on the behavior of the $\dot{\lambda} = 0$ locus and, more important, on the behavior of the equilibrium trajectory. As demonstrated in the appendix (available on request), $\dot{\lambda} = 0$ is upward sloping and behaves asymptotically like the power function $\lambda = Bk^{\nu+\gamma-1}$ for some constant B. For this economy, the equilibrium trajectory will lie above the $\dot{\lambda} = 0$ locus, so it is convenient to define an additional curve that will trap the equilibrium trajectory from above. For an appropriate choice of the constant A, the line L_2 defined by $\lambda = Ak^{\nu+\gamma-1}$ will lie above $\dot{\lambda} = 0$ and will have the property that trajectories must cross it from below (see fig. 4). Since trajectories must cross $\dot{\lambda} = 0$ from above, the same geometric argument as used in the last example demonstrates that there exists a trajectory that remains between these two lines. Consequently it must also behave asymptotically like $k^{\nu+\gamma-1}$. Since $k(t)$ can grow no faster than $e^{\alpha t}$, the product $\lambda(t)k(t)$ will be bounded along such a trajectory by a function of the form $e^{\alpha(\nu+\gamma)t}$. Since $\delta > (\nu + \gamma)\alpha$, this trajectory satisfies the transversality condition and corresponds to an equilibrium.

Along the equilibrium trajectory, λ behaves asymptotically like

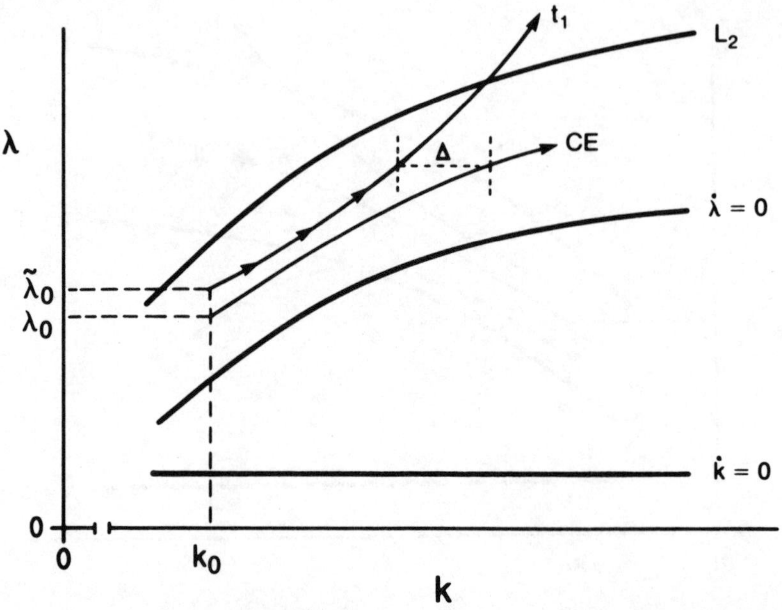

FIG. 5.—Geometry for the economy in example 2 when an exogenous increase of size Δ in the stock of knowledge is known to occur at a time $T > 0$. The equilibrium trajectory moves along t_1 until time T, at which point it is Δ units to the left of the trajectory CE. At time T, the economy jumps horizontally to CE with the change in the capital stock, but the path for $\lambda(t)$ is continuous. The equilibrium then proceeds along CE. $\tilde{\lambda}_0$ denotes the initial shadow price of knowledge in the case in which the exogenous increase will take place; λ_0 denotes the lower value that obtains in an economy in which no exogenous increase will take place.

$k^{\nu+\gamma-1}$. Given the expression noted above for c in terms of λ and k, c behaves asymptotically like $k^{\nu+\gamma} - \alpha k^{1+(.5)(\nu+\gamma-1)}$ and $I = f - c$ behaves like $k^{1+(.5)(\nu+\gamma-1)}$. Then c, I, C/k, and I/k go to infinity with k. By the assumptions on the research technology, I/k going to infinity implies that $\dot{k}/k$ approaches its upper bound α. Consequently, the percentage rate of growth of output and of consumption will be increasing, both approaching the asymptotic upper bound $\alpha(\nu + \gamma)$.

Because the equilibrium trajectory is upward sloping, this economy will exhibit different stability properties from either the conventional model or the economy with logarithmic utility described above. Figure 5 illustrates a standard exercise in which a perfect-foresight equilibrium is perturbed. Suppose that at time 0 it is known that the stock of knowledge will undergo an exogenous increase of size Δ at time T and that no other exogenous changes will occur. Usual arbitrage arguments imply that the path for any price like $\lambda(t)$ must be continuous at time T. The path followed by the equilibrium in the phase plane starts on a trajectory like t_1 such that at time T it arrives at a point exactly Δ units to the left of the trajectory CE from figure 4, which would have been the equilibrium in the absence of any exogenous change in k. As the economy evolves, it moves along t_1 then jumps Δ units to the right to the trajectory CE at time T. Since $e^{-\delta t}\lambda(t)$ can be interpreted as a time 0 market price for knowledge, a foreseen future increase in the aggregate stock of knowledge causes a time 0 increase in the price for knowledge and a consequent increase in the rate of investment in knowledge. Because of the increasing returns, the private response to an aggregate increase in the stock of knowledge will be to reinforce its effects rather than to dampen them. Since the rate of growth of the stock of knowledge is increasing in the level, this kind of disturbance causes the stock of knowledge to be larger at all future dates. Moreover, the magnitude of the difference will grow over time. Thus small current or anticipated future disturbances can potentially have large, permanent, aggregate effects.

As a comparison with the first example shows, this result requires not only that increasing returns be present but also that marginal utility not decrease too rapidly with the level of per capita consumption. If we had restricted attention to the class of bounded, constant elasticity utility functions, $[c^{(1-\theta)} + 1]/(1 - \theta)$ with $\theta > 1$, this phenomenon would not be apparent. The specific example here uses linear utility for convenience, but similar results will hold for constant elasticity utility function $[c^{(1-\theta)} - 1]/(1 - \theta)$ for values of θ close enough to zero.

C. *Example 3*

The analysis of the previous example suggests a simple multicountry model with no tendency toward convergence in the level of per capita output. Suppose each country is modeled as a separate closed economy of the type in example 2. Thus no trade in goods takes place among the different countries, and knowledge in one country has external effects only within that country. Even if all countries started out with the same initial stock of knowledge, small disturbances could create permanent differences in the level of per capita output. Since the rate of growth of the stock of knowledge is increasing over time toward an asymptotic upper bound, a smaller country s will always grow less rapidly than a larger country l. Asymptotically, the rates of growth $(\dot{k}/k)_s$ and $(\dot{k}/k)_l$ will both converge to α, but the ratios k_l/k_s and c_l/c_s will be monotonically increasing over time, and the differences $k_l(t) - k_s(t)$ and $c_l(t) - c_s(t)$ will go to infinity.

It is possible to weaken the sharp separation assumed between countries in this discussion. In particular, neither the absence of trade in consumption goods and knowledge nor the sharp restriction on the extent of the externalities is essential for the divergence noted above. As in the Arrow (1962) learning-by-doing model, suppose that all knowledge is embodied either in physical capital or as human capital. Thus k denotes a composite good composed of both knowledge and some kind of tangible capital. In this embodied form, knowledge can be freely transported between two different countries. Suppose further that the external effect of knowledge embodied in capital in place in one country extends across its border but does so with diminished intensity. For example, suppose that output of a representative firm in country 1 can be described as $f(k, K_1, K_2) = k^{\nu}(K_1^a + K_2^b)$, where k is the firm's stock of the composite good, K_1 and K_2 are the aggregates in the two countries, and the exponent a on the domestic aggregate K_1 is strictly greater than the exponent b on the foreign aggregate K_2. Production in country 2 is defined symmetrically. Then for a specific form of the research technology, Romer (1983) shows that the key restriction on the equilibrium paths Sk_1 and Sk_2 in the two countries comes from the equality of the marginal product of private knowledge imposed by the free mobility of the composite good k:

$$D_1 f(k_1, Sk_1, Sk_2) = D_1 f(k_2, Sk_2, Sk_1). \qquad (1)$$

With the functional form given above, it is easy to verify that, in addition to the symmetric solution $k_1 = k_2$, there exists an asymmetric solution. In that solution, if k_1 is larger than k_2 and growing (e.g., country 1 is industrialized and country 2 is not), the path for k_2 that satisfies this equation either can grow at a rate slower than that for country 1 or may shrink, exporting the composite good to the more developed country.[12]

This kind of steady, ongoing "capital flight" or "brain drain" does not require any fundamental difference between the two countries. They have identical technologies. If we assume that there is perfect mobility in the composite k, it can even take place when both countries start from the same initial level of k. If all agents are convinced that country 2 is destined to be the slow-growing country in an asymmetric equilibrium, a discrete amount of the composite good will jump immediately to country 1. Thereafter, the two countries will evolve according to equation (1), with country 2 growing more slowly than country 1 or possibly even shrinking.

This kind of model should not be taken too literally. A more realistic model would need to take account of other factors of production with various degrees of less than perfect mobility. Nonetheless, it does suggest that the presence of increasing returns and of multiple

[12] Details are available in an app. available from the author.

equilibria can introduce a degree of instability that is not present in conventional models. This identifies a second sense in which small disturbances can have large effects. In addition to the multiplier-type effect for a closed economy as described in the last example, a small disturbance or a small change in a policy variable such as a tax rate could conceivably have a decisive effect on which of several possible equilibria is attained.

VII. Conclusion

Recent discussions of growth have tended not to emphasize the role of increasing returns. At least in part, this reflects the absence of an empirically relevant model with increasing returns that exhibits the rigor and simplicity of the model developed by Ramsey, Cass, and Koopmans. Early attempts at such a model were seriously undermined by the loose treatment of specialization as a form of increasing returns with external effects. More recent attempts by Arrow, Levhari, and Sheshinski were limited by their dependence on exogenously specified population growth and by the implausible implication that the rate of growth of per capita income should be a monotonically increasing function of the rate of population growth. Incomplete models that took the rate of technological change as exogenously specified or that made it endogenous in a descriptive fashion could address neither welfare implications nor positive implications like the slowing of growth rates or the convergence of per capita output.

The model developed here goes part way toward filling this theoretical gap. For analytical convenience, it is limited to a case that is the polar opposite of the usual model with endogenous accumulation of physical capital and no accumulation of knowledge. But once the operation of the basic model is clear, it is straightforward to include other state variables. The implications for a model with both increasing marginal productivity of knowledge and decreasing marginal productivity of physical capital can easily be derived using the framework outlined here; however, the geometric analysis using the phase plane is impossible with more than one state variable, and numerical methods for solving dynamic equation systems must be used.[13] Since the model here can be interpreted as the special case of the two-state-variable model in which knowledge and capital are used in fixed

[13] For an example of this kind of numerical analysis in a model with a stock of knowledge and a stock of an exhaustible resource, see Romer and Sasaki (1985). As in the growth model, increasing returns associated with knowledge can reverse conventional presumptions; in particular, exhaustible resource prices can be monotonically decreasing for all time.

proportions, this kind of extension can only increase the range of possible equilibrium outcomes.

References

Arrow, Kenneth J. "The Economic Implications of Learning by Doing." *Rev. Econ. Studies* 29 (June 1962): 155–73.

———. "Applications of Control Theory to Economic Growth." In *Mathematics of the Decision Sciences,* vol. 1, edited by George B. Dantzig and Arthur F. Veinott. Providence, R.I.: American Math. Soc., 1967.

Aubin, J. P., and Clarke, F. H. "Shadow Prices and Duality for a Class of Optimal Control Problems." *SIAM J. Control and Optimization* 17 (September 1979): 567–86.

Baumol, William J. "Productivity Growth, Convergence and Welfare: What the Long Run Data Show." Research Report no. 85-27. New York: New York Univ., C. V. Starr Center, 1985.

Bernstein, J. I., and Nadiri, M. Ishaq. "Research and Development, Spillovers and Adjustment Costs: An Application of Dynamic Duality at the Firm Level." Working paper. New York: New York Univ., 1983.

Blitch, Charles P. "Allyn Young on Increasing Returns." *J. Post Keynesian Econ.* 5 (Spring 1983): 359–72.

Brock, William A. "A Simple Perfect Foresight Monetary Model." *J. Monetary Econ.* 1 (April 1975): 133–50.

———. "A Polluted Golden Age." In *Economics of Natural and Environmental Resources,* edited by Vernon L. Smith. New York: Gordon and Breach, 1977.

Brock, William A., and Gale, David. "Optimal Growth under Factor Augmenting Progress." *J. Econ. Theory* 1 (October 1969): 229–43.

Cass, David. "Optimum Growth in an Aggregative Model of Capital Accumulation." *Rev. Econ. Studies* 32 (July 1965): 233–40.

Cass, David, and Shell, Karl. "Introduction to Hamiltonian Dynamics in Economics." *J. Econ. Theory* 12 (February 1976): 1–10. (*a*)

———. "The Structure and Stability of Competitive Dynamical Systems." *J. Econ. Theory* 12 (February 1976): 31–70. (*b*)

Chipman, John S. "External Economies of Scale and Competitive Equilibrium." *Q.J.E.* 84 (August 1970): 347–85.

Dechert, W. Davis, and Nishimura, Kazuo. "A Complete Characterization of Optimal Growth Paths in an Aggregated Model with a Non-concave Production Function." *J. Econ. Theory* 31 (December 1983): 332–54.

Dixit, Avinash K.; Mirrlees, James A.; and Stern, Nicholas. "Optimum Saving with Economies of Scale." *Rev. Econ. Studies* 42 (July 1975): 303–25.

Ekeland, Ivar, and Scheinkman, José A. "Transversality Conditions for Some Infinite Horizon Discrete Time Maximization Problems." Technical Report no. 411. Stanford, Calif.: Stanford Univ., IMSSS, July 1983.

Ethier, Wilfred J. "National and International Returns to Scale in the Model Theory of International Trade." *A.E.R.* 72 (June 1982): 389–405.

Hansen, Lars Peter; Epple, Dennis; and Roberds, William. "Linear-Quadratic Duopoly Models of Resource Depletion." In *Energy, Foresight and Strategy,* edited by Thomas J. Sargent. Washington: Resources for the Future, 1985.

Helpman, Elhanan. "Increasing Returns, Imperfect Markets, and Trade Theory." In *Handbook of International Economics,* vol. 2, edited by Ronald W. Jones and Peter B. Kenen. New York: North-Holland, 1984.

Hicks, John R. "Thoughts on the Theory of Capital: The Corfu Conference." *Oxford Econ. Papers* 12 (June 1960): 123–32.

Hochman, Oded, and Hochman, Eithan. "Regeneration, Public Goods, and Economic Growth." *Econometrica* 48 (July 1980): 1233–50.

Kaldor, Nicholas. "The Role of Increasing Returns, Technical Progress and Cumulative Causation in the Theory of International Trade and Economic Growth." *Écon. Appl.* 34, no. 4 (1981): 593–617.

Kendall, M. G. *Rank Correlation Methods.* New York: Hafner, 1962.

Kendrick, John W. *The Formation and Stocks of Total Capital.* New York: Columbia Univ. Press (for N.B.E.R.), 1976.

Knight, Frank H. "On Decreasing Cost and Comparative Cost: A Rejoinder." *Q.J.E.* 39 (February 1925): 331–33.

Koopmans, Tjalling C. "On the Concept of Optimal Economic Growth." In *The Econometric Approach to Development Planning.* Amsterdam: North-Holland (for Pontificia Acad. Sci.), 1965.

Kuznets, Simon. "Notes on the Pattern of U.S. Economic Growth." In *The Reinterpretation of American Economic History,* edited by Robert W. Fogel and Stanley L. Engerman. New York: Harper and Row, 1971.

Levhari, David. "Extensions of Arrow's 'Learning by Doing.'" *Rev. Econ. Studies* 33 (April 1966): 117–31. (*a*)

———. "Further Implications of Learning by Doing." *Rev. Econ. Studies* 33 (January 1966): 31–38. (*b*)

McKenzie, Lionel W. "On the Existence of General Equilibrium for a Competitive Market." *Econometrica* 27 (January 1959): 54–71.

Maddison, Angus. "Per Capita Output in the Long Run." *Kyklos* 32, nos. 1, 2 (1979): 412–29.

———. *Phases of Capitalist Development.* New York: Oxford Univ. Press, 1982.

Majumdar, Mukul, and Mitra, Tapan. "Intertemporal Allocation with a Non-convex Technology: The Aggregative Framework." *J. Econ. Theory* 27 (June 1982): 101–36.

———. "Dynamic Optimization with a Non-convex Technology: The Case of a Linear Objective Function." *Rev. Econ. Studies* 50 (January 1983): 143–51.

Phelps, Edmund S. "Models of Technical Progress and the Golden Rule of Research." *Rev. Econ. Studies* 33 (April 1966): 133–45.

Ramsey, Frank P. "A Mathematical Theory of Saving." *Econ. J.* 38 (December 1928): 543–59.

Reynolds, Lloyd G. "The Spread of Economic Growth to the Third World: 1850–1980." *J. Econ. Literature* 21 (September 1983): 941–80.

Rockafellar, R. Tyrrell. *Convex Analysis.* Princeton, N.J.: Princeton Univ. Press, 1970.

Romer, Paul M. "Dynamic Competitive Equilibria with Externalities, Increasing Returns and Unbounded Growth." Ph.D. dissertation, Univ. Chicago, 1983.

———. "Cake Eating, Chattering and Jumps: Existence Results for Variational Problems." *Econometrica,* vol. 54 (July 1986).

Romer, Paul M., and Sasaki, Hiroo. "Monotonically Decreasing Natural Resource Prices under Perfect Foresight." Working Paper no. 19. Rochester, N.Y.: Univ. Rochester, Center Econ. Res., 1985.

Shell, Karl. "A Model of Inventive Activity and Capital Accumulation." In *Essays on the Theory of Optimal Growth,* edited by Karl Shell. Cambridge, Mass.: MIT Press, 1967. (*a*)

———. "Optimal Programs of Capital Accumulation for an Economy in Which There Is Exogenous Technological Change." In *Essays on the Theory of Optimal Growth,* edited by Karl Shell. Cambridge, Mass.: MIT Press, 1967. (*b*)

Sheshinski, Eytan. "Optimal Accumulation with Learning by Doing." In *Essays on the Theory of Optimal Growth,* edited by Karl Shell. Cambridge, Mass.: MIT Press, 1967.

Skiba, A. K. "Optimal Growth with a Convex-Concave Production Function." *Econometrica* 46 (May 1978): 527–39.

Streissler, Erich. "Growth Models as Diffusion Processes: II. Empirical Illustrations." *Kyklos* 32, no. 3 (1979): 571–86.

Weitzman, Martin L. "Optimal Growth with Scale Economies in the Creation of Overhead Capital." *Rev. Econ. Studies* 37 (October 1970): 555–70.

von Weizsäcker, Carl C. "Tentative Notes on a Two Sector Model with Induced Technical Progress." *Rev. Econ. Studies* 33 (July 1966): 245–51.

Young, Allyn A. "Increasing Returns and Economic Progress." In *Readings in Welfare Economics,* edited by Kenneth J. Arrow and Tibor Scitovsky. Homewood, Ill.: Irwin (for American Econ. Assoc.), 1969.

Uzawa, Hirofumi. "Optimum Technical Change in an Aggregative Model of Economic Growth." *Internat. Econ. Rev.* 6 (January 1965): 18–31.

Part II
Models with Two or More Sectors

[6]

On a Two-Sector Model of Economic Growth [1]

1. In the present paper we are interested in the growth process in a two-sector model of capital accumulation and show that balanced growth equilibria are globally stable under the neoclassical hypotheses.

The neoclassical model of economic growth, as it has been developed by Solow [5] and Swan [6], is formulated in terms of the aggregate production function. The aggregate production function specifies the relationship between output and factors of production, and output is assumed to be composed of homogeneous quantities identical with capital, or at least price ratios between output and capital are assumed constant. The economy we are concerned with in this paper, on the other hand, consists of two types of goods, investment-goods and consumption-goods, to be produced by two factors of production, capital and labor; prices of investment-goods and consumption-goods are determined so as to satisfy the demand requirements.[2] It will be assumed that capital depreciates at a fixed rate, the rate of growth in labor is constant and exogenously determined, capitalists' income is solely spent on investment-goods, that of laborers on consumption-goods, and production is subject to the neoclassical conditions. Under such hypotheses, then, it will be shown that the state of steady growth exists and the growth process, starting at an arbitrary capital and labor composition, approaches some steady growth. If the consumption-goods sector is always more capital-intensive than the investment-goods sector, then the steady growth is uniquely determined and it is stable in the small as well as in the large.

2. We consider an economic system consisting of investment-goods and consumption-goods sectors, labelled 1 and 2, respectively. It is assumed that in both sectors production is subject to constant returns to scale, marginal rates of substitution are positive and diminishing, and there exist neither joint products nor external (dis-)economies.

The production processes in each sector are summarized by specifying each sector's production function; let $F_1(K_1,L_1)$ be the production function for the investment-goods sector, and $F_2(K_2,L_2)$ for the consumption-goods sector. $F_1(K_1,L_1)$ represents the quantity of the investment-goods, Y_1, produced by employing capital and labor by the quantities K_1 and L_1; and similarly for the consumption-goods sector's production function, $F_2(K_2,L_2)$.

In terms of production functions, the assumptions indicated above may be formulated as:

(1) $F_i(\lambda K_i, \lambda L_i) = \lambda F_i(K_i, L_i)$, $F_i(K_i, L_i) > 0$, for all K_i, $L_i > 0$, and $\lambda > 0$;

[1] This work was in part supported by the Office of Naval Research under Task NR-047-004. I owe much to Professor Robert M. Solow and the referees for their valuable comments and suggestions.

[2] Shinkai [4] has investigated the structure of growth equilibria in a two-sector model of growth in which technical coefficients are all constant. Our two-sector model presented here is a neoclassical version of Shinkai's model.

(2) $F_i(K_i, L_i)$ is twice continuously differentiable;

(3) $\partial F_i/\partial K_i > 0,\ \partial F_i/\partial L_i > 0,\ \partial^2 F_i/\partial K_i^2 < 0,\ \partial^2 F_i/\partial L_i^2 < 0$ for all $K_i, L_i > 0$.

In view of the constant-returns-to-scale hypothesis (1), the output-labor ratio y_i is a function of the capital-labor ratio k_i:

(4) $y_i = f_i(k_i)$,

where

$$y_i = Y_i/L_i,\ k_i = K_i/L_i,\ f_i(k_i) = F_i(k_i, 1),\quad i = 1, 2.$$

The assumptions (2-3) are then equivalent to:

(5) $f_i(k_i)$ is twice continuously differentiable;

(6) $f_i(k_i) > 0,\ f_i'(k_i) > 0,\ f_i''(k_i) < 0$, for all $k_i > 0$.

3. Let K and L be the aggregate quantities of capital and labor at time t; these quantities of the two factors of production are allocated competitively among the two sectors, and prices of goods are determined so as to satisfy the demand conditions. In what follows, we assume that both capital and labor are always fully employed and both goods are produced in positive quantities.

Let K_i and L_i be the quantities of capital and labor allocated to the i-th sector, P_1 and P_2 the price of investment-goods and of consumption goods, and r and w the returns to capital and the wage rate, respectively. Then we have,

(7) $Y_i = F_i(K_i, L_i)$,

(8) $P_i \dfrac{\partial F_i}{\partial K_i} = r,\ P_i \dfrac{\partial F_i}{\partial L_i} = w,\quad i = 1, 2.$

(9) $K_1 + K_2 = K,\ L_1 + L_2 = L$,

(10) $P_1 Y_1 = rK, \qquad P_2 Y_2 = wL.$

The condition (8) is familiar marginal productivity conditions, and (10) formulates the hypothesis that labor does not save and capital does not consume.

Let

$$\begin{aligned} k &= K/L \\ k_i &= K_i/L_i,\ y_i = Y_i/L_i,\ \rho_i = L_i/L,\quad i = 1, 2. \\ \omega &= w/r. \end{aligned}$$

Then conditions (7-10) may be reduced to:

(11) $y_i = f_i(k_i),\quad i = 1, 2.$

(12) $$\omega = \frac{f_i(k_i)}{f_i'(k_i)} - k_i, \quad i = 1, 2.$$

(13) $$\rho_1 k_1 + \rho_2 k_2 = k,$$

(14) $$\rho_1 + \rho_2 = 1,$$

(15) $$\rho_1 f_1 (k_1) = f_1'(k_1)k.$$

Differentiating (12) with respect to k_i, we have:

(16) $$\frac{d\omega}{dk_i} = \frac{-f(k_i)\, f_i''(k_i)}{[f_i'(k_i)]^2}$$

which is always positive in view of (6). Hence: *For any wage-rentals ratio* ω, *the optimum capital-labor ratio* k_i *in each sector is uniquely determined by the relation* (12), *provided:*

(17) $$\underline{\omega}_i = \lim_{k_i \to 0} \left[\frac{f_i(k_i)}{f_i'(k_i)} - k_i\right] < \omega < \overline{\omega}_i = \lim_{k_i \to \infty} \left[\frac{f_i(k_i)}{f_i'(k_i)} - k_i\right]$$

The optimum capital-labor ratio k_i corresponding to the wage-rentals ratio ω, uniquely determined by (12), will then be denoted by $k_i = k_i(\omega)$, $i = 1, 2$. The determination of the optimum capital-labor ratio $k_i(\omega)$ may be illustrated by the diagram:

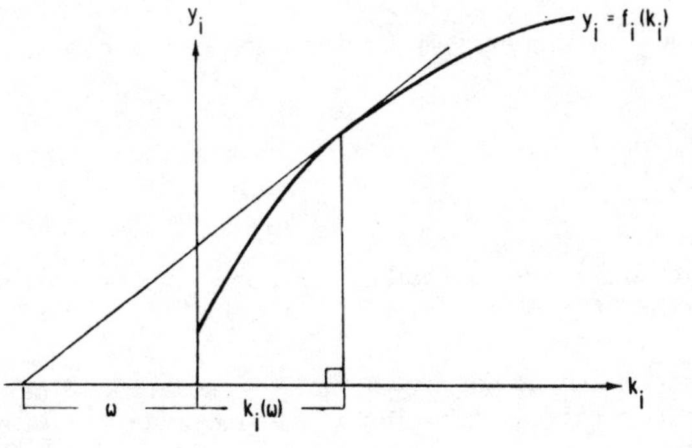

We have from (16) that:

(18) $$\frac{dk_i}{d\omega} = \frac{[f_i'(k_i)]^2}{-f_i(k_i)f_i''(k_i)} > 0,$$

with $k_i = k_i(\omega)$, $i = 1, 2$.

In view of (12), the labor allocation ρ_1 to the investment-goods sector, determined by (15), may be written as:

(19) $$\rho_1 = \frac{k}{\omega + k_1(\omega)}$$

Substituting (14) and (19) into (13) and rearranging, we have

$$(20) \quad k = \frac{\omega + k_1(\omega)}{\omega + k_2(\omega)} k_2(\omega)$$

The equilibrium wage-rentals ratio ω is obtained by solving the equation (20).

4. Let the rate of growth in labor be a positive constant, say λ, and μ be the instantaneous rate of depreciation in capital. Then the growth process in the two-sector model we have described is formulated by the following differential equations:

$$(21) \quad \frac{\dot{K}}{K} = \frac{r}{P_1} - \mu,$$

and

$$(22) \quad \frac{\dot{L}}{L} = \lambda,$$

where r is the equilibrium return to capital and P_1 the equilibrium price of the investment-goods, both at time t.

The equations (21) and (22), together with the equilibrium condition (8), imply that:

$$(23) \quad \frac{\dot{k}}{k} = f_1'(k_1) - \lambda - \mu,$$

where $k_1 = k_1(\omega)$ and ω is an equilibrium wage-rentals ratio corresponding to the aggregate capital-labor ratio.

An aggregate capital-labor ratio k^* may be termed a *balanced capital-labor ratio* if

$$(24) \quad f_1'(k_1^*) = \lambda + \mu,$$

where $k_1^* = k_1(\omega^*)$ and ω^* is an equilibrium wage-rentals ratio corresponding to the aggregate capital-ratio k^*.

It is easily shown that at the growth process starting at a balanced capital-labor ratio k^*, the aggregate capital-labor ratio $k(t)$ and equilibrium wage-rentals ratio $\omega(t)$ both remain constant.

5. Suppose that the consumption-goods sector is always more capital-intensive than the investment-goods sector;[1] namely,

$$(25) \quad k_1(\omega) < k_2(\omega), \text{ for all } \omega \text{ such that } \max\,[\underline{\omega}_1, \underline{\omega}_2] < \omega < \min\,[\bar{\omega}_1, \bar{\omega}_2].$$

Let

$$\Psi(\omega) = \frac{\omega + k_1(\omega)}{\omega + k_2(\omega)} k_2(\omega).$$

[1] The concept of relative factor intensities was introduced by Samuelson in the context of international trade theory; see, e.g., [3], p.9.

Differentiating $\log \Psi(\omega)$ with respect to ω, we have

$$\frac{1}{\Psi(\omega)} \frac{d\Psi}{d\omega} = \frac{1 + \frac{dk_1}{d\omega}}{\omega + k_1(\omega)} - \frac{1 + \frac{dk_2}{d\omega}}{\omega + k_2(\omega)} + \frac{\frac{dk_2}{d\omega}}{k_2(\omega)}$$

$$= \left[\frac{1}{\omega + k_1(\omega)} - \frac{1}{\omega + k_2(\omega)}\right] + \frac{\frac{dk_1}{d\omega}}{\omega + k_1(\omega)}$$

$$+ \frac{dk_2}{d\omega}\left[\frac{1}{k_2(\omega)} - \frac{1}{\omega + k_2(\omega)}\right],$$

which, by (18) and (25), is always *positive*.

Therefore, we have

(26) $\frac{d\Psi}{d\omega} > 0$, for all ω satisfying $\max [\omega_1, \omega_2] < \omega < \min [\bar{\omega}_1, \bar{\omega}_2]$.

The equation (20) has a positive solution ω if and only if:

(27) $\Psi(0) < k < \Psi(\infty)$,

and the solution ω is uniquely determined by k. The equilibrium factor-price ratio ω may be denoted by $\omega = \omega(k)$.

From (20) and (26), we have

(28) $\frac{d\omega}{dk} > 0$ for all k satisfying (27).

In view of conditions (6), (18), and (28), the function

$$f_1'[k_1(\omega(k))]$$

is a strictly decreasing function of the aggregate capital-labor ratio k.

Hence, the balanced capital-labor ratio k^* always exists and is uniquely determined if the following condition is satisfied :

(29) $\lim_{k_1 \to 0} f_1' (k_1) > \lambda + \mu > \lim_{k_1 \to \infty} f_1' (k_1)$.

It is easily shown that, for the growth process starting at an arbitrary initial capital-labor composition, the capital-labor ratio $k(t)$ approaches the balanced capital-labor ratio k^*.[1]

The results in this section may be summarized as:

Existence Theorem: Let the consumption-goods sector be more capital-intensive than the investment-goods sector for all relevant factor-price ratios ω. *Then for any given aggregate capital-labor ratio* k, *the equilibrium factor-price ratio* $\omega = \omega(k)$, *the optimum capital-labor ratios* $k_1 = k_1(\omega)$ *and* $k_2 = k_2(\omega)$ *in both sectors, and the equilibrium outputs per head for investment-goods and consumption-goods,* $y_1 = y_1(k)$ *and* $y_2 = y_2(k)$, *are all uniquely determined, provided the aggregate capital-labor ratio* k *satisfies the relation* (29).

Stability Theorem: Let λ *and* μ *be respectively the growth rate in labor and the instantaneous depreciation in capital; and the balanced capital-labor ratio* k^* *exist. Then, for the growth process starting at an arbitrary initial position, the capital-labor ratio* $k(t)$ *approaches the balanced capital-labor ratio* k^* *as* t *tend to infinity.*

6. The uniqueness of the balanced capital-labor ratio and its stability crucially hinge on the hypothesis that the consumption-goods sector be more capital-intensive than the investment-goods sector. In this section, we shall construct an example of the two-sector growth model in which the capital-intensity hypothesis above is not satisfied and there is an unstable balanced capital-labor ratio.

Let the production functions be:

$$y_1 = f_1(k_1) = \tfrac{1}{1000}\,(k_1^{-3} + 7^{-4})^{\frac{1}{3}},\; y_2 = f_2(k_2) = (k_1^{-3} + 1)^{\frac{1}{3}}.$$

The optimum capital-labor ratios are then given by:

$$k_1 = k_1(\omega) = 7\omega^{\frac{1}{4}},\; k_2 = k_2(\omega) = \omega^{\frac{1}{4}};$$

hence,

$$k_1(\omega) > k_2(\omega), \text{ for all } \omega > 0.$$

For aggregate capital-labor ratio k the equilibrium factor-price ratio ω is determined by:

$$k = \frac{\omega + 7\omega^{\frac{1}{4}}}{\omega + \omega^{\frac{1}{4}}}\,\omega^{\frac{1}{4}};$$

hence,

$$\frac{1}{k}\frac{d\omega}{dk} = \frac{1 + \frac{7}{4}\omega^{-\frac{3}{4}}}{\omega + 7\omega^{\frac{1}{4}}} - \frac{1 + \frac{7}{4}\omega^{-\frac{3}{4}}}{\omega + \omega^{\frac{1}{4}}} + \frac{\omega}{\frac{1}{4}}.$$

Let us consider the case in which the sum $\lambda + \mu$ of the rate of growth in labor and the rate of depreciation is

$$\frac{7\sqrt[3]{7}}{1600} \doteqdot .8\%.$$

[1] See, e.g. Arrow and Hurwicz [2], p. 540.

Then $k^* = 4$ is a balanced capital-labor ratio and $\omega^* = 1$ is the corresponding wage-rentals ratio.

But

$$\left(\frac{1}{k}\ \frac{dk}{d\omega}\right)_{\omega=1} = -\tfrac{1}{32} < 0;$$

hence, the balanced capital-labor ratio $k^* = 4$ is not stable.

7.[1] Let us now consider the general case in which the capital-intensity hypothesis is not necessarily satisfied. In this case, the balanced capital-labor ratio may be no longer uniquely determined for given rates of labor growth and of depreciation; hence, there may exist unstable balanced capital-labor ratios, as was discussed in the previous section.

If, however, the conditions (29) and

$$(30) \quad f_1(0) = 0,\ f_2(0) = 0,$$

are satisfied, then it is possible to show that the growth process represented by (21) and (22) is *globally stable* in the sense introduced by Arrow, Block and Hurwicz ([2], p. 85); namely, given any initial condition, the aggregate capital-labor ratio $k(t)$ converges to some balanced capital-labor ratio.

To see the global stability of the process (23), it suffices to show that[2]

$$(31) \quad \lim_{k\to\infty} [f_1'(k_1) - \lambda - \mu] < 0,$$

$$(32) \quad \lim_{k\to 0} [f_1'(k_1) - \lambda - \mu] < 0.$$

The relation (31) may be seen from the assumption (29) and the inequality:

$$k < \omega + k_1$$

which is derived from (20). On the other hand, to see the relation (32), let k tend to zero. Then the corresponding wage-rentals ratio ω converges to zero also; otherwise, the relation (20) would imply

$$0 = \frac{\bar{\omega} + k_1(\bar{\omega})}{\bar{\omega} + k_2(\bar{\omega})}\, k_2(\bar{\omega})$$

for some positive wage-rentals ratio $\bar{\omega}$, contradicting the assumption (30). Hence the corresponding capital-labor ratio $k_1 = k_1(\omega)$ converges to zero, again in view of (30). The relation (32) is then implied by the condition (29).

[1] This section has been written after I have read Professor Solow's note which suggests that the stability property of the growth equilibrium as discussed in the present paper may not depend on the capital-intensity hypothesis.

[2] See, e.g., Arrow and Hurwicz [2], p. 540.

We may summarize our results as:

Let the growth rate in labor λ *and the depreciation rate in capital* μ *satisfy the conditions* (29) *and* (30). *Then there exists at least one balanced capital-labor ratio, and, for the growth process starting an arbitrary initial capital-labor composition, the aggregate capital-labor ratio* $k(t)$ *converges to some balanced capital-labor ratio.*

Stanford. HIROFUMI UZAWA.

REFERENCES

[1] Arrow, K. J., H. D. Block, and L. Hurwicz. " On the Stability of the Competitive Equilibrium, II ", *Econometrica*, Vol. 27 (1959), pp. 82-109.

[2] Arrow, K. J., and L. Hurwicz. " On the Stability of the Competitive Equilibrium, I ", *Econometrica*, Vol. 27 (1958), pp. 522-552.

[3] Samuelson, P. A. " Prices of Factors and Goods in General Equilibrium," *Review of Economic Studies*, Vol. 21 (1953-54), pp. 1-20.

[4] Shinkai, Y. " On the Equilibrium Growth of Capital and Labor," *International Economic Review*, Vol. 1 (1960), pp. 107-111.

[5] Solow, R. M. " A Contribution to the Theory of Economic Growth," *Quarterly Journal of Economics*, Vol. 70 (1956), pp. 65-94.

[6] Swan, T. W. " Economic Growth and Capital Accumulation," *Economic Record* Vol. 32 (1956), pp. 334-361.

[7]

INTERNATIONAL ECONOMIC REVIEW
Vol. 9, No. 2, June, 1968

THE ROLE OF THE JACOBIAN DETERMINANT IN THE TWO-SECTOR MODEL*

BY EDWIN BURMEISTER[1]

1. INTRODUCTION

AS PROFESSOR HAHN has written, "The two-sector growth story has been unwinding slowly and is not always easy to read." [6, (339)]. The confusion has been compounded by the fact that the literature contains some false and/or misleading theorems. One of my goals, therefore, is to state clearly the most important theorems concerning *causality* (uniqueness of short-run equilibrium) and *stability* which have appeared in numerous other papers (e. g., [5], [7], [8], [11], [14] and [15]).

I have found it convenient to depart from the usual approaches and to introduce the Jacobian determinant J of the entire system of simultaneous equations which determine short-run equilibrium, and I have shown that the two-sector model is causal if and only if J does not change sign. Theorem 5 provides necessary and sufficient conditions for *local* stability, a problem which has been somewhat neglected in previous work; a numerical example is given to illustrate that local stability is sometimes sufficient for the stronger conclusion that there exists a *unique* balanced growth path. Finally, global stability and Harrod-neutral technical progress are discussed briefly.

2. BRIEF DESCRIPTION OF THE TWO-SECTOR MODEL

Investment goods Y_1 and consumption goods Y_2 are produced by two factors of production, homogeneous labor L and malleable capital K. It is assumed that capital depreciates at a fixed rate μ which is independent of use, that the rate of growth of labor is an exogenous constant λ, and that the production processes satisfy the usual neoclassical assumptions (i. e., constant-returns-to-scale, diminishing returns, etc.). It is also assumed that the average and marginal saving propensities from profit income s_r and from wage income s_w are constants.

We define

$$y_i \equiv Y_i/L_i = F_i(K_i/L_i, 1) \equiv f_i(k_i)\,, \qquad i = 1, 2\,,$$

where $k_1 \equiv K_1/L_1$ and $k_2 \equiv K_2/L_2$; since full-employment is assumed, $K_1 + K_2 = K$ and $L_1 + L_2 = L$. The ratio of labor employed in the capital-goods sector

* Manuscript received November 24, 1965, revised October 6, 1966.

[1] I wish to express my appreciation to Professor Paul A. Samuelson whose original insight into the structure of two-sector growth models led me to the approach taken in this paper. Professors Robert M. Solow and Edwin Kuh also provided helpful guidance in my earlier work on this subject, and I have benefitted from conversations with Professors Pranab Bardhan, A. R. Dobell, Ivor Pearce and Robert A. Pollak. Appreciation is also extended to the National Science Foundation for a Graduate Fellowship and for support from Research Grants GS-95 and GS-571.

to total labor is denoted by $\rho \equiv L_1/L$, and thus the full-employment assumption is expressed by the equation $\rho k_1 + (1-\rho)k_2 = k$ where k is equal to the total capital-labor ratio K/L. The growth of the capital stock is given by

$$\dot{K} \equiv Y_1 - \mu K ,$$

where μ is the depreciation rate of capital and is independent of use. Finally, ω is the ratio of the wage rate W to the gross rental rate for a unit of capital R.

For a *given* value of the capital-labor ratio k, the competitive short-run equilibrium conditions may be written as $\Psi(x; k) = 0$ where the vector $x \equiv (y_1, y_2, k_1, k_2, \omega, \rho)$ and

$$\Psi^1 = f_1(k_1) - y_1 = 0$$

$$\Psi^2 = f_2(k_2) - y_2 = 0$$

$$\Psi^3 = \frac{f_1(k_1)}{f_1'(k_1)} - k_1 - \omega = 0$$

$$\Psi^4 = \frac{f_2(k_2)}{f_2'(k_2)} - k_2 - \omega = 0$$

$$\Psi^5 = \rho k_1 + (1-\rho)k_2 - k = 0$$

$$\Psi^6 = \rho f_1(k_1) - f_1'(k_1)(s_r k + s_w \omega) = 0.^2$$

The Jacobian determinant of the above system of simultaneous equations is

$$J = \det\left[\frac{\partial(\Psi^1, \cdots, \Psi^6)}{\partial(y_1, \cdots, \rho)}\right].$$

3. CAUSALITY: UNIQUENESS OF SHORT-RUN EQUILIBRIUM

It is possible to define numbers a and b such that a solution to $\Psi(x; k) = 0$ is possible for all $k \in (a, b)$.[3] If $k \leq a$ or $k \geq b$, it may be necessary to examine corner solutions obtained by replacing the equalities in the system $\Psi = 0$ with appropriate inequalities; to avoid such difficulties, it will be assumed that k is restricted to the domain $a < k < b$. It is important to note, however, that if $f_i(k_i)$ are both constant-elasticity-of-substitution (CES) production functions, then $a = 0$ and $b = \infty$. Likewise $a = 0$ and $b = \infty$ if the Inada derivative conditions [7] $f_i'(\infty) = 0$ and $f_i'(0) = \infty$, $i = 1, 2$, are satisfied.[4]

We wish to determine conditions which imply that the competitive short-run equilibrium is unique for *any* given value of k in the interval (a, b), i.e., the vector x must be uniquely determined by k. At any point (x, k) for which $J(x, k) \neq 0$, we can apply the implicit function theorem and obtain a *local* (vector) function $x = \Phi(k)$. However, the special economic structure of our model and the assumptions which have been made allow us to obtain the following result:

THEOREM 1. *Let $S = \{(x, k) \mid \Psi(x, k) = 0, a < k < b\}$ where $\Psi(x, k)$ is the system of equations given above, and assume that the roots of $J(x, k) = 0, (x, k) \in S$,*

[2] The reader is referred to [4], [5], or [15] for a derivation of these equations.
[3] See [5, (220-21)].
[4] See, e.g., [5] and [15].

are isolated. There exists a solution $x = \Phi(k)$ which is globally unique $(a < k < b)$ if and only if $J(x, k)$ does not change sign for all $(x, k) \in S$.

PROOF. It is well-known that $\Psi(x, k) = 0$ may be written as $k = k(\omega)$ and $x = x(\omega)$; thus for $(x, k) \in S$ we may write $J = J(\omega)$ where $J(\omega)$ is continuous by assumption. Let $(\tilde{w}, \tilde{k}) \in S$ be any point for which $J(\tilde{\omega}) \neq 0$. Then by the implicit function theorem,[5] (1) $dy_1/dk = N_1/J, \cdots, d\rho/dk = N_6/J$ where the determinant N_j is the Jacobian determinant with the j-th column replaced by $[-\Psi_k^i] = [0, 0, 0, 0, 1, s_r f_1'(k_1)]$, and (2) in a neighborhood of $(\tilde{x}, \tilde{k})$ there exist (local) functions $y_1 = \Phi^1(k), \cdots, \rho = \Phi^6(k)$ or $x = \Phi(k)$. Observe that $k(\omega)$ can (cannot) be inverted if $dk/d\omega$ is strictly of one sign (changes sign). Since it is easily shown that $N_1, \cdots, N_5$ are all positive for all $(x, k) \in S$, $\text{sgn}\,(d\omega/dk) = \text{sgn}\,(N_5/J) = \text{sgn}\, J, J \neq 0$. It follows immediately that $x = \Phi(k)$, $k \in (a, b)$, exists (does not exist) if J is *strictly of one sign* (if *J changes sign*) for $(x, k) \in S$.

We must now consider the case in which J vanishes but does not change sign (otherwise Theorem 1 must be stated in a slightly weaker form). By assumption the roots of $J(\omega) = 0$ are isolated, i. e. if ω^* is any root of $J(\omega) = 0$, there exists a deleted neighborhood of ω^* on which $J(\omega) \neq 0$. (If, for example, the function $J(\omega)$ is *analytic* and is not identically zero, the roots ω^* are isolated.)[6] It is then easily shown that $x = \Phi(k)$, $k \in (a, b)$, exists if J *does not change sign* for all $(x, k) \in S$. QED.

We may thus take the view that it is the Jacobian determinant which plays a "fundamental" role, and due to the specific economic structure which is assumed, $\text{sgn}\, J = \text{sgn}\,(dy_1/dk) = \cdots = \text{sgn}\,(d\omega/dk), J \neq 0$. It would be interesting to explore the relationship between my Theorem 1 and Professor Hahn's necessary and sufficient condition for causality [6, (341)], but I will not do so here.

If $x = \Phi(k)$ exists for all $k \in (a, b)$, the model is called *causal* for the following reason. The capital-labor ratio grows according to the differential equation $\dot{k} = f_1'(k_1)(s_r k + s_w \omega) - nk$, $n \equiv \lambda + \mu$, or $\dot{k} = f(x, k)$. For any given value of the capital-labor ratio $k \in (a, b)$, the latter may be written as $\dot{k} = f(\Phi, k) \equiv h(k)$. However, if x is not uniquely determined by k, then $\dot{k}$ is not uniquely determined by k and the system is not causal.

It is natural to wonder "how indeterminate" the system may be, or more precisely, how many short-run equilibrium values of x are possible for a given $k = \bar{k}$. Figures 1 a, 1 b and 1 c illustrate the nature of the problem. In Figure 1 a the Jacobian determinant is always positive, and ω is uniquely determined by k; in 1 b J changes sign twice and at most three short-run

[5] For a clear statement of the implicit function theorem, see [2, (141-48)].

[6] See [2, (518-19, theorems 16-9 and 16-11)]. While the assumption that $J(\omega)$ is an analytic function is quite restrictive, it does not seem unreasonable since the production functions $f_i(k_i)$ are analytic for most of the meaningful examples one can imagine. In any event the matter is of little practical significance since Theorem 1 may be stated in slightly weaker form (ignoring all points for which $J = 0$) without any additional assumptions, and therefore a more detailed investigation does not seem justified.

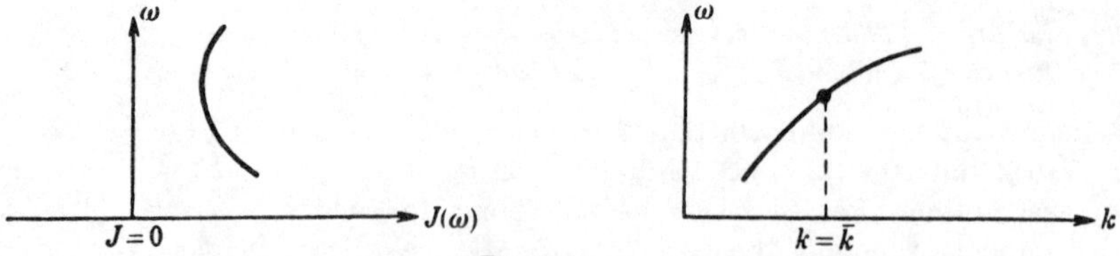

FIGURE 1 a

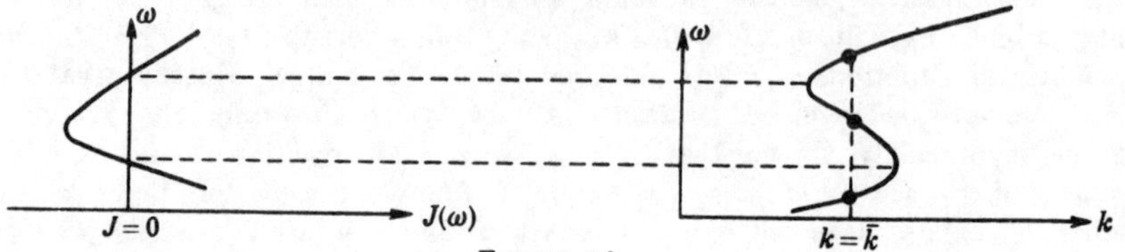

FIGURE 1 b

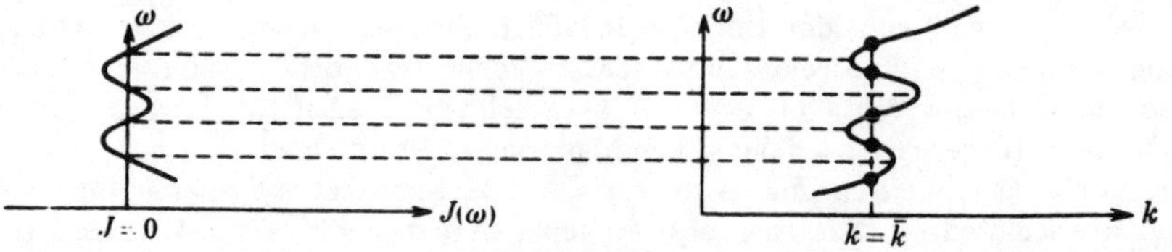

FIGURE 1 c

equilibrium configurations are possible for a given $k = \bar{k}$; and in 1 c the numerous changes in the sign of J allow the possibility of more than three equilibrium positions for a given $k = \bar{k}$. A numerical example shows that the behavior illustrated in Figure 1 b is not only possible, but it definitely exists.[7] The following theorem allows us to rule out the behavior illustrated in Figure 1 c for a special case.

THEOREM 2. *If both $f_1(k_1)$ and $f_2(k_2)$ are constant-elasticity-of-substitution production functions, then the Jacobian determinant either never changes sign or it changes sign exactly twice.*

PROOF. The proof will only be sketched. We construct a function $u(\omega)$ with the property $\operatorname{sgn} u(\omega) = \operatorname{sgn} J$ and show that (1) $u'(\omega) \leq 0 \Rightarrow u''(\omega) > 0$, and (2) $u(\omega) > 0$ for both sufficiently small and sufficiently large ω.[8] From

[7] Following closely an original example by Uzawa [14, (45-6)], let

$$y_1 = f_1(k_1) = 0.001(k_1^{-3} + 7^{-4})^{-1/3}$$

and

$$y_2 = f_2(k_2) = (k_2^{-3} + 1)^{-1/3},$$

with $s_r = 1$, $s_w = 0$, and $\sigma_1 = \sigma_2 = 1/4$. It is easily verified that J changes sign and that three short-run equilibria are possible for $3 < k < 4.5$.

[8] For CES production functions, Ψ^3 and Ψ^4 may be written as $k_i = \alpha_i \omega^{\sigma_i}$ where α_i are positive constants and the Hicksian elasticities of substitution between capital and labor are $\sigma_i = (\omega/k_i)(dk_i/d\omega)$. It may be shown that $k(\omega) = N(\omega)/D(\omega)$ where $N(\omega) = s_w\alpha_1\omega^{\sigma_1+1} + (1 - s_w)\alpha_2\omega^{\sigma_2+1} + \alpha_1\alpha_2\omega^{\sigma_1+\sigma_2}$, and $D(\omega) = \omega + (1 - s_r)\alpha_1\omega^{\sigma_1} + s_r\alpha_2\omega^{\sigma_2}$. We define $u(\omega) = D^2(dk/d\omega) = D^2J/N_5 = DN' - ND'$.

(1) we see that $u(\omega)$ can cross the ω-axis at most twice; and if it crosses once, from (2) we conclude that it *must* cross twice. QED.

Finally, the following theorem gives sufficient conditions for casuality; the reader is referred to [4] and [5] for proofs.

THEOREM 3. *If any of the following five conditions hold for all $(x, k) \in S$, then J is strictly positive and the system is causal.*[9]

$$\text{(i)}\quad s_r = s_w = s\,, \qquad \text{(ii)}\quad s_r > s_w \text{ and } k_1 < k_2\,,$$
$$\text{(iii)}\quad s_r < s_w \text{ and } k_1 > k_2\,, \qquad \text{(iv)}\quad k_1 = k_2\,, \text{ or}$$
$$\text{(v)}\quad \sigma_1 + \sigma_2 \geq 1\,,$$

where $\sigma_i \equiv (\omega/k_i)(dk_i/d\omega)$.

4. STABILITY OF THE SYSTEM

The growth equation $\dot{k} = f_1'(k_1)(s_r k + s_w \omega) - nk$ may be written as

$$\frac{\dot{k}}{k} = f_1'(k_1)\frac{s_r k + s_w \omega}{k} - n \qquad \text{for } k > 0\,.$$

(Recall that k has been restricted to the domain $a < k < b$.) We will assume that the system is causal; thus there exists a function $x = \Phi(k)$ and the latter growth equations may be written as $\dot{k} = h(k)$ or $\dot{k}/k = h(k)/k \equiv g(k)$. In passing we may note that if the system is *not* causal, then $k(t)$ may asymptotically approach a limit cycle with perpetual oscillations in the capital-labor ratio.[10]

Denoting a root of $g(k) = 0$ by k^*, in general there need not exist *any* $k^* \in (a, b)$ unless some restrictions are placed on $n \equiv \lambda + \mu$. However, the Inada derivative conditions $f_i'(\infty)=0$ and $f_i'(0) = \infty$, $i = 1, 2$, are sufficient for the existence of at least one root k^* for *all n*. If $g'(k) < 0$ *for all* $a < k < b$, then clearly any root k^* (if it exists) is unique and the system is stable, i.e., starting from any initial value $k(0) \in (a, b)$, $k(t)$ asymptotically approaches a unique constant k^*. We may thus state the following stability theorem; the reader is referred to [4], [5], [7], [14] and [15] for proofs.

THEOREM 4. *Assume there exists at least one root k^* such that $g(k^*) = 0$, $a < k^* < b$. If any of the following conditions hold for all $k \in (a, b)$, then $g'(k) < 0$ and the system is stable*:

$$\text{(i)}\quad s_r \geq s_w \text{ and } k_1 \leq k_2\,, \qquad \text{(ii)}\quad \sigma \equiv \frac{\omega}{k}\frac{dk}{d\omega} \geq 1\,,$$
$$\text{(iii)}\quad \sigma_2 \geq 1\,, \qquad \text{(iv)}\quad s_r = 1 \text{ and } J > 0\,, \text{ or}$$
$$\text{(v)}\quad s_w = 0 \text{ and } J > 0\,.$$

It is important to note that the sufficiency conditions given in Theorem 4

[9] If $f_i(k_i)$ are CES production functions, Theorem 2 assures that J is positive for both sufficiently small and sufficiently large ω. Thus it is impossible to derive sufficient conditions which imply $J < 0$ for all $a < k < b$ unless some restriction is placed on the production functions ruling out the CES case. However, I have not constructed a meaningful example in which $J < 0$, $a < k < b$.

[10] See [4] and [7].

imply $g'(k) < 0$ *for all* $a < k < b$ and are thus overly strong. Moreover, it is often interesting to know if the model is stable when k is restricted to an interval contained in (a, b); hence the following theorem and its corollary are useful.

THEOREM 5. *Let k^* denote a root (not necessarily unique) of $g(k) = 0$. k^* is locally stable (i.e., for $k(0)$ sufficiently near to k^*, $k(t)$ will converge to k^*) if and only if there exists a deleted neighborhood of k^* for which $g'(k) < 0$. It is sufficient for the local stability of k^* that $g'(k^*) < 0$ because $g(k)$ is a continuous function.* *Assuming* $J(k^*) > 0$, let $x^* = (y_1^*, y_2^*, k_1^*, k_2^*, \omega^*, \rho^*) = \Phi(k^*)$; *if either*

(i)
$$\frac{s_w}{n} \leq \frac{k^*}{f_1(k_1^*)}$$

or

(ii)
$$\frac{s_r}{n} \geq \frac{k_1^*}{f_1(k_1^*)}$$

(= *capital-output ratio in the investment-goods sector*),

then $g'(k^*) < 0$.

PROOF.[11] It may established that $g'(k) \lesseqgtr 0$ if and only if

$$(s_w - \rho)\frac{d\omega}{dk} - s_w\frac{\omega}{k} \lesseqgtr 0\,.$$

Thus $s_w \leq \rho^*$ implies $g'(k^*) < 0$, and from $\dot{k} = h(k) = 0$, $\rho^* = nk^*/f_1(k_1^*)$. Substitution of the latter in the former gives (i). Using Ψ^3 and Ψ^6, we may derive that $s_w - \rho = [\rho k_1 - s_r k]/\omega$; thus $\rho^* k_1^* \leq s_r k^*$ implies $g'(k^*) < 0$, and substitution for ρ^* as above gives (ii). QED.

It is clear that if k^* is locally stable and if k^* is the *unique* root of $g(k) = 0$, then the model is stable even if $g'(k) > 0$ for some values of k. The following obvious corollary extends this idea.

COROLLARY. *Suppose that $J(k) > 0$ for $k \in (\underline{k}, \bar{k})$, $a < \underline{k}$ and $\bar{k} < b$, and assume that* $g(\underline{k}) > 0$ and $g(\bar{k}) < 0$. *If either*

(i)
$$\frac{s_w}{n} \leq \frac{\underline{k}}{f_1(\bar{k}_1)}$$

or

(ii)
$$\frac{s_r}{n} \geq \frac{\bar{k}_1}{f_1(\underline{k}_1)}\,,$$

then starting from any initial $k(0) \in (\underline{k}, \bar{k})$, $k(t)$ will asymptotically converge to a unique k^*, $\underline{k} < k^* < \bar{k}$.

There is good reason for confusion about exactly what sufficient stability conditions are valid for the two-sector model. For example, Drandakis writes, "Finally, in our main stability theorem we establish that if the elasticity of

[11] Professor Bardhan has observed that sufficient conditions (i) and (ii) given in Theorem 5 may both be written as $s_r k^* \geq s_w k_1^*$ and thus may be derived from condition (i) in Theorem 4. However, I believe that the way I have stated Theorem 5 is more convenient, especially if there are *a priori* restrictions on n, s_r and/or s_w.

factor substitution of *either one of the production functions* is greater than or equal to one, then the stability of the balanced growth path is obtained without regard to other conditions."[12] Likewise Takayama has stated the theorem: "If the over-all saving-income ratio is kept constant over time, then . . . there is asymptotic stability of a balanced growth path."[13]

In order to end any doubt, I have constructed a counter-example to *both* of the above assertions; in Example 2 below $\sigma_1 = 1$ and $s_r = s_w = s$, but there exists an *unstable* root to the equation $\dot{k} = h(k) = 0$. Example 1 illustrates that Theorem 5 has some content.

Example 1. Let $y_1 = k_1^{1/2}$ and $y_2 = (k_2^{-1} + 2^{-2})^{-1}$ where $\sigma_1 = 1$ and $\sigma_2 = 1/2$, and assume that $s = 2/5$ and $n = 1/3$. From Ψ^3 and Ψ^4 it is easily verified that $k_1 = \omega$ and $k_2 = 2\omega^{1/2}$, and then using Ψ^5 and Ψ^6, one may derive

$$\rho(\omega) = \frac{2 + \omega^{1/2}}{2 + 4\omega^{1/2}} \quad \text{and} \quad k(\omega) = \frac{8\omega + \omega^{3/2}}{2 + 4\omega^{1/2}} \, .$$

Thus $\dot{k} = \rho y_1 - nk = 0$ if and only if $\omega + 5\omega^{1/2} - 6 = (\omega^{1/2} - 1)(\omega^{1/2} + 6) = 0$. Since the only admissible root of the latter equation is $\omega^* = 1$, we find $k^* = 3/2$. Likewise $x^* = \Phi(k^*) = \Phi(3/2) = (1, 4/3, 1, 2, 1, 1/2)$. Both conditions (1) and (2) of Theorem 5 are satisfied since

$$\frac{k_1^*}{y_1^*} = 1 < \frac{s}{n} = \frac{6}{5} < \frac{3}{2} = \frac{k^*}{y_1^*} \, .$$

Thus the system is stable, and starting from any initial capital-labor ratio $k(0)$, $k(t)$ will asymptotically converge to the unique value $k^* = 3/2$. However, *all* of the sufficient stability conditions given in Theorem 4 are violated; in particular, note that $k_1 = \omega > 2\omega^{1/2} = k_2$ if $\omega > 4$ (i.e., for ω or k sufficiently large).

Example 2. Consider the production functions $y_i = \beta_i[k_i^{-\rho_i} + \alpha_i^{-\rho_i - 1}]^{-1/\rho_i}$ where $\sigma_i \equiv 1/(1 + \rho_i)$, $i = 1, 2$. Setting $\beta_1 = \alpha_1 = \sigma_1 = \alpha_2 = 1$, $\sigma_2 = 1/4$, and $s = n = 1/28$, we may derive, as above, that $k_1 = \omega$, $k_2 = \omega^{1/4}$, and $\dot{k} = h(k) = 0$ when

$$\omega^{5/4} - 28\omega^{3/4} + 55\omega^{2/4} - 28 = 0 \, .$$

Two roots of the latter equation are $(\omega^*, \omega^{**}) = (1, 16)$, and $\omega^* = 1$ is locally stable since it satisfies the sufficient conditions given in Theorem 5. We wish to show that there exists an unstable root. If ω^{**} is unstable (and ω^{**} does violate Theorem 5's sufficient conditions), there is nothing left to prove. Assume ω^{**} is stable with $h'[k(\omega^{**})] < 0$; then there must exist another unstable root ω^{***} with $h'[k(\omega^{***})] > 0$, $\omega^* < \omega^{***} < \omega^{**}$, since $h[k(\omega)]$ is a continuous function.

5. GLOBAL STABILITY

The model is called *globally stable* if starting from *any* initial value

[12] [5, (217)], italics added. However, the stability theorem on page 225 is correct where for $\sigma_1 \geq 1$, s_r must be sufficiently near one or s_w must be sufficiently near zero.

[13] [12, (100)]. I recently learned that Takayama has acknowledged his error in a footnote to a subsequent article (see [13, (253, footnote 3)]).

$k(0) \in (a, b)$, $k(t)$ asymtotically approaches *some* constant value $k^*, k^{**}, \cdots, k^{*\cdots*}$. *If* the system is causal, we can write

$$\frac{\dot{k}}{k} = g(k) \qquad \text{for } 0 \leq a < k < b \leq \infty ,$$

where $g(k)$ is a continuous function. Now if $\lim_{k \to a} g(k) > 0$ and $\lim_{k \to b} g(k) < 0$, there must exist *at least one* root k^* such that $g(k^*) = 0$, $g'(k^*) < 0$, and $a < k^* < b$. If we assume the Inada conditons [7] that $f_i'(k_i) > 0$, $f_i''(k_i) < 0$, $0 < k_i < \infty$, and $f_i'(0) = \infty$, $f_i'(\infty) = 0$, $i = 1, 2$, then it is easily shown that the indicated limits on $g(k)$ are valid where $a = 0$ and $b = \infty$.[14] Thus the Inada conditions *and* causality imply that the model is globally stable for all $0 < s_r$, $s_w < 1$ and for all $n > 0$. Example 2 in the previous section clearly illustrates that the Inada conditions are not necessary for global stability.[15]

6. HARROD-NEUTRAL TECHNICAL PROGRESS

The results of this paper can be extended to the case in which there is purely labor augmenting or Harrod-neutral technical progress present in each sector. We then write $Y_i = F_i(K_i, l_i)$ where the labor-efficiency units l_i are defined by $l_i = L_i e^{g_i t}$ and g_i is the rate of technical progress in the i-th sector, $i = 1, 2$; we will assume $g_1 = g_2 = g$. New variables are now defined in terms of *labor-efficiency* units, i.e., $\tilde{k}_i \equiv K_i/l_i$, $\tilde{y}_i \equiv Y_i/l_i$, $\tilde{\omega} = \omega e^{-gt}$, $\tilde{\rho} \equiv l_i/l$, and $\tilde{k} \equiv K/l = (K_1 + K_2)/(l_1 + l_2)$. As $t \to \infty$, $\tilde{y}_i \to \tilde{y}_i^*$, $\tilde{k}_i \to \tilde{k}_i^*$, $\tilde{\rho} \to \tilde{\rho}^*$, etc., *if the system is stable*. Therefore, the output-capital ratios are *constants* given by

$$\frac{Y_i}{K_i} = \frac{Y_i/l_i}{K_i/l_i} = \frac{\tilde{y}_i^*}{\tilde{k}_i^*} , \qquad i = 1, 2 .$$

The *real* capital-labor ratio is given by

$$\frac{K}{L}(t) = \tilde{k}^* e^{gt} .$$

Similarly, *real* per capita output in each sector grows according to

$$\frac{(\dot{Y_i/L})}{Y_i/L} = \frac{\dot{Y}_i}{Y_i} - \frac{\dot{L}}{L} = (g + \lambda) - \lambda = g , \qquad i = 1, 2 .$$

University of Pennsylvania, U. S. A.

REFERENCES

[1] AMANO, AKIHIRO, "A Further Note on Professor Uzawa's Two-Sector Model of Economic Growth," *Review of Economic Studies*, XXXI (April, 1964), 97-102.

[2] APOSTOL, TOM M., *Mathematical Analysis* (Reading, Massachusetts: Addison-Wesley Publishing Company, 1957).

[3] ARROW, K. J., H. B. CHENERY, B. S. MINHAS and R. M. SOLOW, "Capital-Labor Substitution and Economic Efficiency," *The Review of Economics and Statistics*, XLIII (August, 1961), 225-50.

[14] See, e.g., [5] and [15].

[15] Obviously, however, the system must be causal at least in a neighborhood of every root k^* if there is global stability.

[4] BURMEISTER, EDWIN, "Stability and Causality in Two-Sector Models of Economic Growth," Massachusetts Institute of Technology Ph.D. thesis (May, 1965).
[5] DRANDAKIS, EMANUEL M., "Factor Substitution in the Two-Sector Growth Model," *Review of Economic Studies*, XXX (October, 1963), 217-28.
[6] HAHN, F. H., "On Two-Sector Growth Models," *Review of Economic Studies*, XXXII (October, 1965), 339-46.
[7] INADA, KEN-ICHI, "On a Two-Sector Model of Economic Growth: Comments and a Generalization," *Review of Economic Studies*, XXX (June, 1963), 119-27.
[8] ———, "On the Stability of Growth Equilibria in Two-Sector Models," *Review of Economic Studies*, XXXI (April, 1964), 127-42.
[9] KURZ, M., "A Two-Sector Extension of Swan's Model of Economic Growth," *International Economic Review*, IV (January, 1963), 68-79.
[10] SAMUELSON, PAUL A., "The Canonical Model of Capital," unpublished.
[11] SOLOW, ROBERT M., "Note on Uzawa's Two-Sector Model of Economic Growth," *Review of Economic Studies*, XXIX (October, 1961), 48-50.
[12] TAKAYAMA, AKIRA, "On a Two-Sector Model of Economic Growth: A Comparative Statics Analysis," *Review of Economic Studies*, XXX (June, 1963), 95-104.
[13] ———, "On a Two-Sector Model of Economic Growth with Technological Progress," *Review of Economic Studies*, XXXII (July, 1965), 251-262.
[14] UZAWA, HIROFUMI, "On a Two-Sector Model of Economic Growth," *Review of Economic Studies*, XXIX (October, 1961), 40-47.
[15] ———, "On a Two-Sector Model of Economic Growth: II," *Review of Economic Studies*, XXX (June, 1963), 105-18.

[8]

EQUILIBRIUM DYNAMICS WITH HETEROGENEOUS CAPITAL GOODS *

F. H. HAHN

INTRODUCTION

It is now almost ten years since Solow [1] showed that in a one-good world with a "well-behaved" neoclassical production function, all full employment equilibrium paths approach the steady state path. An equilibrium path is one where at all times there is no *ex-ante* excess demand in the markets for goods and factors and where producers have at all times that combination of inputs which they would wish to have at the going prices. Indeed, it is what Harrod called a "warranted" path. The possibility of factor substitution means that there is a variety of warranted paths depending on initial conditions and Solow showed that all such paths would, under suitable assumptions, approach a particular one.

Solow's work was soon extended to an economy producing one capital, and one consumption good.[2] Once again, for all cases where the initial conditions defined a unique path and where production functions were "well behaved" it could be shown that all equilibrium paths would converge to one particular such path (the "golden age" path).

It is widely believed that these results are crucially related to the postulate that factor proportions are variable. No doubt in the context of these models this is so. But it would appear that the assumption that there is only one single capital good is of equal importance. Indeed, it is the purpose of this paper to show that the "Solowesque" results for equilibrium paths do not extend to a world with heterogeneous capital goods. I postpone until the end of the exercise a more general discussion of why this should be the case.

* I am much indebted to discussions with Professors Meade and Solow and with Dr. J. A. Mirrlees. They cleared away cobwebs and nonsense. They are not responsible for what remains.

1. R. M. Solow, "A Contribution to the Theory of Economic Growth," this *Journal*, LXX (Feb. 1956).

2. F. H. Hahn and R. C. O. Matthews, "The Theory of Economic Growth — A Survey," *Economic Journal*, LXXIV (Dec. 1964).

The Assumption

A.1: There is one consumption good and there are m different kinds of capital goods.

A.2: The production functions everywhere are Cobb-Douglas. No output of any good is possible without the input of some labor and the input of at least one capital good. Every capital good is used in at least one industry and there is no joint production.

A.3: Capital lasts forever and there are no intermediate goods.

A.4: The labor force grows at a constant proportionate rate n.

A.5: Workers do not save; capitalists do not consume.

Some of these assumptions are stronger than strictly required. Thus if there is more than one consumption good but the proportion of wage income spent on each is constant the story would not be much changed. Again A.3 could be replaced by the supposition of "radio-active" decay and A.4 by the postulate of uniform "Harrod-neutral" technical change everywhere. But not much would be gained and some simplicity lost.

A.2 has been introduced for two reasons. Firstly, the Cobb-Douglas production function is a "well-behaved" neoclassical function and it allows substitution between all finite levels of input, and since we wish to concentrate on the consequences of heterogeneity of capital goods, these are desirable properties. Secondly, although the differential equations we shall have to consider are by no means simple, they are a great deal simpler than they would have been for a less special class of production function. Moreover it is my strong impression that nothing of what follows is crucially dependent on the special form of production function chosen and should carry over to other "well-behaved" functions.

Notation

We shall give the consumption good the subscript 0 and let $i = 1 \ldots m$ be the subscripts of the capital goods. A Latin symbol without a subscript always denotes an m-vector with components whose subscripts run from 1 to m. We take the wage as identically equal to unity, (labor is the *numéraire*) and we write P_i as the *supply* price of the ith good in terms of labor and Q_i as the *demand* price of the ith good in terms of labor. R_i will be the rate of profit on the ith capital good.

One defines Y_i as the output *per man* employed in the ith industry and K_{ij} as the amount of the jth capital good used in the ith industry *per worker* employed there. Also K_i is the total amount of the ith kind of capital divided by the total labor force, while L_i is the *proportion* of the labor force employed in the ith industry.

We adopt the following conventions:

(a) Small letters denote the log of capital letters; e.g., $p_i = \log P_i$; $p = \{\log P_1 \ldots \log P_m\}$.

(b) All summation are over $i = 1 \ldots m$ or $j = 1 \ldots m$.

(c) A dot over a symbol denotes the operation d/dt.

Other notation will be introduced as required.

The Model

In the notation just introduced, A.2 is formulated as:

(1) $$y_i = \sum_j a_{ij} k_{ij} \qquad i = 0 \ldots m,\ a_{ij} \geqq 0 \text{ all } j$$

$$a_{ij} > 0 \text{ some } j,\ \sum_j a_{ij} + a_{i0} = 1.$$

Suppose that inputs are bought at the "demand" price Q. Then cost minimization gives for $P_i > 0$, $Q_i > 0$,

(2) $$p_i + y_i = \text{constant } i = 0 \ldots m$$

(3) $$k_{ij} + r_j + q_j = \text{constant } i = 0 \ldots m,\ j = 1 \ldots m.$$

Here (2) and (3) are the usual marginal product-reward relationships for a Cobb-Douglas world. Substituting for k_{ij} in (1) from (3) and the result into (2) gives

(4) $$p_i - \sum_j a_{ij}\, q_j - \sum_j a_{ij}\, r_j = \text{constant} \qquad i = 0 \ldots m.$$

The last m equations of (4) may be written more compactly. Let $e_i + q_i = p_i$ and let $e = \{e_1 \ldots e_m\}$. Then if A is the $(m \times m)$ matrix (a_{ij}) we obtain

(5) $$e + (I - A)q - Ar = \text{vector of constant, say } b.$$

If a good is to be newly produced, then its supply price cannot be more than its demand price. Indeed, because of perfect competition considerations we shall require $e_i = 0$ when $L_i > 0$ and $e_i > 0$ if and only if $L_i = 0$. That is we shall require

(6) $$e_i L_i = 0,\ e_i \geqq 0 \qquad i = 1 \ldots m).$$

Since, (as we shall see), $L_0 > 0$ always, we also require

(7) $$P_0 = Q_0.$$

We now turn to the market for goods. The markets for capital goods are cleared when

$$K_i = \sum_j K_{ji}\, L_j + K_{0i}\, L_0 \qquad i = 1 \ldots m.$$

Multiplying both sides by $R_i\, Q_i$ this becomes:

(8) $R_i Q_i K_i = \sum_j c_{ji} L_j + c_{0i} L_0 \qquad i = 1 \ldots m$

where

$$c_{ji} = R_i Q_i K_{ji} = \frac{a_{ji}}{a_{j0}}.$$

The labor market is cleared when

(9) $\sum_j L_j + L_0 = 1.$

Lastly the market for consumption goods is cleared when

(10) $L_0 = a_{00}.$

This last equation follows from A.6 whereby the proportion of labor employed in the consumption goods industry is equal to labor's share in that industry which by A.2 is constant.

If we consider equation (4) with $i = 0$, and then the equations (5), (6), (7), (8), (9) and (10) we find that we have $3(m + 1) + 1$ relationships. Our unknowns are $q, e, r, L, L_0, p_0, q_0$ i.e., there are $4(m + 1) - 1$ of these. Hence we have $(m - 1)$ degrees of freedom. This is just as it should be since precisely $(m - 1)$ demand conditions have remained unspecified by our savings assumption.

Now the rate of return on holding the ith capital good is given by

$$R_i + \dot{q}_i \qquad i = 1 \ldots m.$$

In a world of perfect competition which is also in equilibrium individuals must be indifferent between the various capital goods they hold and so one has:

(11) $R_1 + \dot{q}_1 = R_2 + \dot{q}_2 = \ldots R_m + q_m = \mu$ (say)

or

$$R_i = \mu - \dot{q}_i \qquad i = 1 \ldots m.$$

Here q_i, etc., must be interpreted as the expected rate of change in the ith price. However, when attention is focused on equilibrium paths; expected and actual prices coincide. The model will tell us at a moment of time $t = 0$ that given, say the expectations: $(\dot{q}_i - \dot{q}_m)$, $i = 1 \ldots m - 1$, what the capital/labor ratios in various activities must be in order that for all newly produced goods production costs be covered and also for (11) to be satisfied. However, once initial expectations have been specified, since they must be fulfilled, the development of the system through time should also be determined.

This will become clearer when the main equations have been cast into recursive form. Here we simply note that when the story starts we are given no information as to the distribution of investment between the various capital assets. If such information were to be provided by, say, the introduction of suitable investment demand functions, then this would "close" the system, but by the same token it would determine what price expectations would have to be.

Balanced Growth

We consider a path for which (a) $e = 0$ all t, i.e., $P_i = Q_i$ all i; (b) $\dot{p} = 0, \dot{p}_0 = 0$, and (c) $\dot{K} = 0$. We call this the balanced growth path.

From (11) one has $R_1 = R_2 = \ldots = R_m$ along such a path. By A.6 the common rate of profit is equal to n, the rate of population growth. Let r^* be a vector with all components equal to log n. Then we solve

(5′) $\quad (I = A)\, p^* - A\, r^* = b$

for the prices ruling on a balanced growth path. Since the matrix A satisfies the Hawkins-Simon condition[3] by A.2, $(I - A)^{-1}$ exists and is a positive matrix. The typical component of the vector of constants on the right-hand side of 5′ is easily found to be

$$= \sum_j a_{ij} \log a_{ij} - a_{i0} \log a_{i0}\,.$$

On solving we find that the system determines a unique strictly positive P^*. Substituting this and r^* in the equation $i = 0$ of (4) we solve for $P^*_0 > 0$.

Next we note that

$$L_j / a_{j0} = L_j P_j Y_j \quad j = 1 \ldots m\,.$$

So that (8), in view of the definition of c_{ji} may also be written

(8′) $\quad R_i P_i K_i = \sum_j a_{ji} L_j P_j Y_j + c_{0i} L_0\, i = 1 \ldots m\,.$

But on any equilibrium path one has

$$L_j P_j Y_j = P_j (\dot{K}_j + n K_j) \qquad j = 1 \ldots m.$$

Substituting this into (8′) and using (10) one has

(8″) $\quad R_i P_i K_i = \sum_j a_{ji} P_j (\dot{K}_j + n K_j) + c_{0i}\, a_{00},\, i = 1 \ldots m.$

On a balanced growth path $R_i = n$ all i and $\dot{K}_j = 0$ all j. Using this and the P^* already solved for, (8″) can be used to find K^*, the vector of balanced growth capital/labor ratios. In matrix notation this is found from:

$$\{P^*_i K^*_i\} = \frac{1}{n} (I - A')_o^{-1}$$

where the left-hand side is the vector with components $P^*_i K^*_i$ and

3. Hahn and Matthews, *op. cit.*

c is the vector with components $c_{0i}\, a_{00}$. Since c is semipositive, $(I - A')^{-1}$ is a positive matrix, and $P_i^* > 0$, we find $K_i^* > 0$ all i.

That the balanced growth path is unique seems self-evident. In particular there cannot be another path in which some of the capital goods are not produced. For suppose the rth kind of capital not to be produced. Then if it is used in the production of, say, the sth kind which is produced, the marginal product of the rth kind of capital in the production of the sth would tend to infinity which is impossible. But if the sth kind of capital is not produced then a similar argument applies to say the tth kind, into the production of which s enters. Proceeding in this way and recalling that the production of the consumption good requires some kind of capital, we easily see that all types of capital goods must be produced on a balanced growth path.

Momentary Equilibrium

We consider a moment $t = 0$ with an arbitrarily given capital/labor ratio vector $K(0)$. We wish to examine the equilibrium at this moment of time. To do so, we already know that $(m - 1)$ unknowns of the model must be arbitrarily specified. Let us do so by fixing:

$$R_i(0) - R_m(0) \; i = 1 \ldots m - 1, R_i > 0 \text{ all } i,$$
$$R_m(0) \leqq R_i(0) \text{ all } i.$$

This then is equivalent to supposing that at $t = 0$ there are given certain expectations of changes in the relative prices of capital goods. The first question we consider is the existence of an equilibrium at $t = 0$.

Although it is tiresome, it will be convenient and necessary to have further notation. We shall write $\hat{R}(0)$ for the $(m - 1)$ vector with components $(R_i(0) - R_m(0))$ and we write $V_i \equiv R_i Q_i, v = \{v_1 \ldots v_m\}$. One also defines the set S by

$$S = \{L/L_i \geqq 0, \Sigma L_i = 1 - a_{00}\}$$

and C as the $m \times m$ matrix $[c_{ji}]$ and c as the m – vector: $\{c_{01} \ldots c_{0m}\}\, a_{00}$. We continue to use small letters to denote the log of capital letters.

For what follows we shall now suppose that c is a strictly positive vector. This, of course, means that the consumption good sector uses every capital good in its production. This is less restrictive than appears at first sight since we can think of the consumption good as a composite good in which the various individual goods are in fixed proportions.

The argument establishing the existence of momentary equilibrium now proceeds by stages. Since $\hat{R}(0)$ and $K(0) > 0$ are constant, they will be omitted as arguments from functions which depend on them.

(a) Combining (8) and (10) yields:

(12) $\{V_i K_i(0)\} = CL + c.$

Evidently for every $L \epsilon S$ there exist values of V_i, call them $V_i(L)$ such that (12) is satisfied and $V(L) > 0$ since $c > 0$.

(b) We may write (5) as

(5″) $a + q - Av(L) = b$

where V takes the value determined by (a). For L fixed, $V(L)$ is fixed. Since $\hat{R}(0)$ is given, knowledge of R_m determines $R_1 \ldots R_{m-1}$. From the definition of $V(L)$, knowledge of R_m gives Q. Hence we may write:

(13) $Q = Q(R_m, L).$

Since $R_i > 0$ all i, $V(L) > 0, Q > 0$ and is strictly diminishing in R_m. We may now write (5″) as

(14) $a(R_m, L) + q(R_m, L) - Av(L) = b.$

By the above argument e is strictly increasing in R_m.

(c) Consider the function

(15) $F_i(L_i, R_m) = \max(0, L_i + (1 - E_i(R_m, L)))$

(where, of course, $\log E_i = e_i$). Clearly $F_i \geqq 0$ all i. We wish to confirm that for some value of R_m one has $F(L, R_m) \epsilon S$, i.e.,

$$\sum_i F_i(R_m, L_i) = 1 - a_{00}.$$

By our choice of R_m such that $\hat{R}_i \geqq 0$ all i we may let $R_m \to 0$. But then $Q_m(R_m, L) \to +\infty$ and so by (14) $E_m(R_m, L) \to 0$. But then certainly there is some value of R_m small enough[4] so that $\sum F_i(L_i, R_m) > 1 - a_{00}$ On the other hand, as $R_m \to \infty$, $Q_i(R_m, L) \to 0$ all i and by the same argument as before, $E_i(R_m, L) \to +\infty$. Hence for some R_m large enough:

(16) $\sum_i F_i(L_i, R_m) < 1 - a_{00}.$

Since E is monotonic in R_m we know that there is only one value of R_m satisfying (16). Since $V(L)$ is evidently continuous in L and Q is continuous in R_m, one has $R_m(L)$ continuous in L.

(d) Consider now the mapping

(17) $f_i(L) =$

$$\max(0, L_i + (1 - E_i(R_m(L), L), L)) i = 1 \ldots m.$$

Then, by construction, $L \epsilon S$, implies $f(L) \epsilon S$. Thus (17) is a continuous map of S into itself and so there is a fixed point L^* such that

$$L^*_i = \max(0, L^*_i + (1 - E_i(R_m(L^*), L^*)) i = 1 \ldots m.$$

4. Since then $F_m(\;) \to L_m + 1$ and all $F_i(\;) > 0$.

If $L^*_i > 0$ then it must be that $E_i = 1$ (and so $Q^*_i = P^*_i$).
If $L^*_i = 0$ then it must be that $E_i > 1$ (and so $Q^*_i < P^*_i$).

All this is just as it should be to satisfy (5) and (6). By inserting Q^*, r^*, into the equation $i = 0$ in (4) we obtain $P^*_0 > 0$, the price of the consumption good. Thus on our assumptions a momentary equilibrium does indeed exist.

Now let us suppose (we return to the point shortly) that the equilibrium for $K(0)$, $\hat{R}(0)$ is unique at $t = 0$, and let us consider the system at a very short interval after $t = 0$, i.e., at $t = 0 + \epsilon$.

From (11) we know that the equilibrium of $t = 0$ has determined $\dot{q}_i(0) - \dot{q}_m(0)$, $(i = 1 \ldots m - 1)$, and since expectations are to be correct, this means that $q_i(0 + \epsilon) - q_m(0 + \epsilon)$, $(i = 1 \ldots m - 1)$, are also fully determined. Moreover, since the equilibrium at $t = 0$ determined $\dot{K}_i(0)$ $(i = 1 \ldots m)$, we also know $K_i(0 + \epsilon)$, $i = 1 \ldots m$. It follows that at $t = 0 + \epsilon$ we have lost the $(m - 1)$ degrees of freedom we had at $t = 0$. We conclude that once the expectations at $t = 0$ are known, and provided equilibrium is unique at every moment of time, the whole subsequent development of the system is known.

Quite clearly the uniqueness assumption is crucial here (as indeed it was found to be in the "two-sector" models). Unfortunately there seems to be no simple economically meaningful or appealing restriction available to ensure that the initial conditions determine a unique path.

For instance, suppose $K(0)$, $\hat{R}(0)$ to be such as to yield one momentary equilibrium with L^* strictly positive (all goods are newly produced). The question asked may now be: does there exist some other equilibrium L^{**} where once again all goods are newly produced? Since we are only interested in situations where $Q_i = P_i$ all i, one has $e = 0$ in (5) and each $R_i Q_i K_i$ may be written as a function of R_m, say $\pi_i(R_m)$, since (5) determines Q as a function of R_m. We may then write (12) as

(12′) $\pi_i(R_m) - C\,L = c.$

Moreover, we are only interested in situations for which

(18) $\Sigma L_i = 1 - a_{00}.$

We are told that (12′) and (18) have at least one solution R^*_m and $L^* >> 0$. The question of whether this type of solution is unique turns then on the global properties of the Jacobian

(19) $$\begin{bmatrix} \left\{ \dfrac{\partial \pi_i(R_m)}{\partial R_m} \right\} & -C \\ 0 & i' \end{bmatrix}$$

where $\left\{ \frac{\partial \pi_i}{\partial R_m} \right\}$ is an m vector and i' the unit row vector. It is known for instance that if the principal minors of (19) are all one-signed over a given domain then the solution over a specified range will also be unique. Inspection of (19) quickly convinces one that there just are no simple or appealing assumptions to make on C and the functions $\pi_i(\ )$ to ensure this result. Since only (rather strong) sufficient conditions for uniqueness (univalence), are available, nothing much further can be said. However, it should be noted that one may readily construct theoretical examples of the model here presented, where equilibrium is definitely not unique.

In the "two-sector" story (i.e., $m = 1$), since the savings assumption fixes L_0, (18) means that L_1 is also fixed, and it is then easy to see that the system would have only one solution. Here, however, there is always the possibility of a reallocation of production between the various capital goods so that multiple equilibria cannot be excluded. Moreover, of course, we may have to take account of situations where equilibrium gives $L_i = 0$ for some i, so that the equilibrium price of that good is not equal to its unit cost of production.

Since there may be a number of equilibrium solutions one cannot predict future events from initial conditions and given expectations. But we shall now simplify sufficiently drastically to remove this difficulty and show that we are even then not much better off.

Two Capital Goods

We shall now suppose there to be two capital goods only and we shall introduce an assumption which allows us to suppose for $0 \leqq t \leqq T$, a unique momentary equilibrium in which both capital goods are newly produced.

From (12′) we have:

(12″) $CL = \{\pi_i (R_m) - c_i\}$

where it will be recalled that $\pi_i (R_m) = V_i K_i$ on the supposition that the price of i just covers its unit costs and $R(0)$, $K(0)$ are given. It is easily verified that $\pi_i (R_m)$ is strictly increasing in R_m and so we may always find R_m such as to give $\pi_i (R_m) > c_i$ $(i = 1, 2)$.

Now if (12″) has a solution with $L >> 0$ and $\Sigma L_i = 1 - a_{00}$ and if we suppose $\frac{c_{ii}}{c_{ji}} < 1$, $(i = 1, 2)$, then in view of the monotonicity of π_i in R_m, that solution must be unique. For if both R^*_m and R^{**} are equilibria with, say, $R^{**}_m > R^*_m$ then $\pi_i(R^{**}_m) -$

$c_i > \pi_i (R^*_m) - c_i$ $(i = 1, 2)$ and we easily find that on this assumption

$$C(L^{**} - L^*) > > 0$$
$$i'(L^{**} - L^*) = 0$$

has no solution.

We therefore stipulate:

A.6 There are only two capital goods ($m = 2$). Each of these two capital goods industries always uses the output of the other more intensively than it does its own. Moreover $K(0) > > 0$ and $\hat{R}(0)$ are such as to allow our equilibrium with $L > > 0$ at $t = 0$.

Occasionally we shall wish to vary the first part of A.6 to read:

A.7: The elasticity of production of each capital good with respect to an input of itself is less than the elasticities with respect to the input of the other capital good.

Neither of these assumptions are particularly "reasonable" or the reverse. They are made to permit us to continue the story which in any case is coming to a sad end.

We are now supposing that the initial conditions and price expectations allow us to determine a unique equilibrium path for $0 \leqq t \leqq T$ where the prices of capital goods continuously cover unit production costs. To see what happens let us differentiate (5), with $e = 0$, with respect to t to obtain:

$$A^{-1}(I - A)\,\dot{p} = \dot{r}. \tag{20}$$

Let the left-hand matrix be written as G having elements g_{ij}. Routine calculations give

$$g_{11} - g_{21} = \frac{1 - a_{20}}{/A/} - 1$$

$$g_{12} - g_{22} = \frac{a_{10-1}}{/A/} + 1\,.$$

Suppose for a moment that $a_{10} = a_{20}$, so that A.6 implies A.6′. Then in subtracting the second from the first equation in (20) we obtain

$$\left(\frac{1 - a_{20}}{/A/} - 1\right)(\dot{p}_1 - \dot{p}_2) = \dot{r}_1 - \dot{r}_2\,.$$

Or using (11):

$$\left(1 + \frac{a_{20-1}}{/A/}\right)(R_1 - R_2) = \dot{r}_1 - \dot{r}_2\,. \tag{21}$$

Let us call the coefficient of $(R_1 = R_2)$, h and note that $h > 0$ since certainly $a_{20} < 1$ and $/A/ < 0$ by A.6.

Now consider the expression:

$$W = 1/2\,({}^{R_1}/_{R_2} - 1)^2 \qquad R_1 > 0, R_2 > 0.$$

Evidently $W > 0$ for all $R_1 \neq R_2$. Certainly also in the vicinity of a balanced growth path we may take $R_1 > 0, R_2 > 0$. Using (21) we find

(22) $\dot{W} = (R_1/R_2 - 1)h\,R_1/R_2(R_1 - R_2) > 0$ for $R_1 \neq R_2$.

It follows that if the two rates of profit diverge at $t = 0$ and both goods continue to be produced, then they cannot come together again and the balanced growth path will not be attained, nor can it be approached asymptotically.

Similar conclusions can be derived from rather less special examples. By suitable manipulations we may cast (20) into the following form:

(23) $R_1 - R_2 = f_1\dot{r}_1 - f_2\dot{r}_2$

where taking $f = \dfrac{|1 - A|}{|A|}$ one defines

$$f_1 = -\frac{1}{f}\left(\frac{a_{11} - a_{21}}{/A/} - 1\right)$$

$$f_2 = -\frac{1}{f}\left(\frac{a_{22} - a_{12}}{/A/} - 1\right).$$

Given A.6′ one has $-^1/f > 0$. The first term in brackets is also positive and if a_{11} is small we may take the whole expression as positive which we proceed to do.

Suppose $f_1 \leqq f_2$. Then $R_1^{f_1} > R_2^{f_2}$ implies $R_1 > R_2$. If $R_1^{f_1}(0) \geqq R_2^{f_2}(0)$, it then follows from (23) that $\dfrac{R_1^{f_1}}{R_2^{f_2}}$ is increasing, and so the two rates of profits continue to diverge. Suppose $f_1 > f_2$. Then $R_1^{f_1}(0) < R_2^{f_2}(0)$ implies $R_1(0) < R_2(0)$ and again by (23) the two rates of profit will continue to diverge. We conclude that, as in the more special case, there is a wide class of initial conditions for which, on the supposition that we may determine prices by unit production costs, the system does not approach a balanced state.

Lastly let us consider what happens if at some $t = T$ one or the other of the capital goods ceases to be produced and its unit production costs exceeds its market (demand) price.

Let us now use $V_i = R_i Q_i$ and suppose $L_2(T) = 0$ (henceforth we omit time subscripts). Then evidently (8, 9 and 10) determine V_1 and V_2. Moreover, as long as L_2 remains zero it must be true that

$$V_i K_i = \text{constant } i = 1; 2.$$

But since the second good is not produced, we have $\dot{k}_1 = -n$ and so

(24) $\dot{v}_2 + \dot{k}_2 = \dot{v}_2 - n = 0\,.$

So the rental-wage ratio of the nonproduced good must be rising. Subtracting (24) from $\dot{v}_1 + \dot{k}_1 = 0$, and noting that $\dot{k}_1 + n > 0$, since the first good is produced, we have using (11)

(25) $\dot{v}_1 - \dot{v}_2 + \dot{k}_1 + n = 0$

or $$\begin{aligned}\dot{v}_1 - \dot{v}_2 &= (\dot{r}_1 - \dot{r}_2) + (\dot{p} - \dot{q}_2)\\ &= (\dot{r}_1 - \dot{r}_2) - (R_1 - R_2) < 0\,.\end{aligned}$$

Now it follows from (25) that if $R_1(T) < R_2(T)$ and $f_1 > f_2$ then the rates of profit will continue to diverge even when the second good is no longer being produced. There is nothing in the story to prevent $L_2\,(T) = 0$ being a solution for $R_2(T) > R_1(T)$. For instance suppose $a_{ii} = 0$ $(i = 1.2)$. Then A.6 and A.6′ certainly hold. One has $a_{12} > g_{21}$ when $f_1 > f_2$. The rate of change of production costs is given by

(26) $\dot{p}_i(T) = a_{ij}\,\dot{v}_j \qquad i = 1, 2, j \neq i\,.$

Evidently $\dot{p}_1(T) - \dot{p}_2(T) > 0$, since $\dot{v}_2 - \dot{v}_1 > 0$. At the point of time at which the second good ceases to be produced $P_2(T) = Q_2(T)$, and if thereafter the production cost exceeds the demand price, $\dot{P}_2(T) > \dot{Q}_2(T)$ so $\dot{p}_1(T) - \dot{q}_2(T)$ certainly > 0 and $R_1(T) - R_2(T) < 0$.

If at (T) the first good ceases to be produced then if $R_1(T) > R_2(T)$, the reader can verify that the same unpleasant conclusions emerge for $f_1 < f_2$.

In contrast to the two-sector case, (one consumption and one capital good), one must therefore conclude that not all equilibrium paths, where they exist, approach a balanced growth path. Indeed many behave in a way which puts considerable strain on one's credulity and raises considerable doubts concerning the model.

Some Comments

It is time to take stock and to interpret the results. There are two main conclusions to be considered. First, in the case of heterogeneous capital goods the problem of the nonuniqueness of momentary equilibrium is much more acute than in the two-sector case. Even when the initial expectations are given the system may pursue a variety of equilibrium paths. Second, even when (in the two-capital case) a single equilibrium path is found, there is a wide class of initial conditions and values of the parameters for which such equilibrium paths do not approach the balanced growth path.

The first conclusion is largely ascribable to the fact that neoclassical growth models do not incorporate any explicit investment functions. The condition that the holding of all assets should be equally profitable (11) does not determine how much of each asset should be produced. It is thus possible that a given volume of savings may find a widely different allocation between the different kinds of investment at different price constellations, which are compatible with equilibrium. When there is only one capital good and we are concerned with full employment equilibrium paths an investment function is not only unnecessary but may actually prevent the system having a solution. The question asked is: what must investment be in order to take up full employment savings; having found it, since there is only the asset to hold, we may presume that that amount of investment will take place. With two capital goods this procedure is evidently not possible.

However, it is not clear how "investment functions" can be grafted on to the model. The world considered is one of perfect competition, so that individual producers have no "volume of demand for their product" to estimate, on which to base their investment decisions. At the same time households, providing only the rate of return of holding any asset is that of any other, must be regarded as indifferent whether their savings are invested in one or the other direction. Having stated this we have also already provided sufficient reason for regarding the neoclassical equilibrium path as not very interesting as a description of the world and it does not seem worthwhile pursuing the story much further.

On the other hand, if we consider an economy which is planned,[5] then many of these difficulties would disappear — and we return to this point presently.

The second of our conclusions is essentially ascribable to the fact that an equilibrium with heterogeneous capital goods is not specified for any moment of time unless it also includes expectations as the relative capital goods prices at a subsequent moment of time. Given an investment allocation we can find a set of expectations which must rule if equilibrium is to be possible. Alternatively given the expectations we can find a set of consistent investment allocations. The fact that the description of the present involves the future

5. See P. A. Samuelson, "Efficient Paths of Capital Accumulation in Terms of the Calculus of Variations," *Mathematical Methods in the Social Sciences*, 1959, Symposium, Stanford University (Stanford: Stanford University Press, 1960). Here it is shown that the balanced growth path is a local saddle-point (in phase space) for all finite horizon efficient paths. Evidently this result is closely related to the one of the previous section — but the problem is different.

in an essential way must bear the responsibility for the unsatisfactory behavior of the equilibrium path. For if expectations should turn out to be correct then this requirement by itself to a large extent determines the subsequent evolution of the system. But, not surprisingly, there is only a restricted set of expectations for every given situation which are consistent with an evolution of the system towards the balanced growth path. Once again the supposition that expectations are not only correct but consequently that they are identical for all economic agents is a hard postulate to swallow, and undoubtedly makes equilibrium dynamics less attractive once we admit that there are hoes as well as shovels.

There remains an alternative interpretation, used by Meade in the two-sector case, of equilibrium paths. On this interpretation the government somehow ensures that the economy always follows a full employment path with planned savings equal to planned investment. In the two-sector case this is not entirely unacceptable; in our case we must evidently suppose the government to be involved in far greater detail in the economy. In particular if the government were to enforce any particular, detailed, accumulation plan which is also "efficient," then associated with such a plan will be a set of shadow prices (including their rate of change), which will satisfy the relationships of our model. If the efficient plan is one for which the balanced growth path is approached, then one particular equilibrium path out of a large number of possible ones has been chosen. This, however, is quite another story.

Churchill College
Cambridge University

[9]

Chapter 6 Money and Economic Growth

Excerpt from E. Burmeister and A.R. Dobell, *Mathematical Theories of Economic Growth*

6–1. Introduction

Thus far our study of economic growth has been based upon models in which only actual flows of goods and actual stocks of a single capital good have appeared. Yet, much theorizing about economic issues focuses on the fact that in modern economies there exist financial assets, paper claims that offer alternative forms in which to hold wealth. Indeed, it might be argued that all of the central Keynesian problems of deficient aggregate demand and unemployment have relevance only to an economy in which there exists a money supply whose value can be augmented without giving rise to employment. In this chapter we will continue to avoid the problems of capacity utilization and unemployment by continuing to assume that there are no independently determined investment desires, but rather that all saving plans are realized. We shall, however, introduce some of the features of a monetary economy by assuming the presence of a paper currency in addition to a single capital good. Such a model was introduced by Tobin [21, 22].

One feature of the resulting model is that wealth may be held in alternative forms, so that some specification of portfolio behavior is necessary. Further, the production side of the model is taken to be identical to the one-sector models discussed in Chapter 2, in that the capital good combines with labor to produce a homogeneous output that can be used either for consumption or for gross capital formation.

On the other hand, it should be emphasized that the following model omits a number of features that probably would be of real importance in a monetary economy—disequilibrium phenomena involving unemployment, short-run adjustments of asset prices to equilibrium levels, and requirements for financing temporary shortfalls in liquid balances due to timing of transactions are all among the possible examples. Explicit treatment of portfolio demands for money requires consideration of the problems of risk and uncertainty.

Incorporating such considerations, however, necessitates paying attention to the institutional peculiarities of the economic community and the special characteristics of financial markets. In particular, a realistic treatment is impossible without the recognition of other financial assets that differ in liquidity from money, e.g., time deposits and bonds.

We cannot aspire to this degree of realism for present objectives, but rather limit ourselves to the fairly abstract issues arising from use of a nonproduced paper asset in the system. This asset, termed money, is issued costlessly by the government. It serves as *numeraire* and is desired for both transactions and investment purposes.

It should be noted that our analysis is based on a differential equation structure. We take a price level and capital stock to be given by the past. Then all that we may choose is the rate of change of the price level and of the capital stock, and we choose these so as to satisfy a money market equilibrium condition and a saving hypothesis. These choices determine the new values of the price level and the capital stock for the "next instant," and the process is repeated.

Our procedure thus appears to say nothing directly about the level of prices, as opposed to the rate of price inflation. It is therefore in marked contrast to the usual theorizing about money market equilibrium that purports to determine the equilibrium price level. But we must remember that this traditional theorizing is based on comparative statics, and it corresponds to a comparison of different stationary solutions to our differential equation system (possibly with the capital stock taken as fixed).

That is, much of the usual theorizing about money markets and price level determination is based on a Keynesian structure, with the time period short enough so that the capital stock may be treated as fixed, but long enough so that adjustments in employment and prices may be accomplished. In this context we study equilibrium configurations in which prices have adjusted fully to a stationary equilibrium value. Such theorizing leads to conclusions about the neutrality of money, the dichotomy of the real and monetary systems, and so on. But since it fails to take capital gains and losses explicitly into account in the formal equation structure, the analysis is really quite difficult. It has to deal implicitly with qualifications arising from changing prices without having an explicit mechanism for incorporating these in the model studied.

The present model does circumvent some of this difficulty. By determining the rate of price change so as to achieve equilibrium in portfolios and in the money market, we continue to deal with a full equilibrium model in which the price level and price change are just appropriate to induce portfolio managers to hold the existing supplies of money and capital goods. We are thus able to incorporate explicitly the dynamic considerations that are implicit, for example, in Keynesian liquidity preference arguments. As in all such models our argument continues to be crucially based on the requirement that at each moment all existing asset stocks must be willingly held in their given proportions, and this condition suffices to determine the required rate of capital gain. Note, finally, that the discussion of the chapter also reflects the traditional distinction between the decision to accumulate wealth, described by a saving hypothesis, and the decision on the composition of wealth, described by a portfolio management rule or liquidity preference function.

6–2. Demand for Money

In general, the demand for money must be sensitive to the distribution of income and wealth. However, neglecting these influences we postulate, for purposes of aggregate analysis, that the per capita demand for money is a function only of per capita money income, per capita money wealth, and the expected yield on capital (the only other asset). We further assume money demand per capita (m^d) always equals the actual money supply per capita (m), and, consequently, we assume that the equilibrium condition[1]

$$m^d = G(y, w, r) = m \tag{1}$$

is always satisfied where

$m \equiv M/L =$ per capita money stock
$p =$ price of output in terms of money as *numeraire*[2]
$y \equiv pF(K, L)/L$
$\equiv pf(k) =$ per capita value of output
$k \equiv K/L =$ capital/labor ratio
$w \equiv \overline{W}/L \equiv (pK + M)/L = pk + m =$ per capita money wealth
$r \equiv f'(k) - \delta + E(\dot{p}/p)$
$=$ expected money yield on the capital good.[3]

Absence of "money illusion" would require that (1) be homogeneous of degree one in its first two arguments. Consequently we may write

$$m/p = G(y/p, w/p, r)$$

[1] This equation could in principle be derived by aggregating the money demand functions of individuals having identical tastes, income, and wealth. More forthrightly, it may be assumed that the aggregate relationship will be of the same form as the individually determined demand functions.

[2] The price of money in terms of output is $p_m \equiv 1/p$.

[3] As in previous chapters, we assume that capital decays physically at the exponential rate δ, and $f'(k) - \delta$ is thus the net own rate of return on capital. The *expected* rate of inflation is denoted by $E(\dot{p}/p)$.

or

$$x = G[f(k), k + x, r] \tag{2}$$

where $x \equiv m/p$ denotes *per capita real money balances.*

We assume $G_1 > 0$, $1 > G_2 > 0$,[4] and $G_3 < 0$ (where G_i is the partial derivative of G with respect to its ith argument) for variables in the relevant ranges. Thus there exists a function

$$x = g(k, r), \tag{3}$$

describing the per capita real cash balances consistent with equilibrium at various levels of capital stock and yield (with $g_1 > 0$, $g_2 < 0$), and another function

$$r = \varphi(k, x), \tag{4}$$

which determines the yield necessary to maintain equilibrium with various portfolios of cash and real capital (with $\varphi_1 > 0$, $\varphi_2 < 0$)[5] (Exercise 1).

Various monetary models depend crucially on alternative forms and properties of (1) and hence of (3) and (4), including the ranges of the variables for which they are defined. In particular, we may identify the following cases.

Case 1 Assume we have the form

$$m^d = G(pk, w, r) = m \tag{1a}$$

instead of (1), with $G_1 > 0$, $1 > G_2 > 0$, and $G_3 < 0$, and assume further that (1a) is homogeneous of degree one in its first two arguments. We may again solve for (3), and it may be proved that the latter function is homogeneous of degree one in k; hence we have

$$x/k = g(1, r) \equiv \mathscr{L}(r) \tag{5}$$

with $\mathscr{L}'(r) < 0$. Thus the ratio M/pK is a declining function of the expected money yield on capital, which is exactly the liquidity preference model introduced by Tobin [21, 22] and later studied by Sidrauski [16], Nagatani [9], and others.

[4] The assumption $1 > G_2$ simply implies that an extra dollar of wealth will not all be held in the form of money balances.

[5] It should be emphasized that equations (3) and (4) are derived from equation (1), which explicitly assumes money market equilibrium.

Case 2 Suppose a second alternative to (1) is

$$m = m(y, r) \tag{1b}$$

where m is homogeneous of degree one in y, $\partial m/\partial y > 0$, and $\partial m/\partial r < 0$. Clearly then,

$$m/y = m/pf(k) = m(1, r) \equiv 1/v(r)$$

or

$$Mv(r) = pF(K, L) \tag{6}$$

where $v'(r) > 0$. Obviously (6) represents a standard transactions demand equation in which the velocity of circulation is an increasing function of r.[6] The classic Cambridge form of equation (6) assumed that $1/v(r)$ is an institutionally determined constant.

Case 3 Monetary models in which the demand for money is purely speculative have been studied by Shell, Sidrauski, and Stiglitz [15] and Hahn [5]. If money is held only for asset purposes, then the expected money yield on capital, r, must equal zero, the money yield on money. For if $r > 0$, and if the variance of expected returns does not matter, as it would not in a model with perfect certainty, then everyone would want to hold all his wealth in the form of capital, whereas if $r < 0$, desired portfolios would consist only of money.[7] Consequently, pure speculation models are equivalent to the special case in which (4) becomes

$$r = \varphi(k, x) \equiv 0. \tag{4a}$$

Case 4 If money is desired both for speculative and transaction purposes, as in the Keynesian tradition, then $g(k, r)$ is not necessarily homogeneous of degree one in k. The dynamic characteristics of a complete growth model will depend on the properties of $g(k, r)$. In the next section we will assume certain specific properties; these properties, which may have some economic justification, enable us to provide a complete description of the dynamic characteristics of our model.

[6] See, e.g., Modigliani [8] pp. 104–105.

[7] Since $r = f'(k) - \delta + E(\dot{p}/p)$, $r = 0$ implies $f'(k) - \delta = -E(\dot{p}/p)$. But, as $p_m \equiv 1/p$, the latter implies $f'(k) - \delta = E(\dot{p}_m/p_m)$, an equation that says that the net real rate of return on capital must equal the expected real rate of return on money. See Samuelson [14], pp. 488–496, for the observation that these conditions are characteristic of perfect capital markets under perfect certainty.

It is important to realize that Cases 1–4 represent different assumptions about economic behavior, and in principle one or more of them could be rejected or accepted for either theoretical or empirical reasons. In Case 1 the concern is with portfolio balance as first discussed by Tobin [21, 22], whereas Case 2 can be regarded as a modified version of the quantity theory of money. Case 3 is very special, and we examine it separately in Section 5-10.

Our preference, therefore, is Case 4, which is not only in the Keynesian tradition but which also provides most general representation in the sense that it includes all the behavioral motivations that underlie the other cases.

6–3. Behavioral Hypotheses

As already noted the equilibrium condition (1) may be taken to yield functions

$$x = g(k, r) \tag{3}$$

and

$$r = \varphi(k, x) \tag{4}$$

defined for relevant ranges of the variables k, x, and r. In all that follows, we shall assume that the capital/labor ratio is bounded away from zero, i.e.,

$$k \geqq \varepsilon > 0. \tag{7}$$

We assume also $g(k, r)$ has the property, that, given any k, $0 < \varepsilon \leqq k < \infty$, there exists a sufficiently large finite value $\bar{r} = \bar{r}(k)$ such that

$$g[k, \bar{r}(k)] = 0. \tag{8}$$

Since

$$r = f'(k) - \delta + E(\dot{p}/p), \tag{9}$$

this assumption states that corresponding to any finite, positive value of the capital/labor ratio k there exists some expected rate of price inflation, $E(\dot{p}/p)$, at which the per capita demand for real money balances is zero. In other words, given a fixed k, we assume there exists a yield $\bar{r}(k)$ on the alternative asset so large that no money balances are desired and the economy resorts to barter or manages to synchronize payments and purchases perfectly.

We further assume that the function $\bar{r}(k)$ has the shape illustrated in Figure 18 with $\infty > \bar{r}(k) > 0$, $\bar{r}'(k) > 0$, $0 < \varepsilon \leqq k < \infty$ and $\lim_{k\to\infty} \bar{r}(k) \equiv \bar{R} \leqq \infty$. Note that the condition $\bar{r}(k) > 0$ implies that there is a positive transactions demand for money; the case in which there is no transactions demand is treated as the case of pure speculative demand in Section 6-10.[8]

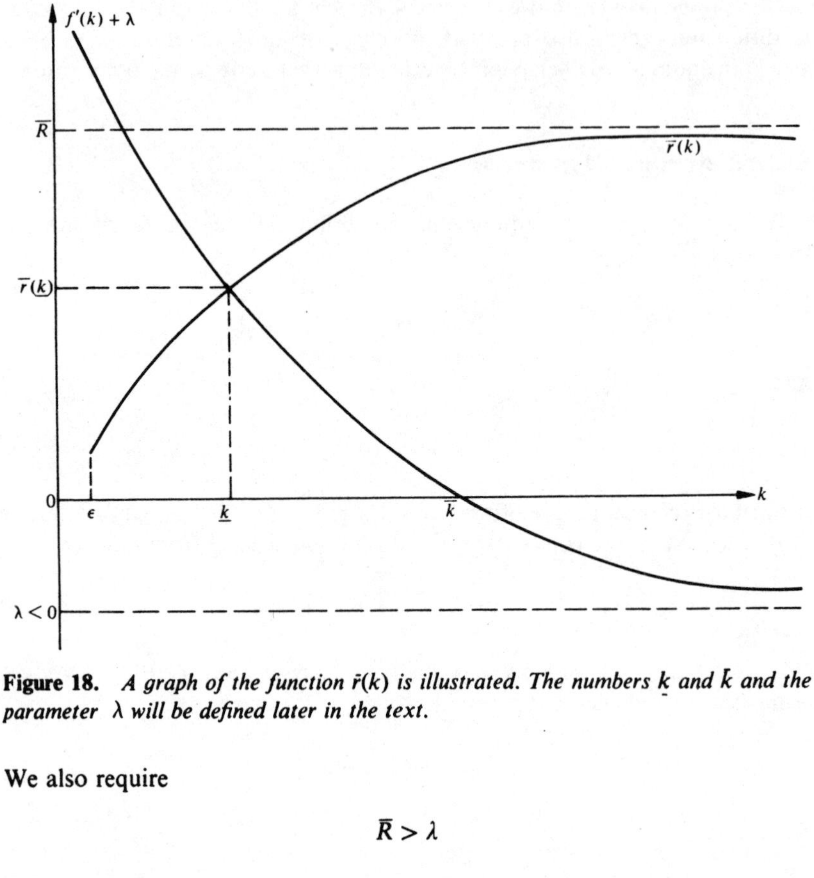

Figure 18. *A graph of the function $\bar{r}(k)$ is illustrated. The numbers $\underline{k}$ and $\bar{k}$ and the parameter λ will be defined later in the text.*

We also require

$$\bar{R} > \lambda$$

where $\lambda \equiv \theta - \delta - n$, $n \equiv \dot{L}/L$, and $\theta \equiv \dot{M}/M$ is the constant rate of increase in the nominal stock of money.[9] Observe that $\bar{R} > \lambda$ whenever $n + \delta$ exceeds θ and λ is negative, the case that seems most likely to prevail for reasonable values of the parameters.

[8] Setting $x = 0$ and $r = \bar{r}(k)$ in (3), we may derive $\bar{r}'(k) = -g_1/g_2 > 0$ as an implication of $g_1 > 0$ and $g_2 < 0$.

[9] It is assumed that the value of θ is set exogenously by the government and maintained constant forever.

The exact role of these assumptions will become clear in the subsequent discussion; essentially it is to ensure the existence and uniqueness of a steady state with positive money balances. Alternative assumptions, e.g., restrictions on the elasticities of x with respect to k and r, serve the same purpose.[10]

Finally, we impose the following commonly invoked regularity conditions on the per capita production function $f(k)$:

$$f(k) > 0, \quad 0 < k < \infty; \qquad f(0) = 0; \qquad f(\infty) = \infty;$$

$$f'(k) > 0, \quad 0 < k < \infty; \qquad f'(0) = \infty;$$

$$f'(\infty) = 0; \qquad f''(k) < 0, \qquad 0 < k < \infty.$$

The latter conditions are not indispensable, but they do avoid difficulties that might arise at boundaries and are therefore convenient for our present expository purposes.[11]

6–4. A Digression: The Liquidity Trap and Disequilibrium Dynamics

For any positive, finite value of the capital/labor ratio there may exist a positive expected yield on capital so low (that is, the expectation of capital losses may be so strong) that no one wishes to hold his wealth in the form of capital. In such a situation the equilibrium level of per capita real money balances becomes indefinitely large, a situation that corresponds to the traditional Keynesian liquidity trap illustrated in Figure 19.

Whether or not such liquidity traps exist for different values of k within the relevant region is of no consequence in our model. The reason for this fact is that we have assumed the money market is always in equilibrium with equality between the exogenously given m and the money demand m^d, as stated by equation (1). This equality must be achieved by instantaneous adjustments in the expected rate of inflation.

The exact mechanism is most easily seen if we take the expected rate of inflation to be always equal to the actual rate of inflation, i.e.,

$$E(\dot{p}/p) = \dot{p}/p. \tag{10}$$

This assumption is sometimes referred to as the assumption of *perfect myopic foresight*, and until stated otherwise we will assume (10) holds. Accordingly,

[10] See, e.g. Sidrauski [16], p. 800.

[11] Chapter 2 has already indicated the type of qualifications necessary to take care of the various boundary cases likely to arise if these assumptions are violated.

we find from (9) that the expected money yield on capital is

$$r = f'(k) - \delta + \dot{p}/p. \tag{11}$$

Consider now any point in time with known k and x. Stock equilibrium in the money market necessitates that (4) be satisfied, which together with (11) implies that the rate of inflation required for portfolio equilibrium is

$$\dot{p}/p = r - f'(k) + \delta = \varphi(k, x) - f'(k) + \delta. \tag{12}$$

Thus, $\dot{p}/p$ is a function only of k and x, and we may view (12) as determining the rate of inflation that establishes stock equilibrium in the money market. Therefore we have assumed implicitly that $\dot{p}/p$ adjusts instantaneously to satisfy (12), and with such perfectly flexible prices a full-employment solution is ensured even if there are liquidity traps.

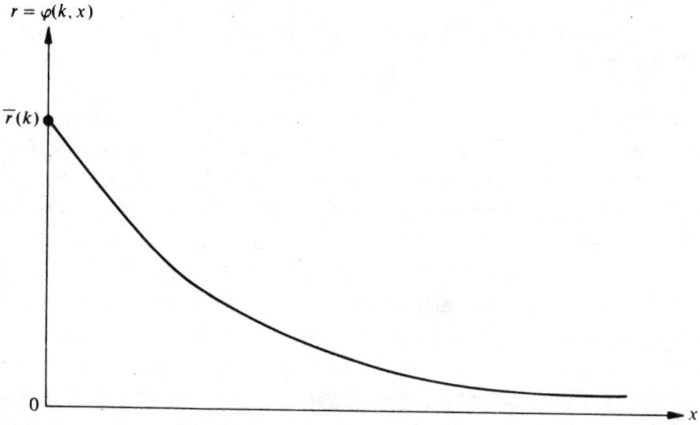

Figure 19. *Consider a fixed value of* k, $0 < \varepsilon \leqq k$. *The equilibrium level of per capita real money balances becomes infinite as* r *decreases toward zero, and everyone then would want to hold all his wealth in the form of money. The latter is possible, of course, for fixed values of* k $(0 < \varepsilon \leqq k < \infty)$ *and* m *only if the price level* p *becomes zero.*

Alternatively, the equilibrium condition (1) may be dropped and a disequilibrium model can be constructed by assuming that the rate of inflation is a function of the excess flow supply of real balances.[12] Suppose, in addition, the excess flow supply is equal to the excess stock supply times an appropriate

[12] The following discussion follows Stein [18].

proportionality factor. We then may assume the rate of inflation is determined by a simple functional form such as

$$\dot{p}/p = \gamma[x - g(k, r)] \quad (13)$$

where $\gamma > 0$ is the finite speed of adjustment.[13] Equation (13) has a simple interpretation, namely when the actual flow supply exceeds the desired flow supply of real balances, then there is inflation; a rising p *lowers* the value of per capita real money balances since $x = m/p$. Accordingly, a positive rate of inflation reduces the excess flow supply of real balances. Similar reasoning applies when the excess supply is negative, and $\dot{p}/p = 0$ if and only if there is equilibrium in the money market with a zero excess flow (and, by assumption, also stock) supply of per capita real balances.

Walras' law implies that the sum of the excess flow supplies must equal zero. Suppose desired net saving and desired net investment in the form of capital are S and I, respectively, and are functions of k, x, and L (population). The excess flow demand for capital is then

$$I - S,$$

and Walras' law is expressed by

$$I - S - (\dot{p}/p)/\gamma = 0. \quad (14)$$

The crucial problem is to determine the actual rate of net capital formation in these circumstances. Stein [18, 19, 20] and Rose [10, 11, 12] impose arbitrarily the hypothesis that the actual rate of net capital formation is some linear function of net desired investment and saving in capital, i.e.,

$$\dot{K} = \alpha I + (1 - \alpha)S \quad (15)$$

where α is an exogenous *constant* between zero and one. On the other hand, Nagatani [9] assumes the investment plan is always realized, which is equivalent to setting $\alpha = 1$ in (15).

If we accept (15), the actual rate of net capital formation is, by substitution from (14),

$$\dot{K} = \alpha(\dot{p}/p)/\gamma + S. \quad (16)$$

Since S is a function of k, x, and L, an equation for the actual change in the capital/labor ratio can be derived from (13) and (16) and is of the form

$$\dot{k} = \dot{k}(k, x). \quad (17)$$

[13] By rescaling the parameter γ, we may always choose the proportionality factor to be unity.

This disequilibrium approach is interesting primarily because the possibility of unemployment can arise in such models; see, e.g., Rose [10, 11, 12]. The serious difficulty, however, is that there is no economic mechanism to determine α, and the assumption that α is an exogenous constant, perhaps determined by the institutional environment, seems most implausible. Indeed, we agree with Hahn when he says,

> One has, in the present state of knowledge, great latitude in the construction of disequilibrium models; that is one of the reasons they are so unattractive and so great a variety of results can be produced.[14]

We therefore analyze a simple dynamic equilibrium model; in so doing we emphasize money market clearing conditions and portfolio balance, thus following the tradition set by Tobin [21, 22].

6–5. The Saving Hypothesis

Following Tobin [21, 22], we define *real wealth* and *real net disposable income*[15] by

$$W = K + M/p \tag{18}$$

and

$$Y = F(K, L) - \delta K + d(M/p)/dt \tag{19}$$

respectively. Since real total output is identically equal to consumption (C) plus depreciation (δK) plus net capital formation ($\dot{K}$), i.e. since

$$F(K, L) \equiv C + \delta K + \dot{K}, \tag{20}$$

we find that

$$Y = \dot{W} + C. \tag{21}$$

In other words, real net disposable income is equal to the change in real wealth plus real consumption, which is the rationale behind the definition (19). We assume that real consumption is always a constant (exogenous) fraction of real net disposable income:

$$C = (1 - s)Y, \qquad 0 < s < 1. \tag{22}$$

[14] Hahn [5].
[15] Note that the term "real" means "deflated by the price level p."

Equation (22) is a flow equilibrium condition satisfied at all points in time; clearly it may be written in the equivalent form

$$\dot{W} = sY. \tag{23}$$

It should be noted that all variables are deflated by the price level and hence are measured in *real* terms. Alternatively, the *money* value of wealth is

$$\overline{W} = pK + M = pW, \tag{24}$$

and if we insist on the flow equilibrium condition

$$\overline{Y} = \dot{\overline{W}} + pC, \tag{25}$$

which is analogous to (21), then the *money* value of net disposable income must equal

$$\overline{Y} = pF(K, L) - p\delta K + \dot{M} + \dot{p}K \neq pY.$$

Consequently, if $pC = (1 - s)\overline{Y}$, we conclude that the capital gains on the capital stock $\dot{p}K$ influence the money value of consumption, and therefore the two foregoing formulations are not equivalent.

Whether or not the savings-consumption behavior of an actual economy is best described in real or money terms is presumably a matter that can be tested empirically. However, behavioral relations cast in money terms may imply the existence of *money illusion*[16]; therefore we will use the Tobin formulation in real terms given by equations (18)–(23).

Finally, it is crucial to realize that equations (18)–(23) may not be consistent with the requirement that total consumption never exceed gross output, i.e., that

$$(1 - s)Y = C \leqq F(K, L). \tag{26}$$

Whenever (26) is violated, the model itself breaks down and must be rejected. We shall return to this observation later in Section 6-7.

6–6. Derivation and Properties of $\dot{x} = \dot{x}(k, x)$

From the definition of real per capita money balances $x \equiv M/pL$, we derive

$$\dot{x} = \left(\frac{\dot{M}}{M} - \frac{\dot{L}}{L} - \frac{\dot{p}}{p}\right)x = (\theta - n - \dot{p}/p)x. \tag{27}$$

[16] See, e.g., Shell, Sidrauski, and Stiglitz [15].

The equation

$$\dot{x} = \dot{x}(k, x) = [f'(k) + \lambda - \varphi(k, x)]x \tag{28}$$

follows by substitution from (12) where $\lambda \equiv \theta - \delta - n$. We should like to know the behavior implied by this equation.

Consider the case $x = 0$; clearly $\dot{x} = 0$ if the bracketed term in (28) is finite, and the latter must equal

$$f'(k) + \lambda - \varphi(k, 0) \equiv f'(k) + \lambda - \bar{r}(k). \tag{29}$$

Since by assumption the terms $\bar{r}(k)$ and $f'(k)$ are both finite for $0 < \varepsilon \leqq k < \infty$, we conclude that

$$\dot{x}(k, 0) = 0, \qquad 0 < \varepsilon \leqq k < \infty. \tag{30}$$

Now consider $x > 0$; then $\dot{x}(k, x) = 0$ if and only if

$$H(k, x) \equiv f'(k) + \lambda - \varphi(k, x) = 0. \tag{31}$$

Because

$$H_x = -\varphi_x > 0,$$

$H(k, x) = 0$ may be solved for

$$x = h(k) = g[k, f'(k) + \lambda] \tag{32}$$

where $h'(k) > 0$ (Exercise 2). A solution to (32) is meaningful only if $x > 0$, which necessitates $f'(k) + \lambda < \bar{r}(k)$. Accordingly, $\dot{x} = 0$, $x > 0$, whenever

$$x = h(k), \qquad k > \underline{k}, \tag{33}$$

where $\underline{k}$ is defined as the root to

$$f'(k) + \lambda = \bar{r}(k).$$

Clearly such a $\underline{k} > 0$ exists and is unique, as shown in Figure 18.

The complete locus of points along which $\dot{x} = 0$ is illustrated by the heavy lines in Figure 20. If there exists a liquidity trap and

$$g[\bar{k}, f'(\bar{k}) + \lambda]$$

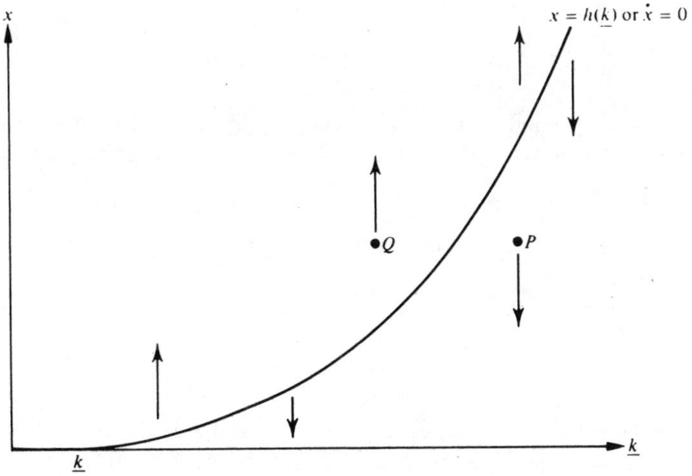

Figure 20

becomes *infinite* as k approaches some sufficiently large value $\bar{k}$, then the curve $h(k)$ has an asymptote at $k = \bar{k}$ and is defined only for $\underline{k} < k < \bar{k}$.[17] However, as already noted, this issue is of no consequence for our model.

Consider any point

$$(k, x) > [h^{-1}(x), 0]$$

which is to the right of $h(k)$ and above the k-axis, as is point P in Figure 20. Examination of (28) reveals that $\dot{x} < 0$ at any such point, as indicated by the arrows in Figure 20. Similarly, $\dot{x} > 0$ at any point such as Q, to the left of $x = h(k)$.

6–7. Derivation and Properties of $\dot{k} = \dot{k}(k, x)$

Manipulation of (18)–(23) and (27) yields

$$\dot{k} = sf(k) - (n + s\delta)k - (1 - s)(\theta - \dot{p}/p)x \qquad \textbf{(34a)}$$

$$= sf(k) - (n + s\delta)k - (1 - s)(\dot{x} + nx) \qquad \textbf{(34b)}$$

(Exercise 3), and substituting (12) in (34a) we obtain

$$\dot{k} = \dot{k}(k, x) = sf(k) - (n + s\delta)k - (1 - s)[f'(k) - \delta + \theta - \varphi(k, x)]x. \qquad \textbf{(35)}$$

[17] If λ is in fact negative, then there presumably will exist such a $\bar{k}$, no larger than the value of k satisfying $f'(k) + \lambda = 0$; see Figure 18.

Let k^{**} be defined as the root to

$$sf(k) - (n + s\delta)k = 0.$$

The regularity conditions imposed on $f(k)$ in Section 6-3 guarantee that a *unique* root exists satisfying $0 < \varepsilon \leqq k^{**} < \infty$ for sufficiently small ε. Consequently, since

$$f'(k^{**}) - \delta + \theta - \varphi(k^{**}, 0) = f'(k^{**}) - \delta + \theta - \bar{r}(k^{**})$$

is finite, we conclude that

$$\dot{k}(k^{**}, 0) = 0.$$

The behavior of the model for any initial conditions $k^0 \geqq \varepsilon > 0$ and $x^0 = 0$ is completely determined, and, except for interpretation, is identical to the one-sector model discussed in Chapter 2.[18]

A simple one-sector model without money in which *net* capital formation is a constant fraction (s) of *net* income implies the differential equation

$$\dot{k} = sf(k) - (n + s\delta)k = \dot{k}(k) \tag{36}$$

with $\dot{k}(k^{**}) = 0$ (Exercise 4). The behavior of such a model is completely illustrated in Figure 21; note that k^{**} is a stable equilibrium.

Our objective is to find a solution $(k^*, x^*) > (0, 0)$ for which

$$\dot{k}(k^*, x^*) = \dot{x}(k^*, x^*) = 0.$$

Since for $k \leqq \underline{k}$, $\dot{x} = 0$ only if $x = 0$ (see Figure 20), we need deal only with the case where

$$\underline{k} < k^{**}. \tag{37}$$

(We know that if (37) is not satisfied, then $\dot{x} = 0$ can occur only for $x \equiv 0$; and when $x \equiv 0$, $\dot{k} = 0$ can occur only at $(k^{**}, 0)$. Hence we need consider only the case $\underline{k} < k^{**}$.)

[18] In this case stocks of nominal money are forever zero, and equation (12) yields

$$\dot{p}/p = \bar{r}(k) - f'(k) + \delta.$$

Prices do not themselves affect anything in this model with no money, however; nevertheless, the price change may be interpreted as essential to ensure that the existing capital stock is willingly held and the rate of accumulation dictated by (35) is maintained. It is in this sense that the Solow model of Chapter 2 implicitly involves capital goods prices, and it is this kind of price equation that links the stable Solow model to unstable models of optimal saving. We return to this issue briefly in Chapter 11.

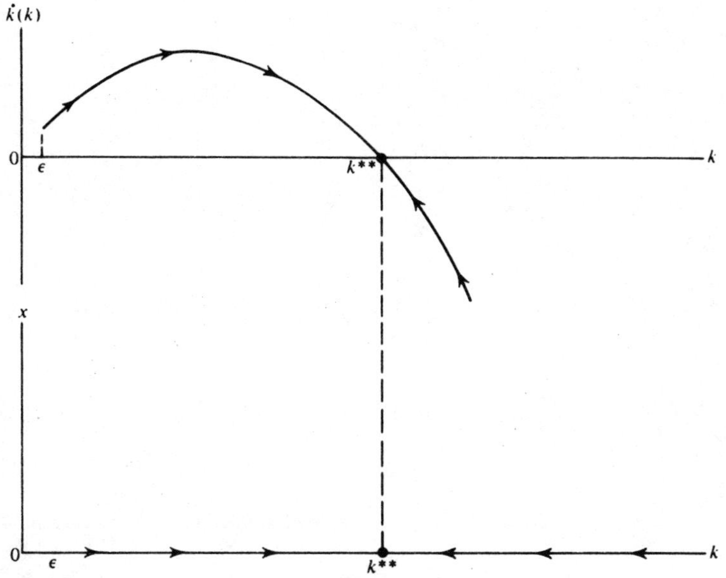

Figure 21. *Behavior of the model with no money balances and $x \equiv 0$ for all t.*

Consider now the equation

$$\dot{k}(k, x) = sf(k) - (n + s\delta)k - (1 - s)[f'(k) - \delta + \theta - \varphi(k, x)]x = 0, \quad x > 0, \quad 0 < \varepsilon \leqq k < k^{**}. \tag{38}$$

Calculating

$$\frac{\partial \dot{k}}{\partial x} = (1 - s)\varphi_x x - (1 - s)[f'(k) - \delta + \theta - \varphi(k, x)],$$

we see that

$$\left.\frac{\partial \dot{k}}{\partial x}\right|_{\dot{k}=0} < 0, \qquad x > 0, \quad 0 < \varepsilon \leqq k < k^{**},$$

because (1) $\varphi_x < 0$, and (2) $f'(k) - \delta + \theta - \varphi(k, x) = [sf(k) - (n + s\delta)k]/(1 - s)x > 0$ when $\dot{k} = 0$, $x > 0$, and $0 < \varepsilon \leqq k < k^{**}$. Thus there exists a function $x = x(k) > 0$, $0 < \varepsilon \leqq k < k^{**}$, $x(k^{**}) = 0$, obtained by solving the implicit equation $\dot{k} = 0$. This function is shown in Figure 22 where the

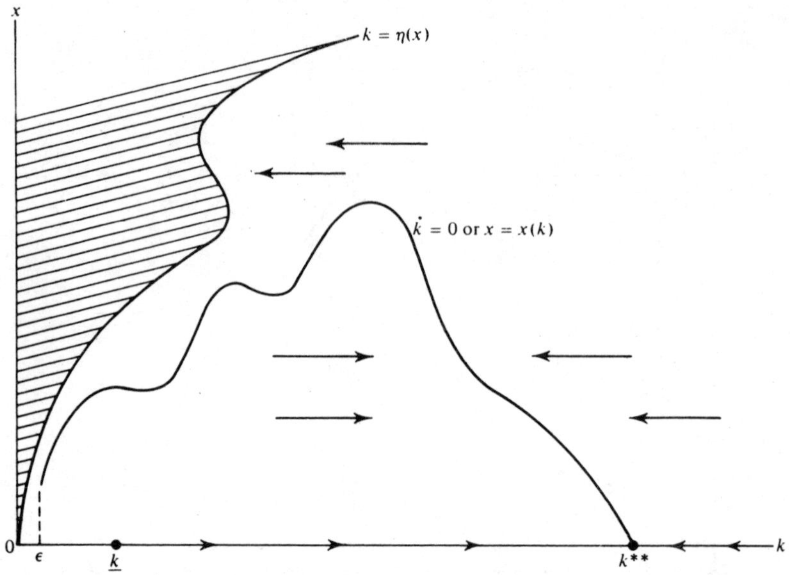

Figure 22

arrows indicate motion in the k-direction at points not on the $x = x(k)$ locus.[19]

We must now return to the important observation made at the end of Section 6-5, namely, consumption can never exceed gross output. Consider first the case in which

$$(1 - s)Y = C = F(K, L)$$

or

$$\Lambda(k, x) = x(\theta - \dot{p}/p) - sf(k)/(1 - s) + \delta k = 0.$$

Since

$$\frac{\partial \Lambda}{\partial k} = x(-\varphi_k + f'') - sf'/(1 - s) - \delta < 0,$$

there exists a function $k = \eta(x)$ along which $C = F(K, L)$, but the sign of

[19] Apparently the possibility of points $(k, x) > (k^{**}, 0)$ at which $\dot{k}(k, x) = 0$ has not been ruled out, but the matter is not sufficiently important to pursue here because there cannot exist an equilibrium point with $\dot{k} = \dot{x} = 0$ for $k > k^{**}$.

$\eta'(x)$ is indeterminate. Moreover, it can be proved that the locus of points for which

$$C \geqq F(K, L),$$

lies entirely above the $\dot{k} = 0$ curve in the k-x plane (Exercise 5).

Accordingly, our model is valid only for points that are on or below the curve $k = \eta(x)$. In other words, there is a region in the k-x plane, indicated by the shaded area in Figure 22, for which our behavioral hypotheses simply are not satisfied and the model ceases to make sense. This situation is not surprising; for "extreme" values of the economic variables, there is every reason to expect that the behavior of the economic agents in the community will change, and then our model is no longer valid. We shall simply avoid this difficulty by invoking the following assumption.

Define the set

$$\Omega \equiv \{(k, x) \mid 0 < \varepsilon \leqq k < \infty \quad \text{and} \quad k \geqq \eta(x)\}.$$

In all our subsequent discussion we shall assume $(k, x) \in \Omega$, *although for expositional convenience we neither mention this fact again nor indicate the set* Ω *in our later illustrations.*

6–8. Existence and Uniqueness of a Positive Equilibrium (k^*, x^*)

The existence of at least one equilibrium solution $(k^*, x^*) > (0, 0)$ satisfying

$$\dot{k}(k^*, x^*) = \dot{x}(k^*, x^*) = 0$$

is already implied by combining Figures 20 and 22. More formally, however, assume $\dot{x} = 0$, $x > 0$; then (31) and (32) must both be satisfied, and substituting these into (35) we find

$$\Psi(k) \equiv \dot{k}\,|_{\dot{x}=0,\,x>0} = sf(k) - (n + s\delta)k - (1 - s)ng[k, f'(k) + \lambda]. \qquad \textbf{(39)}$$

Observe that

(i) $sf(k) - (n + s\delta)k > 0, \qquad 0 < \varepsilon \leqq k < k^{**},$
(ii) $g[\underline{k}, f'(\underline{k}) + \lambda] = 0,$
(iii) $\underline{k} < k^{**}$, by assumption (37).

Consequently,

$$\Psi(\underline{k}) > 0.$$

As $\Psi(k)$ is a continuous function in k, the existence of a root k^* satisfying $\Psi(k^*) = 0$, $\underline{k} < k < k^{**}$, is ensured if

$$\lim_{k \to k^{**}} \Psi(k) < 0.$$

But

$$\lim_{k \to k^{**}} g[k, f'(k) + \lambda] = \lim_{k \to k^{**}} h(k) = h(k^{**}),$$

and $h(k^{**}) > 0$ because $h(\underline{k}) = 0$, $h'(k) > 0$, $\underline{k} < k < \infty$. Thus,

$$\lim_{k \to k^{**}} \Psi(k) = -n(1 - s)h(k^{**}) < 0.$$

The *uniqueness* of such a root k^* is guaranteed if

$$\Psi'(k)|_{\Psi(k)=0} < 0. \tag{40}$$

At the present level of generality, however, it may be impossible to justify (40), and we choose instead to invoke the following assumption: *The elasticity of $x = h(k)$, $\underline{k} < k < \infty$, is larger than one,*[20] i.e.,

$$kh'(k)/h(k) > 1$$

or

$$h'(k) > h(k)/k, \quad \underline{k} < k < \infty. \tag{41}$$

Consider a new function defined by

$$\Gamma(k) \equiv \Psi(k)/(1 - s)n = \frac{sf(k) - (n + s\delta)k}{(1 - s)n} - h(k) \tag{42}$$

and let

$$\gamma(k) \equiv [sf(k) - (n + s\delta)k]/(1 - s)n. \tag{43}$$

[20] This assumption can be illustrated by Figure 20; it implies that a line drawn from the origin to any point on the curve $x = h(k)$ has a slope *less* than that of the tangent to the curve at the corresponding point. See also Sidrauski [16], p. 800. Exercise 17 asks the reader to prove that (41) is always satisfied for the portfolio balance case in which (5) holds.

Clearly any root k^* to $\Psi(k) = 0$ also satisfies $\Gamma(k^*) = 0$. Since the elasticity of $\gamma(k)$ is smaller than one for all $0 < k < k^{**}$ (Exercise 6),

$$\gamma'(k) < \gamma(k)/k. \tag{44}$$

Now the condition

$$\Gamma(k) = \gamma(k) - h(k) = 0$$

for some k satisfying $\underline{k} < k < k^{**}$, together with (41) and (44), implies

$$\gamma'(k) < \gamma(k)/k = h(k)/k < h'(k) \tag{45}$$

at this value of k. Thus,

$$\Gamma'(k)|_{\Gamma(k)=0} = \gamma'(k) - h'(k) < 0,$$

and the uniqueness of a root k^* is proved. The foregoing proof is illustrated by Figure 23; note also that a root to $\Psi(k) = 0$ or $\Gamma(k) = 0$ is impossible for $k > k^{**}$.

Now let

$$x^* = h(k^*)$$

and we have proved Theorem 1.

Theorem 1: *Assume equations* (3), (4), (8), (10), (18)–(23), (26), *and* (41) *are all satisfied, in addition to the regularity conditions stated in the text. Then, there exists a unique root* k^*, $0 < \varepsilon \leqq k^* < k^{**}$, *and a unique corresponding root* $x^* = h(k^*) > 0$ *such that*

$$\dot{k}(k^*, x^*) = \dot{x}(k^*, x^*) = 0.$$[21]

Before turning to the stability properties of (k^*, x^*), we conclude this section with some comparative statics. Suppose the government increases θ, the exogenous rate of growth of the nominal money stock $\dot{M}/M$. If no other parameters change, we may ask the effect on (k^*, x^*). Since (39) implies that

$$sf(k^*) - (n + s\delta)k^* - (1 - s)ng[k^*, f'(k^*) + \lambda] = 0 \tag{46}$$

[21] Observe that $(k^*, x^*) \in \Omega$, the feasible set defined in the previous section for which our behavioral hypotheses are consistent and assumed valid. This conclusion follows directly from (d) in Exercise 5.

and $\lambda = \theta - n - \delta$, we find that

$$\frac{dk^*}{d\theta} = \frac{(1-s)ng_2}{sf' - (n + s\delta) - (1-s)n(g_1 + g_2 f'')}\bigg|_{(k^*,\, x^*)}. \tag{47}$$

However, we have proved $\Gamma'(k^*) < 0$, which implies that $\Psi'(k^*) < 0$. But the denominator of (47) is simply $\Psi'(k^*)$, as seen from (39), whereas g_2 is negative. Thus,

$$\frac{dk^*}{d\theta} > 0.$$

Similarly, it may be proved that

$$\frac{dx^*}{d\theta} \gtreqless 0 \qquad \text{as} \qquad k^* \lesseqgtr \tilde{k},$$

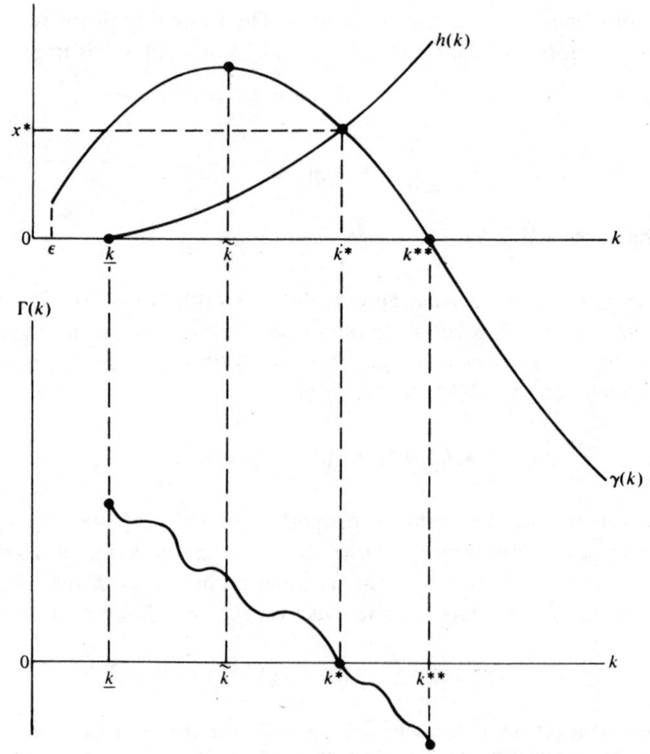

Figure 23

where $\tilde{k}$ is the unique root to both $sf'(k) - (n + s\delta) = 0$ and $\gamma'(k) = 0$ (Exercise 7). When $\dot{x} = 0$, the rate of inflation is

$$\left(\frac{\dot{p}}{p}\right)^* = \theta - n \tag{48}$$

as seen from (27). Thus,

$$d(\dot{p}/p)^*/d\theta = 1.$$

The conclusion, of course, is that "money matters," at least in a comparative statics sense. Comparing only *equilibrium* positions $(k^*, x^*) > (0, 0)$, we have deduced that an increase in the nominal rate of monetary expansion will

(i) Always increase the equilibrium capital/labor ratio k^*,
(ii) Increase or decrease the equilibrium value of per capita real balances x^* as $k^* \lesseqgtr \tilde{k}$, and
(iii) Increase the equilibrium rate of inflation $(\dot{p}/p)^*$.

Two further observations are important.

(iv) In equilibrium the rate of price change $(\dot{p}/p)^*$ may be either positive, negative, or zero, as $\theta \gtreqless n$. Since there is only one policy parameter in this model, once θ is chosen the equilibrium point (k^*, x^*) is completely determined.
(v) The equilibrium point *without* money, $(k^{**}, 0)$, has a higher capital/labor ratio than the equilibrium point with money, $(k^*, x^*) > (0, 0)$, i.e., $k^* < k^{**}$. In this very narrow sense, the existence of a government debt—which in this case consists of only paper currency—is a "burden" because the equilibrium capital/labor ratio k^* is smaller than k^{**}.[22] We note, however, that this burden is negative if k^{**} exceeds the Golden Rule capital/labor ratio, for then per capita consumption is increased by a reduction in the capital/labor ratio.

6–9. Stability Properties of Equilibrium Points

The qualitative behavior of the possible time paths (k^t, x^t) is illustrated in Figure 24. Observe that the (k^*, x^*) equilibrium is a *saddlepoint*, and therefore

[22] Note also that (i) and (ii) above imply that for $k > \tilde{k}$ an increase in θ will increase k^* and decrease x^*. As θ continues to increase, the equilibrium point occurs closer to $(k^{**}, 0)$, and in the limit with infinitely high rates of expansion of the nominal money supply, the rate of price change becomes infinite; apparently the economy then reverts to a situation in which real per capita money balances $x \to 0$ because $p \to \infty$. Alternatively, for sufficiently large θ, we may find a solution to $0 = g[k^{**}, f'(k^{**}) + \theta - n]$. Indeed if $0 = g[k, \bar{r}(k)]$ holds for $k = k^{**}$, which is the barter case, then we can always find a θ so large that $f'(k^{**}) + \theta - n = \bar{r}(k^{**})$ since $f'' < 0$ and $\bar{r}' > 0$.

$\lim_{t\to\infty}(k^t, x^t) = (k^*, x^*)$ only from initial positions (k^0, x^0) lying on the heavy curve labeled AA. On the other hand, the $(k^{**}, 0)$ equilibrium point is stable, and $\lim_{t\to\infty}(k^t, x^t) = (k^{**}, 0)$ starting from all initial positions (k^0, x^0) lying below the AA curve.

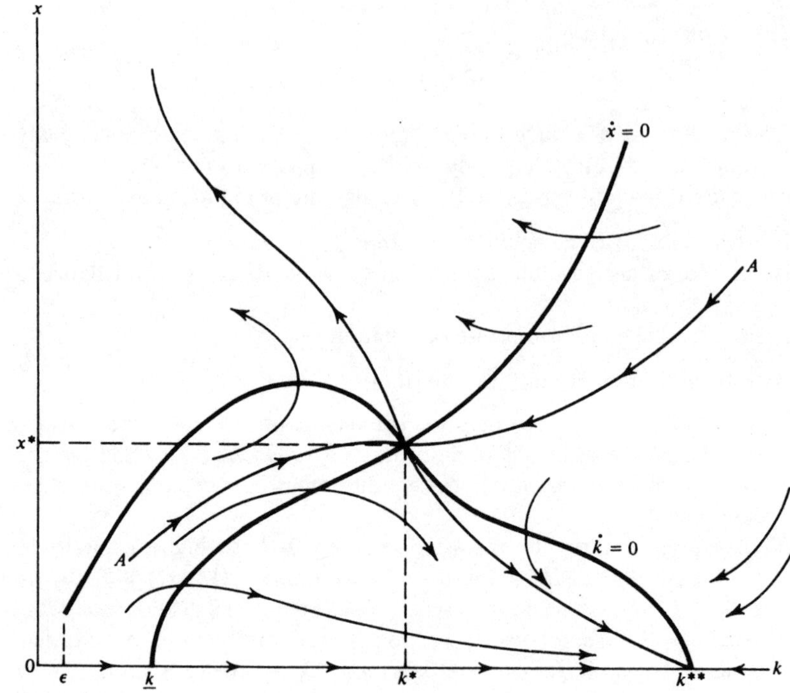

Figure 24

The exact manner in which the economy might approach the $(k^{**}, 0)$ equilibrium depends on the values of the parameters. Of course

$$x^t = (M^0/L^0)e^{(\theta - n)t}/p^t \tag{49}$$

is always valid. Now if $(M^0/L^0) > 0$, which is necessary for $x^0 > 0$, and, if further $\theta \geqq n$, then

$$\lim_{t\to\infty} x^t = 0$$

implies

$$\lim_{t\to\infty} p^t = \infty.$$

The reason is simple: if initially M^0 is positive and the government increases the nominal money stock so fast that the per capita money stock rises, then the price level must become infinite if real per capita money balances become zero.

On the other hand, a slower rate of increase in the nominal money stock, with $\theta < n$, implies that

$$\lim_{t\to\infty} x^t = 0$$

for any value of

$$\lim_{t\to\infty} p^t > 0.$$

The asymptotic behavior of the model starting from initial points (k^0, x^0) above the AA curve is not evident. However, this matter is not of sufficient economic interest to pursue here.[23]

For completeness we now show that (k^*, x^*) is locally a saddlepoint. It is sufficient to prove that

$$\det J^* < 0$$

where

$$J^* = \begin{bmatrix} J_{11}^* & J_{12}^* \\ J_{21}^* & J_{22}^* \end{bmatrix}$$

is the Jacobian of the system

$$\dot{k} = \dot{k}(k, x), \qquad \dot{x} = \dot{x}(k, x)$$

evaluated at the equilibrium point (k^*, x^*). It is easily verified (Exercise 8) that

$$(\partial \dot{k}/\partial k)^* = J_{11}^* = sf' - (n + s\delta) - (1 - s)(-\varphi_k + f'')x$$
$$(\partial \dot{k}/\partial x)^* = J_{12}^* = (1 - s)(\varphi_x x - n) < 0$$
$$(\partial \dot{x}/\partial k)^* = J_{21}^* = (f'' - \varphi_k)x < 0$$
$$(\partial \dot{x}/\partial x)^* = J_{22}^* = -\varphi_x x > 0.$$

[23] Apparently all such trajectories eventually pass out of the feasible set Ω, in which case our model no longer makes sense. Exactly the same difficulty arises in the paper by Shell, Sidrauski, and Stiglitz [15], although their interpretation differs slightly from ours. In any event, further discussion of the issue is beyond the scope of this chapter.

-uently, det $J^* < 0$ if and only if

$$= -\varphi_x x[sf' - (n + s\delta)] + (1 - s)nx(f'' - \varphi_k) < 0 \quad \textbf{(50)}$$

ve have proved that

$$sf' - (n + s\delta) - (1 - s)n[g_1 + g_2 f''] < 0 \quad \textbf{(51)}$$

at (k^*, x^*), whereas by straight-forward calculation

$$g_1 + g_2 f'' = (f'' - \varphi_k)/\varphi_x. \quad \textbf{(52)}$$

Multiplying (51) by $-\varphi_x x > 0$ and substituting from (52), we conclude that (50) is valid and det $J^* < 0$, as was to be proven.

6–10. Another Digression: The Pure Speculative Motive

We have already observed in Section 6-2 that in some models there is no transactions demand for money, in which case the existing money stock will be held if and only if the expected yield on the only other asset, capital, is equal to zero, the yield on money. In such instances where "money" is not used for transaction purposes, it may be thought of as the outstanding government debt, which, accordingly, no longer need be nonnegative. Thus, if "per capita real 'money' balances" are negative ($x < 0$), the interpretation is simply that the public is in debt to the government. Under these circumstances it may be convenient to think of "bonds" rather than "money".[24]

Equations (4a), (11), and (27) imply that

$$\dot{x} = \dot{x}(k, x) = [\theta - n - \delta + f'(k)]x = [f'(k) + \lambda]x, \quad \textbf{(53)}$$

while (4a), (11), and (34a) imply

$$\dot{k} = \dot{k}(k, x) = sf(k) - (n + s\delta)k - (1 - s)[f'(k) - \delta + \theta]x. \quad \textbf{(54)}$$

We will confine our attention to $x \neq 0$, and consequently k^* is determined by (53) alone provided that λ is negative, a necessary assumption if this model is to be meaningful. In other words, the rate of nominal money expansion (θ) must be less than the sum of population growth and depreciation ($n + \delta$).

Shell, Sidrauski, and Stiglitz [15] have studied this system, and they have proved that $(k^*, x^*) > 0$ is a saddlepoint, whereas $(k^{**}, 0)$ is locally stable, with $k^* < k^{**}$. These results seem exactly the same as those we obtained in

[24] See [15].

the previous section, but there is one crucial difference, namely, the possibility of an equilibrium point (k^*, x^*) with $k^* > k^{**} > 0$ and $x^* < 0$ cannot be excluded. Moreover, the stability properties of the latter equilibrium point are drastically different.

The phase diagram for the latter situation is pictured in Figure 25. The crucial observations are

(i) The "no money equilibrium" $(k^{**}, 0)$ is now a saddlepoint with the k-axis as the stable arm.
(ii) The equilibrium with *negative* "money" (bonds) is locally stable, and, moreover, $k^* > k^{**}$.[25]

We now turn to the question of when $k^* > k^{**}$ so that Figure 25 prevails. Clearly it suffices to prove that

$$f(k^*)/k^* < f(k^{**})/k^{**}, \tag{55}$$

where as before,

$$f(k^{**})/k^{**} = (n/s) + \delta.$$

Let α be the relative share of capital at the equilibrium point (k^*, x^*), i.e.,

$$\alpha = k^* f'(k^*)/f(k^*);$$

then,

$$(n + \delta - \theta)/\alpha = f'(k^*)/\alpha = f(k^*)/k^*$$

at (k^*, x^*). Clearly, (55) holds if

$$(n + \delta - \theta)/\alpha < (n/s) + \delta$$

or if

$$\theta > \frac{n}{s}(s - \alpha) + (1 - \alpha)\delta. \tag{56}$$

For "reasonable" values of the parameters, we would certainly expect the right-hand side of (56) to be negative.[26] Accordingly, unless the government

[25] See Exercise 10.
[26] For example, $n(s - \alpha)/s + (1 - \alpha)\delta = 0.04(0.1 - 0.2)/0.1 + (1 - 0.2)(0.03) = -0.016$.

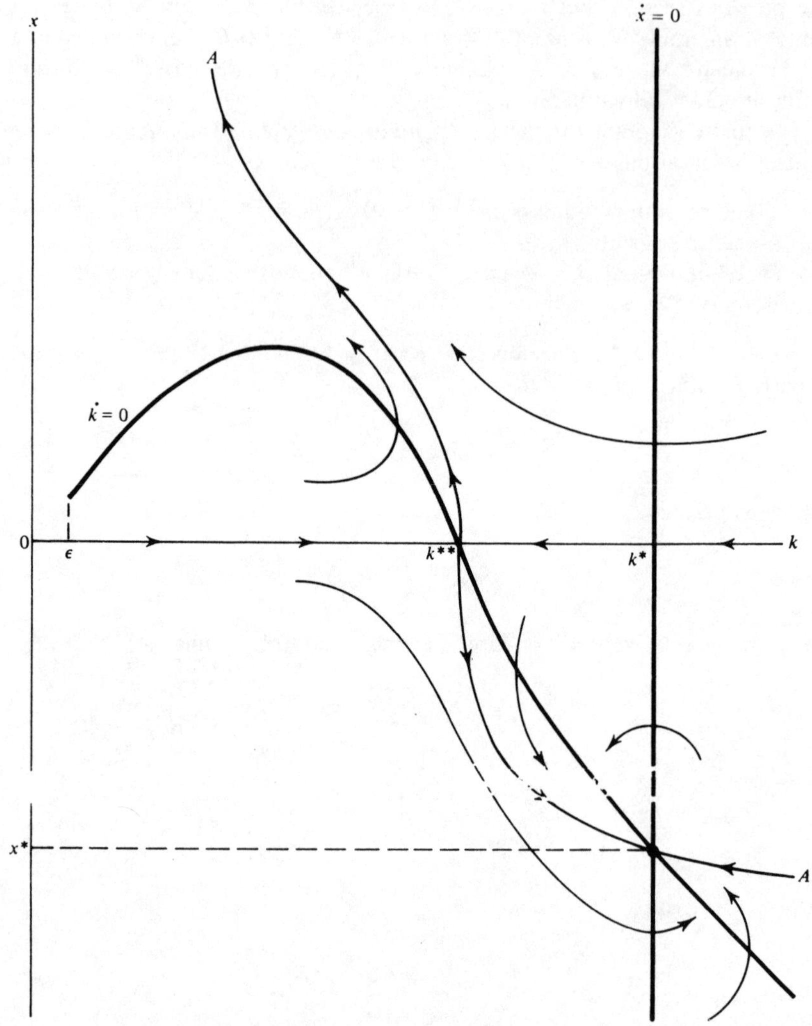

Figure 25. *The equilibrium point* (k^{**}, 0) *with no money is now a saddlepoint, and the point* (k^*, x^*), $x^* < 0$, $k^* > k^{**}$, *is locally stable.*

selects a negative value of θ, we would expect that the situation depicted by Figure 25 is valid.

Given these observations, we reject the pure speculation money models as economically meaningless. Indeed, in such models money has no important role to perform, and it is not surprising that nonsensical conclusions can result.

6–11. Stability in a Simplified Model

In general there is a real balance effect—or, in other words "money matters"—if the equilibrium value of k^* is influenced by the monetary policy of the government, which in our case is represented by a single parameter θ. In our preceding discussion we have found that money does matter and that $dk^*/d\theta > 0$. This result, however, need not hold if the equation for $\dot{k}$ is independent of x (or θ).

For example, suppose that we postulate a simple rule: desired and realized net saving is a constant fraction (s) of net income and always equals realized net investment. This rule, although consistent with the one-sector models studied in Chapter 2, is unlike the more sophisticated saving behavior discussed in Section 6-5. For under this postulate,

$$\dot{k} = sf(k) - (n + s\delta)k, \tag{57}$$

and consequently $\dot{k}$ is independent of θ or x. Indeed, if (57) holds, then $\dot{k} = \dot{k}(k^*) = 0$ if and only if

$$f(k^*)/k^* = (n + s\delta)/s, \tag{58}$$

and by our previous notational convention we find that $k^* \equiv k^{**}$.[27] However, for analytical convenience it is useful at the moment to consider a model composed of (57) and (28), i.e.,

$$\dot{k} = \dot{k}(k) = sf(k) - (n + s\delta)k \tag{57}$$

and

$$\dot{x} = \dot{x}(k, x) = [f'(k) + \lambda - \varphi(k, x)]x. \tag{28}$$

We retain the assumptions previously stated in Sections 6-3, 6-4, and 6-6.[28]

We emphasize that the reason for substituting equation (57) in place of (35) is convenience alone. Real balance effects may be theoretically and/or empirically important, but their exclusion is a great analytical convenience in studying the present stability questions. Moreover, as the zealous reader

[27] The use of (57) led Johnson [6] into an error which has been corrected by Tobin [23], Nagatani [9], and others.

[28] However, it is important to realize that for this special case in which our model consists of (57) and (28), the set of (k, x) consistent with the behavioral equations is $\overline{\Omega} \equiv \{(k, x) | 0 < \varepsilon \leq k < \infty \text{ and } 0 \leq x < \infty\} \supset \Omega$. In this sense also the version now being discussed is a simplification.

may verify, the qualitative conclusions that follow are not sensitive to our simplification, excepting the qualification made in the preceding footnote. Although we now consider (57) and (28), exactly the same results would be obtained in our more general model comprised of equations (35) and (28).

The new phase diagram is illustrated in Figure 26, but we leave its derivation as Exercise 11. The root k^* is now defined by (58), and as already noted, it is identical to k^{**} in our previous notation.

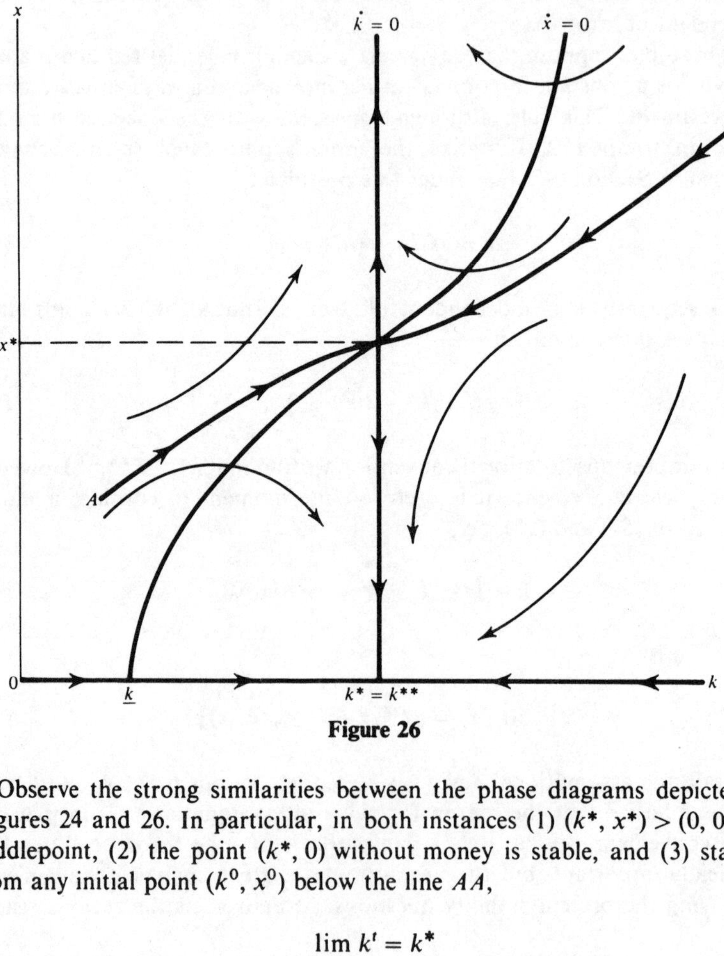

Figure 26

Observe the strong similarities between the phase diagrams depicted by Figures 24 and 26. In particular, in both instances (1) $(k^*, x^*) > (0, 0)$ is a saddlepoint, (2) the point $(k^*, 0)$ without money is stable, and (3) starting from any initial point (k^0, x^0) below the line AA,

$$\lim_{t \to \infty} k^t = k^*$$

and

$$\lim_{t \to \infty} x^t = 0.$$

We now wish to answer two crucial questions.

(i) Retain the perfect myopic foresight assumption $\dot{p}/p = E(\dot{p}/p)$. Is there any government policy $\theta = \theta^t$ that will result in a stable equilibrium $(k^*, x^*) > (0, 0)$?
(ii) Retain the assumption that the government sets $\theta = constant$. Is there any behavioral hypothesis about expectations for which $(k^*, x^*) > (0, 0)$ is stable?

The first question is easy to answer. Consider, for example, the policy

$$\theta^t = n + \delta + qr^t$$

where q is an exogenous constant; as before $\lambda \equiv \theta - \delta - n$ and

$$r^t = \varphi(k^t, x^t) = f'(k^t) - \delta + (\dot{p}/p)^t.[29]$$

The system of equations now becomes

$$\begin{aligned} \dot{k} &= \dot{k}(k) = sf(k) - (n + s\delta)k \\ \dot{x} &= \dot{x}(k, x) = [f'(k) + (q - 1)\varphi(k, x)]x. \end{aligned} \qquad \textbf{(59)}$$

The derivation of (59) is Exercise 12.

Consider now the Jacobian determinant of the system (59) evaluated at the equilibrium point $(k^*, x^*) > (0, 0)$:

$$\det J^* = \det\begin{bmatrix} sf'(k^*) - (n + s\delta) & 0 \\ [f''(k^*) + (q - 1)\varphi_k(k^*, x^*)]x^* & (q - 1)\varphi_x(k^*, x^*)x^* \end{bmatrix}$$

with $\det J^* = J^*_{11} J^*_{22}$. Clearly, (k^*, x^*) is (locally) stable if both J^*_{11} and J^*_{22} are negative, for then

$$\text{(i)}\ \det J^* > 0,$$

and

$$\text{(ii)}\ \text{Trace}\ J^* = J^*_{11} + J^*_{22} < 0,$$

which are sufficient conditions. However, it is easy to show that $J^*_{11} < 0$ (Exercise 13), and clearly $J^*_{22} < 0$ for all $q > 1$ because $\varphi_x < 0$.

[29] As previously, the superscripts t denote time and are not exponents.

Closer examination of this stablizing policy is of interest. From (59) we see that

$$\frac{\dot{M}}{M} - \frac{\dot{p}}{p} - n \equiv \frac{\dot{x}}{x} = f'(k) + (q-1)\varphi(k, x) \tag{60}$$

and

$$\theta' = \frac{\dot{M}}{M} = q(\dot{p}/p) + qf'(k) + (1-q)\delta + n \tag{61}$$

may be derived (Exercise 14).

Such a stabilizing policy may seem "perverse" because in times of "excessive" inflation, the stock of money is also increasing. Note, however, that the perversity is a consequence of the fact that p is an asset price—a perfect asset price—and p is only coincidentally a goods price because of the one-sector assumption. When should there be excessive inflation in this model? It is when the yield required on capital (required if the existing portfolios, i.e., capital and money stocks, are to be willingly held) is so high that it must consist primarily of expected capital gains. That is, people would really wish more money, but they are persuaded to hold the existing capital stock by the promise of very high capital gains. This situation can be interpreted as a case in which money is scarce relative to capital goods in the eyes of the portfolio managers. The stabilizing policy calls for the government to supply cash in these times of scarcity. What is perverse about that? Remember, there is simply no way a demand inflation can occur in this model because the goods market always clears.

Possible confusion about this issue may arise from a failure to distinguish goods prices and asset prices, and from a mistaken identification of this situation as an inflation resulting from rising goods market prices because people are trying to substitute money for goods. Here prices are rising because people have to be persuaded to hold goods as assets. Inflation in this model is a sign of scarcity of cash, high demand for money, and is not a sign of too many dollars chasing too few goods.

In the next section we turn to our second question, namely, is there a behavioral hypothesis other than perfect myopic foresight for which $(k^*, x^*) > (0, 0)$ is stable?

6–12. Adaptive Expectations

If we reject perfect myopic foresight, a behavioral replacement for

$$\dot{p}/p = E(\dot{p}/p) \tag{10}$$

must be found. We have already rejected a flow (or stock) adjustment mechanism of the form

$$\dot{p}/p = \gamma[x - g(k, x)] \tag{13}$$

(see Section 6-4). However, it is possible to retain the spirit of a dynamic equilibrium model without (10), and the *adaptive expectations* postulate is most convenient.

This postulate, used by Cagan [2], states that *the rate of adjustment in the current expected rate of inflation depends on the error made in predicting the current rate of change.* If we denote $E(\dot{p}/p)$ by π, the latter assumption is expressed in symbols by

$$\dot{\pi} = \beta(\dot{p}/p - \pi) \tag{62}$$

where $\beta \geqq 0$ is the speed of adjustment in expectations. We may note that $\beta = 0$ and $\beta = \infty$ are analogous to "static expectations" and "perfect myopic foresight," respectively. In other words, larger values of β imply smaller time lags in the adjustment of expectations.

It is now convenient to work with the variables (k, π) instead of (k, x). We may calculate

$$\dot{x} = d[g(k, r)]/dt = [g_k \dot{k} + g_r \dot{r}]. \tag{63}$$

Similarly, we differentiate

$$r \equiv f'(k) - \delta + \pi,$$

and substituting into (63), obtain

$$\dot{x} = g_k \dot{k} + g_r[f''(k)\dot{k} + \dot{\pi}]. \tag{64}$$

However,

$$\dot{p}/p = \theta - n - \dot{x}/x, \tag{65}$$

and combining (62), (64), and (65), we may derive

$$\dot{\pi} = \frac{\beta x(\theta - n - \pi) - \beta[g_k + g_r f''(k)]\dot{k}}{\beta g_r + x} \tag{66}$$

(Exercise 15).

Since $\dot{k} = \dot{k}(k)$, given by (57), our final system is of the form

$$\dot{k} = \dot{k}(k, \pi), \qquad \dot{\pi} = \dot{\pi}(k, \pi) \tag{67}$$

and again we seek the existence, uniqueness, and stability of a point $(k^*, \pi^*) > (0, 0)$.[30]

We ignore the questions of existence and uniqueness of an equilibrium point $(k^*, \pi^*) > (0, 0)$; reasoning similar to that employed in the previous sections reveals identical conclusions. The local stability of (k^*, π^*), on the other hand, can be shown to hinge solely on the sign of

$$\left.\frac{\partial \dot{\pi}}{\partial \pi}\right|_{(k^*, \pi^*)} = -\frac{\beta x^*}{\beta g_r + x^*} \tag{68}$$

which must be negative for stability (Exercise 16).

Thus a sufficient local stability condition is

$$\beta < -x^*/g_r(x^*, r^*). \tag{69}$$

Since g_r is negative and likely to be small in absolute value, at least as suggested by empirical evidence, condition (69) may not be too restrictive. In any event, the important conclusion is that sufficiently large values of β (very high speeds of adjustment in expectations) lead to

$$\left.\frac{\partial \dot{\pi}}{\partial \pi}\right|_{(k^*, \pi^*)} > 0$$

and a saddlepoint equilibrium.

Again, comparative statics of equilibrium positions are of some interest. Since $\dot{\pi} = 0$ in equilibrium, we conclude that

$$\beta(\dot{p}/p - \pi^*) = 0 \tag{70}$$

or

$$(\dot{p}/p)^* = \theta - n, \tag{71}$$

as might be expected. If the rate of increase in the nominal stock of money $(\theta \equiv \dot{M}/M)$ exceeds the rate of growth of the labor force, $(n \equiv \dot{L}/L)$, then there is inflation in equilibrium.

[30] Observe that $x = g(k, r) = g[k, f'(k) - \delta + \pi]$ implies the existence of $x = x(k, \pi)$.

We have already stressed that monetary policy cannot affect k^* because we have made a simplifying assumption in this section that serves to expedite the analysis. In general, however, the real balance effect is important even in stable models using the adaptive expectations postulate. As in our previous model (Section 6-8) $dk^*/d\theta > 0$, so that a rise in the rate of increase in the money supply has a stimulating effect on the economy. However, as is clear from (70) and (71), this result is achieved only with a higher value of $(\dot{p}/p)^*$.

Moreover, although $dk^*/d\theta > 0$ in a *comparative statics sense*, the motion from k_1^* to k_2^* $(k_2^* > k_1^*)$ due to an increase in θ from θ_1 to θ_2 *may not be monotonically increasing in* k^t. The latter observation, which was also made by Sidrauski ([16], pp. 805–807) in the context of a similar model, could conceivably play a most crucial role in choosing between expansionary policy alternatives.

6–13. Additional Policy Parameters

Many monetary growth models are exceedingly limited in their policy implications because they assume that there is only one parameter under government control, namely $\theta = \dot{M}/M$. A common assumption is that the government creates money in only one way: it distributes it as "gifts" to the public. Clearly there are simple alternatives. The government might create money to purchase new capital goods that would then be rented to firms in the private sector at the competitive rental rate. The latter may be interpreted as an "open market operation." In this section we will briefly analyze a model built upon this possibility, and then comment on the implications.

The following model was suggested by Hahn [5], and we have introduced only minor modifications. In this model the government always owns a constant fraction α of the capital stock, $0 \leqq \alpha < \bar{\alpha} \leqq 1$, where $\bar{\alpha}$ will be defined precisely in footnote 32; however, the selection of some $\alpha \in [0, \bar{\alpha})$ is a matter of government choice. Constancy of α means that the government must purchase capital at the flow rate $\alpha\dot{K}$ for all points in time. As before, we assume the nominal money stock increases at the constant rate θ, but we may identify two distinct roles by writing

$$\theta = \dot{M}/M = \dot{M}_1/M + \dot{M}_2/M; \tag{72}$$

here we interpret $\dot{M}_1/M$ as the flow rate of money "gifts," whereas $\dot{M}_2/M$ is the rate of change in the money supply required to purchase capital at the *net* flow rate $\alpha\dot{K}$, thereby keeping α constant. Consequently, we have

$$\dot{M}_2 = \alpha p(\dot{K} + \delta K),$$

or, equivalently,

$$(\dot{M}_2/M)(M/pL) = (\dot{M}_2/M)x = \alpha(\dot{K}/L + \delta K/L) = \alpha[\dot{k} + (n + \delta)k]. \quad (73)$$

Further assumptions are needed regarding the government's use of its capital and the savings behavior of individuals when $\alpha > 0$. Suppose all the rentals received on the capital stock owned by the government, αK, are distributed to the public as transfer payments; then net disposable income includes the term

$$\alpha F_K K + (1 - \alpha)F_K K + F_L L - \delta K = F_K K + F_L L - \delta K = F(K, L) - \delta K, \quad (74)$$

as before.[31]

However, *real net disposable income* is no longer

$$Y = F(K, L) - \delta K + d(M/p)/dt \quad (19)$$

since $\dot{M}_2/p$ does not add to disposable income—it is not a "gift" but rather a "trade"—net government purchases of capital must be subtracted to give

$$Y(\alpha) = F(K, L) - \delta K + d(M/p)/dt - \alpha\dot{K}. \quad (75)$$

Furthermore, our basic flow equilibrium condition which is analogous to (23), is

$$\dot{W}(\alpha) = sY(\alpha) \quad (76)$$

where

$$W(\alpha) \equiv (1 - \alpha)K + M/p = \textit{real private wealth}. \quad (77)$$

Manipulation of (75), (76), and (77) yields the differential equation

$$\dot{k} = \frac{sf(k) - [s\delta + (1 - \alpha)n + s\alpha n]k - (1 - s)(\theta - \dot{p}/p)x}{(1 - \alpha) + s\alpha}; \quad (78)$$

observe that (78) and (34a) are equivalent when $\alpha = 0$.

[31] Thus we are assuming that individuals are indifferent as to whether (1) they own the entire capital stock and receive all rental payments $F_K K$ directly, or, alternatively (2) the government owns a fraction α of the capital stock, but turns back all rental income to the public as transfers with individuals still receiving exactly the same total income.

As before,

$$\begin{aligned} r &= f'(k) - \delta + E(\dot{p}/p) \\ &= f'(k) - \delta + \dot{p}/p \end{aligned}$$

under the assumption of perfect myopic foresight. However, it is reasonable to suppose that the demand for money depends on privately owned wealth, and hence, (2) must be replaced by

$$x = G[f(k), (1 - \alpha)k + x, r] \tag{79}$$

where $(1 - \alpha)k + x \equiv w(\alpha)$ is *real per capita private wealth*. Again we may solve (79) for x and r, but now we obtain

$$x = g(k, r; \alpha) \tag{80}$$

with

$$g_\alpha \equiv \left.\frac{\partial x}{\partial \alpha}\right|_{k,\,r} = -kG_2/(1 - G_2) < 0 \tag{81}$$

and

$$r = \varphi(k, x; \alpha) \tag{82}$$

with

$$\varphi_\alpha \equiv \left.\frac{\partial r}{\partial \alpha}\right|_{x,\,k} = kG_2/G_3 < 0. \tag{83}$$

Although (81) and (83) may be derived by calculation, economic intuition will suffice here. Consider (81); with k and r fixed, so is $\dot{p}/p = r - f'(k) + \delta$. Hence, an increase in α decreases $(1 - \alpha)k$, which tends to decrease the demand for money x, and feedback effects can only tend to decrease x further because $0 < G_2 < 1$ by assumption. Similarly, consider (83); if the demand for money x is to remain constant with constant k as α increases, the expected yield on the alternative asset r surely must fall.

Consequently, (12) must be replaced by

$$\dot{p}/p = \varphi(k, x; \alpha) - f'(k) + \delta, \tag{84}$$

and analogously to (32), we may conclude that $\dot{x} = 0$, $x \neq 0$, whenever

$$x = h(k; \theta, \alpha) = g[k, f'(k) + \lambda; \alpha], \tag{85}$$

where $0 < \varepsilon \leqq k(\alpha) \leqq \underline{k}$, $d\underline{k}(\alpha)/d\alpha > 0$, $0 \leqq \alpha < \bar{\alpha} \leqq 1$, and with

$$\left.\frac{\partial h}{\partial \alpha}\right|_{k,\theta} < 0 \tag{86}$$

implied by (81).[32] Accordingly, the curve $h(k; \theta, \alpha)$ shifts downward and to the right with an increase in α.

In summary, we may again derive a differential equation system

$$\begin{aligned} \dot{k}(k, x; \theta, \alpha) &= \{sf(k) - \xi k - (1-s)[f'(k) - \delta + \theta - \varphi(k, x; \alpha)]x\}/[(1-\alpha)+s\alpha], \\ \xi &= s\delta + (1-\alpha)n + s\alpha n, \\ \dot{x}(k, x; \theta, \alpha) &= [f'(k) + \lambda - \varphi(k, x; \alpha)]x. \end{aligned} \tag{87}$$

Now (87) is written in a form that indicates explicitly that θ and α enter as government policy parameters subject to choice, but assumed constant. The existence and uniqueness of an equilibrium point $(k^*, x^*) > (0, 0)$ for $\alpha \in (0, \bar{\alpha})$ are proved in the same manner as in Section 6-8 under exactly analogous assumptions, and we need not repeat the argument here.

A glance at the system of differential equations (87) shows that the stability properties are the same for all $\alpha \in [0, \bar{\alpha})$, and the case $\alpha = 0$ has already been treated in detail. Similarly, a stable model with adaptive expectations and sufficiently slow speeds of adjustment will have properties analogous to those stated in Section 6-12 where $\alpha = 0$. Since the comparative static properties of such a stable model are qualitatively identical to the system (87) with a

[32] Observe that $\underline{k}$ is determined by the intersection of the curves $\bar{r}(k)$ and $f'(k) + \lambda$ where $\bar{r}(k)$ is the solution to

$$0 = g[k, \bar{r}(k); \alpha],$$

and where, as assumed previously, $\bar{r}'(k) > 0$ (see Figure 18). Hence,

$$0 = g_1\, dk + g_2\, d\bar{r} + g_\alpha\, d\alpha$$

or

$$\left.\frac{\partial \bar{r}}{\partial \alpha}\right|_k = -g_\alpha/g_2 < 0.$$

The latter means that the $\bar{r}(k)$ curve shifts downward with an increase in α, implying the stated conclusion $d\underline{k}(\alpha)/d\alpha > 0$.

Finally, recall that the assumption $\underline{k} < k^{**}$ was required for the existence of a root $(k^*, x^*) > (0, 0)$ when $\alpha = 0$; see (37) and the subsequent discussion. Therefore, for any fixed θ it is necessary to restrict our attention to $\alpha \in [0, \bar{\alpha})$ where $\bar{\alpha}$ is defined as the root to $\underline{k}(\bar{\alpha}) = k^{***}$ and k^{***} satisfies $sf(k^{***}) - \xi k^{***} = 0$, where ξ is a parameter representing $s\delta + (1-\alpha)n + s\alpha n$. It is important to realize that $\bar{\alpha}$ may be substantially less than one, depending, of course, upon the function $f(k)$ and the exogenous parameters s, δ, and n.

For similar reasons very high values of θ may preclude the existence of an equilibrium point $(k^*, x^*) > (0, 0)$, as was true in the model with $\alpha = 0$.

saddlepoint equilibrium, we need only investigate the comparative statics of (87).

We have already stated that the curve $x = h(k; \theta, \alpha)$, along which $\dot{x} = 0$, $x \neq 0$, shifts downward and to the right for increases in either θ or α. Now, analogously to (43), define

$$\gamma(k; \alpha) \equiv [sf(k) - \xi k]/(1 - s)n; \tag{88}$$

clearly

$$\left.\frac{\partial \gamma}{\partial \alpha}\right|_k = k > 0. \tag{89}$$

Likewise, $d\tilde{k}/d\alpha = -n(1 - s)/sf''(\tilde{k}) > 0$, where $\tilde{k}$ is the root to $sf'(k) - \xi = 0$. Consequently the curve $\gamma(k; \alpha)$, pictured in Figure 23 for $\alpha = 0$, shifts upward and to the right for increases in α.

All the features just discussed are illustrated in Figure 27. The policy implications are immediately evident. For example, suppose the government insists upon zero inflation in equilibrium, which necessitates fixing $\theta = n = \dot{L}/L$. If $\alpha = 0$, as in our previous models, the equilibrium point (k^*, x^*) is completely determined and no further government control is possible. For illustrative purposes, suppose the equilibrium point A depicted in Figure 27 is possible with $\alpha = 0$ and $\theta = n$. By choosing a value of $\alpha \in [0, \bar{\alpha})$ a whole locus of equilibrium points is now possible. For example, any point on the curve labeled AB in Figure 27 is now a feasible equilibrium position.[33] (In Figure 27 it has been assumed that $\alpha < \bar{\alpha}$.)

[33] The proper slope of the AB curve in Figure 27 is not evident either graphically or intuitively. However, it is clear that any root k^* must satisfy

$$\Psi(k^*; \theta, \alpha) = sf(k^*) - \xi k^* - (1 - s)ng[k^*, f'(k^*) + \lambda; \alpha] = 0,$$

and the proof that (k^*, x^*) is unique implies

$$D^* \equiv \partial\Psi(k^*; \theta, \alpha)/\partial k^* < 0.$$

Consequently we find

$$\left.\frac{\partial k^*}{\partial \alpha}\right|_\theta = [g_\alpha - (1 - s)nk^*]/D^*,$$

which is clearly positive because g_α is negative; see (81).

Since $x^* = g[k^*, f'(k^*) + \lambda; \alpha]$, we may calculate

$$\left.\frac{\partial x^*}{\partial \alpha}\right|_\theta = [g_1 + g_2 f''(k^*)](\partial k^*/\partial \alpha) + g_\alpha,$$

and although the first term of the latter expression is clearly positive, g_α is negative. Therefore an increase in α, for any fixed θ, may either increase or decrease x^*.

However, observe from (81) that $g_\alpha^* = -k^*G_2/(1 - G_2)$ where G_2 represents the partial derivative of the demand for real per capita money balances with respect to real per capita private wealth. We may anticipate that G_2 is very near zero, in which case it is likely that $\partial x^*/\partial\alpha|_\theta$ is positive, as implied by the upward-sloping AB curve in Figure 27.

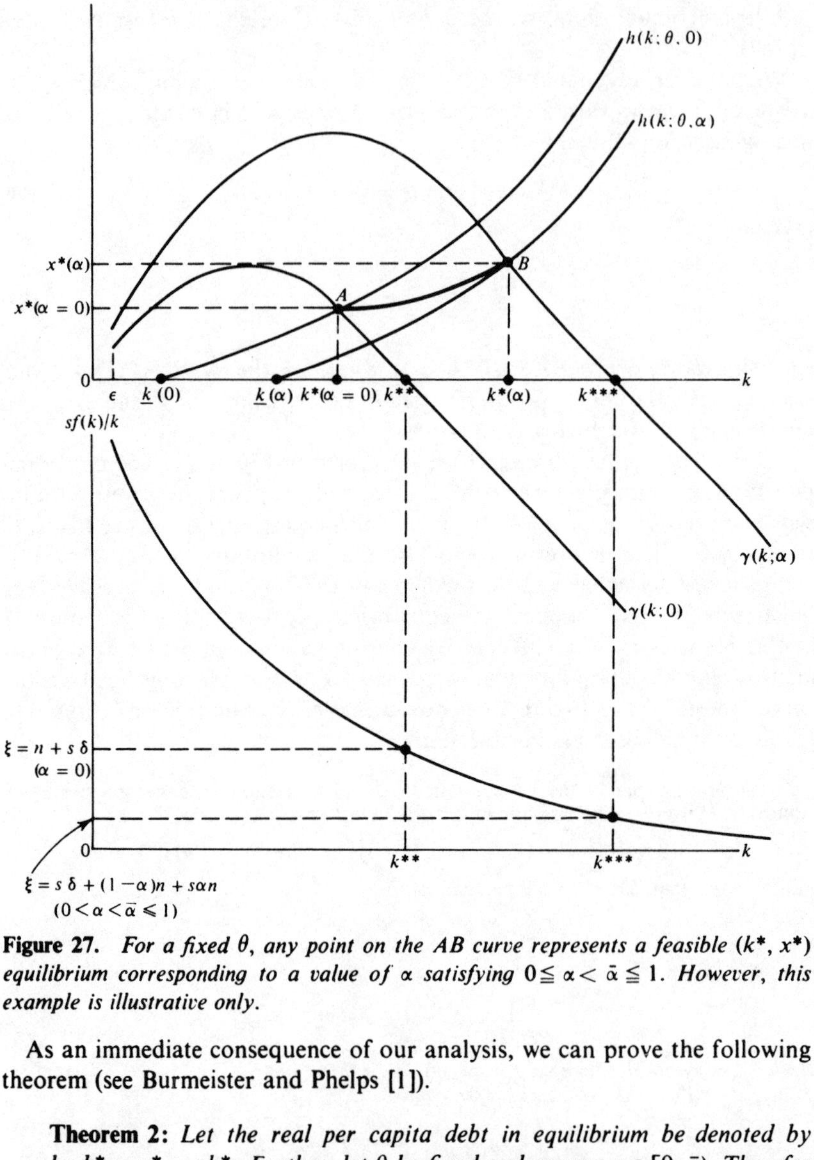

Figure 27. *For a fixed θ, any point on the AB curve represents a feasible (k^*, x^*) equilibrium corresponding to a value of α satisfying $0 \leq \alpha < \bar{\alpha} \leq 1$. However, this example is illustrative only.*

As an immediate consequence of our analysis, we can prove the following theorem (see Burmeister and Phelps [1]).

Theorem 2: *Let the real per capita debt in equilibrium be denoted by by $b^* \equiv x^* - \alpha k^*$. Further, let θ be fixed and assume $\alpha \in [0, \bar{\alpha})$. Then for any feasible equilibrium value of the capital/labor ratio k^* there corresponds one and only one value of the real per capita debt b^*. The exact relationship is*

$$b^* = \gamma(k^*; 0) = [sf(k^*) - (n + s\delta)k^*]/(1 - s)n$$

where $\gamma(k; \alpha)$ is defined by (88).

Proof: Equilibrium prevails if and only if $sf(k^*) - \xi k^* - (1 - s)nx^* = 0$, where $\xi = s\delta + (1 - \alpha)n + s\alpha n$. Substituting $x^* = b^* + \alpha k^*$ into the latter and simplifying yield the conclusion. QED.

As an immediate consequence of Theorem 2 we have Corollary 2.1.

Corollary 2.1: *Let the conditions stated in Theorem 2 be satisfied. Further, assume that for some fixed* θ *there exists a value of* $\alpha \in (0, \bar{\alpha})$ *for which* $k^* = k^{**}$ *is the equilibrium capital/labor ratio, i.e., assume* k^{**} *is a feasible equilibrium value. Then* $k^* = k^{**}$ *if and only if* $b^* = 0$, *where* k^{**} *is the no-money Solow equilibrium point at which*

$$sf(k^{**}) - (n + s\delta)k^{**} = 0.$$

As suggested in Section 6-11, the government may pursue policies that stabilize the system. Thus we have a second corollary of Theorem 2.

Corollary 2.2: *Any stabilizing policy for which*

$$\lim_{t\to\infty} k^t = k^{**} \Rightarrow \lim_{t\to\infty} b^t = 0.$$

Conversely, any stabilizing policy for which

$$\lim_{t\to\infty} b^t = 0 \Rightarrow \lim_{t\to\infty} k^t = k^{**}.$$

From Corollary 2.1 we conclude that the Solow point capital/labor ratio k^{**} represents an equilibrium if and only if the net indebtedness of the government (in the sense defined earlier) is zero. More generally, this analysis suggests that the additional policy instrument arising from government ownership of a portion of the capital stock provides, as expected, additional freedom in influencing the location of the equilibrium points for the system, but does not alter the structure of the system itself in any drastic fashion.

6-14. Conclusions and Other Issues

Let us summarize briefly the results of this chapter. In Section 6-2 we introduced a function describing the level of money balances desired (for speculative, as well as for transactions, purposes) in the economy. From the beginning we assumed that the yield on capital is always at the level required to bring about equilibrium on the money market (and hence on both asset markets).

That is, we have in the system at any time stocks of two assets, capital goods and paper money, and we assumed that the money yield on the capital good is uniquely determined at each instant by the requirement that the existing stocks be willingly held. Since the real rental on the capital good is determined by the stock of capital (and the known depreciation rate), and the price of the capital good is fixed at each instant, the requirement of money market equilibrium suffices to determine the rate of asset price inflation (the rate of capital gain on the capital good) each instant. With both the nominal stock of money and the labor force expanding at exogenously determined constant rates, the rate of change of real balances per capita is determined directly by the rate of asset price inflation. As in our previous models, a saving hypothesis determines the rate of change in the capital labor ratio. Hence the model may be reduced to two differential equations determining real balances per capita and capital per capita.

Section 6-3 elaborates properties of the demand for money function, while Section 6-4 indicates one approach to models in which money market clearing may not always be realized, either as a result of a conventional liquidity trap or otherwise. Though such models are important because of their relevance to situations of unemployment, we do not pursue them here. Instead we specify a saving hypothesis in Section 6-5, and develop the properties of the resulting differential equation system in Sections 6-6, 6-7, 6-8, and 6-9.

The central result is that there apparently exist two equilibrium points for the system, a saddlepoint equilibrium with positive real balances, and a stable equilibrium with zero real balances. (The fact of the saddlepoint equilibrium confirms results of Tobin [22] and Nagatani [9] in a slightly different context, but for the whole class of paths approaching the stable no-money equilibrium, it appears that money is indeed neutral in the long run). Section 6-10 analyzes a particularly special case where money is desired only as an asset, and hence will only be held if the rate of price deflation brings the money yield on capital down to zero.

The only policy instrument available in these models (apart from the saving rate which we have discussed before) is the rate of expansion of the nominal money supply. The only policy question at which the models can be directed is the effect of the paper asset on the real accumulation of the system. Interestingly, the analysis suggests that the presence of the paper asset does reduce the equilibrium capital labor ratio for the system (in this sense conferring a burden on later generations), but that, given a positive money stock, a higher rate of nominal money expansion raises saving rates and thus leads to higher capital/labor ratios in equilibrium.

Slightly richer policy choices may also be considered. Given the saddlepoint character of the equilibrium with positive real balances, one may ask whether a policy permitting changing rates of growth of the money supply might change that equilibrium to a stable one. Section 6-11 shows (in a simplified model) that a policy relating the rate of growth of the money supply to the revealed desire for money to hold does indeed stabilize the system, a result which should hardly be startling. (One must, however, ask whether this stabilizing policy is desirable, since the stable no-money Solow point may be a preferable target at which to be aiming.) It is also true that sluggish adjustment of expectations serves to stabilize the system as Section 6-12 shows (again in the context of a simplified model). Finally, Section 6-13 analyzes a model similar to that of Sections 6-7 to 6-9, but in which the government is imagined to own a fraction of the capital stock, and this fraction is itself a policy parameter. The additional instrument does yield additional scope for policy, but the structure of the model is not much altered.

As we stated in the introductory section to this chapter, the models we have presented and analyzed relate to somewhat subordinate aspects of the role of money in economic theory. In particular, we have retained the hypothesis that runs through our entire book, namely the assumption that there are no aggregate demand deficiencies and labor is fully employed. Section 6-4 mentions some of the serious pitfalls that may be encountered when more general models are attempted.

Our models also suffer from a defect noted in another context by Sidrauski:[34]

> The major limitation of this analysis is given by the fact that we have postulated a saving function and a demand function for real cash balances that are not explicitly derived from the maximizing behavior of the individual economic units of the economy. A more reasonable procedure would be to consider a representative economic unit in this simplified world and to analyze first how this economic unit would behave in a monetary economy if it attempted to maximize its well-being over its economic horizon. Once this is done, demand functions for assets and real consumption can be derived on the basis of which one could build a macroeconomic model that will describe the economy's time path under different assumptions about the behavior of the monetary authority.

The difficulty is to develop a satisfactory treatment of *uncertainty*. Other work by Sidrauski [17] and more recently by Levhari and Patinkin [7] attempts to circumvent the uncertainty problem in part by including real money balances in the utility functions of individuals and/or the production functions of firms. Samuelson [13] has also introduced money into the utility function, because, as he writes, "... one can put M into the utility function,

[34] [16], pp. 809–810.

along with other things, as a real convenience in a world of stochastic uncertainty and indivisible transaction charges."[35]

Undoubtedly, there is a great deal of merit to these heuristic arguments, but a rigorous uncertainty framework is beyond our reach at this moment. Hence we have followed simple saving-consumption hypotheses, and these at least have some empirical support, even if they do not rest upon an explicit derivation from a foundation of individual preference orderings.

The role of money in society is rather complex, but we see that to a substantial extent it serves as a mediating entity necessary because barter is not feasible and capital markets are not perfect or frictionless. In a world with institutional restrictions on modes of financing, where bankruptcy and liquidity crises may be real threats to firms with quite promising prospects of future earnings, money serves as a buffer stock smoothing transactions and providing liquidity. Thus, "money" is more than the artificial "outside" money considered in the previous pages; to deal adequately with important aspects of monetary problems we would have to examine descriptions of financial markets and financial institutions. Perhaps we also should question the assertion that some part of government liabilities can be treated as outside money. Why outside? Is it really accurate to suggest that government operations can be separated so thoroughly that agents in the economy do not see the government as conforming to the same double-entry accounting requirements as other economic institutions? Perhaps we require a descriptive theory bringing government decisions into the model on the same basis as other institutions that can borrow now only against future power to obtain earnings (through tax levies or otherwise).

To the extent these issues are important, the foregoing models fail to deal adequately with important features of a monetary economy. We can argue for our analysis only as a starting point. In the long run, we may hope that results are little changed from the real models earlier studied. Certainly this might be expected as a consequence of the emphasis on the simple mediating role played by money stocks.[36] On the other hand, we must remember that the presence of money offers an alternative form in which to hold wealth. To the extent that a saving flow is diverted in part from accumulation of physical assets to the acquisition of paper claims on an outside government, the equilibrium of the system and associated per capita income levels clearly may be affected, as demonstrated by this chapter.

[35] Samuelson [13], p. 8.

[36] The expectation is reinforced by the fact that in most of these monetary growth models there is a stable equilibrium (at the Solow point) which can be attained from a whole range of initial positions. Convergence to this point, where money balances effectively become irrelevant, is in these models a perfectly feasible and acceptable outcome, with none of the difficulties associated in recent growth models with divergence from the balanced growth (saddlepoint) equilibrium.

Exercises

1. Show that if $x = G[f(k), k + x, r]$ has $G_1 > 0$, $1 > G_2 > 0$, and $G_3 < 0$, then there exists a function of the form $x = g(k, r)$ with $g_1 > 0$ and $g_2 < 0$. Likewise, prove the existence of a function $r = \varphi(k, x)$ with $\varphi_1 > 0$, $\varphi_2 < 0$.
2. Prove that (31) may be solved for $x = h(k)$ with $h'(k) > 0$.
3. Derive the equations 34(a) and 34(b).
4. Show that a simple one-sector model without money in which net capital formation is a constant fraction (s) of net income implies the differential equation

$$\dot{k} = sf(k) - (n + s\delta)k = \dot{k}(k)$$

with

$$\dot{k}(k^{**}) = 0.$$

5. (a) Prove that $(1 - s)Y = C = F(K, L)$ if and only if $\Lambda(k, x) = x(\theta - \dot{p}/p) - sf(k)/(1 - s) - \delta k = 0$.
   (b) Show that there exists a function $k = \eta(x)$ such that $C \gtreqqless F(K, L)$ as $k \gtreqqless \eta(x)$.
   (c) Show $\eta'(x)$ is of indefinite sign in general.
   (d) Prove $k \leqq \eta(x)$ implies $\dot{k}(k, x) < 0$.
6. Show that the elasticity of $\gamma(k)$ is less than one for all $0 < \varepsilon \leqq k < k^{**}$.
7. Show that $dx^*/d\theta \gtreqqless 0$ as $k \gtreqqless \tilde{k}$ where $\tilde{k}$ is defined by $sf'(\tilde{k}) - (n + s\delta) = 0$.
8. Obtain expressions for J^*_{11}, J^*_{12}, J^*_{21}, J^*_{22}.
9. Derive equation (50).
10. Derive equations (53) and (54), and prove assertions (i) and (ii) on p. 181 of the text.
11. Derive the phase diagram illustrated in Figure 26.
12. Derive the equation $\dot{x} = \dot{x}(k, x)$ in (59).
13. Show that $J^*_{11} < 0$ for the simplified model discussed in Section 6-11.
14. Derive the equation (61).
15. Derive the expression for $\dot{\pi}$ given in equation (66).
16. Prove that $(k^*, \pi^*) > (0, 0)$ is locally stable if and only if $\partial\dot{\pi}/\partial\pi\,|_{(k^*, \pi^*)}$, given by equation (68), is negative.
17. Prove that equation (41) is always satisfied when (5) holds.

Answers and Hints

PROBLEM 3. Substitute into (20) $C = (1 - s)Y$, using the expression for Y given in (19).

PROBLEM 5.

(b) $\dfrac{\partial\Lambda}{\partial k} = x(-\varphi_k + f'') - sf'/(1 - s) - \delta < 0.$

(d) It suffices to prove that $(1-s)Y = C \geqq F(K, L)$ implies $\dot{k} < 0$. But, from (a) and (b) of this problem, $C \geqq F(K, L)$ if and only if $\Lambda(k, x) \geqq 0$, which in turn holds if and only if $(1-s)x(\theta - \dot{p}/p) \geqq sf(k) + (1-s)\delta k$. Therefore

$$\dot{k} = sf(k) - (n + s\delta)k - (1-s)(\theta - \dot{p}/p)x$$
$$\leqq sf(k) - (n + s\delta)k - sf(k) - (1-s)\delta k = -(n+\delta)k < 0.$$

PROBLEM 6. Derive an expression for the elasticity of $\gamma(k)$ and show that it is less than 1 as long as $f'(k)k < f(k)$ (which always holds).

PROBLEM 15. Derive an expression for $\dot{x}$ in terms of x, $\dot{\pi}$, π by combining (62) and (65); then equate the latter to the formulation for $\dot{x}$ given in (64).

References

[1] BURMEISTER, E., and E. S. PHELPS, "Money, Public Debt, Inflation and Real Interest," Discussion Paper No. 122, Department of Economics, University of Pennsylvania, Philadelphia, Pa. (June, 1969).

[2] CAGAN, P., "The Monetary Dynamics of Hyperinflation," in *Studies in the Quantity Theory of Money* (M. Friedman, Ed.). Chicago: University of Chicago Press, 1956, pp. 25–117.

[3] FOLEY, D., K. SHELL, and M. SIDRAUSKI, "Optimal Fiscal and Monetary Policy, and Economic Growth," *Journal of Political Economy*, **77**, *4*, Part 2 (July–August, 1969), pp. 698–719.

[4] — and M. SIDRAUSKI, *Monetary and Fiscal Policy in a Growing Economy*. New York: Macmillan, to be published in 1970.

[5] HAHN, F. H., "On Money and Growth," *Journal of Money, Credit and Banking* **I**, *2* (May, 1969), pp. 172–187.

[6] JOHNSON, H. G., "The Neoclassical One-Sector Growth Model: A Geometrical Exposition and Extension to a Monetary Economy," *Economica*, **XXXIII**, *131* (August, 1966), pp. 265–287.

[7] LEVHARI, D., and D. PATINKIN, "The Role of Money in a Simple Growth Model," *American Economic Review*, **LVIII**, *4* (September, 1968), pp. 713–753.

[8] MODIGLIANI, F., "The Monetary Mechanism and Its Interaction with Real Phenomena," *Review of Economics and Statistics*, **XLV**, *1* (February, 1963), pp. 79–107.

[9] NAGATANI, K., "Professor Tobin on Money and Economic Growth," forthcoming in *Econometrica*.

[10] ROSE, H., "On the Non-Linear Theory of the Employment Cycle," *Review of Economic Studies*, **XXXIV**, *98* (April, 1967), pp. 153–174.

[11] — "Real and Monetary Factors in the Business Cycle," *Journal of Money, Credit and Banking*, **I**, *2* (May, 1969), pp. 138–152.

[12] — "Unemployment in a Theory of Growth," *International Economic Review*, **7**, *3* (September, 1966), pp. 260–282.

[13] SAMUELSON, P. A., "What Classical and Neoclassical Monetary Theory Really Was," *The Canadian Journal of Economics*, **I**, *1* (February, 1968), pp. 1–15.

[14] — "Some Aspects of the Pure Theory of Capital," *Quarterly Journal of Economics*, **LI** (May, 1937), pp. 469–496.
[15] SHELL, K., M. SIDRAUSKI, and J. E. STIGLITZ, "Capital Gains, Income and Saving," *Review of Economic Studies*, **XXXVI**, *105* (January, 1969), pp. 15–26.
[16] SIDRAUSKI, M., "Inflation and Economic Growth," *Journal of Political Economy*, **75**, *6* (December, 1967), pp. 796–810.
[17] — "Rational Choice and Patterns of Growth in a Monetary Economy," *American Economic Review*, **LVII**, *2* (May, 1967), pp. 534–544.
[18] STEIN, J. L., "Growth in a Monetary Economy: Comment," *American Economic Review*, **LVIII**, *4* (September, 1968), pp. 944–950.
[19] — "Money and Capacity Growth," *Journal of Political Economy*, **LXXXIV**, *5* (October, 1966), pp. 451–465.
[20] — "Neoclassical and Keynes-Wicksell Monetary Growth Models," *Journal of Money, Credit and Banking*, **I**, *2* (May, 1969), pp. 153–171.
[21] TOBIN, J., "A Dynamic Aggregative Model," *Journal of Political Economy*, **LXIII**, *2* (April, 1955), pp. 103–115.
[22] — "Money and Economic Growth," *Econometrica*, **33**, *4* (October, 1965), pp. 671–684.
[23] — "The Neutrality of Money in Growth Models: A Comment," *Economica*, **XXXIV**, *133* (February, 1967), pp. 69–72.

[10]

Econometrica, Vol. 41, No. 1 (January, 1973)

THE "SADDLEPOINT PROPERTY" AND THE STRUCTURE OF DYNAMIC HETEROGENEOUS CAPITAL GOOD MODELS

BY EDWIN BURMEISTER, CHRISTOPHER CATON, A. RODNEY DOBELL, AND STEPHEN ROSS[1]

The topological properties of dynamic heterogeneous capital good models are examined, and it is found that the savings hypothesis crucially influences the dimension of the manifold consisting of the locus of backward solutions from stationary equilibrium. If not all capital gains are saved, the convergent manifold is generally of higher dimension than it is if no income from capital gains is spent on consumption. Accordingly, the characteristic equation for the associated linear system near stationary equilibrium may have more than half its roots with negative real parts, and thus in general the model does not possess a "regular saddlepoint property."

1. INTRODUCTION AND SUMMARY

MUCH RECENT WORK on the dynamics of heterogeneous capital models has emphasized that the unique stationary equilibrium for the models under study is a "saddlepoint" in price-quantity space. Generally one speaks of a saddlepoint in E^{2n} as a critical point with the property that the locus of backward solutions from equilibrium is a manifold of dimension n; thus, given any initial vector of capital stocks, there exists a unique initial price vector that will bring the system asymptotically to the stationary equilibrium.[2] *However, this saddlepoint property does not hold for many heterogeneous capital models*; we have found a class of counterexamples in which the equilibrium point is approached along a manifold of dimension greater than n. Thus, given an initial vector of per capita capital stocks, there exist many assignments of initial prices for which the system converges asymptotically to its unique stationary equilibrium.[3] This result, which is valid for many technologies not studied here, depends crucially upon the assumption that not all capital gains are saved.

This result suggests that general stability theorems may be difficult to obtain for dynamic heterogeneous capital good models because no model of our class

[1] The authors wish to acknowledge, with thanks, the programming and computational assistance of Imre Farkas and Michael Wolfson, both of the University of Toronto. The research of E. Burmeister and S. Ross was supported by the National Science Foundation, and that of A. R. Dobell by the Canada Council under a grant from the Izaak Walton Killan Memorial Fund. An earlier version of this paper was presented at the Second World Congress of the Econometric Society, Cambridge, England, September 8–14, 1970.

[2] More precisely, existence of a unique price vector with this property depends also upon the manifold "covering" the capital space. We shall also follow a convenient precedent and call a stationary point for which the characteristic equation of the associated linear system has k roots with negative real part and $n - k$ roots with positive real part a stationary point of type k or a k-saddle. (See [4].)

[3] Hahn has conjectured that "it may be that there are a number of accumulation paths which converge" [7, p. 180] in a heterogeneous capital good model with "no saving out of wages and no consumption out of profit" [7, p. 176]. However, we do not use this savings assumption.

Likewise, Samuelson's work [10 and 11] indicates that the dynamic equilibrium of heterogeneous capital good models may be a "regular" saddlepoint of type n under very general assumptions, but *only* when all capital gains are saved. Also, in unpublished work Stiglitz has indicated that with finitely-lived capital goods the equilibrium point may not be a saddlepoint.

has a saddlepoint of type n, and hence none can ever be viewed as a "regular Hamiltonian system" resulting from an optimization problem. Given an initial vector of (per capita) capital stocks $k(0)$, however, it is still not true that the assignment of any arbitrary initial price vector $p(0)$ will yield asymptotic convergence to equilibrium. Furthermore, in a specific example given below, all paths which do not converge to equilibrium have the property that at least one price becomes zero in finite time, and hence such paths are revealed to be inconsistent with perfect competition.[4] The presence of this result is important because the models studied by Shell-Stiglitz [**12**] and Caton-Shell [**3**] (in which this property was previously demonstated) have two important special features: (i) total consumption equals total wage income, and (ii) the production possibility frontier in output space is not strictly concave. One might suspect that the finite time property depends crucially on (i), (ii), or both, but our example demonstrates that this is not the case.

2. THE TECHNOLOGICAL STRUCTURE OF A GENERAL CLASS OF HETEROGENEOUS CAPITAL GOOD MODELS

Consider a model with one (possibly composite) consumption good and n different capital goods. Denoting the outputs of these by $Y_0, Y_1, \ldots, Y_n$, respectively, the capital stocks by $K_1, \ldots, K_n$, and the labor supply by $L \equiv K_0$, there exists a production possibility frontier

$$Y_0 = T(Y_1, \ldots, Y_n; K_0, K_1, \ldots, K_n) \tag{1}$$

or, using lower case letters for per capita quantities,

$$y_0 = P(y_1, \ldots, y_n; 1, k_1, \ldots, k_n). \tag{2}$$

For mathematical simplicity we introduce the following assumption: *For any given k_i's > 0, the function T defines a strictly concave hypersurface in the space of admissible* $(y_0, y_1, \ldots, y_n)$. We emphasize, however, that our results do not depend upon this assumption as was indicated in an earlier and longer version of this paper. Note that the function T embodies all the usual static efficiency conditions of pure competition or Lerner-Lange socialism. In particular

$$\partial T/\partial Y_i \equiv T_i = -p_i \qquad (i = 1, \ldots, n) \tag{3}$$

are the competitive prices of the respective outputs, while

$$\partial T/\partial K_i \equiv T_{n+i+1} = w_i \qquad (i = 0, 1, \ldots, n) \tag{4}$$

are the competitive gross rental rates of the respective factor inputs; the lower case letters now indicate that prices and rental rates are in terms of the consumption good numeraire.

[4] This example satisfies all the usual neoclassical assumptions and also possesses the following properties: (i) All prices (in terms of the consumption good as numeraire) and capital stocks (per capita) can take on any value in the open interval $(0, \infty)$; (ii) momentary equilibrium is always unique for any assigned vectors of prices and capital stocks p and k respectively; (iii) the differential equations for p and k are always causal; and (iv) there exists a unique stationary equilibrium (p^*, k^*).

Consider now given k_i's and given p_i's, say $p_i = \bar{p}_i > 0$ and $k_i = \bar{k}_i > 0$ $(i = 1, \ldots, n)$. Provided equations (3) can be satisfied with equality, clearly momentary (static) equilibrium is completely determined and is unique. Since by assumption T defines a strictly concave hypersurface in the space of admissible $(y_0, y_1, \ldots, y_n)$, the tangency conditions (3) uniquely determine the corresponding outputs $(\bar{y}_0, \bar{y}_1, \ldots, \bar{y}_n)$. Finally, since the w_i given by (4) depend only on $(\bar{y}_1, \ldots, \bar{y}_n)$ and $(\bar{k}_1, \ldots, \bar{k}_n)$, these too are uniquely determined.[5]

The dynamics of the system is determined by $2n$ differential equations in the k_i's and p_i's. We assume that the labor supply grows at the exponential rate g and that the ith capital good depreciates at the exponential rate δ_i; hence the capital accumulation equations are simply

$$(5) \qquad \dot{k}_i = y_i - (g + \delta_i)k_i \qquad (i = 1, \ldots, n).$$

Likewise it is well-known that the capital accumulation process is efficient only if

$$(6) \qquad \dot{p}_i = -w_i + (r_0 + \delta_i)p_i \qquad (i = 1, \ldots, n)$$

where r_0 is the common interest or profit rate; these familiar conditions are also necessary for profit maximization in a world of pure competition, perfect capital markets, and perfect myopic foresight. (We will omit the index t for time where no confusion is possible; however, when clarity is needed we will write $y_i(t)$, $k_i(t)$, etc.)

Our primary concern is the evolution of the system governed by equations (5) and (6). As shown above, both the y_i's and the w_i's are functions of $(p_1, \ldots, p_n)$ and $(k_1, \ldots, k_n)$. Thus *if* we can determine the interest or profit rate endogenously—i.e., if there exists a function

$$(7) \qquad r_0 = r_0(p_1, \ldots, p_n; k_1, \ldots, k_n),$$

then (5) and (6) may be written in the causal, autonomous form

$$(8) \qquad \begin{aligned} \dot{k}_i &= f^i(k_1, \ldots, k_n; p_1, \ldots, p_n), \\ \dot{p}_i &= h^i(k_1, \ldots, k_n; p_1, \ldots, p_n), \end{aligned} \qquad (i = 1, \ldots, n),$$

with initial conditions $k_i(0) = \bar{k}_i$ and $p_i(0) = \bar{p}_i$. We now turn to the question of when r_0 can be determined by an equation such as (7).[6]

[5] Of course, for some sets of exogenous $\bar{k}_i$'s and $\bar{p}_i$'s, conditions (3) may not have a solution with equalities, and in this case it becomes necessary to study "corner solutions." When the problem of "corner solutions" exists, the dynamics of the model cannot be expressed as causal differential equations of the usual kind, but rather the model must be studied as a more complex "dynamical system." Such problems are of interest, but for our purposes we wish to avoid them and to concentrate on the properties of a simpler system. Accordingly, we assume that for *any* positive values of the p_i's and k_i's, equations (3) can all be satisfied with equalities and hence momentary (static) equilibrium is always unique. In the examples given below this assumption is satisfied.

[6] Hahn's model [6] implicitly assumes that all capital gains are saved, so that the relationship equating realized investment to desired saving does not explicitly involve the yield r_0. It is this that accounts for the fact that only $n - 1$ prices may be chosen initially to be consistent with momentary equilibrium. So long as some income from capital gains is consumed, the saving equation can be solved directly for r_0, the common yield or profit rate on assets. We shall elaborate upon this observation below.

The basic flow equilibrium condition asserts that $\dot{V} = S$ where $\dot{V}$ is the realized change in the real value of capital (wealth) and S is desired saving.[7] On the assumption that the propensities to save from the three components of an income stream—capital gains, net rentals, and wages—are given constants s_c, s_r, and s_w, respectively, we obtain

$$(9) \qquad S = s_c \sum_{i=1}^{n} \dot{p}_i K_i + s_r \sum_{i=1}^{n} (w_i K_i - p_i \delta_i K_i) + s_w w_0 K_0$$

and

$$(10) \qquad \dot{V} = \frac{d}{dt}\left(\sum_{i=1}^{n} p_i K_i\right) = \sum_{i=1}^{n} \dot{p}_i K_i + \sum_{i=1}^{n} p_i \dot{K}_i.$$

Substituting $\dot{p}_i$ from (6), using $\dot{K}_i = Y_i - \delta_i K_i$, and manipulating the income identity $\Sigma_{i=0}^{n} p_i Y_i = \Sigma_{i=0}^{n} w_i K_i$, we find that (9) and (10) can be solved for r_0 provided $s_c < 1$. For example, if $0 \leqslant s_r = s_c < 1$ and $s_w = 0$, we may solve explicitly for

$$(11) \qquad r_0 = \frac{\sum_{i=1}^{n} (w_i K_i - p_i Y_i)}{(1 - s_c) \sum_{i=1}^{n} p_i K_i} = \frac{Y_0 - w_0 K_0}{(1 - s_c)V}$$

or, in per capita terms,

$$(12) \qquad r_0 = (y_0 - w_0)/(1 - s_c)v$$

where $v \equiv V/K_0$ is the per capita value of wealth in terms of the consumption good as numeraire. Since all the variables on the right-hand side of (12) are functions only of $(p_1, \ldots, p_n; k_1, \ldots, k_n)$, this relationship implicitly defines (7).

Similarly suppose $s_c = s_r = s_w \equiv s$ where $0 < s < 1$; then we have

$$(13) \qquad r_0 = [Y_0 - (1 - s)w_0 K_0]/(1 - s)V$$

or

$$(14) \qquad r_0 = [y_0 - (1 - s)w_0]/(1 - s)v,$$

and again r_0 is determined endogenously as a function of the p_i's and k_i's.

3. A SPECIFIC MODEL

We can now apply the above to a specific model. Let $n = 2$ and assume that the production possibility frontier is given by

$$(15) \qquad (Y_0^2 + Y_1^2 + Y_2^2)^{\frac{1}{2}} = K_0^{\alpha_0} K_1^{\alpha_1} K_2^{\alpha_2}$$

[7] This equilibrium condition is found in the writings of many neoclassical authors. An economic justification in the context of this model is given by Burmeister and Dobell [2, pp. 297–298 and 303–304].

where $\alpha_0 + \alpha_1 + \alpha_2 = 1$. Thus equation (1) becomes

(16) $$Y_0 = T(Y_1, Y_2; K_0, K_1, K_2) = (K_0^{2\alpha_0} K_1^{2\alpha_1} K_2^{2\alpha_2} - Y_1^2 - Y_2^2)^{\frac{1}{2}}.$$

We may take the viewpoint that

(17) $$Z = K_0^{\alpha_0} K_1^{\alpha_1} K_2^{\alpha_2}$$

is the production function for an intermediate product Z. Then Z is "split" or "cracked" in accordance with

(18) $$Z = (Y_0^2 + Y_1^2 + Y_2^2)^{\frac{1}{2}},$$

i.e., Z is the radius of a ball in E^3 with its center at the origin; the radius of the ball is determined by factor endowments. Thus relative prices, which determine a hyperplane tangent to $(Y_0^2 + Y_1^2 + Y_2^2)^{\frac{1}{2}}$ when conditions (3) are satisfied, can assume *any* positive values for any positive k_i's. However, the production process given by (18) and its associated cost function are self-dual, so that

(19) $$(P_0^2 + P_1^2 + P_2^2)^{\frac{1}{2}} = P_Z$$

or

(20) $$(1 + p_1^2 + p_2^2)^{\frac{1}{2}} = P_Z/P_0 \equiv p_Z.$$

Of course, p_Z is simply the price of the intermediate product in terms of the consumption good as numeraire. Since the cost function for the Cobb-Douglas production function is

(21) $$\left(\frac{W_0}{\alpha_0}\right)^{\alpha_0}\left(\frac{W_1}{\alpha_1}\right)^{\alpha_1}\left(\frac{W_2}{\alpha_2}\right)^{\alpha_2},$$

in equilibrium we have

(22) $$(1 + p_1^2 + p_2^2)^{\frac{1}{2}} = p_Z = \left(\frac{w_0}{\alpha_0}\right)^{\alpha_0}\left(\frac{w_1}{\alpha_1}\right)^{\alpha_1}\left(\frac{w_2}{\alpha_2}\right)^{\alpha_2}.$$

In the next section we will see that the relationship (22) appears in many calculations.

In order to simplify the calculations which follow, we shall suppose $\alpha_1 = \alpha_2 \equiv \alpha$ and $\alpha_0 = 1 - 2\alpha$. We also adopt the "neoclassical savings assumption" $s_c = s_r = s_w \equiv s, 0 < s < 1$, and we assume that both capital goods depreciate at the common rate, δ. It should be noted that, given our assumptions, this model may behave as a one capital good, two-sector model which is known to be stable. In particular, this result follows when $k_1(t) = k_2(t)$ and $p_1(t) = p_2(t)$ for all t and "aggregation" is possible. Nevertheless, our model is continuous in the parameters α_1 and α_2, so certainly our qualitative results remain valid when α_1 and α_2 differ slightly, although in such cases *no* aggregation is possible. Indeed, computer calculations of the growth paths when $\alpha_1 \neq \alpha_2$ verify the natural global extension of an important local stability property discussed below, namely in a neighborhood of equilibrium three characteristic roots have negative real parts and only one has a positive real part.

Finally, it should be stressed again that although the technology we have specified allows us to avoid all "corner solution" problems, the assumption that such problems do not exist in general is quite unfounded. When such problems occur, of course, they are not important for local analysis provided the equilibrium point is interior. Likewise, uniqueness of both momentary (static) and dynamic equilibria cannot, in general, be ensured without strong regularity conditions such as those we have imposed.

4. DETERMINATION OF UNIQUE MOMENTARY AND DYNAMIC EQUILIBRIA

The production possibility frontier for this model can now be written as

$$Y_0 = [K_0^{2(1-2\alpha)}K_1^{2\alpha}K_2^{2\alpha} - Y_1^2 - Y_2^2]^{\frac{1}{2}} \tag{23}$$

or in intensive form

$$y_0 = (k_1^{2\alpha}k_2^{2\alpha} - y_1^2 - y_2^2)^{\frac{1}{2}}. \tag{24}$$

From (3) we know that

$$\partial y_0/\partial y_i = -p_i \qquad (i = 1, 2). \tag{25}$$

Thus

$$\begin{aligned} p_1 &= -(k_1^{2\alpha}k_2^{2\alpha} - y_1^2 - y_2^2)^{-\frac{1}{2}}(-y_1) \\ &= y_1/y_0, \end{aligned} \tag{26}$$

and, similarly,

$$p_2 = y_2/y_0. \tag{27}$$

Combining these with (24), one obtains

$$\begin{aligned} y_0 &= \frac{k_1^\alpha k_2^\alpha}{p_Z}, \\ y_1 &= \frac{p_1 k_1^\alpha k_2^\alpha}{p_Z}, \\ y_2 &= \frac{p_2 k_1^\alpha k_2^\alpha}{p_Z}, \end{aligned} \tag{28}$$

where p_Z is defined by (20). Thus, for initial factor endowments and prices, the outputs of the consumption good and of the two capital goods are each uniquely determined.

Equations (4) enable us to evaluate the gross rental rates of the factor inputs at any point of time:

$$\begin{aligned} w_i &= \partial y_0/\partial k_i \qquad (i = 1, 2), \\ w_0 &= \partial Y_0/\partial K_0. \end{aligned} \tag{29}$$

It can be shown that (29) yields

$$
\begin{aligned}
&w_1 = \alpha k_1^{\alpha-1} k_2^{\alpha} p_Z, \\
(30)\quad &w_2 = \alpha k_1^{\alpha} k_2^{\alpha-1} p_Z, \quad \text{and} \\
&w_0 = (1 - 2\alpha) k_1^{\alpha} k_2^{\alpha} p_Z,
\end{aligned}
$$

which, in turn, satisfy (22).

We now seek the solutions to the equations

$$\dot{k}_i = 0,$$

and

$$\dot{p}_i = 0 \qquad (i = 1, 2).$$

Combining (5), (6), (14), (28), and (30), we require

$$(31) \qquad \dot{k}_i = \frac{p_i k_1^{\alpha} k_2^{\alpha}}{p_Z} - (g + \delta) k_i = 0$$

and

$$(32) \qquad \dot{p}_i = p_i(r_0 + \delta) - \alpha \frac{k_1^{\alpha} k_2^{\alpha}}{k_i} p_Z = 0,$$

where the common net own-rate of return is

$$r_0 = \frac{k_1^{\alpha} k_2^{\alpha}[1 - (1 - s)(1 - 2\alpha)p_Z^2]}{p_Z(1 - s)(p_1 k_1 + p_2 k_2)}.$$

Now, from the symmetry which has been introduced for computational convenience, it is obvious that $k_1^* = k_2^* \equiv k^*$ and $p_1^* = p_2^* \equiv p^*$ where the starred variables represent equilibrium values. Thus in equilibrium (33) and (34) will hold:

$$(33) \qquad \dot{k} = pk^{2\alpha}(1 + 2p^2)^{-\frac{1}{2}} - (g + \delta)k = 0$$

and

$$
\begin{aligned}
&\dot{p} = \frac{k^{2\alpha}(1 + 2p^2)^{-\frac{1}{2}}[1 - (1 - s)(1 - 2\alpha)(1 + 2p^2)]}{2(1 - s)k} \\
(34)\quad &\qquad -\alpha k^{2\alpha-1}(1 + 2p^2)^{\frac{1}{2}} + p\delta = 0.
\end{aligned}
$$

From (33)

$$k^{2\alpha-1}(1 + 2p^2)^{-\frac{1}{2}} = (g + \delta)/p;$$

substituting this in (34), one obtains

$$\frac{g + \delta}{2p(1 - s)}[1 - (1 - s)(1 - 2\alpha)(1 + 2p^2)] - \frac{\alpha(g + \delta)(1 + 2p^2)}{p} + p\delta = 0,$$

from which one finally derives

$$(35)\qquad p^* = \sqrt{\frac{s(g+\delta)}{2(1-s)g}},\qquad k^* = \left(\sqrt{\frac{2(g+\delta)(g+s\delta)}{s}}\right)^{1/(2\alpha-1)}.$$

The $\alpha_1 \neq \alpha_2$ case is a straightforward generalization of the above but is not necessary for our purposes. Thus equilibrium values for prices and capital stocks are defined and uniquely determined in terms of the parameters of the system.

5. ANALYSIS OF LOCAL STABILITY

In this section we examine the stability properties of the equilibrium point of the system. The analysis will reveal that the particular saddlepoint property found in previous heterogeneous capital good models is not generally valid, i.e., there are not always n roots with positive real part and n with negative real part in the neighborhood of the equilibrium point. On the contrary, in our example there are, in fact, three stable directions of approach to equilibrium and only one unstable direction.

We begin by expanding the system linearly about the equilibrium point (p^*, k^*). Considerations of symmetry yield a perturbed system of the form

$$(36)\qquad \begin{bmatrix}\dot{\xi}\\ \dot{\eta}\end{bmatrix} = \begin{bmatrix} a & b & c & d\\ b & a & d & c\\ e & f & j & h\\ f & e & h & j\end{bmatrix}\begin{bmatrix}\xi\\ \eta\end{bmatrix},$$

where

$$\xi \equiv \begin{bmatrix}p_1\\ p_2\end{bmatrix} - \begin{bmatrix}p^*\\ p^*\end{bmatrix},$$

$$\eta \equiv \begin{bmatrix}k_1\\ k_2\end{bmatrix} - \begin{bmatrix}k^*\\ k^*\end{bmatrix},$$

$$a \equiv \left.\frac{\partial \dot{p}_1}{\partial p_1}\right|_{(p^*,k^*)} = \left.\frac{\partial \dot{p}_2}{\partial p_2}\right|_{(p^*,k^*)},$$

and

$$b \equiv \left.\frac{\partial \dot{p}_1}{\partial p_2}\right|_{(p^*,k^*)} = \left.\frac{\partial \dot{p}_2}{\partial p_1}\right|_{(p^*,k^*)},$$

with obvious notation for the remaining terms.

The partitioned property of the system matrix can be exploited to simplify the computation of both the eigenvectors and the characteristic roots of the linear system. Notice first that the eigenvectors are of the two types:

$$\text{(37)} \qquad \begin{bmatrix} 1 \\ 1 \\ \beta_1 \\ \beta_1 \end{bmatrix}, \begin{bmatrix} 1 \\ 1 \\ \beta_2 \\ \beta_2 \end{bmatrix}; \quad \text{and} \quad \begin{bmatrix} 1 \\ -1 \\ \theta_3 \\ -\theta_3 \end{bmatrix}, \begin{bmatrix} 1 \\ -1 \\ \theta_4 \\ -\theta_4 \end{bmatrix}.$$

By substitution into the original system, (36), the eigenvectors of the first type yield

$$\lambda = (a + b) + \beta(c + d)$$

and

$$\lambda\beta = (e + f) + \beta(j + h),$$

and upon eliminating β we obtain an equation for two of the characteristic roots,

$$\text{(38)} \qquad [\lambda - (a + b)][\lambda - (j + h)] = (c + d)(e + f);$$

similarly for the second type of eigenvector we obtain

$$\text{(39)} \qquad [\lambda - (a - b)][\lambda - (j - h)] = (c - d)(e - f).$$

The discriminant of equation (38) is given by

$$\begin{aligned} \Delta &= [(a + b) + (j + h)]^2 - 4[(a + b)(j + h) - (c + d)(e + f)] \\ &= [(a + b) - (j + h)]^2 + 4(c + d)(e + f) \\ &\geqslant 4(c + d)(e + f). \end{aligned}$$

Now,

$$\begin{aligned} c + d &\equiv \left.\frac{\partial \dot{p}_1}{\partial k_1}\right|_{(p^*,k^*)} + \left.\frac{\partial \dot{p}_1}{\partial k_2}\right|_{(p^*,k^*)} \\ &= -\frac{(2\alpha - 1)(g + \delta)}{2k^*p^*(1 - s)} \frac{s\delta}{g}, \end{aligned}$$

and

$$\begin{aligned} e + f &\equiv \left.\frac{\partial \dot{k}_1}{\partial p_1}\right|_{(p^*,k^*)} + \left.\frac{\partial \dot{k}_1}{\partial p_2}\right|_{(p^*,k^*)} \\ &= \frac{k^*}{p^*} \frac{(g + \delta)(1 - s)g}{g + s\delta}. \end{aligned}$$

Therefore,

$$\text{(40)} \qquad (c + d)(e + f) = \frac{(1 - 2\alpha)(1 - s)g(g + \delta)\delta}{g + s\delta} > 0.$$

It follows that the roots of equation (38) are both real and distinct. By a similar calculation

$$(c - d)(e - f) = \frac{2\alpha(g + s\delta)(g + \delta)}{s} > 0, \tag{41}$$

which implies that the discriminant of (39) is also positive and, hence, it too has real and distinct roots.

To determine the signs of the roots we need only note that the sign of the product of the roots of (38) is given by

$$\begin{aligned} \operatorname{sign} \lambda_1\lambda_2 &= \operatorname{sign} \{(a + b)(j + h) - (c + d)(e + f)\} \\ &= \operatorname{sign} \left\{ -\left[\frac{g(g + \delta)}{(g + s\delta)} + g\right][(g + \delta)(2\alpha - 1)] \right. \\ &\qquad \left. - \frac{(1 - 2\alpha)(1 - s)g(g + \delta)\delta}{(g + s\delta)} \right\} \\ &= \operatorname{sign} \{(1 - 2\alpha)(g + \delta)g(2g + (s + 1)\delta) \\ &\qquad -(1 - 2\alpha)(1 - s)g(g + \delta)\delta\} \\ &= \operatorname{sign} \{2g + (s + 1)\delta - (1 - s)\delta\} \\ &= \operatorname{sign} \{2g + 2s\delta\} = (+). \end{aligned} \tag{42}$$

It follows that both roots have the same sign. Since the sum of the roots is given by

$$\begin{aligned} \lambda_1 + \lambda_2 &= (a + b) + (j + h) \\ &= -\frac{g(g + \delta)}{(g + s\delta)} - g + (g + \delta)(2\alpha - 1) < 0, \end{aligned} \tag{43}$$

both roots are negative. The product of the roots of equation (39), however, is given by

$$\begin{aligned} \operatorname{sign} (\lambda_3\lambda_4) &= \operatorname{sign} \{(a - b)(j - h) - (c - d)(e - f)\} \\ &= \operatorname{sign} \left\{\frac{1}{s}2\alpha(g + s\delta)[-(g + \delta)] - \frac{1}{s}2\alpha(g + s\delta)(g + \delta)\right\} \\ &= (-), \end{aligned} \tag{44}$$

and, hence, one root will be negative and one will be positive. Thus we have proved that three of the four characteristic roots are negative and only one is positive.

Since the roots of (38) and (39) are distinct, it follows from (37) that the eigenvectors are all linearly independent. Consequently, the four eigenvectors span E^4 and the solution to the differential system local to (p^*, k^*) may be written as

$$\begin{bmatrix} \xi \\ \eta \end{bmatrix} = c_1 X_1 e^{\lambda_1 t} + c_2 X_2 e^{\lambda_2 t} + c_3 X_3 e^{\lambda_3 t} + c_4 X_4 e^{\lambda_4 t}, \tag{45}$$

where X_i is the eigenvector associated with λ_i, the c_i are constants determined by the initial conditions, and λ_4 is the positive root. Hence for any initial (p_1, p_2, k_1, k_2) such that the deviation vector (ξ, η) lies in the subspace spanned by the vectors associated with the negative characteristic roots,

$$\begin{bmatrix} 1 \\ 1 \\ \beta_1 \\ \beta_1 \end{bmatrix}, \quad \begin{bmatrix} 1 \\ 1 \\ \beta_2 \\ \beta_2 \end{bmatrix}, \quad \text{and} \quad \begin{bmatrix} 1 \\ -1 \\ \theta_3 \\ -\theta_3 \end{bmatrix},$$

the system will converge to (p^*, k^*). What is required is simply that (ξ, η) be orthogonal to the independent direction provided by the eigenvector of the positive root,

$$X_4 = \begin{bmatrix} 1 \\ -1 \\ \theta_4 \\ -\theta_4 \end{bmatrix}.$$

Moreover, these local properties generalize: the subspace spanned by the three stable eigenvectors, X_1, X_2, and X_3 will be tangent in E^4 at the stationary point, (p^*, k^*), to the three dimensional manifold along which solutions converge to equilibrium. A proof of this global dynamic property is given in Section 7 below.

6. GENERALIZATION TO n CAPITAL GOODS

The results of Section 5 also serve as a counterexample to any conjecture that in a heterogeneous capital good model, given the n initial capital stocks, there always exists a *unique* choice of the remaining free prices that will allow the system to converge to the equilibrium Golden Age growth path. In our above example there is, in fact, an entire three dimensional manifold containing paths that converge to the equilibrium point. Given an initial $(k_1(0), k_2(0))$ we can choose either of the other prices, say $p_1(0)$, and a value for the remaining price, $p_2(0)$, can be found that will enable the system to converge to (p^*, k^*).[8]

This property is shared by all models that allow consumption out of capital gains but not by models where all gains are saved. One way to see the distinction between implications of the two savings hypotheses is to rewrite (5) and (6) as

$$\dot{k} = F(p, k)$$

and

$$\dot{p} = H(p, k, r_0)$$

[8] Strictly speaking we have not verified that the three dimensional manifold may be extended globally in a non-pathological manner, but it seems highly unlikely that the dimensionality of the manifold will be altered as we move from (p^*, k^*). Calculations have verified this global property for particular examples, and it is proved for a special case in the next section.

where $k = (k_1, \ldots, k_n)$ and $p = (p_1, \ldots, p_n)$. To close the model we need an equation which allows us to solve for the common interest rate r_0. When consumption out of capital gains is allowed, the equilibrium condition $S = \dot{V}$ can be solved directly for

$$r_0 = r_0(p, k)$$

which allows us to write the dynamic equations in the causal form of (8). Thus, for example, (14) implies (7).

On the other hand, when capital gains are all saved, the savings hypothesis takes the form $\Psi(p, k) = 0$ and *does not* contain r_0 explicitly. Differentiating the function $\Psi(p, k)$ allows us to again find a function $r_0 = r_0(p, k)$, as in (7). Notice, however, that $\Psi(p, k) = 0$ imposes *one additional* restriction on the economy. In particular, given the initial capital stocks, $k(0)$, not all choices of $p(0)$ are admissible, only those for which $\Psi(p(0), k(0)) = 0$.

Consequently, when all capital gains are saved, the system is restricted to motions along a manifold of dimension $2n - 1$, and if n initial capital stocks are given, only $n - 1$ prices are open to choice. It is not surprising, then, that in the specialized two capital good models that have employed such savings hypotheses, there is a unique choice of the initial price vector which allows convergence to the equilibrium growth path. Given the $n + 1(=3)$ restrictions in such models, the specification of $(k_1(0), k_2(0))$ leaves only one price free. Once $p_1(0)$ is chosen, the savings relation determines $p_2(0)$ and future development of the economy. In effect, then, it would be impossible to have convergence along a manifold unless the economy were actually stable.

When capital gains enter into the savings relation in a meaningful way, we actually gain a degree of freedom since we now no longer are imposing any restriction on the initial price choices. As a result, we are free to choose both $p_1(0)$ and $p_2(0)$, although only a restricted set of such choices will allow convergence.

In a general n capital good model where not all capital gains are saved, we can freely choose all of the n initial prices. Furthermore, we are led to conjecture that for a wide class of models there will be $n + 1$ stable directions of approach to equilibrium and $n - 1$ unstable ones, and the stationary point will be approached along paths lying in a manifold of dimensionality $n + 1$; in other words, having chosen any one initial price, there exists a unique choice of the remaining $n - 1$ prices for which the model converges.

This conjecture is consistent with the work of Samuelson [**11**] who has proved that if consumption is given by a general consumption function of the form

$$y_0 = \varepsilon h(k_1, \ldots, k_n; \dot{k}_1, \ldots, \dot{k}_n),$$

then for ε sufficiently small, the model behaves like a closed von Neumann model and has the usual (generalized) saddlepoint of type n. However, this analogy to the von Neumann model does *not* follow when capital gains terms involving $\dot{p}_i$'s enter the $h(\cdot)$ consumption function since $\dot{p}_i = d(-T_i)/dt$, $y_i = \dot{k}_i + (g + \delta_i)k_i$ (and thus $\dot{p}_i$ depends upon terms which include $\ddot{k}_i$'s).

7. GLOBAL RESULTS AND NONCOMPETITIVE PATHS

In the example studied in Sections 3, 4, and 5 we have shown that, given an initial vector of per capita capital stocks $k(0)$, there are many possible initial price vectors $p(0)$ which will yield asymptotic convergence to equilibrium, but it is still not true that any arbitrary $p(0)$ will lead to such convergence. We turn now to the question of how the system develops when it is off the convergent manifold. It is proved below that all paths not converging to equilibrium will have the property that at least one price becomes zero in finite time, and hence such paths will be revealed (eventually) to be inconsistent with perfect competition, free disposability of capital goods, and equilibrium in the markets for capital assets. (See, e.g., [3, pp. 19–20] for the details of this argument.) Given the fiction of Walrasian markets for all periods into the future, the economy will never follow such errant paths, and convergence to equilibrium will be assured.

For the purposes of this section alone, we define two new variables, $k \equiv k_1/k_2$ and $p \equiv p_1/p_2$. We can then study the development of the model in the (k, p) plane of Figure 1.[9] For convenience we also set α_1 and α_2 equal although the argument of this section depends upon this equality in no essential way and the generalization is trivial. As before $p_Z = (1 + p_1^2 + p_2^2)^{\frac{1}{2}}$ and is, in effect, the price of undifferentiated

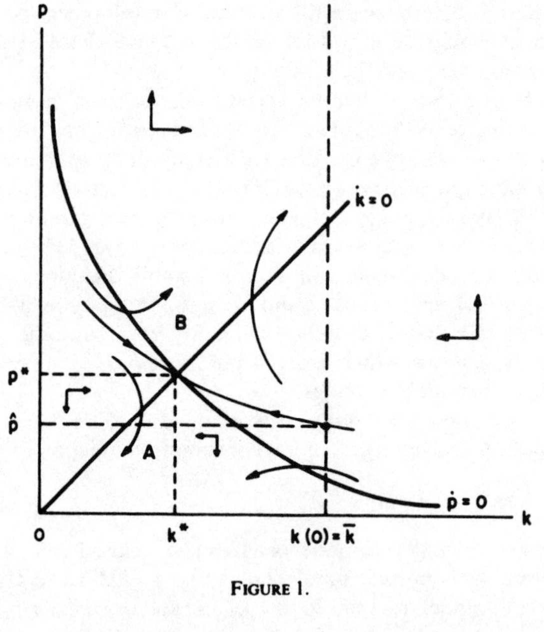

FIGURE 1.

[9] This figure, originally suggested by Atkinson [1], is identical to Figure 1 of [3], but as we discuss below, the interpretation and analysis of the figure is quite different.

output. Now

$$\begin{aligned}\frac{\dot{k}}{k} &= \frac{\dot{k}_1}{k_1} - \frac{\dot{k}_2}{k_2} \\ &= \frac{k_1^{\alpha}k_2^{\alpha}}{p_Z}\left[\frac{p_1}{k_1} - \frac{p_2}{k_2}\right] = \frac{p_2 k_1^{\alpha-1}k_2^{\alpha}}{p_Z}(p - k),\end{aligned} \tag{46}$$

and hence $\dot{k} = 0$ requires $k = p$. Likewise, using (30),

$$\begin{aligned}\frac{\dot{p}}{p} &= \frac{\dot{p}_1}{p_1} - \frac{\dot{p}_2}{p_2} \\ &= (r_0 + \delta) - \frac{w_1}{p_1} - (r_0 + \delta) + \frac{w_2}{p_2} \\ &= \frac{w_2}{p_2} - \frac{w_1}{p_1} = \frac{w_1}{p_1}(pk - 1),\end{aligned} \tag{47}$$

so that $\dot{p} = 0$ requires that $pk = 1$. To determine $\dot{k}$ and $\dot{p}$ given k and p, we must also know one of k_1 or k_2, and one of p_1 or p_2. But we can say that above the $\dot{k} = 0$ ray k is rising, and below it k is falling; similarly, above the $\dot{p} = 0$ hyperbola p is rising, and below it p is falling. Consequently, we can examine some *qualitative properties* of the system in (p, k) space. In particular, the intersection of the $\dot{k} = 0$ and $\dot{p} = 0$ curves defines a saddlepoint equilibrium, and there exists a unique locus of p and k values along which the system converges in (p, k) space.[10]

In fact, if we are on this stable arm in Figure 1, then it will also be the case that the global system in (p_1, p_2, k_1, k_2) space will be stable, but this does not follow directly from the observation that the ratio system in (p, k) space is stable. It does follow from the analysis of local stability in Section 5, where we showed that the system in E^4 has only a single unstable direction. These global properties are verified further by the numerical results presented in Section 8. In the Caton-Shell model, since one functional restriction on the prices (at any moment of time) held as a direct consequence of the savings hypothesis, a particular value of p implied particular values for p_1 and p_2 and convergence in the ratio space insured that the global system also converged. In our model, however, it is at least a priori possible that even though the price ratio has converged the individual prices may not have done so, and, thus, we require the additional analysis of the other

[10] This statement and the preceding paragraph must be interpreted with great care. Clearly, the complete behavior of a four-dimensional system in general cannot be depicted by a two-dimensional figure. Suppose, however, we take as given one of the k_i's and one of the p_i's at time $t = 0$, say $k_1(0) = \bar{k}_1 > 0$ and $p_1(0) = \bar{p}_1 > 0$. Likewise, assume $k(0) \equiv k_1(0)/k_2(0) = k > 0$ is given (which, of course, implies that $k_2(0) = \bar{k}_2 > 0$ is also known).

As stated, the *qualitative behavior* of the system is illustrated in Figure 1. The initial condition $\bar{k}$ determines a vertical line, and there exists one and only one value of $p(0)$ on this line, namely $p(0) = \hat{p}$, such that $(p(t), k(t))$ asymptotically approach (p^*, k^*) equilibrium.

Alternatively, let the initial conditions $\bar{k}_1, \bar{k}_2$, and $\bar{p}_1$ be given; then there exists a $p_2(0) = \bar{p}_2 > 0$ (such that $\bar{p}_1/\bar{p}_2 = \hat{p}$) for which the system converges. In other words, the manifold containing convergent paths is (globally) of dimension $n + 1 (= 3)$ in $2n (= 4)$-dimensional space (p_1, p_2, k_1, k_2).

sections to exclude this possibility. Now consider those paths that are off the stable arm of Figure 1.

We wish to prove that on any path not tending to equilibrium, some price will become zero in finite time. But any non-convergent path at some finite time must enter either region A (where $\dot{k} < 0$, $\dot{p} < 0$) or B (where $\dot{k} > 0$, $\dot{p} > 0$), as the directional arrows in Figure 1 indicate. (This result follows from the fact that the adjustment coefficients for equations (46) and (47), i.e.,

$$\frac{p_2 k_1^{\alpha} k_2^{\alpha-1}}{p_Z} \quad \text{and} \quad \frac{w_1}{p_2},$$

respectively, are appropriately bounded; see, e.g., footnote 11 below.) Therefore, we need only show that for any trajectory entering region A, the price ratio p becomes zero in finite time, and this conclusion is easily provided.[11] By symmetry, for trajectories entering region B, $1/p$ becomes zero in finite time.

In conclusion, we have shown that the violation of non-negativity in finite time holds for some neoclassical models with *strictly* concave transformation surfaces and that this result does not depend on either of two specific properties of earlier models, i.e., (i) the equality of total consumption and total wage income, or (ii) the existence of ruled segments on the production possibility frontier in output space.

8. NUMERICAL RESULTS

To confirm the above analysis and to explore the sensitivity of these results to the choice of parameters, a computer was used to generate representative trajectories for the model under alternative types of specifications. The numerical results may be quickly summarized.

(i) For various selections of the parameter values, it has been possible to impose three initial conditions upon a fourth order problem and select the fourth

[11] From equation (47)

$$\dot{p} = p\left[\frac{w_2}{p_2} - \frac{w_1}{p_1}\right] = \frac{w_1}{p_2}(pk - 1),$$

and since $(pk - 1)$ is negative and falling in the interior of region A, it is sufficient to show that w_1/p_2 is bounded away from zero in region A. By direct calculation

$$\begin{aligned} \frac{w_1}{p_2} &= \alpha \frac{p_Z}{p_2} \frac{k_1^{\alpha} k_2^{\alpha}}{k_1} \\ &= \alpha \frac{p_Z}{p_2} k^{\alpha-1} k_2^{2\alpha-1}. \end{aligned} \qquad (*)$$

We know that p_Z is not less than p_2, and k is bounded above in region A. Also, k_2 is bounded above, as shown by the following argument. From (31)

$$\dot{k}_i = \frac{p_i}{p_Z} k_1^{\alpha} k_2^{\alpha} - (g + \delta) k_i,$$

and since $1 > 2\alpha$, $\dot{k}_i < 0$ for k_i sufficiently large. Hence for any initial $k_i(0)$ there is a $\bar{k}_i$ such that $k_i(t) < \bar{k}_i < \infty$, $i = 1, 2$. Thus all three non-constant terms on the right-hand side of (*) are positive and bounded away from zero, and accordingly so is w_1/p_2.

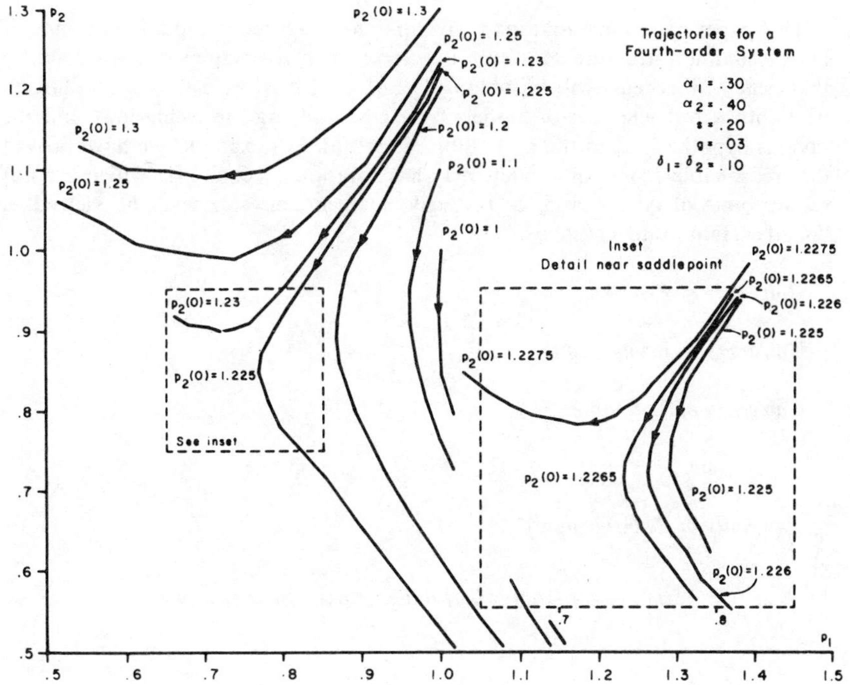

FIGURE 2.

initial condition so as to achieve convergence to the stationary equilibrium of the system.

(ii) The solution procedure (which determined the unique value for the fourth component of the vector of initial values associated with any selection of the other three components) was significantly simplified by virtue of the fact that values departing only slightly from the correct one lead very quickly to violation of non-negativity constraints. Apart from simplifying the computations, this result is itself of economic importance.

The situation is well depicted in Figure 2 which shows trajectories in the (p_1, p_2) space for given initial values of k_1 and k_2 and the arbitrary selection of one further initial condition $p_1(0) = 1$. Figure 2 indicates that the present fourth order example possesses a saddlepoint in the price space, so that for any choice of one initial price, there will be some unique initial value of the other price that will drive the system to equilibrium. Thus, although the local analysis undertaken in Section 5 employed the simplifying assumption that the capital elasticities were equal, the numerical results demonstrate that such symmetry is not essential to our conclusions.

9. CONCLUDING REMARK

This paper has shown that many dynamic heterogeneous capital good models share a common structure. However, that structure is so complex it seems doubtful that general theorems will be obtained easily—at least unless one is willing to deal with a restricted set of models by, e.g., specifying the technology and the savings hypothesis as in the first Hahn model [**6**]. For example, we have proved that reasonable economic models may have stationary equilibria which are not saddlepoints of type *n*, and, accordingly, such models can never be viewed as "regular Hamiltonian systems."

University of Pennsylvania,

University of Pennsylvania,

University of Toronto,

and

University of Pennsylvania

Manuscript received October, 1970; revision received June, 1971.

REFERENCES

[1] Atkinson, A. B.: "The Timescale of Economic Models: How Long is the Long Run?" *Review of Economic Studies*, 36 (1969), 137–152.

[2] Burmeister, Edwin, and A. Rodney Dobell: *Mathematical Theories of Economic Growth*. New York: Macmillan, 1970

[3] Caton, Christopher, and Karl Shell: "An Exercise in the Theory of Heterogeneous Capital Accumulation," *Review of Economic Studies*, 38 (1971), 13–22.

[4] El'sgol'c. L. E.: *Qualitative Methods in Mathematical Analysis*, AMS Translation of Mathematical Monographs, Vol. 12. Providence, R.I.: American Mathematical Society, 1964.

[5] Furaya, H., and K. Inada: "Balanced Growth and Intertemporal Efficiency in Capital Accumulation," *International Economic Review*, 3 (1962), 94–107.

[6] Hahn, F. H.: "Equilibrium Dynamics with Heterogeneous Capital Goods," *The Quarterly Journal of Economics*, 80 (1966), 633–646.

[7] ———: "On Warranted Growth Paths," *Review of Economic Studies*, 35 (1968), 175–184.

[8] Kurz, M.: "The General Instability of a Class of Competitive Growth Processes," *Review of Economic Studies*, 35 (1968), 155–174.

[9] Liviatan, N., and P. A. Samuelson: "Notes on Turnpikes: Stable and Unstable," *Journal of Economic Theory*, 1 (1969), 455–474.

[10] Samuelson, Paul A.: "Indeterminacy of Development in a Heterogeneous Capital Model with Constant Savings Propensity," in *Essays on the Theory of Optimal Growth*, ed. K. Shell. Cambridge: MIT Press, 1967.

[11] ———: "Uniqueness of Permanent Competitive Equilibrium in Low-Consuming Economies," paper presented at the Second World Congress of the Econometric Society, Cambridge, England, September 8–14, 1970.

[12] Shell, K., and Joseph E. Stiglitz: "The Allocation of Investment in a Dynamic Economy," *The Quarterly Journal of Economics*, 81 (1967), 592–609.

Part III
Capital Deepening, Reswitching and Neo-Austrian Models

[11]

THE NATURE AND IMPLICATIONS OF THE RESWITCHING OF TECHNIQUES *

MICHAEL BRUNO, EDWIN BURMEISTER, AND EYTAN SHESHINSKI

I. INTRODUCTION

By reswitching of techniques we mean the recurrence at different rates of interest of a whole matrix of activities or a "technique of production." The "Ruth Cohen Curiosum" may be considered a special case where only a *single* activity recurs.[1] We have analyzed the conditions under which reswitching can occur, which are perfectly general, the conditions under which it cannot occur, which are quite restrictive, and some of the important implications for capital theory.

In a paper read to the Econometric Society meeting in Rome in September 1965, Luigi Pasinetti [2] was the first to question seriously the validity of Levhari's nonswitching theorem.[3] It is this challenge that gave us the immediate inspiration for our own work. However, Pasinetti's earlier Rome discussion seemed incomplete to us because there was no clear indication whether or not Levhari's

* We are greatly indebted to Paul A. Samuelson and Robert M. Solow for their helpful leads, insights, and numerous discussions. Frank M. Fisher and Robert M. Solow have also given us very helpful comments on an earlier draft.

Likewise we are indebted to the Center for International Affairs, Harvard University, for partial support of M. Bruno's research, to the National Science Foundation for partial support of E. Burmeister's research under Grant GS-571 and to the Irwin Foundation for a Fellowship supporting E. Sheshinski's Ph.D. thesis at Massachusetts Institute of Technology, of which his present contribution forms a part.

1. Joan Robinson, *Accumulation of Capital* (London: Macmillan, 1956); Piero Sraffa, *Production of Commodities by Means of Commodities* (Cambridge: Cambridge University Press, 1960); and M. McManus, "Process Switching in the Theory of Capital," *Economica*, XXX (May 1963). The reswitching phenomenon has also been discussed by Michio Morishima in "Mrs. Robinson's New Book and Professor Leontief's Dynamic System," mimeographed paper, Feb. 1958; "Refutation of the Nonswitching Theorem," this *Journal*, this issue; and *Equilibrium, Stability, and Growth* (Oxford: Clarendon Press, 1964), p. 126.

2. Luigi L. Pasinetti's present paper "Changes in the Rate of Profit and Switches of Techniques," this *Journal*, this issue, is a revised version of the paper he presented in Rome.

3. David Levhari, "A Nonsubstitution Theorem and Switching of Techniques," this *Journal*, LXXIX (Feb. 1965), 98–105.

theorem was in fact wrong and therefore the primary issue was still unresolved.[4] In our subsequent work we have individually and jointly discovered in various ways that the theorem is indeed wrong; the credit, however, goes to Pasinetti's lead. Pasinetti's present paper is a considerable modification and revision of his earlier analysis and now touches on a number of aspects which we have ourselves analyzed in the meantime. We shall nonetheless risk minor repetition for the sake of clarification and proceed with our own discussion as originally envisaged.

Numerical examples and the realization that switching points are roots of n-th degree polynomials (and therefore numerous) have convinced us that reswitching may well occur in a general capital model. A seemingly small alteration in the fundamental lemma can be shown to make Levhari's theorem and its original proof formally correct, but unfortunately the class of cases for which it would remain valid is thereby restricted quite heavily. We have analyzed some alternative sufficiency conditions for non-switching which are of interest in themselves, especially for the two-sector case, but such analyses only help to convince one of their highly restrictive nature.

Two points must be clarified at the outset: (1) There is no essential difference between the circulating-capital and fixed-capital models as far as the important capital-theoretic issues are concerned. One, in fact, includes the other as a special case. (2) Indecomposability of the technique matrix is essentially irrelevant for the reswitching discussion. A short digression on the various capital models and a clarification of their relationships follows in Section II of this paper.

In Section III we use Samuelson's two-sector canonical model of capital to show that there are simple classes of cases in which both reswitching and no reswitching can occur, and we give simple sufficiency conditions for either to take place. It is also shown that in any n-sector model having only one capital good, reswitching cannot occur; difficulties arise with two capital goods. There follows a simple two-sector numerical example to serve as a definite proof that reswitching can occur.

In Section IV we discuss the n-sector model, showing that in general there can be n switching points between any two techniques. We then use Descartes' rule of signs to formulate and interpret a

4. E.g., the modified numerical counterexample produced by Pasinetti in his Rome paper did not satisfy the indecomposability on the whole technique matrix as required by the conditions of Levhari's theorem.

sufficiency condition for nonswitching, which turns out to be extremely restrictive in nature.

Once the reswitching phenomenon is acknowledged, it is important to realize its implications for capital theory. As is often the case after the fact, one finds it hard to differentiate between reswitching and another well-known phenomenon, namely the existence of multiple rates of return to investment in present value calculations.

Perhaps the most interesting and most important finding of our analysis concerns the behavior of consumption and the rate of interest (profit) in steady states. The reswitching phenomenon implies the existence of "perverse behavior" where it is *not* true that steady-state consumption *always rises* as the rate of interest *falls*.[5] Rather for certain ranges of the interest rate, steady-state consumption may *rise* when the rate of interest rises. Moreover, although the reswitching phenomenon alerted us to this possibility, we find that such "perverse behavior" can exist *even when no reswitching occurs on the factor-price frontier*. The latter and related issues form the subject of Section V.

II. Alternative Discrete Capital Models

Various discussions of the reswitching phenomenon employ a great variety of capital models differing with respect to such assumptions as depreciation, timing of wage payments, and the time structure of inputs in the production of capital goods. Pasinetti has illustrated his arguments with a Sraffa model in which capital goods essentially consist of "maturing" labor inputs at different time periods; Levhari considered another Sraffa model with one-period circulating capital.[6] Naturally, one prefers to think in terms of more general fixed-capital models which include the former as special cases. Since all of these alternative models basically lead to the same theoretical conclusions, it seems useful to begin our discussion with a short classification. We try to minimize confusion by indicating how they all relate to each other and how the present issue can be discussed in terms of any of the models and therefore is best analyzed in greatest generality. An issue somewhat related to the same question is the irrelevance of decomposability or indecomposability of the technology matrix.

5. The possibility of such "perverse behavior" was pointed out without proof by Professor Morishima in *Equilibrium, Stability, and Growth*, *op. cit.*, p. 126.

6. Pasinetti, *op. cit.*, Levhari, *op. cit.*, and Sraffa, *op. cit.*

1. Consider an n-sector fixed-proportions technology (a_{ij}) using and producing n capital goods (prices P_j) and using one primary factor, labor (a_{oj}) commanding a nominal wage w.

Denoting the depreciation rate for the j-th capital good by μ_j and the rate of interest by r, and supposing wages are paid during the production period, we have:

(II.1) $$P_j = wa_{oj} + \sum_{i=1}^{n} (\mu_i + r) P_i a_{ij}; \quad j = 1, \ldots, n,$$

or in vector notation

(II.2) $$p = a_o [\mathrm{I} - \rho a]^{-1}$$

where $p = \left(\frac{P_j}{w}\right)$ and $\rho = [\mu + r]$, a diagonal matrix whose i-th diagonal entry is $(\mu_i + r)$. We must assume that the maximal interest rate, r^*_a, is positive and that $a_{oj} \geqq 0$ to have $p_j \geqq 0$.

There are some obvious special cases of this model which are used often and which we shall at times mention. All of these involve the assumption of a uniform depreciation rate:

$$\mu_i = \mu \text{ and } \rho = r + \mu, \text{ a scalar.}$$

The two extreme subcases here are:

(i) $\mu = 0, \quad \rho = r$ (capital is infinitely durable),

and

(ii) $\mu = 1, \quad \rho = r + 1$ (there is only circulating capital).

2. Next suppose we slightly alter our above assumptions and have wages paid at the *beginning* of the production period. The only change required in equations (II.2) is that a factor $(1 + r)$ now must multiply a_o, i.e., we have

(II.3) $$p = (1 + r)\, a_o\, [I - \rho a]^{-1}.$$

Now if we consider the special case $\mu = 1$ $(\rho = r + 1)$, we get the Sraffa circulating-capital model used by Levhari, i.e.,

(II.4) $$p = a_o[\lambda I - a]^{-1} \text{ where } \lambda \equiv \frac{1}{1+r}.$$

Other than a factor $(1 + r)$ due to a different assumption about wage payments, there is no real difference between the two models except that (II.1) is more general. Clearly the nonsubstitution theorem as well as the discussion of the switching problem could be conducted equally well in terms of the fixed-capital model.

3. Now suppose there are some goods that take more than one period to produce. One can either treat goods-in-process of different ages as different goods (with different activities) or else calculate directly the implied price relationships. For example, if a commodity available at present requires an input a_{oj} of labor t periods

earlier, then that input's contribution to present cost must be $w\, a_{oj}\, (1 + r)^t$. The Pasinetti-Sraffa numerical example uses precisely the latter type of capital model. Clearly a further generalization would have not only labor but also capital inputs required in earlier periods. All of these ideas could be incorporated without difficulty in a modified expression for (II.1) or (II.2). For simplicity we shall confine our discussion to the models that can be derived from (II.2) or (II.3).

There is one general common characteristic of all these models from which reswitching and other properties can be shown to follow. Under some quite unrestrictive assumptions,[7] we can always expand the price vector (in terms of labor units) as a convergent power series in r, i.e.,

(II.5) $$p = g_o + g_1 r + g_2 r^2 + \ldots + g_n r^n + \ldots$$

where g_i are nonnegative vectors whose elements eventually approach zero as n increases. (II.5) is the equation of the factor-price frontier (FPF) in terms of p instead of $1/p$. In Section IV we shall have occasion to examine (II.5) for the general fixed-capital model (II.1) and to provide the economic interpretation of the g_i's. Let us only note here that these vectors can be interpreted in terms of the direct and indirect use of labor in production. The price of any product is thus positive if it uses directly or indirectly some of the primary factor labor.[8] As long as one of these vectors (for $i \geqq 1$) is not zero, we obtain a downward sloping factor-price frontier i.e., $\frac{dp}{dr} > 0$, from (II.5). At the same time we cannot generally say whether the FPF when expressed as $1/p(r)$ will be convex or concave unless we know something about the coefficients.[9]

Finally consider another generalization. Suppose that in addition to fixed-capital goods and consumption goods, we have Leontief-type intermediate goods in the system. We propose to show that the formal properties of the system (II.2) remain unchanged.

Suppose that in addition to a fixed-capital matrix a there is an ordinary input-output matrix $\bar{a}$ (assume a and $\bar{a}$ are defined so as

7. Some variant of the Hawkins-Simon conditions.

8. This, incidentally, does not require indecomposability of the technique matrix.

9. $\frac{d^2(1/p)}{dr^2} = -p^{-2}\left(\frac{d^2p}{dr^2}\right) + 2p^{-3}\left(\frac{dp}{dr}\right)^2$. Even though $\frac{d^2p}{dr^2} > 0$ so that $p(r)$ will always be convex to the origin, $\frac{d^2\left(\frac{1}{p}\right)}{dr^2}$ is a difference of two positive terms and may be either positive or negative.

to be conformable).[1] The price equations must now be modified as follows:

(II.2′) $p = a_o\,[I - \bar{a} - \rho a]^{-1}$.

But this can also be written in the form

$$p = a_o S[I - \rho a S]^{-1} \qquad \text{where } S = [I - \bar{a}]^{-1}.$$

Now define

$$A_o = a_o[I - \bar{a}]^{-1} \qquad (= \text{"total" labor input}),$$
$$A = a[I - \bar{a}]^{-1} \qquad (= \text{"total" capital matrix}),$$

and we have

$$p = A_o[I - \rho A]^{-1}$$

which is formally equivalent to (II.2).

This derivation has two corollaries. First, for purposes of exposition we can ignore the existence of intermediate inputs since they do not alter the formal structure of the capital model. The second, somewhat more interesting, is that there is a sense in which the distinction between decomposable and indecomposable models is artificial. For example, suppose that the "total" capital matrix A is decomposable while the input-output matrix $\bar{a}$ is indecomposable; then it may be misleading to term the model either decomposable or indecomposable. This ambiguity should be an additional indication that decomposability is not an important property in the present context.[2]

III. Reswitching in Two-Good Technologies

Before returning to a more general discussion of n-sector models, it seems helpful to use a simpler two-sector technology to illustrate the switching problem.

Consider a technique a producing two goods, a capital good (subscript 1) and a consumption good (subscript 2). The capital good is assumed to depreciate at a fixed rate μ_a, and labor (subscript 0) is the only primary input. If we denote the fixed coefficients for this technique by a_{ij} ($i = 0, 1$; $j = 1, 2$) and express the wage rate w and price of capital good P_K in terms of the consumption good as *numéraire*, we get the following price equations: [3]

1. See, e.g., Morishima, *Equilibrium, Stability, and Growth, op. cit.*, Chaps. III and IV, and Jacob T. Schwartz, *Lectures on the Mathematical Method in Analytical Economics* (New York: Gordon and Breach, 1961), Chap. I.

2. Samuelson has suggested an alternative argument using the fact that any decomposable capital matrix can be turned into an indecomposable one by adding some arbitrarily small elements in the right places thereby causing only an infinitesimal change in the FPF.

3. This so-called canonical model was introduced by Samuelson, "Parable and Realism in Capital Theory: The Surrogate Production Function," *Review of Economic Studies*, XXIX (June 1962), 193–207.

(III.1) $P_K = a_{01}w + a_{11}\,(r + \mu_a)\,P_K$

(III.2) $1 = a_{02}w + a_{12}(r + \mu_a)P_K,$

from which the following equation for the factor-price curve FPC_a (Figure I) can be derived:

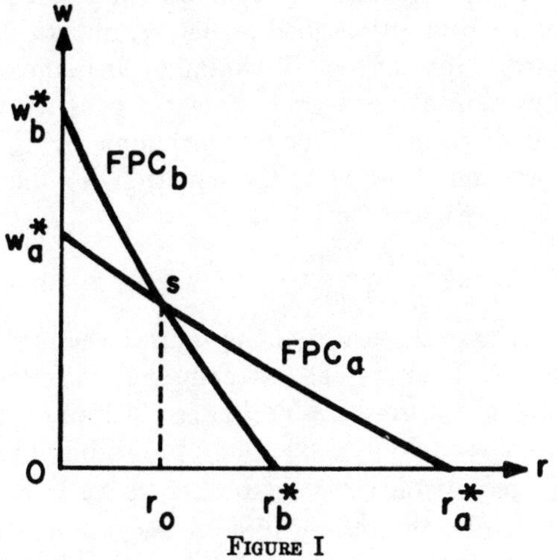

FIGURE I

(III.3) $$w = \frac{1 - (\mu_a + r)a_{11}}{a_{02} + (\mu_a + r)G_a}$$

where

$$G_a = \det \begin{bmatrix} a_{01} & a_{02} \\ a_{11} & a_{12} \end{bmatrix}.$$

This downward sloping *FPC* will be convex or concave to the origin according to whether $G_a > 0$ or < 0, namely according to whether the consumption good industry is more capital-intensive or more labor-intensive than the capital good industry. For our purposes this distinction is unimportant, and the curve in Figure I is drawn with the assumption $G_a > 0$. Next we note that the *FPC* intersects both the w and the r axes at w^*_a and r^*_a respectively, where:

$$w^*_a = \frac{1 - \mu_a a_{11}}{a_{02} + \mu_a G_a}$$ = "net"[4] labor productivity in the consumption good sector

4. "Net labor productivity" is the quantity of consumption goods produced per unit of labor after taking into account the indirect labor embodied in the current replacement cost of capital. Perhaps this interpretation can be seen better by rewriting this expression in the form:

$$w^*_a = \frac{1}{a_{02} + \dfrac{a_{01}\mu_a a_{12}}{1 - \mu_a a_{11}}}.$$

and

$$r_a^* = \frac{1}{a_{11}} - \mu_a \quad = \text{"net" capital productivity in the capital good sector.}$$

Consider now an alternative technique b, again producing two goods, the same consumption good as before, but a *different* capital good with depreciation rate μ_b. Technique b is assumed to use only the second type capital good (but the same primary factor labor). Denoting the fixed coefficients for this technique by b_{ij}, we can write analogous expressions leading to the equation for the *FPC* for this case (see FPC_b in Figure I):

$$\text{(III.4)} \qquad w = \frac{1 - (\mu_b + r)b_{11}}{b_{02} + (\mu_b + r)G_b}.$$

Suppose our hypothetical economy must select one of two alternative techniques. There is one switching point S corresponding to the critical rate of interest r_o. Technique b is more profitable for $0 \leq r < r_o$, and technique a is more profitable for $r_o < r < r_a^*$; thus the factor price frontier is the broken curve $w_b^* S r_a^*$. The techniques are ordered by the rate of interest because as r falls below r_o and the economy switches from technique a to technique b, technique a will never recur if r falls further. But is this feature inherent in the model? The answer turns out to be negative even in this highly simplified model. Figure II illustrates a case where the

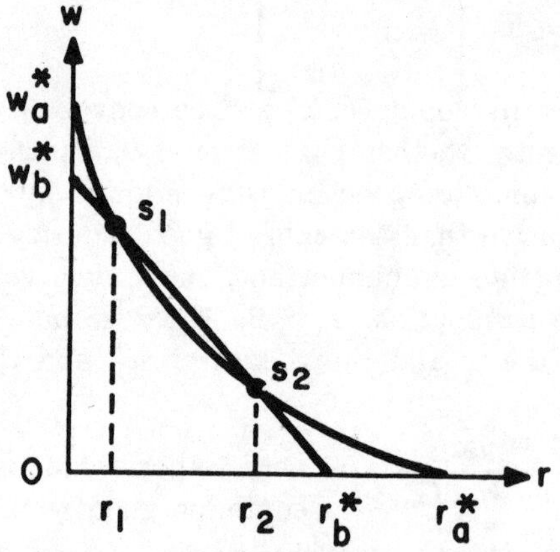

FIGURE II

(When $\mu_a = 0$, $w_a^* = \frac{1}{a_{02}}$). w_a^* will also correspond to the total consumption per capita in a stationary state, a fact that we shall use in subsequent discussion.

two curves cross twice. When r becomes less than r_1, the economy switches back to technique a. Technique a is profitable for two disjoint intervals of r, $0 < r < r_1$ and $r_2 < r < r^*_a$, and the two techniques cannot be ordered. That either one of the cases is in general possible can readily be seen by equating w in equations (III.3) and (III.4) and solving for r. We obtain a quadratic equation for r which, in principle, can easily have two roots in the positive quadrant. A condition for that occurrence can be formulated in terms of the coefficients a_{ij} and b_{ij}. Similarly we can use some known method, such as Descartes' rule of signs, to determine a sufficiency condition which prevents that occurrence. In the next section we shall take the latter approach in the discussion of the general n-sector case. Here a more straightforward and economically meaningful condition can be formulated. (The latter does not, unfortunately, hold in the n-sector case.)

Since we know that there are at most two switching points in this simplified model, we can state the following obvious sufficiency condition for unique switching:

Theorem: If either $r^*_a > r^*_b$ and $w^*_a < w^*_b$
or $r^*_a < r^*_b$ and $w^*_a > w^*_b$,
then there exists only one switching point in the positive quadrant.

In other words, whenever the technique which has a higher capital/output ratio in the capital good industry is also more labor-productive in the consumption good industry, then these techniques can be ordered in an unambiguous manner. (See, e.g., Figure I.)

A number of remarks are now in order:

1. The class of cases which are excluded by this sufficiency condition includes:

(a) Cases in which no switching point exists (i.e., where one technique completely dominates the other).

(b) Cases with multiple roots or cases in which the curves cross only at end points (i.e., $w^*_a = w^*_b$ or $r^*_a = r^*_b$). These again are cases in which one technique can be ignored since it is dominated.

Both (a) and (b) can be classified as irrelevant since the FPF (envelope) is unchanged by their exclusion.

(c) Cases which have two separate crossings inside the positive quadrant, as illustrated in Figure II.[5]

5. After we had completed our analysis, we became aware of the recent book by Professor John R. Hicks, *Capital and Growth* (Oxford: Oxford University Press, 1965); there he has discussed this two-sector model and the reswitching phenomenon. The sufficiency condition which Hicks derives for

2. This sufficiency condition applies to an economy with any number of alternative two-sector techniques all using *different* capital goods and having the same properties as a and b, if the condition of the theorem holds for any pair of techniques a and b. It is sufficient for no reswitching that the ordering of techniques by r^* is exactly the reverse of the ordering by w^*.

3. This sufficiency condition is *not a necessary condition* for nonswitching.

Figure III illustrates an example with three techniques (1, 2 and 3) where *each pair* satisfies the sufficiency condition; yet technique 2 is irrelevant since it is dominated by the combination of 1

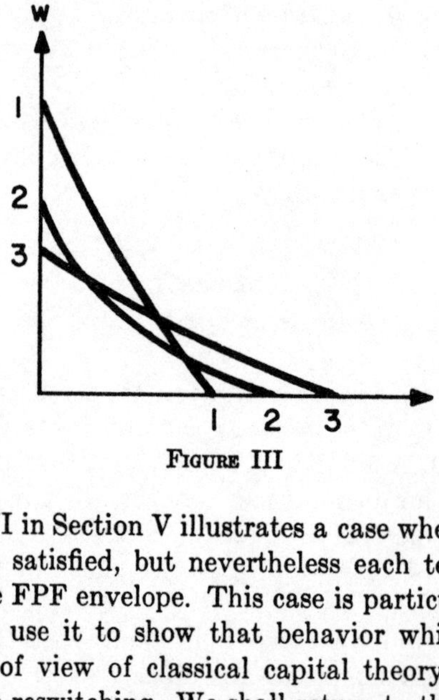

FIGURE III

and 3. Figure VI in Section V illustrates a case where the sufficiency condition is not satisfied, but nevertheless each technique appears only once on the FPF envelope. This case is particularly interesting because we can use it to show that behavior which is "perverse" from the point of view of classical capital theory can occur even when there is no reswitching. We shall return to this point later.[6]

4. We have thus far assumed that $G \neq 0$ for all techniques. Obviously reswitching can also occur when $G = 0$ for some but not all techniques. When $G = 0$ for *all* techniques, factor proportions in the two industries are equal. Then the *FPC*'s are straight lines and the system degenerates to Samuelson's simple surrogate capital model[7] in which reswitching obviously cannot occur.

nonswitching is that the ratio of factor intensities must be the same for all techniques (see p. 154). However, this condition is overly strong since it also includes cases of complete dominance which are irrelevant.

6. See Sec. V below and Pasinetti, *op. cit.*, fn. 14.

7. Samuelson, *op. cit.*

5. It should be stressed that the model discussed above is extremely simplified and that the sufficiency condition given does not lend itself to easy generalization if activities use more than one capital good. The latter fact can be seen by considering a case with one consumption good and two capital goods where prices are clearly equations of the third degree. Thus in general there may be three switching points and we can no longer formulate any simple sufficiency condition for nonswitching. We shall return to this problem in the next section.

An interesting question arises at this point. How crucial is the assumption that the two (or more) capital goods in our simplified model are *different*, i.e., nontransferable between activities? Can we get reswitching if all activities use the *same* capital good? The answer to this question turns out to be negative, and we have the following theorem:

Theorem: In a two-sector economy with many alternative independent techniques for producing the two goods, if there is *only one* capital good in the system, reswitching cannot occur.

Proof: Since there is only one capital good (let it be of type a), there is only one P_K in the system. From equation (III.1) we can see that for any given r, there will be only one most efficient activity for producing the one capital good and it cannot recur. Looking at the factor-price frontier in the $\frac{w}{P_K} - r$ plane, we find an envelope of straight line segments. We now need only show that within the range of r *for any one* such segment, an activity for the production of the consumption good cannot recur. This problem, however, is equivalent to that of finding switching points in the previous model for the case in which there is only one way of producing the capital good. From previous considerations we can immediately deduce that for any two *FPC*'s in the $w - r$ plane, there can be at most one switching point in the range $0 < r < r_a^*$ (because there is already one common intersection at $r_a^* = \frac{1}{a_{11}} - \mu_a$). Thus even though a single activity for producing the consumption good may recur, in this case we cannot have the *simultaneous* recurrence of two activities (for the two goods). Thus reswitching in the sense of Levhari cannot occur. Q.E.D.

The above theorem also holds for a multisector economy producing many intermediate (or consumption) goods as long as there is only *one capital good* (i.e., only one interest earning asset).[8]

All the above examples fail to meet Levhari's indecomposability assumption and thus may be deemed irrelevant for his nonswitching theorem. (Note that our examples are decomposable because the consumption good uses capital goods in its production but is not itself used in the production of capital goods.)[9]

For the sake of completeness, we end this section with a numerical example as a definite proof that reswitching can occur despite indecomposability. Although we do not think that indecomposability has any relevance to the switching problem, it is pedagogically preferable and logically crucial to choose an example which satisfies *every* assumption of the theorem to be disproved.[1] The following is a two-sector indecomposable example with circulating capital (i.e., $\mu = 1$) in full conformity with Levhari's model:

The economy produces two goods labeled 1 and 2. Good 1 has two alternative activities while good 2 can be produced by only one available activity:

	Sector 1		Sector 2
	Activity 1	Activity 2	
Labor	0.66	0.01	1.0
Good 1	0.3	0	0.1
Good 2	0.02	0.71	0

Thus there are two possible techniques of production:

$$\text{technique } a = \left[\begin{array}{c} a_o \\ \hline a \end{array}\right] = \left[\begin{array}{cc} 0.66 & 1.0 \\ \hline 0.3 & 0.1 \\ 0.02 & 0 \end{array}\right]$$

and

$$\text{technique } b = \left[\begin{array}{c} b_o \\ \hline b \end{array}\right] = \left[\begin{array}{cc} 0.01 & 0.1 \\ \hline 0 & 0.1 \\ 0.71 & 0 \end{array}\right].$$

Notice that both techniques are indecomposable.

Some values of $\frac{P_1}{w}$ and $\frac{P_2}{w}$ for both techniques are computed in Table I.

8. This is the obvious case in which the concept of "capital-intensity" can be defined unambiguously.

9. Nothing, however, is changed in our analysis if the consumption good is also used as an intermediate good in the Leontief sense; then the technique matrix may *appear* indecomposable. But this is obviously not the kind of indecomposability that Levhari had in mind.

1. Pasinetti's numerical example is thus, strictly speaking, not a valid counterexample to Levhari's theorem.

TABLE I

$\lambda = \frac{1}{1+r}$	r	Technique a		Technique b	
		$\frac{P_1}{w}$	$\frac{P_2}{w}$	$\frac{P_1}{w}$	$\frac{P_2}{w}$
1.	0.	0.9742	1.0974	0.7750	1.0775
0.95	0.053	1.0512	1.1633	0.8653	1.1437
0.90	0.111	1.1413	1.2379	0.9729	1.2192
0.85	0.176	1.2481	1.3233	1.1028	1.3062
0.80	0.250	1.3769	1.4221	1.2619	1.4077
0.75	0.333	1.5350	1.5380	1.4598	1.5279
0.70	0.429	1.7338	1.6763	1.7112	1.6730
0.65	0.538	1.9911	1.8448	2.0384	1.8521
0.60	0.667	2.3371	2.0562	2.4775	2.0796
0.55	0.818	2.8266	2.3321	3.0907	2.3801
0.50	1.000	3.5714	2.7143	3.9944	2.7989
0.45	1.222	4.8397	3.2977	5.4335	3.4296
0.40	1.500	7.4737	4.3684	8.0225	4.5056
0.35	1.857	16.1936	7.4839	13.8544	6.8155

It is seen that technique b is selected for very low and for very high rates of interest, while for interest rates in the interval (approximately) $r = 0.45$ to $r = 1.79$, technique a is optimal.

IV. Reswitching in a General Capital Model

We now focus our attention on a general model with n capital goods and examine the reswitching phenomenon for this case. Obviously, if reswitching can occur in special two-sector technologies, it will be the rule rather than the exception with any larger number of sectors. We have investigated reswitching where there are a number of alternative activities to produce each good. Subsequently we discuss a general sufficiency condition for nonswitching which, as expected, is very restrictive and is most probably not a realistic assumption in any practical situation.

Consider, as in Levhari's analysis, a general model of an economy using one primary good, labor, and producing n (capital) goods, each one of which can be produced by k_i alternative activities ($i = 1, 2, \ldots$, n). We thus have $\prod_{i=1}^{n} k_i$ alternative technique matrixes $\begin{bmatrix} a_o \\ \vdots \\ a \end{bmatrix}, \begin{bmatrix} b_o \\ \vdots \\ b \end{bmatrix}, \ldots$, which constitute the economy's "book of blue prints" or its technology. To make our discussion sufficiently general, suppose these n goods can be fixed-capital goods. Then, for example, prices using technique a are given by the vector equation

(IV.1) $\frac{P}{w} = a_o [\mathrm{I} - (\mu + r)a]^{-1} = p_a(r)$, where $(\mu + r)$ is a diagonal matrix with the element in the i-th row and i-th column equal to $(\mu_i + r)$.[2] From the subsequent analysis it will be clear that everything discussed for this general model is *a fortiori* applicable to the Levhari-Sraffa model with circulating capital.[3]

We will find it convenient to express the price vector in the following form:

(IV.2) $$p_a(r) = \frac{T_a(r)}{Q_a(r)}$$

where $T_a(r)$ is a *vector* of polynomials, each of degree at most $(n - 1)$, and $Q_a(r) > 0$ is a polynomial of degree n.[4]

Suppose that technique a is preferred to any other technique b for $r_1 < r < r_o$, and suppose that $r = r_1$ is a genuine switching point (i.e., ties are excluded). For the open interval $r_1 < r < r_o$, we must have

$$p_a(r) \leqq p_b(r),$$

from which it follows that

(IV.3) $$p_a(r)(\mu + r)[a - b] + (a_o - b_o) \leqq 0.$$[5]

Now define

(IV.4) $$G(r) \equiv T_a(r)(\mu + r)[a - b] + Q_a(r)(a_o - b_o) \leqq 0.$$

Note that $G(r)$ is a vector of polynomials whose elements denoted by $G_i(r)$ are linear combinations of the polynomials $T_a(r)$ and $Q_a(r)$; thus $G_i(r)$ is in general a polynomial of degree n.

We next observe that the i-th column of $[a - b]$ will consist of either zeros or a *mixture* of both positive and negative (and possibly zero) elements. The same applies to the augmented matrix when labor inputs are included.[6] It follows that for all r such that

2. We note that if, as in the two-sector model, there is also an $(n + 1)$th good which uses all other inputs but is not used by any other activity, its price equation will be $\frac{P_{n+1}}{w} = a_{o,\, n+1} + (\mu + r)p_a(r)a_{n+1}$.

3. Observe that $\mu_i = 1$, $i = 1, 2, \ldots, n$, is simply a special case.

4. (IV.2) may be easily derived from (IV.1) by using the familiar adjoint method to calculate the inverse of $[I - (\mu + r)a]$. $Q_a(r)$ is equal to det $[I - (\mu + r)a]$. Since $[I - (\mu + r)a]$ has rank n, it is a polynomial of degree n. Every $(n - 1) \times (n - 1)$ minor of $[I - (\mu + r)a]$ is a polynomial of degree at most $(n - 1)$, and every component of the vector $T_a(r)$ is a linear combination of the latter polynomials and hence also of degree at most $(n - 1)$. $Q_a(r) > 0$ by the Hawkins-Simon condition.

5. If there were only circulating capital, $(\mu + r)$ would be replaced by $(1 + r)$ in (IV.3), an inequality obtained by Levhari, *op. cit.*, p. 104.

6. The case of an *all* (semi) positive or *all* (semi) negative column can be excluded since it would indicate that one of the matrixes has been chosen inefficiently, i.e., it is dominated by some other matrix for all r.

$r_1 < r < r_o$ and for each i, we must have *either* $G_i(r) \equiv 0$ or $G_i(r) < 0$. An intermediate case in which $G_i(r) \leqslant 0$ (e.g., a multiple root inside the interval) can be ruled out by making the interval $r_1 < r < r_o$ small enough. A candidate for switching must obviously come from an activity (or activities) for which $G_i(r) < 0$.

Since r_1 is defined as a switching point, there exists at least one index, say $i = q$, and a vector $\begin{bmatrix} b_o \\ \cdots \\ b \end{bmatrix}_q$ for which

(IV.5) $\quad G_q(r_1) = 0$ and $G_q(r) > 0$

for some interval $r_2 < r < r_1$. (The latter follows from the polynomial property of G.) [7]

If q is the only index for which (IV.5) holds, we can readily see that our choice of the new technique b (at least for the interval $r_2 < r < r_1$) will be a change of q-th activity from $\begin{bmatrix} a_o \\ \cdots \\ a \end{bmatrix}_q$ to $\begin{bmatrix} b_o \\ \cdots \\ b \end{bmatrix}_q$, while all other activities remain the same as those in $\begin{bmatrix} a_o \\ \cdots \\ a \end{bmatrix}$. Without loss of generality we can assume $q = 1$ and write

$$\begin{bmatrix} a_o \\ \cdots \\ a \end{bmatrix} - \begin{bmatrix} b_o \\ \cdots \\ b \end{bmatrix} = \begin{bmatrix} d_o \\ \cdots \\ d \end{bmatrix}$$

$$= \begin{bmatrix} d_{o1} & 0 & 0 & & 0 \\ \cdots\cdots & \cdots & \cdots & & \cdots \\ & , \; 0 & , \; 0 & , \ldots ; , & 0 \\ d_1 & & & & \end{bmatrix}.$$

Thus for all r such that $r_2 < r < r_1$ we have

(IV.6) $\quad G_1(r) > 0$ and $G_i(r) \equiv 0$ for all $i > 1$.

Consider the new price vector $p_b(r)$ given by

$$\begin{aligned} p_b(r) &= b_o[I - (\mu + r)b]^{-1} \\ &= (a_1 - d_o)[I - (\mu + r)(a - d)]^{-1} \\ &= (a_o - d_o)R_a[I + (\mu + r)dR_a]^{-1} \end{aligned}$$

where $R_a \equiv [I - (\mu + r)a]^{-1}$.

Expanding in a power series we get:

(IV.7) $$p_b(r) = [p_a(r) - d_oR_a]\,\{I - (\mu + r)dR_a + [(\mu + r)\,dR_a]^2 - \ldots\}.$$

7. $G_q(r)$, being an n-th degree polynomial, will have up to n roots and thus in principle there *will be up to n switching points*. By assumption r_1 is the root closest to r_o. It may be noted that here is a case where one recurring activity is synonymous with the recurrence of the entire technique matrix (suppose these are the only two matrixes available). Thus the existence of a "Ruth Cohen Curiosum" for one activity also implies the reswitching phenomenon.

Ignoring second order terms we obtain

(IV.8) $$p_b(r) = p_a(r) - [p_a(r)(\mu + r)d + d_o]R_a = p_a(r) - \frac{G(r)}{Qa}R_a.$$

Since (1) $G_1(r) > 0$, (2) $G_i(r) = 0$ for $i > 1$, and (3) $R_a > 0$, we have

$$p_b(r) < p_a(r) \text{ for } r_2 < r < r_1,$$

as we would expect. At the same time $(r_1 - r_2)$ can be made sufficiently small so that the constructed matrix b is preferable to any other matrix in that interval.

Clearly if $G_i(r) = 0$ for more than one index i, say for $i = 1, \ldots, m$, then we switch m activities and keep the other $(n\text{-}m)$ fixed; i.e., we take

$$\begin{bmatrix} d \\ \cdots \\ d_o \end{bmatrix} = \begin{bmatrix} d_1 & 0 & & 0 \\ \cdots & \cdots & & \cdots \\ d_o & 0 & \ldots & 0 \end{bmatrix} + \ldots + \begin{bmatrix} 0 & & d_m & 0 & & 0 \\ \cdots & & \cdots & \cdots & & \cdots \\ 0 & \ldots & d_{om} & 0 & \ldots & 0 \end{bmatrix}.$$

From previous considerations we find that minimizing $p_b(r)$ in the same interval $r_2 < r < r_1$ would necessitate bringing *all* m new activities into the matrix.

Since $[p_a(r)(\mu + r)d + d_oR_a] > 0$ for $d_1, d_2, \ldots, d_m$, $p_b(r)$ in (IV.8) will be smallest if all m activities are introduced simultaneously.

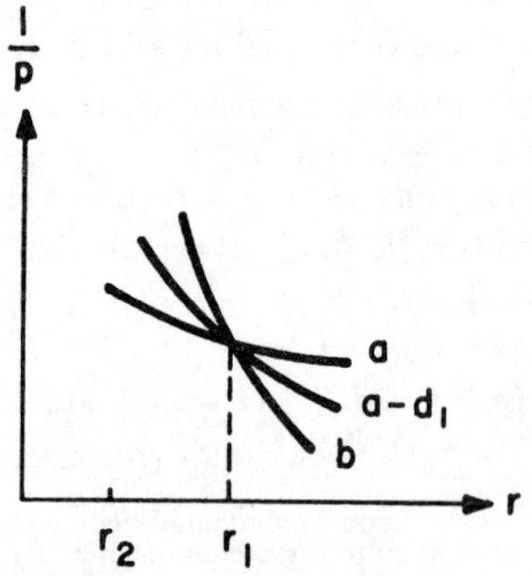

FIGURE IV

r_1 is a common switching point for m activities when the m polynomials $G_i(r)$, $i = 1, 2, \ldots, m$, all happen to have a root at $r = r_1$. If by coincidence *all* n polynomials $G_i(r)$, $i = 1, \ldots, n$, vanish at r_1, then and only then can we say that matrixes a and b which are "adjacent" on the factor-price frontier have no common column, i.e., $(a - b)$ will not contain a zero column vector. For completeness we consider the special case where $G_s(r) \equiv 0$ and

$$\begin{bmatrix} a_o \\ \vdots \\ a \end{bmatrix}_s - \begin{bmatrix} b_o \\ \vdots \\ b \end{bmatrix}_s \neq 0$$

for some index $i = s$. In this case prices are left unaltered by keeping $\begin{bmatrix} a_o \\ \vdots \\ a \end{bmatrix}_s$ in the matrix or by switching to $\begin{bmatrix} b_o \\ \vdots \\ b \end{bmatrix}_s$ i.e., $p_a(r)(\mu + r)d + d_o \equiv 0$ and $p_b(r) = p_a(r)$. Clearly, the above cannot hold for *all* $s = 1, 2, \ldots, n$.

Our results may be summarized by the following theorem:

Theorem: (1) In the general n-sector capital model there may be up to n switching points between any two techniques, and thus a technique may recur up to $(n - 1)$ times. (2) "Adjacent" techniques on two sides of a switching point will usually differ from each other only with respect to *one activity*.[8] Techniques in general may differ with respect to m *activities* $(n \geq m > 1)$ only if certain m independent n-th degree polynomials happen to have a common root at that switching point.

It should be noted that we have confined our discussion to reswitching between pairs of techniques, although the problem of reswitching as originally stated involved only intersection points which lie on the FPF *envelope*. It is clear that there may be no reswitching even if two or more curves intersect several times *below* the envelope.[9] It is important to keep this distinction in mind when discussing sufficiency conditions for nonswitching; assuming that *any two FPC's* can intersect only once is almost certainly an overly strong sufficient condition for nonswitching. In the next section, however, it will become clear why only such strong restrictions (rather than merely nonswitching on the envelope) might ensure "classical behavior" of consumption and capital across steady states with different interest rates.

The second part of the above theorem helps to clarify discussions about the wrong step in Levhari's proof, namely his funda-

8. This particular result is also stated without proof by Pasinetti, *op. cit.*
9. See Figure VI in Section V below.

mental lemma.[1] His lemma is wrong, but some of the criticism about it is also wrong.

Solow has rightly pointed out that one cannot in general find a semipositive vector x such that either $[a - b]x \geqq 0$, $[a - b]x \leqq 0$, or $[a - b]x = 0$.[2] The second part of our above theorem shows that the lemma will "almost" always work, but only trivially. In other words, we can "almost" always find $x \geqq 0$ such that $[a - b]x = 0$.[3] We agree with Pasinetti[4] that despite this fact, Levhari's proof is incorrect because we could always select a vector x with zeros that correspond precisely to those activities in which switching had taken place. Suppose, however, that we were to *assume* that there exists a vector x (it can be *any* vector!) such that either $[a - b]x \geqq 0$ or $[a - b]x \leqq 0$ for *any* pair of matrices a and b with associated positive price vectors. Strangely enough, Levhari's nonswitching theorem would *then be correct*!

Proof: Suppose there exist two distinct switch points r_1 and r_2. Define the vector function $f(r) \equiv p_a(r)(\mu + r)[a - b] + (a_o - b_o)$. By assumption, $f(r_1) = f(r_2) = 0$ where $r_1 \neq r_2$. Also $p_a'(r) > 0$. Now define the *scalar function*

$$\phi(r) \equiv f(r)x$$

where $\phi(r_1) = \phi(r_2) = 0$. Differentiating $\phi(r)$ we obtain

$$\phi'(r) = [p_a(r) + p_a'(r)(\mu + r)]\,[a - b]x.$$

Thus *for all* r $\phi'(r) > 0$ *if* $[a - b]x \geqq 0$ and $\phi'(r) < 0$ *if* $[a - b]x \leqq 0$. Thus we cannot have $\phi(r_1) = \phi(r_2) = 0$ unless $r_1 = r_2$, which provides a contradiction, and hence two (or more) distinct switch points cannot exist. Q.E.D.

At first glance one might mistakenly conclude that the assumption (that there exists a vector x such that $[a - b]x$ semipositive or seminegative) is only a minor restriction. However, it is a *very* restrictive assumption: it rules out (at least) all switches which involve only one activity and which we considered the "normal" case.[5] Economically the sufficiency condition implies (after some

1. Levhari, *op. cit.*, pp. 104–5.

2. Any (2×2) numerical example in which one row of $[a - b]$ is positive and the other is negative will suffice.

3. If $m < n$, we can always choose an x with zeros in the first m columns and positive elements in the remaining n-m columns; thus $[a - b]x = 0$. Even if $m = n$, there may be cases where the lemma is valid and thus we could claim that it is indeed valid except for extreme coincidences.

4. Pasinetti, *op. cit.*

5. If $[a - b]$ has one column of mixed positive and negative elements and $(n - 1)$ zero columns, then there does not exist *any* vector x such that either $[a - b]x \geqq 0$ or $[a - b]x \leqq 0$. This sufficiency condition can apply

manipulation) that there exists one level of operation for which one technique uses at least as much of all inputs as the other technique and definitely more of at least one input; moreover, the latter must hold for *any* pair of techniques that appear on the factor-price frontier.

We end this section by presenting an alternative sufficiency condition which is again highly restrictive. The price vector for technique a is given by (IV.1). For simplicity we assume that all goods depreciate at the same rate and define the scalar $\rho \equiv \mu + r$. Then

(IV.9) $$p_a(\rho) = a_o[I - \rho a]^{-1}.$$

Likewise

(IV.10) $$p_b(\rho) = b_o[I - \rho b]^{-1}$$

gives the price vector when technique b is used. If $\rho = \rho_1$ is a switching point, it follows that

(IV.11) $$p_a(\rho_1) - p_b(\rho_1) = a_o[I - \rho_1 a]^{-1} - b_o[I - \rho_1 b]^{-1} = 0.$$

(IV.11) is a polynomial of degree at most n, and a simple condition for the existence of at most one positive root can be provided by Descartes' rule of signs. The latter states that the number of positive real roots is equal to the number of variations in sign of the coefficients of the polynomial or is less than this number by a positive integer.[6]

We can obtain the economic interpretation of an analogous sufficiency condition by expanding (IV.9) and (IV.10) in a (convergent) vector power series:

(IV.12) $$p_a(\rho) = \alpha_o + \alpha_1\rho + \alpha_2\rho^2 + \ldots$$

where $\alpha_o = a_o$, $\alpha_1 = a_o a$, $\alpha_2 = a_o a^2$, . . . ; likewise

(IV.13) $$p_b(\rho) = \beta_o + \beta_1\rho + \beta_2\rho^2 + \ldots$$

where $\beta_o = b_o$, $\beta_1 = b_o b$, $\beta_2 = b_o b^2$, ... Thus (IV.11) becomes

(IV.14) $$p_a(\rho_1) - p_b(\rho_1) = (\alpha_o - \beta_o) + (\alpha_1 - \beta_1)\rho_1 + (\alpha_2 - \beta_2)\rho_1^2 + \ldots = 0.$$

Note that α_o is the vector of direct labor inputs; α_1 is the first round of indirect labor; and α_2 is the second round of indirect labor, etc. The β's have the same interpretation in terms of technique b.

Assume that there is only one sign variation in (IV.14). Assume, for example that the first term in (IV.14) is negative for the i-th good ($\alpha_{oi} \leq \beta_{oi}$), while all the other coefficients are positive

only when there are at least two nonzero columns in $[a - b]$, which in the present model, as we have seen, is not a general case. This might, however, be relevant in an 'Austrian'-type capital model, in which activities are not chosen independently.

6. See, for example, L.E. Dickson, *New First Course in the Theory of Equations* (New York: Wiley, 1939), p. 76.

($\alpha_{ji} \geqq \beta_{ji}$ for $j = 1, 2, \ldots, n$). The first derivative of $p_a(\rho) - p_b(\rho)$ will then be positive for $\rho > 0$, and therefore (IV.14) can have at most one root. This condition on the coefficients has a simple economic interpretation. Recall that α_{oi} and β_{oi} are the *direct* labor inputs per unit of the i-th good, that α_{1i} and β_{1i} are the first round of indirect labor needed to produce a unit of the i-th good, and that α_{2i} and β_{2i} are the second round of indirect labor needed to produce the i-th good, etc.[7] Hence, while activity a_i uses less direct labor than activity b_i, it embodies more indirect labor than activity b_i. If it is desired, one can substitute the word "capital" for "indirect labor," and conclude that activity a_i is more "capital-intensive" than activity b_i.[8]

We conclude that if for any pair of relevant techniques a and b, all pairs of corresponding activities a_i and b_i can be ranked in terms of "capital intensity" (in the above sense, which is independent of the rate of interest), then reswitching cannot occur.[9]

Although the latter sufficiency condition is again highly restrictive, it may be somewhat less restrictive than the former one: note the latter allows changes of single activities while the former does not. We might also observe that the latter condition seems to be the most natural extension of our previous two-sector nonswitching theorem (see Section III). Let us again stress that, except for highly exceptional circumstances, techniques cannot be ranked in order of capital intensity.[1] We thus conclude that reswitching is, at least theoretically, a perfectly acceptable case in the discrete capital model.[2]

Finally, let us note the crucial role of discreteness of activities

7. In the general case where the μ_i are unequal, the price vectors p_a is a polynomial in r. One can show that the first coefficient in that polynomial will be $a_o' = a_o\,[I - \mu_a]^{-1}$ = direct "embodied" labor input. The next terms have somewhat more complicated coefficients but have an analogous interpretation in terms of direct and indirect labor costs.

8. One can show that if we measure aggregate capital in each activity in value (or labor unit) terms, then this interpretation is precise.

The fact that the variations in signs of the input streams are related to the possibility of reswitchings (multiple roots) suggests that reswitching is similar to the problem of an investment option having more than one internal rate of return. (See also Section V below.) That any number of zeros can occur in the present value function was pointed out by Samuelson, "Some Aspects of the Pure Theory of Capital," this *Journal*, LI (May 1937), 469–96.

9. Note that we do not require pairs of activities to be ordered in the *same* way across the two matrixes, i.e., we need not have $a_{oi} \geqq b_{oi}$ or $a_{oi} \leqq b_{oi}$ for all i.

1. We are thus in agreement with Morishima, *Equilibrium, Stability, and Growth*, *op. cit.*, and Pasinetti, *op. cit.*

2. There is an open empirical question as to whether or not reswitching is likely to be observed in an actual economy for reasonable changes in the interest rate.

for obtaining the reswitching result. This is best exhibited by the following interesting theorem due to both M. Weitzman and Solow: In a general n capital good economy, suppose there is at least one capital good that is produced by a smooth neoclassical production function. In such an economy reswitching cannot occur provided that labor and each good are inputs in one or more of the goods produced neoclasically.

Setting the various marginal productivity conditions and supposing that at two different rates of interest the *same* set of input-output coefficients holds, the proof follows by contradiction.

V. Some Additional Implications for Economic Theory

A. *Expressions for National Product*

In order to facilitate the exposition, we assume a circulating-capital technology, although the results can be generalized to include the fixed-capital case without difficulty. Let $X = (X_1, \ldots, X_n)$ denote the output vector. The dynamics of the model are described by

(V.1) $$X(t) - C(t) = aX(t+1),$$

a difference equation with the interpretation that the part of *this* period's output which *is not* consumed must be equal to the input requirements for *next* period. We also assume that the labor supply is exogenously given, does not grow, and is fully employed.[3] A steady-state solution $X(t) = X(t+1) = X$ must satisfy the balance relationship

(V.2) $$X = aX + C$$

or

(V.2a) $$X = [I - a]^{-1}C$$

where the labor constraint is

(V.2b) $$L = a_0X.$$

The price vector now is (as in Levhari):

(V.3) $$P(r) = (1+r)wa_0[I - (1+r)a]^{-1}.$$

Manipulation of (V.2a), V.2b), and (V.3) yields the following expressions for gross national product and net national product:

(V.4a) $$GNP \equiv P(r)X = (1+r)wL + (1+r)P(r)aX$$

and

(V.4b) $$NNP \equiv P(r)C = wL + r[wL + P(r)aX].$$

Since labor and circulating capital are paid for at the beginning of

3. We could also generalize the results to the case where L grows according to $\dot{L}/L = n$, an exogenous constant. Here we take $n = 0$, and consider steady states which are in fact stationary states.

the production period, capitalists must advance an amount equal to $[wL + P(r)aX]$, on which they earn a net profit equal to $r[wL + P(r)aX]$ where r is the one-period rate of interest or the profit rate.

Under the simplifying assumption that all wage income is consumed, the quantity $[wL + P(r)aX]$ has a simple interpretation. Then all saving is done by capitalists who must save-invest enough to maintain the value of circulating capital required for the steady state, namely $P(r)aX$.

Let C^* and C^- denote capitalists' and workers' consumption, respectively. Capitalists and workers are faced with their respective budget constraints: [4]

(V.5) $\quad P(r)C^* = r[wL + P(r)aX]$

and

(V.6) $\quad P(r)C^- = wL = \text{constant}.$

The latter is what Samuelson has called net-net national product; it is that part of net national product left over for the primary factor (labor) after the other factors have been paid.[5] Note that $C \equiv C^* + C^-$.

It is easily seen from (V.2a), (V.2b), and (V.3) that there exists a *technical* constraint

(V.7) $\quad L = P(0)C$

where $P(0) = a_0[I - a]^{-1}$. Thus for a given technique $\begin{bmatrix} a_0 \\ \cdots \\ a \end{bmatrix}$, an equilibrium consumption vector C must satisfy (V.7), the equation of a hyperplane; such a C also satisfies (V.4b), and vice versa.

$P(r)C^-$ does *not* depend on tastes because wL is a fixed number and workers are free to choose any point C^- which satisfies their budget constraint (V.6); thus (V.6) is indeed the consumption possibility schedule for workers. But $P(r)C^*$ *does* depend on tastes. Suppose, for example, that C^- is fixed and equilibrium is established with $C^* = \hat{C}^*$. At first glance, one might think that capitalists are free to move to another point C^* (remember that r is fixed) provided that

$$P(r)\hat{C}^* = P(r)\tilde{C}^*.$$

4. As we will see, it is misleading to call both (V.5) and (V.6) consumption possibility schedules. Note also that the interpretation of C^* and C^- must change if the saving assumption is dropped. In fact, C^- is the *maximum* steady-state consumption for workers, and C^* is the *minimum* steady-state consumption for capitalists. It would be an easy matter to alter the discussion which follows to include any case.

5. Paul A. Samuelson, "A New Theorem on Nonsubstitution," in H. Hegeland (ed.), *Money, Growth, and Methodology; and Other Essays in Economics in Honor of Johan Akerman* (Lund: C. W. K. Gleerup, 1961).

But such a movement is in general impossible because the budget equation for capitalists (V.5) depends on X, and X depends on $C \equiv C^* + C^-$ via (V.2a). Hence (V.5) must be interpreted as a *virtual* consumption possibility schedule. Capitalists are *actually* constrained to a choice of C^* which satisfies

$$\text{(V.8)} \qquad \{P(r) - rP(r)a[I - a]^{-1}\}C^* \\ = r\{wL + P(r)a[I - a]^{-1}C^-\}.$$

With r fixed, we conclude that $P(r)C^*$ and thus $P(r)C$ are not invariant to a change in tastes of *either* workers *or* capitalists, even though $P(r)C^- = wL = constant$ is obviously invariant.[6]

B. Steady-state Consumption Patterns

We now wish to consider a finite set of alternative techniques $\begin{bmatrix} & a_0 & \\ \cdot & \vdots & \cdot \\ & a & \end{bmatrix}$, $\alpha = a, b, c, \ldots$. The fact that a technique can recur now alerts us to the existence of a "perverse case" in which a low rate of interest is not always associated with high consumption.[7]

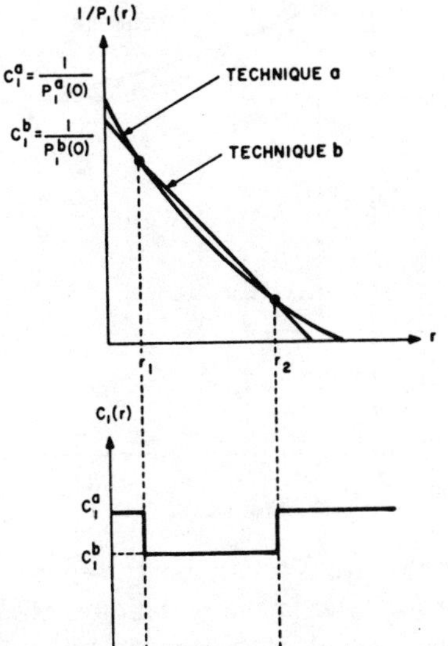

FIGURE V

This fact may be seen most easily by setting $C_2 = \cdots = C_n = 0$ and observing the behavior of C_1 in different steady states. We may

6. *Ibid.*
7. This fact was pointed out by Morishima, *Equilibrium, Stability, and Growth, op. cit.*, p. 126.

solve (V.7) for

$$\text{(V.9)} \qquad C_1{}^a = \frac{L}{P_1{}^a(0)}$$

where $P_1{}^a$ (0) is the price of good 1 when $r = 0$ and technique a is employed. We lose no generality by setting $w = L = 1$; then the height at $r = 0$ of the factor-price frontier *for technique* a is equal to $C_1{}^a$. A "perverse case" is illustrated in Figure V.

It is crucial to realize that while reswitching tells us that such behavior exists, the phenomenon illustrated in Figure V exists *without* reswitching, as shown in Figure VI. The cause of the "per-

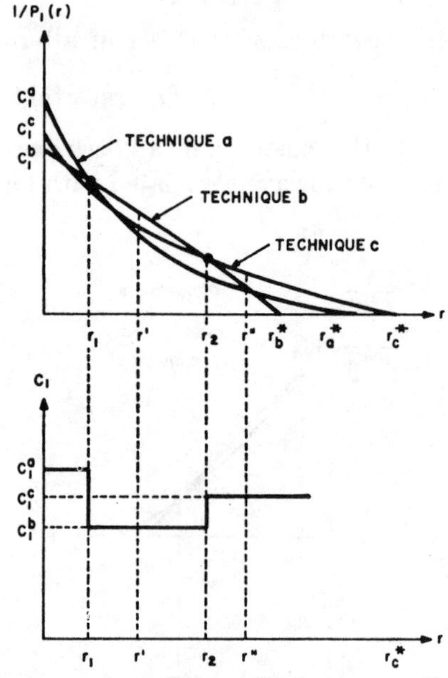

FIGURE VI

verse behavior" in Figure VI can be traced to the fact that the factor-price curves for alternative techniques cross *below* the outer envelope. Thus even though there are no multiple crossings on the outer envelope (the economy's factor-price frontier) and reswitching does not occur, we still find that C_1 *rises* when r is increased from r' to r'' where $r_1 < r' < r_2$ and $r_2 < r'' < r^*_c$.

We note that the sufficiency conditions for nonswitching which we have stated and proved in Sections III and IV may be, in general, overly strong to preclude reswitching on the FPF envelope. However, these same conditions may be *necessary* if the monotonicity of $C(r)$ is to be preserved.

The problem is a bit harder to analyze when there is positive consumption of more than one good, but the same qualitative behavior is possible. With alternative techniques the hyperplane equation (V.7) becomes a set of equations:

(V.10) $\quad L = P^{\alpha}(0)c^{\alpha},\ \alpha = a, b, c, \ldots\ .$

For a two-good economy (V.10) become the equations of straight lines in the $C_1 - C_2$ plane, as illustrated in Figure VII for alter-

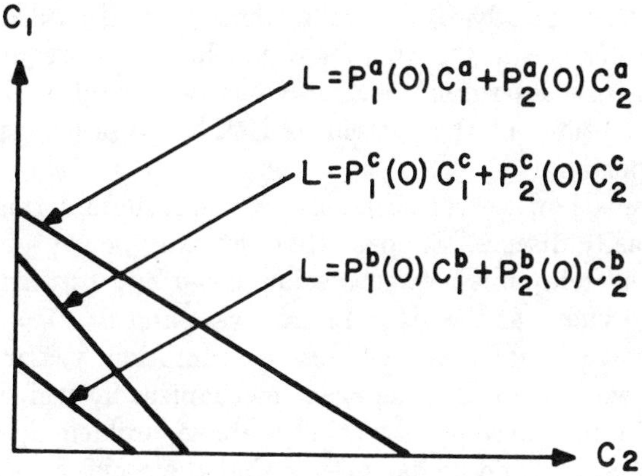

FIGURE VII

native techniques a, b, and c.[8] If, as in Figure VI, technique a is used for $0 \leq r \leq r_1$, b for $r_1 \leq r \leq r_2$, and c for $r_2 \leq r \leq r^*_c$ where $r_1 < r_2$, we can unambiguously say that steady-state consumption is high for low r, then lower for higher r, but higher again for still higher r.

Other conclusions follow from the above analysis. First, since (1) the nonsubstitution theorem tells us that the real wage in terms of every good is always maximized for a given r, and (2) the economy's factor-price frontier is downward sloping, it follows that consumption is maximized when $r = 0$, although that maximum may not be unique.[9] Second, workers' consumption *is* always higher for lower r, a conclusion which follows immediately from (V.6) and the fact that prices *always* increase when r is increased. Finally, the steady-state *value* of circulating capital $P(r)aX$ is not a

8. The three lines in Figure VII are parallel if we have the Marx case of "equal organic composition of capital." The nonsubstitution theorem guarantees that the lines can never cross because *all* prices are simultaneously minimized.

9. If we were to assume $\dot{L}/L = n > 0$, per capita consumption would be maximized when the Golden Rule condition $r = n$ is satisfied.

monotonic function of r, a fact also stated by Pasinetti, Morishima, and others.[1]

C. Transitions between Steady States

We have completely ignored how the economy moves from one steady state to another. It is as if there were different planets possessing the same book of blueprints (set of techniques) but which were in different steady states that correspond to different exogenously given r's. We then would observe each planet and compare their steady-state equilibriums. To discuss a movement from one steady state to another would in general require a theory of interest rate determination. Moreover, we would need to examine dynamic motions of the system and stability problems might become important.

There is, however, a special case which is illuminating and which we can easily discuss. Suppose that the exogenously given interest rate is a switch point between techniques a and b; then both techniques are viable at the given interest rate and $P^a(r) = P^b(r)$. The economy can usually move from consumption vector C^a to C^b, although we shall ignore the exact mechanism by which the movement is in fact accomplished. The above problem has been discussed by Solow, and he has proved that the social rate of return to saving, ρ, is equal to the switch-point interest rate r; a brief discussion of Solow's proof follows.

Suppose that the economy initially uses only technique a and has a corresponding consumption vector C^a. If the economy is able to move in one period to an equilibrium where only technique b is used, there must exist a consumption vector $\bar{C} \geq 0$ which satisfies

$$X = \bar{C} + bY \tag{V.11}$$

where bY is the vector of input requirements using technique b.[2] If such a $\bar{C}$ can be found, the economy may consume $\bar{C}$ for one period and then move into steady-state equilibrium with technique b and consumption C^b. Defining the social rate of return

$$\rho \equiv \frac{P(C^b - C^a)}{P(C^a - \bar{C})},$$

Solow proved that $\rho = r$.[3]

1. Morishima, *Equilibrium, Stability, and Growth, op. cit.*, and Pasinetti, *op cit.*

2. Solow has also considered a more complicated case in which a one-period transition is impossible because there does not exist a solution to $X = \bar{C} + bY$ with $\bar{C} \geqq 0$. The conclusion $\rho = r$ may remain valid even when more than one period is required to complete the transition.

3. From (V.4a) and (V.4b) we have $PC^a = (1 + r)wL + rPaX$, $PC^b =$

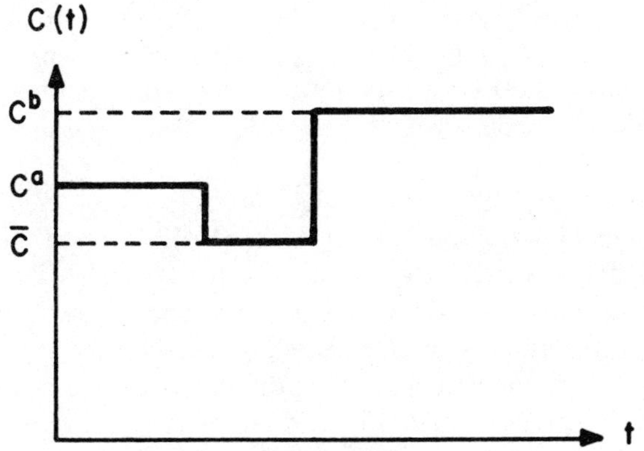

FIGURE VIII

In a well-behaved case $C^a > \overline{C}$ and $C^b > C^a$, and the time path of consumption appears as in Figure VIII. But in a "perverse" case, $C^a < \overline{C}$ and $C^b < C^a$ as illustrated in Figure IX.

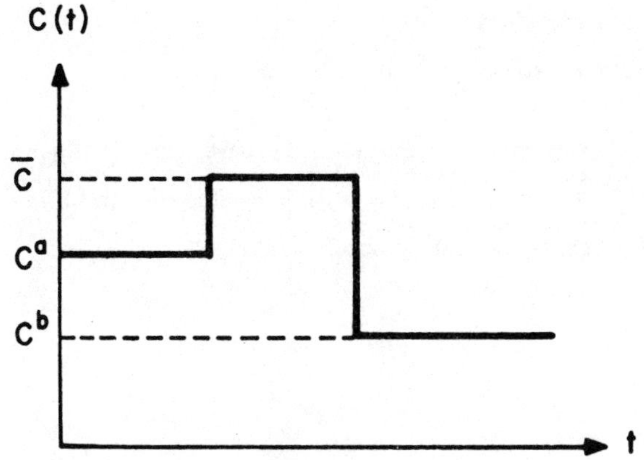

FIGURE IX

What can be concluded?

Since $P^a(r) = P^b(r)$, workers are not affected by the change: they may still consume C^- where $PC^- = wL$. But the story is not the same for capitalists. As $C \equiv C^* + C^-$, it is C^* which changes when the economy moves from technique a to b. If $C^{*b} < C^{*a}$, can we conclude that capitalists have been hurt? The answer is most

$(1+r)wL + rPbY$, and $PX = (1+r)wL + (1+r)PaX$. Then from (V.11) we obtain $PC^a - P\overline{C} = PbY - PaX$. Likewise, $PC^b - PC^a = r(PbY - PaX)$, and the conclusion $\rho = r$ follows immediately.

certainly "no," for it is the capitalists who enjoyed a splash of consumption $\bar{C}^* > C^{*a}$, and the extra consumption in which they indulged for one period is exactly equal to the value of their forever-lower consumption stream $C^{*b} < C^{*a}$ discounted at the social rate of return.[4]

Finally let us point out a corollary of Solow's theorem. If there are a number of switching points, then at all of them the rate of interest (usually) equals the rate of return to saving. The *physical acts* of moving back and forth from one consumption "plateau" to the other as the rate of interest changes will be identical at every switch point, but the interest rate is different at each switch point. In other words, here is a clear illustration of the analogy between the reswitching problem and the existence of multiple rates of return in investment profitability calculations.

One may recall that we have been warned long ago that "there is no new thing under the sun." [5]

MASSACHUSETTS INSTITUTE OF TECHNOLOGY
AND HEBREW UNIVERSITY, JERUSALEM

UNIVERSITY OF PENNSYLVANIA

MASSACHUSETTS INSTITUTE OF TECHNOLOGY AND
HARVARD UNIVERSITY

4. The above argument depends on keeping r fixed. As pointed out by Samuelson, *op. cit.*, when $r = 0$, workers get all of NNP with $P(O)C^- = P(O)C$ and $C^* = 0$; and when $r = r^*$, the maximum rate of interest where $w = 0$, $P(0)C^* = PC$ and $C^- = 0$.

5. *Bible*, Ecclesiastes 1.9 (about B.C. 977).

[12]

M. Brown, K. Sato and P. Zarembka (eds.), *Essays in Modern Capital Theory*

REAL WICKSELL EFFECTS AND REGULAR ECONOMIES*

Edwin Burmeister

1. Introduction and summary

The real Wicksell effect equals the price-weighted changes in the per capita stocks of capital goods across steady-state equilibria, and an economy is termed *regular* if the real Wicksell effect is negative at every steady-state interest or profit rate. This concept of a regular economy, introduced by Burmeister and Turnovsky (1972), does not depend upon either (i) the differentiability of neoclassical production functions or (ii) the possibility of boundary or 'corner solutions'. Moreover, the basic theorem we will prove below, which excludes certain 'paradoxical behavior', is valid both in models with many consumption goods and when joint production exists. It will be shown that the qualitative conclusions of the 'neoclassical one-sector parable' are valid only for regular economies, and we will argue that there is no logical necessity for 'capital aggregation' in microeconomic theory and general equilibrium analysis.

2. Description of the technology

Consider an economy with one primary factor (labor, L) and n heterogeneous commodities. Labor grows at the exogenous rate g, and every commodity can serve as both a consumption and capital good; the (gross) output of the ith commodity and the stock of the ith capital good are denoted by Y_i and K_i, respectively, $i = 1, \ldots, n$.

*I am grateful for a fellowship from the John Simon Guggenheim Memorial Foundation and to the Australian National University for a most enjoyable visit during 1974–1975. Comments from Ngo Van Long, Peter Hammond and Paul Zarembka on an earlier version of this paper are greatly appreciated.

The feasible technology can be represented by either a *production possibility frontier*

$$Y_1 = T(Y_2, \ldots, Y_n; L, K_1, \ldots, K_n) \tag{1}$$

or by a *technology set*

$$S = \{(Y, L, K): Y_1 \leqq T(\cdot), (Y, L, K) \geqq 0\}. \tag{2}$$

As usual, it is assumed that S is a closed, convex cone, that fıee disposal is possible, and that positive outputs of every commodity can be produced when every input is positive (see, for example, Burmeister and Dobell (1970, pp. 208–209). If T is twice continuously differentiable, our assumptions imply that the Hessian matrix $[T_{ij}]$ is singular (because there are constant returns to scale and S is a cone). Moreover, it will be negative semi-definite with a rank that varies according to the degree of joint production in the economy (Samuelson, 1966; Burmeister and Turnovsky, 1971; Kuga, 1973). The assumption that S exhibits strong superadditivity[1] (or an assumption that S is strictly convex except along rays through the origin) implies that $[T_{ij}]$ has rank $(2n - 1)$, in which case *all* commodities are produced jointly (Burmeister and Turnovsky, 1971; Samuelson, 1966).

We first proceed on the assumption that $T(\cdot)$ is twice continuously differentiable, and then we will turn to the non-differentiable case in which S is a polyhedral cone exhibiting 'flats' or facets.

3. The differentiable case

In steady-state equilibrium all quantities must grow at the rate g. Let output Y_i equal consumption plus net capital formation, i.e.

$$Y_i = C_i + \dot{K}_i, \qquad i = 1, \ldots, n. \tag{3}$$

Substituting the steady-state requirements

$$Y_i = C_i + gK_i, \qquad i = 1, \ldots, n, \tag{4}$$

[1]Let $Y = (Y_1, \ldots, Y_n)$ and $Z = (L, K_1, \ldots, K_n)$. The technology set S is *strongly superadditive* provided $(Y', Z') \in S$, $(Y'', Z'') \in S$, and $Z' \neq \lambda Z''$ for any $\lambda > 0$, imply that there exists a process $(Z' + Z'', Y''') \in S$ with $Y''' \geqq Y' + Y''$ and $Y_i''' > Y_i' + Y_i''$ for at least one i.

into (1), we derive

$$C_1 + gK_1 = T(C_2 + gK_2, \ldots, C_n + gK_n; L, K_1, \ldots, K_n), \quad (5)$$

or, using lower-case letters to denote per capita quantities,

$$c_1 + gk_1 = T(c_2 + gk_2, \ldots, c_n + gk_n; 1, k_1, \ldots, k_n). \quad (6)$$

Likewise, steady-state price equilibrium requires that

$$w_i = rp_i, \qquad i = 1, \ldots, n, \quad (7)$$

where r is the interest or profit rate, prices of goods and factors in terms of the wage rate as *numéraire* are denoted by lower case p_i's and w_i's, respectively, and w_i is the net (of depreciation) factor price or rental rate for the ith capital good. Since

$$\frac{\partial T}{\partial(c_i + gk_i)} = -\frac{P_i}{P_1} = -\frac{P_i/W}{P_1/W} = -\frac{p_i}{p_1}, \qquad i = 1, \ldots, n, \quad (8)$$

and

$$\frac{\partial T}{\partial k_i} = +\frac{W_i}{P_1} = \frac{W_i/W}{P_1/W} = \frac{w_i}{p_1}, \qquad i = 1, \ldots, n, \quad (9)$$

a vector

$$(c^*, k^*; r^*, p^*) = (c_1^*, \ldots, c_n^*, k_1^*, \ldots, k_n^*; r^*, p_1^*, \ldots, p_n^*) \geqq 0$$

satisfying (6)–(9) represents a steady-state solution. We then say that p^* supports (c^*, k^*) at the interest or profit rate r^*, and given r^* and p^*, the corresponding equilibria points c^* and k^* are determined.

Although derivatives such as $\mathrm{d}y_1/\mathrm{d}r|_{(r^*, p^*)}$ may not exist unless steady-state quantities are uniquely determined by r^*, from (6) we may calculate that almost everywhere

$$\begin{aligned}
\left.\frac{\mathrm{d}y_1}{\mathrm{d}r}\right|_{(r^*, p^*)} &= \left.\frac{\mathrm{d}(c_1 + gk_1)}{\mathrm{d}r}\right|_{(r^*, p^*)} \\
&= \left.\left[\sum_{i=2}^{n} \frac{\partial T}{\partial(c_i + gk_i)}\left(\frac{\mathrm{d}c_i}{\mathrm{d}r} + g\frac{\mathrm{d}k_i}{\mathrm{d}r}\right) + \sum_{i=1}^{n} \frac{\partial T}{\partial k_i}\left(\frac{\mathrm{d}k_i}{\mathrm{d}r}\right)\right]\right|_{(r^*, p^*)} \\
&= \left.\left[-\sum_{i=2}^{n}\left(\frac{\mathrm{d}c_i}{\mathrm{d}r} + g\frac{\mathrm{d}k_i}{\mathrm{d}r}\right)\frac{p_i}{p_1} + \sum_{i=1}^{n}\left(\frac{\mathrm{d}k_i}{\mathrm{d}r}\right)\frac{rp_i}{p_1}\right]\right|_{(r^*, p^*)}
\end{aligned}$$

or

$$\sum_{i=1}^{n} p_i \left(\frac{\mathrm{d}c_i}{\mathrm{d}r}\right)\bigg|_{(r^*, p^*)} = (r - g) \sum_{i=1}^{n} p_i \left(\frac{\mathrm{d}k_i}{\mathrm{d}r}\right)\bigg|_{(r^*, p^*)}. \tag{10}$$

Here every expression is evaluated at the steady-state equilibrium point corresponding to (r^*, p^*).

Note that (10) does not depend on the choice of *numéraire*; every p_i in (10) can be multiplied by any positive number without changing the basic relationship, namely:

Theorem 1.

$$\operatorname{sgn} \sum_{i=1}^{n} p_i \left(\frac{\mathrm{d}c_i}{\mathrm{d}r}\right)\bigg|_{(r^*, p^*)} = \operatorname{sgn}(g - r^*) \neq 0 \quad \text{at } r^* \neq g$$

if, and only if,

$$\sum_{i=1}^{n} p_i \left(\frac{\mathrm{d}k_i}{\mathrm{d}r}\right)\bigg|_{(r^*, p^*)} < 0.$$

Proof. The result follows immediately from (10). Q.E.D.

In particular, in the context of an optimal growth model

$$\max \int_0^\infty U(c_1, \ldots, c_n)\, \mathrm{e}^{-\rho t}\, \mathrm{d}t, \qquad \rho > 0, \tag{11}$$

at a steady-state (rest point) solution to (11), we have

$$\sum_{i=1}^{n} p_i \left(\frac{\mathrm{d}c_i}{\mathrm{d}r}\right)\bigg|_{(r^*, p^*)} = \frac{\mathrm{d}U}{\mathrm{d}r}\bigg|_{(r^*, p^*)}, \qquad r^* = \rho + g, \tag{12}$$

a fact which follows directly from the necessary optimality conditions

$$p_i = \partial U / \partial c_i = U_i, \qquad i = 1, \ldots, n; \tag{13}$$

see Brock (1973), especially pp. 546–547[2].

Corollary 1.1. Let $U^* = U(c_1^*, \ldots, c_n^*)$ represent a rest-point solution to (11) with $r^* = \rho^* + g$. This equilibrium utility level increases

[2]Throughout this paper we assume that $U(c_1, \ldots, c_n)$ is strictly concave and twice continuously differentiable.

(decreases) with a decrease (increase) in the discount rate $\rho^* > 0$ *if, and only if,*

$$\sum_{i=1}^{n} p_i \left(\frac{\mathrm{d}k_i}{\mathrm{d}r}\right)\bigg|_{(r^*=\rho^*+g,\, p^*)} < 0.$$

Corollary 1.2. Suppose $c_2 = \cdots = c_n = 0$. *The steady-state level of per capita consumption* c_1 *increases (decreases) with a decrease (increase) in* $r^* > g$ *if, and only if,*

$$\sum_{i=1}^{n} p_i \left(\frac{\mathrm{d}k_i}{\mathrm{d}r}\right)\bigg|_{(r^*>g,\, p^*)} < 0.$$

4. Real and price Wicksell effects

For expositional simplicity consider models without joint production, in which case all steady-state equilibrium prices and quantities are functions of only the interest or profit rate r (see, for example, Burmeister and Dobell (1970, chs. 8, 9). In particular, the value of capital in terms of the wage rate as *numéraire* is given by

$$v = v(r) = \sum_{i=1}^{n} p_i(r) k_i(r). \tag{14}$$

As the interest rate varies, the change in the value of capital across steady-state equilibria is composed of the sum of two terms:

$$\frac{\mathrm{d}v}{\mathrm{d}r} = \sum_{i=1}^{n} \left(\frac{\mathrm{d}p_i}{\mathrm{d}r}\right) k_i + \sum_{i=1}^{n} p_i \left(\frac{\mathrm{d}k_i}{\mathrm{d}r}\right). \tag{15}$$

The first term on the right-hand side of (15) is the *price Wicksell effect*, and it is always positive because steady-state equilibrium prices always increase with an increase in the interest rate, i.e. $\mathrm{d}p_i/\mathrm{d}r > 0$, $i = 1, \ldots, n$.[3] The second term on the right-hand side of (15) is the *real Wicksell effect*; it equals the price-weighted sum of the changes in physical capital stocks, and, in general, it may be either negative or positive.

[3]We assume that no commodity is produced using only labor.

What is crucial, the change in the value of capital [$\mathrm{d}v/\mathrm{d}r$] or the real Wicksell effect just defined [$\Sigma_{i=1}^{n} p_i(\mathrm{d}k_i/\mathrm{d}r)$]? An example due to Burmeister and Dobell demonstrates that it is the real Wicksell effect which is of economic significance for answering questions about changes in the steady-state levels of utility or consumption. This conclusion stems from the fact that $\mathrm{d}v/\mathrm{d}r$ may be *positive* while $\Sigma_{i=1}^{n} p_i(\mathrm{d}k_i/\mathrm{d}r)$ is always negative, even though the example is constructed with neoclassical production functions of the simple Cobb–Douglas form (Burmeister and Dobell, 1970, pp. 291–292).

Of course, if $\mathrm{d}v/\mathrm{d}r$ is negative, then the real Wicksell effect must be negative; this fact is obvious from (15) since the price Wicksell effect must always be positive. Thus, the example just cited demonstrates the possibility of situations in which the positive price Wicksell effect outweighs a negative real Wicksell effect, implying that the change in the value of capital is positive.

A crucial observation is that the *sign* of the expression

$$\sum_{i=1}^{n} p_i\left(\frac{\mathrm{d}k_i}{\mathrm{d}r}\right)\Bigg|_{(r^*,\,p^*)}$$

is independent of the choice of *numéraire*. Thus, for example, we may set the price of any commodity or the wage rate at unity, or, alternatively, normalize prices by setting $\Sigma_{i=1}^{n} p_i = 1$. In all instances the *sign* of the real Wicksell effect is invariant, which, of course, justifies the use of our term *real* Wicksell effect. On the other hand the sign of $\mathrm{d}v/\mathrm{d}r$ definitely depends upon the choice of *numéraire* through the influence of price changes $\mathrm{d}p_i/\mathrm{d}r$.

Definition 1. An economy is called regular if

$$\sum_{i=1}^{n} p_i\left(\frac{\mathrm{d}k_i}{\mathrm{d}r}\right)\Bigg|_{(r^*,\,p^*)} < 0$$

at every steady-state equilibrium point (r^*, p^*), $r^* \neq g$.

Definition 2. An economy is said to exhibit *paradoxical consumption behavior* at the steady-state equilibrium point (r^*, p^*) if

$$\operatorname{sgn} \sum_{i=1}^{n} p_i\left(\frac{\mathrm{d}c_i}{\mathrm{d}r}\right)\Bigg|_{(r^*,\,p^*)} = \operatorname{sgn}(r^* - g) \neq 0 \quad \text{at } r^* \neq g.$$

In particular, suppose $c_2 = \cdots = c_n = 0$; then an economy exhibits paradoxical consumption behavior at an interest rate $r^* > g$ if $\mathrm{d}c_1/\mathrm{d}r\,|_{(r^*, p^*)} > 0$. The word 'paradoxical' is appropriate because, although the steady-state interest rate exceeds the growth rate ($r^* > g$), an *increase* in the interest rate (which *increases* the gap $r^* - g$) will lead to a new steady-state equilibrium with a *higher* level of per capita consumption of commodity 1. Such paradoxes are possible in models without joint production only when more than one physical type of capital good exists. However, paradoxical consumption behavior definitely *can* occur in models with only one physical type of capital good, provided joint production is admitted (Burmeister and Turnovsky, 1972). Therefore, one cannot unequivocally assert that 'The presence of heterogeneous capital goods is the (only) cause of paradoxes in capital theory.' Rather, paradoxical consumption behavior occurs when our index of the *change* in capital

$$\sum_{i=1}^{n} p_i\left(\frac{\mathrm{d}k_i}{\mathrm{d}r}\right)\bigg|_{(r^*, p^*)}$$

is positive, an observation we return to in section 8. Theorem 1 may be stated now in the following equivalent form.

Theorem 1(a). An economy never exhibits paradoxical consumption behavior if, and only if, the economy is regular.

5. A non-differentiable case: the generalized von Neumann model

In this section we adopt the generalized von Neumann model described by Burmeister (1974). There are m alternative activities for producing the n different commodities ($m \gtreqless n$), and activity j operating at the unit intensity level requires a labor input a_{0j} and a vector of commodity inputs $(a_{1j}, \ldots, a_{nj})$ to produce a vector of commodity outputs $(b_{1j}, \ldots, b_{nj})$. There is only one primary factor, labor, and the row vector $A_0 = (a_{01}, \ldots, a_{0m})$ designates the labor requirements for the m alternative activities. The input matrix is

$$A = \begin{bmatrix} a_{11} & \cdots & a_{1m} \\ \vdots & & \vdots \\ a_{n1} & \cdots & a_{nm} \end{bmatrix},$$

the output matrix is

$$B = \begin{bmatrix} b_{11} & \cdots & b_{1m} \\ \vdots & & \\ b_{n1} & \cdots & b_{nm} \end{bmatrix},$$

and the column vector

$$x = \begin{bmatrix} x_1 \\ \vdots \\ x_m \end{bmatrix}$$

designates the intensity levels at which each of the m activities is operated. In general, some of the a_{0j}'s, a_{ij}'s, and b_{ij}'s may be zero, but we will ignore this technical detail here (or the reader may assume that they are all positive).

The column vector

$$C = \begin{bmatrix} C_1 \\ \vdots \\ C_n \end{bmatrix}$$

represents consumption of final commodities, and we assume that labor grows at the exogenous rate $g \geqq 0$. The economy is capable of growth at rate g provided the inequalities

$$(1+g)\sum_{j=1}^{m} a_{ij}x_j \leqq \sum_{j=1}^{m} b_{ij}x_j - C_i, \qquad i = 1, \ldots, n, \tag{16}$$

have a solution with both $x_j \geqq 0$ and $C_i \geqq 0$, and with not all $x_j = 0$, not all $C_i = 0$. Eq. (16) has the straightforward interpretation that the part of this period's output which is *not* consumed must equal or exceed the input requirements to produce output (allowing for growth at rate g) in the next period. In standard vector–matrix notation, the quantity system (16) is written as

$$(1+g)Ax \leqq Bx - C, \qquad C, x \geqq 0, \qquad C, x \neq 0, \tag{17}$$

while the labor constraint takes the trivial form

$$(1+g)A_0x = (1+g)A_0x. \tag{18}$$

Prices of the n commodities are given by the row vector

$$p = (p_1 \ldots p_n), \qquad \sum_{i=1}^{n} p_i = 1,$$

the wage rate is w_0, and the steady-state profit or interest rate is $r \geqq 0$. Analogous to (17) and (18), the economy can achieve a steady-state equilibrium at a given value of r if the 'dual' von Neumann price system has a solution satisfying

$$w_0A_0 + (1+r)pA \geqq pB, \qquad w_0, p \geqq 0, \qquad p \neq 0. \tag{19}$$

Moreover, if the cost of operating an activity exceeds its revenue, that activity is shut down (is operated at a zero intensity level). Thus,

$$x_j = 0 \quad \text{if } w_0a_{0j} + (1+r)\sum_{i=1}^{n} p_ia_{ij} > \sum_{i=1}^{n} p_ib_{ij}, \qquad j = 1, \ldots, m. \tag{20}$$

Similarly, if an activity is operated at a positive intensity level, then revenue must exactly cover cost and

$$w_0a_{0j} + (1+r)\sum_{i=1}^{n} p_ia_{ij} = \sum_{i=1}^{n} p_ib_{ij} \qquad \text{if } x_j > 0, \qquad j = 1, \ldots, m. \tag{21}$$

Likewise, the price of a commodity is zero if it is in excess supply; and if a commodity has a positive price, its supply and demand are equal. Thus,

$$p_i = 0 \quad \text{if } (1+g)\sum_{j=1}^{m} a_{ij}x_j < \sum_{j=1}^{m} b_{ij}x_j - C_i, \qquad i = 1, \ldots, n, \tag{22}$$

and

$$(1+g)\sum_{j=1}^{m} a_{ij}x_j = \sum_{j=1}^{m} b_{ij}x_j - C_i \quad \text{if } p_i > 0, \qquad i = 1, \ldots, n. \tag{23}$$

Combining (20)–(23), we see that in steady-state equilibrium,

$$p(1+g)Ax + pC = pBx = w_0A_0x + p(1+r)Ax. \tag{24}$$

Since $A_0x = L$, note that $pAx/A_0x = v$ is the per capita value of capital, while $pC/A_0x = pc$ is the per capita value of consumption. Hence, (24) may be rewritten as

$$pC = w_0A_0x + (r-g)pAx \tag{25}$$

or

$$pc = w_0 + (r-g)v. \tag{26}$$

Suppose that (c^1, x^1) and (c^2, x^2) both represent von Neumann equilibria with respect to a price vector p^*, the wage rate w_0^*, and the interest rate r^*.[4] Both (c^1, x^1) and (c^2, x^2) then satisfy eq. (26) with $p = p^*$, $w_0 = w_0^*$, and $r = r^*$, and we say that (w_0^*, p^*) *supports* the von Neumann activity vectors x^1 and x^2 with corresponding consumption vectors c^1 and c^2. Define the per capita value of capital in these two equilibria by

$$v_i^* = p^*Ax^h/A_0x^h, \qquad h = 1, 2. \tag{27}$$

From eq. (24) or (26) we conclude that

$$(1+g)v_i^* + p^*c^h = w_0^* + (1+r^*)v_h^*, \qquad h = 1, 2. \tag{28}$$

The following result is immediate.

Theorem 2.

$$\operatorname{sgn}(p^*\Delta c) = \operatorname{sgn}(g - r^*) \neq 0 \quad \text{at } r^* \neq g$$

if, and only if,

$$\Delta v^* = p^*\Delta k^* < 0,$$

[4]Recall that the price normalization in this section is $\Sigma_{i=1}^n p_i = 1$, and w_0 denotes the normalized wage rate.

where

$$\Delta c = c^1 - c^2, \qquad \Delta v^* = v_1^* - v_2^*, \qquad \Delta k^* = k_1^* - k_2^*,$$

$$k_1^* = p^*Ax^1/A_0x^1, \quad \text{and} \quad k_2^* = p^*Ax^2/A_0x^2.$$

Whenever inequalities are binding (for example, when $x_i^1 = 0$, but $x_i^2 > 0$ for at least one i) it is *not* true that real Wicksell effects cannot be measured. The appropriate prices are provided by the support vector p^*. Therefore, the familiar model discussed in Zarembka (1975, p. 16) can be handled in a straightforward manner using this generalized von Neumann model. In particular, we now may define the input matrix

$$A = \begin{bmatrix} a_{11} & \cdots & 0 & a_{1,n+1} & \cdots & 0 \\ \vdots & & \vdots & \vdots & & \vdots \\ 0 & \cdots & a_{nn} & 0 & \cdots & a_{n,n+n} \\ 0 & \cdots & 0 & 0 & \cdots & 0 \end{bmatrix},$$

the output matrix

$$B = \begin{bmatrix} 1 & \cdots & 0 & 0 & \cdots & 0 \\ \vdots & & \vdots & \vdots & & \vdots \\ 0 & \cdots & 1 & 0 & \cdots & 0 \\ 0 & \cdots & 0 & 1 & \cdots & 1 \end{bmatrix},$$

and the labor input vector

$$A_0 = (b_1 \ldots b_n \, a_{1c} \ldots a_{nc}).$$

In this notation, row $(n + 1)$ designates the consumption good, b_i is the labor requirement to produce one unit of the ith capital good (also using a_{ii} machines of type i), and a_{ic} is the labor requirement to produce one unit of the single consumption good (also using $a_{i,n+i}$ machines of type i).

Except at r's corresponding to switch points, a unique choice of i (type of machine) will be most profitable and satisfy the von

Neumann *inequalities* (20)–(23). Accordingly, the intensity vector is

$$x = \begin{bmatrix} x_1 \\ \vdots \\ x_n \\ \vdots \\ x_{2n} \end{bmatrix} = \begin{bmatrix} 0 \\ \vdots \\ 0 \\ x_i > 0 \\ 0 \\ \vdots \\ 0 \\ x_{n+i} > 0 \\ 0 \\ \vdots \\ 0 \end{bmatrix}$$

if, and only if, only capital of type i is employed in the economy. At a switch point r^* two (or more) types of capital can co-exist in equilibrium at the support prices p^*. For this model, therefore, the following corollary to theorem 2 is evident.

Corollary 2.1. There is no reswitching of techniques if $\Delta v^* = p^* \Delta k^* < 0$ *at every switch point* r^*.

(The notation $\Delta z = z^1 - z^2$ must follow the convention that z^h represents an equilibrium variable at the interest rate r^h and $r^1 > r^2$ so that $\Delta r = r^1 - r^2 > 0$. At r^*, $r^1 > r^* > r^2$, both z^1 and z^2 represent equilibrium variables by virtue of the switch point definition.)

This result is easily generalized to more complex von Neumann or Leontief–Sraffa models.

6. Negativity of the real Wicksell effect at $r = g$

Because the underlying technology (1) is concave, maximization of steady-state per capita consumption yields a unique golden rule solution $c = c^*$, $k = k^*$. For a discrete technology consumption may have a 'flat' at $r = g$ with $c = c^*$, $k = k^*$ for all r in a neighborhood of g, $N(g)$. In such cases, of course, $p\Delta k = 0$ for changes near $r = g$.

If there is a continuum of techniques and the production possibility frontier is twice continuously differentiable, weak additional conditions assure that the golden rule point with $c = c^*$ at $r = g$ is a *unique* maximum. However, even in this case

$$pk' \equiv \sum_{i=1}^{n} p_i\left(\frac{dk_i}{dr}\right)$$

may be zero at $r = g$, where primes denote differentiation with respect to r across steady-state equilibria. To see this possibility, differentiate (10) to obtain

$$pc'' = (r - g)(p'k' + pk'') + pk' - p'c' = pk' \quad \text{at } r = g. \tag{29}$$

Since c'' may be zero at a unique, regular maximum, the possibility that $pk' = 0$ at $r = g$ is not precluded.

We suppose, as in section 5, that the underlying technology is comprised of m 'industries' constrained by the technological relationships

$$F^j(b_{1j}, \ldots, b_{nj}; a_{0j}, a_{1j}, \ldots, a_{nj}) = 0, \qquad j = 1, \ldots, m. \tag{30}$$

Corresponding to (30) there are m dual profit functions

$$\Pi^j(p_1, \ldots, p_n; w_0, w_1, \ldots, w_n) = 0, \qquad j = 1, \ldots, m, \tag{31}$$

where w_0 is the wage rate and w_i is the rental rate for the ith factor input, $i = 1, \ldots, n$. The dual functions $F^j(\cdot) = 0$ and $\Pi^j(\cdot) = 0$ are concave and homogeneous of degree one with

$$\begin{aligned} &\partial F^j/\partial b_{ij} = -p_i, i = 1, \ldots, n; \partial F^j/\partial a_{hj} = w_h, h = 0, 1, \ldots, n; \\ &\partial \Pi^j/\partial p_i = b_{ij}, i = 1, \ldots, n; \partial \Pi^j/\partial w_h = -a_{hj}, h = 0, 1, \ldots, n. \end{aligned} \tag{32}$$

We now postulate:

The matrices

$$[\Pi^j_{ih}] \equiv \left(\frac{\partial^2 \Pi^j}{\partial_{w^2}}\right) = \begin{bmatrix} \dfrac{\partial^2 \Pi^j}{\partial w_1 \partial w_1} & \cdots & \dfrac{\partial^2 \Pi^j}{\partial w_1 \partial w_n} \\ \vdots & & \vdots \\ \dfrac{\partial^2 \Pi^j}{\partial w_n \partial w_1} & \cdots & \dfrac{\partial^2 \Pi^j}{\partial w_n \partial w_n} \end{bmatrix} \tag{A}$$

are negative definite, $j = 1, \ldots, m$.

Note that (A) asserts strong diminishing returns of profits with respect to decreases in non-labor input prices $(w_1, \ldots, w_n)$ measured in terms of the wage rate as *numéraire*. It will be satisfied for any non-joint technology having neoclassical production functions as defined by Burmeister and Dobell (1970, pp. 9–10) since the dual cost functions will have negative semi-definite Hessians of one less than full rank.

We also require the following assumptions:

$$\left.\begin{array}{ll}\text{(i)} & a_{0j} > 0 \textit{ for all } r \in N(g) \textit{ and for all } j. \\ \text{(ii)} & \textit{If } a_{hj} = 0 \textit{ at } r = g, \textit{ then it is zero for all } r \in N(g). \\ \text{(iii)} & \textit{If } b_{hj} = 0 \textit{ at } r = g, \textit{ then it is zero for all } r \in N(g). \end{array}\right\} \quad \text{(B)}$$

The first condition assumes that the labor input is positive in every industry (process), while (ii) and (iii) serve to rule out corner or boundary solutions that might occur at only particular prices near $r = g$. Thus, while some inputs and outputs may be zero in certain processes, in a neighborhood of $r = g$ there are no 'corner switches' in which the equilibrium value of an input or output *changes* from positive to zero with changes in r. Also note that (iii) is trivially satisfied in a non-joint production technology where the output matrix is $B = I$.

We may now prove that $pk' < 0$ at $r = g$ if (A) and (B) hold.

Theorem 3. Assume (A) and (B). Then the real Wicksell effect is negative at $r = g$, i.e.

$$pk' \equiv \sum_{i=1}^{n} p_i \left(\frac{dk_i}{dr}\right) < 0 \quad \textit{at } r = g.$$

Proof. As we now have a differentiable technology and (B) assures interior solutions, we may work with equalities rather than inequalities for $r \in N(g)$. Thus the full-employment conditions

$$Bx = C + (1+g)Ax, \qquad A_0 x = L \equiv 1,$$

may be solved for the intensity vector

$$x = [B - (1+g)A]^{-1} c, \tag{33}$$

where $c \equiv C/A_0x$ denotes the per capita consumption vector. From (33) we calculate

$$x' = -[B-(1+g)A]^{-1}[B'-(1+g)A'][B-(1+g)A]^{-1}c$$
$$= -[B-(1+g)A]^{-1}[B'-(1+g)A']x, \qquad r=g. \tag{34}$$

Similarly, prices in terms of the nominal wage rate ($w_0 \equiv 1$) are

$$p = A_0[B-(1+r)A]^{-1} \tag{35}$$

with

$$p' = pA[B-(1+r)A]^{-1}. \tag{36}$$

(Warning: In section 5 prices were normalized by $\Sigma_{i=1}^{n} p_i = 1$, while here p_i denotes the price of commodity i relative to the nominal wage rate ($w_0 = 1$). As already noted, the *sign* of expressions such as pk' is independent of price normalizations.) The derivation of (36) from (35) uses the envelope result that $w_0A'_0 + wA' = pB'$.

Steady-state factor rentals are

$$w = p(1+r) \tag{37}$$

with

$$w' = p + (1+r)p', \tag{38}$$

and using (35) and (36), (38) is written as

$$w' = A_0[B-(1+r)A]^{-1} + (1+r)pA[B-(1+r)A]^{-1}$$
$$= [A_0 + (1+r)pA][B-(1+r)A]^{-1} = p[B-(1+r)A]^{-1}. \tag{39}$$

Now we take the last duality relationships in (32) and differentiate:

$$a'_{ij} = \sum_{h=1}^{n} \Pi^{j}_{ih} w'_h \quad \text{where } a'_{ij} \equiv 0 \quad \text{if } a_{ij} = 0 \text{ by (B).} \tag{40}$$

For $i = 1, \ldots, n$, (40) may be written as

$$\begin{bmatrix} a_{ij} \\ \vdots \\ a_{ni} \end{bmatrix} = [\Pi^j_{ih}] \begin{bmatrix} w'_1 \\ \vdots \\ w'_n \end{bmatrix}. \tag{41}$$

Thus since $[\Pi_{ih}]$ is negative definite by (A), we have

$$(w'_1, \ldots, w'_n) \begin{bmatrix} a_{1j} \\ \vdots \\ a_{nj} \end{bmatrix} = (w_1, \ldots, w_n)[\Pi^j_{ih}] \begin{bmatrix} w'_1 \\ \vdots \\ w'_n \end{bmatrix} < 0, \quad j = 1, \ldots, m, \tag{42}$$

or

$$w'A' < 0. \tag{43}$$

Similarly, using the third duality relationship in (32) plus the fact that the matrices $[\partial^2 \Pi^j/(\partial p_i \, \partial p_h)]$ are negative semi-definite because $\Pi^j(\cdot)$ are concave, it may be proved that

$$p'B' \geqq 0. \tag{44}$$

Since the per capita capital vector is Ax with $A_0 x = 1$, we have

$$pk' = p(Ax' + A'x). \tag{45}$$

At $r = g$ we use (34) to write (45) as

$$\begin{aligned} pk' &= p\{-A[B-(1+g)A]^{-1}[B'-(1+g)A'] + A'\}x \\ &= -\{p'[B'-(1+r)A'] - pA'\}x \quad \text{using (35)} \\ &= -p'B'x + [p'(1+r) + p]A'x \quad \text{using (38)} \\ &= -p'B'x + w'A'x < 0, \end{aligned} \tag{46}$$

where the last inequality follows from (43), (44), and $x \geqq 0$, $x \neq 0$. Q.E.D.

Thus we have proved that, under our assumptions, the real

Wicksell effect is always negative at $r = g$, and by continuity it must remain negative for all $r \in N(g)$.

7. General results

The von Neumann example in section 5 is a freak because the change in the value of capital, at constant prices, is obviously equal to the price-weighted sum of the capital increments. However, as we have already discussed in section 4, in general when $\Delta v \neq p\Delta k$, it is the real Wicksell effect ($p\Delta k$) which is important for the economic questions under investigation here.

If $T(\cdot)$ in (6) is not differentiable, the expressions in (8) and (9) must be replaced by the zero-profit support prices used in section 5. This device enables us to handle all cases involving any degree of joint production and allows the possibility that S is not a polyhedral cone, but still possesses some 'flats' or facets. When derivatives exist and $\mathrm{d}p_i/\mathrm{d}r \neq 0$, theorem 1 follows from an envelope theorem (see Burmeister and Dobell (1970, corollary 3.4, p. 278, and theorem 7, p. 286)). Accordingly, with the appropriate interpretation, theorem 2 may be regarded as a special case of theorem 1, where in theorem 1 the prices must be zero-profit support prices and where the vector $(\mathrm{d}k/\mathrm{d}r)|_{(r^*, p^*)}$ is replaced by the appropriate Δk^* defined in theorem 2 whenever the analogous derivatives do not exist (Samuelson, 1966, p. 40). Finally, recall that an economy is *regular* if

$$\sum_{i=1}^{n} p_i\left(\frac{\mathrm{d}k_i}{\mathrm{d}r}\right)\bigg|_{(r^*, p^*)} < 0$$

for all equilibria where $r^* \in [0, \bar{r})$, and where $\bar{r} \leqq \infty$ is the maximum rate of profit consistent with non-negative steady-state prices (and $w_0 > 0$). We then have

Theorem 4. Let $g = 0$ (for convenience) and assume that the technology is continuously differentiable. (The non-differentiable case can be handled with a separate argument.) Then if the economy is 'regular', any optimal rest point solution to (11) is 'unique' for all $\rho \in [0, \bar{r})$.

Proof. Differentiability of the technology and $U(c)$ guarantees that the implicit function

$$\phi(U,\rho) \equiv \phi[U(c),\rho] = 0$$

is differentiable. Thus if the economy is regular, from (10) and (12) we have

$$\frac{\mathrm{d}U}{\mathrm{d}\rho} = -\frac{\phi_\rho(U,\rho)}{\phi_U(U,\rho)} = \rho\sum_{i=1}^{n} p_i\left(\frac{\mathrm{d}k_i}{\mathrm{d}\rho}\right)\Bigg|_{(r^*=\rho,\, p^*)} < 0 \quad \text{for } \rho > 0.$$

Since U is unique at the golden rule point $\rho = 0$ and falls monotonically with ρ, U is unique for all $\rho \in [0, \bar{r})$. Q.E.D.

Note that this theorem applies for an economy with any degree of joint production *and* with any number of consumption goods[5].

8. Concluding remarks

The real Wicksell effect,

$$\sum_{i=1}^{n} p_i\left(\frac{\mathrm{d}k_i}{\mathrm{d}r}\right)\Bigg|_{(r^*,\, p^*)},$$

is *not* an index of 'aggregate capital', but rather it is one measure of the *change* in 'capital' as an economy moves across steady-state equilibria. Moreover, we may define the change in net output divided by the change in 'capital' as the 'marginal product of capital'. For changes across steady states, eq. (10) is valid and

$$\frac{\text{change in net output}}{\text{change in 'capital'}} = \left[\sum_{i=1}^{n} p_i\left(\frac{\mathrm{d}c_i}{\mathrm{d}r}\right)\Bigg|_{(r^*,\, p^*)} + g\sum_{i=1}^{n} p_i\left(\frac{\mathrm{d}k_i}{\mathrm{d}r}\right)\Bigg|_{(r^*,\, p^*)}\right] \Bigg/ \sum_{i=1}^{n} p_i\left(\frac{\mathrm{d}k_i}{\mathrm{d}r}\right)\Bigg|_{(r^*,\, p^*)} \tag{47}$$

[5]Uniqueness of rest points for dynamic systems is obviously a prerequisite for proving any global convergence theorems, either in optimal or descriptive economic models.

$$= r = \text{`marginal product of capital'}. \tag{48}$$

In this very limited sense, we may conclude that the 'marginal product of capital' is equal to the steady-state equilibrium profit or interest rate r.

Of course, an index of the change in capital can be used to construct an index of 'aggregate capital'. However, such an index will not be well behaved in general[6]. For example, a well-behaved (in the sense of not contradicting one-sector neoclassical results) index of 'aggregate capital' would exhibit diminishing returns, implying that

$$\sum_{i=1}^{n} p_i \left(\frac{\mathrm{d}c_i}{\mathrm{d}r}\right)\Bigg|_{(r^*, p^*)} + g \sum_{i=1}^{n} p_i \left(\frac{\mathrm{d}k_i}{\mathrm{d}r}\right)\Bigg|_{(r^*, p^*)} < \sum_{i=1}^{n} p_i \left(\frac{\mathrm{d}k_i}{\mathrm{d}r}\right)\Bigg|_{(r^*, p^*)}. \tag{49}$$

It can be shown that (49) holds in a neighborhood of $r^* = g$, but the inequality in (49) may be reversed if $|r^* - g|$ is large (see Burmeister and Turnovsky (1972, pp. 848–899) and von Weizsäcker (1971, pp. 62–63)).

Even if we rule out joint production, it is not true that our measure of the change in 'capital' must fall with a rise in the steady-state interest or profit rate r^*. It is only for regular economies – economies in which the real Wicksell effect is negative at *every* steady-state equilibrium point – that the qualitative results of one-sector neoclassical parables stand without contradiction.

Finally, it is important to recognize that the non-existence of an index of an 'aggregate capital' index is a serious problem for much empirical work and for some macroeconomic theories. However, for microeconomic theory and general equilibrium analysis, no logical difficulties arise because 'capital' may be represented – indeed, it *should* be represented – by a vector of *physically different* capital stocks, $k = (k_1, \ldots, k_n)$. There is no need for aggregation in pure microeconomic theory and general equilibrium analysis.

[6]Champernowne (1953–1954) introduced a chain-index method of measuring aggregate 'capital', and each unit quantity of 'capital' earns a 'marginal product' which equals the interest rate in steady-state equilibria. However, the existence of this chain-index neither implies nor is implied by a regular economy.

References

Brock, W. A. (1973), Some results on the uniqueness of steady states in multisector models of optimum economic growth when future utilities are discounted, *International Economic Review*, 14 (3) (Oct.) 535–559.

Bruno, M., Burmeister, E. and Sheshinski, E. (1966), The nature and implications of the reswitching of techniques, *Quarterly Journal of Economics*, 80 (Nov.) 526–553.

Burmeister, E. (1974), Synthesizing neo-Austrian and alternative approaches to capital theory: a survey, *The Journal of Economic Literature*, June.

Burmeister, E. and Dobell A. R. (1970), *Mathematical Theories of Economic Growth*, Macmillan: New York.

Burmeister, E. and Turnovsky, S. J. (1971), The degree of joint production, *International Economic Review*, 12 (Feb.) 99–105.

Burmeister, E. and Turnovsky, S. J. (1972), Capital deepening response in an economy with heterogeneous capital goods, *American Economic Review*, 62 (Dec.) 842–853.

Champernowne, D. G. (1953–1954), The production function and the theory of capital: a comment, *Review of Economic Studies*, 21, 112–135.

Karlin, S. (1959), *Mathematical Methods and Theory in Games, Programming, and Economics*, vols. I and II, Addison-Wesley: Reading, Massachusetts.

Kuga, K. (1973), More about joint production, *International Economic Review*, 14 (1) (Feb.) 196–210.

Samuelson, P. A. (1966), The fundamental singularity theorem for non-joint production, *International Economic Review*, 7 (Jan.) 34–41.

von Neumann, J. (1938), Über ein Ökonomisches Gleichungssystem und eine Verallgemeinerung des Brouwerschen Fixpunktsatzes, *Ergebuisse eines Mathematischen Seminars*, Menger, K. (Ed.), Morgenstern, G. (Trans.), Vienna, English translation: A model of general economic equilibrium, *Review of Economic Studies*, 13 (1945–1956), 1–9; reprinted in *Readings in Mathematical Economics*, Newman, P. (Ed.), vol. II, Johns Hopkins Press: Baltimore (1968), 221–229.

von Weizsäcker, C. C. (1971), *Steady State Capital Theory*, Springer-Verlag: New York.

Zarembka, P. (1975), 'Real' capital and the neoclassical production function, In *On the Measurement of Factor Productivities: Theoretical Problems and Empirical Results*, Altmann, F. L., Kyn, O. and Wagener, H.-J. (Eds.) Vandenhoeck and Rupprecht: Göttingen. Forthcoming.

[13]

Synthesizing the Neo-Austrian and Alternative Approaches to Capital Theory: A Survey

By EDWIN BURMEISTER
University of Pennsylvania

I wish to thank George Adams, Christopher Bliss, William A. Brock, Meyer Burstein, Wilfred J. Ethier, Walter P. Heller, Edward Nell, Carl Palash, Karl Shell, Peter Simon, C. C. von Weizsäcker, and Gary Yohe for their very helpful comments, and I have benefited greatly from conversations with Daniel A. Graham, John R. Hicks, Stephen A. Ross, Paul A. Samuelson, Robert M. Solow, and Sidney Weintraub.

CAPITAL theory involves many complex issues which have generated heated debates within the profession,[1] and no one survey can treat the subject exhaustively. However, *Capital and time: A neo-Austrian theory* [27, Hicks, 1973], the third book John R. Hicks has written about capital,[2] serves to provide a manageable list of topics for discussion. Since the neo-Austrian approach to capital theory is unfamiliar to most students of economics, especially in America, I have elected to discuss this method in detail, and the following sections are ordered approximately in accordance with the progression of ideas in *Capital and time*. As major issues of capital theory arise in this discussion, I have attempted to provide clear and simple expositions, including the following items:

(1) truncation of production processes and uniqueness of the internal rate of return;
(2) factor-price curves and the factor-price frontier;
(3) reswitching (both as usually defined and along a dynamic path);
(4) duality results;
(5) determination of relative factor shares;
(6) complications arising from joint production (including an example showing why the nonsubstitution theorem is invalid when certain types of joint production exist);
(7) technological change and the relationship of Hicks' old classification, his new classification, and Harrod neutrality;
(8) a clarification of the famous "Ricardo on Machinery" dispute;
(9) dynamic paths and stability (or the Traverse) when problems of uncertainty are circumvented;
(10) two numerical examples illustrating full-employment transitions;
(11) a simple demonstration that the neo-Austrian method is a special case of the more general von Neumann approach;
(12) an interpretation of a neo-Austrian example without joint production as a specialized Leontief-Sraffa model;

[1] See, for example, Harcourt's survey and the list of references cited there [21, 1969].

[2] His two previous books about capital are *Value and capital* [23, 1939] and *Capital and growth* [25, 1965].

(13) the problem of substitution and a brief explanation of i) stability results from other sectoral models, and ii) the similarity of the strong assumptions which are sufficient for convergence;

(14) a very short summary of the subjects which traditionally have been controversial in capital theory (including a paradox revealed by the reswitching controversy); and

(15) a generalized von Neumann model with consumption and a primary factor (presented in the Appendix).

Three issues which have been central to the Cambridge, U.K.–Cambridge, Mass., controversies are omitted, namely alternative theories of income distribution, the social rate of return to savings-investment, and disequilibrium adjustment mechanisms.[3] Space does not permit an adequate discussion of these topics. I have also ignored questions of efficiency and optimal capital accumulation programs, although the latter are of fundamental importance in normative economic theory and are the subject of much current research. Here I concentrate on descriptive (positive) capital models.

I. *Three Alternative Capital Models*

Hicks distinguishes three economic models according to their degree of disintegration: 1) the Method of Sectoral Disintegration, 2) the Method of J. von Neumann, and 3) the Neo-Austrian Method which forms the foundation of *Capital and time*. Hicks finds the first approach "treacherous," and this is no doubt correct when one admits only two sectors, a "machine-building sector" and a "machine-using" or "consumption-good sector."[4] His view of the von Neumann method is that it is logically elegant, but that ". . . the categories with which it works are not very recognizable as economic categories; so to make economic sense of its propositions translation is required. One has got so far away from the regular economic concepts that the translation is not at all an easy matter" [27, 1973, p. 6]. This provides Hicks' motivation for the neo-Austrian approach in which every production process consists of a specified time profile of inputs and outputs, an approach which is viewed as a polar opposite to the von Neumann model [27, 1973, p. 6]. In the latter, all production activities have only a one-period duration, and each activity requires a vector of inputs to produce (jointly) a vector of outputs. Since one type of output may be considered used capital equipment, the model generates equilibrium prices for *all* economic goods (including one-year-old machines, two-year-old machines, etc.) at the end of every time period. Thus we arrive at the Hicks statement:

> The von Neumann method is the extreme of disintegration; there is a complete reference back to the market in every period, a period which can be made as short as we like. Ours, on the other hand, is the extreme of (vertical) integration. There is no 'intermediate' reference back to the market. The production process, over time, is taken as a whole [27, 1973, p. 6].

However, an economic model in which there are no markets for any used capital equipment is exceptionally restrictive. Such an assumption has two equally dubious justifications.

First, one may believe that in reality used capital equipment is not traded. Nevertheless, if trade is feasible at finite cost, a formulation which *assumes* that certain markets do not exist is incomplete and, more

[3] In many interpretations of Keynesian models, it is the precise assumptions about disequilibrium adjustment mechanisms which play a crucial role in the determination of actual employment, actual capital accumulation, etc. In addition to the numerous articles by Cambridge, U.K., authors, see Solow and Stiglitz [45, 1968].

[4] Later we shall see that with an apparently minor modification of Hicks' Standard Assumptions, the neo-Austrian model becomes a special case of a general n-sector model [27, 1973, p. 5].

importantly, it may be inconsistent with profit maximization. Logical completeness demands a justification of why markets for some economic goods do not exist,[5] especially since there are examples where it pays for a firm to sell its used capital equipment.

Second, trading of certain commodities may be assumed technologically infeasible; new capital equipment, once installed, may be "bolted down" and unmovable to another process at any finite cost. This assumption is extreme, and it raises the related question of whether or not a time process may be freely terminated (or "truncated"). We will return to this issue in Section V below.

A theory of transaction and other adjustment costs apparently is required to explain adequately whether or not trade in used capital equipment will exist, and such problems lie on the frontiers of economic theory. However, as we will demonstrate in following sections, Hicks' assumption of complete vertical integration is not essential because the neo-Austrian model can be incorporated into the von Neumann framework, thereby allowing us to assume that competitive markets exist for all economic goods. Thus even if certain capital goods are not traded, we may impute shadow prices to them which would be used by both a central planner and by a profit-maximizing manager who must calculate the appropriate present discounted value of a production process.

II. *The Hicks Neo-Austrian Model*

The Hicks approach, based on the Austrian tradition associated with Böhm-Bawerk, K. Wicksell, and Hayek, is a generalization of the idea that a time flow of inputs produces current output.[6] In his "neo-Austrian" model there exist production processes by which a time sequence of inputs $\{a_t\}$ yields an associated time sequence of outputs $\{b_t\}$. The story is simplified drastically since each input a_t and each output b_t are assumed to be *scalars* (rather than vectors of heterogeneous commodities) and there exist only two economic commodities, one type of homogeneous input and one type of homogeneous output. We identify the homogeneous final output as a consumption good, or, as Hicks prefers, simply *goods* [27, 1973, p. 37]. Using goods as the standard of value, b_t represents both the physical quantity of output and its value. Likewise we identify the homogeneous inputs as labor and define w_t as the wage rate of workers in terms of goods during period t—*i.e.*, the real wage rate during period t.

A particular production process yields a net output stream measured in goods $q_0 = b_0 - w_0a_0$, $q_1 = b_1 - w_1a_1, \ldots, q_n = b_n - w_na_n$. We denote this sequence by

$$\{q_t\} = \{(b_t - w_ta_t)\}_{t=0}^{n},$$

where the process is operated during periods $1, \ldots, n, n+1$. The feasible technology for the neo-Austrian model consists of a set of such processes, *i.e.*, the set of alternative time sequences of net outputs which are technologically feasible. During any time period, one or more of these alternative processes may be employed, and as an economy evolves over time, it may or may not converge to a steady-state equilibrium in which a single (most profitable) process is operated. We will turn to this stability question in sections XVI, XVIII, and XXIII.

Following the Austrian tradition of production requiring time, it is assumed that every process

$$\{(a_t, b_t)\}_{t=0}^{n} = \{(a_0, b_0), (a_1, b_1), \ldots, (a_n, b_n)\}$$

has the properties that $a_t > 0$ and $b_t = 0$ for $t = 0, 1, \ldots, m-1$. Thus for the first m production periods, the labor inputs are

[5] See, for example, George A. Akerlof [1, 1970].

[6] See David Cass for an exposition of the Wicksell model and its relationship to the neoclassical one-sector model [17, 1973]. Also see C. C. von Weizsäcker for a modern survey of Austrian capital theory [50, 1971].

positive, but there is no output of final goods; Hicks calls this time duration the "construction period" [27, 1973, p. 15].

This description of the feasible technology is incomplete and objectionable. It is incomplete because, as the word "construction" implies, workers presumably are producing *something* during the first m periods, but that something is never specified. It is as if the economy were contained in a black box; we observe only a time flow of labor inputs and a time flow of final outputs, without ever observing what intermediate goods or capital equipment may have been produced and utilized inside the black box. Clearly such a description is incomplete—and fatally so if one of our primary concerns is capital theory and we cannot observe any capital goods in the economy!

One can provide a trivial interpretation which does admit the existence of capital goods. Suppose that a_0 workers produce one "machine of type 1;" a_1 workers plus one "machine of type 1" produce one "machine of type 2;" . . . ; and a_{m-1} workers plus one "machine of type $m-1$" produce one "machine of type m." Then for $t \geq m$, suppose a_t workers plus one "machine of type t" produce b_t units of final consumption goods plus one "machine of type $t+1$."

Later we shall use precisely this scheme to demonstrate that the neo-Austrian model in fact is a very special case of the von Neumann approach. Here, however, note that the technology just described has a triangular structure in which the production of new capital goods requires only older machines. For example, during the first period the production of a machine of type 1 requires *only* labor (and no capital goods of any type). Surely this is unreasonably restrictive; does the technology not contain *some* process whereby labor working with, for example, a hammer can produce a machine of type 1?

It is sometimes argued that if history could be traced back far enough, the production of every capital good must be explained by labor inputs alone. This argument, which is reminiscent of a labor theory of value, is entirely fallacious for the issue at hand. While one may admit that there exists a process by which a hammer *could* be produced by labor alone, this fact may be irrelevant. Thus once labor working with one hammer produces a machine of type 1, *it may never again be efficient to produce hammers by the process which uses labor alone*. All that is required is the existence of a (sufficiently productive) alternative process for producing hammers using labor *and* a machine of type 1. When such realistic simultaneity is admitted, the neo-Austrian description of the feasible technology becomes inadequate.

Stated in another way, the issue is whether or not the stock of capital goods available in period one allows an unrestricted choice of production processes. If such an unrestricted choice is not possible, then the most efficient processes may become available to the economy only after the stocks of various capital goods (various types of machines) have been built up using other processes that can be operated from the given initial conditions. The assumption that there are *no* capital goods available at the beginning of the first production period is very special.

These serious objections can be circumvented by allowing a_t and b_t to represent vectors of heterogeneous inputs and outputs, a modification which will again lead us to adopt a von Neumann approach. But we are getting ahead of our story; and the neo-Austrian model at least does have the virtue that it is easily analyzed using only elementary methods.

III. *Timing of the Production Processes and an Ante versus Post Factum Wage*

The exact timing of the flow of inputs and outputs and their payments is always a source of some difficulty since the end of one time period coincides with the beginning of the next. It is best to quote Hicks directly on this matter:[7]

> Let us further suppose that all the payments 'of' the week (either way) are made at the beginning of the week. The counting-house, say, is only open on Mondays; it is on Mondays that both inputs and outputs are paid for. Let k_t be the capital value of the process (the remainder of the process) at the beginning of week t; at the moment, that is, when the counting-house opens.
>
> Let r be the rate of interest for one week, and write $R = 1 + r$. So R is the interest multiplier for one week, and R^{-1} is the discount factor. Then (by the discounted value formula)
>
> $$k_t = q_t + q_{t+1}R^{-1} + q_{t+2}R^{-2} + \ldots + q_n R^{-(n-t)}.$$
>
> From this, and from the corresponding formula for k_{t+1}, we have at once
>
> $$k_t = q_t + k_{t+1}R^{-1}. \qquad (2.1)$$
>
> The capital value at the beginning of week t equals the net output of week t (undiscounted, because it comes in immediately) plus the capital value at the end of the week, discounted for that one week [27, 1973, p. 20].

With the wage rate equal in every week ($w_t = w$), Hicks' equation (2.1) can be written as[8]

$$k_0 = \sum_{t=0}^{n} q_t R^{-t} = \sum_{t=0}^{n} (b_t - wa_t)R^{-t}. \qquad (2)$$

Is the model formulated with an *ante factum* or *post factum* real wage rate w? The matter is easiest to discuss using a two-period example with

$$\{(a_0, b_0), (a_1, b_1)\} = \{(a_0, 0), (a_1, 1)\}.$$

If we denote calendar time by τ, the time interval from $\tau = 0$ to $\tau = 1$ is "period one" and the time interval from $\tau = 1$ to $\tau = 2$ "period two." One interpretation of the production process is straightforward: the employment of a_0 workers during period one and a_1 workers during period two yields one unit of goods output at the *end* of period two.[9] Since in equilibrium the present discounted capital value for a unit process must equal zero at time $\tau = 0$, *i.e.*, at the beginning of period one, we have the condition

$$-\frac{wa_0}{(1+r)} + \frac{1 - wa_1}{(1+r)^2} = 0 \qquad (3a)$$

where w is the wage rate paid to workers at the *end* of each production period.[10]

Possible confusion arises because the index t denotes the t-th period of production in which inputs at calendar time $\tau = t - 1$ produce real output at calendar time $\tau = t$. In our above example, if workers hired to work during periods one and two are paid at the *beginning* of the periods one and two (at calendar times $\tau = 0$ and $\tau = 1$, respectively), the capital value must reflect the interest cost on advanced wages, and the equilibrium condition (3a) must be replaced by

$$-wa_0 - \frac{wa_1}{(1+r)} + \frac{1}{(1+r)^2} = -\frac{w(1+r)a_0}{(1+r)} + \frac{1 - w(1+r)a_1}{(1+r)^2} = 0 \qquad (3b)$$

[7] The interest or profit rate r is in terms of goods (it is a real rate of interest), and Ω denotes the terminal *economic* lifetime of the production process; *i.e.*, Ω is the time at which it is no longer profitable to continue the project. The time interval from 0 to Ω is divided into $(n + 1)$ weeks.

[8] Hicks also assumes that the rate of interest is expected to remain unchanged; see [27, 1973, pp. 16–17].

[9] This interpretation of the timing process appears inconsistent with the preceding quotation from Hicks and his statement at the bottom of p. 21. However, the alternative interpretation that the output b_t appears at the *beginning* of period t, *i.e.*, at calendar time $\tau = t - 1$, does not seem legitimate unless production can be instantaneous, which surely violates the Austrian tradition of production requiring time. The difficulty can be seen by considering the terminal pair (a_n, b_n). If the output b_n appears at time $\tau = n$, what is the function of the a_n workers during the terminal period? The convention $a_n = 0$ will not work because it contradicts Hicks' Standard Case described later.

However, as Professor Hicks has pointed out to me, when his "weeks" are aggregated into "years," continuity arguments suggest that setting $a_n = 0$ for each week will not influence the results substantially.

[10] Throughout *Capital and time*, Hicks assumes that capital markets are in equilibrium, which implies that $k_0 = 0$ at the equilibrium rate of interest; see [27, 1973, p. 32]. Equivalently we assume that there is free entry, implying that the beginning capital value of any production process must equal zero in equilibrium.

The important observation is that (3a), but *not* (3b), defines the same relationship between w and r as does

$$\sum_{t=0}^{n} (b_t - wa_t)R^{-t} = 0,$$

which is the equilibrium condition $k_0 = 0$ with k_0 defined by equation (2). Thus, given our interpretation of the production process timing, we have justified the equilibrium condition $k_0 = 0$ on the assumption that workers are paid at the *end* of the production period in which they have been employed.

The correct interpretation of the timing mechanism is important for at least two reasons. First, in most classical models, capitalists advanced a subsistence wage to workers at the beginning of the production period. This notion provides one traditional justification for a model in which the (short-run) wage rate is determined via a wage fund mechanism, and Hicks does use a wage fund theory to determine the short-run wage rate in the full employment version of this model [27, 1970, p. 60]. Second, the Piero Sraffa results concerning a Standard Commodity depend upon a *post factum* wage; the simple linear relationship between the real wage rate, measured in terms of a Standard Commodity, is lost with an *ante factum* wage [47, Sraffa, 1960; 8, Burmeister, 1968]. Thus the issue of an *ante* versus *post factum* real wage may be a matter of economic consequence in some contexts, although it is not crucial for any of the results we will discuss.

IV. *Three Types of Joint Production*

It is evident that the Hicks modification of the classical Austrian tradition—what he has called the neo-Austrian approach—does provide insights of considerable economic importance. For example, clearly Böhm-Bawerk's notion of "roundaboutness" collapses when output occurs in more than one time period [27, 1973, p. 9]. Likewise the model captures one essential aspect of capital theory: a capital good yields its services over time, and if a process is viewed as an entity, outputs are produced *jointly*.

Jointness of production is a necessary characteristic of any durable capital good. Machines manned by workers for one production period produce both output *and* one-period-older machines—an obvious instance of joint production. But one should not make too much of durable machines if they are the *only* source of joint production. Under such circumstances, it is reasonable to assume that capital goods of different ages (vintages) may be compared in terms of efficiency in production. Certainly this comparison is always possible if the technology allows the production of output using either new machines or older machines, while holding every other input fixed. It then is possible to define an efficiency index which expresses a new machine in terms of the number of old machines of a specific age which are equivalent in production. Such an efficiency index may depend upon the industry in which a machine is employed; for example, a modern computer may be superior to an older one in the aerospace industry where computational speed is important, but the difference may be negligible for other businesses. The important conclusion is that this specific kind of joint production (where output and older machines of different productivity are produced jointly) need not alter the familiar results which are proved for the case of no-joint production. In particular, the concept of a factor-price frontier and Paul A. Samuelson's nonsubstitution theorem both remain valid when the efficiency indices I have described exist.[11]

Joint production involving outputs of final consumption goods, as in wool-mutton examples, are fundamentally more impor-

[11] Proofs are in Burmeister and Eytan Sheshinski [9, 1969]. J. A. Mirrlees proves a nonsubstitution theorem under very general conditions [31, 1969]; also see Stiglitz [48, 1970].

tant in that this change will negate nearly all of the conclusions which stem from the existence of a factor-price frontier.[12] When no joint production exists, a steady-state equilibrium point must lie on the factor-price frontier, and given a value of the real wage or interest rate, relative prices are determined independently of demand. If joint production of the wool-mutton type is present, the equilibrium position depends on the pattern of demand (between wool versus mutton, for example). We will return to this issue in Section XII.

The third type of joint production arises when we consider the whole time profile $\{(a_t, b_t)\}_{t=0}^{n}$ of a unit process. Now we not only have the joint production of output and "older machines," but also the *intertemporal joint production* of final output at different dates. In general, with these complications, one might expect that a factor-price frontier does not exist, but as we shall see below, the difficulties are circumvented when the internal rate of return for every process is unique.

V. *Truncation of Production Processes and Uniqueness of the Internal Rate of Return*

How is the economic life, Ω, of a project to be determined? Equation (2) is a special case of

$$k_0 = \sum_{t=0}^{n} q_t R_t^{-t} = \sum_{t=0}^{n} (b_t - w_t a_t) R_t^{-t} \quad (4)$$

where w_t is the real wage rate paid to the workers a_t, r_t is the real rate of interest in period t (*i.e.*, the prevailing rate over the time interval from calendar time $\tau = t$ to $\tau = t + 1$), and $R_t = (1 + r_t)$.[13] A steady-state equilibrium in which $w_t = w$ and $r_t = r$ for all t is the easiest case to analyze. Under these circumstances Hicks proves that if there exists a positive rate of interest $r = r^*$ for which $k_0 = 0$, then r^* is *unique*.[14] Moreover, such an r^* must exist if the process is viable at the prevailing wage, and it is the internal rate of return for the process $\{(a_t, b_t)\}_{t=0}^{n}$.

The fact that the internal rate of return is unique depends crucially on the fact that truncation is possible, *i.e.*, the terminal time n is selected to maximize the present discount capital value of the process, k_0 [27, 1973, pp. 18–21].[15] The possibility of truncation, in turn, is a severe restriction on the technology; it is equivalent to the assertion that if the process

$$\{(a_t, b_t)\}_{t=0}^{n}$$

is feasible, then the truncated process

$$\{(a_t', b_t')\}_{t=0}^{n} = \{(a_0, b_0), (a_1, b_1), \ldots, (a_m, b_m), (0, 0), \ldots, (0, 0)\}$$

is also feasible for all $m < n$.[16] There are two obvious instances in which this assumption is not reasonable.

1) Even though a process is terminated, certain consequences which the firm cannot avoid may occur after the truncation time. Damage lawsuits are one example.[17] However, if such consequences are unknown at the beginning of period zero, as seems likely with examples such as law-

[12] There does exist an analogous concept which I have called the *minimum wage frontier;* see Burmeister and K. Kuga [12, 1970] and Burmeister and A. R. Dobell [11, 1970, pp. 296–97]. We will return to this point in Section X.

[13] Recall that the time interval from $\tau = 0$ to $\tau = \Omega$ is divided into $(n + 1)$ weeks.

[14] Hicks calls this a "Fundamental Theorem." See [27, 1973, p. 19] and footnote 19, below.

[15] The uniqueness of the internal rate of return for an investment project in which truncation is possible has also been proved by Kenneth J. Arrow and David Levhari [2, 1969].

[16] Truncation is not implied by the conventional free disposal assumption, which asserts that if a net output vector $y = \{(-a_0, b_0), (-a_1, b_1), \ldots, (-a_n, b_n)\}$ is feasible, then any vector $y' \leqq y$ is also feasible. In the example just cited, $-a_{m+1}' = 0$, and since $-a_{m+1} < 0$ $(a_{m+1} > 0)$ is not precluded, free disposal does not imply truncation. In other words, free disposal implies that less output can be produced with additional input, but it implies nothing about what can be produced with less input.

[17] Of course, some (but not necessarily all) lawsuits may be avoided if a firm legally is allowed to dissolve.

suits, the *existence of uncertainty* becomes a separate issue as important as truncation.

2) Truncation is not an appropriate assumption if important externalities continue after the operation of a process has stopped; the permanent effects of strip mining provides an example. However, externalities are an issue with or without the truncation assumption. We have ignored the fact that certain effects (pollution, for example) are *produced jointly* with the final output of goods; such simplifications are justified if the produced effects are costless to the firm (*i.e.*, if polluting is a free activity).[18] If such jointly-produced effects are not costless, then the description of the technology must reflect this fact.

If one is willing to assume the absence of both uncertainty and externalities, the possibility of costless truncation becomes more reasonable. However, we may capture some of the effects of externalities by assuming that every process has associated "clean-up costs" which are known with certainty. For example, we may presume that by law a firm incurs non-negative clean-up costs (measured in terms of final goods)

$$\{e_t\}_{t=0}^{n}$$

which must be paid at the end of every production period a process is operated (a "pay-as-you-go" anti-pollution scheme). Let $w_t = w$, $r_t = r$, and $R = (1 + r)$; then the problem of the firm at time zero is to select a truncation time n such that the present discounted value

$$k_0 = \sum_{t=0}^{n} (b_t - e_t - wa_t)R^{-t}$$

is maximized. Clearly the maximized present discounted value depends on the rate of interest, and as in the case without clean-up costs (where $e_t = 0$), it is a decreasing monotonic function of r.[19] Thus any solution of $k_0(r) = 0$, *i.e.*, the internal rate of return r^*, is unique even in the presence of these clean-up costs. When only e_0 is positive, we can interpret that single cost as the price of a license to operate a particular process. Of course, if the e_t's are sufficiently large, the process will not be operated at all.

It is important to note that this formulation of clean-up costs is distinctly different from the alternative assumption that costs are incurred only *after* truncation. For example, one might formulate a model in which there is a penalty imposed at the end of the truncation period; such a penalty may be a once-and for-all shut-down cost (which in general would vary with the choice of n). However, such a shut-down cost is logically identical to a *negative* scrap value for the firm, in which case the internal rate of return for the process need not be unique.[20]

We will assume that truncation is possible, although we allow for clean-up costs at the end of every period of operation. Now consider a process which is profitable to operate at some non-negative wage rate and at some non-negative interest rate. For every such fixed wage rate, it follows from Hicks' Fundamental Theorem that the internal rate of return which renders $k_0 = 0$ is unique. The set of such wage and interest rates defines a function

$$r = f(w) \tag{5}$$

[18] Likewise costless inputs (such as the air workers breathe) can be ignored when describing the feasible technology.

[19] See Hicks [27, 1973, pp. 18–21] and Arrow and Levhari [2, 1969]. J. S. Flemming and J. F. Wright have proved more general results when $r_t \neq r$ for all t and when there is a net cash flow after the truncation period [19, 1971]; recently Amartya Sen has proved further generalizations [43, 1973].

[20] While the condition that the maximized present discounted value of a process be a decreasing monotonic function of r is sufficient for the uniqueness of the internal rate of return (assuming existence), clearly it is not a necessary condition. Thus a process might have a unique positive internal rate of return despite the presence of shut-down costs. See Arrow and Levhari [2, 1969, pp. 563–64].

for the process, and this curve is downward sloping with $f'(w) < 0$. In Hicks' earlier work he called this relationship the *wage-interest curve* or the *wage-curve* [25, 1965], but in *Capital and time* he has renamed it the *efficiency curve;* he objects to the name *factor-price curve* on the valid grounds that the rate of interest is not the price of a "factor." However, consistent terminology is also an advantage and I will continue to refer to the relationship $r = f(w)$ as the factor-price curve.

VI. *The Factor-Price Frontier, the Choice of Technique, and Reswitching*

In general the feasible technology set for a neo-Austrian model consists of many alternative production processes, but for simplicity assume there exist only two. Let $\{(a_t, b_t)\}_{t=0}^{n}$ and $\{(a'_t, b'_t)\}_{t=0}^{n'}$ be labeled process A and process B, respectively, with corresponding factor-price curves $r = f_A(w)$ and $r = f_B(w)$. Although both factor-price curves are necessarily downward sloping with $f'_A(w) < 0$ and $f'_B(w) < 0$, it is nevertheless true that the equation

$$f_A(w) - f_B(w) = 0 \tag{6}$$

may have two distinct roots $w_1 \neq w_2$, as pictured in Figure 1.

Which process or technique will be selected in a steady-state equilibrium? The answer depends upon the real wage rate. For any given value of w, the technique that maximizes the rate of profit r will be chosen. The outer envelope of the factor-price curves generated by the alternative production processes forms the *factor-price frontier* for the technology (depicted by the heavy line in Figure 1) and defines the function

$$r = F(w); \tag{7}$$

it is also a downward-sloping curve with $F'(w) < 0$.[21]

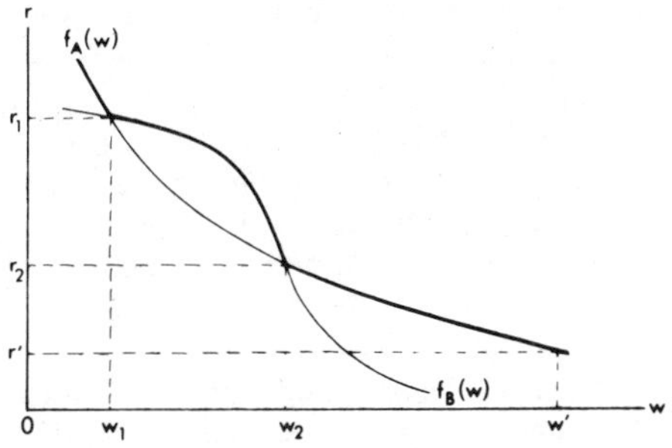

Figure 1.

An illustration of the reswitching of techniques. The outer envelope for the factor-price curves $f_A(w)$ and $f_B(w)$ for techniques A and B, respectively, is the factor-price frontier for the technology. It is the heavy line in Figure 1 and is denoted by the function $r = F(w)$.

Figure 1 illustrates reswitching the techniques:[22] at sufficiently high wage rates ($w > w_2$), process A is more profitable than B; at intermediate wage rates ($w_1 < w < w_2$), process B is more profitable than process A; and for sufficiently low wage rates ($0 \leqq w < w_1$), process A is most profitable again. Thus consider alternative steady-state equilibria points (which must lie on the economy's factor-price frontier)

[21] Hicks calls $F(w)$ the efficiency curve of the technology, and he sometimes refers to it as the technology frontier; see pages 40 and 49, respectively [27, 1973].

The derivative $F'(w)$ does not exist at switch points such as (w_1, r_1) in Figure 1. However, at such points the left-hand derivative is less (more negative) than the right-hand derivative, *i.e.*, $F'(w-) < F'(w+)$. Hicks makes an equivalent statement: "It is of course true that whenever a rise in the wage induces a change in technique, the change must be such that, at the switch point, the new efficiency curve has the greater slope" [27, 1973, p. 45].

[22] Although the reswitching controversy has received considerable attention in the literature, misunderstandings remain and controversy about related issues continues to flourish in the profession. The first comprehensive series of articles about reswitching are contained in "Paradoxes in Capital Theory: A Symposium" [36, 1966].

at different wage rates; when the steady-state wage rate rises from values near zero, we first switch from *A* to *B* as we pass through the *switch point* (w_1, r_1), and then we "switch back" or reswitch from *B* to *A* again as we pass through the second switch point (w_2, r_2); process *A* is then said to *recur*[23] [6, Bruno, Burmeister, and Sheshinski, 1966; 11, Burmeister and Dobell, 1970, p. 246].

In general, reswitching is possible within the framework of the neo-Austrian model. However, most of the results obtained in *Capital and time* depend upon restrictive assumptions. I quote directly:

> Suppose that each of the techniques that are in question are of the following *simple* form. There is a construction period, lasting *m* weeks, in which labour is applied at a constant rate but in which there is no final output. It is followed by a utilization period, lasting a further *n* weeks, in which labour is applied at a constant (but different) rate, and in which final output appears at a constant rate. I shall describe this form as a *Simple Profile*. We shall subsequently make much use of it, as an instrument of exploration; we can use it to great advantage, provided we recognize its limitations.
>
> We may choose the constant rate of output as unit of quantity; so the Simple Profile may be written:

weeks	0 to $m-1$	m to $m+n-1$
inputs	a_c	a_u
outputs	0	1 [27, 1973, p. 41].

Hicks proves that reswitching is impossible when all processes have this Simple Profile [27, 1973, p. 42].

While reswitching is a complication, it is *per se* uninteresting; rather it is the possibilities which are revealed by reswitching (and which can exist in its absence) that are significant. One such example is discussed in Section XIV.

[23] It should be noted that since $f'(w) < 0$, there exists an inverse function to $f(w)$, say $w = \phi(r)$, and many authors prefer to work with this equivalent representation of the factor-price curve.

VII. *The Optimal Transformation Curve*

A study of steady states is no more than a means to an end, and as Hicks notes, we should not expect any surprises from a steady-state analysis:

> . . . we are ourselves on the way to a steady state theory, which is not substantially different from that which has become conventional; for in the steady state, where the structure of the economy is the same in every time-period, time has been so nearly abolished that the passage from the assumption of a "sectoralized" technique to our assumption of a technique that is time-articulated cannot make much difference. So in our steady state theory we shall do little more than confirm well-established results. I wish, however, to present those results in a new way; and for that I need some additional preparation [27, 1973, p. 47].

Hicks considers two distinct assumptions, first his *Fixwage* theory, and second, the standard *Full Employment* theory.[24] In the Fixwage theory, employment may vary, but the real wage rate is fixed in the manner of David Ricardo, Malthus, or Arthur Lewis, the last being the primary justification:

> We may regard our model economy as a representation of the "developed" sector of such a country, there being a subsistence sector outside it. Labour can be drawn from the subsistence sector, and will be drawn from it quite freely, as soon as the wage that is offered in the developed sector is marginally above what can be earned in the subsistence sector. The presence of the subsistence sector prevents the wage in the developed sector from rising above this basic level; so, to the developed sector, the supply of labour is perfectly elastic. This is no doubt an over-simplification of what actually happens in any actual economy; but it is near enough to what sometimes happens to be of some interest [27, 1973, p. 49].

This assumption of a fixed, exogenous real wage rate is extremely convenient because, for any given *w*, the equilibrium technique of production is uniquely determined (except for the razor's edge case

[24] There is full employment of a labor supply which grows at an exogenous rate.

of ties) via the factor-price frontier, and this dominant technique will not change unless an innovation alters the set of technically feasible production processes. Likewise the equilibrium rate of interest is determined from the factor-price frontier and is equal to the yield on the technique which is employed.[25]

We must develop some notation before proceeding, and we shall follow *Capital and time* whenever possible. Processes may be replicated – the economy exhibits constant returns to scale – and x_{T-t} represents the number of unit production processes of a particular type which began operation t weeks ago, where the capital letter T designates the current week (period of production). (For example, x_T denotes the number of unit production processes which begin operation in the current week, or simply the current number of *starts*.) When the single process $\{(a_t, b_t)\}_{t=0}^{n}$ is employed, we have the following definitions.

Total labor input during the current week, period T, is

$$A_T = x_T a_0 + x_{T-1} a_1 + \ldots + x_{T-n} a_n = \sum_{t=0}^{n} x_{T-t} a_t. \quad (8a)$$

The current value of capital is

$$K_T = 0 + x_{T-1} k_1 + \ldots + x_{T-n} k_n = \sum_{t=0}^{n} x_{T-t} k_t. \quad (8b)$$

Finally, output and net output (or *Take-out* as Hicks calls it) are

$$B_T = \sum_{t=0}^{n} x_{T-t} b_t \quad (8c)$$

and

$$Q_T = B_T - wA_T = \sum_{t=0}^{n} x_{T-t} q_t = \sum_{t=0}^{n} x_{T-t}(b_t - wa_t). \quad (8d)$$

In a steady-state only one production process is employed and the number of starts during each period must grow at a constant rate. The last condition is expressed by the equation

$$x_T = x_0 G^T,$$

where the number of starts grows at the rate of g per period, $G = (1 + g)$ is the growth factor, and x_0 is a constant reflecting the scale of the system. As is usual in growth theory, the scale of the economy and hence the *level* of output is indeterminate; we only can solve for rates of growth and magnitudes measured per worker. In a steady-state the total number of workers employed is

$$A_T = \sum_{t=0}^{n} x_0 G^{T-t} a_t = x_0 \Big(\sum_{t=0}^{n} a_t G^{-t} \Big) G^T \quad (9)$$

and the output of final goods is

$$B_T = \sum_{t=0}^{n} x_0 G^{T-t} b_t = x_0 \Big(\sum_{t=0}^{n} b_t G^{-t} \Big) G^T. \quad (10)$$

Both A_T and B_T grow at the same rate g because the terms in parentheses in equations (9) and (10) are constants.

A special case of a very general and important duality theorem follows almost trivially. For a specified production process $\{(a_t, b_t)\}_{t=0}^{n}$, recall that the factor-price curve $r = f(w)$ or its inverse $w = \phi(r)$ was derived from equation (4) with $k_0 = 0$, $w_t = w$, and $r_t = r$. Therefore from (4) we find

[25] Some economists have taken the rate of interest to be exogenous, assuming that it is determined by "animal spirits." Alternatively, one may assume that there is some mechanism which eliminates any possible discrepancy between private and social rates of return so that the rate of interest must always equal a fixed (exogenous) social rate of time preference. Although the choice of technique is also unique (excepting ties) for any given r, the Hicks assumption has the additional feature of eliminating any labor constraint.

$$w = \frac{\sum_{t=0}^{n} b_t R^{-t}}{\sum_{t=0}^{n} a_t R^{-t}} = \phi(r) \qquad (11)$$

where, as before, $R = (1 + r)$. But from (9) and (10)

$$c = B_T/A_T = \frac{\sum_{t=0}^{n} b_t G^{-t}}{\sum_{t=0}^{n} a_t G^{-t}} = \phi(g). \qquad (12)$$

In other words, w depends on r in *exactly* the same way that the ratio B_T/A_T depends on g. Hicks calls the ratio $B_T/A_T = B/A$ the *efficiency* of the technique since it is the output of final goods per worker. However, the close relationship between Hicks' results and the existing literature is clarified if we think of B/A as *consumption per worker*, which I have denoted by c. Indeed, my terminology is consistent with Hicks' chapter on social accounting [27, 1973, Ch. III, pp. 27–36]. In a steady state profits are rK and net investment is gK; thus the social accounting equation

Wages + Profits = Consumption + Net Investment

becomes

$$wA + rK = B + gK, \qquad (13)$$

and clearly B/A represents consumption per worker [27, 1973, p. 67].[26] The function $\phi(g)$ is usually referred to as *the optimal transformation curve*.

VIII. *The Factor-Price Frontier and Restricted Factor-Price Curves*

Since it is a well-known fact that in general the internal rate of return for an investment project is not unique,[27] it may seem strange that there exists a function $r = f(w)$, the factor-price curve for a particular process $\{(a_t, b_t)\}_{t=0}^{n}$. However, *the duration of the process* (n) *is not constant along the factor-price curve* $r = f(w)$; as discussed in Section V, we have assumed that truncation is possible. Thus for any assigned value of the real wage rate, say $w = w_1$, there exists an optimal lifetime of the project, say $(n_1 + 1)$ "weeks" or production periods, and a unique value of the interest rate, r_1, for which the present discounted value of the project equals zero. We have already noted that the set of such pairs (w_i, r_i) defines the factor-price curve $r = f(w)$, and it is downward sloping with $f'(w) < 0$.[28]

There is, however, a further complication. Let the lifetime of the process $\{(a_t, b_t)\}_{t=0}^{n}$ be fixed at $(n_1 + 1)$ weeks, the duration optimal for a real wage rate equal to $w = w_1$. The unique equilibrium rate of interest is then $r_1 = f(w_1)$. Now consider

$$\sum_{t=0}^{n_1} (b_t - wa_t)(1 + r)^{-t} = 0,$$

which defines the function

$$w = \frac{\sum_{t=0}^{n_1} b_t R^{-t}}{\sum_{t=0}^{n_1} a_t R^{-t}} = \psi(r). \qquad (14)$$

The crucial and perhaps somewhat

[26] Note that workers may or may not own capital; equation (13) is valid for any pattern of factor ownership, *e.g.*, a "two-class model" with one class identified as "workers" and another as "capitalists."

[27] Consider the following simple example with a three-period production process: $\{(a_0, b_0), (a_1, b_1), (a_2, b_2)\} = \{(1.00, 0), (2.00, 4.30), (2.00, 0.68)\}$. The equation $\sum_{t=0}^{2} (b_t - wa_t)R^{-t} = 0$ with $w = 1$ implies $R^2 - 2.30R + 1.32 = (R - 1.2)(R - 1.1) = 0$. Thus there are two values for the internal rate of return $(r = R - 1)$, namely 10 percent and 20 percent, and the present discounted value of the process is positive for all rates of interest satisfying $0.10 < r < 0.20$.

[28] The proofs of these results are contained in two passages and they represent Hicks at his best; the arguments are clear, elegant, and, above all, based on economic principles [27, 1973, pp. 17–22 and 38–39].

subtle observation is that the function $\psi(r)$ in equation (14) is *not* equivalent to the function $\phi(r)$ in equation (11). Since n_1 is optimal for $w = w_1$,

$$\psi(r) \leq \phi(r),$$

with equality holding for $r = r_1$. As illustrated in Figure 2, $\psi(r)$ is tangent to $\phi(r)$ at the point (r_1, w_1); at any value of the real wage rate not equal to w_1, it would be more profitable to be at a point on the unrestricted curve $\phi(r)$ along which the duration of the project may vary. Thus we call $\psi(r)$ the *restricted factor-price curve* for a particular process, while the dual function $c = \psi(g)$ is the corresponding *restricted transformation curve* (for the same process).[29]

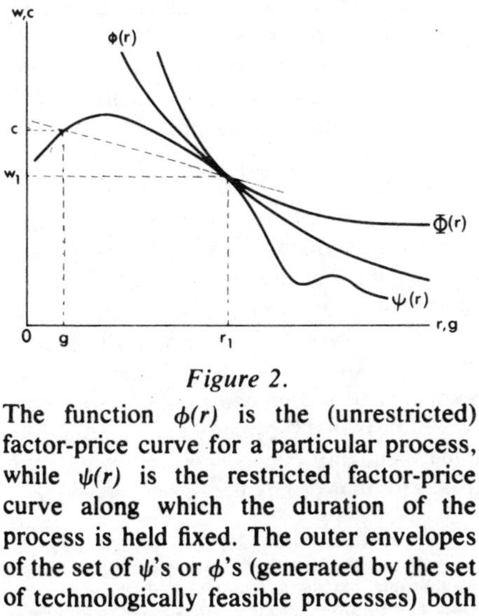

Figure 2.

The function $\phi(r)$ is the (unrestricted) factor-price curve for a particular process, while $\psi(r)$ is the restricted factor-price curve along which the duration of the process is held fixed. The outer envelopes of the set of ψ's or ϕ's (generated by the set of technologically feasible processes) both define the function $w = \Phi(r)$, the factor-price frontier for the economy.

[29] Hicks calls $\psi(g)$ a *restricted efficiency curve;* see [27, 1973, p. 66].

Recall that the restricted factor-price curve for a given process, $\psi(r)$, was defined with the duration fixed at $(n_1 + 1)$ weeks, the optimal lifetime when the real wage rate was w_1. If we repeat this procedure for other real wage rates w_i and correspondingly optimal n_i, we will produce a set of ψ's, the outer envelope of which is the factor-price curve $w = \phi(r)$. Now the factor-price frontier for the technology is the outer envelope of the factor-price curves for the alternative feasible processes. In other words, each feasible process generates a factor-price curve, $r = f(w)$, and the factor-price frontier, $r = F(w)$, is the outer envelope of this set of factor-price curves.

But $F(w)$ also has an inverse, and equivalently we could have defined the factor-price frontier for the economy as $w = \Phi(r)$, the outer envelope of the set of functions $w = \phi(r)$. Finally, it is clear that the factor-price frontier for the economy is also the outer envelope of the restricted factor-price curves generated by the technologically feasible production processes [27, 1973, p. 68].

IX. *Determination of Relative Factor Shares in Steady-State Equilibrium*

Figure 2 illustrates how the ratio of factor shares can be determined. Assume the economy is in a steady-state equilibrium with a real wage rate w_1 and a growth rate g. We know that the optimal technique is $\{(a_t, b_t)\}_{t=0}^{n}$ with $n = n_1$. Thus from equations (11), (12), and (14), it is easily seen that steady-state consumption per worker is $c = \psi(g)$. Draw a straight line through the points (r_1, w_1) and (g, c), as illustrated in Figure 2. This line has a slope

$$-\frac{c - w_1}{r_1 - g}. \qquad (15)$$

If we let v denote the per capita[30] value of capital, in competitive equilibrium the accounting relation

$$w + rv = c + gv \qquad (16)$$

must hold. Rewriting the latter, we have

$$-v = -\frac{c - w_1}{r_1 - g}. \qquad (17)$$

Thus the arc elasticity of the restricted factor-price curve $w = \psi(r)$ calculated between the two points (r_1, w_1) and (g, c) is an approximate measure of the ratio of relative shares

$$\frac{r_1 v}{w_1} = \frac{\text{per capita profits}}{\text{per capita wages}}.^{31}$$

The approximation vanishes if $r_1 = g$ and we calculate the point elasticity of any of the three curves $\psi(r)$, $\phi(r)$, or $\Phi(r)$ at (r_1, w_1). Alternatively, we could calculate the elasticity of the indicated straight line at the point (r_1, w_1) and obtain an exact measure even if $r_1 \neq g$.

One additional observation is evident from Figure 2. It is impossible that $c = \psi(g) < w_1$ with $r_1 > g$, for in this case equation (17) implies that v is negative, which is inconsistent with a steady-state equilibrium [27, 1973, p. 67].

X. *A Fundamental Duality Theorem*

The duality relationship between the real wage rate and per capita consumption —*i.e.*, the relationship between equations (11) and (12)—is a fundamental theorem which is only exemplified by this neo-Austrian model. This result was originally proved by C. C. von Weizsäcker [49, 1963], and subsequently it was developed by Michael Bruno [5, 1969] and Hicks [25, 1965] for discrete Leontief technologies.[32] Burmeister and Kuga proved analogous results for a neoclassical multi-sector model [13, 1970].[33]

It is well known that there does not exist a factor-price frontier if the technology admits joint production [41, Samuelson, 1962, p. 205, f. 2].[34] However, there does exist an even more general concept, the *minimum wage frontier* [12, Burmeister and Kuga, 1970]. Where there is no joint production, the minimum wage frontier and the factor-price frontier coincide.

The more general theorem is proved by considering a von Neumann model modified to allow for a single primary factor (labor) and a single consumption good or a fixed basket of consumption goods. We wish to find the maximum per capita consumption given an assigned growth rate g for the economy (the exogenous growth rate of labor). Thus the primal problem is *maximize* c subject to the inequality constraints imposed by the feasible technology. The solutions for different g's define a function

$$c = E(g) \qquad (18)$$

which is the *optimal transformation frontier* for the economy; it gives the maximum per capita consumption which can be produced at alternative growth rates.[35]

The dual problem is to minimize the real wage rate when a rate of profit r is assigned. The reason we *minimize* the real wage rate is that the mathematical programming inequality constraints are formulated to assure that profits for every process are

[30] Here, as elsewhere in this paper, the term "per capita" means "per worker employed."

[31] The ratio of factor shares is the ratio of two types of income, and it is determined *independently* of factor ownership; see footnote 26.

[32] See especially Hicks [25, 1965, pp. 317–19].

[33] The generalization from Leontief to neoclassical technologies entails a familiar mathematical difficulty, namely proof of the existence and uniqueness of steady-state equilibria.

[34] See Samuelson [41, 1962, p. 205, f. 2]. This example is elaborated in more detail by Burmeister and Dobell [11, 1970, pp. 280–82].

[35] Of course, the optimal transformation frontier for an economy, $E(g)$, is the outer envelope of the set of optimal transformation curves (the set of $\phi(g)$'s).

non-positive and that the actual rate of profit is *less than or equal to r*. The solutions to the dual problem for different r's define a function

$$w = H(r), \tag{19}$$

the minimum wage frontier. The usual mathematical programming duality theorem implies

$$c = E(g) = H(r) = w \tag{20}$$

for all $g = r$ restricted to a suitable domain.[36]

The above provides a proof of the familiar Golden Rule result for this model with joint production.

The important distinction between the minimum wage frontier in a model with joint production and the factor-price frontier in a model without joint production will become clear in the next two sections where I will discuss how a steady-state equilibrium point is determined and the nonsubstitution theorem.

XI. *Determination of Steady-State Equilibria*

We need to assume some relationship between r and g, or between c and w, to completely determine a steady state equilibrium.[37] For example, one might assume that employment grows at the exogenous rate g and the rate of profit is exogenous. If, then, we take r' as given in Figure 1, the optimal (most profitable) technique, including its duration, is determined from the factor-price frontier.[38] Thus $\psi(r)$ is the corresponding restricted factor-price curve, and the real wage rate is

$$w' = \psi(r') = \phi(r') = \Phi(r').$$

Since a particular process and its duration are now fixed, consumption per worker must be

$$c = \psi(g).$$

Hicks proceeds in two different manners; in both instances, however, he assumes that saving is a fixed percentage of profits. Since investment must equal saving, in a steady-state equilibrium we have

$$gv = s_r rv$$

or

$$s_r = g/r \tag{21}$$

where in my notation v is the per capita value of capital (it is K/A in Hicks' notation) and s_r is the saving proportion out of profit income.

Suppose we follow the Hicks Fixwage model with a perfectly elastic supply of labor. Let the exogenous real wage rate be w'; now the rate of interest is determined from the factor-price frontier and is

$$r' = F(w'),$$

where F is the inverse of Φ. Since s_r is given, from (21) we see that the growth rate of the economy must be

$$g = s_r r',$$

and consequently, for the same reasons stated in the previous case, consumption per worker is

$$c = \psi(g) = \psi(s_r r'). \tag{22}$$

If the actual growth rate of the population, g_p, is less than g, then the difference between the number of workers and the population will grow. Conversely, if $g > g_p$, at some finite time the economy will reach full employment and the Fixwage model with a perfectly elastic supply of labor breaks down.

[36] The domain must be restricted to insure the existence and uniqueness of a steady-state equilibrium. The necessity of this restriction is obvious since one could assign a growth rate so high that the technology would not be productive enough to produce positive consumption.

[37] See, for example, [27, 1973, p. 69].

[38] The optimal technique, which is the most profitable to operate at the prevailing real wage and interest rates, is selected from the given set of feasible techniques (or production processes). Possible ties at switch points are ignored here; see Figure 1 where process A is most profitable when either $r = r'$ or $w = w'$.

Finally, suppose the labor force is fully employed and grows at a constant exogenous rate g. Now if s_r is fixed, equation (21) determines the equilibrium rate of profit, and we can proceed to determine the steady-state equilibrium point exactly as we did in my first example (where r' was exogenous).

XII. *Joint Production and the Nonsubstitution Theorem*

Although the neo-Austrian model—either with Hicks' Fixwage or Full Employment assumption—involves joint production, this aspect is not an *essential* feature. This fact is evident because the point (r, w) representing a steady-state equilibrium always lies *on* the factor-price frontier.[39] On the other hand, consider examples which do involve joint production in an essential manner,[40] and assume full employment with labor growing at the constant rate g. The steady-state value of consumption must satisfy the inequality

$$c \leqq E(g). \tag{23}$$

However—and this is the crucial observation—the equilibrium pair (r, w) will lie *on* the minimum wage frontier $w = H(r)$ *if, and only if,*[41] $s_r = 1$. Of course, when $s_r = 1$, the saving hypothesis—equation (21)—implies that $r = g$; then equation (20) is valid and

$$c = E(g) = H(r) = w, \; r = g. \tag{24}$$

But for all $s_r < 1$, the equilibrium real wage rate satisfies the inequality

$$w > H(r); \tag{25}$$

that is, the real wage rate *lies above* the minimum wage frontier. As s_r rises toward one, r and w both fall. The real wage rate reaches a point on the minimum wage frontier only when s_r reaches one and $r = g$. It follows immediately that the standard nonsubstitution theorem (which asserts that steady-state equilibrium prices are *independent of the pattern of final demand* for a given value of w or r) is not valid for this example.[42] In this example (cited in the preceding footnote) it is *not* true that the real wage rate is determined *only* by the interest rate r; it also depends on the savings ratio s_r and hence on the pattern of demand between the consumption and investment goods.

Consideration of joint production also leads to a generalization of the von Weizsäcker result that the elasticity of the factor-price frontier equals the ratio of factor shares when $r = g$ [49, 1963]. There is a more general theorem which does not depend on the absence of joint production: *the elasticity of the minimum wage frontier equals the ratio of factor shares when* $r = g$.[43]

[39] This issue also arises in subsequent sections dealing with dynamics.

[40] See Burmeister and Kuga [13, 1970, pp. 16–18]. Also see footnote 34.

[41] In general, necessity requires regularity conditions on the feasible technology. For our present purposes, we need only consider Example 2 in Burmeister and Kuga [13, 1970, pp. 17–18].

[42] It can be proved that when the rate of interest plus the depreciation rate on the capital good is equal to $\frac{1}{2}$, the equilibrium value of the real wage rate in a steady state is

$$w = \frac{2}{[s_r(2 - s_r)]^{1/2}}$$

with $dw/ds_r < 0$. Moreover, the equilibrium real wage rate w (for a given interest rate r) is not independent of the relative price of investment to consumption goods; see Burmeister and Kuga [13, 1970, p. 18], and Burmeister and Dobell [11, 1970, pp. 280–82].

[43] A brief proof is easily sketched. Let $c = T(y_1, \ldots, y_n; 1, x_1, \ldots, x_n)$ be the per capita production possibility frontier summarizing the feasible technology for the economy. Here c, y_i, and x_i denote per capita consumption, output of the i-th type machine, and the stock of the i-th type machine, respectively. Let fully-employed labor grow at the exogenous rate g, so that a steady-state condition is

$$c = T(gx_1, \ldots, gx_n; 1, x_1, \ldots, x_n). \tag{*}$$

The outer envelope of (*) as the parameters $x_1, \ldots, x_n$ vary defines the optimal transformation frontier $c = E(g)$. We know from (20) that $c = E(g) = H(r) = w$ when $r = g$. But the slope of $E(g)$ can be calculated from (*):

$$E'(g) = \partial c/\partial g = \sum_{i=1}^{n} T_i x_i = -v.$$

If one attempts to generalize the neo-Austrian model and treat (a_t, b_t) as an input-output vector, the complexities discussed in this section are certain to arise because then joint production will become an essential feature of the model.

XIII. *The Saving Hypothesis and Capital Gains*

The assumption that saving is a constant proportion of profit income is expedient for illustrative purposes.[44] However, existing empirical evidence does not support this hypothesis,[45] and it is a dangerous assumption to make about an economy out of steady-state equilibrium with changing prices. For example, it has been proved that the dynamic behavior of an economy with many capital goods is significantly altered provided not all capital gains are saved [15, Burmeister, Caton, Dobell, and Ross, 1973][46] and this underscores my warning: Because capital gains are zero in a steady state, its characteristics remain unchanged, but in general the stability properties of a dynamic path do not.

The issue is clarified with a simple example. Let upper case and lower case letters denote magnitudes and per capital magnitudes, respectively, and assume there exists a single consumption good which we take as *numeraire*. Define *real income* in terms of the returns to labor, L, and the value of capital, V, by

$$\text{Real Income} = Y = wL + rV, \quad (26)$$

and assume net saving is a constant fraction, s, of real income.[47] It is convenient here to work in continuous time, and a dot over a variable signifies total differentiation with respect to time. The condition for momentary equilibrium is that saving must equal the change in the value of capital, *i.e.*,

$$sY = \dot{V}. \quad (27)$$

It then follows that

$$\begin{aligned} Y &= sY + C \\ &= wL + rV = \dot{V} + C. \end{aligned} \quad (28)$$

Finally, expressing (28) in per capita terms, we obtain

$$\dot{v} = (r - g)v + (w - c), \quad (29)$$

i.e., the growth in the per capita value of the capital stock is equal to the return on the capital stock, adjusted for labor growth, plus the excess of the real wage rate over per capita consumption. With more manipulation we can rewrite (29) in the form

$$\dot{v} = sy - gv, \quad (30)$$

strongly reminiscent of the equation for the growth of the capital stock in a model with one type of machine (capital good).[48]

Now, along a steady-state growth path where $\dot{v} = 0$,

$$c = (r - g)v + w \quad (31)$$

or

$$\begin{aligned} \text{Consumption} + \text{Net Investment} &= c + gv \\ &= w + rv = \text{Wages} + \text{Profits}. \end{aligned}$$

---

where $-T_i$ is the price of the i-th output in terms of the consumption good and v is the value of capital (the stock of machines) in terms of the consumption good.

Thus we have proved that $H'(r) = E'(g) = -v$ at $r = g$, and consequently the elasticity of the minimum wage frontier at $r = g$ is

$$-\frac{rH'(r)}{w} = \frac{rv}{w} = \frac{\text{per capita profits}}{\text{per capita wages}}. \quad \text{Q.E.D.}$$

[44] Hicks is clear about his intentions in the case of steady states; see [27, 1973, p. 69].

[45] See, for example, Burmeister and Taubman and the references cited there [10, 1969].

[46] Capital gains are *net* and may be negative if prices fall.

[47] The value of capital in terms of the (single) consumption good as *numeraire is* $\sum_{i=1}^{n} p_i K_i$ where $K_1, \ldots, K_n$ denote the physical stocks of the n different types of machines. Thus there is no issue of capital aggregation.

[48] Except in a fictional world with only one type of machine (capital good), v is a *value* measure which does not represent any physical stock of capital and which definitely should *not* be the independent variable of any "aggregate production function." The reminiscence I have mentioned is potentially dangerous and may have been the cause of some misunderstandings.

Obviously (31) is equivalent to (13) and (16) obtained previously, but we have arrived at it via a completely different route. We should be alerted that a mere comparison of alternative steady states may obscure important aspects of the underlying economic structure. In particular, alternative saving hypotheses—and especially the treatment of capital gains—may have important influences on the dynamic behavior of any economy.

XIV. *Technological Change and Biased Innovations*

For a fixed technology we have seen that there exists an optimal transformation frontier $c = E(g)$ and a minimum wage frontier $w = H(r)$. In technologies without joint production, and in the neo-Austrian model we have described, the situation is simplified and we need only consider a factor-price frontier $w = \Phi(r)$. Any steady-state equilibrium point (r, w) must lie on this curve.

Now suppose there is an invention which alters the feasible technology. How does the factor-price frontier change? Assuming that the old technology is still available—which it must be if technical knowledge about methods of production can be remembered—an invention must shift the factor-price frontier outward for at least some values of the real wage rate. In other words, at some wage rates any viable invention must yield *higher* rates of profits than were possible previously.

We follow Hicks' notation and use asterisks to designate the old (pre-invention) steady state. Consider an economy which is in a steady-state equilibrium at a point (r^*, w^*) using a technique $\{(a_t^*, b_t^*)\}_{t=0}^{n^*}$, and then at time zero a new technique is invented which is optimal at the existing rate of profit. If we assume full employment with labor growing at the exogenous rate g, the equilibrium rate of profit in the new steady state must remain at r^* under the savings hypothesis that $gK = s_r rK$ (or $g = s_r r$) where s_r is the fixed saving ratio out of profits [27, 1973, p. 73].

This observation leads Hicks to define

$$I(r) = \frac{w(r)}{w(r^*)} \tag{32}$$

"as an Index of Improvement in Efficiency, *in one sense or another* (italics in the original)" [27, 1973, p. 75].[49] He then argues that $I(r)$ can be used as an index to classify innovations, or, more accurately, to compare two alternative processes in the tradition of his classic *Theory of wages* [24, 1932].[50]

> It is at once suggested that we should classify Improvements, according to the effect on the Index, when the rate of interest varies. We find no difficulty in saying that an Improvement is *neutral*, if a change in the interest rate has no effect on the Index; that, as we have seen, is in line with Harrod. But when there are effects, it is not *necessary* that they should be simple effects; it is possible, for instance, that a fall in interest from 10 to 9 percent might raise the index, while a further fall from 5 to 4 percent might lower it. (This, in another way, is what the re-switching controversy is about.) But perhaps the reader will be willing to accept that *most* technical changes are not infected by this difficulty. It is usually possible to give a straight answer to the question: would such and such an improvement offer a larger, or a smaller, saving in cost if the rate of interest were lower? An answer that does not depend on the size of the reduction, nor on the level of the rate of interest from which it is made. This may not be so; but the cases in which it is so are surely sufficiently important for us to need a classification which applies to them [27, 1973, p. 76].
>
> . . .
>
> Looking again at the case in which the output streams are the same, we see that $I(r)$ rises with a fall in r when the main cost-saving comes *late;* when the later sectoral ratios (a_t^*/a_t) are systematically larger than the earlier. It would then seem appropriate to say that the improvement is

[49] In our notation the efficiency index is $I(r) = \psi(r)/\psi^*(r^*)$, where $\psi^*(r)$ is the restricted factor-price curve for the old process.

[50] He clearly states that his 1973 classification bears no relationship to the 1932 notion of "Hicks neutrality." See [27, 1973, pp. 182–84].

forward-biased. Similarly, when a fall in r lowers $I(r)$, I shall say that the improvement is *backward-biased*. Though the names are derived from the case in which the output streams are the same, they will serve us well as general descriptions. We shall make much use of them in what follows [27, 1973, p. 77].

One warning is appropriate. It is only in exceptional circumstances that the factor-price frontier for a newly invented process will dominate the old factor-price curve at *every* rate of interest. A more realistic assumption is that the index $I(r)$ rises as the rate of interest falls for all r less than some value $\bar{r}$, where $I(\bar{r}) = 1$. Or, conversely, an invention may be more profitable only for rates of profits larger than some prescribed value. This issue is not of any consequence for the uses to which Hicks puts his efficiency index (and in his hands it becomes a powerful weapon), but others should be cautious.[51]

In Section VI above we have defined a process with a Simple Profile. In addition, assume that the length of the utilization period is an integral multiple of the length of the construction period. Then by defining "*m* weeks" as "one year," we have a construction period one "year" in length and a utilization period *n* "years" in length. Every economic variable is now defined with one "year" as the unit time period, and the Simple Profile takes the following form:[52]

	construction period	*utilization period*
years	0	1 to n
inputs	a_0	a_1
outputs	0	1
net output	$-wa_0$	$1 - wa_1$

[27, 1973, p. 84].

All processes considered have Simple Profiles of the above form, and the dynamic properties of paths for this *Standard Case* are easy to study in detail.

In the Standard Case, the equilibrium condition $k_0 = 0$ takes the form

$$\frac{1}{w} = a_1 + a_0 r_n \tag{33}$$

where $r_n = r/(1 - R^n) \geq 1/n$; see equation (2). Thus we have

$$I(r) = \frac{w}{w^*} = \frac{a_0^* r_n + a_1^*}{a_0 r_n + a_1}, \tag{34}$$

and we see immediately that the efficiency index $I(r)$ must lie between the two ratios $(a_0^*/a_0) = h$ and $(a_1^*/a_1) = H$. (Warning: the latter H is a constant and should not be confused with my previous functional notation for the minimum wage frontier.) Clearly h measures improvement (cost saving) in the construction period, and H measures improvement in the utilization period.

A *neutral* or *unbiased* innovation has the property that

$$h = H = I(r) \text{ for all } r. \tag{35}$$

When $h < H$, a fall in the rate of interest raises $I(r)$ and the innovation is *forward-biased*. Finally, because $I(r) > 1$ for any profitable innovation, Hicks introduces the term *strong forward bias* for the case $h < 1$. A technological invention which is strongly forward biased has the property that it must be profitable to operate at sufficiently low rates of profit. It is very important to realize that the definitions of neutrality and bias just stated should not be identified with the older notions of "neutral," "capital-saving," and "labor-saving" innovations [27, 1973, pp. 86–87].[53]

Our discussion of technological change would be incomplete without mentioning "Harrod neutrality." If the ratio of profit to labor income remains constant before and after an innovation, and provided the rate of interest remains constant, the shift is termed "Harrod neutral." Suppose the new Hicks

[51] The issue is clarified in the context of Hicks' Standard Case; see [27, 1973, pp. 86–88].

[52] Every process has a fixed duration of $(n + 1)$ weeks.

[53] Also see footnote 62.

efficiency index is constant so that an innovation is unbiased, at least over a range including r^* and g. Then by definition [27, 1973, pp. 72–75][54]

$$I(g) = \frac{c}{c^*} = I(r) = \frac{w}{w^*}. \tag{36}$$

If saving is a constant proportion of income,

$$gv = s(w + rv), \tag{37}$$

and combining the accounting relationship

$$c + gv = w + rv \tag{38}$$

with (37), we derive

$$c = w + rv - s(w + rv) = (1 - s)(w + rv). \tag{39}$$

Then, using (36), we find

$$\frac{c}{c^*} = \frac{w}{w^*} = \frac{w + rv}{w^* + rv^*}$$

or

$$\frac{w}{w + rv} = \frac{w^*}{w^* + rv^*}$$

or

$$\frac{w}{rv} = \frac{w^*}{rv^*}. \tag{40}$$

The conclusion—that the ratio of wage to profit income is constant for unbiased inventions—is also valid when saving is a constant proportion of profit income and $g = s_r r$.

Thus, as Hicks states, "From one steady state to another the Harrod condition is satisfied, for a change in technique which exhibits (our) lack of bias. That is how the Harrod classification fits in" [27, 1973, p. 183].[55]

[54] See footnote 49.

[55] See Hicks for a discussion of an important difference between "Harrod neutrality" and Hicks' new definition of an unbiased innovation [27, 1973, p. 74].

XV. *Dynamic Paths and Uncertainty*

We now turn our attention to questions of dynamics, to an examination of an economy which is not in steady-state equilibrium. The traditional approach proceeds in three steps: 1) the *existence* of a steady-state equilibrium is established; 2) the *uniqueness* of steady-state equilibrium is investigated; 3) *starting from arbitrary initial conditions*, the question of whether or not the economy asymptotically approaches a (perhaps unique) steady-state equilibrium is studied.

Hicks adopts an alternative approach taken in his *Capital and growth* and considers an economy which initially is in a steady-state equilibrium at a real wage rate w^* and a rate of interest r^*. Thus our attention is limited to initial conditions which represent a steady-state equilibrium, rather than taking arbitrary initial conditions. Then at time zero there is an "invention" which causes a new technique to become the most profitable at the prevailing point (r^*, w^*). Therefore the new process is introduced, but the old process also continues to operate until it no longer is profitable. In general there may be induced changes in the wage rate along the dynamic path the economy generates, and such changes may alter the selection of the optimal (most profitable) technique. It is only under additional restrictions that the economy will move from the initial steady state and converge asymptotically to a new steady-state equilibrium.

Hicks calls the equilibrium path from one steady state to another a *Traverse*, and he clearly states that his study of such paths is exploratory in nature:

> The task thus outlined is formidable. I do not pretend that I have been able to complete it. Most of what I can offer is no more than a fairly full solution for a quite Special Case, which I shall call the Standard Case. Even that, we shall find, gives a good deal of trouble.
>
> It may well be felt that this Standard Case is so special as to be uninteresting. It is indeed true

that it excludes complications, which have received much attention, and to which attention has been given in the earlier chapters of this book. It is a narrow front on which to advance. It may nevertheless be claimed that on that narrow front we can advance a long way. As a general theory, it is clearly inadequate; but as an instrument of exploration, it will serve [27, 1973, p. 82].[56]

Since we are no longer concerned only with steady-state equilibria, we must recognize that the future is uncertain. If one wishes to avoid all problems of uncertainty, there is an alternative, the favorite alternative for optimal control theorists, but it is one which Hicks explicitly rejects:

> There is indeed an alternative—the sequence which is based on correct expectations, expectations of the wages and interest which in the course of the Traverse will be realized. But the place of this is in optimum theory; and that is not the kind of theory with which in this book we are concerned. In positive economics we must not endow our actors with perfect foresight; for to do so would abolish Time, which is our subject [27, 1973, p. 172].

We must deal with uncertainty in some manner, and its presence is a severe complication in most all economic models. The way is opened for a host of important questions: What is the appropriate definition of "equilibrium," both for a single period and for a time sequence of periods? What is the probability distribution for an expected event or an expected price? How do economic agents behave when faced with risk, and how do they revise their expectations as actual events unfold over time?

A discussion of these and other related issues, however interesting and important they may be, would lead us far astray from our central theme. We will not discuss the general problem of "decision-making under uncertainty," but rather follow Hicks and circumvent problems associated with uncertainty in a most straight-forward manner:

> Since each individual process extends over time, the choice should in general depend on expected wages as well as on current wages; but as I have previously explained, I shall in this book leave that complication out of account. I shall assume *static expectations*—that the wage that is ruling at time T is expected to remain unchanged, at least so long as the processes started at time T are expected to continue. Since these expectations are "wrong," the path that is chosen will not be an optimum path; it may sometimes behave in curious ways that are to be attributed to its non-optimality. But in positive economics it has its place; there is no simple assumption which throws more light on the kinds of things that are likely to happen [27, 1973, p. 110].[57]

Of course static expectations is an extreme case of the familiar adaptive expectations mechanism. Alternatively, we may postulate that price forecasts are derived from more sophisticated behavior as exemplified by rational expectations in J. F. Muth [34, 1961] or by William A. Brock [3, 1972]. Space does not permit a discussion of such alternative specifications which allow a much more satisfactory treatment of uncertainty.

XVI. *Stability with a Fixed Wage Rate*

It is now apparent why the Fixwage model is so convenient. Since the wage rate is exogenous, it remains constant at w^* (the old equilibrium value) no matter how the feasible technology may change through inventions. Consequently, the new optimal process

$$\{(a_t, b_t)\}_{t=0}^{n} = \{(a_0, 0), \overbrace{(a_1, 1), \ldots, (a_1, 1)}^{n \text{ periods}}\}$$

is immediately determined from the factor-price frontier of the new (post-invention) technology. With free entry of firms, capital markets adjust instantaneously (or at least within one period) to equilibrium, and

[56] Two of the most important simplifications under the Standard Case are 1) reswitching is impossible, and 2) once a project is started, it will never be truncated, provided the wage rate is less than $(1/a_1)$ and $(1 - wa_1)$ is positive; [27, 1973, p. 83].

[57] For Hicks' views on the uncertainty issue in a similar context, see [25, 1965, pp. 69–72].

the new rate of interest, also determined from the factor-price frontier, is

$$r = F(w^*). \tag{41}$$

This value of r will render the present discounted value of the new process equal to zero. And now, with w and r fixed at their new equilibrium values, predictions based on static expectations prove correct.

With the labor supply completely elastic, there is no question of full employment in the Fixwage model. However, there is an analogous concept which Hicks calls Full Performance [27, 1973, p. 52]. Recall that x_{T-t} denotes the number of processes started t periods ago; x_T is the number of starts in the current period.[58] If we take past starts $x_{T-n}, \ldots, x_{T-1}$ as given, the number of new starts determines the actual number of workers employed in the current period; see equation (8a). The highest value of x_T consistent with current saving sets an upper limit for economic activity and defines Full Performance.

> At Full Performance the rate of starts is at its maximum—at the maximum permitted by the share of current output that is not absorbed by consumption out of wages paid to labour engaged on old processes, and not absorbed in consumption of other kinds. So at Full Performance activity is limited by saving—just as the older economists (*classical* economists in the usual sense, not specifically in Keynes's sense) supposed it to be [27, 1973, p. 52].

One additional relationship—an assumption about total saving—is required to complete the system, and Hicks chooses a convenient, albeit unusual, method:

> What is fairly easy, in the present case, is to make the other assumption that was mentioned in Chapter V—that the Take-out (Q_T), considered as "consumption out of profits," is unaffected by the change in technique. It is the same as it would have been if the change had not occurred. In order to get the *effect* of the change, we must compare what actually happens with what would have happened otherwise; that is to say, we compare the actual path with a continuation of the old path, the *reference path* we may call it. We shall thus assume that $Q_T = Q_T^*$, where Q_T^* is the take-out at time T on the reference path [27, 1973, p. 90].

As Hicks notes, his assumption that consumption out of profit income remains constant is reasonable enough when total profits first change, but it is "rather ridiculous" after profits have changed substantially [27, 1973, pp. 90 and 95]. He argues, however, that the results he has proved probably remain substantially valid, although the system would converge to a new steady-state with a lower rate of growth [27, 1973, pp. 96–97].

The Traverse is divided into three parts:

1) The *Preparatory Phase,* during which new machines are constructed, but still produce no output. This is period 1 in the Standard Case.

2) The *Early Phase,* during which both modern machines and pre-invention machines produce output. This phase lasts from periods 2 to $(n + 1)$.

3) The *Late Phase,* starting in period $(n + 2)$, during which pre-invention machines no longer exist (remember they were not produced after the invention and have a lifetime of n periods), and all output is from modern machines.

The paths of employment and output depend upon the parameter h. If $h \geq 1$, employment and output grow faster than on the reference path (for $n \geq 1$), and they converge asymptotically to a path with a growth rate r, the new equilibrium rate of interest.

If, however, $h < 1$—if the invention is strongly forward biased in Hicks' language—output and employment *fall* compared with the reference path. Eventually the actual path intersects and then rises above the reference path, converging again to a path with growth rate r. Hicks provides proofs of these results in a mathematical appendix, and for his Fixwage model, the conclusions do not depend upon the Standard Case assumptions. However, convergence to a steady-state equilibrium path

[58] See Section VII.

does depend upon an assumption that constructional labor requirements do not increase between any two periods in the preparatory phase [27, 1973, pp. 205–210]. Without such a restriction, the economy may converge to a cycle—at least that possibility has not been ruled out.

XVII. *The Question of "Ricardo on Machinery"*

The effects on labor due to the introduction of a new (more roundabout? more mechanized?) process has been a subject of debate since at least the early 1800's. The third edition of Ricardo's *Principles* contains his famous chapter entitled "On Machinery," where he takes the position that the introduction of machinery could have an adverse effect on employment *in the short run*.[59] Wicksell, however, stated that Ricardo's argument was "erroneous."[60] In particular, he asserted that Ricardo's position is "theoretically untenable" and that, "A diminution in the gross product, or in its value (assuming, as before, that prices of commodities are given and constant), is scarcely conceivable as a result of technical improvements—under free competition" [51, 1934, p. 137]. But this criticism results from a simple misunderstanding of terminology. Ricardo's statement that "gross revenue" may fall in the short-run should be interpreted as the valid assertion that the demand for labor (and also the final output of consumption goods) temporarily may be diminished due to the introduction of machinery. Wicksell's conclusion that an innovation must increase the economy's potential output (*i.e.*, the outputs of consumption plus investment goods which may be produced) is correct; thus *if* employment is maintained, the actual output of consumption plus investment goods must increase, although its distribution may be changed. However, these conclusions in no way contradict Ricardo once his peculiar language is properly understood.[61]

The logically possible effects of an innovation on labor were clarified further by A. C. Pigou and Hicks in 1932. Pigou showed that an innovation might decrease the absolute level of the real wage rate, a case which is now called an "absolute–labor-saving invention" [37, 1932]. Hicks generalized this concept and demonstrated that workers could be harmed by an invention in the sense that the ratio of total wage to profit income may fall, the case now termed a "labor-saving invention" [24, 1932; 11, Burmeister and Dobell, 1970, Chapter 3, pp. 68–69].[62] Ricardo was essentially correct.

In 1969 and 1973, Hicks has again come to Ricardo's defense, but for entirely different reasons [26, 1969, pp. 151–54 and pp. 168–71; 27, 1973, pp. 97–99]. The 1973 Hicks Fixwage model provides almost an exact replication of Ricardo's assumptions; the real wage rate is fixed, labor supply is perfectly elastic, and employment (g) varies positively with saving.[63] Thus

[59] See Chapter XXXI in Ricardo [38, 1911]. With the real wage rate fixed, a reduction in employment is equivalent to a reduction in the total wage bill.

It should be noted that the neo-Austrian and Ricardian models are completely aggregative; when an "innovation" occurs, it is in fact a "technological revolution" influencing the whole economy. Innovations solely at the firm or industry level involve micro-economic effects which need not lead to dramatic changes in the equilibrium values of macro-economic variables.

[60] See Wicksell [51, 1934, pp. 133–44, especially p. 135].

[61] Likewise Ricardo's term "net incomes" is what we mean by "profits," etc.

[62] There, a classification of technological change is given, and it is shown that a particular innovation may be labor saving along one time path, but labor using (capital saving) along a different path. The notion of a "labor-saving invention" becomes precise only if we agree to limit our attention to a certain class of paths, *e.g.* time paths along which the capital-labor ratio remains constant.

[63] For this model the long-run effect of an invention is clear. Since $g = s_r r$, s_r is fixed, and r must rise after an innovation, it follows that g and hence the total wage bill must rise. But, as stated in the previous section, the *short-run effects* of an innovation depend on the parameter h [27, 1973, p. 98].

we have Hicks' most recent interpretation of Ricardo:

> I think we must remember how the problem presented itself to him. He was becoming conscious of the Industrial Revolution; rather late, some would say, but no one, at that depth, had thought it out earlier. What, in that context, he will surely have had in mind is not "improved machinery" (though he says "improved machinery") but the introduction of machinery: the introduction of a strongly fixed-capital-using technique in place of one which, as an approximation, could be regarded as circulating-capital-using only. The latter, in terms of our model, would be represented by a profile in which a_0^* and a_1^* were much the same. To pass from that to a technique in which fixed capital was substituted for circulating must involve a *rise* in the "constructional" or preparatory coefficient ($a_0 > a_0^*$, so that $h < 1$). The *introduction* of machinery must, almost inevitably, be a switch with a strong forward bias. May it not be that this is what Ricardo (mainly) meant? [27, 1973, pp. 98–99].

There is another aspect of this debate which seems more important than whether or not h exceeds unity.[64] A crucial feature of Ricardo's work is the existence of a single primary factor, *land*. If the wage rate is fixed at $w = w^*$, there will still exist a curve which represents the possible steady-state equilibrium values of the profit rate, r, and the competitive real rental rate on (homogeneous) land, π. Denote this function by

$$r = \Gamma(\pi; w^*); \tag{42}$$

the $\pi - r$ curve is downward sloping with

$$\left.\frac{\partial r}{\partial \pi}\right|_{w^*} < 0. \tag{43}$$

We know that any viable invention must shift this curve outward, but, without additional assumptions, no more can be predicted about the post-invention steady-state equilibrium. Now suppose, as Samuelson does in his exposition of Ricardo, the profit or interest rate is also fixed at a level r^* [39, 1959; 40, 1959, especially pp. 227–28]. Clearly with these restrictions an invention *must raise* π, the real rental rate for land.

Apparently Hicks had this fact in mind when later in *Capital and time* he again comments on Ricardo:

> One can perhaps go a little further. When the theory of this chapter is re-thought in Ricardo-Mill terms, it suggests an interesting conclusion. For wages we are now to read rents. What we shall then learn from our Principal Proposition is that induced invention, though it may very probably cause a fall in rents in the short run, must in the longer run raise them. The same will apply to any autonomous invention, which raises the rate of profit. It will thus apply to any "economically desirable" improvement, even (for instance) to Free Trade in Corn. All the gains from the efforts of business men and inventors—and even of economists—must ultimately go nowhere else but into the landlord's pocket.[1]
>
> ([1] As an owner of building land, if not of agricultural!) [27, 1973, pp. 123–24].

One must interpret these words with great care. While Hicks' exegesis of Ricardo is correct, the conclusion is surely false if *both* labor and land are treated as primary factors, fixed in supply, and if the rate of interest is not fixed. With this alternative formulation of a Ricardian model, equation (42) becomes

$$r = \Gamma(\pi, w), \tag{44}$$

which defines a factor-price frontier *surface* when the fixed quantities of labor and land are both fully employed.[65] An inven-

[64] Note that the possibility $h > 1$ is not logically precluded.

[65] Processes which involve joint production in an essential manner—as discussed in section IV—must again be ruled out if all steady-state equilibrium points (π, w, r) are to lie *on* the surface $r = \Gamma(\pi, w)$. We have seen that the production of older machines jointly with new output usually does not necessarily alter the conclusions derived from a model in which there is no joint production.

Note, however, the qualification that the two primary factors are fully employed *simultaneously* is a strong restriction if the technology contains only a few feasible processes with fixed coefficients. For example, consider production processes of one-period duration, and suppose it takes 1 worker + 1 unit of land + 1 unit of "capital" to produce 1 unit of final output ("consumption"). Suppose also 1 unit of "new

tion must again shift the frontier *outward*, but now there is an extra degree of freedom; it is possible that the new wage rate may *rise* while *both* r and π fall. And, contrary to the last quotation from Hicks, such an invention most definitely is "economically desirable" and would be introduced under pure competition.

In summary, the incidence of an invention cannot be easily determined without restrictive assumptions. Hence I am in complete agreement with the concluding sentence of the Hicks' text: "A reminder that the Distribution of Income is not, in the short-run, a well-founded economic concept is perhaps not the least important point which has emerged from our enquiry" [27, 1973, p. 184]. But I wish to add that the long-run problem is only slightly easier!

XVIII. *Stability in the Full Employment Model*

An analysis of the dynamic behavior in the Full Employment model is much more difficult than in the Fixwage model because the real wage rate may vary, and, accordingly, changes in the real wage rate can induce switches in the optimal (*i.e.*, most profitable) technique along the full employment path. The assumption of static price expectations was quite acceptable for the Fixwage model since the expectations are fulfilled (except for an initial jump in the rate of profit). The problem of expectations is vital for the full employment model because it is the *expected* values of w_t and r_t which should be used to calculate the *expected* present discounted value of a process, and the expectation mechanism has a crucial influence upon which new techniques are introduced.

The general problem is almost intractable, and Hicks first studies the Traverse from one given (old) technique to another given (new) technique. I too will confine my attention to this special case for the moment.

Table 1 illustrates two transitions, both beginning from a steady-state equilibrium with a two-period process

$$\{(a_t^*, b_t^*)\}_{t=0}^{1} = \{(2, 0), (2, 1)\} \quad (45)$$

for an economy with a fixed labor supply of 4 workers ($g = 0$). First consider transition A, a Traverse to a new steady-state equilibrium using the process

$$\{(a_t, b_t)\}_{t=0}^{1} = \{(1, 0), (1, 1)\}. \quad (46)$$

Because $h = a_0^*/a_0 = H = a_1^*/a_1$, the innovation is *neutral;* the number of workers displaced from the old process (which is abandoned) are exactly equal to the number of workers hired during the construction period for the new process. Note that the transition to the new steady-state equilibrium actually is completed in two time periods.

Transition B uses the new process

$$\{(a_t, b_t)\}_{t=0}^{1} = \{(2, 0), (1, 1)\} \quad (47)$$

with $h = 1$, $H = 2$, and $a_0 = 2 > a_1 = 1$. The economy follows a full-employment path which asymptotically approaches a new

capital" (a new machine) can be produced by 1 worker alone. Assume the machines ("capital") employed to produce the consumption good are exhausted during the single production period. With labor and (or) land fixed in supply, the only feasible steady state is stationary with a growth rate $g = 0$. But if the technology consists only of the two processes just described—*i.e.* the single process to produce the consumption good and the single process to produce the capital good—then both labor and land can be fully employed in steady-state equilibrium only if the (fixed) number of available workers is exactly twice the (fixed) number of units of available land. When labor to land supplies stand in any other proportion, either (but not both) the equilibrium real rental rate for land π or the equilibrium real wage rate w is zero because that factor will be in excess supply. However, these complexities only serve to underscore my main conclusion and do not detract from its validity.

[The problem of zero factor prices may be avoided if the feasible technology set contains a sufficient number (perhaps infinite as in the neoclassical case) of alternative techniques and "substitution" is therefore possible; this condition may also be expressed in terms of some strict convexity restrictions on the feasible technology set.]

TABLE 1

Transition A	(a)	(b)	(c)	(d)	(e)	(f)	(g)	(h)	(i)	(j)	(k)
Old Equilibrium	2	1	2	1	0	0	0	0	4	1	1/8
Period 0	0	0	2	1	2	2	0	0	4	1	1/8
Period 1 = New Equilibrium	0	0	0	0	2	2	2	2	4	2	1/8
Transition B											
Old Equilibrium	2	1	2	1	0	0	0	0	4	1	1/8
Period 0	0	0	2	1	2	1	0	0	4	1	1/8
Period 1	0	0	0	0	3	3/2	1	1	4	1	1/8
Period 2	0	0	0	0	5/2	5/4	3/2	3/2	4	3/2	1/4
Period 3	0	0	0	0	11/4	11/8	5/4	5/4	4	5/4	3/16
.	.	.	.	.	.	.	.	.	.	.	.
.	.	.	.	.	.	.	.	.	.	.	.
.	.	.	.	.	.	.	.	.	.	.	.
Period t	0	0	0	0	$4 - C_t$	$(4 - C_t)/2$	C_t	C_t	4	C_t	$(C_t - \frac{1}{2})/4$
New Equilibrium	0	0	0	0	8/3	4/3	4/3	4/3	4	4/3	5/24

where $C_t = 2[1 - \frac{1}{2} + (\frac{1}{2})^2 - (\frac{1}{2})^3 + (\frac{1}{2})^4 + \ldots + (-1)^t(\frac{1}{2})^t]$ and $\lim_{t \to \infty} C_t = 2[(4/3) - (4/6)] = 4/3$.

Explanation of columns:

(a) Workers producing machines of old type
(b) Output of machines of old type
(c) Workers producing consumption goods using old machines
(d) Output of consumption goods using old machines
(e) Workers producing machines of new type
(f) Output of new machines
(g) Workers producing consumption goods using new machines
(h) Output of consumption goods using new machines
(i) Total employment = *(a)* + *(c)* + *(e)* + *(g)*
(j) Total output of consumption goods = *(d)* + *(h)*
(k) The real wage rate $w_t = (B_t - Q_t)/A_t = [(j) - \frac{1}{2}]/4$, where the "Take-out" Q_t is set at $\frac{1}{2}$.

steady-state equilibrium. Because $h = 1$, the transfer of workers to the production of new machines does not create any fall in final consumption output along the full employment path. Consumption remains constant during periods 1 and 2, and it then begins to increase and asymptotically approaches its new steady-state value (4/3). The time pattern of the wage rate depends on the value of the Take-out; assuming the latter is constant at 1/2, the wage rate first remains constant, then falls, and finally rises asymptotically to its new (higher) equilibrium value, as indicated in column *(k)* of Table 1.

These two examples are simple enough. The situation is more complicated when $h < 1(a_0^* < a_0)$—the case of a strong forward bias. Consumption must initially fall along a transition path to the new steady-state equilibrium. As we have learned to expect, Hicks provides a verbal explanation of this result to reinforce the mathematical proof in the appendix [27, 1973, pp. 103–107 and pp. 189–98]. Space limitations preclude a discussion of this case here.

A full-employment transition is not always possible. Consider, for example, a simple two-period example with a fixed labor force L. Since the old process is abandoned after the innovation, workers are employed only on new machines after period 0. Thus for periods 1, 2, . . . , the full employment condition is

$$a_0 x_{T+1} + a_1 x_T = L \tag{48}$$

where x_0 is an initial condition. Equation (48) may be rewritten as

$$x_{T+1} = \frac{L}{a_0} - \frac{a_1}{a_0} x_T \tag{49}$$

or

$$x_{T+1} = \alpha + \beta x_T. \tag{50}$$

Clearly (50) has a steady-state solution

$$x_T = x_{T+1} = \bar{x} = \frac{L}{a_0 + a_1}. \tag{51}$$

The system is stable and the new steady state is approached asymptotically if

$$\lim_{T\to\infty} x_T = \bar{x}. \tag{52}$$

But the solution to (50) is

$$x_T = \alpha[1 + \beta + \beta^2 + \ldots + \beta^{T-1}] + \beta^T x_0. \tag{53}$$

Now provided $-1 < \beta < 1$,

$$\lim_{T\to\infty} [1 + \beta + \beta^2 + \ldots + \beta^{T-1}] = \frac{1}{1-\beta}, \tag{54}$$

$$\lim_{T\to\infty} \beta^T x_0 = 0, \tag{55}$$

and

$$\lim_{T\to\infty} x_T = \frac{\alpha}{1-\beta} = \frac{L/a_0}{1 + (a_1/a_0)} = \frac{L}{a_0 + a_1} = \bar{x}.$$

Therefore the condition

$$-1 < -\frac{a_1}{a_0}$$

or

$$a_0 > a_1 \tag{56}$$

is sufficient. Moreover, this condition is also necessary except in the razor's edge case when $a_0 = a_1$ and $x_0 = \bar{x}$. This exception is possible for neutral innovations, as exemplified above by transition *A;* in all other cases the condition $a_0 > a_1$ is necessary as well as sufficient.[66]

It is important to understand that when $a_0 < a_1$, Traverses from the old steady-state equilibrium to a new equilibrium do exist, but none of them has the property that workers are fully employed for every period along the path. In more complicated models there may not exist *any* transition paths from an equilibrium using one technique to another equilibrium using a different technique. But the existence of feasible transition paths for the neo-Austrian model is not an issue; it is always possible to achieve a new steady-state equilibrium in $(n + 1)$ production periods.[67]

XIX. *Substitution and Dynamic Reswitching*

Every physical quantity along a Traverse is known in the Full Employment model. It is the specified properties of the technology, combined with the assumption that there is no unemployment of labor, which determines the entire time paths for such variables as the number of new starts, the number of workers employed on machines of various ages, and, most importantly, the final output of consumption goods. The questions of production and distribution are quite independent along a Traverse between two given techniques.

An assumption about saving is required to determine the path of the real wage rate and, consequently, the distribution of final consumption goods. Since expectations are static, at any moment in time the equilibrium rate of profit must be such that

[66] Hicks also considers more general processes than the Standard Case, and he proves i) that a Full Employment model will converge provided $a_0 > a_1 > a_2 > \ldots > a_n$, and ii) the restriction $a_0 > a_n$ is necessary. See [27, 1973, p. 136 and pp. 205–210].

[67] For example, consider a path (starting from the old equilibrium position at time zero) along which all workers are employed *only* on the new process and the rate of starts is set at its new steady-state equilibrium value. Given the triangular structure of the neo-Austrian technology discussed in Section II, the capital equipment appropriate for the new steady-state equilibrium can be attained in $(n + 1)$ production periods. Thus the path described provides one feasible transition from the old to the new steady-state equilibrium.

the present discounted value of the new process equals zero. Almost any saving behavior will suffice to form a logically complete model.

The situation is complicated considerably when we allow for the possibility that the optimal technique – that is, the technique used for new starts – may change because the real wage rate changes. But now the questions of production and distribution are both linked to saving behavior because saving influences what technique is optimal in the final steady-state equilibrium position when the real wage and interest rates have converged to (perhaps) new values. The assumption that saving is a constant proportion of profit income provides an easy example, for then the rate of profit in the final equilibrium must equal its original (pre-invention) value and

$$r = r^* = g/s_r.\text{[68]} \qquad (57)$$

Since the factor-price frontier must shift outward with an innovation, we also conclude that the real wage rate must have risen ($w > w^*$).

Hicks argues that the existence of many alternative techniques which may be used along a dynamic path – that is, the possibility of "substituting" one process for another – has a predictable influence:

> The function of substitution, in an expanding economy, is to slow up the rises in wages that come from technical improvement; but the effect of the retardation is to stretch out the rise, making it a longer rise, so that a larger rise, than would otherwise have occurred, is ultimately achieved. That is the Principal Proposition I am advancing in this chapter. It is surely an important proposition, perhaps the most important in all this book. But it has taken a long series of specializing assumptions for it to be reached. It is only on the basis of those assumptions that we have established it. On more general assumptions it will probably be subject to exception, or at least to qualification. Something should be said on possible qualifications before going further [27, 1973, p. 115].
>
> . . .
>
> None of this changes our proposition seriously; the main effect of substitution, in a growth process, appears as stated. But what would happen if we went outside the Standard model? That is a large question, which I am quite unable to discuss at all adequately; it may however be suggested that the specialized assumptions of that model may not, after all, have been so restrictive. The Efficiency curve diagram is not in itself dependent on the Simple Profile assumption; it is indeed so general that it makes little use of our general "Austrian" assumption of the separable processes [27, 1973, p. 116].

Complications can arise because, in general, "reswitching" is possible not only as we have defined it (see Section VI above), but also in the following sense. Consider an economy in steady-state equilibrium using technique α, and then suppose *two* new techniques are invented, β and γ. It is *possible* that the economy may follow a dynamic path along which technique β is used first. There is then a "switch" to technique γ, and, finally, a "reswitch" back to technique β, which is optimal in the final steady-state equilibrium. I will call the later behavior *dynamic reswitching*. [*Warning:* "Dynamic reswitching," which occurs along a time path, is *not* the same as the ordinary reswitching defined in Section VI, which involves only steady-state comparisons. An economy exhibiting ordinary reswitching may or may not also exhibit dynamic reswitching, depending upon the saving behavior and other assumptions.]

Clearly, dynamic reswitching contradicts the assertion that the possibility of substitution results in a higher real wage rate than would have been possible otherwise; in the example stated, the real wage rate attained in the final equilibrium position is that appropriate to technique β, and it is no higher because technique γ exists. Hicks rejects this possibility: "It seems safe to regard the exception, just defined,

[68] See Hicks [27, 1973, pp. 112–13].

as so extreme that it can be disregarded" [27, 1973, p. 118]. I remain skeptical.[69]

XX. *A von Neumann Interpretation of the Neo-Austrian Model*

It is well known that the cost of production for a commodity in a static Leontief model can be expressed "as the sum of direct labor congealed in an infinite number of previous stages" where "if we insist on giving a calendar-time interpretation we must think of the Gaitskell process as going *backward* in time and the Cornfield process as showing how much production must be started many periods back if we are to meet the new consumption targets today" [18, Dorfman, Samuelson, and Solow, 1958, pp. 253–54]. The reswitching controversy has involved different capital models, but many have structures which are logically equivalent.[70] In particular, if there are goods that take more than a single period to produce, one can either 1) calculate the price relationships directly, or 2) treat "goods-in-process" of different ages as different goods [7, Bruno, Burmeister, and Sheshinski, 1968, pp. 529–30]. Although the Leontief-Sraffa formulation excludes joint production, goods which require more than one production period and which do involve joint production can still be treated by the procedure of identifying "older machines" as *different* commodities; but now we must do so in a context which does admit joint production, as do models of the von Neumann type [33, Morishima, 1969, pp. 91–94].

Our understanding both of the neo-Austrian model and of the von Neumann method will be deepened by studying a simple example. Consider the process

$$\{(a_t, b_t)\}_{t=0}^{2} = \{(a_0, 0), (a_1, b_1), (a_2, b_2 = 1)\}. \quad (58)$$

The present discounted value of this process (for a given real wage and interest rate) must equal zero if there is free entry and if capital markets are to be in equilibrium. Here we will take an alternative approach and will treat "goods-in-process" as different goods.

Before proceeding, two observations are important. First, if $a_1 \neq a_2$ or if $b_1 \neq b_2$, the process described by (58) violates the assumptions of Hicks' Standard Case. Second, since the process terminates at the end of the third production period, we may set $b_2 = 1$, or, alternatively, we may modify the price normalization introduced below and define a "consumption basket" containing b_2 units of consumption goods.

We now interpret the production process described by (58) as a von Neumann model.[71] Activity 1 produces 1 new machine from a_0 workers employed for one period. Let the price of such a new machine be p_1; the equilibrium price must equal the unit cost of production. But since wages are paid at the end of the period (see Section III),

$$p_1 = wa_0. \quad (59)$$

Activity 2 produces b_1 units of final consumption goods jointly with one "one-year-old machine" (a machine which has been operated for one period) by employing a labor input of a_1 workers, for one production period, together with one new machine. Let p_2 be the price of a one-year-old machine. In equilibrium its price must equal the cost of "producing" a one-year-old machine, *minus* the value of any

[69] Morishima's discussion of technological invention and "trigger effects" is relevant to this issue; see Morishima [32, 1964, pp. 116–22].

[70] See Section II, "Alternative Discrete Capital Models," in Bruno, Burmeister, and Sheshinski [6, 1966, pp. 528–31].

[71] Strictly speaking, von Neumann did not allow either primary factors such as labor or final consumption, but this detail is of no consequence for our discussion. The model discussed in this section, which is elaborated in the Appendix, could be presented within the framework of Malinvaud's pioneering work [29, 1953; 30, 1962], but the von Neumann method has more structure and its economic interpretation is better suited for our purposes here.

consumption output created jointly by the process. Thus

$$p_2 = wa_1 + p_1(1+r) - p_3 b_1$$
$$= wa_1 + p_1(1+r) - b_1 \qquad (60)$$

where we may select the consumption good as our *numeraire* commodity and set $p_3 = 1$. Note that $p_1(1+r)$ reflects the original price plus interest on one new machine, which must be purchased at the *beginning* of the production period.

Finally, activity 3 uses a_2 workers plus one one-year-old machine to produce one unit of final consumption goods. We may assume either that the one-year-old machine is completely exhausted by activity three, or that a two-year-old machine—one which has been operated for two production periods—cannot be used in any other production activity and consequently is worthless. Either interpretation leads to the same equilibrium condition for activity 3:

$$p_3 = 1 = wa_2 + p_2(1+r). \qquad (61)$$

What do equations (59), (60), and (61) imply? We may proceed sequentially and first substitute the value for p_1 given by (59) into (60); this yields

$$wa_1 + wa_0(1+r) = p_2 + b_1. \qquad (62)$$

We then solve (62) for p_2 and substitute the result into (61):

$$1 = wa_2 + [wa_1 + wa_0(1+r) - b_1](1+r). \qquad (63)$$

Finally, we rewrite (63) and find

$$1 + b_1(1+r) = wa_2 + wa_1(1+r) + wa_0(1+r)^2$$

or

$$\frac{1}{(1+r)^2} + \frac{b_1}{(1+r)} = \frac{wa_2}{(1+r)^2} + \frac{wa_1}{(1+r)} + a_0$$

or

$$0 = [0 - wa_0] + \left[\frac{b_1 - wa_1}{(1+r)}\right] + \left[\frac{1 - wa_2}{(1+r)^2}\right]. \qquad (63a)$$

But (63a) is *equivalent* to Hicks' equilibrium condition that the present discounted value of the production process (58), k_0, must equal zero! (See equation (2) in Section III.)

It is evident that the interpretation just described is valid for any process $\{(a_t, b_t)\}_{t=0}^{n}$, as discussed in Section II. However, some care must be taken when we write the system in the usual vector-matrix notation for a von Neumann model. The *input matrix* is

$$\begin{bmatrix} a_0 & a_1 & a_2 \\ - & - & - \\ 0 & 1 & 0 \\ 0 & 0 & 1 \\ 0 & 0 & 0 \end{bmatrix} = \begin{bmatrix} A_0 \\ A \end{bmatrix}. \qquad (64)$$

Columns represent activities 1, 2, and 3, respectively, and rows represent the inputs required to operate the respective activities at the unit intensity level. Such labor requirements are designated by the row vector $A_0 = (a_0, a_1, a_2)$, while rows 1, 2, and 3 of the matrix A represent requirements of new machines, one-year-old machines, and consumption goods, respectively. Row 3 of A is (0, 0, 0) because consumption goods are not inputs for any production activity.

The corresponding *output matrix* is

$$\begin{bmatrix} 1 & 0 & 0 \\ 0 & 1 & 0 \\ 0 & b_1 & 1 \end{bmatrix} = B. \qquad (65)$$

An element b_{ij} of B represents the output of commodity i from the j-th activity operated at the unit intensity level. Note that activity 2 involves joint production; one-year-old machines and consumption goods are produced together.

Let the row vector

$$p = (p_1 \;\; p_2 \;\; 1)$$

designate the prices defined previously. In a steady-state equilibrium (when commodities 1, 2, and 3 are produced in positive quantities), if all three activities are operated at positive intensity levels, then the von Neumann inequalities

$$wA_0 + p(1+r)A \geqq pB \quad (\text{with } p \geqq 0, p \neq 0) \tag{66}$$

are replaced by equalities and the condition

$$wA_0 = p[B-(1+r)A] \quad (\text{with } p > 0) \tag{67}$$

must be satisfied. Provided $[B-(1+r)A]^{-1}$ exists, we may calculate the equilibrium price vector

$$p = wA_0[B-(1+r)A]^{-1}. \tag{68}$$

For this example,

$$[B-(1+r)A]^{-1} = \begin{bmatrix} 1 & \frac{(1+r)}{1+b_1(1+r)} & \frac{(1+r)^2}{1+b_1(1+r)} \\ 0 & \frac{1}{1+b_1(1+r)} & \frac{(1+r)}{1+b_1(1+r)} \\ 0 & -\frac{b_1}{1+b_1(1+r)} & \frac{1}{1+b_1(1+r)} \end{bmatrix}, \tag{69}$$

and we find, from (68), that

$$p_1 = wa_0, \tag{70}$$

$$p_2 = \frac{wa_0(1+r)}{1+b_1(1+r)} + \frac{wa_1}{1+b_1(1+r)} - \frac{wb_1a_2}{1+b_1(1+r)}, \tag{71}$$

and

$$p_3 = 1 = \frac{wa_0(1+r)^2}{1+b_1(1+r)} + \frac{wa_1(1+r)}{1+b_1(1+r)} + \frac{wa_2}{1+b_1(1+r)}. \tag{72}$$

Clearly (59) and (70) are identical, and it is quickly verified that (72) is equivalent to (63) or (63a). But what are we to make of (71)? The mathematical operation of calculating $[B-(1+r)A]^{-1}$ tends to obscure the economic meaning of the production process; equations (71) and (72) must be considered *simultaneously* because activity 2 involves the joint production of one-year-old machines *and* consumption goods. The appropriate value of a one-year-old machine therefore must reflect *its* value, properly discounted, in the production of consumption goods using activity 3. Thus combining (71) and (72) we can derive

$$p_2 + \frac{wb_1a_2}{1+b_1(1+r)} = \frac{wa_0(1+r)}{1+b_1(1+r)} + \frac{wa_1}{1+b_1(1+r)} = \frac{1}{1+r}\left[1 - \frac{wa_2}{1+b_1(1+r)}\right]$$

or

$$p_2 = \frac{1}{1+r} - \frac{\frac{wa_2}{(1+r)} + \frac{wb_1a_2(1+r)}{(1+r)}}{1+b_1(1+r)}$$

or

$$p_2 = \frac{1}{1+r} - \frac{wa_2}{1+r}. \tag{73}$$

Now, just as (60) explains the equilibrium price of a one-year-old machine in terms of "cost," (73) tells us that the price p_2 must equal the present discounted value of the future *net* output which a one-year-old machine can produce. To prove the equivalence of these two interpretations, take (72) and derive

$$1+b_1(1+r) = wa_0(1+r)^2 + wa_1(1+r) + wa_2$$

or

$$\frac{1}{1+r} + b_1 = wa_0(1+r) + wa_1 + \frac{wa_2}{1+r}$$

or

$$\frac{1}{1+r} + b_1 - \frac{wa_2}{1+r} = wa_0(1+r) + wa_1. \tag{74}$$

Then combining (73) and (74), we obtain

$$p_2 + b_1 = wa_0(1+r) + wa_1, \tag{75}$$

which is identical with (62).

Several important conclusions emerge from this discussion:

1) The alternative interpretations of

the price p_2 are analogous to Hicks' forward-looking and backward-looking measures of capital.[72] These two measures must be equal in a steady-state equilibrium [27, 1973, p. 23 and p. 167].

2) We can now appreciate the Hicks' remarks, quoted earlier, about the von Neumann model:

> the categories with which it works are not very recognizable as economic categories; so to make economic sense of its propositions translation is required. One has got so far away from the regular economic concepts that the translation is not at all an easy matter [27, 1973, p. 6].

Hopefully this simple example helps provide an appropriate translation of a few economic concepts.

3) The neo-Austrian model is a very special case of a general von Neumann approach.[73]

4) The "new machine" produced by activity 1, as well as the "one-year-old machine" produced by activity 2, may be purely fictitious in nature [33, Morishima, pp. 91–94, especially the bottom of p. 92].[74]

5) Even if machines do exist in a physical sense, there need not be any market for them. Nevertheless, a firm operating the process described by equation (58) must impute shadow prices equal to the p_1 and p_2 we have calculated; otherwise the process would not have a zero present discounted value in steady-state equilibrium.

6) Once the appropriate economic translation has been completed, we are in a position to apply all the mathematical results which have been proved for the von Neumann case to the neo-Austrian model. This feature becomes especially important if one attempts a generalization of the neo-Austrian model to include many heterogeneous inputs and outputs. Such a generalization is more technical, and a brief sketch is given in the Appendix.

XXI. *An Interpretation of a Neo-Austrian Model as a Sectoral Leontief-Sraffa Model*

In the mathematical appendix to *Capital and time,* Hicks derives the dynamic difference equations which govern the motion of the system during the Preliminary Phase, the Early Phase, and the Late Phase. In the Standard Case, every process has a construction period lasting m weeks and a

[72] See p. 23, Chapter III, and most importantly, the discussion in Chapter XIV, "The Accumulation of Capital" [27, 1973].

[73] The neo-Austrian approach implies that the von Neumann input and output matrices must have a very specialized and restrictive pattern of zero elements.

[74] Presumably a "fictitious" capital good is one which need not exist in a physical sense. If this meaning is intended, it is dubious whether or not the concept is useful in capital theory. Consider the common example of a wine-aging process. Suppose that plentiful grape juice is free, but it takes one unit of labor working one time period to prepare grape juice for aging; then, without further labor inputs, aging for two additional time periods yields one unit of wine. In the notation of the neo-Austrian model, this production process is represented by

$$\{(a_t, b_t)\}_{t=0}^{n} = \{(1, 0), (0, 0), (0, 1)\}$$

where $a_0 = 1$ is the initial input of labor and $b_2 = 1$ is the final output of wine at the end of the third period; since raw grape juice is free, labor is the only factor of production with a positive price.

As before, suppose this process is started at calendar time $\tau = 0$; consider time $\tau = 2$, the end of the second production period. At time $\tau = 2$ the grape juice has been aged for one time period. Do we require any "fictitious" capital good? The answer is clearly, "No," because "grape juice aged-for-one-period" is a perfectly well-defined commodity which exists in a physical sense and which in principle could be traded in a competitive market.

Sometimes a model is formulated with the implicit (or perhaps explicit) assertion that some "fictitious" goods do not exist. Thus consider the example discussed in Sections II and XX where a_0 workers produced one "machine of type 1" in the first period. Must some "machine of type 1" exist? Suppose not. The a_0 workers are employed for one time period (from calendar time $\tau = 0$ to $\tau = 1$), and assume there is an explosion (any physically-destructive natural disaster will serve for my purposes) at time $\tau = 1$. Is the destruction of workers the *only* conceivable eventuality which would harm the production process, *i.e.*, which would diminish the feasible future stream $\{(a_t, b_t)\}$ for $t > 0$? In every realistic case I can imagine, the a_0 workers must produce *some* physical commodity which is in existence at time $\tau = 1$ and which, in principle, could be destroyed by an explosion; we are free to name this commodity a "machine of type 1."

utilization period lasting $(\Omega - m)$ weeks; moreover, Ω is an integral multiple of m. This enables Hicks to cast his three difference equations in an especially convenient form where the construction period is one "year" and the utilization period is n "years" in length, each year consisting of m "weeks."[75]

Alternatively, suppose the construction period of m weeks is longer than the utilization period of $(\Omega - m)$ weeks, and assume that m is an integral multiple of $(\Omega - m)$. We may then define $(\Omega - m)$ weeks as one "year" and consider a constructional period of n "years."[76] With this (apparently) minor change, the Simple Profile is:

	construction period	*utilization period*
years	0 to $n - 1$	n
inputs	a_0	a_1
outputs	0	1
net output	$-wa_0$	$1 - wa_1$

Thus Hicks' equations (5.4) become

$$\text{(EP)} \qquad a_0 x_0 = a_0^* x_0^*, \qquad T = 0, \qquad (76)$$

$$\text{(PP)} \quad a_0 \sum_{t=T-n+1}^{T} x_t + a_1 \sum_{t=0}^{T-n} x_t = a_0^* \sum_{t=T-n+1}^{T} x_t^* + a_1^* \sum_{t=0}^{T-n} x_t^*, \qquad (77)$$

$$T = 1, 2, \ldots, n-1,$$

and

$$\text{(LP)} \quad a_0 \sum_{t=T-n+1}^{T} x_t + a_1 x_{T-n} = A_T^*, \qquad (78)$$

$$T = n, n+1, n+2, \ldots$$

[27, 1973, p. 187].

Although this modification may appear minor, in fact it is not; now *all* problems of joint production can be avoided. We can follow the approach taken in Section XX, but with the additional simplification that the output matrix, B, is an identity matrix. Hence we have a Leontief-Sraffa technology in which every column of the input matrix unambiguously can be associated with a single output; column 1 is the activity for producing "new machines," column j is the activity for producing "machines of age $(j - 1)$," and column n is the activity producing final consumption goods (using machines of age $(n - 1)$ and labor). With this modification of Hicks' Standard Case, the neo-Austrian approach becomes a special case of a standard Leontief-Sraffa model, and the latter, in turn, is a special no-joint production case of the von Neumann approach.

XXII. *Joint Production and Merger*

Of course, a Leontief-Sraffa model also has an interpretation as a sectoral model because, as already noted, each column of the input matrix can be associated with a single output. We may choose to identify outputs with "sectors" of the economy, as we do when speaking of a "consumption-good sector;" but this is not necessary. Nothing precludes the possibility that a single competitive "firm" may produce two (or more) different commodities. However, in the absence of joint production, such integration entails no cost-saving because a "firm" producing two commodities behaves identically to the simple aggregation of two different "firms," each producing a single commodity.

It must be emphasized that the assumption of no-joint production is indeed very strong, and sometimes it may be inconsistent with the existence of strictly intermediate factors which are used only for the production of a final consumption good. For example, when the activity $(a_{01}, a_{11}, \ldots, a_{n1}) = (a_{i1})$ is employed to produce commodity 1 if, and only if, commodity 2

[75] See equations (5.4) [27, 1973, p. 187].

[76] This redefinition of time units, while simple in principle, is potentially confusing. Hicks assumes that $(\Omega - m) = nm$ for some integer $n \geqq 1$; equivalently, $\Omega = (n + 1)m$. Then he defines m weeks = 1 year and $(\Omega - m)$ weeks = n years.

I have assumed $m = n(\Omega - m)$ for some integer $n \geqq 1$. Then defining $(\Omega - m)$ weeks = 1 year, it follows that m weeks = n years.

is produced by the activity $(a_{02}, a_{12}, \ldots, a_{n2}) = (a_{i2})$, the technological necessity that these two input vectors—(a_{i1}) and (a_{i2})—always appear as a pair entails essential joint production. This difficulty is avoided if we can construct a *new* technology (which is free of joint production) by merging the activities for producing the various commodities. And the situation just described certainly provides an example of an economically natural vertical integration.

A specific example is easier to understand. Suppose that the three activities

$$\begin{bmatrix} a_{01} \\ \hline a_{11} \\ a_{21} \\ a_{31} \\ a_{41} \end{bmatrix} = \begin{bmatrix} .3 \\ \hline .2 \\ .1 \\ .3 \\ 0 \end{bmatrix}, \quad \begin{bmatrix} a_{02} \\ \hline a_{12} \\ a_{22} \\ a_{32} \\ a_{42} \end{bmatrix} = \begin{bmatrix} .3 \\ \hline .4 \\ .3 \\ .1 \\ 0 \end{bmatrix},$$

and

$$\begin{bmatrix} a_{03} \\ \hline a_{13} \\ a_{23} \\ a_{33} \\ a_{43} \end{bmatrix} = \begin{bmatrix} .31 \\ \hline .2 \\ .2 \\ .1 \\ 0 \end{bmatrix}$$

must always be used in combination. Likewise assume that the three alternative activities

$$\begin{bmatrix} a'_{01} \\ \hline a'_{11} \\ a'_{21} \\ a'_{31} \\ a'_{41} \end{bmatrix} = \begin{bmatrix} .3 \\ \hline .2 \\ 0 \\ .3 \\ .2 \end{bmatrix}, \quad \begin{bmatrix} a'_{03} \\ \hline a'_{13} \\ a'_{23} \\ a'_{33} \\ a'_{43} \end{bmatrix} = \begin{bmatrix} .3 \\ \hline .2 \\ 0 \\ .1 \\ .4 \end{bmatrix},$$

and

$$\begin{bmatrix} a'_{04} \\ \hline a'_{14} \\ a'_{24} \\ a'_{34} \\ a'_{44} \end{bmatrix} = \begin{bmatrix} .25 \\ \hline .1 \\ 0 \\ .1 \\ .2 \end{bmatrix}$$

also must always be used in combination. There are two alternative production techniques open to the economy, namely

$$\begin{bmatrix} .3 & .3 & .31 & 0 \\ \hline .2 & .4 & .2 & 0 \\ .1 & .3 & .2 & 0 \\ .3 & .1 & .1 & 0 \\ 0 & 0 & 0 & 0 \end{bmatrix} \quad (\text{technique } \alpha)$$

and

$$\begin{bmatrix} .3 & 0 & .3 & .25 \\ \hline .2 & 0 & .2 & .1 \\ 0 & 0 & 0 & 0 \\ .3 & 0 & .1 & .1 \\ .2 & 0 & .4 & .2 \end{bmatrix} \quad (\text{technique } \beta).$$

Steady-state prices (with the wage rate as *numeraire*) of commodities one and three using technique α are denoted by $p_1^\alpha(r)$ and $p_3^\alpha(r)$, while the corresponding prices using technique β are $p_1^\beta(r)$ and $p_3^\beta(r)$. If a value of r is given, will technique α or β be employed? Suppose that the only final output is commodity one (the single good which can be used for consumption), and consequently only *its* cost of production, $p_1(r)$, determines the choice of technique.

For this example it is easily calculated that

$$p_1^\alpha(0) = .7714 < p_1^\beta(0) = .7727 \tag{79}$$

and

$$p_3^\alpha(0) = .7323 > p_3^\beta(0) = .7273; \tag{80}$$

thus technique α will be selected when $r = 0$.[77] Although $p_3^\alpha(0) > p_3^\beta(0)$, this fact is irrelevant for the choice of technique because commodity three is a strictly intermediate factor of production. In general, technique α will be selected for all values of r such that $p_1^\alpha(r) < p_1^\beta(r)$, while technique β will be selected for all values of r such that $p_1^\alpha(r) > p_1^\beta(r)$. Because the other "industries" do not matter for production decisions, we may "aggregate" the technology into two alternative activities for producing commodity one.

[77] I am grateful to Carl Palash and Peter Simon of the University of Pennsylvania for calculating this numerical example.

The essence of this example is joint production; without joint production, *the activity columns of the technique matrix always can be selected independently*. Here this possibility is denied, and techniques such as

$$\begin{bmatrix} .3 & .3 & .3 & .25 \\ \hdashline .2 & .4 & .2 & .1 \\ .1 & .3 & 0 & 0 \\ .3 & .1 & .1 & .1 \\ 0 & 0 & .4 & .2 \end{bmatrix} \quad \text{(technique } \gamma\text{)}$$

are excluded.[78]

XXIII. *Substitution and Stability*

Either with or without joint production, the possibility of substitution—that is, the possibility that there may exist many alternative production processes or activities—is a serious complication. For simplicity, I will restrict my remarks to models without joint production, and as we have seen in Section XXI, some special cases of the neo-Austrian model can be interpreted within this framework.

How should we depict the feasible set of input vectors which can be used to produce the j-th commodity? Neoclassical theory provides one convenient representation. Any input vector $(a_{0j}, a_{1j}, \ldots, a_{ij}, \ldots, a_{nj})$ must satisfy

$$1 = F^j(a_{0j}, a_{1j}, \ldots, a_{nj}), \quad j = 1, \ldots, n, \quad (81)$$

where a_{ij} is the quantity of the i-th input required to produce a unit output of commodity j, and where $F^j(\cdot)$ is a neoclassical production function.[79] While there is an extensive literature on this subject, almost all of it is concerned with optimizing models.[80] Most descriptive economic models are in the tradition of Hahn's seminal contribution and incorporate the assumption that price expectations always are correct;[81] as Hicks has stated, such an assumption is most dubious in positive economics.[82]

Unfortunately, many of the viable alternatives are not very palatable either, but I can briefly sketch a few preliminary results for a model which, at least in some respects, is similar to Hicks' and which combines some features of the Fixwage model with others from the Full Employment model.[83] Assume that the labor supply grows at an exogenous rate g and is fully employed, and let the saving hypothesis set the rate of interest at a constant value, γ. Of course, no simple saving rule will generate a dynamic path along which the rate of interest is constant, but this simplification allows an analysis which is tractable, and it does provide a firm basis for comparing future results derived with alternative assumptions. All prices are measured in terms of the (single) consumption good as *numeraire*. At any moment in time prices are known, while expected future prices determine the current production decisions. It is convenient to work in con-

[78] If the quantity produced of a commodity is not positive, we may adopt the convention that its steady-state equilibrium cost of production and price are zero. With this convention we must modify the wording of the standard nonsubstitution theorem to assert that the prices of all goods *produced in positive quantities* are simultaneously minimized (except for possible ties) in steady-state price equilibrium. In this example, technique γ provides such a simultaneous minimum to $p_1(r), \ldots, p_4(r)$ at $r=0$. While $p_4^\alpha = p_2^\beta = 0$ because commodity 4 is not produced when technique α is employed and commodity 2 is not produced when technique β is employed, we have $p_i^\gamma(r) < p_i^\alpha(r)$ and $p_i^\gamma(r) < p_i^\beta(r)$ at $r = 0$ for commodities $i = 1, 3$. Likewise $p_4^\gamma(r) < p_4^\beta(r)$ and $p_2^\gamma(r) < p_2^\alpha(r)$ at $r = 0$.

A more satisfactory treatment of commodities which are not produced is possible using the von Neumann approach described in the Appendix. We can then avoid the convention of zero prices for non-produced commodities; if the cost of operating an activity exceeds its revenue, then that activity is shutdown. (In this example an activity can be associated unambiguously with the production of a single commodity.)

[79] See Burmeister and Dobell for a definition of a neo-classical production function [11, 1970, pp. 8–10].

[80] See Burmeister and Dobell, Chapter 11, for a list of references [11, 1970].

[81] See Hahn and Burmeister, Caton, Dobell, and Ross, and the references cited there [20, 1966; 15, 1973].

[82] See the quotation and footnote 57.

[83] The results reported below are proved in Burmeister and Graham [16, 1974].

tinuous time, but this necessitates a fundamental change in the usual adaptive-type expectation mechanism which generates expected price levels [16, Burmeister and Graham, 1974].

With sufficiently strong assumptions, rental rates and the wage rate (or factor prices) are determined uniquely by commodity prices.[84] Under these exceptional conditions, the movement of expected prices is determined simultaneously from the expectation equations and portfolio equilibrium equations. Thus the paths of expected and actual prices are independent of the quantity equations, and provided initial prices lie in a certain set, the price system will converge asymptotically to a unique steady-state equilibrium.

As noted, along the actual path factor prices are determined, and these in turn determine the optimal activity vectors $(a_{0j}, a_{1j}, \ldots, a_{nj}), j = 1, \ldots, n$, which must satisfy (81). Because prices converge, the activity vectors converge to a technique matrix. But now, provided the initial quantities also lie in a specified set, quantities will converge to their unique steady-state equilibrium values.[85]

The stability results just described necessitate very strong assumptions which bear a striking resemblance to those which Hicks makes. First, expectations must not adjust too fast, which is a slightly weaker version of his static expectations. Second, the activity vectors form a matrix of input coefficients which must satisfy certain "capital intensity" restrictions at *every* point along the dynamic path; the latter restrictions seem analogous to the Hicks stability condition $a_0 > a_1$. These facts again suggest that alternative capital models share a common underlying logical structure. The problem is to isolate those common features which are of economic significance.

XIV. *Traditional Controversies*

The concluding three chapters in *Capital and time* contain discussions of three controversies in capital theory: the measurement of capital, the accumulation of capital, and the production function. Hicks now reveals his sympathy for the macro theorist and the applied economist:

> Consider (for a closed economy) the stock of real goods, commodities having value, that exists at a moment of time. Many economists would be prepared to identify that stock with the Capital of the economy; all, I think, would admit that the Capital stands in some relation to it. But even those who accept the identification will grant that for macroeconomic purposes we need some single measure, by which the stock can be represented. All that we get from the physical goods is a list – so much of this, so much of that; for macroeconomics there must be aggregation [27, 1973, p. 151].

Hicks discusses index number problems associated with the concepts of *capital value* and *capital volume*. He then proceeds to demonstrate how these aggregates behave along particular Traverses for which the actual microeconomic behavior is known. Finally, he turns to what he regards as "the nub of the Controversy: the Production Function itself" [27, 1973, p. 177]. While at one time the existence of an aggregate production function may have been a central issue, it is difficult to maintain that view today. Certainly an aggregate production function is not accepted as a rigorous theoretical concept, and perhaps the matter of its empirical usefulness is best resolved by the econometricians. My own view coincides with Solow's, expressed in his 1966 review of Hicks' *Capital and growth:*

[84] The conditions which are sufficient for this result imply that certain severe capital intensity restrictions are satisfied at all factor price ratios.

[85] Note that these stability results fall short of Hicks' analyses of Traverses in his neo-Austrian models. First, we do not (necessarily) start from an initial steady-state equilibrium, but rather asymptotic convergence to a steady-state equilibrium is proved provided initial prices and quantities belong to a specified set. Second, we only prove stability and do not solve explicitly for the dynamic path. See Burmeister and Graham [16, 1974].

> I have never thought of the macroeconomic production function as a rigorously justifiable concept. In my mind it is either an illuminating parable, or else a mere device for handling data, to be used so long as it gives good empirical results, and to be abandoned as soon as it doesn't, or as soon as something better comes along [46, 1966, pp. 1259–60].

There is one controversial issue which Hicks does not mention. If an economy is in a steady-state equilibrium with the rate of interest exceeding the rate of growth ($r > g$), and if the economy completes a Traverse to a new steady-state equilibrium with a higher rate of interest, is it true that steady-state per capita consumption must always fall? Or is "paradoxical consumption behavior" possible, *i.e.*, can the second steady-state equilibrium with a higher rate of interest also have a higher level of per capita consumption? One of the few positive conclusions emerging from the discussions of reswitching is a definite answer to this question. "Paradoxical consumption behavior," as just defined, *is* possible; moreover, it is possible *without* reswitching [6, Bruno, Burmeister, and Sheshinski, 1966, pp. 546–53].[86]

However, it can be proved that such paradoxical consumption behavior is impossible if, and only if, the sum of the changes in per capita stocks, weighted by equilibrium prices, is always negative (or nonpositive) across steady-state equilibria with higher rates of interest.[87] Unfortunately, movements in the measure of the change in capital just described do not necessarily bear any simple relationship to movements in the value of capital, even in models with only two capital goods and Cobb-Douglas production functions [11, Burmeister and Dobell, 1970, Tables 2 and 3, pp. 291–92]. Without severe restrictions, one must be brave indeed to work with a macroeconomic "capital" aggregate!

XXV. *Conclusion*

Alternative approaches to capital theory – the Leontief-Sraffa sectoral models, joint production models in the von Neumann tradition, and the neo-Austrian formulations – share numerous common features. In all instances, we have found concepts such as the factor-price frontier and price-quantity duality relationships, as well as complications such as the existence of joint production and reswitching. The selection of an appropriate model depends upon the particular set of economic problems under investigation. If our attention is focused only on steady-state properties, the most important issue is whether or not the technology involves (essential) joint production. The analysis of dynamic paths and their stability is more difficult, and conclusions may be acutely sensitive to the exact specification of the model; in particular, the savings hypothesis and the formation of price expectations are both crucial.

The primary advantage of the neo-Austrian approach is pedagogical; the analysis of simple problems using Hicks' Standard Case serves to deepen our comprehension of many economic principles. Thus, for example, within this context, we have again demonstrated the validity of a fundamental duality relationship between the factor-price frontier (or the minimum wage frontier) and the optimal transformation frontier. Likewise, we have discussed a new classification for inventions which enables us to study the incidence of technological change, and although no definitive conclusions emerged,

[86] Here "consumption" refers to either a single commodity or a fixed basket of commodities.

[87] More formally, let $x_i > 0$ denote the per capita stock of the i-th capital good, and let c denote per capita consumption. Then $sgn(dc/dr) = sgn(g - r) \neq 0$ at $r \neq g$ *if, and only if,*

$$\sum_{i=1}^{n} p_i(dx_i/dr) < 0.$$

See Burmeister and Turnovsky [14, 1972, especially p. 846].

it does provide a basis for further work. Similarly the stability results established for the neo-Austrian Standard Case are not of general validity, but they are suggestive of the extreme complexity one would encounter without simplifying assumptions.

When interpreted properly—"When translated into economic terms," Hicks might say—the von Neumann approach yields all the insights derived from both the neo-Austrian and Leontief-Sraffa models (see Section XX and the Appendix). Moreover, the extreme generality of the von Neumann formulation, modified to include primary factors and final consumption, makes this approach preferable for reasons other than its logical elegance; the von Neumann method allows us to study important aspects of capital theory which are impossible to capture in a neo-Austrian model (see Section II and the Appendix). Finally a variation of Hicks' Standard Case excluding joint production can be interpreted as a specialized Leontief-Sraffa sectoral model (Section XXI), and the latter, in turn, is also a special case of a generalized von Neumann model (in which joint production is excluded).

In our effort to attain an understanding of the most basic fundamentals of pure capital theory, many topics have been omitted. There is no quarrel with those who believe that transaction costs, uncertainty, non-competitive behavior, unemployment, disequilibrium adjustment mechanisms, and the distribution of income are significant issues. For example, the existence of uncertainty about both new commodities and the feasible technology set (the set of production processes) that will be available in the future presents a formidable problem which is crucial for the development of capital theory and which involves aspects of all the above issues. In general, the invention of a new commodity or a new production process will create proprietary information held by a subset of economic agents. Such situations can be exploited by non-competitive actions; indeed, the very concept of competitive behavior (*and* of intertemporal efficiency) becomes ambiguous. Under these circumstances the initial disequilibrium and the resulting non-competitive profits may disappear over time as knowledge of the new technology diffuses throughout the economy, thereby justifying Schumpeter's notion of entrepreneurial profits. However, no matter where we focus our attention, the generalized von Neumann model not only facilitates our comprehension of theoretical principles, but it also provides a promising framework within which to analyze more complex economic phenomena.

APPENDIX

A Generalized von Neumann Model

The von Neumann approach discussed in Section XX is easily generalized.[1] We now suppose that there are m alternative activities for producing the n different commodities ($m \gtreqless n$). Activity j operating at the unit intensity level requires a labor input a_{0j} and a vector of commodity inputs $(a_{1j}, \ldots, a_{nj})$ to produce a vector of commodity outputs $(b_{1j}, \ldots, b_{nj})$. In this generalization only one primary factor, labor, is admitted, and the row vector

$$A_0 = (a_{01}, \ldots, a_{0m})$$

designates the labor requirements for the m alternative activities.[2] The input matrix is

$$A = \begin{bmatrix} a_{11} & \cdots & a_{1m} \\ \cdot & & \cdot \\ \cdot & & \cdot \\ \cdot & & \cdot \\ a_{n1} & \cdots & a_{nm} \end{bmatrix},$$

the output matrix is

$$B = \begin{bmatrix} b_{11} & \cdots & b_{1m} \\ \cdot & & \cdot \\ \cdot & & \cdot \\ \cdot & & \cdot \\ b_{n1} & \cdots & b_{nm} \end{bmatrix},$$

and the column vector

$$x = \begin{bmatrix} x_1 \\ \cdot \\ \cdot \\ \cdot \\ x_m \end{bmatrix}$$

gives the intensity levels at which each of the m activities are operated. While in general some of the a_{0j}'s, a_{ij}'s, and b_{ij}'s may be zero, for expositional simplicity I assume here that they are all positive.[3]

[1] The original von Neumann model appeared in the German article [35, 1938]. A modern exposition is contained in Burmeister and Dobell [11, 1970, Chapters 8 and 10], and references are cited there to numerous mathematical and economic refinements. Morishima provides more detailed analyses of various economic models formulated in a von Neumann framework [33, 1969].

Karlin generalized the von Neumann model to admit nonlinear joint production functions and gave a simple proof of the von Neumann theorem [28, 1959]; a summary is contained in Burmeister and Dobell [11, 1970, pp. 207–213].

[2] Several primary factors easily can be incorporated into this framework. The model given here is similar to that in Burmeister and Kuga [12, 1970], and it may be regarded as a special case of Malinvaud's approach; see footnote 71.

[3] Of course, this simplification precludes an intertemporal néo-Austrian interpretation which necessitates a special pattern of zero elements in the A and B matrices; see footnote 73.

In particular, an intertemporal interpretation (as given in Section XX) is possible when we can identify activity j with the j-th period of production. However, caution is required. Activity j "precedes" activity $(j + 1)$ by one time period if

$$a_{iu} = 0,\ u \neq j + 1;\ a_{i,j+1} > 0$$

and

$$b_{ij} > 0;\ b_{iu} = 0,\ u \neq j,$$

for at least one commodity i, say $i = s$. Thus commodity s is unique to activities j and $(j + 1)$; it is produced only by activity j and is used as an input only by activity $(j + 1)$. One-year-old wine can exemplify such a commodity if it is produced only by activity one in the first time period and is used only by activity two in the second time period (to produce two-year-old wine).

Again note that unless such a commodity s exists in a physical sense, there is no logical reason why activity $(j + 1)$ must "follow" activity j. In other words, if activity one (operated in period one) produces *no* commodity which is required for the operation of activity α in period two, *then activity α could be operated in period one*. Note also that such a commodity s cannot be identified as "knowledge" because the model is free of technological uncertainty; the entire feasible technology set is known at time zero and cannot be changed.

This discussion leads to another important observation. The assumption that the von Neumann activities may be operated at zero intensity levels implies that truncation is possible. Thus consider the numerical example in Section XX and suppose $a_2 > (1/w)$. From equation (73) we see that the price of a one-year-old machine would be negative, which is im-

Finally, let the column vector

$$C = \begin{bmatrix} C_1 \\ \cdot \\ \cdot \\ \cdot \\ C_n \end{bmatrix}$$

represent consumption of final commodities, and let the single primary factor (labor) grow at the exogenous rate $g \geqq 0$.

The economy is capable of growth at the rate g provided the inequalities

$$(1+g)\sum_{j=1}^{m} a_{ij}x_j \leqq \sum_{j=1}^{m} b_{ij}x_j - C_i, \quad i = 1, \ldots, n, \qquad \text{(A1)}$$

have a solution with both $x_j \geqq 0$ and $C_i \geqq 0$, and with not all $x_j = 0$, not all $C_i = 0$. Equation (A1) has the straight-forward interpretation that the part of this period's output which is *not* consumed must equal or exceed the input requirements to produce output (allowing for growth at the rate g) in the next period. In standard vector-matrix notation, the quantity system (A1) is written as

$$(1+g)Ax \leqq Bx - C, \quad C, x \geqq 0, \; C, x \neq 0, \qquad \text{(A2)}$$

while the labor constraint takes the trivial form

$$(1+g)A_0x = (1+g)A_0x. \qquad \text{(A3)}$$

Prices of the n commodities are given by the row vector

$$p = (p_1, \ldots, p_n), \quad \sum_{i=1}^{n} p_i = 1,$$

the wage rate is w, and the steady-state profit or interest rate is $r \geqq 0$. Analogous to (A2) and (A3), the economy can achieve a steady-state equilibrium at a given value of r if the "dual" von Neumann price system has a solution satisfying

$$wA_0 + (1+r)pA \geqq pB, \quad w, p \geqq 0, \; p \neq 0. \qquad \text{(A4)}$$

Moreover, if the cost of operating an activity exceeds its revenue, that activity is shut-down (is operated at a zero intensity level). Thus

$$x_j = 0 \text{ if } wa_{0j} + (1+r)\sum_{i=1}^{n} p_i a_{ij} > \sum_{i=1}^{n} p_i b_{ij}, \quad j = 1, \ldots, m. \qquad \text{(A5)}$$

Similarly, if an activity is operated at a positive intensity level, then revenue must exactly cover cost and

$$wa_{0j} + (1+r)\sum_{i=1}^{n} p_i a_{ij} = \sum_{i=1}^{n} p_i b_{ij} \text{ if } x_j > 0, \quad j = 1, \ldots, m. \qquad \text{(A6)}$$

Likewise the price of a commodity is zero if it is in excess supply; and if a commodity has a positive price, its supply and demand are equal. Thus

$$p_i = 0 \text{ if } (1+g)\sum_{j=1}^{m} a_{ij}x_j < \sum_{j=1}^{m} b_{ij}x_j - C_i, \quad i = 1, \ldots, n, \qquad \text{(A7)}$$

---

possible. Thus if $a_2 > (1/w)$, we cannot replace (66) by (67); the correct steady-state solution involves essential inequalities. The price of a one-year-old machine is zero ($p_2 = 0$), while one-year-old machines are not used because the third activity is not operated ($x_3 = 0$). Therefore the process is truncated at the end of the second production period.

A similar result holds in general. Given the structure of zeros we have imposed for our intertemporal interpretation, $x_j = 0$ for activity j implies that $x_u = 0$ for all $u = j+1, \ldots, m$. This result follows immediately from the fact that activity $(j+1)$ requires an output produced by, and only by, activity j. Accordingly, the process is truncated at the end of period $(j-1)$ where $x_{j-1} > 0$ and $x_u = 0$, $u = j, j+1, \ldots, m$.

Finally, here we have considered only a time sequence of single activities. The von Neumann model allows a further generalization, and we may define a set of activities J which precedes a set of activities $(J+1)$ by one time period. In this case, of course, some activities in a particular set may be operated at zero intensity levels in a steady-state von Neumann equilibrium.

and

$$(1+g)\sum_{j=1}^{m} a_{ij}x_j = \sum_{j=1}^{m} b_{ij}x_j - C_i \text{ if } p_i > 0, \quad i = 1, \ldots, n. \qquad (A8)$$

In the model just described we have not specified any mechanisms to determine final consumption, savings and investment, or the wage rate. Here we will leave the formulation of a general equilibrium model incomplete. But in whatever manner this model is closed, we can be certain that the presence of heterogeneous capital goods will create severe stability problems, unless, of course, we consider models with an infinite time horizon or unless we abandon descriptive economics and confine our attention to dynamic paths which are in some sense optimal or efficient.[4]

Even without a complete general equilibrium specification, this generalization of the von Neumann model confirms familiar results. Thus combining (A5), (A6), (A7), and (A8) we see that in steady-state equilibrium

$$p(1+g)Ax + pC = pBx = wA_0x + p(1+r)Ax. \qquad (A9)$$

Since $A_0x = L$, note that

$$\frac{pAx}{A_0x} = v$$

is the per capita value of capital, while

$$\frac{pC}{A_0x} = pc$$

is the per capita value of consumption. Hence (A9) may be rewritten as

$$pC = wA_0x + (r-g)pAx \qquad (A10)$$

or

$$pc = w + (r-g)v. \qquad (A11)$$

Clearly (A11) is the generalization of (31), derived in Section XIII, to this von Neumann case with many different consumption goods.

Similarly, suppose (C^1, x^1) and (C^2, x^2) both represent von Neumann equilibria with respect to the price vector p, the wage rate w, and the interest rate r; then (A9) implies

$$p(1+g)Ax^i + pC^i = pBx^i = wA_0x^i + p(1+r)Ax^i, \quad i = 1, 2. \qquad (A12)$$

Let K denote a column vector of capital goods, and define $\Delta C = C^1 - C^2$, $\Delta x = x^1 - x^2$, $K^1 = Ax^1$, $K^2 = Ax^2$, and $\Delta K = K^1 - K^2 = A\,\Delta x$. It follows that

$$p\Delta C = (r-g)p\Delta K, \qquad (A13)$$

and we conclude

$$sgn(p\Delta C) = sgn(g-r) \neq 0 \;\; at \;\; r \neq g \;\; \textit{if, and only if,} \;\; p\Delta K < 0. \qquad (A14)$$

At the end of Section XXIV we discussed paradoxical consumption behavior in models with either a single consumption good or a fixed consumption basket. It is now evident from (A14) that analogous conclusions are valid for a generalized von Neumann model with joint production and heterogeneous consumption goods.[5]

References

1. Akerlof, G. A. "The Market for 'Lemons': Quality Uncertainty and the Market Mechanism," *Quart. J. Econ.*, August 1970, *84*(3), pp. 488–500.
2. Arrow, K. J. and Levhari, D. "Uniqueness of the Internal Rate of Return with Variable Life of Invest-

[4] See, for example, Hahn [20, 1966], Samuelson [42, 1967], Shell and Stiglitz [44, 1967], Heller [22, 1971], Burmeister, Caton, Dobell, and Ross [15, 1973], and Burmeister and Graham [16, 1974].

[5] The statement in footnote 87 is analogous to (A14). Also see Burmeister and Turnovsky [14, 1972, especially p. 846 and pp. 851–53], as well as Brock [4, 1973, pp. 546–47].

ment," *Econ. J.*, Sept. 1969, *79*, pp. 560–66.

3. BROCK, W. A. "On Models of Expectations that Arise From Maximizing Behavior of Economic Agents over Time," *J. Econ. Theory*, Dec. 1972, *5*(3), pp. 348–76.
4. ———, "Some Results on the Uniqueness of Steady States in Multisector Models of Optimum Economic Growth When Future Utilities Are Discounted," *Int. Econ. Rev.*, Oct. 1973, *14*(3), pp. 535–59.
5. BRUNO, M. "Fundamental Duality Relations in the Pure Theory of Capital and Growth," *Rev. Econ. Stud.*, Jan. 1969, *36*(1), No. 105, pp. 39–53.
6. ———; BURMEISTER, E. AND SHESHINSKI, E. "The Nature and Implications of the Reswitching of Techniques," *Quart. J. Econ.*, Nov. 1966, *80*(4), pp. 526–53.
7. ———; ——— AND ———, "The Badly Behaved Production Function: Comment," *Quart. J. Econ.*, August 1968, *82*, pp. 524–25.
8. BURMEISTER, E. "On a Theorem of Sraffa," *Economica*, N.S., Feb. 1968, *35*, pp. 83–87.
9. ——— AND SHESHINSKI, E. "A Nonsubstitution Theorem in a Model with Fixed Capital," *Southern Econ. J.*, Jan. 1969, *35*(3), pp. 273–76.
10. ——— AND TAUBMAN, P. "Labour and Non-labour Income Saving Propensities," *Can. J. Econ.*, Feb. 1969, *2*(1), pp. 78–89.
11. ——— AND DOBELL, A. R. *Mathematical theories of economic growth*. New York: Macmillan, 1970.
12. ——— AND KUGA, K. "The Factor-Price Frontier, Duality and Joint Production," *Rev. Econ. Stud.*, Jan. 1970, *37*(109), pp. 11–19.
13. ——— AND ———, "The Factor-Price Frontier in a Neoclassical Multi-Sector Model," *Int. Econ. Rev.*, Feb. 1970, *11*(1), pp. 162–74.
14. ——— AND TURNOVSKY, S. J. "Capital Deepening Response in an Economy with Heterogeneous Capital Goods," *Amer. Econ. Rev.*, Dec. 1972, *62*(5), pp. 842–53.
15. ———; CATON, C.; DOBELL, A. R. AND ROSS, S. A. "The 'Saddlepoint Property' and the Structure of Dynamic Heterogeneous Capital Good Models," *Econometrica*, Jan. 1973, *41*(1), pp. 79–95.
16. ——— AND GRAHAM, D. A. "Multi-Sector Economic Models with Continuous Adaptive Expectations," *Rev. Econ. Stud.*, forthcoming.
17. CASS, D. "On the Wicksellian Point-Input, Point-Output Model of Capital Accumulation: A Modern View (or Neoclassicism Slightly Vindicated)," *J. Polit. Econ.*, Jan./Feb. 1973, *81*(1), pp. 71–97.
18. DORFMAN, R.; SAMUELSON, P. A. AND SOLOW, R. M. *Linear programming and economic analysis*. New York: McGraw-Hill, 1958.
19. FLEMMING, J. S. AND WRIGHT, J. F. "Uniqueness of the Internal Rate of Return: A Generalisation," *Econ. J.*, June 1971, *81*(322), pp. 256–63.
20. HAHN, F. H. "Equilibrium Dynamics with Heterogeneous Capital Goods," *Quart. J. Econ.*, Nov. 1966, *80*(4), pp. 633–46.
21. HARCOURT, G. C. "Some Cambridge Controversies in the Theory of Capital," *J. Econ. Lit.*, June 1969, *7*(2), pp. 369–405.
22. HELLER, W. P. "Disequilibrium Dynamics of Competitive Growth Paths," *Rev. Econ. Stud.*, Oct. 1971, *38*(4), No. 116, pp. 385–400.
23. HICKS, J. R. *Value and capital*. New York and London: Oxford University Press, 1939.
24. ———, *Theory of wages*. 2nd edition. London: Macmillan, [1932] 1963.

25. ———, *Capital and growth.* New York and London: Oxford University Press, 1965.
26. ———, *A theory of economic history.* New York and London: Oxford University Press, 1969.
27. ———, *Capital and time: A neo-Austrian theory.* New York and London: Oxford University Press, 1973.
28. KARLIN, S. *Mathematical methods and theory in games, programming, and economics.* Vols. I and II. Reading, Mass.: Addison-Wesley, 1959.
29. MALINVAUD, E. "Capital Accumulation and Efficient Allocation of Resources," *Econometrica,* April 1953, *21*(2), pp. 233–68.
30. ———, "Efficient Capital Accumulation: A Corrigendum," *Econometrica,* July 1962, *30*(3), pp. 570–73.
31. MIRRLEES, J. A. "The Dynamic Nonsubstitution Theorem," *Rev. Econ. Stud.,* Jan. 1969, *36*(1), pp. 67–76.
32. MORISHIMA, M. *Equilibrium, stability, and growth: A multi-sectoral analysis.* Oxford: Clarendon Press, 1964.
33. ———, *Theory of Economic Growth.* Oxford: Clarendon Press, 1969.
34. MUTH, J. F. "Rational Expectations and the Theory of Price Movements," *Econometrica,* July 1961, *29*(3), pp. 315–35.
35. VON NEUMANN, J. "Über ein Okonomisches Gleichungssystem und eine Verallgemeinerung des Brouwerschen Fixpunktsatzes," *Ergebuisse eines mathematischen seminars.* Edited by MENGER, K., MORGENSTERN, G., translator. Vienna: 1938. English translation: "A Model of General Economic Equilibrium," *Rev. Econ. Stud.,* 1945–46, *13,* pp. 1–9. Reprinted in *Readings in mathematical economics.* Edited by PETER NEWMAN. Vol. II. Baltimore: Johns Hopkins University Press, 1968. Pp. 221–29.
36. "Paradoxes in Capital Theory: A Symposium," *Quart. J. Econ.,* Nov. 1966, *80*(4), pp. 503–83.
37. PIGOU, A. C. *The economics of welfare.* 4th edition. London: Macmillan, 1932.
38. RICARDO, D. *The principles of political economy and taxation.* London: [1911], 1960.
39. SAMUELSON, P. A. "A Modern Treatment of the Ricardian Economy: I. The Pricing of Goods and of Labor and Land Services," *Quart. J. Econ.,* Feb. 1959, *73*(1), pp. 1–35. Reprinted in *The collected scientific papers of Paul A. Samuelson.* Cambridge, Mass.: M.I.T. Press, 1966.
40. ———, "A Modern Treatment of the Ricardian Economy: II. Capital and Interest Aspects of the Pricing Process," *Quart. J. Econ.,* May 1959, *73*(2), pp. 217–31. Reprinted in *The collected scientific papers of Paul A. Samuelson.* Cambridge, Mass.: M.I.T. Press, 1966.
41. ———, "Parable and Realism in Capital Theory: The Surrogate Production Function," *Rev. Econ. Stud.,* June 1962, *29*(3), No. 80, pp. 193–206. Reprinted in *The collected scientific papers of Paul A. Samuelson.* Cambridge, Mass.: M.I.T. Press, 1966.
42. ———, "Indeterminacy of Development in a Heterogeneous-Capital Model with Constant Saving Propensity." In *Essays on the theory of optimal economic growth.* Edited by KARL SHELL. Cambridge: M.I.T. Press, 1967. Pp. 219–31.
43. SEN, A. "The Monotonicity of Capital Value." Mimeographed manuscript, December 1973.
44. SHELL, K. AND STIGLITZ, J. E. "The Allocation of Investment in a Dynamic Economy," *Quart. J. Econ.,* Nov. 1967, *81*(4), pp. 592–609.

45. SOLOW, R. M. AND STIGLITZ, J. E. "Output, Employment, and Wages in the Short Run," *Quart. J. Econ.*, Nov. 1968, *82*(4), pp. 537–60.
46. ———, "*Capital and growth* by John Hicks," *Amer. Econ. Rev.*, Dec. 1966, *61*, pp. 1257–60.
47. SRAFFA, P. *Production of commodities by means of commodities: Prelude to a critique of economic theory.* Cambridge: Cambridge University Press, 1960.
48. STIGLITZ, J. E. "Non-Substitution Theorems with Durable Capital Goods," *Rev. Econ. Stud.*, Oct. 1970, *37*(4), No. 112, pp. 543–70.
49. VON WEIZSÄCKER, C. C. "Bemerkungen zu einem 'Symposium' Über Wachstrumstheorie und Produnktionfunktionen," *Kyklos*, 1963, *16*, pp. 438–57.
50. ———, *Steady state capital theory.* New York: Springer-Verlag, 1971.
51. WICKSELL, K. *Lectures on political economy.* Translated from Swedish by E. CLASSEN. 2 vols. London: Routledge & Kegan Paul, 1934; Clifton, N.J.: Augustus M. Kelley, 1967.

Part IV
Technological Change

[14]

Disembodied Technical Change in a Two-Sector Model[1]

1. *Introduction*

There are two aspects of technical change that are essential for a description of the behavior of an economy over time. These are the rate of technical progress and the bias of the change. For a twice-differentiable production function, $F(K, L, t)$ homogeneous of the first degree, with positive marginal products and a diminishing marginal rate of substitution everywhere, where K is capital; L, labor; t, time; these two aspects can be characterized by two indices:[2]

$$(1) \qquad T = \frac{F_t}{F} = \frac{KF_{Kt} + LF_{Lt}}{KF_K + LF_L},$$

$$(2) \qquad D = \frac{\partial(F_K/F_L)}{\partial t} \Big/ \frac{F_K}{F_L} = \frac{F_{Kt}}{F_K} - \frac{F_{Lt}}{F_L}.$$

Both indices, in general, are functions of both the capital-labor ratio, $k\left(=\frac{K}{L}\right)$, and time.

In a two-sector model the conditions necessary to preserve equilibrium in the factor markets can be expressed in terms of these aspects of the production functions of the two sectors. These conditions can then be used to characterize those types of technical change which permit steady exponential growth, in the labor force, and capital stock in both sectors.

2. *Economic Growth*

In order to describe the time profile of various economic variables, two standard characteristics of a production function will also be used. These are the elasticity of substitution, σ, and the share of capital, π; both of which, in general, are functions of both k and t.

$$(3) \qquad \sigma = -\frac{(dK/L)}{d(F_K/F_L)} \Big/ \frac{K/L}{F_K/F_L} = \frac{F_K F_L}{F F_{KL}},$$

$$(4) \qquad \pi = \frac{F_K K}{F}.$$

A dot over a variable will denote its time derivative.

The definitions of T and D can be solved for F_{Kt} and F_{Lt} giving:

$$(5) \qquad \frac{F_{Kt}}{F} = T + (1 - \pi)D, \quad \frac{F_{Lt}}{F_L} = T - \pi D.$$

[1] The author is indebted to Robert M. Solow for lengthy discussions on this paper. Financial support by the Ford Foundation is gratefully acknowledged. Views and remaining errors are solely the author's.

[2] These are the natural counterparts for a study of economic growth of the indices used to describe changes in unit costs in [5]. For other uses of similar indices see [1], [2].

From the definition of σ we have:

$$\text{(6)} \qquad \frac{\partial F_K}{\partial k} \bigg/ F_K = -\frac{(1-\pi)}{\sigma k}, \quad \frac{\partial F_L}{\partial k} \bigg/ F_L = \frac{\pi}{\sigma k}.$$

Equations (5) and (6) can now be combined to give the rate of growth of the marginal products in terms of the two indices of technical change and the rate of growth of the capital-labor ratio.

$$\text{(7)} \qquad \frac{\dot{F}_K}{F_K} = T + (1-\pi)D - \frac{(1-\pi)}{\sigma}\frac{\dot{k}}{k},$$

$$\text{(8)} \qquad \frac{\dot{F}_L}{F_L} = T - \pi D + \frac{\pi}{\sigma}\frac{\dot{k}}{k}.$$

From equations (7) and (8) can be derived the rates of growth of output and the share of capital.

$$\text{(9)} \qquad \frac{\dot{F}}{F} = T + \pi\frac{\dot{k}}{k} + \frac{\dot{L}}{L},$$

$$\text{(10)} \qquad \frac{\dot{\pi}}{\pi} = (1-\pi)\left(D + \left(1 - \frac{1}{\sigma}\right)\frac{\dot{k}}{k}\right).$$

These relationships between the indices of technical change and the rates of growth of output and marginal products will hold for a one-sector model or for any sector of a multi-sector model of an economy.

These equations can be used to examine the maintenance of factor market equilibrium For the consumption good sector, let $C = F(K_1, L_1, t) = L_1 f(k_1, t)$, $f_k > 0$, $f_{kk} < 0$. For the investment good sector, let $I = G(K_2, L_2, t) = L_2 g(k_2, t)$, $g_k > 0$, $g_{kk} < 0$, both f and g twice differentiable. Let p be the price of the investment good in terms of the consumption good.[1] Preservation of equilibrium in the factor markets requires that the ratios of marginal products for the two sectors remain equal. Since $\frac{1}{\sigma}\frac{\dot{k}}{k} - D$ is the rate of change of this ratio, this condition is:

$$\text{(11)} \qquad \frac{1}{\sigma_1}\frac{\dot{k}_1}{k_1} - D_1 = \frac{1}{\sigma_2}\frac{\dot{k}_2}{k_2} - D_2.$$

Preservation of factor market equilibrium also requires that the wage in consumption units be the same in both sectors. This implies:

$$\text{(12)} \qquad \frac{\dot{p}}{p} = T_1 - T_2 + D_2(\pi_2 - \pi_1) - \frac{(\pi_2 - \pi_1)}{\sigma_2}\frac{\dot{k}_2}{k_2}.$$

[1] Note that the equations in this section will hold for any depreciation assumption for which the rate of depreciation is independent of the use of the capital.

From (9), (11), and (12), the remaining variables can be expressed:

$$\frac{\dot{C}}{C} = \sigma_1\pi_1(D_1 - D_2) + \frac{\pi_1\sigma_1}{\sigma_2}\frac{\dot{k}_2}{k_2} + T_1 + \frac{\dot{L}_1}{L_1}, \tag{13}$$

$$\frac{\dot{I}}{I} = \pi_2\frac{\dot{k}_2}{k_2} + T_2 + \frac{\dot{L}_2}{L_2}, \tag{14}$$

$$\frac{\dot{(pI)}}{pI} = (\pi_2 - \pi_1)D_2 + \left(\frac{\pi_1 - \pi_2}{\sigma_2} + \pi_2\right)\frac{\dot{k}_2}{k_2} + T_1 + \frac{\dot{L}_2}{L_2}. \tag{15}$$

For the gross saving rate, $s = \frac{pI}{C + pI}$:

$$\frac{\dot{s}}{s} = (1 - s)\left(\frac{\dot{p}}{p} + \frac{\dot{I}}{I} - \frac{\dot{C}}{C}\right) \tag{16}$$

$$= (1 - s)\left(\frac{\pi_1(1 - \sigma_1) - \pi_2(1 - \sigma_2)}{\sigma_2}\frac{\dot{k}_2}{k_2} + (\pi_2 - \pi_1)D_2 - \sigma_1\pi_1(D_1 - D_2) + \frac{\dot{L}_2}{L_2} - \frac{\dot{L}_1}{L_1}\right).$$

Thus, the difference in the rates of technical change of the two sectors is reflected in the changing price ratio, implying that the change in the value of new investment (in terms of consumption goods) and the change in the saving rate depend on the economy's decisions as to changes in k_2, L_1, and L_2 and the biases of the change in the two production functions but not the difference in the rates of technical progress.

3. "*Harrod*" *Neutrality*

In a two-sector model, the natural counterpart of Harrod neutrality, which will be called " Harrod " neutrality, is the constancy of the capital-output ratio in value terms at a constant rate of interest. For the economy, the capital-output ratio depends on the capital-output ratios in the two sectors and, except when the two ratios are equal, on the relative outputs of the two sectors. Expressed in terms of the share of capital

$$\pi = (1 - s)\pi_1 + s\pi_2 \text{ where } s \text{, as above, equals } \frac{pI}{C + pI}. \tag{17}$$

Thus if π_1 and π_2 are unequal, π is not uniquely related to the rate of interest, but depends on r and a decision variable, s. Thus, as a definition of the character of technical change, " Harrod " neutrality cannot be applied to the entire economy, but must be applied to the two sectors separately.

From (7) and (11) the constancy of the rate of interest implies:

$$\frac{\dot{k}_1}{k_1} = \frac{\sigma_1 T_2}{1 - \pi_2} + \sigma_1 D_1; \quad \frac{\dot{k}_2}{k_2} = \frac{\sigma_2 T_2}{1 - \pi_2} + \sigma_2 D_2. \tag{18}$$

From (10) the constancy of π_2 implies

$$\frac{\dot{k}_2}{k_2} = -\frac{D_2}{1 - \frac{1}{\sigma_2}}, \text{ for } \sigma_2 \neq 1; \quad D_2 = 0 \text{ for } \sigma_2 = 1. \tag{19}$$

Equating (18) and (19) gives the condition for " Harrod " neutrality in the investment good sector:

$$(20) \qquad \left(1 - \frac{1}{\sigma_2}\right)T_2 + (1 - \pi_2)D_2 = 0.$$

Since the rate of interest is the marginal product of capital in the investment good sector and since the capital-output ratio is the same in both value and physical units for this sector, equation (20) is the same as the condition for Harrod neutrality in a one-sector model (see [1]). This implies that $G(K, L, t)$ can be written as $H(K, A(t)L)$ and $\frac{T_2}{1 - \pi_2} = \frac{A'}{A}$. Harrod neutrality is equivalent to the independence of $\frac{T_2}{1 - \pi_2}$ of k.

For the consumption good sector the price of capital appears both in the equation relating the marginal product of capital and the interest rate and in the expression for the capital-output ratio in value terms. This causes the condition for " Harrod " neutrality for this sector to depend on the nature of the change in both sectors. The constancy of π_1 implies:

$$(21) \qquad \frac{\dot{k}_1}{k_1} = \frac{-D_1}{1 - \frac{1}{\sigma_1}}, \text{ for } \sigma_1 \neq 1, \; D_1 = 0 \text{ for } \sigma_1 = 1.$$

Equating (18) and (21) gives the condition for " Harrod " neutrality in the consumption good sector:

$$(22) \qquad \left(\frac{1}{1 - \sigma_1}\right)T_2 + (1 - \pi_2)D_1 = 0.$$

Thus, neutral technical change for the consumption good sector depends on characteristics of both production functions.

As an example consider the constant elasticity production functions:

$$C = (\beta_{1t}K_1{}^{-\rho_1} + \alpha_{1t}L_1{}^{-\rho_1})^{-\frac{1}{\rho_1}},$$

$$I = (\beta_{2t}K_2{}^{-\rho_2} + \alpha_{2t}L_2{}^{-\rho_2})^{-\frac{1}{\rho_2}}.$$

Then, for either sector:

$$T = -\frac{\dot{\beta}k^{-\rho} + \dot{\alpha}}{\rho(\beta k^{-\rho} + \alpha)},$$

$$D = \frac{\dot{\beta}}{\beta} - \frac{\dot{\alpha}}{\alpha},$$

$$\sigma = \frac{1}{1 + \rho},$$

$$\pi = \frac{\beta k^{-\rho}}{\beta k^{-\rho} + \alpha}.$$

Equation (20) becomes:

$$\dot{\beta}_2\left(k_2^{-\rho} + \frac{\alpha_2}{\beta_2}\right) = 0$$

which implies $\dot{\beta}_2 = 0$ for " Harrod " neutrality for all capital-labor ratios. This and (22) imply that $\frac{\rho_1}{\rho_2}\left(\frac{\dot{\alpha}_2}{\alpha_2}\right) + \frac{\dot{\beta}_1}{\beta_1} - \frac{\dot{\alpha}_1}{\alpha_1} = 0$ is the condition on the consumption good sector for " Harrod " neutrality in both sectors.

4. *Kennedy's Theorem*

Kennedy [3], [4], has shown the equivalence of Hicks neutrality in the consumption good sector, which is equivalent to $D_1 = 0$, and " Harrod " neutrality in that sector when there is no technical change in the investment good sector. The absence of technical change in the investment good sector implies that $T_2 = 0$. From equation (22) we see that $D_1 = 0$ is then the condition for both Hicks and " Harrod " neutral change. It is also seen from (22) that, except for the unit elasticity of substitution case, the presence of technical change in the investment good sector prevents the equivalence of the two types of change.

5. *Exponential Growth*

For a two-sector model to exhibit exponential growth, in addition to the equation relating the growth of the capital stock and the growth of output of the investment good sector, it is necessary to satisfy equation (11) relating the rates of growth of the capital-labor ratios of the two sectors. We will first consider the case where capital and labor grow at the same rates in both sectors with the rates independent of the initial conditions and then relax these assumptions.

Assume $\frac{\dot{L}_1}{L_1} = \frac{\dot{L}_2}{L_2} = \gamma$, $\frac{\dot{K}_1}{K_1} = \frac{\dot{K}_2}{K_2} = \rho$, and depreciation equals δ times the capital stock.[1]

Equation (11) expressing factor market equilibrium becomes:

$$(23) \qquad (\rho - \gamma) = \frac{\sigma_1(D_1 - D_2)}{1 - \frac{\sigma_1}{\sigma_2}} \text{ for } \sigma_1 \neq \sigma_2; \; D_1 = D_2 \text{ for } \sigma_1 = \sigma_2.$$

Equation (9) relating the growth of investment and capital good production is expressed as:

$$(24) \qquad (\rho - \gamma) = \frac{T_2}{1 - \pi_2}.$$

While growth is feasible for only certain initial capital-labor ratios, it is assumed that these equations hold for all initial capital-labor ratios, not just those with a sufficiently small capital-output ratio to permit growth.

Equation (24) imposes the same condition on the investment good production function as is imposed in a one-sector model for exponential growth in the case of a constant savings ratio. The independence of $\frac{T_2}{1 - \pi_2}$ of k_2 implies that the investment good production function is Harrod neutral $G(K, L, t) = \hat{G}(K, A(t)L)$. This permits the use of equation (20), the

[1] Any depreciation function independent of the use of the capital and not affecting the rate of growth of capital on the growth path could be used here; the one-hoss shay assumption for example.

equation for Harrod neutrality, which may be solved for D_2 in terms of T_2. Equating (23) and (24), using this substitution, gives the equation for " Harrod " neutrality in the consumption good sector, equation (22). Thus for an economy growing along such an exponential path, both production functions are " Harrod " neutral and, from (7), (20), and (24), the rate of interest and relative shares in both sectors are constant.

The rate of growth of the output of consumption goods can be derived from (13):

$$\frac{\dot{C}}{C} = T_1 + (\rho - \gamma)\pi_1 + \gamma. \tag{25}$$

$\left(\text{For } \frac{\dot{C}}{C} \text{ to equal } \frac{\dot{I}}{I}\text{, this equation would imply Harrod neutrality, } F(K, L, t) = F(K, B(t)L), \text{ with } \frac{A'}{A} = \frac{B'}{B}\right).$

The change in the price ratio can be derived from (12):

$$\frac{p}{\dot{p}} = T_1 - (1 - \pi_1)(\rho - \gamma) = T_1 - (1 - \pi_1)\frac{T_2}{1 - \pi_2} \tag{26}$$

$$= (1 - \pi_1)\left(\frac{T_1}{(1 - \pi_1)} - \frac{T_2}{(1 - \pi_2)}\right).$$

Thus, the sign of the price change depends on the relative rates of technical change, $\frac{T_1}{1 - \pi_1} - \frac{T_2}{1 - \pi_2}$. Thus, the amount of capital which may be purchased by the sacrifice of a unit of consumption changes over time with the changing input requirements for unit production.

This equation can also be used to derive the consumption stream which may be obtained by sacrificing one unit of consumption, at $t = 0$, for example. One unit of consumption purchases $\frac{1}{p_0}$ units of capital which gives a stream of $(r - \delta)\frac{1}{p_0}$ units of capital. This is worth $(p_t/p_0)(r - \delta)$ units of consumption at time t for all $t \geqq 0$. In the general case p_t changes irregularly over time. The instantaneous rate of return on a unit of consumption, that is the own rate of return of consumption goods, is $(r - \delta) + \frac{\dot{p}}{p}$, which, in general, will not equal the net interest rate, $(r - \delta)$.

Equations (25) and (26) imply that the gross savings rate, $s = \frac{pI}{C + pI}$, is constant. This constancy, and those of π_1 and π_2, imply constant relative shares for the entire economy. This also implies that the value of *GNP* in consumption units grows at the same rate as consumption.

From (8) the growth of the real wage, w, satisfies:

$$\frac{\dot{w}}{w} = T_1 + \pi_1(\rho - \gamma). \tag{27}$$

Thus, the real wage rises at the same rate as the average product of labor in the consumption sector, which is also the rate of growth of consumption per head.

While still assuming $\frac{\dot{K}_1}{K_1} = \frac{\dot{K}_2}{K_2} = \rho$, we shall now assume $\frac{\dot{L}_1}{L_1} = \gamma_1$ and $\frac{\dot{L}_2}{L_2} = \gamma_2$, with γ_1 and γ_2 not necessarily equal. Equations (23) and (24) now become:

$$(\rho - \gamma_1) = \sigma_1(D_1 - D_2) + \frac{\sigma_1}{\sigma_2}(\rho - \gamma_2); \tag{28}$$

$$(\rho - \gamma_2) = \frac{T_2}{1 - \pi_2}. \tag{29}$$

If these two equations hold for all initial capital-labor ratios, equation (29) and the constancy of the growth rate again imply Harrod neutrality in the investment good sector. As before, the growth of the other variables can be derived.

Equating (28) and (29), using (22), gives:

$$D_1 = \frac{1}{\sigma_1}(\rho - \gamma_1) - (\rho - \gamma_2). \tag{30}$$

For " Harrod " neutrality in the consumption sector D_1 would have to equal $\frac{1}{\sigma_1}(\rho - \gamma_2) - (\rho - \gamma_2)$. Thus, for $\gamma_1 \neq \gamma_2$, there is not " Harrod " neutrality in the consumption good sector.

As before, the interest rate and relative shares in the investment good sector are constant. The share of capital in the consumption good sector satisfies:

$$\frac{\dot{\pi}_1}{\pi_1} = (1 - \pi_1)(\gamma_2 - \gamma_1). \tag{31}$$

Thus, the sign of the change depends on the relative rates of growth of labor inputs.

The equation for the growth in the output of consumption goods becomes:

$$\frac{\dot{C}}{C} = T_1 + (\rho - \gamma_1)\pi_1 + \gamma_1. \tag{32}$$

(For $\frac{\dot{C}}{C} = \frac{\dot{I}}{I}$, this implies Harrod neutrality, $F(K, L, t) = \hat{F}(K, A(t)L)$, with $\frac{A'}{A} + \gamma_1 = \frac{B'}{B} + \gamma_2$.)

The price change equation remains essentially the same:

$$\frac{\dot{p}}{p} = T_1 - (1 - \pi_1)(\rho - \gamma_2) = T_1 - \frac{(1 - \pi_1)}{(1 - \pi_2)} T_2. \tag{33}$$

The rate of change of the gross savings rate can be derived from (16), (32), and (33):

$$\frac{\dot{s}}{s} = (1 - s)(1 - \pi_1)(\gamma_2 - \gamma_1). \tag{34}$$

Since the price ratio reflects the differences in technical change, the sign of the change in the savings rate depends on the difference in the growth of labor inputs.

The equation for the growth of the real wage becomes:

$$\frac{\dot{w}}{w} = T_1 + \pi_1(\rho - \gamma_2). \tag{35}$$

Thus, the average and marginal products in the consumption good sector no longer grow at the same rate.[1, 2]

[1] If the rates of growth of the capital inputs are different for the two sectors, $\frac{\dot{I}}{I} \neq \frac{\dot{K}_2}{K_2}$. Let $\rho = \frac{\dot{I}}{I}$, $\rho_2 = \frac{\dot{K}_2}{K_2}$, $\gamma_2 = \frac{\dot{L}_2}{L_2}$. Then the relation between inputs and outputs in the investment good sector is:

$$(\rho_2 - \gamma_2) = \frac{T_2}{1 - \pi_2} + \frac{\rho_2 - \rho}{1 - \pi_2}.$$

This is similar to the expression for a one-sector model with a changing savings rate with $\rho_2 - \rho = \frac{\dot{s}}{s}$.

[2] As in a one-sector model, see [1], it is possible to describe the movement of the factor-price frontier over time. The frontier has the form $w = \psi(\varphi_1^{-1}(\varphi_2(g_k^{-1}(r))))$, where r is the interest rate, $\varphi_2(k_2) = \frac{g_k}{g - k_2 g_k}$, $\varphi_1(k_1) = \frac{f_k}{f - k_1 f_k}$, and $\psi(k_1) = f(k_1) - k_1 f_k(k_1) = w$. Over time the movement of the frontier along lines of constant interest rate satisfies $\frac{\dot{w}}{w} = T_1 + \frac{\pi_1 T_2}{1 - \pi_2}$ while the movement along radii through the origin satisfies $\frac{\dot{r}}{r} = \frac{\dot{w}}{w} = \frac{\pi_1 T_2 + (1 - \pi_2) T_1}{1 + \pi_1 - \pi_2}$.

University of California, Berkeley. PETER A. DIAMOND.

REFERENCES

(1) Diamond, P. A. " Disembodied Technical Change in a One-Sector Model ", unpublished.

[2] Fei, J. C. H. and Ranis, G. " Capital Accumulation and Economic Development ", *American Economic Review*, 53 (1963), pp. 283-313.

[3] Kennedy, C. " Harrod on ' Neutrality ' ", *Economic Journal*, 1962, pp. 249-250.

[4] Kennedy, C. " The Character of Improvements and of Technical Progress ", *Economic Journal*, 1962, pp. 899-911.

[5] Salter, W. E. G. *Productivity and Technical Change*, Cambridge, 1960.

[15]

The Review *of* Economics *and* Statistics

VOLUME XLVII | NOVEMBER 1965 | NUMBER 4

A THEORY OF INDUCED INNOVATION ALONG KENNEDY–WEISÄCKER LINES*

Paul A. Samuelson

1. For 30 years economists have toyed with the notion that innovation, along with its purely random component, has a bias toward being labor saving in some sense. Very little definite has been demonstrated in this area, suggesting that the subject can use more careful economic analysis.

Suppose we have a neoclassical production function in two factors subject to technical change. Its general form will be $F(V_1,V_2;t)$. A special ("factor-augmenting") form will be $F[V_1/\lambda_1(t),V_2/\lambda_2(t)]$, where a decrease in λ_i means a saving of the amount of the V_i factor needed to produce any given output. (Think of V_1 as "labor" and V_2 as "capital.")

Presumably a limited amount of resources available for research and development can be used to get a larger decrease in $\lambda_1(t)$ only at the expense of a slower decrease in $\lambda_2(t)$. Thus, we might experiment with the hypothesis that the rates of improvement; $-\frac{1}{\lambda_i}(d\lambda_i/dt) = -\dot{\lambda}_i/\lambda_i = q_i$, are related by a transformation function with the usual convexity properties of a production possibility frontier as shown in figure 1

$$q_2 = f(q_1),\ f'(q_1) < 0,\ f''(q_1) < 0. \qquad (1)$$

For each set of factor prices (W_1,W_2), at any stage there will be a minimum unit cost of production, which can be written in the form

$$M[W_1\lambda_1(t),W_2\lambda_2(t)]$$

where

$$M(W_1,W_2) = \underset{[V_j]}{\text{Min}} \sum_1^2 W_jV_j \text{ subject to}$$
$$F(V_1,V_2) = 1 \qquad (2)$$

and the partial derivatives of M, $M_i(W_1,W_2)$, are proportional to the V_i's, being equal to the $V_i/F = a_i$ input requirements per unit of product. (The $M(W_1,W_2)$ function is completely "dual" to $F(V_1,V_2)$ having the same homogeneous concavity;[1] $1 = M(W_1,W_2)$ defines the important factor-price frontier, giving the trade-off between one real factor price in terms of another; the dual relations, $(\partial F/\partial V_i)/(\partial F/\partial V_j) = -W_i/W_j$ and $(\partial M/\partial W_i)/(\partial M/\partial W_j) = -V_i/V_j$ hold.)

2. The instantaneous rate of reduction in unit cost is given by differentiating M to get

$$\frac{-\dot{M}}{M} = -\left(a_1\frac{\dot{\lambda}_1}{\lambda} + a_2\frac{\dot{\lambda}_2}{\lambda}\right) + \text{terms involving } W \text{ changes} \qquad (3)$$
$$= a_1q_1 + a_2q_2 + \ldots$$

where the relative shares of the factors are defined by marginal productivities

$$\frac{W_iV_i}{MF} = a_i = \frac{W_i}{M}\frac{\partial M(W_1\lambda_1,W_2\lambda_2)}{\partial W_i}$$
$$= \frac{V_i}{F}\frac{\partial F(V_1/\lambda_1,V_2/\lambda_2)}{\partial V_i}. \qquad (4)$$

Provided the f transformation function is

* Although the formulation here is my own, the original idea was given to me by Dr. Christian Weizsäcker during his 1962–1963 sojourn at M.I.T., and by an informal seminar paper given at M.I.T. on May 28, 1964 by Professor Charles Kennedy of the University of the West Indies, a preview of C. Kennedy, "Induced Bias in Innovation and the Theory of Distribution," *Economic Journal*, LXXIV (Sept. 1964), 541–547. What the theories of Weizsäcker and Kennedy have in common is a transformation trade-off relating the technical improvements in input requirements of the respective factors of production. A similar idea, but not so explicit, can be found in the writings of many modern writers, most notably Professor William Fellner of Yale in W. Fellner, "Two Propositions in the Theory of Induced Innovations," *Economic Journal*, LXXI (June 1961), 305–308.

Finally, I should like to acknowledge financial aid from the Carnegie Corporation and the research assistance of Mrs. Felicity Skidmore.

[1] See P. A. Samuelson, "Parable and Realism in Capital Theory: The Surrogate Production Function," *Review of Economic Studies*, XXIX, No. 3 (1962), 193–206.

FIGURE 1. — The heavy concave technical frontier, $q_2 = f(q_1)$, is tangential to the equi-unit-cost contours of $M = a_1q_1 + a_2q_2$ at A, whose tangency gives $-f'(q_1) = a_1/a_2$.

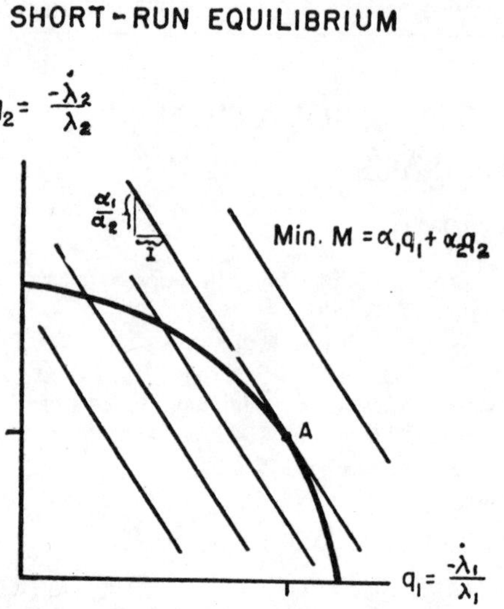

suitably concave (like a quarter circle or the usual production-possibility frontier of economics), the firm maximizes its instantaneous rate of cost reduction in (3), subject to (1), by finding a tangency position at which

$$\frac{a_1}{a_2} = -f'(q_1). \tag{5}$$

(Figure 1 shows the short-term equilibrium tangency.) But for fixed (W_i) or (V_i) ratios, the a's themselves depend on the λ_1/λ_2 ratio in accordance with the formulas in (4) or (2). Making the necessary substitution of (4) into the inversion of (5) leads us ultimately to the differential equations of the simple Weizsäcker-Kennedy (W-K) process

$$\frac{-\dot{\lambda}_1}{\lambda_1} = g\left[\frac{\lambda_1}{\lambda_2}\frac{W_1}{W_2}\right] \qquad \frac{-\dot{\lambda}_2}{\lambda_2} = f\left[\frac{-\dot{\lambda}_1}{\lambda_1}\right] \tag{6}$$

where the sign of $g'(\cdot)$ can be shown to depend on the relation of the elasticity of substitution to unity, namely

$$g' \gtrless 0 \longleftrightarrow \sigma \lessgtr 1. \tag{7}$$

3. The condition that $\lambda_1(t)/\lambda_2(t)$ remains constant, with both factors being "augmented" by innovation in equal degree and thereby being Hicks-neutral, is that we find the following q^* root of (6) or (1)

$$\frac{-\dot{\lambda}_1}{\lambda_1} = \frac{-\dot{\lambda}_2}{\lambda_2} = q^* = f(q^*). \tag{8}$$

If it be the case that (8) hold and

$$\lambda_i(t) = \lambda_i(t_0)e^{-q^*t}, \tag{9}$$

either asymptotically or from the beginning, then from (5) we deduce the corresponding asymptotic (or invariant, equilibrium) value for relative shares

$$\frac{a_1^*}{a_2^*} = -f'(q^*). \tag{10}$$

Equations (8) and (10) constitute a "theory of relative shares" (described in figure 2), but the marginal productivity equation, (4) above, warns us that this is in no genuine sense an "alternative theory" of distribution to the neoclassical one. Nor have we yet established the fact that the states defined by (8)–(10) will in fact be realized initially or asymptotically. We must now analyze the dynamic properties of (6).

4. Let us first look briefly at the Cobb-Douglas (C-D) case where relative shares are constant and $\sigma \equiv 1$. In this case there is no unique way of splitting change into its labor-augmenting and capital-augmenting components, since the $\lambda_i(t)$ function can be factored out of the C-D expressions and divorced from either input. Specifically, either of the following are equivalent

$$F(V_1,V_2;t) = b\left(\frac{V_1}{\lambda_1}\right)^{3/4}\left(\frac{V_2}{\lambda_2}\right)^{1/4} = b\left(\frac{V_1}{\gamma_1}\right)^{3/4}\left(\frac{V_2}{\gamma_2}\right)^{1/4}, \tag{11}$$

$\lambda_i \neq \gamma_i$, but $\gamma_1^{3/4}\,\gamma_2^{1/4} = \lambda_1^{3/4}\,\lambda_2^{1/4}$.

None the less a technical constraint like (1) could hold for a particular choice of $[\lambda_1(t), \lambda_2(t)]$. A director of research and development, who had to make a decision about innovational effort, would find it valuable to know about the feasible effects on $-\dot{\lambda}_i/\lambda_i$. So let us examine the implications of (6) for C-D functions.

In this singular case, where the relative shares, a_i, are strict constants independent of the λ's, W's, or V's, $g' \equiv 0$ and $g(\cdot)$ is a strict

FIGURE 2. — In the long run, if $q_1{}^* = q_2{}^* = q^*$ at E, Hicks-neutral technical change will persist, with relative shares given by $a_1{}^*/a_2{}^* = -f'(q^*)$.

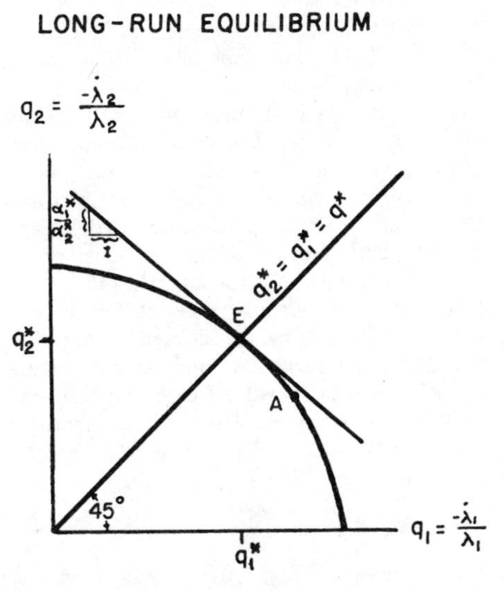

constant. Hence, (6) leads, in general, to endless divergence of the rates of improvement of the λ's, namely

$$-\frac{\dot{\lambda}_1}{\lambda_1} = \beta_1 \neq \beta_2 = -\frac{\dot{\lambda}_2}{\lambda_2} \qquad (12)$$

so that the ratio (λ_2/λ_1) is proportional to $\exp(\beta_1 - \beta_2)t$, which goes to zero or infinity depending on whether β_2 exceeds or falls short of β_1.

There seems to be no *a priori* presumption that β_2 be greater or less than β_1. However, if we get tempted into making the "equal-ignorance" assumption that f in (1) is a *symmetric* transformation function

$$q_2 = f(q_1) \longleftrightarrow q_1 = f(q_2) \qquad (13)$$
$$q^* = f(q^*) \longleftrightarrow -f'(q^*) = 1,$$

then the factor with the highest relative share (say $a_1 = \frac{3}{4}$, labor's share) will have its requirement-per-unit improving faster forever than will the capital factor whose $a_2 < \frac{1}{2}$. However, the steady augmentation of labor, even if it exceeds the rate at which capital (in efficiency units) is being deepened relative to labor population, cannot make labor's relative share deteriorate, because nothing can in the Cobb-Douglas case.

The C-D case is significant because in it the alleged Kennedy distribution-of-income condition given in my equation (10) has no relevance to actual income determination. Except by fluke, the actual ($\frac{3}{4}$,$\frac{1}{4}$) income distribution dictated by C-D marginal productivity will differ from the Kennedy distribution of ($\frac{1}{2}$, $\frac{1}{2}$) given by equation (13)'s symmetric specification of (10).

5. Equations (6) by themselves constitute an incomplete system, unless like Kennedy we are content to consider the W's, or their ratio, as constants.

Even though each small entrepreneur may take the factor prices W_i as given parameters subject to time trends he cannot appreciably affect, for the system as a whole, relative factor supplies V_i and the effectiveness factors λ_i are prime determinants of factor prices. Still, let us examine the general properties of (6) on the assumption that the W's or their ratio can be treated as constants (or on the less monstrous assumption that their ratio changes very slowly compared to λ_i/λ_j changes). Subtract (6)'s second equation from its first, to get

$$\frac{1}{(\lambda_2/\lambda_1)}\frac{d(\lambda_2/\lambda_1)}{dt} = \frac{-\dot{\lambda}_1}{\lambda_1} - \frac{-\dot{\lambda}_2}{\lambda_2}$$
$$= \frac{-\dot{\lambda}_1}{\lambda_1} - f\left(\frac{-\dot{\lambda}_1}{\lambda_1}\right) = \phi\left(\frac{-\dot{\lambda}_1}{\lambda_1}\right)$$
$$= \phi\left[g\left(\frac{\lambda_2}{\lambda_1}\frac{W_2}{W_1}\right)\right] = \psi(\lambda_2/\lambda_1);$$

or

$$\frac{1}{(\lambda_2/\lambda_1)}\frac{d(\lambda_2/\lambda_1)}{dt} = \psi(\lambda_2/\lambda_1), \text{ for fixed } W_2/W_1, \qquad (14)$$

where

$$\text{sign } \psi' = \text{sign } (1 - f') \text{ sign } g'$$
$$= \text{sign } (\sigma - 1). \qquad (15)$$

Equation (14) is a first-order differential equation for λ_2/λ_1. If its left-hand side vanishes at $(\lambda_2/\lambda_1)^*$, where

$$\psi\left(\frac{\lambda_2}{\lambda_1}\right)^* = 0,$$

there is a possible state of Hicks-neutral technical progress at which both factors have equal-percentage augmentation, with $\lambda_i(t)$ proportional to $\exp\text{-}q^*t$. This Kennedy configuration may or may not be stable, depending on whether

$$\psi'(\lambda_2^*/\lambda_1^*) \lesseqgtr 0 \longleftrightarrow g'\left(\frac{\lambda_2^*}{\lambda_1}\frac{W_2}{W_1}\right) \lesseqgtr 0 \longleftrightarrow (\sigma^* - 1) \lesseqgtr 0. \quad (16)$$

Theorem: If for fixed W_2/W_1 a Kennedy neutral-change state exists, at it

$$\frac{-\dot{\lambda}_1}{\lambda_2} = \frac{-\dot{\lambda}_2}{\lambda_2} = q^*,\ \lambda_2/\lambda_1 = \frac{c_1 e^{q^* t}}{c_2 e^{q^* t}} = (\lambda_2/\lambda_1)^*;$$

it will be stable (unstable) if the elasticity of substitution there is less than (greater than) unity.

6. I conclude this section with two warnings. First, it is not legitimate to neglect the *induced* changes in factor prices W_2/W_1. (Thus, my (6) was deduced using (4)'s imputation equations, which imply that the W's are variables determined by relative effective factor scarcities $(V_1,V_2,\lambda_1,\lambda_2)$ and are not parameters.)

Waiving this fundamental objection, we must recognize that there may be no equilibrium configuration compatible with the Kennedy condition (10) and the competitive market imputation (4). We saw this in the C-D case, but there are other counter-examples even when $\sigma \not\equiv 1$. (For example, let $q_2 = f(q_1)$ be a symmetric function, calling in the Kennedy theory for $-f'(q^*) = a_1^*/a_2^* = 1$, or equal factor shares. But suppose $F(V_1,V_2) = V_1^{.8}V_2^{.2} + V_1^{.7}V_2^{.3}$, with factor shares always between 70 and 80 per cent for labor. Then Kennedy will find endlessly divergent rates of growth for the λ's and no Hicks-neutral equilibrium state. We shall see that the Solow constant-elasticity-of-substitution family, $F(V_1,V_2) = [(a_1V_1)^b + (a_2V_2)^b]^{1/b}$, whose σ can always be bounded *away* from unity, avoids this paradox; but economists should not emancipate themselves from the tyranny of Cobb-Douglas only to enchain themselves in a new Solow *CES* tyranny.)

II

7. It is time now to drop the assumption that factor prices are constant. Instead they are deducible, as will be relative shares, from the marginal productivities of the factors, being dependent only upon the effective factor supplies $(V_1,V_2,\lambda_1,\lambda_2)$. Hence, our earlier differential equations of (1) and (5) will enable us to express the percentage rate of change of the ratio (λ_2/λ_1) in terms of this ratio itself, or more precisely in the form

$$\frac{d(\lambda_2/\lambda_1)}{(\lambda_2/\lambda_1)dt} = G\left[\frac{\lambda_2}{\lambda_1}\frac{V_1}{V_2}\right],$$
$$\text{sign } G' = \text{sign } (\sigma - 1). \quad (17)$$

To derive this, use (4) to express a_2/a_1 in terms of $(V_2/\lambda_2)/(V_1/\lambda_1)$ and substitute this into the inversion of (5).

If the factors in natural units are constant, or grow in the same ratio, we can look for a fixed ratio λ_2/λ_1 that will satisfy this equation. In such a regime, the induced inventions will have become neutral in the 1932 sense of Hicks, augmenting both factors at the same percentage rate. Equation (17) is a logical, and needed, fulfillment of the Kennedy-Weizsäcker theories.

8. Now in the case of assumed symmetry of the $q_i = f(q_j)$ technical-improvement frontier (which might be called the case of a "neutral" technical-improvement frontier), it is evident from the symmetry of equation (8), that (5) can be rewritten as

$$q_1^* = q_2^* = q^* \longleftrightarrow \frac{a_2^*}{a_1^*} = -f'(q^*) = 1 = \frac{a_1^*}{a_2^*}.$$

Hence, only for relative shares equal to one-half (or to 1/n in the case of n factors) can the system with a neutral technical-improvement frontier settle down to a steady state of balanced technical change.

I call this paradoxical tendency for factor shares to become absolutely equal the Kindleberger Effect, because my colleague Professor Charles P. Kindleberger conjectured that this empirically bizarre result was implied by the present theory.

9. Until we are told something about the determination of V_1/V_2, (17) constitutes an incomplete system for the unknowns $(\lambda_2/\lambda_1, V_1/V_2)$. If the V's are assumed constant as in a stationary state, or if they grow always in the same proportion so that their ratio stays constant at $(V_1/V_2)^*$, (17) becomes a complete system. A stationary solution for $(\lambda_2/\lambda_1)^*$, in which both factors are augmented in accordance with Hicks-neutral change, is possible wherever

$$0 = G\left(\frac{\lambda_2^*}{\lambda_1}\frac{V_1^*}{V_2}\right) = G(X^*), \quad (18)$$

an equation which may have no roots at all (as in the C-D and related cases), which may have exactly one root (as in the CES case, $\sigma \neq 1$), or may have multiple roots (as in cases where

σ varies above and below unity as factor proportions change).

10. A well-behaved example would be a CES function with $1 > \sigma = 1/(1-b)$, $b < 0$, say $b = -1$:

$$F(V_1,V_2) = [(a_1V_1)^{-1} + (a_2V_2)^{-1}]^{-1}, \quad (19)$$

a weighted "harmonic mean" of the inputs. For it,

$$G(X^*) = 0 \quad (20)$$

will have the single root X^*, with $G' < 0$. Hence, for all initial conditions with $(V_1/V_2)^*$ constant, the system will approach ultimately an asymptotic state

$$\lim_{t\to\infty} \frac{\lambda_2(t)}{\lambda_1(t)} = \frac{X^*}{(V_1/V_2)^*}, \quad (21)$$

and induced technical change becomes asymptotically Hicks-neutral.

11. Now consider a CES case with $\sigma > 1$, say $\sigma = 2$, $b = \frac{1}{2}$,

$$F(V_1,V_2) = [(a_1V_1)^{\frac{1}{2}} + (a_2V_2)^{\frac{1}{2}}]^2. \quad (22)$$

As did (19), with $\sigma \neq 1$, (20) has a unique root X^*, but now $G'(X^*) > 0$. Hence, $X^*/(V_1/V_2)^*$ is an equilibrium state that will persist forever if not at all perturbed. However, for the slightest deflection of the system from equilibrium, the system will move ever further away in a cumulative self-reinforcing flight from equilibrium. Using the convention that initially $\lambda_i(0) = 1$, we consider the two cases where $(\lambda_2/\lambda_1)^* > 1$ or < 1. If the former holds, the unstably-diverging system must move ever further from equilibrium with $\lambda_1/\lambda_2 \rightarrow 0$: if only λ_1 is being reduced, we have purely labor-augmenting technical change of the Harrod-neutral variety; because $\sigma > 1$, this Harrod-neutral change is definitely Hicks capital-saving with labor's share of product going to *100* per cent and the profit rate going to zero! The reader can work out the opposite case where the system diverges on the other side of $(\lambda_2/\lambda_1)^*$ and approaches pure capital-augmentation.

If σ oscillates around unity for different values of $(V_2/\lambda_2)/(V_1/\lambda_1)$, there may be multiple equilibrium values for X^* and $(\lambda_2^*/\lambda_1^*)$. These will be alternately stable and unstable, depending on the negatives of the sign of $G'(X^*)$, which in turn depends upon the sign of $\sigma(X^*) - 1$. (If for $\sigma(X^*) = 1$ there should happen to be an equilibrium, it will be stable (unstable) on any side where σ turns less (more) than unity.)

We can now state the correct version of our previous theorem, removing the blemish of self-contradiction in assuming factor prices as parameters of the problem.

Basic Theorem: If $(V_2/V_1)^*$ is constant, the process of selecting among alternative inventions,

$$\frac{-\dot{\lambda}_2}{\lambda_2} = f\left(\frac{-\dot{\lambda}_1}{\lambda_1}\right), f' < 0, f'' < 0,$$

the optimal combination that minimizes instantaneous unit costs (of consumption and capital goods interchangeably) will involve

$$\frac{a_1}{a_2} = -f'\left(\frac{-\dot{\lambda}_1}{\lambda_1}\right)$$

and (expressing relative shares a_1/a_2 in terms of effective factor ratios)

$$\frac{1}{(\lambda_2/\lambda_1)} \frac{d(\lambda_2/\lambda_1)}{dt} = G\left[\frac{\lambda_2}{\lambda_1}\frac{V_2^*}{V_1}\right] = G(X),$$

where

sign $[G'(X)]$ = sign $[\sigma(X) - 1]$.

Then if $\sigma(X)$ is sufficiently bounded away from unity (or some other sufficient conditions are postulated),

$$0 = G(X^*)$$

may have one (or more) equilibrium roots at which the system undergoes Hicks-neutral technical change, with

$$\left(\frac{\lambda_2}{\lambda_1}\right)^* = \frac{X^*}{(V_2/V_1)^*}, \quad \frac{-\dot{\lambda}_1^*}{\lambda_1^*} = q^* = \frac{-\dot{\lambda}_2^*}{\lambda_2},$$

$$\lambda_i(t)^* = c_ie^{-q^*t}$$

$$q^* = f(q^*), \quad \frac{a_1^*}{a_2^*} = \frac{a_1^*}{1-a_1^*} = -f'(q^*).$$

Each equilibrium state will be stable (or unstable) depending upon whether $\sigma(X^*) <$ (or $>$) 1. However, the multiplicity of X^* does not imply any multiplicity of relative shares (a_1^*, a_2^*) since q^* is always unique. Should $\sigma > 1$ always, as in the CES case, it is virtually certain that the system will diverge from the (a_1^*, a_2^*) equilibrium toward a pure capital- or pure labor-augmenting state where one factor gets all the product and the other has a zero price.

For the symmetric $f(\cdot)$ frontier, we have the Kindleberg Paradox.

Corollary: If by the Principle of Insufficient Reason, we posit that the technology of labor augmentation is likely to be symmetric with that of capital augmentation so that

$$q_2 = f(q_1) \longleftrightarrow q_1 = f(q_2) \longleftrightarrow -f'(q^*) = 1 \text{ where } q^* = f(q^*)$$

Kennedy-Weizsäcker induced technical change will be in a permanent Hicks-neutral state only when labor and property incomes have become equalized (or, if we call male labor, female labor, and property the three factors, when their shares are all $a_i = 1/3$ — or $a_i = 1/n$ in the general case of n specified factors). But only if the E of S departs sufficiently from unity need there even exist such an equilibrium state, and if one or more such equilibrium states does exist, only for $\sigma^* < 1$ will a particular state be (locally) stable and be asymptotically approached from near-by initial conditions.

12. We ought now to drop the assumption of fixed factor ratio V_1/V_2, replacing it by the more realistic recognition that capital is "deepening relative to labor," with the $K/L = V_2/V_1$ ratio growing exponentially at around two or three per cent per year. Indeed, the rate of technical progress has to be postulated to have been just enough to offset neoclassical diminishing returns if we are to be consistent with a fairly constant profit or interest rate and a fairly constant capital-output ratio.

What does this imply for the (λ_1,λ_2) model? Unless the production function of that model is Cobb-Douglas, we know that realism requires that the technical change be Harrod-neutral and nothing else. There is no other way of ensuring a constant profit rate and constant capital-output ratio. But Harrod Neutrality implies for the (λ_1,λ_2) model that λ_1 only changes! Only an invention that can be regarded as purely labor-augmenting can be persistently Harrod Neutral.[2]

I conclude from this that the (λ_1,λ_2) theory outlined in this paper fails to account for one of the stylized facts of modern development, namely that the interest or profit rates show no clear trend upward or downward.[3]

13. I shall now give an extension of the Kennedy theory that helps bring it into agreement with the Hicks and Fellner emphasis on labor saving rather than neutral invention.

Assuming a constant V_2/V_1 ratio ignores the fundamental fact that historical development has involved an accumulation of capital relative to labor. If V_2/V_1 grows exponentially as capital "deepens," there will be a powerful tendency to lower interest rates and raise real wages even in the absence of technical change. Moreover, as Marx, Hicks, and Fellner have argued, this very fact should bias technical change in some kind of a labor-saving (or factor-that-can-be-expected-to-become-dear) direction. Can my basic equation (17) justify any such conclusion? The answer is a qualified yes.

The intuitive explanation of my theory would run as follows. How could relative shares remain constant as capital deepens relative to labor even when the elasticity of substitution is less than unity and is tending to raise labor's relative shares? Answer: If, and only if, the induced technical change is relatively labor-augmenting in comparison with capital-augmentation — so that λ_1/λ_2 moves in the same direction as V_2/V_1, ensuring that the ratio of effective factor supplies, in "efficiency units" as measured by $(V_2/\lambda_2)/(V_1/\lambda_1)$, remains unchanged. For all this to be the case, we must have

$$\frac{-\dot\lambda_1}{\lambda_1} - \frac{-\dot\lambda_2}{\lambda_2} = q_1^{**} - q_2^{**} = \gamma = \frac{d(V_2/V_1)}{(V_2/V_1)dt}, \tag{23}$$

or

$$f(q_1^{**}) = q_1^{**} - \gamma, \quad \frac{a_1^{**}}{a_2^{**}} = -f'(q_1^{**}). \tag{24}$$

Figure 3 shows how the Hicks-neutral equilibrium of Kennedy, corresponding to q_1^* and $\gamma = 0$, is displaced southeast in the labor-saving direction by the capital-deepening factor $\gamma > 0$. This moves labor's equilibrium share, a_1^{**}/a_2^{**}, upward, and, hence, in the equal-ignorance case of $f(\cdot)$ symmetry, it pushes the share of the factor that is showing most rapid

[2] Of course, the C-D case requires separate formulation. Here the distinction between Harrod and Hicks evaporates along with the possibility of distinguishing between the amount of augmentation of specific factors.

[3] Both Kennedy and Weizsäcker have variant models which do deduce an ultimate state that is purely labor-augmenting (and, with $\sigma < 1$, is Hicks labor-saving). In Kennedy's case, this is supposed to come about when he drops his assumption (which has *not* been mine) that technical progress takes place only in the consumption goods sector, and replaces it by the ". . . much-analysed one-product model in which the single product can be used equally well as a consumption good or as a capital good." This model, which I would write after conventional change of units in the Ramsey-Solow form, $dV_2/dt = F(t;V_1,V_2)$ — Consumption Output, is the one I have been analyzing, and for it I do not reach the Kennedy conclusion $-\dot\lambda_2/\lambda_2 = q_2 = 0$, corresponding to Harrod-neutrality.

FIGURE 3. — If capital grows relative to labor (in natural units) at 2 per cent per year or at rate $\gamma = .02$, any long-run equilibrium has to be at E', where $f(q_1^{**}) = q_1^{**} - \gamma$ and $a_1^{**}/a_2^{**} = -f'(q_1^{**})$ and technical change is persistently "relatively labor-augmenting." If, at E', $\sigma < 1$, change will be Hicks labor saving and E' will be the stable equilibrium asymptote. But the interest rate will be ever-rising.

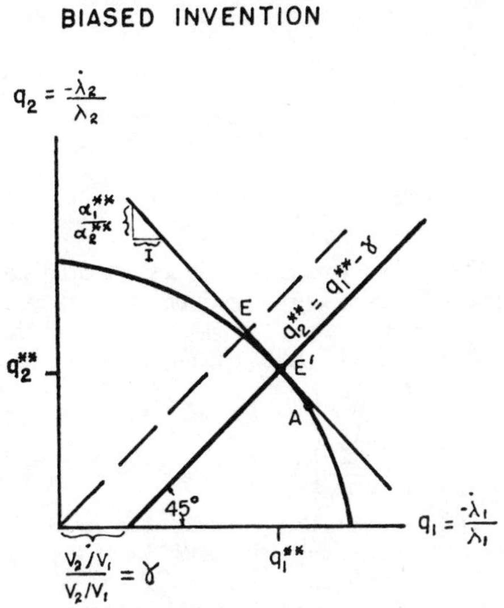

relative growth (i.e., capital) down below ½. Qualitatively, this agrees with the fact that property gets only about 20 rather than 50 per cent of total product. But one must reserve doubt that so severe a reduction could be attributable to the rather mild secular rate of capital deepening.

Substitute $V_1/V_2 = C \exp - \gamma t$ into (17), to get

$$\frac{d(\lambda_2/\lambda_1)}{(\lambda_2/\lambda_1)dt} = G\left[\frac{\lambda_2}{\lambda_1} Ce^{-\gamma t}\right]; \tag{25}$$

and try for a possible solution of the form $\lambda_2/\lambda_1 = Y \exp - \gamma t$, to get

$$\frac{\dot{Y}}{Y} = G[CY] + \gamma \tag{26}$$

the steady state of which is given by $Y = Y^{**}$ in

$$-\gamma = G(CY^{**}) = G(X^{**}). \tag{27}$$

Just as (18) can be solved uniquely for X^* if σ is always bounded away from unity, so can (27) be solved for a unique X^{**} under these conditions.[4] If $\sigma < 1$, as in the CES case, this "equilibrium state" — in which the bias of induced technical factor augmentation just offsets the bias toward capital/labor accumulation — will in fact be approached asymptotically from any initial conditions.

14. The time has come to summarize the results. In the end, even in a model where no one looks forward to future increases in wages relative to interest or capital rents, we have been able to develop a model in which the accumulation of capital relative to labor does, with the help of a Kennedy-Weizsäcker technical change frontier, generate a steady state of induced labor-saving (or, more precisely, relative labor-augmenting) invention.

Be it noted that the argument does not rest upon wages being in some sense "high." High compared to what? Compared to marginal physical productivity? Obviously not, since in least-cost equilibrium all factors are equally productive, dear, or cheap, per dollar spent at the margin. Nor does the argument apply to a land-rich country like America, which is alleged to have higher wages than those it sees abroad, and is supposed, therefore, to have some special inducement to introduce labor-saving inventions. (Actually, if America is self-sufficient in the products in question, why should it look abroad and be interested in lower wage rates abroad? And if it is not self-sufficient, why should comparative advantage leave it producing goods with high labor content?) To repeat, the Fellner emphasis, upon a reasonable expectation on the part of non-myopic entrepreneurs that wage rates will be rising in the future (which we shall touch on in the next sections), is not at all involved in the present model.

Only the following elements are involved:

A. The explicit assumption, for which evidence is not at all copious, that the elasticity of substitution is less than unity, so that an increase in capital relative to labor would tend, statistically, to raise labor's relative share.

[4] The usual multiplicity (stable and unstable) on nonexistence of solution can hold for (27) if σ is not bounded away from unity. However, the a_1^{**}/a_2^{**} level is unique by virtue of the uniqueness of (24)'s solution. But unless it is compatible with (4)'s marginal productivity relations, (27) will have no root and my K-W model fails to give a theory of long-run distribution.

B. A factual assumption that capital, in natural units, is accumulating relative to labor in natural units.

C. A hypothetical assumption that, other things being equal, the larger the fraction of costs going to a factor, the more it will pay inventors to work to reduce the physical requirement of that input in production. This is what is involved in the time-invariant technical progress frontier as specified in equation (1).

Then the content of figure 3 and the equations leading up to (26) can be stated intuitively, as follows.

The accumulation of capital tends to raise labor's share. The increased labor share accelerates the successful search for labor-saving inventions. The process reaches steady-state equilibrium when the increase in the capital/labor ratio in natural units is just being offset by relatively labor-augmenting or labor-saving invention at a pace that makes the effective requirements ratio λ_1/λ_2 grow exactly as fast as V_2/V_1.

III

15. I shall now give a natural generalization to the problem. Why should we want to maximize the *instantaneous* rate of unit cost reduction? This could appear to be a rather myopic procedure. Instead of maximizing $-\dot{M}$, suppose we sought to act now to minimize unit cost at some future date, say five years from now. Or more generally, act to take account of the effect that alternative choices of present $\dot{\lambda}_i/\lambda_i$ will have on some weighted average of future unit costs. Thus, instead of maximizing $-\dot{M}$ at each instant, we set up the calculus of variations problem

$$\text{Maximize} - \int_{t_0}^{t_1} J[M(W_1\lambda_1, W_2\lambda_2)]dt \qquad (28)$$

subject to (1)

$$\frac{-\dot{\lambda}_2}{\lambda_2} = f\left(-\frac{\dot{\lambda}_1}{\lambda_1}\right).$$

By the usual technique of Lagrange multipliers, this leads to the Euler differential equations for an optimal path. I leave this to the reader, and work out only the special case where we aim to minimize unit cost at a time T periods from now. Our problem can be written

$$\text{Maximize} \int_0^T -\frac{d\log M}{dt}dt = \int_0^T -\frac{\dot{M}}{M}dt$$

$$= -\int_0^T \sum_1^2 \frac{\dot{\lambda}_j}{\lambda_j} a_j dt \qquad (29)$$

subject to the above constraint on the $\dot{\lambda}_j/\lambda_j$.

We write down the usual variation condition on the Lagrangian integrand, using the more convenient variables $-\dot{\lambda}_i/\lambda_i = d\log\lambda_i/dt = \dot{y}_i$

$$L = \sum_1^2 \dot{y}_j a_j + \mu[f(\dot{y}_1) - (\dot{y}_2)]. \qquad (30)$$

The resulting Euler equations

$$\frac{d}{dt}\frac{\partial L}{\partial \dot{y}_i} - \frac{\partial L}{\partial y_i} = 0$$

become

$$\frac{d}{dt}[a_1 + \mu f'(\dot{y}_1)] = \dot{y}_1\frac{\partial a_1}{\partial y_1} + \dot{y}_2\frac{\partial a_2}{\partial y_1}$$

$$\frac{d}{dt}[a_2 - \mu] = \dot{y}_1\frac{\partial a_2}{\partial y_1} + \dot{y}_2\frac{\partial a_2}{\partial y_2} \qquad (31)$$

$$\dot{y}_2 - f(\dot{y}_1) = 0.$$

To these extremal conditions must be adjoined transversality conditions to determine the terminal values of (y_i) which maximize $-M(T)$. These can be written as

$$\frac{-\partial M}{\partial y_1(T)} = \left.\frac{\partial L}{\partial \dot{y}_1}\right]_T = a_1 + \mu f' = 0$$

$$\frac{-\partial M}{\partial y_2(T)} = \left.\frac{\partial L}{\partial \dot{y}_2}\right]_T = a_2 - \mu = 0. \qquad (32)$$

It is evident that eliminating μ gives the optimality tangency condition (5) of the myopic theory. This is as it should be since, at the end of the period planned for, it pays to be myopic!

In the special Cobb-Douglas case where the a's are constants, the right-hand side of (31) vanishes and the left-hand side integrates to

$$a_1 + \mu f'(\dot{y}_1) = c_1, \text{ a constant}$$

$$a_2 - \mu = c_2, \text{ a constant.}$$

The terminal condition (32) assures us that these constants are zero.

Thus, in the C-D case, myopia has no penalty and farsightedness confers no advantages. Again, this is as it should be. For, wherein lies the advantage of planning ahead? Obviously, if we know that present decisions concerning the direction of research effort will affect the weight of labor costs relative to other costs in the future, we should prudently take into account that influence and not operate, as in the simplest W-K theory, completely in terms of curent a weights.

The general theory sketched here would seem distinctly superior to the myopic theory if it were really a question of managerial planning by a single monopoly firm. But, in the context of Darwinian perfect competition, there is something to be said for the myopic theory. Each competitor must minimize cost for the moment because it is only in the transient moment when he has a cost advantage that he can make any profit above the competitive minimum. The competitive system as a whole then gives the appearance of being run by an *Invisible Hand* which acts in the manner postulated by the myopic model.

Until we redo the problem, as we did the myopic version, in terms of a growing $V_2(t)/V_1(t)$ ratio and deduce from this fact the expected decline in W_2/W_1, our general formulation is still symmetric in its formulation of the variables. Hence, it is still subject to the defect of displaying the Kindleberger Effect, a tendency for relative shares to become absolutely equal (or, in the case where $\sigma > 1$, for one factor to gobble all the totals). But taking account of an expected rise in real wage will tend (with $\sigma < 1$ and an unchanged frontier) to bias the final equilibrium in the labor-saving direction.[5]

IV

16. The situation is not changed in essentials if we study more than two factors. If the transformation function of (1) is written as a symmetric function of many variables

$$T(q_1, q_2, \ldots, q_n) = 0, \tag{33}$$

and if there are no systematic changes in V_i/V_j proportions, the Kindleberger Effect will continue to hold, with $a_i = 1/n$ the ultimate steady state.[6]

Again, if every elasticity of substitution has $\sigma_i < 1$, an accumulation of any factor or subset of factors relative to the rest will tend to lower its relative share a_i^{**}.

17. I shall not attempt here an extended critique of the theories under discussion. A few dogmatic remarks must suffice. In situations involving imperfect knowledge there is a danger in thinking up new concepts. Definition should be harmless, but the human tendency to presuppose constancy in some new brain child puts the scientist at the mercy of the random walk of his thoughts.

Once I write down a transformation function between improvements in input requirements, I forget to make it so general as to be compatible with all behavior. It would be all right, indeed salutary, to put restrictions on behavior if such restrictions grew out of empirical observations, but if they grow merely out of the happenstance of definition, the result can be harmful.

18. To be sure, altering the specification of the transformation function can undo the harm, at the possible cost of introducing new arbitrary errors. Suppose, for example, that employers have learned from experience that any dollar of costs is as promising an object for research improvement as any other dollar. Then the boss may wisely decree that mobile research resources will be allocated to each input *ex ante* in direct proportion to its cost. This means that a factor like labor, or like unskilled female labor, will get the same research and development *per dollar of cost* that any other factor gets. Such a theory seems fatal to any simple notion of induced and biased technical change.

This is what the late W. E. G. Salter of Australia seems to have had in mind in his valuable *Productivity and Technical Change* (Cambridge University Press, 1960), when he put matters thus:

> The entrepreneur is interested in reducing costs in total, not particular costs such as labour costs or capital costs. When labour costs rise any advance that reduces total cost is welcome, and whether this is achieved by saving labour or capital is irrelevant. There is no reason to assume that attention should be concentrated on labour-saving techniques.
>
> . . .
>
> The above arguments make it difficult to accept any *a priori* reason for labour-saving biases. . . . (pp. 43–44).

It is certainly what I had in mind in the latest edition of my text, *Economics*, 6th Edition (McGraw-Hill, 1964):

[5] In W. Fellner's cited 1961 *Economic Journal* paper, his Figure 1 shows that an expected rise in the wage relative to the interest rate will cause firms, other things being equal, to choose of two improvements the one with relatively low labor requirements. This somewhat reinforces the previous section's non-expectational results.

[6] Even if we deem it more realistic to put into the transformation function, along with $\dot{\lambda}_i/\lambda_i$, the attained levels of the λ_i themselves, the equal-ignorance assumption of the Principle of (In)Sufficient Reason will still imply the Kindleberger Effect — both in the myopic theory and the version involving the calculus of variations.

> . . . we must recognize that *any* invention which lowers cost of production can benefit the first competitor who introduces it. Furthermore, since the relative share of wages in total costs has been approximately constant for a century, any employer who is planning his research expenditures over the coming years will reasonably take this into account and will do well to spend now the same number of pennies on experimentation designed to save a dollar of future cost, whatever its source. (pp. 738–739).

Kennedy, recognizing that the Salter argument is inconsistent with his own, regards his own argument as so ". . . indisputable that it is difficult to see how Mr. Salter, in the passage quoted above, persuaded himself otherwise. . . . reaching a conclusion that conflicts with common sense. For if the reduction in unit costs is the same whatever the character of the innovation, then there is no reason why the entrepreneur should search for one type of improvement rather than another." [7]

As is argued in the last footnote, this misinterprets the nature of the argument that ". . . in the absence of specific knowledge about possible innovation, any dollar of expenditure is as likely a candidate for innovational economy as any other." We embody this insight, and emasculate the Kennedy-Weizsäcker formulations, by rewriting the transformation function (1) so that it ***involves relative shares directly***

$$q_2 = f(q_1;a_1) \tag{34}$$

subject to the specific property that at $q_1 = q_2 = q$, we have the slope property

$$\frac{a_1}{1-a_1} \equiv -\frac{\partial f(q;a_1)}{\partial q_1},\quad q = f(q;a_1) = q(a_1). \tag{35}$$

The whole point of this reformulation is to get away from the implicit theorizing by which one assumes that the entrepreneur can have knowledge that the transformation function remains invariant over time and has naught to do with the costs and shares of the factors themselves. There is no necessity to agree with my formulation. (If there were, this would be an empty tautology. Indeed, if it were the case, as engineers tell me it is not, that innovational research aimed at reducing labor costs could concentrate on improving processes that are inherently human, and that have a transfer value for all laborers whether they be violin players or typists, one would not want to specify a transformation function with (34)'s properties.)

By virtue of (35)'s definition, the minimization of unit costs is achieved at the following tangency point, which represents a simple generalization of the Kennedy condition (5)

$$\frac{-\dot{M}}{M} \text{ is at a minimum where } q_1 = q_2 = q \text{ and}$$

$$\frac{a_1}{a_2} = \frac{-\partial f(q;a_1)}{\partial q_1}. \tag{36}$$

This says that, in the absence of special knowledge, induced technical change is presumably Hicks-neutral. Note that the common q is not q^*, an asymptotic state, but rather one that holds all the time.

What are the fundamental equations of dynamic development of this Samuelson-Salter process? When we substitute (36) into (34) we get the following counterpart to (6) and (17)

$$\frac{-\dot{\lambda}_1}{\lambda_1} = \frac{-\dot{\lambda}_2}{\lambda_2} = q(a_1)$$

$$a_1 = \frac{\partial F[1,V_2(t)/V_1(t)]}{\partial V_1} F[1,V_2(t)/V_1(t)]^{-1}.$$

[7] Kennedy, *op. cit.*, p. 543. Kennedy goes on to interpret, in his equation (3), Salter as having to assume that the transformation schedules in the diagrams or in my (1) have to be a straight line with slope that happens to be the same as the relative shares. This would indeed make the entrepreneur ***indifferent*** to the degree of q_1 augmentation chosen. But Kennedy has not understood the nature of the common-sense argument made by Salter and me. It is not that we assume straight-line transformation schedules and indifference, but rather that the entrepreneur, by the principle of Sufficient Reason and in the absence of some special knowledge about exogenously given trends of innovation, has no reason to expect that the tangency equation of my diagrams and equation (5) comes with $q_2 > q_1$ rather than with $q_1 < q_2$. To render this fundamental insight mathematically, we assume that the form of the transformation function itself depends upon relative shares, a_1/a_2, and in such a way that at the root $q_1 = q_2 = q$, the slope equals the ratio of relative shares. All this is embodied in my subsequent equations and in figure 4. That common sense lies in this direction is made more clear when we realize that redefinition of what we specify as "a factor of production," so that unskilled, male labor becomes a different factor from a violin player and from a carpenter, leaves the Salter-Samuelson formation invariant, while it seems to make nonsense of the Kennedy-Weizsäcker formulation. The objection I have made here is the familiar one that probability theorists have always made to the lack of invariance of *a priori* probabilities to changes in what is specified as equally-likely. A modern Bayes approach avoids fallacy but achieves results only by stipulation of believed knowledge, not of ignorance.

FIGURE 4. — If the firm's best policy is to spend on research equal sums to reduce each dollar of expense, the $(q_1 . q_2)$ transformation function depends on relative share a_1 in such a way as to make the slope at E always equal to $-a_1/a_2$. No bias results.

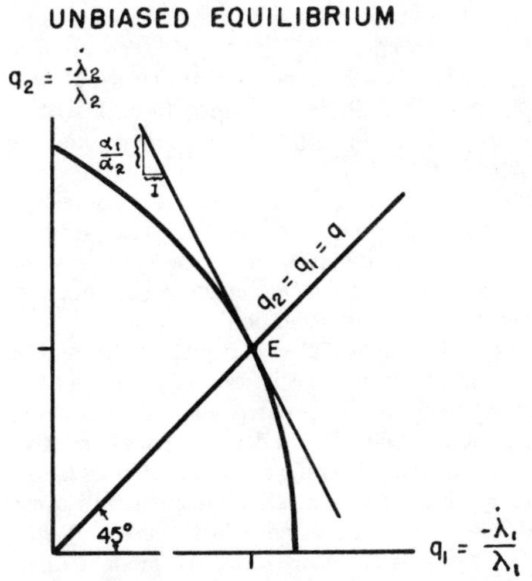

This says that, in the absence of special knowledge about technical change, labor's relative share develops in dependence upon relative factor supplies, going with capital deepening up (or down) if $\sigma < 1$ (or > 1), and with induced technical change *not* being presumed to alter the probabilities.

19. Until now, I have gone along with the assumption that there are no discernible exogenous trends in technical development. This is of course not true. Any scientist can tell you, after some breakthrough has been made, that there is likely to be "pay-dirt" in pursuing a certain line of invention rather than another. Indeed, the whole art of decision-making in creative science is to discern such promising developments. Nor is there, as has sometimes been argued by means of shallow semantics, a contradiction in terms in being able to know in advance of the development or discovery of as yet unknown phenomena. What we have in advance are probability judgments about the general character of promising findings. To know the answer to a question is, of course, to deny that it is still a question. But to have a flair for asking the right question at the right time is part of what is meant by being a creative scientist.

Hence, it is not realistic to assume that new discoveries are "random." Indeed, as in the theory of Darwinian evolution that is supposed to take place by virtue of "random mutation conditioned by selective survival," one finds on deeper analysis that one cannot even define the notion of random mutation precisely. (This does not drive one to the alternative of believing that if I play tennis hard my offspring will be better tennis players, but it does recognize that if I play with X-rays my children may be likely to have certain forms of pathology predictable in advance.)

We might in a formal way allow for a "natural drift" of technical change by introducing exogenous functions $\lambda_i^{\dagger}(t)$, with certain specifiable properties, and then rewrite (1) or (34) in the form

$$\frac{-\dot{\lambda}_2/\lambda_2}{-\dot{\lambda}_2^{\dagger}/\lambda_2^{\dagger}} = f\left[\frac{-\dot{\lambda}_1/\lambda_1}{-\dot{\lambda}_1^{\dagger}/\lambda_1^{\dagger}}; a_1\right]. \qquad (37)$$

Then certain patterns of $-\dot{\lambda}_i/\lambda_i$ become more profitable than others, depending on what is known about $\lambda_i^{\dagger}(t)$. (An interesting hypothesis might make the latter neutrally exponential.) I shall not explore this important matter of natural drift of technology further.[8]

V

After these extensive researches, some historical conclusions can be briefly summarized:

i. Ricardo, to the disgust of some of his disciples (such as McCulloch), noted that invention of machines might hurt wages. Wicksell corrected what appears to be one of Ricardo's rare outright errors — namely the view that an invention might harm all of a competitive society. In resurrecting Ricardo's discussion of invention, Wicksell called attention to the passages in which Ricardo is all but recognizing that labor's share is affected in accordance with what today would be described as how the relative shift and twist in labor's Clarkian marginal-product diagram ends up changing the ratio of its marginal-product rectangle to its residual-rent triangle.[9]

[8] The absence of zero serial correlation in innovation gives this notion of natural drift operational content.

[9] K. Wicksell, *Lectures on Political Economy, Vol. I: General Theory* (London: Routledge & Kegan Paul, 1934),

ii. Wicksell gives the first modern discussion of technical change and distribution, although applied primarily to labor and land rather than to land and capital. Hick's 1932 treatment is more like that of Wicksell than anybody else, but the influence of Edwin Cannan and of Pigou is also evident.[10]

iii. Hicks, like Marx before him, ends up with a vague notion that innovation tends to be biased in a labor-saving direction. Numerous authors, including economic historians, have pursued this vague line of reasoning.[11] But in what sense any factor price can be said to be "high" was insufficiently explored. Fellner, at least, tried to make the Hicks analysis dynamic and expectational, utilizing (as Kennedy never does) the Hicksian insight that capital tends to grow (in some kind of natural units) relative to labor. All that Fellner seems to end up showing is that, if two improvements seem equally easy to make, the one which involves the least labor will tend to be introduced with greater probability the greater is the expectation of the entrepreneur that wage rates will rise relative to other factors. This near tautology, by itself, conveys little to my mind.

iv. Kennedy, although he thinks he is fulfilling the Hicks program of labor-saving bias, in fact deduces an asymptotic state of Hicks-neutral technical change [12] (which I show to be stable if, and only if, the elasticity of substitution can be assumed to be less than unity). This is not a theory of constant relative shares so much as a theory that technical change itself will not ultimately contribute toward a change in relative shares when the ratio of factor prices or of factor supplies is not exogenously changing.

v. When I postulate a deepening of capital relative to labor, so that V_2/V_1 tends to rise and to raise labor's relative share (if the elasticity of substitution is presumed to be less than unity), I am able to deduce an asymptotic steady state of induced labor-augmenting (and also, with $\sigma < 1$, Hicks labor-saving) technical change, by virtue of the fact that every increase in labor's relative share increases the inducement to augment its technical effectiveness by purposive invention.

This is demonstrated in my basic theorem of section 11. In the special case of assumed symmetry, my corollary shows that we can avoid the Kindleberger paradox of equal relative shares as the deepening of capital induces labor-saving invention at a rate large enough to cause labor to have the larger relative share. While this agrees with broad facts, the model cannot explain the approximate constancy of the rate of profit over long periods of time.

Having entrepreneurs show prevision and minimize costs over a future period of time in which wage rates can be presumed to rise does give a Fellner reinforcement to the above conclusion.

vi. However, all of the above is emasculated if we should postulate that a rational entrepreneur will, other things being equal, have no reason to expend more effort to reduce one dollar of expenditure than another. As soon as we make the technical transformation function of (1) depend upon factor shares in the way stipulated in (35), so that cost minimization is as likely to take place with either factor augmented more than the other, the Principle of Sufficient Reason makes induced technical change Hicks-neutral at every instant no matter what the relative shares. Hence, induced invention has no systematic bias, and the drift of relative shares depends upon the drift of exogenous technical changes and upon the change of factor proportions (as affected by the relevant elasticity of substitution).

vii. Final analysis shows factor shares free to drift as the wind listeth. As a matter of his-

143–144; David Ricardo, *Principles of Political Economy* (Sraffa edition), Chapter XXXI; N. Kaldor, "A Case Against Technical Progress?" *Economica*, 12 (1932), 180–196; P. A. Samuelson, "Wages and Interest: A Modern Dissection of Marxian Economic Models," *American Economic Review*, 47 (1957), 884–912, particularly 894.

[10] J. R. Hicks, *The Theory of Wages* (London: Macmillan, 1932 and 1963), Chapter 5; E. Cannan, *The Economic Outlook*, p. 215ff; A. C. Pigou, *Economics of Welfare*, 4th ed. (London: Macmillan, 1960), Part IV, Chapter IV; W. Fellner, *op. cit.*

[11] Cf. E. Rothbart, "Causes of the Superior Efficiency of U.S.A. Industry as Compared with British Industry," *Economic Journal*, 56 (Sept. 1946), 383–390, and H. J. Habakkuk, *American and British Technology in the Nineteenth Century* (Cambridge University Press, 1962). Professor Kindleberger is correct is his famous quotation that economic history is great fun but [often] can not be taken seriously. It is even more comical when it degenerates into inconclusive anecdotes purporting to verify ill-formulated economic theorizing.

[12] See however, my qualification in footnote 3.

torical fact and reasonable expectation, the purely exogenous drift of invention need not be "random" in any easily defined sense. Informed technologists in any era and area have good hunches concerning the natural drift of productive invention, all of which can be formally embodied in the basic technical transformation functions.

viii. For the most part, labor-saving innovation has a spurious attractiveness to economists because of a fortuitous verbal muddle. When writers list inventions, they find it easy to list labor-saving ones and exceedingly difficult to list capital-saving ones. (Cannan is much quoted for his brilliance in being able to think up wire*less* as a capital-saving invention, the syllable "less" apparently being a guarantee that it does save capital!) That this is all fallacious becomes apparent when one examines a mathematical production function and tries to decide in advance whether a particular described invention changes the partial-derivatives of marginal productivity imputation one way or another.

Thus, consider a locomotive. It is big and heavy. So the literary mind thinks that it must correspond to a capital-using invention and hence to a labor-saving invention. Or think of a complex Rube Goldberg-like modern contraption. It is intricate and round about. So it must be regarded as labor saving and capital using. And yet there is not the slightest pretext for such an inference. In the steady state, when human labor is organized through time with locomotives rather than without them, there is no way to tell in advance whether the relative share of labor in comparison with property has gone up or down in the steady state with production at all the stages vertically integrated.

We have the unfortunate tendency to use labor as the denominator in making productivity statements. *Any* invention, whether capital saving or labor saving, just by virtue of its definition as an invention rather than a disimprovement will, other things being equal, result in more output with the same labor or the same output with less labor. *That* could be said with *any* factor substituted for labor. But we know how difficult it is in a changing technology to get commensurable non-labor factors to put in the denominator of a productivity comparison. So we tend to concentrate on labor. and then we fall for the pun, or play on words, which infers a labor-saving invention whenever there is an invention! [13]

Thus, consider a simple case where output acts as if it were produced by a Cobb-Douglas function with coefficients ¾ and ¼. Now let the locomotive, or the wheel, or fire, or the calculus be invented. Now can one have the least idea whether the function is merely increased in scale as against being twisted one way or the other in terms of its C-D coefficients? And when one considers embodied technical change, and changing elasticities of substitution, as one must be prepared to do, how far from intuitive inference the problem becomes.

VI

The following summary may help the understanding of this intricate analysis.

Since the 1932 publication of J. R. Hicks' *Theory of Wages* there has been the vague notion that high wages somehow induce "labor-saving" inventions. Rothbarth, Kaldor, and Habbakuk have attempted to use this theory to interpret the history of American prosperity. Since at minimum-cost equilibrium, all inputs are equally marginally dear and productive, the simplest interpretation of the high-wage theory of induced innovation is ill-founded. Fellner has added the dynamic consideration that, the steady accumulation of capital (somehow defined) relative to labor can be expected to continue in the future as in the past. It is reasonable for firms, therefore, to extrapolate a rising trend of (money and real) wage rates, and not unreasonable for them to extrapolate the historical lack of trend of the profit rate, and the concomitant downward trend in rental rates for equipment of the same technical type. This dynamic expectational effect of relatively high wage rates should, other things equal, pro-

[13] Even Pigou (p. 675) is capable of this gem: "Probably, however, the majority of inventions in the narrower sense would have to be reckoned as 'labor-saving,' because as Cassel has observed, 'almost all the efforts of inventors are directed toward finding durable instruments to do work which has hitherto been done by hand'." As if inventors wanted durability for its own sake, or that one could legitimately make inferences about labor share from the natural desire to economize on payrolls.

mote inventions designed to lower labor-input requirements.

The present paper carries the analysis further. Based upon the Kennedy-Weizsäcker notion of a (time-invariant) trade-off frontier between innovational reductions in labor versus capital-input requirements, then the theorem is proved that a long-run equilibrium of constant relative shares will exist, and that, provided the elasticity of substitution is less than unity, the equilibrium will be stably approached i.e., any initial tendency for the share of labor to drift upward will make it especially profitable to introduce relatively labor-augmenting innovations, thereby (with $\sigma < 1$) bringing labor's share back to the equilibrium level. If factor supplies remain in balance, my theory deduces an equilibrium of Hicks-neutral technical change. (Under a special symmetry assumption, the model would lead to equal factor shares for two factors or for n factors, a rather bizarre result.) Then the theorem is proved that steady growth of the capital/labor ratio will lead to a long-run equilibrium in which there is induced relatively greater labor-augmenting or labor-saving inventions to just the degree needed to keep the ratio of capital (in efficiency units) to labor (in efficiency units) constant. This equilibrium, which would be unstable if the elasticity of substitution were greater than one, provides a theory of stable relative shares with the testable implication that an increase in thrift relative to labor growth will increase the share of labor relative to property. This conclusion is independent of Fellner expectational effects, but reinforced by them. The model leading to this conclusion is shown to be only one of a number of economically important models — as, for example, the simple view that each dollar of cost tends to merit an equal research effort toward cost reduction, with *no* implied bias of innovation.

[16]

On Putty-Clay[1]

I. INTRODUCTION

1. *The Model*

Following on the work of Johansen [3] and Salter [8] a number of writers (e.g. [2], [4], [6], [7] and [10]) have investigated various properties of a model of economic growth which is characterized by a variable capital-labour ratio at the moment that investment occurs (putty), and a fixed capital-labour ratio thereafter (clay). Technical progress takes the form of a flow of new ideas for the construction of investments, but it does not include any new ideas for the more efficient employment of existing investments. In the now standard terminology, technical change is all " embodied ". The term " putty-clay ", coined by Phelps [7], neatly describes these assumptions. The aim of this paper is to provide a fairly complete and rigorous treatment of the balanced and the efficient growth paths of the model without recourse to unnecessarily restrictive assumptions such as Cobb-Douglas. This task, among others, has already been completed by Solow, Tobin, von Weizsäcker and Yaari [9] for the case in which the capital-labour ratio is fixed even at the moment of investment. Such a case is a limiting and special case of the model of this paper, so that the results of Solow and his colleagues have provided a useful check on my results. The same is true of Phelps' results on the Cobb-Douglas case.

It turns out that there are certain problems to be faced in a rigorous treatment whose existence has not been noted in the literature. For example, even under the usual assumption of " diminishing returns ", the relation between the rate of profit and the balanced growth state need not be one-to-one; indeed, unless some care is taken with assumptions and proof, there may be no balanced growth path at all for some values of the rate of profit. This will all be demonstrated below. In the remainder of this introduction the assumptions are carefully stated, and critically evaluated. Then the notion of balanced growth is introduced, and certain consequences of the definition noted. Next comes an intensive examination of the state of a balanced growth economy at one moment of time, a discussion of the existence and uniqueness of profit maximizing investment choices, and an existence theorem. In balanced growth conditions there is a known relationship between the capital intensity of an investment designed to employ one man and the difference between its present value and its cost (the net present value). If net present value has a maximum for a unique investment decision then, in competitive conditions with perfect foresight, the type of investment is uniquely determined. But, unfortunately, there is nothing to guarantee a unique net present value maximizing decision, and the discussion has to take account of this fact. If the reader bears this in mind he will more readily follow where the argument is going. After the existence theorem, the proof of which is given in an appendix, there is a general discussion of comparative dynamics results under a special uniqueness assumption designed to eliminate the above problem. Finally there is a section on efficient growth paths in which the usual relation between efficiency and equilibrium under a shadow price system is shown to hold in the putty-clay model.

2. *Assumptions*

There is only one kind of output flow, whose level at time t is denoted $Y(t)$. This is divided into consumption, $C(t)$, and gross investment, $I(t)$. Thus

$$Y(t) = C(t)+I(t). \qquad \text{...(1)}$$

[1] I am greatly indebted to D. G. Champernowne, F. M. Fisher, F. H. Hahn and J. A. Mirrlees for helpful advice and criticism of earlier drafts. None of these bear any responsibility for errors in this version.

Total output is the sum of outputs obtained from investments of various " vintages ", or past dates. Let $X(t, \theta)$ be the amount of output obtained at time t from investments initiated at, of vintage, θ. Then

$$Y(t) = \int_{-\infty}^{t} X(t, \theta)d\theta. \qquad \ldots(2)$$

$X(t, \theta)$ depends upon four things: the level of gross investment at time θ, the extent to which this investment has survived physically to time t, the amount of employment which investments of vintage θ were designed to offer (represented, given $I(\theta)$, by the investment-employment ratio), and the amount of labour applied to these investments at time t. Let us dispose of the problem of physical depreciation of capital by supposing that none occurs. This is unrealistic; but the inclusion of physical depreciation would not greatly enrich the model, while its exclusion serves to highlight important features of this vintage technology, in particular the central role of economic obsolescence. Let $L(t, \theta)$ be the amount of labour applied at time t to investments of vintage θ. Assume that at the instant at which an investment is undertaken it is fully manned, so that $L(\theta, \theta)$ represents the employment-capacity of investments of vintage θ. Later it will be seen that this assumption is justified under competition or on an efficient path. Now $X(\theta, \theta)$ is the capacity-output of investments of vintage θ and, assuming away gestation lags for investment, this is related to gross investment and capacity-employment by a production function.

$$X(\theta, \theta) = F[I(\theta), L(\theta, \theta), \theta]. \qquad \ldots(3)$$

In fact writing $X(\theta, \theta)$ as a function of $I(\theta)$, $L(\theta, \theta)$ and θ, as in (3), involves an important, so far unstated, assumption. This is that at most one kind of investment is constructed at θ, i.e. all investments of vintage θ share a common investment-labour ratio. Although it seems to be widely assumed that this will always be the case in a competitive economy with perfect foresight about future wage and interest costs, there is in fact no reason why investments of a particular vintage need be homogeneous in this manner. This will become clear below. Fortunately, there is no need to introduce a more general expression for $X(\theta, \theta)$, for the equations derived on the assumption of a unique investment-labour ratio turn out to be valid anyway. Where multiple investment-labour ratios occur the equations will have multiple solutions.

It is now necessary to specify the short-run, or ex-post, relation between labour input and output on existing investments—the utilization function. The easiest assumption, and the one that will be adopted, is that this relation is linear up to the employment-capacity. Then on applying any fraction, less than one, of capacity-labour to an investment one obtains the same fraction of capacity-output. Thus

$$X(t, \theta) = X(\theta, \theta)\frac{L(t, \theta)}{L(\theta, \theta)}; \qquad \ldots(4)$$

$$\left.\begin{array}{ll} L(t, \theta) \leq L(\theta, \theta) & t \geq \theta \\ L(t, \theta) = 0 & t < \theta \end{array}\right\}. \qquad \ldots(5)$$

However, convenient though it is, this assumption should not be allowed to pass unnoticed. There is no reason why there has to be constant-returns in this sense, anymore than there is ever any reason why there has to be constant returns-to-scale. Suppose, for example, that plant warmed up during use and operated more efficiently when hot. Then if a fraction of capacity-labour were applied to an investment by operating the plant for a fraction of the normal working day, (which might be the only feasible way of having labour below capacity), the plant would operate at a lower average temperature and might produce less than the given fraction of capacity output. The utilization function would, in this case, be strictly convex. In the present continuous time formulation this question is not critically involved because $L(t, \theta)$ will be equal either to $L(\theta, \theta)$ or to zero almost everywhere. But in a more realistic discrete time model one might have to modify (4).

Let $N(t)$ denote total employment at time t, and note that

$$N(t) = \int_{-\infty}^{t} L(t, \theta) d\theta. \qquad \text{...(6)}$$

Finally, define $s(t)$, the gross saving-investment ratio, as

$$s(t) = I(t)/Y(t) \qquad \text{...(7)}$$

and $k(t)$, *per capita* investment at time t, as

$$k(t) = I(t)/L(t, t). \qquad \text{...(8)}$$

3. *Returns-to-Scale*

Equations (1) to (7) make no assertion about, and do not in any way depend upon, the homogeneity of degree one of the production function F. However, we must at some stage concern ourselves with the question of returns-to-scale. There are at least two ways in which increasing, or decreasing, returns-to-scale could be represented in this model, plus another which my formulation has virtually excluded. The latter is considered first. The technology is specified as though investment consisted entirely of the construction of a number of plants each completely independent of all existing plant. This formulation makes it hard to find a way of representing the kinds of returns-to-scale which neo-classical writers have had in mind when suggesting that the aggregate production function might exhibit increasing returns; namely the view that there may be returns-to-scale associated with the level of activity in the whole economy. Such returns-to-scale might derive from those of individual firms, or they might be Marshallian external economies. But they are not associated with the size of investment projects of particular dates. Yet such returns-to-scale may be of considerable importance.

The scale effects that might be more readily considered are of two types. One that has been discussed already is convexity of the utilization function of a particular plant. A different kind of increasing returns would be present if (3) were to exhibit increasing returns-to-scale. This would mean that there are returns to designing and building a large plant; or, more accurately, there are returns to having a large current investment project.

Thus there are numerous possibilities, and it should by now be clear that the whole question of returns-to-scale is very much more complex in the case of vintage models than it is in the straight non-vintage theory. Having said all this I shall from now on assume that (3) is homogeneous of degree one. Balanced growth theory requires, at the very least, homogeneity, not necessarily of degree one. The interested reader will however be able to confirm that my theorem on efficient paths of economic growth can easily be restated and proved, by the same methods, for the case of increasing returns.

There is another property of the production function that has to be considered. This is what is usually called diminishing returns. Suppose the amount of labour to be allocated to new investments (of one type) is fixed at a certain level. This eliminates pure scale effects. The capacity output of these investments now depends only upon *per capita* gross investment. Let

$$X(\theta, \theta)/L(\theta, \theta) = f(k(\theta), \theta). \qquad \text{...(9)}$$

The function f will be said to satisfy the property of diminishing returns if it is a strictly concave function of k. Later a slightly stronger condition proves to be useful.

Definition 1. The function $f(k(\theta), \theta)$ will be said to be regularly strictly concave if for each $h>0$ there exists a value of k, denoted k_h, such that $f(k_h, \theta)<h.k_h$.

This is equivalent to saying that the investment output ratio increases without limit as $k \to \infty$. A sufficient condition for this is the right-hand Inada condition:

$$\lim_{k \to \infty} \frac{\partial f}{\partial k} = 0. \qquad \text{...(10)}$$

Another condition sufficient to guarantee that Definition 1 be satisfied, due to Koopmans [5], is that the production function be strictly concave and that positive output cannot be produced without labour. An example of a function that is strictly concave, but not regularly strictly concave, is provided by the function:

$$f(k, \theta) = \frac{k(k+5)}{2(k+1)}. \qquad \text{...(11)}$$

4. *Competitive Equilibrium and Efficiency*

Consider a time path of the economy satisfying equations (1) to (7), where $N(t)$ is a given function of time. Such a path will be said to be feasible.

Definition 2. A growth path of the economy will be said to be efficient if it is feasible and if there exists no other distinct feasible growth path, with consumption stream $C'(t)$, such that $C'(t) \geqq C(t)$, and $C'(t) > C(t)$ on a set of t whose measure is not zero.

The definition has of necessity to admit cases in which $C'(t)$ exceeds $C(t)$ at moments of time so sparse that they can be neglected for the purpose of integration. With that proviso, Definition 2 states that, essentially, no other feasible path dominates the efficient path with consumption stream $C(t)$.

On an efficient path investments are manned up in descending order of output per man. Thus if $f[k(\theta), \theta] > f[k(\theta'), \theta']$, then $L(t, \theta') > 0$ at $t \geqq \theta$ only if $L(t, \theta) = L(\theta, \theta)$. This leads naturally to the following definitions

$$S_t = \{x \mid x = f[k(\theta), \theta] \text{ for } \theta \leqq t \text{ such that } L(t, \theta) < L(\theta, \theta)\},$$
$$S_t' = \{x \mid x = f[k(\theta), \theta] \text{ for } \theta \leqq t \text{ such that } L(t, \theta) = L(\theta, \theta)\}. \qquad \text{...(12)}$$

S_t is the set of all *per capita* outputs of investments that are not fully manned at time t. S_t' is the set of all *per capita* outputs of investments that are fully manned at time t. If a small amount of extra labour were to be made available to the economy and found employment then output could increase at a rate indicated by the least upper bound of S_t, while if labour available fell then output would decrease at a rate indicated by the greatest lower bound of S_t'. The shadow wage rate is a function satisfying at each t the following condition.

$$\sup S_t \leqq w(t) \leqq \inf S_t'. \qquad \text{...(13)}$$

In most of the cases that we shall want to study S_t and S' will contain every value in a certain interval, in which case the sup and the inf of (13) will be equal, and $w(t)$ will be unique. But that cannot be guaranteed in general, and the definition has to cover the general case.

Definition 3. The function $r(t)$ will be said to be the rate of return on an efficient growth path if it satisfies the relation

$$-k(\theta) + \int_\theta^\infty \{f[k(\theta), \theta] - w(t)\} \frac{L(t, \theta)}{L(\theta, \theta)} \exp\left(-\int_\theta^t r(z)dz\right) dt = 0. \qquad \text{...(14)}$$

for some $w(t)$ satisfying (13). (14) says that the investment cost of one man-place is equal to the value of all future quasi-rents discounted at an instantaneous rate which is $r(t)$ at time t. The existence and uniqueness of $r(t)$ will be established below. The fact that the path is required to be efficient plays no part in the definition, but the rate of return as defined would not correspond to the ordinary notion of a rate of return were the path inefficient.

Definition 4. A growth path of the economy will be said to be a competitive equilibrium if there exists $r(t)$ such that, for each θ, and for each type of investment constructed,

$$-k(\theta)+\int_\theta^\infty \{f[k(\theta),\theta]-w(t)\}\frac{L(t,\theta)}{L(\theta,\theta)}\exp\left(-\int_\theta^t r(z)dz\right)dt$$

$$=\max_{\substack{k\\ L(t,\theta)}}\left[-k+\int_\theta^\infty \{f(k,\theta)-w(t)\}\frac{L(t,\theta)}{L(\theta,\theta)}\exp\left(-\int_\theta^t r(z)dz\right)dt\right]=0. \quad \text{...(15)}$$

This corresponds to the ordinary notion of an intertemporal competitive equilibrium. The capital intensity of each type of investment and the plan for manning it are chosen so as to maximize the net present value of an investment designed to employ one man (one man-place), and this present value is zero; there is no pure profit.

There are two conditions that are clearly necessary for (15) to be satisfied for a positive k. In the first place, $L(t, \theta)$ should be zero whenever $f(k, \theta)<w(t)$ (neglecting cases where this condition is violated on sets of t of zero measure). This simply states that present value cannot be maximized if the investment is manned when the output produced is not sufficient to pay shadow wage costs. The second condition is that the derivative of (15) with respect to k should vanish; net present value should be stationary with respect to variations in capital intensity alone. In certain cases these two necessary conditions may together be sufficient for (15), but they are not in general sufficient for a maximum of net present value. This is a basic problem of which our analysis has to take account. It is therefore useful to have to hand a piece of terminology to cover the case in which we know that necessary conditions for a maximum of net present value are satisfied, but we do not wish to prejudge the question as to whether (15) is satisfied.

Definition 5. A growth path of the economy will be said to be a first-order competitive equilibrium if there exists $r(t)$ such that (14) is satisfied and such that

$$L(t,\theta)=0 \text{ whenever } f[k(\theta),\theta]<w(t);$$

$$\frac{\partial f}{\partial k}\int_\theta^\infty \frac{L(t,\theta)}{L(\theta,\theta)}\exp\left(-\int_\theta^t r(z)dz\right)dt-1=0 \quad \text{...(16)}$$

for each θ, and for each type of investment constructed.

II. BALANCED GROWTH

1. *Definition*

The economy is in a state of balanced growth if all the variables grow through time at constant exponential rates, some of which are zero. This idea is given a precise formulation in the following definition.

Definition 6. A growth path will be said to be a balanced growth path if there exist scalars a and b such that: (i) b is positive; (ii) Y and I both grow at exponential rate $a+b$; (iii) N and $L(t, t)$ both grow at exponential rate a.

An immediate consequence of Definition 6 is that s, the gross saving-investment share is also a constant.

Theorem 1. *If Definition 6 is satisfied by an efficient path one of the following conditions is satisfied:* either *all investments, however old, are in use;* or *there exists T, a constant, such that an investment of vintage θ is in use if and only if $t \leq \theta+T$.*

Proof. The definition of balanced growth clearly implies technical progress, rather than regress, since Y increases faster than N and $L(\theta, \theta)$. Thus the *per capita* output of investments is a monotonically increasing function of θ, the date of the investment. Hence, at any t, either all investments are in use or there exists a T satisfying the requirement of the theorem. It is only necessary to show that this T is invariant with time. Note that

$$N(t) = \int_{t-T(t)}^{t} L(\theta, \theta)d\theta = L_0 \int_{t-T(t)}^{t} e^{a\theta}d\theta = L_0 e^{at}\frac{1-e^{-aT(t)}}{a}; \qquad \text{...(17)}$$

$$\dot{N}(t) = L(t, t) - L(t-T, t-T)[1-\dot{T}(t)]$$
$$= L_0 e^{at}[1-e^{-aT(t)} + \dot{T}(t)e^{-aT(t)}]. \qquad \text{...(18)}$$

From which it follows at once that N is growing at rate a only if $\dot{T} = 0$.

2. *Existence of Balanced Growth Paths*

Balanced growth is only possible if technical change takes a particular form. Even if technical change is such as to permit balanced growth, such growth will not be possible if the labour supply does not expand or contract in such a manner as to permit balanced growth. Finally, even if the labour supply grows at a constant exponential rate it may grow so rapidly that it does not all find employment. There is no need to discuss all these questions in this paper. The condition for balanced growth with full employment of the labour force to be possible has been derived by Solow and colleagues [9] for the fixed investment-labour ratio model as

$$s \geqq \frac{g}{\mu_0(1-e^{-gT})} \qquad \text{...(19)}$$

where $g = a+b$ and μ_0 is the given constant output-investment ratio. (19) has to hold for some $T \leqq +\infty$. In the present model the condition is clearly the same with μ_0 interpreted as the supremum of the set of output-investment ratios available. Less obvious perhaps is the following theorem.

Theorem 2. *Balanced growth is technically possible, given sufficient labour supply, if and only if technical progress is Harrod-neutral at a constant positive exponential rate.*

Proof. (i) Sufficiency. Without loss of generality, let technical change be Harrod-neutral at rate 1. This is a choice of time units. Then the production function takes the form

$$X(\theta, \theta) = F[I(\theta), L(\theta, \theta)e^{\theta}]. \qquad \text{...(20)}$$

$L(\theta, \theta)$ grows at rate a. Then if $I(\theta)$ grows at rate $a+1$, and given the homogeneity of degree one of F, $X(\theta, \theta)$ will grow at rate $a+1$. But

$$Y(t) = \int_{t-T}^{t} X(\theta, \theta)d\theta, \qquad \text{...(21)}$$

where T is to be read as " $+\infty$ " if all investments are in use. Thus Y grows at rate $a+1$ and growth is balanced as required.

(ii) Necessity. Without loss of generality write the production function in the form

$$X(\theta, \theta) = F[I(\theta), L(\theta, \theta)e^{\theta}, \theta], \qquad \text{...(22)}$$

where units for time have been chosen so as to make b of Definition 6 equal 1. Derivatives with respect to various arguments of F will be denoted F_1, F_2 and F_3 to avoid confusion. Then

$$\dot{X}(\theta) = F_1(\theta)\dot{I}(\theta) + F_2(\theta)[\dot{L}(\theta, \theta)e^{\theta} + L(\theta, \theta)e^{\theta}] + F_3(\theta) \qquad \text{...(23)}$$
$$= (1+a)F_1(\theta)I(\theta) + (1+a)F_2(\theta)L(\theta, \theta)e^{\theta} + F_3(\theta). \qquad \text{...(24)}$$

But $\dot{X}(\theta) = (1+a)X(\theta)$ and, by constant returns-to-scale

$$X(\theta) = F_1(\theta)I(\theta)+F_2(\theta)L(\theta, \theta)e^{\theta}. \quad ...(25)$$

Hence

$$F_3(\theta) = (1+a)X(\theta)-(1+a)F_1(\theta)I(\theta)-(1+a)F_2(\theta)L(\theta, \theta)e^{\theta} = 0. \quad ...(26)$$

So that, at least at the point at which balanced growth takes place, the production function has the Harrod-neutral form. If balanced growth could take place on a whole range of values of the investment-output ratio at the same rate then technical change is Harrod-neutral everywhere on this range. The proof of Theorem 2 is now complete.

3. *Competitive Balanced Growth*

Consider now balanced growth paths that are also competitive equilibria in the sense of Definition 4. A balanced path is fully characterised by its state at time zero and by the numbers a and b. From now on units for measuring time will always be chosen so as to make b equal to 1. Thus technical progress is Harrod-neutral at rate 1. The shadow wage rate grows at the same rate as output per man on new investments which is the same as the rate of technical progress which is 1. It is first shown that if a balanced path satisfies Definition 4 then $r(t)$ must be a constant. From now on attention is confined to the case when T is finite.[1]

A necessary condition for positive k and non-negative $L(t, \theta)$ to maximize the present value expression (15) is that (15) be at a maximum for k taken alone, and for this a necessary condition is (16). If growth is balanced (15) and (16) reduce to

$$-k_0e^{\theta}+\int_{\theta}^{\theta+T}\{f_0e^{\theta}-w_0e^{t}\}e^{-\int_0^t r(z)dz}dt = 0 \quad ...(27)$$

and

$$f'(\theta)\int_{\theta}^{\theta+T}e^{-\int_0^t r(z)dz}dt-1 = 0, \quad ...(28)$$

where $f'(\theta)$ denotes the partial derivative of $f[k(\theta), \theta]$ with respect to $k(\theta)$, and where $f_0e^{\theta} = w_0e^{\theta+T}$. The relations (27) and (28) hold identically in θ. Thus the first derivative of (27) with respect to θ is zero.

$$-k_0e^{\theta}-[f_0e^{\theta}-w_0e^{\theta}]+f_0e^{\theta}\int_{\theta}^{\theta+T}e^{-\int_0^t r(z)dz}dt+r(\theta)\int_{\theta}^{\theta+T}\{f_0e^{\theta}-w_0e^{t}\}e^{-\int_0^t r(z)dz}dt = 0. \quad ...(29)$$

Taking into account (27) and (28) this reduces to

$$-k_0e^{\theta}-[f_0e^{\theta}-w_0e^{\theta}]+\frac{f_0e^{\theta}}{f'(\theta)}+r(\theta)k_0e^{\theta} = 0, \quad ...(30)$$

or

$$r(\theta) = 1+\frac{f_0-w_0}{k_0}-\frac{f_0}{k_0f'(\theta)}. \quad ...(31)$$

Since $f'(\theta)$ is a constant on a balanced path it follows that $r(\theta)$ is a constant.

Since a balanced growth path is characterized, given a and b, by its state at time zero it is sufficient for many purposes to develop the theory of competitive investment behaviour at time zero. Competitive behaviour by decision-makers is taken to entail the following; (i) they are price-takers who expect the real wage rate to rise at exponential rate 1, and the rate of discount to remain constant at r, (ii) they choose the capital intensity

[1] My proof that $r(t)$ must be a constant is an alternative proof to that of Solow and colleagues in [9], which would serve as well for this model. Their proof is superior to the present one in that no appeal is made to the maximisation of present value. However, it is also more intricate than the simple proof which a variable proportions model allows.

of new investments so as to maximize the present value, discounting at rate r, of one " man-place ", i.e, an investment designed to employ one man, and (iii) in order to achieve a maximum of present value they plan to retire investments when the cost of manning them has just reached their capacity output level. The maximum net present value is zero. From now on a variable without a time argument will denote the value of that variable at time zero, e.g. $X = X(0, 0)$, and

$$\frac{X}{L} = f[k(0), 0] = f(k). \qquad ...(32)$$

Consider an investor at time zero making a decision as to the type of investment to construct. For the moment it is assumed that only one kind of investment is constructed, and its type is fully specified by the investment-labour ratio k. This investment is one man-place. Suppose that the planned economic lifetime of the investment is T years. Then the net present value net of investment outlay is the following

$$-k+\int_0^T f(k)e^{-rt}dt-\int_0^T we^te^{-rt}dt = -k+f(k)\frac{1-e^{-rT}}{r}-w\frac{1-e^{-(r-1)T}}{r-1}. \qquad ...(33)$$

The expression $\frac{1-e^{-rT}}{r}$ is the discounted value of a stream of one unit of output lasting for T periods of time, the discount rate being r. It is useful to have a shorthand for expressions of this kind, and the following is introduced

$$\text{dis}\,(r, T) = \frac{1-e^{-rT}}{r}. \qquad ...(34)$$

Then the right-hand side of (33) can be written more compactly as

$$-k+f(k)\,\text{dis}\,(r, T)-w\,\text{dis}\,(r-1, T). \qquad ...(35)$$

If the optimal retirement condition is satisfied we also have

$$f(k) = we^T \text{ or } T = \max[\log_e\{f(k)/w\}, 0]. \qquad ...(36)$$

The max operator in (36) reminds us that if an investor were foolish enough to build an investment that could not produce enough to cover wage costs even at their low initial level, then it would be optimal to retire it at once.

Now, given r and w, and taking into account (36), the net present value can be written as a function of k alone. Since the net present value is to be maximised it would be desirable, though by no means necessary, if this function were to be concave on the range of values of k such that $f(k) \geqq w$. Better still, it might be strictly concave. Of course a failure of this function to be concave would mean that on a range on which there was not concavity the net present value of investments in this range could be bettered by convex combinations of investments outside the range. This is illustrated in Fig. 1. On the range AB the net present value of a man-place of capital intensity k, denoted $P(k)$, is non-concave. But the net present value of a convex combination of machines of capital intensity k_A and k_B is clearly the same convex combination of their net present values. Thus the " dip " in the function can always be filled in by building investments of less than one man-place and of differing capital intensities and " mixing " them. Furthermore, as is to be expected, the maximum net present value can always be obtained, given any r and w, with one kind of investment; but that may not be the unique way of obtaining it.

There are two things that I have not yet demonstrated. The first is that the kind of case illustrated in Fig. 1 can in fact arise when the ex-ante production function is subject to the diminishing returns requirement $f''(k)<0$. The second is that this case, should it arise, could occur in the instance that the values of r and w were values consistent with equilibrium, i.e. such that the maximum net present value was zero, and that further there might be more than one equilibrium value of k associated with a particular value of r. All these possibilities occur in the following example.

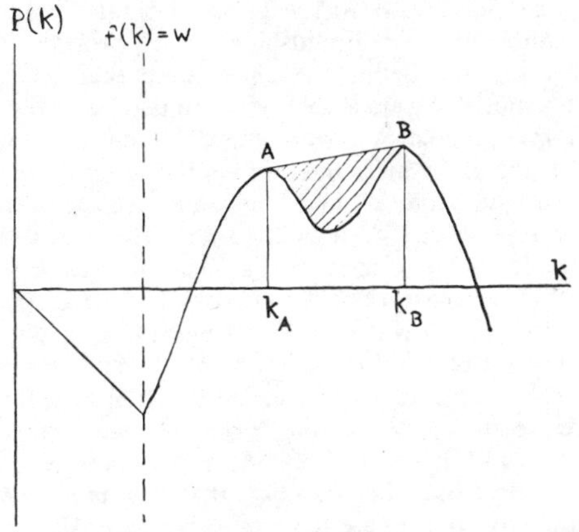

FIGURE 1

Let $r = 0{\cdot}25$ and $w = 1$. Since the production function is monotonic we can work just as well with the inverse of $f(k)$ as with $f(k)$ itself. Thus let $k = f^{-1}(x)$. The function f^{-1} gives the amount of *per capita* investment that is required to obtain a *per capita* output of x. The requirement that $f(k)$ be a strictly concave function now translates into the requirement that f^{-1} be a strictly convex function; the inverse of a monotonic strictly concave function is strictly convex. Now consider this case:

$$k = f^{-1}(x) = \tfrac{4}{3}(1-4x^{0\cdot75}+3x). \qquad \text{...(37)}$$

This function is not very well behaved for low x, but the example does not depend upon the properties of the function for $x<1 = w$. So the function could be modified so as to make it a better text-book production function for low values of x. As it stands $f^{-1}(1) = 0$ so that some output is obtainable with no investment at all, but again it could be easily modified, while still remaining convex, to remove this feature. That the function (37) is indeed strictly convex on the relevant range can be seen as follows.

$$\left.\begin{aligned}\frac{dk}{dx} &= 4(1-x^{-0.25})>0 \text{ for } x>1,\\ \frac{d^2k}{dx^2} &= x^{-1.25}>0.\end{aligned}\right\} \qquad \text{...(38)}$$

Thus f^{-1} is the inverse of a well-behaved production function, at least for x greater than some number greater than one. Now, substituting into (33), obtain the following expression for the net present value as a function of x.

$$-k+x\,\frac{1-e^{-rT}}{r}-x\,\frac{1-e^{-(r-1)T}}{r-1} = -f^{-1}(x)+x\,\frac{1-e^{-0.25\log_e x}}{0\cdot25}+\frac{1-e^{0.75\log_e x}}{0\cdot75}, \qquad \text{...(39)}$$

where T has been eliminated from (36). Simplifying (39) one obtains

$$-f^{-1}(x)+4x(1-x^{-0.25})+\tfrac{4}{3}(1-x^{0.75}) = -f^{-1}(x)+\tfrac{4}{3}(1-4x^{0.75}+3x), \qquad \text{...(40)}$$

which is identically zero from (37). Here then is the ultimate case of multiple equilibrium solutions corresponding to one value of r. If the production function is the inverse of $\frac{4}{3}(1-4x^{0\cdot75}+3x)$ then at $r = 0\cdot25$ every choice of technique such that x exceeds unity is an equilibrium, as is every possible mix of choices on this range, for the net present value function corresponds identically to the horizontal axis. How do such cases arise and how are they compatible with the diminishing returns property of $f(k)$?

The answer to this question lies in the observation that the capital stock has two distinct dimensions in a putty-clay technology, an intensive investment-labour ratio k, and an extensive economic lifetime of investments T. Consider now an investor who is comparing the present value of an investment of capital intensity k^- to one with a larger capital intensity k^+. A switch from k^- to k^+ increases *per capita* output but, because of the concavity of $f(k)$, it does so at a diminishing rate. This effect taken alone makes for concavity of the net present value function $P(k)$. The stronger the effect of diminishing returns manifested in the curvature of $f(k)$ the more this effect makes for concavity in $P(k)$. But, given w, a rise in $f(k)$ will lead to a lengthening of the economic lifetime of investments and this will tend to offset to some extent the tendency of diminishing returns to lead to concavity of $P(k)$. Thus if the production function were linear, so that diminishing returns did not operate at all, $P(k)$ would be everywhere strictly convex. So, in some sense, non-concavity is more " likely " if the effect of diminishing returns is weak, and this would lead one to expect that the condition that $P(k)$ is a strictly concave function will be related in some way to the elasticity of substitution between employment and investment, denoted by σ, at the relevant point. This is indeed the case as the following argument demonstrates.

$P(k)$ is locally concave (strictly concave) if and only if its second derivative is non-positive (negative).[1] From (33) one obtains the first two derivatives of $P(k)$ noting that T is a function of k through (36).

$$\frac{dP(k)}{dk} = -1+f'(k)\frac{1-e^{-rT}}{r} + (f(k)-we^{T})e^{-rT}\frac{f'(k)}{f(k)}$$

$$= -1+f'(k)\left[\frac{1-e^{-rT}}{r}+e^{-rT}\right] - we^{-(r-1)T}\frac{f'(k)}{f(k)}, \qquad \ldots(41)$$

where, from (36), I have obtained the relation $\frac{dT}{dk} = \frac{f'(k)}{f(k)}$. Next note that,

$$\frac{d^2P(k)}{dk^2} = f''(k)\left(\frac{1-e^{-rT}}{r}+e^{-rT}\right) - we^{-(r-1)T}\frac{f''(k)f(k)-f'(k)^2}{f(k)^2}$$

$$+f'(k)\left[e^{-rT}-re^{-rT}+(r-1)e^{-(r-1)T}\frac{w}{f(k)}\right]\frac{f'(k)}{f(k)}. \qquad \ldots(42)$$

From (36) the last term is zero. Hence,

$$\frac{d^2P(k)}{dk^2} = f''(k)\left[\frac{1-e^{-rT}}{r}+e^{-rT}-e^{-rT}\right] + e^{-rT}\frac{f'(k)^2}{f(k)}$$

$$= f''(k)\frac{1-e^{-rT}}{r} + e^{-rT}\frac{f'(k)^2}{f(k)}, \qquad \ldots(43)$$

[1] This statement requires a regularity condition to justify the necessity for the second derivative to be negative. A function can be strictly concave at a point at which its second derivative vanishes provided that higher order derivatives, should they exist, satisfy the requirement that the lowest order non-vanishing derivative that exists be of even order and negative. An example is provided by the function $-x^m$, where m is a positive even integer, at $x = 0$.

$$\frac{d^2P}{dk^2} = \frac{f'(k)\{f(k)-kf'(k)\}}{kf(k)}\left[-\frac{1}{\sigma}\left(\frac{1-e^{-rT}}{r}\right)+\frac{kf'(k)}{f(k)-kf'(k)}e^{-rT}\right], \quad \text{...(44)}$$

where σ, the elasticity of substitution, is given by the usual formula

$$\sigma = -\frac{f'(k)\{f(k)-kf'(k)\}}{kf(k)f''(k)}. \quad \text{...(45)}$$

Thus $P(k)$ will fail to be locally concave when

$$\sigma > \frac{1-e^{-rT}}{re^{-rT}}\left[\frac{f(k)-kf'(k)}{kf'(k)}\right]. \quad \text{...(46)}$$

This is a very important condition, and one that will turn up again in later discussion. It depends of course not simply upon the technology as specified by $f(k)$, but also upon the factor prices r and w.

4. *Existence of Competitive Balanced Growth Paths*

The ground has now been cleared for the existence theorem for a competitive balanced growth equilibrium. The foregoing discussion has given warning that there are certain problems which must be taken into account in the construction of this proof. In the first place we know already that we cannot hope to establish the uniqueness of the competitive equilibrium values corresponding to a particular value of r. But the existence theorem will clair.. to establish no more than the proposition that to each r within a given range there corresponds at least one competitive equilibrium. More important, the argument must take account of the fact that $P(k)$ cannot be assumed in advance to be concave at any particular point. Fortunately, this does not give rise to any great analytical problems.

We are here concerned with the following limited question: given suitable values of w, can the equations expressing the conditions of equilibrium in the investment market (profit maximization and free entry) be satisfied by admissible values of r, k and T? The production function $f(k)$ will be assumed to satisfy the property of regular strict concavity, i.e., for each $h>0$ there exists k_h such that $f(k_h)-hk_h<0$.

Theorem 3. *Either, for each positive w less than a given w_0, or for each positive w, there exists a unique positive r, and positive k and T (not necessarily unique), such that the right-hand side of* (33) *achieves its maximum value for positive k and T, and this maximum value is zero.*

The proof of Theorem 3 is given in the Appendix, together with a discussion of why each requirement on w may be necessary. The essence of Theorem 3 is the assertion that the putty-clay model has a factor-price frontier relating r to w. The factor-price frontier may or may not meet the axes.

5. *Comparative Dynamics of Balanced Growth*

The following is the only comparative dynamic result which has general validity.

Theorem 4. *Let w' and w'' be less than w_0 of Theorem* 3, *if such a bound on w exists, and let r' and r'' be such that the requirements of Theorem* 3 *are satisfied, i.e., at r' and w' the maximum net present value is zero, and the same is true at r'' and w''. Then $w'>w''$ implies $r'<r''$.*

Proof. The proof is almost implicit in the proof of Theorem 3. The right-hand side of (33) is, by inspection, a decreasing function of w. So a fall in w from w' to w'' will raise the net present value of every policy, hence raise the net present value of the most profitable policies, which must then be positive for $r = r'$. Also, the present value of every policy (every choice of k and T) is a monotonically decreasing function of r, the derivative of (33) with respect to r being

$$-\int_0^T \{f(k)-we^t\}te^{-rt}dt<0. \qquad ...(47)$$

Suppose now that $r' \geqq r''$. Then the change from r' to r'' would further increase the net present value of every policy, or at least leave it unchanged. Then the most profitable policy at $w = w''$ would have a positive net present value, so that r'' and w'' would not satisfy the requirements of Theorem 3, contrary to assumption.

The possibility of multiple solutions for k and T given r and w seems to rule out the derivation of further comparative dynamic results. The situation is parallel to that which has emerged in the literature on neo-classical two-sector models, where the derivation of general comparative dynamic results depends upon assumptions sufficient to ensure the uniqueness of the solution to the model. In order to carry the discussion further I need the following assumption.

Uniqueness assumption. To each pair of values of r and w satisfying the requirements of Theorem 3 there correspond unique values of k and T such that the net present value function achieves its maximum.

It would no doubt be more desirable to have a condition, at least a sufficient one, for the uniqueness assumption to be valid. Such a condition is provided by the inequality (46). If this inequality is reversed we have a condition that $P(k)$ is locally strictly concave which, were it to hold everywhere, would guarantee that a unique k would produce a maximum of $P(k)$. The uniqueness of T would then follow from (36). However, (46) is not very satisfactory from this point of view because it is not a direct statement about the shape of $f(k)$ alone, but involves also the factor prices r, and, if T is eliminated, w also. So it is very difficult to apply (46) to some particular function to see if uniqueness can be guaranteed. I have however been unable to obtain a more transparent condition. If the uniqueness assumption, in its admittedly unsatisfactory form, is accepted there are some further comparative dynamic results available. I need the following Lemma. As with Theorem 3, the proof is relegated to the Appendix to avoid filling the text with lengthy arguments.

Lemma 5. *Let* $\frac{1}{w}\frac{dw}{dr}$ *be the proportional change in the wage rate associated with a change in* r. *Then the following inequality is satisfied identically.*

$$-\frac{rT+1-e^{rT}}{r^2} > -\frac{1}{w}\frac{dw}{dr}. \qquad ...(48)$$

The equipment necessary to tackle the question of the relation between r, and k and T, is now to hand. Since net present value is at a maximum it must be stationary with respect to variations in k alone. Hence,

$$-1+f'(k)\frac{1-e^{-rT}}{r} = 0. \qquad ...(49)$$

Taking the total derivative of (49) one obtains

$$-\frac{f''(k)}{f'(k)^2}\frac{dk}{dr} - e^{-rT}\frac{dT}{dr} - \frac{(rT+1)e^{-rT}-1}{r^2} = 0. \qquad ...(50)$$

Similarly, net present value is at a maximum with respect to variations in T alone, so that

$$f(k)-we^T = 0, \qquad ...(51)$$

and a total derivative of (51) gives

$$f'(k)\frac{dk}{dr}-e^{T}\frac{dw}{dr}-we^{T}\frac{dT}{dr}=0. \qquad ...(52)$$

Let $q=-\frac{1}{k}\frac{dk}{dr}$. Then (50) and (52) can be written

$$\frac{dT}{dr}=-\frac{f(k)-kf'(k)}{f'(k)f(k)}\frac{1}{\sigma}e^{rT}q-\frac{rT+1-e^{rT}}{r^2}, \qquad ...(53)$$

$$\frac{dT}{dr}=-\frac{kf'(k)}{f(k)}q-\frac{1}{w}\frac{dw}{dr}, \qquad ...(54)$$

where σ is the elasticity of substitution between investment and employment. (53) and (54) are two linear relations between $\frac{dT}{dr}$ and q, since at any particular equilibrium point r, k and T will all have known values. Clearly if one were to take two arbitrary linear relations between $\frac{dT}{dr}$ and q one could get no information at all about their signs, nor indeed about anything else. This approach is useful because we in fact have, already, two important restrictions on (53) and (54). Consider first the difference between their slopes, given by

$$-\frac{f(k)-kf'(k)}{f'(k)f(k)}\frac{1}{\sigma}e^{rT}+\frac{kf'(k)}{f(k)} \qquad ...(55)$$

The sign of (55) is the same as the sign of

$$\sigma-\frac{f(k)-kf'(k)}{kf'(k)^2}e^{rT}. \qquad ...(56)$$

At an equilibrium, taking into account (49), this can be written

$$\sigma-\frac{f(k)-kf'(k)}{kf'(k)}\frac{1-e^{-rT}}{re^{-rT}}. \qquad ...(57)$$

Now compare this to the concavity condition (46). If local strict concavity, and hence the uniqueness assumption, is not to be violated (57) must be negative. Thus the uniqueness assumption guarantees that the slope of (53) will be less than the slope of (54). Next consider the relationship between the vertical intercepts of these two lines; these are

$$-\frac{rT+1-e^{rT}}{r^2} \quad \text{and} \quad -\frac{1}{w}\frac{dw}{ar}.$$

But Lemma 5 is concerned with the relationship between these two expressions and it asserts that the first is strictly greater than the second.

In Fig. 2 the lines (53) and (54) are illustrated taking into account the restrictions on slopes and intercepts already noted. The figure also illustrates the effect on the intersection of the two lines of changes in σ and the rotation of (53) through its intercept that results. A number of results that are obtained immediately from this Figure are collected together in the next theorem.

Theorem 6. *Let r, w, T and k be equilibrium values of the variables at time zero. Let the uniqueness assumption hold, and let* $\frac{dT}{dr}$ *be the slope of the function relating T to r evaluated at this equilibrium point, let* $\frac{dk}{dr}$ *be the slope of the function relating k to r evaluated at this equilibrium point, and let q be* $-\frac{1}{k}\frac{dk}{dr}$. *Then;*

(i) *q is positive for every positive value of σ consistent with the concavity condition, and hence the uniqueness assumption.*

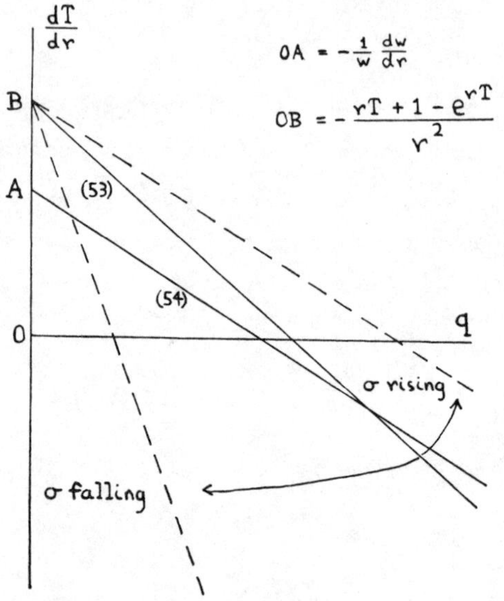

FIGURE 2

(ii) *q is a monotonically increasing function of σ, and* $q \to +\infty$ *as* $\sigma \to \sigma^*$, *where* σ^* *is the least upper bound of the values of σ consistent with the concavity condition.* $q \to 0$ *as* $\sigma \to 0$.

(iii) *The sign and magnitude of* $\frac{dT}{dr}$ *are determined by the magnitude of σ.* $\frac{dT}{dr}$ *is a monotonically decreasing function of σ.* $\frac{dT}{dr} \to -\infty$ *as* $\sigma \to \sigma^*$. $\frac{dT}{dr} \to -\frac{1}{w}\frac{dw}{dr}$ *as* $\sigma \to 0$.

Proof. Earlier arguments and inspection of Fig. 2.

While Theorem 6 provides us with a considerable amount of information about the form of the function relating T to r, and the dependence of that function upon the elasticity of substitution, it does not elucidate the global properties of that function. The following analysis shows what form the function relating T to r will take in various cases, always assuming the uniqueness assumption to hold. As is to be expected, the magnitude of σ plays a crucial role.

In equilibrium the present value of one man-place is zero.

$$-k+f(k)\,\text{dis}\,(r, T)-w\,\text{dis}\,(r-1, T) = 0. \qquad ...(58)$$

Multiplying (49) by $kf'(k)$ and adding the resulting equation to (58).

$$\{f(k)-kf'(k)\}\,\text{dis}\,(r, T)-w\,\text{dis}\,(r-1, T) = 0. \qquad \ldots(59)$$

Rearranging, and taking into account (36).[1]

$$\frac{f(k)-kf'(k)}{f(k)} = e^{-T}\frac{\text{dis}\,(r-1, T)}{\text{dis}\,(r, T)} \qquad \ldots(60)$$

The equation (60) is an extremely useful relation, because the left-hand side depends upon k only, while the right-hand side depends only on r and T. The right-hand side of (60) is graphed as a function of r, for various values of T, in Fig. 3. As the Figure shows it is a monotonically descreasing function of both r and T, and for all positive values of r and T it has a value between zero and one. The maximum value ($r = 0$) is $(1-e^{-T})/T$, and the limit as $r\to\infty$ is e^{-T}.

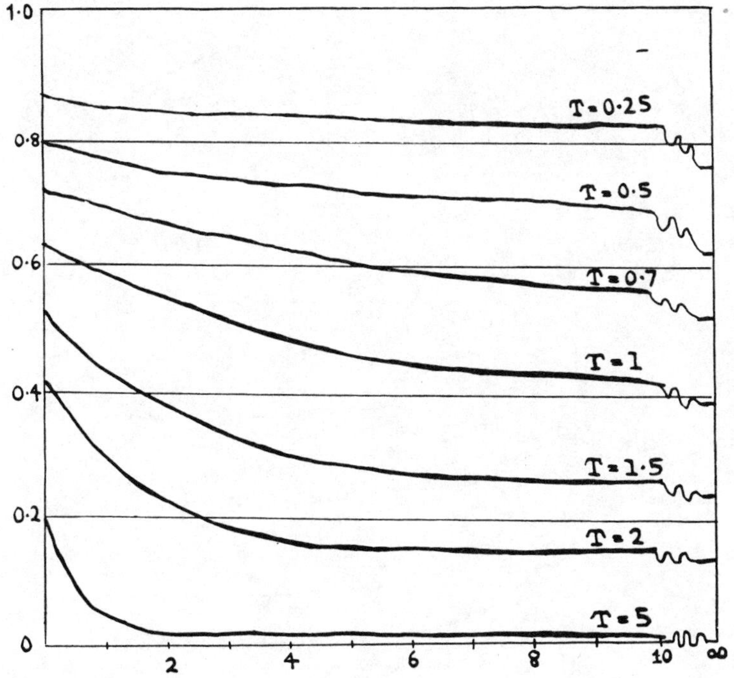

FIGURE 3

Graphs of the function $\frac{r}{r-1}\,e^{-T}\,\frac{1-e^{-(r-1)T}}{1-e^{-rT}}$

Now consider the left-hand side of (60) regarded as a function of r. From Theorem 6 we know that k is a decreasing function of r, i.e. q is positive. But the response of

$$\{f(k)-kf'(k)\}/f(k)$$

[1] The reader who knows R. C. O. Matthews' paper [6] will recognise the tactics that I am adopting here, and will appreciate the extent of my debt to that paper. His argument is open to certain objections on account of its lack of rigour, but the faults are fairly easily remedied. More seriously, the argument is conducted on the assumption that a rise in the gross saving-investment share will be associated with a fall in r. This is not in general true; not even if the elasticity of substitution is less than one.

to a fall in k depends upon the elasticity of substitution between employment and investment. There are numerous possibilities here, and I have selected three cases to present. They serve to demonstrate the richness of the model.

(i) The elasticity of substitution is greater than or equal to 1. Then k falls as r increases and the fall in k is associated with a rise, or no change at all, in $\{f(k)-kf'(k)\}/f(k)$.

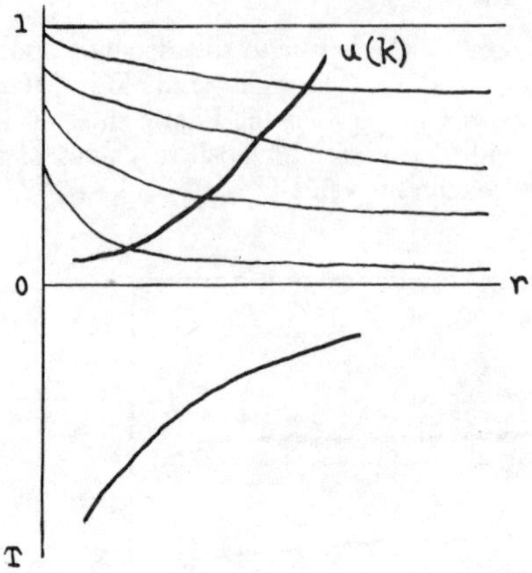

FIGURE 4a

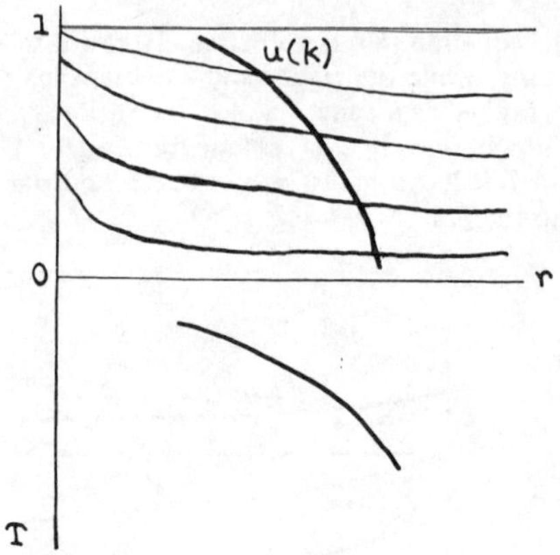

FIGURE 4b

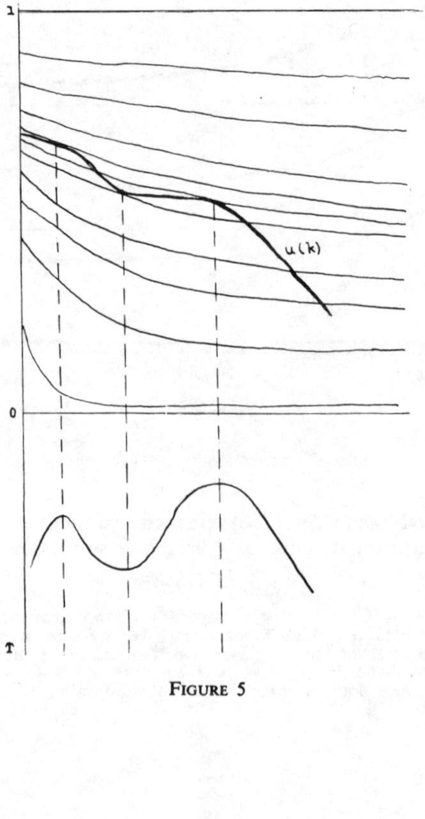

FIGURE 5

Moving along the r axis to the right one travels across curves corresponding to lower and lower values of T. Thus T is a monotonically decreasing function of r. This case is illustrated in Fig. 4(a) in which the function $\{f(k)-kf'(k)\}/f(k)$, denoted $u(k)$, is superimposed upon Fig. 3. In the lower quadrant the resulting relationship between r and T is illustrated.

(ii) The elasticity of substitution is close to zero. In this case k is not very responsive to changes in r, but even a small change in k results in a large movement of $u(k)$, which is an increasing function of k. Hence the curve $u(k)$ falls sharply to the right as one travels along the r-axis, cutting the curves of Figure 3 from above. T is a monotonically increasing function of r. Figure 4(b) illustrates this case.

(iii) The elasticity of substitution is less than one, but is not everywhere very small. Furthermore, it may vary with k, and it is not required to be a monotonic function of k. In this class of cases the curve $u(k)$ is falling as one travels to the right along the r-axis, but it may fall faster or slower than the curves of Figure 3. The slope of the function relating T to r may be either positive or negative, and T may oscillate as r increases. Such an oscillatory case is illustrated in Fig. 5.

Here then is a summary of the above analysis. The effect of a change in r upon T is the outcome of two offsetting influences: (i) a rise in r is associated with a fall in w and this, given $f(k)$, tends to lengthen the economic lifetime of investments, and (ii) a rise in r is associated with a fall in k and this, given w, tends to lower the economic lifetime of investments. The effect that a change in r has on w is independent of the elasticity of substitution (see the proof of Lemma 5), while the effect on k is larger the larger is σ. Hence the second effect tends to dominate when the elasticity of substitution is sufficiently large. In general oscillatory cases cannot be excluded.

6. *Balanced Growth and the Gross Saving-Investment Share*

The ratio of $I(t)$ to $Y(t)$, denoted s, is a constant on a balanced growth path. Let employment grow at rate a; then the natural rate of growth n is $1+a$. Note that

$$Y = Lf(k)\int_0^T e^{-nt}dt = Lf(k)\,\text{dis}\,(n, T). \qquad \text{...(61)}$$

Since $s = I/Y$, one has

$$k = \frac{sY}{L} = sf(k)\,\text{dis}\,(n, T). \qquad \text{...(62)}$$

Thus balanced growth is characterized by the equation

$$s = \frac{k}{f(k)}\frac{1}{\text{dis}\,(n, T)} = \frac{k}{f(k)}\frac{n}{1-e^{-nT}}. \qquad \text{...(63)}$$

Now given n the right-hand side of (63) is a function of r, since k and T depend, given the uniqueness assumption, uniquely on r. In this section I shall be mainly concerned with the following question: is the opposite true; i.e., does a knowledge of s uniquely determine r? Or the same question can be put in somewhat different ways. Is it true, for example, as has sometimes been assumed, that a rise in s will be associated, in a comparative dynamic sense, with a fall in r and a move to investments with a larger k? Rewrite (63) as

$$\frac{k}{f(k)} = s\,\frac{1-e^{-nT}}{n}. \qquad \text{...(64)}$$

The left-hand side of (64) is a decreasing function of r. If the right-hand side were to be an increasing function of r it would follow that there was at most one balanced growth equilibrium consistent with a given value of s. This will be the case if the elasticity of substitution is less than 1 and small; for then, as has been seen, T will be an increasing function of r, and the right-hand side of (64) is an increasing function of T. But in no other case can uniqueness of r, given s, be guaranteed. For if $\sigma>1$ we have seen that T will decrease with r; while if $\sigma<1$ and large T may even oscillate, and in neither case can the possibility of multiple solutions be excluded. Clearly, if several disjoint values of the rate of return are consistent with one value of s, it must follow that s is not a monotonic function of r.

So far nothing has been said about the determinants of the gross saving-investment share s. This number has been treated as parameter, an approach commonly used, though with more justification, in treating the net saving-investment share in neo-classical growth models. Yet s may be affected by any of the variables of the model. The most important relation between s and other variables is likely to be the dependence of s upon the distribution of income between wages and gross profits. To demonstrate the consequences of such a relation I need an expression for the share of wages in gross output. Total employment at time zero is given by

$$N = L\int_0^T e^{-at}dt = L \text{ dis}(a, T). \qquad \text{...(65)}$$

Hence the share of wages in gross output is given by

$$\frac{w.N}{Y} = w\frac{\text{dis}(a, T)}{\text{dis}(n, T)}\frac{1}{f(k)} = e^{-T}\frac{\text{dis}(a, T)}{\text{dis}(n, T)} = e^{-T}\frac{\text{dis}(n-1, T)}{\text{dis}(n, T)}. \qquad \text{...(66)}$$

Now the right-hand side of (66) has precisely the functional form of the right-hand side of (60). Thus one can say at once, or by inspection of Fig. 3, that, given n, the share of wages in gross output is a decreasing function of T. This is not an unnatural result. Now suppose that s is a weighted average of a saving share for wages and a saving share for gross profits, the weights being the relative income shares. Suppose a larger share of gross profits is saved. Then s increases with r if and only if T increases with r. However, allowing s to vary with the distribution of income does not, of necessity, guarantee a unique balanced growth equilibrium. For take the extreme " classical " case, when all gross profits are saved and there is no saving of wage income. This case is surely most favourable to uniqueness of r if income distribution effects are favourable to uniqueness of r, since maximum power is given to these effects. The balanced growth state is now characterised by the condition that s shall be equal to the share of gross profit in gross output.

$$1-e^{-T}\frac{\text{dis}(n-1, T)}{\text{dis}(n, T)} = \frac{k}{f(k)}\frac{1}{\text{dis}(n, T)}, \qquad \text{...(67)}$$

$$\frac{1-e^{-nT}}{n} - e^{-T}\frac{1-e^{-(n-1)T}}{n-1} = \frac{k}{f(k)}. \qquad \text{...(68)}$$

The right-hand side of (68) is a decreasing function of r. The left-hand side depends upon T alone, given n, and its derivative with respect to T is

$$e^{-nT} - e^{-(n-1)T}e^{-T} + e^{-T}\frac{1-e^{-(n-1)T}}{n-1} = e^{-T}\frac{1-e^{-(n-1)T}}{n-1} > 0. \qquad \text{...(69)}$$

So the left-hand side of (68) is an increasing function of T. For uniqueness to be guaranteed one would certainly want to have the left-hand side an increasing function of r. But this is only the case if T is an increasing function of r, as would be the case if σ were small. Otherwise we may again face the possibility that there will be more than one balanced growth equilibrium consistent with pure " classical " saving. If saving is related to net profits and is of the pure classical kind balanced growth equilibrium is unique by the usual argument that the rate of growth of the market value of capital is equal to n, which is equal to r. But even here the uniqueness assumption is still required.

III. EFFICIENT GROWTH

1. *A Theorem on Efficient Growth Paths*

Definition 2 introduced the concept of an efficient growth path.

Theorem 7. *A growth path of the economy is efficient only if it is a first-order competitive equilibrium.*

Proof. A necessary condition for a growth path to be efficient in the sense of Definition 2 is that the infinite integral

$$\int_0^\infty \{C'(t) - C(t)\}dt \qquad \text{...(70)}$$

should achieve a maximum at zero for $C'(t) = C(t)$ when $C'(t)$ is constrained by the feasibility conditions (1) to (7), plus the requirement that

$$C'(t) \geqq C(t).^1 \qquad \text{...(71)}$$

This is virtually a restatement of Definition 2. Thus an efficient path can be regarded as the solution to a problem in the variational calculus. The natural way to proceed now is to introduce the Lagrangean expression

$$\int_0^\infty \Bigg[C'(t) - C(t) + \eta(t)\{C'(t) - C(t)\} + \lambda(t)\left\{\int_{-\infty}^t f[k(\theta), \theta]L(t, \theta)d\theta - k(t)L(t, t) - C(t)\right\} + \mu(t)\left\{N(t) - \int_{-\infty}^t L(t, \theta)d\theta\right\} dt \Bigg]. \qquad \text{...(72)}$$

Not all the feasibility constraints are incorporated into (72). For example, the requirement $L(t, \theta) \leqq L(\theta, \theta)$ is not included. A variation in one of the functions will be said to be admissible if it does not lead to a violation of any of the constraints not included. This is a common way of treating sign constraints in programming problems; they are not included in the Lagrangean, but care is taken to ensure that the variations considered do not lead to their violation. A necessary condition for (70) to achieve a maximum subject to the various constraints involved is that the Lagrangean expression (72) should be locally stationary for any admissible variation. Let $C^v(t)$, $k^v(t)$ and $L^v(t, \theta)$ be admissible variations in C', k and L.

Variations in $k(t)$

If (72) is to be stationary with respect to admissible variations in $k(t)$, and assuming $k(t)$ everywhere positive, so that any variation is admissible, one must have

$$\int_0^\infty \lambda(t)\left\{\int_{-\infty}^t f'[k(\theta), \theta]L(t, \theta)k^v(\theta)d\theta - L(t, t)k^v(t)\right\} dt = 0 \qquad \text{...(73)}$$

for arbitrary $k^v(t)$. Let $k^v(t) = \max(h-t, 0)$, where h is a parameter.[2] Then (73) must be identically zero in h. Substituting one obtains

$$\int_0^h \left[\lambda(t)\left\{\int_{-\infty}^t f'[k(\theta), \theta]L(t, \theta)(h-\theta)d\theta - L(t, t)(h-t)\right\}\right] dt + \int_h^\infty \left[\lambda(t)\left\{\int_{-\infty}^h f'[k(\theta), \theta]L(t, \theta)(h-\theta)d\theta\right\}\right] dt = 0 \qquad \text{...(74)}$$

1 Both the statement that the maximum is achieved at $C'(t) = C(t)$, and the inequality (71), should be interpreted in the almost everywhere sense. I shall dispense with the tiresome reiteration of this qualification. Those who are annoyed by its absence will know where to insert it.

2 This special variation approach is an adaptation of R. Courant's technique for deriving Euler's equation by special variations. An account of that method as applied to traditional variational problems can be found in [1], page 191.

identically in h. Hence, forming derivatives of (74) with respect to h, and identifying them with zero

$$\int_0^h \left[\lambda(t)\left\{\int_{-\infty}^t f'[k(\theta), \theta]L(t, \theta)d\theta - L(t, t)\right\}\right]dt + \int_h^\infty \left[\lambda(t)\left\{\int_{-\infty}^h f'[k(\theta), \theta]L(t, \theta)d\theta\right\}\right]dt = 0, \quad \text{...(75)}$$

all other terms being zero. Then the next derivative with respect to h is

$$-\lambda(h)L(h, h) + \int_h^\infty \lambda(t)f'[k(h), h]L(t, h)dt = 0, \quad \text{...(76)}$$

or, rearranging (76)

$$f'[k(h), h]\int_h^\infty \frac{\lambda(t)}{\lambda(h)}\frac{L(t, h)}{L(h, h)}dt - 1 = 0. \quad \text{...(77)}$$

Compare this to (16).

Variations in $L(t, \theta)$:

First note, by inspection of (72), that the Lagrange multiplier $\mu(t)$ must be equal, for each t, to $\lambda(t).w(t)$, where $w(t)$ is the shadow wage rate as defined in (13). Thus suppose, for example, that on a set of values of t we have $\mu(t) < \lambda(t)w(t)$. Then an increase in $L(t, \theta)$ on this set for vintages θ satisfying $f[k(\theta), \theta] = w(t)$ would increase the value of (72). Then a variation in $L(t, \theta)$ yields

$$\int_0^\infty \lambda(t)\left\{\int_{-\infty}^t [f\{k(\theta), \theta\} - w(t)]L^v(t, \theta)d\theta - k(t)L^v(t, t)\right\}dt = 0 \quad \text{...(78)}$$

for all admissible variations $L^v(t, \theta)$. Now choose $L^v(t, \theta)$ to be

$$L^v(t, \theta) = \begin{cases} \min(\theta - h, 0)L(t, \theta) & \text{if } t \geq \theta \\ 0 & \text{if } t < \theta \end{cases}. \quad \text{...(79)}$$

Then $L^v(t, \theta)$ is an admissible variation. For by definition it satisfies the restriction $L(t, \theta) = 0$ for all $\theta > t$. Furthermore, when $L(t, \theta)$ is zero, in which case one has to worry about variations that would decrease $L(t, \theta)$, $L^v(t, \theta)$ is zero by definition. Finally, when $L(t, \theta)$ is positive $L^v(t, \theta)$ is non-positive, so that there is no danger that the condition $L(t, \theta)$ not greater than $L(\theta, \theta)$ will be violated. Then (78) becomes

$$\int_0^h \lambda(t)\left\{\int_{-\infty}^t [f(\theta) - w(t)](\theta - h)L(t, \theta)d\theta - L(t)L(t, t)(t - h)\right\}dt + \int_h^\infty \lambda(t)\left\{\int_{-\infty}^h [f(\theta) - w(t)]L(t, \theta)(\theta - h)d\theta\right\}dt = 0, \quad \text{...(80)}$$

which is true identically in h. Then again all derivatives with respect to h must vanish, so that

$$-\int_0^h \lambda(t)\left\{\int_{-\infty}^t [f(\theta) - w(t)]L(t, \theta)d\theta - k(t)L(t, t)\right\}dt - \int_h^\infty \lambda(t)\left\{\int_{-\infty}^h [f(\theta) - w(t)]L(t, \theta)d\theta\right\}dt = 0, \quad \text{...(81)}$$

all other terms being zero. And another derivative yields

$$k(h)L(h, h)\lambda(h) - \int_h^\infty \lambda(t)[f(h) - w(t)]L(t, h)dt = 0, \quad \text{...(82)}$$

or, rearranging (82)

$$-k(h)+\int_h^\infty \frac{\lambda(t)}{\lambda(h)}[f(h)-w(t)]\frac{L(t, h)}{L(h, h)}dt=0. \qquad ...(83)$$

Compare this expression to (15). Now define $r(t)$ as

$$r(t)=-\frac{d}{dt}\log\lambda(t), \qquad ...(84)$$

and the solution to this differential equation is

$$\frac{\lambda(t)}{\lambda(h)}=e^{-\int_h^t r(z)dz}. \qquad ...(85)$$

Now substituting (85) into (77) and (83) the latter are seen to be the equations defining a first-order competitive equilibrium. This completes the proof of Theorem 7.

Now (16) by no means implies that the present value of investments is actually maximized on an efficient path. This has been demonstrated by the earlier discussion of the concavity of the net present value function. However, it is clear from general considerations of programming theory, and from the fact that (72) is concave in the choice functions, that in fact net present value must be maximized (not necessarily strictly) on an efficient path. Then the lesson to be drawn from the possibility of a locally non-concave net present value function is not that efficient growth may not involve the maximization of shadow net present values, but rather that the satisfaction of necessary conditions for the maximization of net present values may not be sufficient for efficient growth.

In order to make these points clear, I shall shift the formulation of the model to one to which standard theorems in programming can be more readily applied. Instead of continuous time let time be divided into discrete periods, numbered by t, t = 0, 1, 2, ... where period " 0 " is a fictitious period, beyond our control, whose history is such as to give the model suitable initial conditions. At each period of time there are only M types of investment to be constructed, numbered by m, m = 1, 2, ..., M. The following notation is used.

$L_{m\theta t}$ = number of men assigned to investments of type m, vintage θ, at time period t.
I_{mt} = number of man places of type m constructed at t.
C_t = consumption at t.
$\bar{z}_{mt}$ = output required to construct one man-place of type m at t.
$\bar{x}_{mt}$ = output of one man-place of type m, vintage t.
$\bar{N}_t$ = total labour available at t.
$\bar{C}_t$ = actual consumption at t on an efficient path.
$C_t^* = C_t - \bar{C}_t$.

Then the analogue to the Lagrangean form (72) is

$$\sum_{t=1}^{\infty}\left[C_t^*+\lambda_t\left\{\sum_{\theta=0}^{t-1}\sum_{m=1}^{M}L_{m\theta t}\bar{x}_{m\theta}-\sum_{m=1}^{M}I_{mt}\bar{z}_{mt}-C_t^*-\bar{C}_t\right\}\right.$$
$$\left.+\mu_t\left\{\bar{N}_t-\sum_{\theta=0}^{t-1}\sum_{m=1}^{M}L_{m\theta t}\right\}+\sum_{\theta=0}^{t-1}\sum_{m=1}^{M}\pi_{m\theta t}\{I_{m\theta}-L_{m\theta t}\}\right]. \qquad ...(86)$$

The choice variables are by definition non-negative, the non-negativity of C_t^* indicating that C_t must be chosen not less than $\bar{C}_t$. In (86) the constraints on the maximum amount of labour that can be allocated to an investment have been included explicitly. (86) is the Lagrangean form of a linear programme, though one with infinitely many variables and infinitely many constraints. However, if $\bar{C}_t$, t = 1, 2, ..., is in fact an efficient feasible growth plan, then (86) has the value zero, and the usual programming theorems apply. In particular the derivative of (86) with respect to any variable is non-positive. Differentiation with respect to $L_{m\theta t}$ gives

$$\lambda_t \bar{x}_{m\theta} - \mu_t - \pi_{m\theta t} \leqq 0. \qquad \text{...(87)}$$

A similar argument to that applied to (72) shows that $\mu_t = \lambda_t w_t$, where w_t is the shadow price of labour at t. Or note directly that $\pi_{m\theta t}$ is equal to the rate at which the value of the programme would increase as extra capacity of type m vintage θ became available at t. Then, necessarily,

$$\pi_{m\theta t} = \lambda_t \max (\bar{x}_{m\theta} - w_t, 0), \qquad \text{...(88)}$$

which is equivalent to (87). Now the derivative of (86) with respect to $I_{m\theta}$ gives

$$-\lambda_\theta \bar{z}_{m\theta} + \sum_{t=\theta}^{\infty} \lambda_t \max (\bar{x}_{m\theta} - w_t, 0) \leqq 0, \qquad \text{...(89)}$$

where (89) holds for all θ and all m. Hence, no feasible investment has a positive net present value, and an investment actually constructed has zero net present value. Thus profits, in the sense of net present values, are actually maximized by the efficient path.

Theorem 7, following Definitions 4 and 5, merely asserted the existence of one function $r(t)$ having the properties required of a competitive equilibrium. Will $r(t)$ be unique? The answer in general is no. In defining the shadow wage rate I have already had to take account of some rather pathological and awkward cases in which there is more than one possible shadow wage function. Clearly in such cases we cannot hope to have a unique $r(t)$. However, if the shadow wage function is unique, or anyway, given the shadow wage function, there exists a unique $r(t)$ such that any time function satisfying Definition 4 corresponds to $r(t)$ almost everywhere. Without being at all precise (the footnote points the way to a precise argument) form the derivative of (83) with respect to h to obtain, taking into account (77),[1]

$$-\dot{k}(h) - \{f(h) - w(h)\} + \dot{f}(h)/f'(h) - \frac{\dot{\lambda}(h)}{\lambda(h)} k(h) = 0. \qquad \text{...(90)}$$

Thus,

$$r(h) = \frac{f(h) - w(h)}{k(h)} + \frac{\dot{k}(h)}{k(h)} - \frac{\dot{f}(h)}{k(h) f'(h)}, \qquad \text{...(91)}$$

so that $r(h)$ is unique, as required. Further simplification is possible since

$$\dot{f}(h) = f'(h)\dot{k}(h) + f_h(h),$$

where $f_h(h)$ is the partial derivative of $f\{k(h), h\}$ with respect to its second argument. Then

$$r(h) = \frac{f(h) - w(h)}{k(h)} - \frac{f_h(h)}{k(h) f'(h)}. \qquad \text{...(92)}$$

The first term on the right-hand side of (92) is the ratio of gross profit after paying shadow wage rate to the cost of investment at the instant that the investment starts production. It is sometimes called " the immediate rate of profit ". In an economy with a constant shadow wage rate it would be equal to the rate of profit as usually defined. A remarkable

[1] The lack of precision arises because $L(t, h)/L(h, h)$ is clearly not a differentiable function of h; yet in (90) the derivative of this function " under the integral " has been equated implicitly to zero. However, there is no difficulty in making this precise. There is a sense in which the derivative of $L(t, h)/L(h, h)$ is either zero, or a positive or negative δ-function; and in the latter case one must have $f(h) = w(t)$. So it is not surprising that the integral turns out to be zero. More simply, replace the range of integration by a set of closed intervals representing the set of t for which $f(h) \geqq w(t)$. The end-points of each of these intervals are continuous functions of h. If they are also differentiable functions of h we only have to note that the integrand vanishes by definition at every t which is an end-point, so that the derivative of the integral with respect to an end-point is zero. The set of end-points is at most countable if we exclude degenerate intervals. This is the basis of a precise argument.

consequence of (92) is the following.[1] Suppose there is no technical progress, so that $f_h(h)$ is zero. Then $r(h)$ is equal to the immediate rate of profit, i.e., at the instant that an investment starts production there is no depreciation, the instantaneous loss of value is zero. This must be the case if the rate of return net, r, is equal to the gross immediate rate of return. This result holds even if the shadow wage rate is changing, for example, even if capital deepening is going on.

The necessary conditions for an efficient growth path are by no means sufficient as the discussion of the next section will make clear.

2. *Efficient Balanced Growth: The Golden Rule*

Numerous writers in recent years have provided proofs of the following proposition in the context of various growth models: if there exists an equilibrium balanced growth path, with natural rate of growth n, and rate of return r equal to n, then no other feasible balanced growth path has a higher level of consumption per unit of labour measured in efficiency units. For references, see Hahn and Matthews [2]. The same proposition holds true also for the present model. I give two proofs, each of which is useful in showing the relation of the Golden Rule in this model to the same rule in other cases.

For the first proof, which is an extremely general proof that will do for virtually any model, prices for old investments are introduced. Let $p(x, t)$ be the price at time t of a man-place of productivity x. Then

$$p(x, t) = \int_t^{\infty} \{x - w(h)\}L(h)e^{-\int_t^h r(z)dz}\,dh, \qquad ...(93)$$

where $L(h)$ is the optimal amount of labour, not exceeding one unit, to employ on this investment at time h. For the discussion of balanced growth it is useful to work with a slightly different variable. Thus $p^*(x, t)$ is the price at time t of an investment employing one efficiency unit of labour ($e^{-\gamma t}$ natural units) and producing x units of output, while $q^*(x, t)$ is the number of such units available. On a balanced growth path $p^*(x, t)$ is then independent of t, since $w(t)$ grows at rate γ, while $q^*(x, t)$ grows at rate n. Consider a balanced growth path at time t, and suppose it to be a competitive equilibrium. Then the instantaneous costs of production must be equal to the value of output; the latter is the value of consumption output and the value of the addition to the capital stock.

$$W + r\int_0^{\infty} p^*(x, t)q^*(x, t)dx = n\int_0^{\infty} p^*(x, t)q^*(x, t)dx + C, \qquad ...(94)$$

where C and W are the output of consumption and the wage bill respectively. Now consider an alternative balanced growth path, offering at this instant of time the same total employment. Denote the quantities relevant to this path by the subscript " o ". Then the instantaneous activities of this path cannot be more profitable to the decision-makers of the original path, given the prices that they face, than their own activities. Thus

$$W + r\int_0^{\infty} p^*(x, t)q_0^*(x, t)dx \geqq n\int_0^{\infty} p^*(x, t)q_0^*(x, t)dx + C_0. \qquad ...(95)$$

These two relations together yield

$$(r-n)\int_0^{\infty} p^*(x, t)[q^*(x, t) - q_0^*(x, t)]dx \leqq C - C_0. \qquad ...(96)$$

Now in the case of a balanced growth path for which $r = n$ it follows at once that $C \geqq C_0$. Notice that the argument shows that C is at a global maximum. Furthermore, if there

[1] I am indebted to J. A. Mirrlees for this interpretation of equation (92). Notice that under balanced growth conditions (92) implies (31).

exists an alternative balanced growth path with the same level of consumption as the Golden Rule path, then it must be equally profitable at the Golden Rule prices and, since r is unique to a path, it must itself be a Golden Rule path. Thus consumption is at a maximum if and only if $r = n$.

Another proof follows that provided by Solow and his colleagues [9], for their model with fixed coefficients. This proof has the advantage that it also establishes the proposition that the Golden Rule path can also be characterised by the condition that the gross saving-investment share should be equal to the share of profit in gross output. This result is already obtained by Solow and colleagues for the fixed coefficient case. It only remains to note that it is easily generalized. Choose an arbitrary level of k, investment per man at time zero, within the range of feasible values. Holding this k constant, consumption at time zero is a function of the gross saving share; this is the fixed coefficient case. Thus there exists a curve relating C, consumption at time zero, to s lying between 0 and 1. This curve has a unique maximum for some value of s, call it s_k^*. Now there exists one of these curves for each feasible value of k, and the relation between consumption and the gross saving share which is offered by the model without fixed coefficients is clearly given by the upper envelope of the class of curves corresponding to fixed values of k. Hence, because it is an envelope, it must achieve a maximum at the same value of x as does one of the fixed coefficient curves. It will of course be the curve corresponding to the value of k on the Golden Rule path. Now the maximum of this fixed coefficient curve is achieved when s_k^* is equal to the share of gross profits. This completes the proof. These results are collected together in the next theorem.

Theorem 8. *If there exists a balanced growth path satisfying either of the following properties,*

(i) *it is a competitive equilibrium with rate of return equal to the natural rate of growth,*

or (ii) *the share of gross profit in gross output is equal to the investment-saving share; then this path has a level of consumption per head not less than that of any feasible balanced growth path.*

In the one good neo-classical model the Golden Rule can also be regarded as an efficiency theorem. For a balanced growth path with rate of return less than the natural rate of growth can be readily shown to be inefficient. The same result can be obtained for the putty-clay model, and this will justify an earlier remark that competitive equilibrium is not a sufficient condition for efficiency.

Theorem 9. *A balanced growth path with rate of return r less than the natural rate of growth n is inefficient.*

Proof. It is sufficient to show that the result is true in the case of a fixed coefficient model. For if a balanced growth path is inefficient subject to the constraint that every other path shall have investments, at each t, of the same capital intensity, then it is inefficient *a fortiori* in the case in which this restriction is relaxed. In the discussion of balanced growth I was able to show that T, the economic lifetime of investments, is an increasing function of r in the fixed coefficients case. Then output, at a given t, is a decreasing function of r. The economy with a higher value of r has its labour spread out over a longer set of vintages so that average output, the weights being given, is lower. From this it follows that the economy with a high r has an economy utilization function (economy output related to efficiently allocated labour) which is dominated by the utilization function of the economy with the lower value of r. Suppose then that at a certain moment of time the gross saving share is switched to the Golden Rule gross saving share, and remains at this level thereafter. This entails a once-for-all fall in the saving share. Now, since output is initially higher than the Golden Rule level, investment is larger. Thus, at each t, more men are employed on the latest investments than would be the case on the

Golden Rule path. But then output remains above the Golden Rule level, and hence the same share of it going to consumption gives more consumption than on the Golden Rule path, and hence more than on the original path. So the original path with $r<n$ was certainly inefficient.

It can be easily shown that the path discussed above would in fact approach the Golden Rule path asymptotically; but that is incidental to the proof of Theorem 9, which is now complete.

Christ's College, Cambridge CHRISTOPHER BLISS.

REFERENCES

[1] Courant, R. *Calculus of Variations* (New York University, 1957) (mimeographed).

[2] Hahn, F. H. and Matthews, R. C. O. "The Theory of Economic Growth: A Survey", *Economic Journal* (December 1964).

[3] Johansen, L. "Substitution versus Fixed Production Coefficients in the Theory of Economic Growth: A Synthesis", *Econometrica* (April 1959).

[4] Kemp, M. C., and Thanh, P. C. "On a Class of Growth Models", *Econometrica* (April 1966).

[5] Koopmans, T. C. "The Concept of Optimal Economic Growth", Cowles Foundation Discussion Paper, No. 163.

[6] Matthews, R. C. O. "'The New View of Investment': Comment", *Quarterly Journal of Economics* (February 1964)

[7] Phelps, E. S. "Substitution, Fixed Proportions, Growth and Distribution", *International Economic Review* (September 1963).

[8] Salter, W. E. G. *Productivity and Technical Change* (Cambridge University Press. 1960).

[9] Solow, R. M., Tobin, J., von Weizsäcker, C. C. and Yaari, M. "Neoclassical Growth with Fixed Factor Proportions", *Review of Economic Studies* (April 1966).

[10] Solow, R. M. "Substitution and Fixed Proportions in the Theory of Capital", *Review of Economic Studies* (June 1962).

APPENDIX

Theorem 3. *Either, for each positive w less than a given w_0, or for each positive w, there exists a unique positive r, and positive k and T (not necessarily unique), such that the right-hand side of* (33) *achieves its maximum value for positive k and T, and this maximum value is zero.*

Proof. It is first shown that for each positive r and positive w the right-hand side of (33), here denoted $P(k, T)$, has a maximum on the set of k and T satisfying

$$f(k) \geqq \cdot \quad \text{and} \quad T \geqq 0. \qquad \ldots(97)$$

The optimal retirement condition implies that

$$P(k, T) \leqq P(k, \max\{\log_e f(k)/w, 0\}) = P(k), \qquad \ldots(98)$$

so that $P(k, T)$ fails to achieve a maximum, subject to (97), if and only if $P(k)$ fails to achieve a maximum. But $P(k)$ is a continuous function of k, and as such achieves a maximum on every compact subset of its range. Thus it is enough to show that $P(k)$ is eventually a monotonically decreasing function of k. Now (33) can be rewritten as

$$-k+f(k)\frac{1-e^{-r\log_e f(k)/w}}{r}-w\frac{1-e^{-(r-1)\log_e f(k)/w}}{r-1}$$

$$=-k+\frac{f(k)}{r}\left[1-\left\{\frac{f(k)}{w}\right\}^{-r}\right]-\frac{w}{r-1}\left[1-\left\{\frac{f(k)}{w}\right\}^{-(r-1)}\right]. \quad ...(99)$$

Now (99) is the sum of the term

$$[f(k)-rk]/r \quad ...(100)$$

and terms that reduce to

$$\left\{\frac{f(k)}{w}\right\}^{-(r-1)}\left[\frac{w}{r(r-1)}\right]-\frac{w}{r-1}. \quad ...(101)$$

(101) is always a decreasing function of k, while (100) must eventually decrease with k by the regular strict concavity property of $f(k)$. Thus, for positive r and w, $P(k)$ has a maximum for k and T satisfying (47). Furthermore (100) goes to $-\infty$ as k goes to $+\infty$ so that $P(k)$ is certainly negative for all sufficiently large k.

I am now in a position to introduce the following definition.

$$Q(r, w)=\max_{f(k)\geqq w}\{P(k, \log_e[f(k)/w])\}. \quad ...(102)$$

From the above argument it is known that Q exists for each positive r and positive w.

It is next shown that $Q(r, w)$ is a continuous function of r on the positive r. Denote the net present value with optimal retirement by $P_r(k)$ to remind one of the dependence on r. Suppose that for each $\varepsilon>0$ there were to exist an $\alpha>0$ such that, for all k, $|r'-r|<\alpha$ implied $|P_r(k)-P_{r'}(k)|<\varepsilon$; that is, suppose $P_r(k)$ a continuous function of r uniformly with respect to k. Let $P_r(k_0)=Q(r, w)$ and $P_{r'}(k_0')=Q(r', w)$, and without loss of generality suppose $r'>r$. Then because, as has been noted, the net present value of every policy is a decreasing function of r, $Q(r, w)>Q(r', w)$. Next note that

$$Q(r, w)-Q(r', w)=P_r(k_0)-P_r(k_0')+P_r(k_0')-P_{r'}(k_0'). \quad ...(103)$$

The second difference on the right-hand side of (103) is $<\varepsilon$ by assumption if $|r'-r|<\alpha$, while the first difference is certainly non-positive by the definition of $Q(r, w)$. Thus $|Q(r, w)-Q(r', w)|<\varepsilon$ giving the required continuity with respect to r. It remains to show that $P_r(k)$ is continuous with respect to r uniformly with respect to k, as was assumed above. Now every continuous function of two variables is continuous with respect to one uniformly with respect to the second on a compact subset of its range. In the above argument on the continuity of $Q(r, w)$ the values of k with which the argument was concerned were both values at which $P_r(k)$ achieved a maximum for some value of r in a neighbourhood of the particular value of r at which continuity was to be established. Given any value of r, say $\bar{r}$, we can select a value of k, call it $\bar{k}$, such that for any value of r in an α-neighbourhood of $\bar{r}$, $P_r(k)$ is a monotonically decreasing function of k whenever $k>\bar{k}$. So values of k larger than $\bar{k}$ can be excluded without changing the argument in any way. One is then working on a compact subset of the values of k and r so that the required uniformity with respect to k of the continuity of $P_r(k)$ is obtained.

$Q(r, w)$ is now known to be a continuous monotonically decreasing function of r on the positive r. Then, on account of the monotonicity, one of two things can happen as $r\to 0$. Either $Q(r, w)$ approaches a finite limit from below, or $Q(r, w)$ increases without limit. If a finite limit exists it will be denoted $Q(0, w)$. Now define S_w as

$$S_w=\{w>0\mid Q(0, w)\geqq 0 \text{ or } \lim_{r\to 0} Q(r, w)=+\infty\}. \quad ...(104)$$

S_w is non-empty. For choose r and k such that $f(k) > rk$. Then, as $w \to 0$, $T \to \infty$, and

$$\lim_{w \to 0} P_r(k) = -k + \frac{f(k)}{r} > 0. \qquad \text{...(105)}$$

Furthermore, if w' is in S_w then so is any positive $w < w'$, since a fall in w increases $Q(r, w)$. So S_w is an interval, and if it is bounded it is closed at its upper end-point. If this upper end-point exists, call it w_0. Next note that, for each positive w there exists a positive r such that $Q(r, w)$ is negative. For

$$\lim_{r \to \infty} \left\{ -k + f(k) \frac{1 - e^{-rT}}{r} - w \frac{1 - e^{-(r-1)T}}{r-1} \right\} = -k < 0. \qquad \text{...(106)}$$

Thus $P_r(k)$ is negative eventually for each positive k. But $P_r(k)$ is negative anyway except on the interval $f^{-1}(w) \leqq k \leqq \bar{k}$, and the greatest lower bound of the values of r required to make $P_r(k)$ negative is a continuous function of k on this interval and as such has a maximum. Hence there exists an r that will make $P_r(k)$ everywhere negative, so that $Q(r, w)$ will be negative.[1]

The theorem is now complete. For each positive w we have seen that there exists an r such that $Q(r, w)$ is negative. But

$$\lim_{r \to 0} Q(r, w) > 0, \text{ for } w < w_0,$$

and $Q(r, w)$ is a continuous function of r. Hence there exists a value of r such that $Q(r, w) = 0$. Furthermore this r is unique, since $Q(r, w)$ is monotonic.

The proof of Theorem 3 has left open the question as to whether w_0 always exists; or, equivalently, whether it is possible to have equilibrium with $r = 0$. Equilibrium with $r = 0$ is certainly sometimes possible as, for example, when $f(k)$ is bounded above. But the assumption of regular strict concavity is not alone sufficient to guarantee it, as the following example shows. Let $x = f(k)$ and $k = f^{-1}(x) = g(x)$. Let $r = 0$. Then (33) becomes

$$-k + f(k)T - w(e^T - 1) = -g(x) + x(\log x - \log w) - x + w. \qquad \text{...(107)}$$

Suppose

$$g(x) = \tfrac{1}{2} x \log (x+1). \qquad \text{...(108)}$$

This is the inverse of an acceptable production function since

$$\left. \begin{aligned} & g(0) = 0, \\ & \frac{dg}{dx} = \tfrac{1}{2}\left[\log (x+1) + \frac{x}{x+1} \right], \\ & \frac{d^2 g}{dx^2} = \tfrac{1}{2}\left[\frac{1}{x+1} + \frac{1}{(x+1)^2} \right] \end{aligned} \right\} . \qquad \text{...(109)}$$

Also

$$g(x) - hx = x[\tfrac{1}{2} \log (x+1) - h] \qquad \text{...(110)}$$

is positive for x sufficiently large for each $h > 0$; i.e. $g(x)$ is regularly strictly convex, so that its inverse is regularly strictly concave. Then substituting (108) into (107) one obtains

$$-\tfrac{1}{2} x \log (x+1) + x(\log x - \log w - 1) + w$$
$$= \tfrac{1}{2} x \log x + \tfrac{1}{2} x \log \frac{x}{x+1} - x(\log w + 1) + w, \qquad \text{...(111)}$$

which is unbounded regardless of the size of w.

[1] This statement is not of course true if we admit the case $w = 0$. For then the only lower bound on k is zero, and the argument fails at this point. It may then happen that however large the r chosen there exists a k sufficiently small to make $P(k)$ positive at $w = 0$. An example is provided by the Cobb-Douglas function.

Lemma 5. *Let* $\frac{1}{w}\frac{dw}{dr}$ *be the proportional change in the wage rate associated with a change in r. Then the following inequality is satisfied identically;*

$$-\frac{(rT+1)-e^{rT}}{r^2} > -\frac{1}{w}\frac{dw}{dr}. \qquad ...(112)$$

Proof. Differentiating the present value expression (33) totally with respect to r and equating the resulting expression to zero one obtains

$$\left[-1+f'(k)\frac{1-e^{-rT}}{r}\right]\frac{dk}{dr}+[f(k)-we^{T}]e^{-rT}\frac{dT}{dr}$$

$$-\left[\frac{1-e^{-(r-1)T}}{r-1}\right]\frac{dw}{dr}+\left[-f(k)\int_0^T te^{-rt}dt+w\int_0^T te^{-(r-1)t}dt\right]=0. \qquad ...(113)$$

But since k and T are chosen so as to maximize the present value of a man-place it follows that the terms multiplying $\frac{dk}{dr}$ and $\frac{dT}{dr}$ must be zero, and (113) reduces to

$$-\frac{1}{w}\frac{dw}{dr}=\frac{r-1}{1-e^{-(r-1)T}}\int_0^T te^{-rt}(e^T-e^t)dt, \qquad ...(114)$$

taking into account (36). Now note that

$$-\frac{rT+1-e^{rT}}{r^2}=-e^{rT}\frac{\partial}{\partial r}\left[\frac{1-e^{-rT}}{r}\right]=-e^{rT}\frac{\partial}{\partial r}\left[\int_0^T e^{-rt}dt\right]$$

$$=e^{rT}\int_0^T te^{-rt}dt. \qquad ...(115)$$

Thus the condition that is required can be written

$$\int_0^T te^{-rt}(e^T-e^t)dt<\frac{e^{rT}-e^T}{r-1}\int_0^T te^{-rt}dt, \qquad ...(116)$$

or

$$\int_0^T te^{-rt}\left(\frac{re^T-e^{rT}}{r-1}-e^t\right)dt<0. \qquad ...(117)$$

(117) would be established if it could be shown that

$$\frac{re^T-e^{rT}}{r-1}-e^t<0 \text{ for } 0<t\leqq T, \qquad ...(118)$$

and this would follow at once if it could be shown that

$$\frac{re^T-e^{rT}}{r-1}\leqq 1. \qquad ...(118)$$

It is this condition which will be established. Expanding the exponential expressions in (118),

$$\frac{1}{r-1}\left[r\left(1+T+\frac{T^2}{2\cdot 1}+...+\frac{T^j}{j!}+...\right)-\left(1+rT+\frac{r^2T^2}{2\cdot 1}+...+\frac{r^jT^j}{j!}+...\right)\right], \qquad ...(119)$$

and then,

$$1-r\left(\frac{T^2}{2.1}+\frac{T^3}{3.2.1}\frac{r^2-1}{r-1}+...+\frac{T^j}{j!}\frac{r^{j-1}-1}{r-1}+...\right)\leqq 1, \qquad ...(120)$$

as required.

[17]

The Economic Implications of Learning by Doing

It is by now incontrovertible that increases in per capita income cannot be explained simply by increases in the capital-labor ratio. Though doubtless no economist would ever have denied the role of technological change in economic growth, its overwhelming importance relative to capital formation has perhaps only been fully realized with the important empirical studies of Abramovitz [1] and Solow [11]. These results do not directly contradict the neo-classical view of the production function as an expression of technological knowledge. All that has to be added is the obvious fact that knowledge is growing in time. Nevertheless a view of economic growth that depends so heavily on an exogenous variable, let alone one so difficult to measure as the quantity of knowledge, is hardly intellectually satisfactory. From a quantitative, empirical point of view, we are left with time as an explanatory variable. Now trend projections, however necessary they may be in practice, are basically a confession of ignorance, and, what is worse from a practical viewpoint, are not policy variables.

Further, the concept of knowledge which underlies the production function at any moment needs analysis. Knowledge has to be acquired. We are not surprised, as educators, that even students subject to the same educational experiences have different bodies of knowledge, and we may therefore be prepared to grant, as has been shown empirically (see [2], Part III), that different countries, at the same moment of time, have different production functions even apart from differences in natural resource endowment.

I would like to suggest here an endogenous theory of the changes in knowledge which underlie intertemporal and international shifts in production functions. The acquisition of knowledge is what is usually termed " learning," and we might perhaps pick up some clues from the many psychologists who have studied this phenomenon (for a convenient survey, see Hilgard [5]). I do not think that the picture of technical change as a vast and prolonged process of learning about the environment in which we operate is in any way a far-fetched analogy; exactly the same phenomenon of improvement in performance over time is involved.

Of course, psychologists are no more in agreement than economists, and there are sharp differences of opinion about the processes of learning. But one empirical generalization is so clear that all schools of thought must accept it, although they interpret it in different fashions: Learning is the product of experience. Learning can only take place through the attempt to solve a problem and therefore only takes place during activity. Even the Gestalt and other field theorists, who stress the role of insight in the solution of problems (Köhler's famous apes), have to assign a significant role to previous experiences in modifying the individual's perception.

A second generalization that can be gleaned from many of the classic learning experiments is that learning associated with repetition of essentially the same problem is subject to sharply diminishing returns. There is an equilibrium response pattern for any given stimulus, towards which the behavior of the learner tends with repetition. To have steadily increasing performance, then, implies that the stimulus situations must themselves be steadily evolving rather than merely repeating.

The role of experience in increasing productivity has not gone unobserved, though the relation has yet to be absorbed into the main corpus of economic theory. It was early observed by aeronautical engineers, particularly T. P. Wright [15], that the number of labor-hours expended in the production of an airframe (airplane body without engines) is a decreasing function of the total number of airframes of the same type previously produced. Indeed, the relation is remarkably precise; to produce the Nth airframe of a given type, counting from the inception of production, the amount of labor required is proportional to $N^{-1/3}$. This relation has become basic in the production and cost planning of the United States Air Force; for a full survey, see [3]. Hirsch (see [6] and other work cited there) has shown the existence of the same type of " learning curve " or " progress ratio," as it is variously termed, in the production of other machines, though the rate of learning is not the same as for airframes.

Verdoorn [14, pp. 433-4] has applied the principle of the learning curve to national outputs; however, under the assumption that output is increasing exponentially, current output is proportional to cumulative output, and it is the former variable that he uses to explain labor productivity. The empirical fitting was reported in [13]; the estimated progress ratio for different European countries is about ·5. (In [13], a neo-classical interpretation in terms of increasing capital-labor ratios was offered; see pp. 7-11.)

Lundberg [9, pp. 129-133] has given the name " Horndal effect " to a very similar phenomenon. The Horndal iron works in Sweden had no new investment (and therefore presumably no significant change in its methods of production) for a period of 15 years, yet productivity (output per manhour) rose on the average close to 2% per annum. We find again steadily increasing performance which can only be imputed to learning from experience.

I advance the hypothesis here that technical change in general can be ascribed to experience, that it is the very activity of production which gives rise to problems for which favorable responses are selected over time. The evidence so far cited, whether from psychological or from economic literature is, of course, only suggestive. The aim of this paper is to formulate the hypothesis more precisely and draw from it a number of economic implications. These should enable the hypothesis and its consequences to be confronted more easily with empirical evidence.

The model set forth will be very simplified in some other respects to make clearer the essential role of the major hypothesis; in particular, the possibility of capital-labor substitution is ignored. The theorems about the economic world presented here differ from those in most standard economic theories; profits are the result of technical change; in a free-enterprise system, the rate of investment will be less than the optimum; net investment and the stock of capital become subordinate concepts, with gross investment taking a leading role.

In section 1, the basic assumptions of the model are set forth. In section 2, the implications for wage earners are deduced; in section 3 those for profits, the inducement to invest, and the rate of interest. In section 4, the behavior of the entire system under steady growth with mutually consistent expectations is taken up. In section 5, the divergence between social and private returns is studied in detail for a special case (where the subjective rate of discount of future consumption is a constant). Finally, in section 6, some limitations of the model and needs for further development are noted.

1. The Model

The first question is that of choosing the economic variable which represents " experience ". The economic examples given above suggest the possibility of using cumulative output (the total of output from the beginning of time) as an index of experience, but this does not seem entirely satisfactory. If the rate of output is constant, then the stimulus to learning presented would appear to be constant, and the learning that does take place is a gradual approach to equilibrium behavior. I therefore take instead cumulative gross investment (cumulative production of capital goods) as an index of experience. Each new machine produced and put into use is capable of changing the environment in which production takes place, so that learning is taking place with continually new stimuli. This at least makes plausible the possibility of continued learning in the sense, here, of a steady rate of growth in productivity.

The second question is that of deciding where the learning enters the conditions of production. I follow here the model of Solow [12] and Johansen [7], in which technical change is completely embodied in new capital goods. At any moment of new time, the new capital goods incorporate all the knowledge then available, but once built their productive efficiency cannot be altered by subsequent learning.

To simplify the discussion we shall assume that the production process associated with any given new capital good is characterized by fixed coefficients, so that a fixed amount of labor is used and a fixed amount of output obtained. Further, it will be assumed that new capital goods are better than old ones in the strong sense that, if we compare a unit of capital goods produced at time t_1 with one produced at time $t_2 > t_1$, the first requires the co-operation of at least as much labor as the second, and produces no more product. Under this assumption, a new capital good will always be used in preference to an older one.

Let G be cumulative gross investment. A unit capital good produced when cumulative gross investment has reached G will be said to have *serial number* G. Let

$\lambda(G)$ = amount of labor used in production with a capital good of serial number G,
$\gamma(G)$ = output capacity of a capital good of serial number G,
x = total output,
L = total labor force employed.

It is assumed that $\lambda(G)$ is a non-increasing function, while $\gamma(G)$ is a non-decreasing function. Then, regardless of wages or rental value of capital goods, it always pays to use a capital good of higher serial number before one of lower serial number.

It will further be assumed that capital goods have a fixed lifetime, T. Then capital goods disappear in the same order as their serial numbers. It follows that at any moment of time, the capital goods in use will be all those with serial numbers from some G' to G, the current cumulative gross investment. Then

$$x = \int_{G'}^{G} \gamma(G)\,dG, \tag{1}$$

(2) $$L = \int_{G'}^{G} \lambda(G)dG.$$

The magnitudes x, L, G, and G' are, of course, all functions of time, to be designated by t, and they will be written $x(t)$, $L(t)$, $G(t)$, and $G'(t)$ when necessary to point up the dependence. Then $G(t)$, in particular, is the cumulative gross investment up to time t. The assumption about the lifetime of capital goods implies that

(3) $$G'(t) \geqq G(t - T).$$

Since $G(t)$ is given at time t, we can solve for G' from (1) or (2) or the equality in (3). In a growth context, the most natural assumption is that of full employment. The labor force is regarded as a given function of time and is assumed equal to the labor employed, so that $L(t)$ is a given function. Then $G'(t)$ is obtained by solving in (2). If the result is substituted into (1), x can be written as a function of L and G, analogous to the usual production function. To write this, define

$$\Lambda(G) = \int \lambda(G)dG,$$

(4)

$$\Gamma(g) = \int \gamma(G)dG.$$

These are to be regarded as indefinite integrals. Since $\lambda(G)$ and $\gamma(G)$ are both positive, $\Lambda(G)$ and $\Gamma(G)$ are strictly increasing and therefore have inverses, $\Lambda^{-1}(u)$ and $\Gamma^{-1}(v)$, respectively. Then (1) and (2) can be written, respectively,

(1′) $$x = \Gamma(G) - \Gamma(G'),$$

(2′) $$L = \Lambda(G) - \Lambda(G').$$

Solve for G' from (2′).

(5) $$G' = \Lambda^{-1}[\Lambda(G) - L].$$

Substitute (5) into (1′).

(6) $$x = \Gamma(G) - \Gamma\{\Lambda^{-1}[\Lambda(G) - L]\},$$

which is thus a production function in a somewhat novel sense. Equation (6) is always valid, but under the full employment assumption we can regard L as the labor force available.

A second assumption, more suitable to a depression situation, is that in which demand for the product is the limiting factor. Then x is taken as given; G' can be derived from (1) or (1′), and employment then found from (2) or (2′). If this is less than the available labor force, we have Keynesian unemployment.

A third possibility, which, like the first, may be appropriate to a growth analysis, is that the solution (5) with L as the labor force, does not satisfy (3). In this case, there is a shortage of capital due to depreciation. There is again unemployment but now due to structural discrepancies rather than to demand deficiency.

In any case, except by accident, there is either unemployed labor or unemployed capital; there could be both in the demand deficiency case. Of course, a more neoclassical model, with substitution between capital and labor for each serial number of capital good, might permit full employment of both capital and labor, but this remains a subject for further study.

In what follows, the full-employment case will be chiefly studied. The capital shortage case, the third one, will be referred to parenthetically. In the full-employment case, the depreciation assumption no longer matters; obsolescence, which occurs for all capital goods with serial numbers below G', becomes the sole reason for the retirement of capital goods from use.

The analysis will be carried through for a special case. To a very rough approximation, the capital-output ratio has been constant, while the labor-output ratio has been declining. It is therefore assumed that

(7) $\gamma(G) = a,$

a constant, while $\lambda(G)$ is a decreasing function of G. To be specific, it will be assumed that $\lambda(G)$ has the form found in the study of learning curves for airframes.

(8) $\lambda(G) = bG^{-n},$

where $n > 0$. Then

$$\Gamma(G) = aG,\ \Lambda(G) = cG^{1-n},\ \text{where } c = b/(1-n) \text{ for } n \neq 1.$$

Then (6) becomes

(9) $$x = aG\left[1 - \left(1 - \frac{L}{cG^{1-n}}\right)^{1/(1-n)}\right] \text{ if } n \neq 1.$$

Equation (9) is always well defined in the relevant ranges, since from (2′),

$$L = \Lambda(G) - \Lambda(G') \leqq \Lambda(G) = cG^{1-n}.$$

When $n = 1$, $\Lambda(G) = b \log G$ (where the natural logarithm is understood), and

(10) $x = aG(1-e^{-L/b})$ if $n = 1$.

Although (9) and (10) are, in a sense, production functions, they show increasing returns to scale in the variables G and L. This is obvious in (10) where an increase in G, with L constant, increases x in the same proportion; a simultaneous increase in L will further increase x. In (9), first suppose that $n < 1$. Then a proportional increase in L and G increases L/G^{1-n} and therefore increases the expression in brackets which multiplies G. A similar argument holds if $n > 1$. It should be noted that x increases more than proportionately to scale changes in G and L in general, not merely for the special case defined by (7) and (8). This would be verified by careful examination of the behavior of (6), when it is recalled that $\lambda(G)$ is non-increasing and $\gamma(G)$ is non-decreasing, with the strict inequality holding in at least one. It is obvious intuitively, since the additional amounts of L and G are used more efficiently than the earlier ones.

The increasing returns do not, however, lead to any difficulty with distribution theory. As we shall see, both capital and labor are paid their marginal products, suitably defined. The explanation is, of course, that the private marginal productivity of capital (more strictly, of new investment) is less than the social marginal productivity since the learning effect is not compensated in the market.

The production assumptions of this section are designed to play the role assigned by Kaldor to his " technical progress function," which relates the rate of growth of output per worker to the rate of growth of capital per worker (see [8], section VIII). I prefer to think of relations between rates of growth as themselves derived from more fundamental relations between the magnitudes involved. Also, the present formulation puts more stress on gross rather than net investment as the basic agent of technical change.

Earlier, Haavelmo ([4], sections 7.1 and 7.2) had suggested a somewhat similar model. Output depended on both capital and the stock of knowledge; investment depended on output, the stock of capital, and the stock of knowledge. The stock of knowledge was either simply a function of time or, in a more sophisticated version, the consequence of investment, the educational effect of each act of investment decreasing exponentially in time.

Verdoorn [14, pp. 436-7] had also developed a similar simple model in which capital and labor needed are non-linear functions of output (since the rate of output is, approximately, a measure of cumulative output and therefore of learning) and investment a constant fraction of output. He notes that under these conditions, full employment of capital and labor simultaneously is in general impossible—a conclusion which also holds for for the present model as we have seen. However, Verdoorn draws the wrong conclusion: that the savings ratio must be fixed by some public mechanism at the uniquely determined level which would insure full employment of both factors; the correct conclusion is that one factor or the other will be unemployed. The social force of this conclusion is much less in the present model since the burden of unemployment may fall on obsolescent capital; Verdoorn assumes his capital to be homogeneous in nature.

2. Wages

Under the full employment assumption the profitability of using the capital good with serial number G' must be zero; for if it were positive it would be profitable to use capital goods with higher serial number and if it were negative capital good G' would not be used contrary to the definition of G'. Let

w = wage rate with output as numéraire.

From (1′) and (7)

(11) $$G' = G - (x/a)$$

so that

(12) $$\lambda(G') = b\left(G - \frac{x}{a}\right)^{-n}.$$

The output from capital good G' is $\gamma(G')$ while the cost of operation is $\lambda(G')w$. Hence

$$\gamma(G') = \lambda(G')w$$

or from (7) and (12)

(13) $$w = a\left(G - \frac{x}{a}\right)^{n}/b.$$

It is interesting to derive labor's share which is wL/x. From (2′) with $\Lambda(g) = cG^{1-n}$ and G' given by (11)

$$L = c\left[\, G^{1-n} - \left(G - \frac{x}{a}\right)^{1-n} \right],$$

for $n \neq 1$ and therefore

(14) $$wL/x = a\left[\left(\frac{G}{x} - \frac{1}{a}\right)^{n}\left(\frac{G}{x}\right)^{1-n} - \left(\frac{G}{x} - \frac{1}{a}\right)\right]/(1-n) \text{ for } n \neq 1,$$

where use has been made of the relation, $c = b/(1-n)$. It is interesting to note that labor's share is determined by the ratio G/x.

Since, however, x is determined by G and L, which, at any moment of time, are data, it is also useful to express the wage ratio, w, and labor's share, wL/x, in terms of L and G. First, G' can be found by solving for it from (2′).

(15) $$G' = \left(G^{1-n} - \frac{L}{c}\right)^{1/(1-n)} \text{ for } n \neq 1.$$

We can then use the same reasoning as above, and derive

(16) $$w = a\left(G^{1-n} - \frac{L}{c}\right)^{n/(1-n)}/b,$$

(17) $$\frac{wL}{x} = \frac{\left[\left(\frac{L}{G^{1-n}}\right)^{(1-n)/n} - \frac{1}{c}\left(\frac{L}{G^{1-n}}\right)^{1/n}\right]^{n/(1-n)}}{b\left[1 - \left(1 - \frac{L}{cG^{1-n}}\right)^{1/(1-n)}\right]}.$$

Labor's share thus depends on the ratio L/G^{1-n}; it can be shown to decrease as the ratio increases.

For completeness, I note the corresponding formulas for the case $n = 1$. In terms of G and x, we have

(18) $$w = (aG - x)/b,$$

(19) $$wL/x = \left(\frac{aG}{x} - 1\right) \log \frac{G/x}{(G/x) - (1/a)}.$$

In terms of G and L, we have

(20) $$G' = Ge^{-L/b},$$

(21) $$w = \frac{aG}{be^{L/b}},$$

(22) $$wL/x = \frac{L}{b(e^{L/b} - 1)}.$$

In this case, labor's share depends only on L, which is indeed the appropriate special case ($n=1$) of the general dependence on L/G^{1-n}.

The preceding discussion has assumed full employment. In the capital shortage case, there cannot be a competitive equilibrium with positive wage since there is necessarily unemployment. A zero wage is, however, certainly unrealistic. To complete the model, it would be necessary to add some other assumption about the behavior of wages. This case will not be considered in general; for the special case of steady growth, see Section 5.

3. Profits and Investment

The profit at time t from a unit investment made at time $v \leq t$ is

$$\gamma[G(v)] - w(t)\ \lambda[G(v)].$$

In contemplating an investment at time v, the stream of potential profits depends upon expectations of future wages. We will suppose that looking ahead at any given moment of time each entrepreneur assumes that wages will rise exponentially from the present level. Thus the wage rate expected at time v to prevail at time t is

$$w(v)\ e^{\theta(t-v)},$$

and the profit expected at time v to be received at time t is

$$\gamma[G(v)]\ [1 - W(v)\ e^{\theta(t-v)}],$$

where

(23) $$W(v) = w(v)\ \lambda[G(v)]/\gamma[G(v)],$$

the labor cost per unit output at the time the investment is made. The dependence of W on v will be made explicit only when necessary. The profitability of the investment is expected to decrease with time (if $\theta > 0$) and to reach zero at time $T^* + v$, defined by the equation

(24) $$We^{\theta T^*} = 1.$$

Thus T^* is the expected economic lifetime of the investment, provided it does not exceed the physical lifetime, T. Let

(25) $$T = \min(\bar{T}, T^*).$$

Then the investor plans to derive profits only over an interval of length T, either because the investment wears out or because wages have risen to the point where it is unprofitable to operate. Since the expectation of wage rises which causes this abandonment derives from anticipated investment and the consequent technological progress, T^* represents the expected date of obsolescence. Let

$$\rho = \text{rate of interest.}$$

If the rate of interest is expected to remain constant over the future, then the discounted stream of profits over the effective lifetime, T, of the investment is

(26) $$S = \int_{0}^{T} e^{-\rho t}\, \gamma[G(v)]\,(1 - W e^{\theta t})dt,$$

or

(27) $$\frac{S}{\gamma[G(v)]} = \frac{1 - e^{-\rho T}}{\rho} + \frac{W(1 - e^{-(\rho-\theta)T})}{\theta - \rho}.$$

Let

(28) $$V = e^{-\theta T} = \max(e^{-\theta T}, W),\ \alpha = \rho/\theta.$$

Then

(29) $$\frac{\theta S}{\gamma[G(v)]} = \frac{1 - V^{\alpha}}{\alpha} + \frac{W(1 - V^{\alpha-1})}{1-\alpha} = R(\alpha).$$

The definitions of $R(\alpha)$ for $\alpha = 0$ and $\alpha = 1$ needed to make the function continuous are:

$$R(0) = -\log V + W(1 - V^{-1}),\ R(1) = 1 - V + W \log V.$$

If all the parameters of (26), (27), or (29) are held constant, S is a function of ρ, and, equivalently, R of α. If (26) is differentiated with respect to ρ, we find

$$dS/d\rho = \int_{0}^{T} (-t)e^{-\rho t}\, \gamma[G(v)]\,(1 - W e^{\theta t})dt < 0.$$

Also

$$S < \gamma[G(v)] \int_{0}^{T} e^{-\rho t}dt = \gamma[G(v)]\,(1 - e^{-\rho T})/\rho$$

$$< \gamma[G(v)]/\rho.$$

Since obviously $S > 0$, S approaches 0 as ρ approaches infinity. Since R and α differ from S and ρ, respectively, only by positive constant factors, we conclude

$$dR/d\alpha < 0,\ \lim_{\alpha \to +\infty} R(\alpha) = 0.$$

To examine the behavior of $R(\alpha)$ as α approaches $-\infty$, write

$$R(\alpha) = -\frac{(1/V)^{1-\alpha}}{(1-\alpha)^2}\,[(1-\alpha)V + \alpha W]\left(\frac{1-\alpha}{\alpha}\right) + \frac{1}{\alpha} + \frac{W}{1-\alpha}.$$

The last two terms approach zero. As α approaches $-\infty$, $1 - \alpha$ approaches $+\infty$. Since $1/V > 1$, the factor

$$\frac{(1/V)^{1-\alpha}}{(1-\alpha)^2}$$

approaches $+\infty$, since an exponential approaches infinity faster than any power. From (28), $V \geqq W$. If $V = W$, then the factor,

$$(1-\alpha)V - \alpha W = \alpha(W - V) + V,$$

is a positive constant; if $V > W$, then it approaches $+\infty$ as α approaches $-\infty$. Finally,

$$\frac{1-\alpha}{\alpha}$$

necessarily approaches -1. Hence,

(30) $R(\alpha)$ is a strictly decreasing function, approaching $+\infty$ as α approaches $-\infty$ and 0 as α approaches $+\infty$.

The market, however, should adjust the rate of return so that the discounted stream of profits equals the cost of investment, i.e., $S = 1$, or, from (29),

(31) $R(\alpha) = \theta/\gamma[G(\nu)]$.

Since the right-hand side of (31) is positive, (30) guarantees the existence of an α which satisfies (31). For a given θ, the equilibrium rate of return, ρ, is equal to $\alpha\ \theta$; it may indeed be negative. The rate of return is thus determined by the expected rate of increase in wages, current labor costs per unit output, and the physical lifetime of the investment. Further, if the first two are sufficiently large, the physical lifetime becomes irrelevant, since then $T^* < \bar{T}$, and $T = T^*$.

The discussion of profits and returns has not made any special assumptions as to the form of the production relations.

4. Rational Expectations in a Macroeconomic Growth Model

Assume a one-sector model so that the production relations of the entire economy are described by the model of section 1. In particular, this implies that gross investment at any moment of time is simply a diversion of goods that might otherwise be used for consumption. Output and gross investment can then be measured in the same units.

The question arises, can the expectations assumed to govern investment behavior in the preceding section actually be fulfilled? Specifically, can we have a constant relative increase of wages and a constant rate of interest which, if anticipated, will lead entrepreneurs to invest at a rate which, in conjunction with the exogenously given rate of interest to remain at the given level? Such a state of affairs is frequently referred to as "perfect foresight," but a better term is "rational expectations," a term introduced by J. Muth [10].

We study this question first for the full employment case. For this case to occur, the physical lifetime of investments must not be an effective constraint. If, in the notation of the last section, $T^* > \bar{T}$, and if wage expectations are correct, then investments will disappear through depreciation at a time when they are still yielding positive current profits. As seen in section 2, this is incompatible with competitive equilibrium and full employment. Assume therefore that

(32) $T^* \leqq \bar{T}$;

then from (28), $W = V$, and from (29) and (31), the equilibrium value of ρ is determined by the equation,

(33) $$\frac{1 - W^\alpha}{\alpha} + \frac{W - W^\alpha}{1 - \alpha} = \frac{\theta}{a},$$

where, on the right-hand side, use is made of (7).

From (16), it is seen that for the wage rate to rise at a constant rate θ, it is necessary that the quantity,

$$G^{1-n} - \frac{L}{c},$$

rise at a rate $\theta(1 - n)/n$. For θ constant, it follows from (33) that a constant ρ and therefore a constant α requires that W be constant. For the specific production relations (7) and (8), (23) shows that

$$W = \frac{a\left(G^{1-n} - \frac{L}{c}\right)^{n/(1-n)}}{b} \frac{bG^{-n}}{a} = \left(1 - \frac{L}{cG^{1-n}}\right)^{n/(1-n)},$$

and therefore the constancy of W is equivalent to that of L/G^{1-n}. In combination with the preceding remark, we see that

(34) L increases at rate $\theta(1 - n)/n$, G increases at rate θ/n.

Suppose that

σ = rate of increase of the labor force,

is a given constant. Then

(35) $\theta = n\,\sigma/(1-n)$,

(36) the rate of increase of G is $\sigma/(1-n)$.

Substitution into the production function (9) yields

(37) the rate of increase of x is $\sigma/(1-n)$.

From (36) and (37), the ratio G/x is constant over time. However, the value at which it is constant is not determined by the considerations so far introduced; the savings function is needed to complete the system. Let the constant ratio be

(38) $G(t)/x(t) = \mu$.

Define

$g(t)$ = rate of gross investment at time $t = dG/dt$.

From (36), $g/G = \sigma/(1 - n)$, a constant. Then

(39) $$g/x = (g/G)(G/x) = \mu\,\sigma/(1 - n).$$

A simple assumption is that the ratio of gross saving (equals gross investment) to income (equals output) is a function of the rate of return, ρ; a special case would be the common assumption of a constant savings-to-income ratio. Then μ is a function of ρ. On the other hand, we can write W as follows, using (23) and (13):

(40) $$W = a\frac{\left(G - \frac{x}{a}\right)^n}{b}\;\frac{bG^{-n}}{a} = \left(1 - \frac{x}{aG}\right)^n = \left(1 - \frac{1}{a\mu}\right)^n.$$

Since θ is given by (35), (33) is a relation between W and ρ, and, by (40) between μ and ρ. We thus have two relations between μ and ρ, so they are determinate.

From (38), μ determines one relation between G and X. If the labor force, L, is given at one moment of time, the production function (9) constitutes a second such relation, and the system is completely determinate.

As in many growth models, the rates of growth of the variables in the system do not depend on savings behavior; however, their levels do.

It should be made clear that all that has been demonstrated is the existence of a solution in which all variables have constant rates of growth, correctly anticipated. The stability of the solution requires further study.

The growth rate for wages implied by the solution has one paradoxical aspect; it increases with the rate of growth of the labor force (provided $n < 1$). The explanation seems to be that under full employment, the increasing labor force permits a more rapid introduction of the newer machinery. It should also be noted that, for a constant saving ratio, g/x, an increase in σ decreases μ, from (39), from which it can be seen that wages at the initial time period would be lower. In this connection it may be noted that since G cannot decrease, it follows from (36) that σ and $1-n$ must have the same sign for the steady growth path to be possible. The most natural case, of course, is $\sigma > 0$, $n < 1$.

This solution is, however, admissible only if the condition (32), that the rate of depreciation not be too rapid, be satisfied. We can find an explicit formula for the economic lifetime, T^*, of new investment. From (24), it satisfies the condition

$$e^{-\theta T^*} = W.$$

If we use (35) and (40) and solve for T^*, we find

(41) $$T^* = \frac{-(1 - n)}{\sigma}\log\left[1 - \frac{1}{a\mu}\right]$$

and this is to be compared with T; the full employment solution with rational expectations of exponentially increasing wages and constant interest is admissible if $T^* \leq T$.

If $T^* > T$, then the full employment solution is inadmissible. One might ask if a constant-growth solution is possible in this case. The answer depends on assumptions about the dynamics of wages under this condition.

We retain the two conditions, that wages rise at a constant rate θ, and that the rate of interest be constant. With constant θ, the rate of interest, ρ, is determined from (31); from (29), this requires that

(42) W is constant over time.

From the definition of W, (23), and the particular form of the production relations, (7) and (8), it follows that the wage rate, w, must rise at the same rate as G^n, or

(43) G rises at a constant rate θ/n.

In the presence of continued unemployment, the most natural wage dynamics in a free market would be a decreasing, or, at best, constant wage level. But since G can never decrease, it follows from (43) that θ can never be negative. Instead of making a specific assumption about wage changes, it will be assumed that any choice of θ can be imposed, perhaps by government or union or social pressure, and it is asked what restrictions on the possible values of θ are set by the other equilibrium conditions.

In the capital shortage case, the serial number of the oldest capital good in use is determined by the physical lifetime of the good, i.e.,

$G' = G(t - T)$. From (43),

$$G(t - T) = e^{-\theta T/n} G.$$

Then, from (1′) and (7),

$$x = aG(1 - e^{-\theta T/n}),$$

so that the ratio, G/x, or μ, is a constant,

(44) $\mu = 1/a(1 - e^{-\theta T/n})$.

From (43), $g/G = \theta/n$; hence, by the same argument as that leading to (39),

(45) $g/x = \theta/na(1 - e^{-\theta T/n})$.

There are three unknown constants of the growth process, θ, ρ, and W. If, as before, it is assumed that the gross savings ratio, g/x, is a function of the rate of return, ρ, then, for any given ρ, θ can be determined from (45); note that the right-hand side of (45) is a strictly increasing function of θ for $\theta \geqq 0$, so that the determination is unique, and the rate of growth is an increasing function of the gross savings ratio, contrary to the situation in the full employment case. Then W can be solved for from (31) and (29).

Thus the rate of return is a freely disposable parameter whose choice determines the rate of growth and W, which in turn determines the initial wage rate. There are, of course, some inequalities which must be satisfied to insure that the solution corresponds to the capital shortage rather than the full employment case; in particular, $W \leqq V$ and also the labor force must be sufficient to permit the expansion. From (2′), this means that the labor force must at all times be at least equal to

$$cG^{1-n} - c(G')^{1-n} = cG^{1-n}(1 - e^{-\theta(1-n)T/n});$$

if σ is the growth rate of the labor force, we must then have (46)

$$(46) \qquad \sigma \geqq \theta(1-n)/n,$$

which sets an upper bound on θ (for $n < 1$). Other constraints on ρ are implied by the conditions $\theta \geqq 0$ and $W \geqq 0$ (if it is assumed that wage rates are non-negative). The first condition sets a lower limit on g/x; it can be shown, from (45), that

$$(47) \qquad g/x \geqq 1/aT;$$

i.e., the gross savings ratio must be at least equal to the amount of capital goods needed to produce one unit of output over their lifetime. The constraint $W > 0$ implies an interval in which ρ must lie. The conditions under which these constraints are consistent (so that at least one solution exists for the capital shortage case) have not been investigated in detail.

5. Divergence of Private and Social Product

As has already been emphasized, the presence of learning means that an act of investment benefits future investors, but this benefit is not paid for by the market. Hence, it is to be expected that the aggregate amount of investment under the competitive model of the last section will fall short of the socially optimum level. This difference will be investigated in detail in the present section under a simple assumption as to the utility function of society. For brevity, I refer to the *competitive solution* of the last section, to be contrasted with the *optimal* solution. Full employment is assumed. It is shown that the socially optimal growth rate is the same as that under competitive conditions, but the socially optimal ratio of gross investment to output is higher than the competitive level.

Utility is taken to be a function of the stream of consumption derived from the productive mechanism. Let

$$c = \text{consumption} = \text{output} - \text{gross investment} = x - g.$$

It is in particular assumed that future consumption is discounted at a constant rate, β, so that utility is

$$(48) \qquad U = \int_o^{+\infty} e^{-\beta t} c(t) dt = \int_o^{+\infty} e^{-\beta t} x(t) dt.$$

$$- \int_o^{+\infty} e^{-\beta t} g(t) dt.$$

Integration by parts yields

$$\int_o^{+\infty} e^{-\beta t} g(t) dt = e^{-\beta t} G(t) \Big|_o^{+\infty} + \beta \int_o^{+\infty} e^{-\beta t} G(t) dt.$$

From (48),

(49) $$U = U_1 - \lim_{t \to +\infty} e^{-\beta t}G(t) + G(0),$$

where

(50) $$U_1 = \int_0^{+\infty} e^{-\beta t}[x(t) - \beta\, G(t)]dt.$$

The policy problem is the choice of the function $G(t)$, with $G'(t) \geqq 0$, to maximize (49), where $x(t)$ is determined by the production function (9), and

(51) $$L(t) = L_0 e^{\sigma t}.$$

The second term in (49) is necessarily non-negative. It will be shown that, for sufficiently high discount rate, β, the function $G(t)$ which maximizes U_1 also has the property that the second term in (49) is zero; hence, it also maximizes (49), since $G(0)$ is given.

Substitute (9) and (51) into (50).

$$U_1 = \int_0^{+\infty} e^{-\beta t}G(t) \left[a - \beta - a\left(1 - \frac{L_0 e^{\sigma t}}{cG^{1-n}}\right)^{1/(1-n)}\right] dt.$$

Let $\bar{G}(t) = G(t)\, e^{-\sigma t/(1-n)}$.

$$U_1 = \int_0^{+\infty} e^{-\left(\beta - \frac{\sigma}{1-n}\right)t}\, \bar{G}(t)\left[a - \beta - a\left(1 - \frac{L_0}{c\bar{G}^{1-n}}\right)^{1/(1-n)}\right] dt.$$

Assume that

(52) $$\beta > \frac{\sigma}{1-n};$$

otherwise an infinite utility is attainable. Then to maximize U_1 it suffices to choose $\bar{G}(t)$ so as to maximize, for each t,

(53) $$\bar{G}\left[a - \beta - a\left(1 - \frac{L_0}{c\bar{G}^{1-n}}\right)^{1/(1-n)}\right].$$

Before actually determining the maximum, it can be noted that the maximizing value of $\bar{G}$ is independent of t and is therefore a constant. Hence, the optimum policy is

(54) $$G(t) = \bar{G}\, e^{\sigma t/(1-n)},$$

so that, from (36), the growth rate is the same as the competitive. From (52), $e^{-\beta t}G(t) \longrightarrow 0$ as $t \longrightarrow +\infty$.

To determine the optimal $\bar{G}$, it will be convenient to make a change of variables. Define

$$v = \left(1 - \frac{L_0}{c\bar{G}^{1-n}}\right)^{n/(1-n)}.$$

so that

(55) $$\bar{G} = \left[\frac{L_0}{(1 - v^{(1-n)/n})}\right]^{1/(1-n)}.$$

The analysis will be carried through primarily for the case where the output per unit capital is sufficiently high, more specifically, where

(56) $$a > \beta.$$

Let

(57) $$\gamma = 1 - \frac{\beta}{a} > 0.$$

The maximizing $\bar{G}$, or v, is unchanged by multiplying (53), the function to be maximized, by the positive quantity, $(c/L_0)^{1/(1-n)}/a$ and then substituting from (55) and (57). Thus, v maximizes

$$(1 - v^{(1-n)/n})^{-1/(1-n)} (\gamma - v^{1/n}).$$

The variable v ranges from 0 to 1. However, the second factor vanishes when $v = \gamma^n < 1$ (since $\gamma < 1$) and becomes negative for larger values of v; since the first factor is always positive, it can be assumed that $v < \gamma^n$ in searching for a maximum, and both factors are positive. Then v also maximizes the logarithm of the above function, which is

$$f(v) = -\frac{\log (1 - v^{(1-n)/n})}{1 - n} + \log (\gamma - v^{1/n}),$$

so that

$$f'(v) = \frac{v^{\frac{1}{n} - 2}}{n} \left[\frac{\gamma - v}{(1 - v^{(1-n)/n}) (\gamma - v^{1/n})}\right].$$

Clearly, with $n < 1, f'(v) > 0$ when $0 < v < \gamma$ and $f'(v) < 0$ when $\gamma < v < \gamma^n$, so that the maximum is obtained at

(58) $$v = \gamma.$$

The optimum $\bar{G}$ is determined by substituting γ for v in (55).

From (54), L/G^{1-n} is a constant over time. From the definition of v and (58), then,

$$\gamma = \left(1 - \frac{L}{cG^{1-n}}\right)^{n/(1-n)}$$

for all t along the optimal path, and, from the production function (9),

(59) $$\gamma = \left(1 - \frac{x}{aG}\right)^n \text{ for all } t \text{ along the optimal path.}$$

This optimal solution will be compared with the competitive solution of steady growth studied in the last section. From (40), we know that

(60) $$W = \left(1 - \frac{x}{aG}\right)^n \text{ for all } t \text{ along the competitive path.}$$

It will be demonstrated that $W < \gamma$; from this it follows that *the ratio G/x is less along the competitive path than along the optimal path.* Since along both paths,

$$g/x = [\sigma/(1 - n)]\ (G/x),$$

it also follows that *the gross savings ratio is smaller along the competitive path than along the optimal path.*

For the particular utility function (48), the supply of capital is infinitely elastic at $\rho = \beta$; i.e., the community will take any investment with a rate of return exceeding β and will take no investment at a rate of return less than β. For an equilibrium in which some, but not all, income is saved, we must have

(61) $\rho = \beta$.

From (35), $\theta = n\sigma/(1 - n)$; hence, by definition (28),

(62) $\alpha = (1 - n)\beta/n\sigma$.

Since $n < 1$, it follows from (62) and the assumption (52) that (63)

(63) $\alpha > 1$.

Equation (33) then becomes the one by which W is determined. The left-hand side will be denoted as $F(W)$.

$$F'(W) = \frac{1 - W^{\alpha-1}}{1 - \alpha}.$$

From (63), $F'(W) < 0$ for $0 \geqq W < 1$, the relevant range since the investment will never be profitable if $W > 1$. To demonstrate that $W < \gamma$, it suffices to show that $F(W) > F(\gamma)$ for that value of W which satisfies (33), i.e., to show that

(64) $F(\gamma) < \theta/a$.

Finally, to demonstrate (64), note that $\gamma < 1$ and $\alpha > 1$, which imply that $\gamma^{\alpha} < \gamma$, and therefore

$$(1 - \alpha) - \gamma^{\alpha} + \alpha\gamma > (1 - \alpha)(1 - \gamma).$$

Since $\alpha > 1$, $\alpha(1 - \alpha) < 0$. Dividing both sides by this magnitude yields

$$\frac{1 - \gamma^{\alpha}}{\alpha} + \frac{\gamma - \gamma^{\alpha}}{1 - \alpha} < \frac{1 - \gamma}{\alpha} = \frac{\theta}{a}$$

where use is made of (57), (28), and (61); but from (33), the left-hand side is precisely $F(\gamma)$, so that (64) is demonstrated.

The case $a \leqq \beta$, excluded by (56), can be handled similarly; in that case the optimum v is 0. The subsequent reasoning follows in the same way so that the corresponding competitive path would have $W < 0$, which is, however, impossible.

6. SOME COMMENTS ON THE MODEL

(1) Many writers, such as Theodore Schultz, have stressed the improvement in the quality of the labor force over time as a source of increased productivity. This interpretation can be incorporated in the present model by assuming that σ, the rate of growth of the labor force, incorporates qualitative as well as quantitative increase.

(2) In this model, there is only one efficient capital-labor ratio for new investment at any moment of time. Most other models, on the contrary, have assumed that alternative capital-labor ratios are possible both before the capital good is built and after. A still more plausible model is that of Johansen [7], according to which alternative capital-labor ratios are open to the entrepreneur's choice at the time of investment but are fixed once the investment is congealed into a capital good.

(3) In this model, as in those of Solow [12] and Johansen [7], the learning takes place in effect only in the capital goods industry; no learning takes place in the use of a capital good once built. Lundberg's Horndal effect suggests that this is not realistic. The model should be extended to include this possibility.

(4) It has been assumed here that learning takes place only as a by-product of ordinary production. In fact, society has created institutions, education and research, whose purpose it is to enable learning to take place more rapidly. A fuller model would take account of these as additional variables.

REFERENCES.

[1] Abramovitz, M., "Resource and Output Trends in the United States Since 1870," *American Economic Review, Papers and Proceedings of the American Economic Associations*, 46 (May, 1956): 5-23.

[2] Arrow, K. J., H. B. Chenery, B. S. Minhas, and R. M. Solow, "Capital-Labor Substitution and Economic Efficiency," *Review of Economics and Statistics*, 43 (1961): 225-250.

[3] Asher, H., *Cost-Quantity Relationships in the Airframe Industry*, R-291, Santa Monica, Calif.: The RAND Corporation, 1956.

[4] Haavelmo, T. *A Study in the Theory of Economic Evolution*, Amsterdam: North Holland, 1954.

[5] Hilgard, E. R., *Theories of Learning*, 2nd ed., New York: Appleton-Century-Crofts, 1956.

[6] Hirsch, W. Z., "Firm Progress Radios," *Econometrica*, 24 (1956): 136-143.

[7] Johansen, L., "Substitution vs. Fixed Production Coefficients in the Theory of Economic Growth: A Synthesis," *Econometrica*, 27 (1959): 157-176.

[8] Kaldor, N., "Capital Accumulation and Economic Growth," in F. A. Lutz and D. C. Hague (eds.), *The Theory of Capiatl*, New York: St. Martin's Press, 1961, 177-222.

[9] Lundberg, E., *Produktivitet och räntabilitet*, Stockholm: P. A. Norstedt and Söner, 1961.

[10] Muth, J., " Rational Expectations and the Theory of Price Movements," *Econometrica* (in press).

[11] Solow, R. M., " Technical Change and the Aggregate Production Function," *Review of Economics and Statistics*, 39 (1957): 312-320.

[12] Solow, R. M., " Investment and Technical Progress," in K. J. Arrow, S. Karlin, and P. Suppes (eds.), *Mathematical Methods in the Social Sciences*, 1959, Stanford, Calif.: Stanford University Press, 1960, 89-104.

[13] Verdoorn, P. J., " Fattori che regolano lo sviluppo della produttività del lavoro," *L'Industria*, 1 (1949).

[14] Verdoorn, P. J., " Complementarity and Long-Range Projections," *Econometrica*, 24 (1956): 429-450.

[15] Wright, T. P., " Factors Affecting the Cost of Airplanes," *Journal of the Aeronautical Sciences*, 3 (1936): 122-128.

Stanford. KENNETH J. ARROW.

Name Index